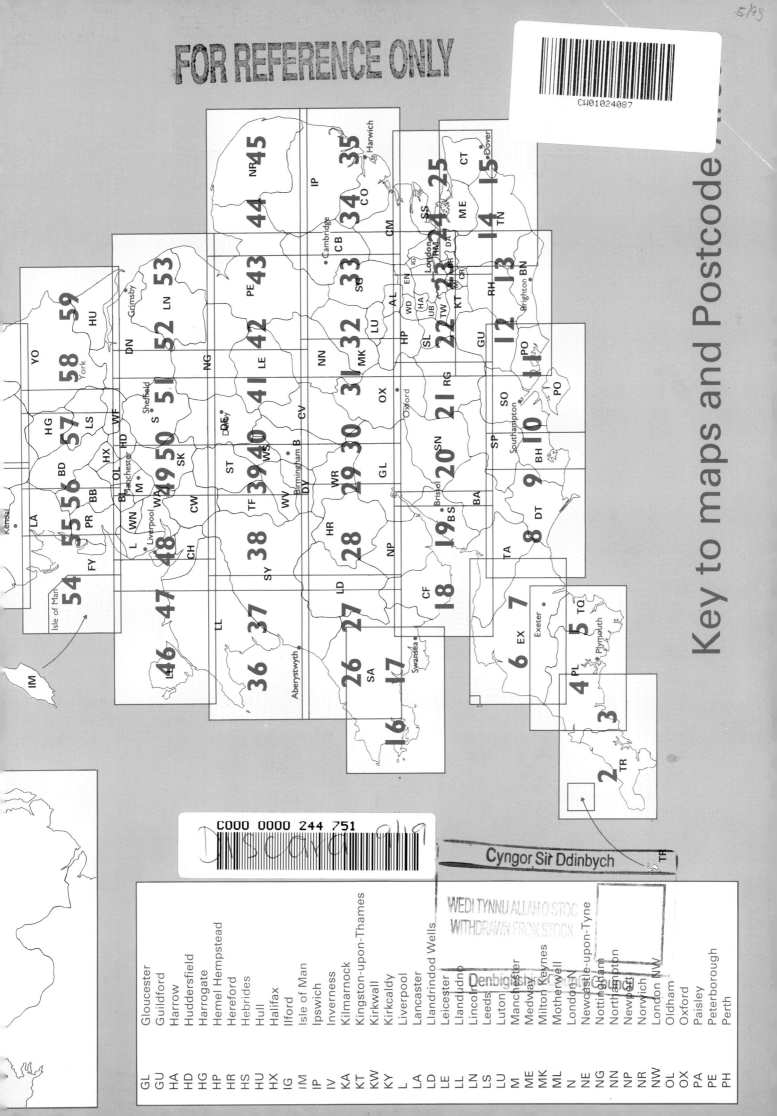

FOR REFERENCE ONLY

Key to maps and Postcode

CW01024087

5/95

C000 0000 244 751

Cyngor Sir Ddinbych

GL Gloucester
GU Guildford
HA Harrow
HD Huddersfield
HG Harrogate
HP Hemel Hempstead
HR Hereford
HS Hebrides
HU Hull
HX Halifax
IG Ilford
IM Isle of Man
IP Ipswich
IV Inverness
KA Kilmarnock
KT Kingston-upon-Thames
KW Kirkwall
KY Kirkcaldy
L   Liverpool
LA Lancaster
LD Llandrindod Wells
LE Leicester
LL Llandudno
LN Lincoln
LS Leeds
LU Luton
M   Manchester
ME Medway
MK Milton Keynes
ML Motherwell
N   London N
NE Newcastle-upon-Tyne
NG Nottingham
NN Northampton
NP Newport
NR Norwich
NW London NW
OL Oldham
OX Oxford
PA Paisley
PE Peterborough
PH Perth

Ru.

•Bartholomew•

Postcode Atlas

of Great Britain
and Northern Ireland

Postcode Area and District Boundaries

Central London Sector Boundaries

Plus Major Cities at improved scale

· Bartholomew ·

Postcode Atlas

of Great Britain
and Northern Ireland

Postcode Area and District Boundaries
Central London Sector Boundaries
Plus Major Cities at improved scale

Bartholomew
An Imprint of HarperCollinsPublishers

Published by Bartholomew
An Imprint of HarperCollins*Publishers*
77-85 Fulham Palace Road, Hammersmith
London W6 8JB

Postcode Atlas Copyright © Bartholomew
Postcode Boundaries & Codes Copyright © The Post Office

First published 1989
New edition 1994
New edition 1995

ISBN 0 7028 2937 4

Printed in Hong Kong

HV 7917

CONTENTS

INDEX OF POSTCODE AREAS

Post-Code	Area	Post-Code	Area	Post-Code	Area
AB	Aberdeen	HA	Harrow	PO	Portsmouth
AL	St. Albans	HD	Huddersfield	PR	Preston
B	Birmingham	HG	Harrogate	RG	Reading
BA	Bath	HP	Hemel Hempstead	RH	Redhill
BB	Blackburn	HR	Hereford	RM	Romford
BD	Bradford	HS	Hebrides	S	Sheffield
BH	Bournemouth	HU	Hull	SA	Swansea
BL	Bolton	HX	Halifax	SE	London SE
BN	Brighton	IG	Ilford	SG	Stevenage
BR	Bromley	IM	Isle of Man	SK	Stockport
BS	Bristol	IP	Ipswich	SL	Slough
BT	Belfast	IV	Inverness	SM	Sutton
CA	Carlisle	KA	Kilmarnock	SN	Swindon
CB	Cambridge	KT	Kingston-upon-Thames	SO	Southampton
CF	Cardiff	KW	Kirkwall	SP	Salisbury
CH	Chester	KY	Kirkcaldy	SR	Sunderland
CM	Chelmsford	L	Liverpool	SS	Southend-on-Sea
CO	Colchester	LA	Lancaster	ST	Stoke-on-Trent
CR	Croydon	LD	Llandrindod Wells	SW	London SW
CT	Canterbury	LE	Leicester	SY	Shrewsbury
CV	Coventry	LL	Llandudno	TA	Taunton
CW	Crewe	LN	Lincoln	TD	Galashiels
DA	Dartford	LS	Leeds	TF	Telford
DD	Dundee	LU	Luton	TN	Tunbridge Wells
DE	Derby	M	Manchester	TQ	Torquay
DG	Dumfries	ME	Medway	TR	Truro
DH	Durham	MK	Milton Keynes	TS	Cleveland
DL	Darlington	ML	Motherwell	TW	Twickenham
DN	Doncaster	N	London N	UB	Southall
DT	Dorchester	NE	Newcastle upon Tyne	W	London W
DY	Dudley	NG	Nottingham	WA	Warrington
E	London E	NN	Northampton	WC	London WC
EC	London EC	NP	Newport	WD	Watford
EH	Edinburgh	NR	Norwich	WF	Wakefield
EN	Enfield	NW	London NW	WN	Wigan
EX	Exeter	OL	Oldham	WR	Worcester
FK	Falkirk	OX	Oxford	WS	Walsall
FY	Blackpool	PA	Paisley	WV	Wolverhampton
G	Glasgow	PE	Peterborough	YO	York
GL	Gloucester	PH	Perth	ZE	Lerwick
GU	Guildford	PL	Plymouth		

BARTHOLOMEW POSTCODE PUBLICATIONS AND DIGITAL DATA

POSTCODE AREA MAP

The Planners Postcode Area Map shows boundaries and code letters for all postcode areas in the UK at a scale of 1:792 000. An index chart to the postcode areas is also shown.

POSTCODE DISTRICT MAPS

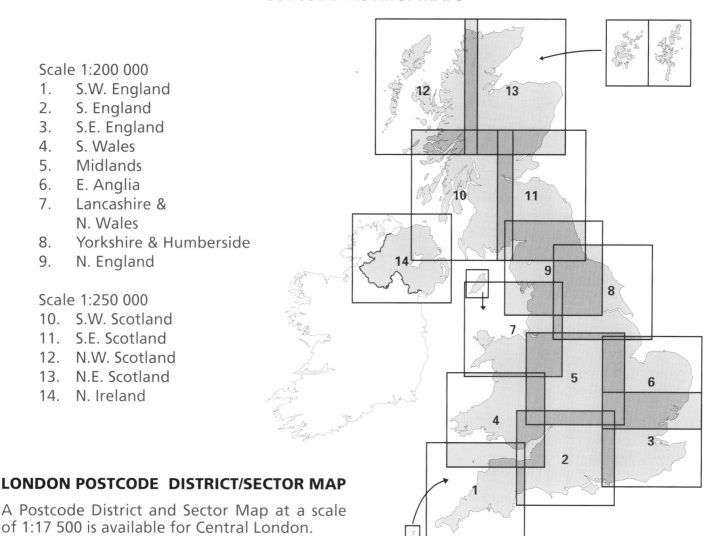

Scale 1:200 000
1.   S.W. England
2.   S. England
3.   S.E. England
4.   S. Wales
5.   Midlands
6.   E. Anglia
7.   Lancashire &
     N. Wales
8.   Yorkshire & Humberside
9.   N. England

Scale 1:250 000
10. S.W. Scotland
11. S.E. Scotland
12. N.W. Scotland
13. N.E. Scotland
14. N. Ireland

LONDON POSTCODE DISTRICT/SECTOR MAP

A Postcode District and Sector Map at a scale of 1:17 500 is available for Central London.

POSTCODE MAPS

Postcode Area and District Maps plus the Central London District and Sector Map are published by Bartholomew and are available from: HarperCollins Distribution Services, PO Box, Glasgow G4 ONB. Tel: 041 772 3200. Fax: 041 762 0584

DIGITAL DATA

Digital data are available for Postcode Sector and District boundaries of the UK.This information is supplied on floppy disks or magnetic tapes in a number of different formats. For further information: Data Sales Co-ordinator, Bartholomew/Times, HarperCollins Publishers, 77-85 Fulham Palace Road, London , W6 8JB. Tel: 081 307 4065. Fax: 081 307 4813.

USES OF POSTCODES

The structure of the Postcode system provides an established grid for the detailed research, analysis and planning involved in modern business management. The system offers a variety of different sized, readily identifiable geographic units ranging from the 121 Postcode Areas illustrated at the beginning of this atlas, down to small groups of individual addresses. It proves a ready made reference base with built-in flexibility.

ADMINISTRATION

For example, a firm's area manager may be responsible for Postcode Area ST (Stoke-on Trent), his district supervisor responsible for Postcode Districts ST1 to ST10 and one representative responsible for Postcode Sectors 1 to 8 within one of these Districts. In this way any customer's Postcode gives a complete and immediate key to all those who handle his account. Whatever the size of the company, and however many representatives it has there are tailor-made geographical units within the Postcode system.

PLANNING

Postcodes are suitable for computer applications and Postcode maps are readily available. Postcode Districts can be grouped together to form sales and marketing areas - the basic units for planning and control. In the same way these units can be used to define distribution or franchise areas.

RESEARCH AND SCHEDULING

Some companies use composite Postcode maps to target customers by market research statistics. A list of prospective customers is sorted by Postcode then penetration is measured in terms of goods sold. Other companies use Postcode District maps to plan optimum delivery routes for their fleets of vans, whilst others organise door drops of advertising material by Postcode Sectors and code response to mail shots by Postcodes. High response Sectors can then be targeted for cold calling.

ANALYSIS

Market analysis in the form of Postcode-related turnover comparisons for different areas is widely used and Postcode-based schemes such as those outlined here allow for much greater accuracy and efficiency.

ADDITIONAL APPLICATIONS

Postcodes are also used for insurance premium assessment and are increasingly used by government departments as units for planning and population census.

ADVANTAGES

The postcode system is well established, universal (every address in the United Kingdom is Postcoded), practical and versatile. It enables analysis of company computerised sales statistical data on a regional or national basis, aids efficiency and is a substantial cost saver. In short, Postcodes make an ideal national reference system on which to base company information.

MAPS AND DATA

Postcode Area and District Maps plus the Central London District and Sector Map are published by Bartholomew. (See page vii for details)

In addition, digital data are available to facilitate the use of Postcodes. (See page vii for details)

STRUCTURE OF POSTCODES

POSTCODE MAPS

Postcodes operate at four levels.

Level 1. Areas are denoted by the first one or two letters of the code, eg **ST**. These areas are broken down into districts.

Level 2. Districts are denoted by the number or numbers in the first part of the postcode. eg ST**4** Districts are subdivided into sectors.

Level 3. Sectors are denoted by the number in the second part of the postcode. eg ST4 **5**

Level 4. This will denote a group of houses or an individual building. eg ST4 5**RD**

All postcode areas and districts are featured in this atlas.

Postcode sectors are not shown on the maps in this atlas with the exception of sectors in Central London.

ST (Stoke-on-Trent) is one of the postcode **areas** in the UK.

ST4 is a district within postcode area ST.

ST4 5 is a sector in ST4 postcode district.

ST4 5RD is the **POSTCODE**. It pinpoints a group of houses and in some cases individual business premises.

KEY TO ATLAS MAPS

Area Code	Boundary	District Code	Boundary
ST	━━	4	──

A

B

C

D

E

F

G

TR

ISLES OF SCILLY

same scale as main map

St Helen's
White Island
Lower Town
Tean
Old Grimsby
St Martin's
Middle Town
KING CHARLES
& CROMWELL
25
New Grimsby
Higher Town
Bryher
24
TRESCO
ABBEY
& GDNS
23
Eastern Isles
Samson
CARN
Crow Sound
CHAMBERED CAIRNS
Maypole
21
St Mary's
Hugh
Town
PORTH HELLICK DOWN
BURIAL CHAMBER
Scilly Isles
Penzance
The Garrison
Old Town
GARRISON
WALLS
Crim Rocks
Broad Sound
22
St Mary's Sound
Annet
Gugh
Western
Rocks
St Agnes
Smith Sound
Bishop Rock

Towan H
Newq
Fistral B
Pentire
Kelsey Head
West Pentire
Holywell
Holywell
Penhale Point
Ligger Pt
Mour
Ligger
or
Perran Bay
Penhale
Sands
Perranporth
Rose
6
Bawden Rocks
or
Man and his Man
Trevella
Bolingey
Perranza
St Agnes Head
Penhallow
St Agnes
Mithian
Calle
5
Goonbell
A3075
Porthtowan
Mount
Hawke
Three
Burrows
Tregavethan
Short
A30
Portreath
Mawla
Blackwater
Chacewater
Three
Crane Islands
Navax Point
Illogan
Bridge
St Day
Baldi
Coombe
Redruth
Cross Lar
Godrevy Island
15
16
Twelveh
Kehelland
Pool
Carharrack
Bisho
Gwithian
BARBARA HEPWORTH
MUSEUM
The Island
St Ives Bay
Roseworthy
Camborne
Lanner
Pennance
Gwennap
A393
Carn Naun
Pt
The Carrack's
26
Halsetown
Carbis Bay
Connor Downs
Four Lanes
Ponsanooth
St Ives
Phillack
Angarrack
Barripper
Troon
Renhalven
Gumard's Head
Zennor
Trendrine
Hill
Towednack
A3074
Gwinear
Carnhell
Green
27
Hayle
Lelant
Roseworne
Praze-an-Beeble
Porthmeor
Amalebra
Trencrom
Hill
St Erth
Praze
Long
Downs
Penryn
Pendeen Watch
Nancledra
Canon's Town
Whitecross
St Erth
Fradden
Leedstown
Burras
Lower Boscaswell
Morvah
20
New Mill
Luggvan
Townshend
Crowan
Porkellis
Name
10
Mabe
Burnthouse
Trewellard
Pendeen
CHYSAUSTER
ANCIENT VILLAGE
Crowlas
Nancegollan
Budock
Water
Botallack
Bojewyan
Madron
A30
Godolphin
Cross
Wendron
Seworgan
Falm
Cape Cornwall
The Brisons
Carnyorth
St Just
Newbridge
Heamoor
Gulval
St Hilary
Goldsithney
Trescowe
Crowntown
13
Brill
11
CARN LESKYS
Bosavern
Tremethick Cross
18
Chyandour
Marazion
GODOLPHIN
HOUSE
Mawnan
Smith
Kelynack
Sancreed
Buryas
Bridge
St Michael's
Mount
Tregonning
Hill
Sithney
Porth Navas
Whitesand
Bay
Barnes
Lowe
Drift
Penzance
17
A394
Germoe
Breage
Constantine
Helston
Gweek
Sennen Cove
19
Catchall
Newlyn
Perranuthnoe
Ashton
Helford
Longships
Sennen
Kerris
Mousehole
Praa Sands
Rinsey
Garras
Mawgan
St Martin
Manaccan
Trevescan
St Buryan
Boleigh
St Clement's Isle
Cudden Point
Porthleven
A3083
Newtown in
St Martin
Tregidden
LAND'S END
BOLEIGH
STONE CIRCLE
Trewavas Head
MOUNT'S
Gunwalloe
Berepper
Cury
St Keverne
Porthcurno
Treen
Lamorna Cove
Crosslanes
12
Traboe
St Levan
Cribba Head
Logan Rock
BAY
Poldhu Cove
Poldhu Point
Mullion
Goonhilly
Downs
Gwennap Head
Mullion Cove
Fenhale
Gwenter
Scilly Isles
Port Mellin
Mullion Island
Ruan
Major
Cov
Predannack Wollas
Koggar
Black Hea
Ruan Minor
Vellan Head
A3083
Grade
Cadgwith
Toll
Wolf Rock
Kynance Cove
Landewednack
Lizard
Hot Point
LIZARD POINT

0 2 4 6 8 10 miles
0 2 4 6 8 10 km

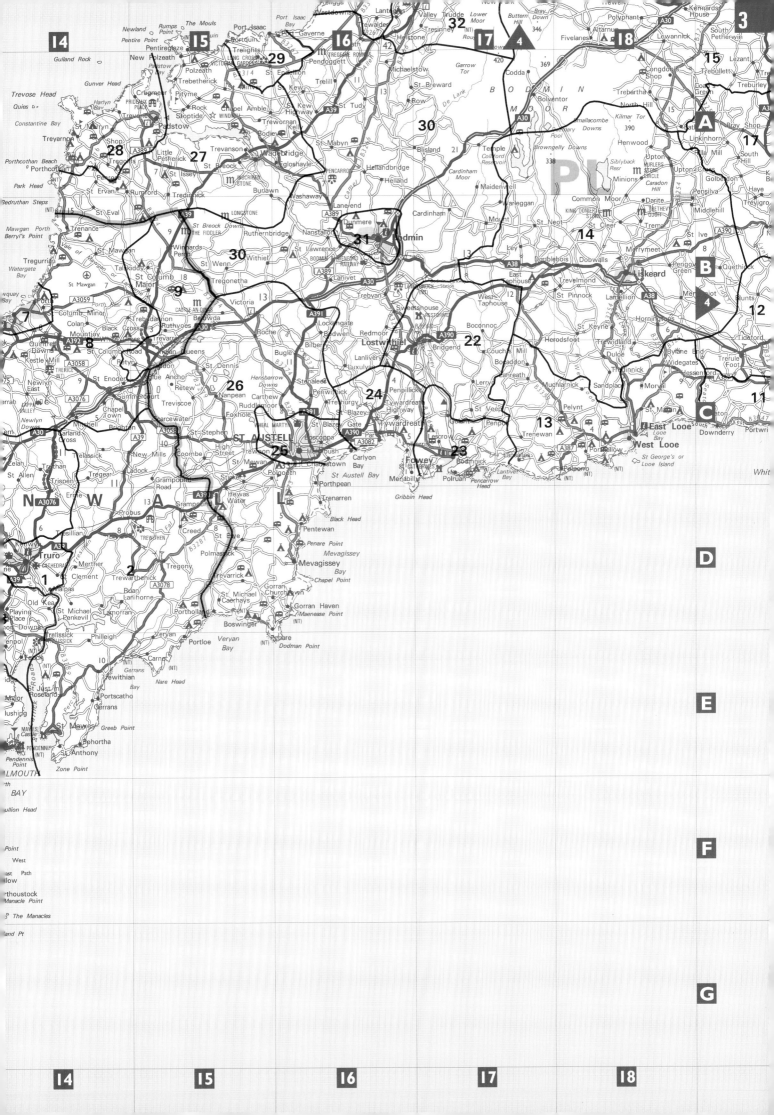

BUCKINGHAM
HIGH WYCOMBE
CHESHAM
Amersham
Beaconsfield
Chorleywood
RICKMANSWORTH
WATFORD
HEMEL HEMPSTEAD
Berkhamsted
Tring
Wendover
Princes Risborough
Thame
Haddenham
Long Crendon
Aylesbury
Great Missenden
Marlow
Henley-on-Thames
MAIDENHEAD
SLOUGH
Eton
WINDSOR
Old Windsor
HILLINGDON
HARROW
Ruislip
Uxbridge
Hayes
Southall
HOUNSLOW
STAINES
SUNBURY
WALTON-ON-THAMES
ESHER
Weybridge
Chertsey
Addlestone
Byfleet
WOKING
Chobham
Bisley
Lightwater
Bagshot
Windlesham
Sunninghill
Ascot
BRACKNELL
Wokingham
Binfield
Twyford
Sonning
READING
Caversham
Whitley
Crowthorne
Sandhurst
CAMBERLEY
FRIMLEY
FARNBOROUGH
FLEET
ALDERSHOT
FARNHAM
Odiham
Hook
GUILDFORD
Godalming
Cranleigh
DORKING
Cobham
Leatherhead
Alton
Stokenchurch
Nettlebed
Purley on Thames
Tilehurst
Mortimer
Wellington
Hartley Wintney
Eversley
Yateley
Frensham
Milford
Shalford
Great Bookham
Effingham
East Horsley
West Horsley
Ripley
Send
Ockham
Shere
Gomshall
Abinger Hammer
Holmbury St Mary
Wotton
Westcott
A40
M40
A404
A404(M)
A4010
A41
A413
A416
A329(M)
M4
M25
M3
A30
A31
A3
A287
A325
A331
A322
A320
A308
A4
A412
43
44
45
46
47
32
21
12

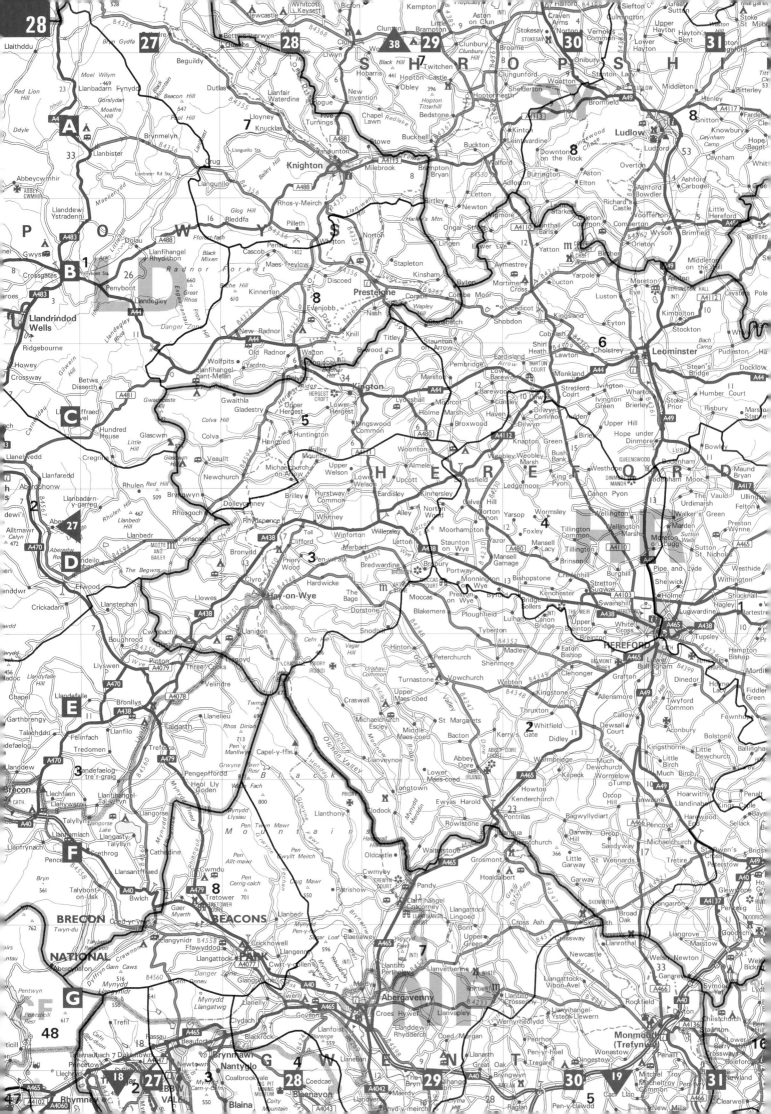

See page 111 for Postcode detail

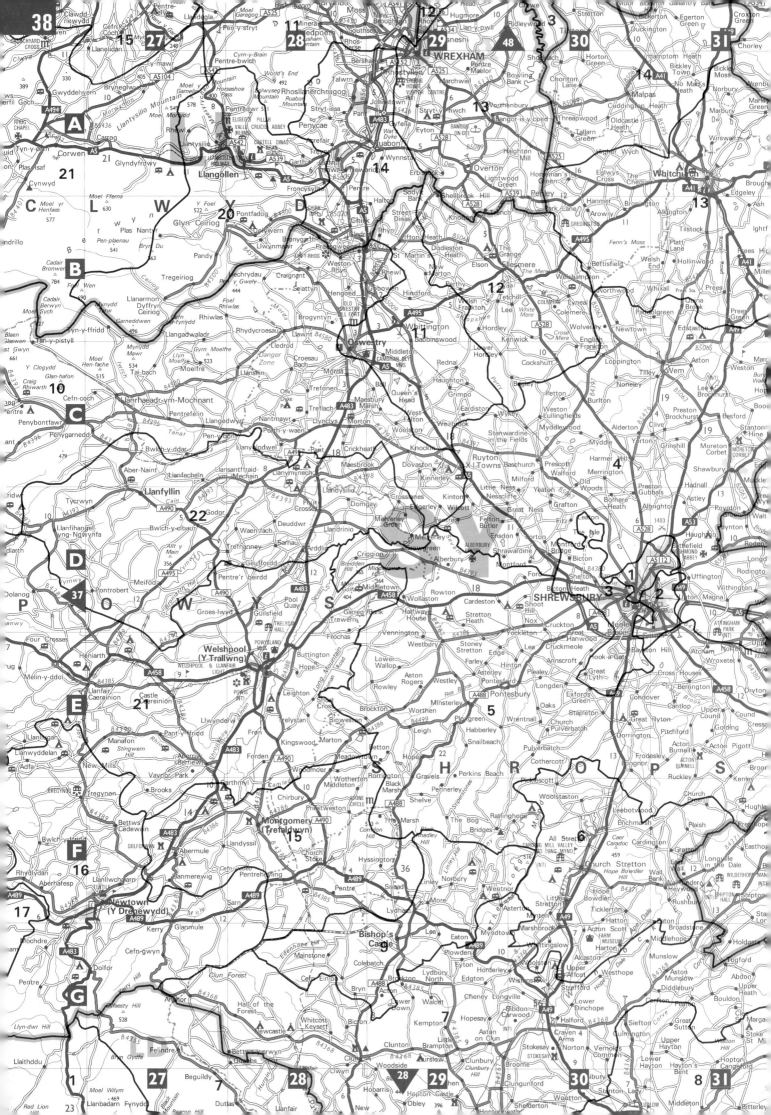

See page 111 for Postcode detail

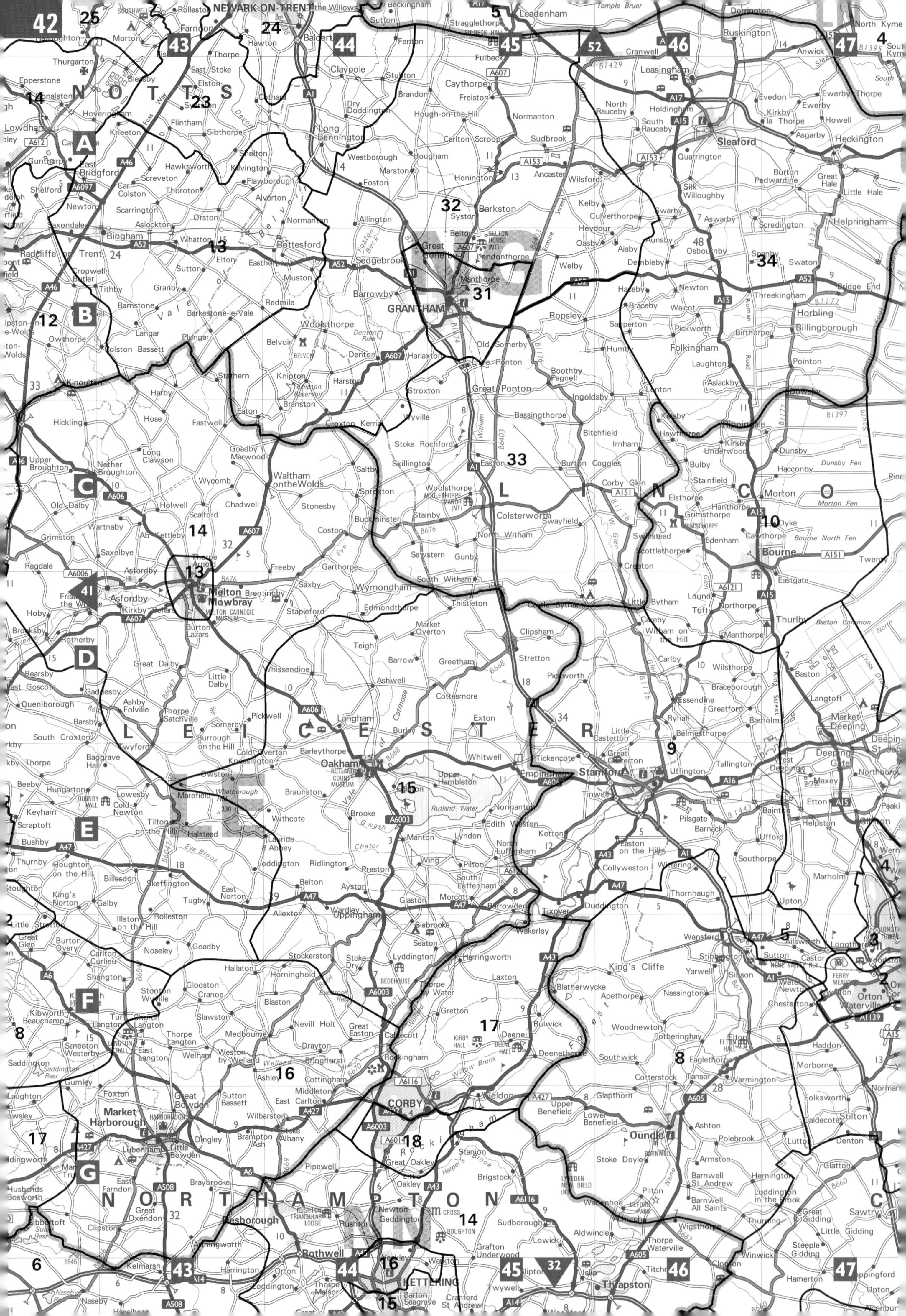

THE WASH

Boston Deeps · **Long Sand** · **Lynn Deeps** · **Roger Sand** · **Toft Sand** · **Gat Sand** · **Black Buoy Sand** · **The Scalp** · **Mare Tail** · **Old South** · **Seal Sand** · **Peter Black Sand** · **Danger Zone** · **Breast Sand** · **Bulldog Sand** · **Old Lynn Channel** · **Great Ouse**

Wildmore Fen · Leake Common Side · Wrangle · Wrangle Bank · Friskney Flats · Brancaster
Gipsey Bridge · Sibsey · Old Leake · Leake Hurn's End · Leverton Outgate · Holme next the Sea · Titchwell · Thornham
Trader Windmill · 53 · 49 · 22 · 50 · 51 · 52
Langriville · Fishtoft Drove · Frith Bank · Hill Dyke · Leverton · Benington Sea End · Ringstead · 36
Amber Hill · Brothertoft · Hubbert's Bridge · BOSTON · GUILDHALL · Halltoft End · Butterwick · Freiston · Benington Sea End · Hunstanton · A149
Holland Fen · Witham · Skirbeck · 21 · Butterwick Low · Freiston Shore · Heacham · Sedgeford · B1454
Swineshead Bridge · Kirton Holme · Frampton West End · Scrane End · Southgate · Snett · Fring · Great
Swineshead · Fenhouses · Kirton End · Wyberton · Sandholme · Frampton · Ingoldisthorpe · Shernborne · Peddars Way
Drayton · Algarkirk · Kirton · Skeldyke · A149 · Dersingham · 31 · Anm
A17 · 20 · A16 · Fosdyke · Holbeach St Matthew · Wolferton · Sandringham · 35 · West Newton · B153 · Flitcham · A148
Church End · Hoffleet Stow · 4 Wigtoft · Holbeach St Marks · Dawsmere · North Wootton · Castle Rising · Hillington
Quadring Eaudike · Sutterton · Surfleet · Holbeach Marsh · Gedney Marsh · Gedney Drove End · Ongar Hill · South Wootton · Babingley · Trinity Hospital · Congham · Roydon
Gosberton · Surfleet Seas End · Whaplode Marsh · Holbeach Hurn · B1359 · Lutton Marsh · King's Lynn · Pott Row · Grimston
Spalding · Moulton Seas End · Holbeach Bank · Gedney Dyke · Fleet Hargate · Chapelgate · Lutton · Guy's Head · Terrington Marsh · Gaywood · Ashwicken
LINCOLNSHIRE · Saracen's Head · Holbeach Clough · Gedney · Fleet · Long Sutton · Little London · Terrington St Clement · Clenchwarton · West Lynn · East Winch · East Walton
Whaplode · Holbeach · 26 · Gedney Broadgate · Sutton Crosses · Sutton Bridge · Walpole Cross Keys · Tilney All Saints · West Winch · Middleton · Blackborough End
Moulton · Weston · Weston Hills · Whaplode St Catherine · Sutton St James · Tydd St Mary · Walpole St Andrew · Walpole St Peter · Tilney High End · Terrington St John · Tilney St Lawrence · Middle Bow · North Runcton · Narborough · Pentney
Little London · Moulton Chapel · Holbeach St Johns · Tydd Gote · Four Gotes · St John's Highway · Tilney · Wiggenhall St Germans · Setchey · Wormegay
Cowbit · Moulton Fen · Tydd St Giles · Newton · West Walton · Walpole Highway · St Lawrence · Wiggenhall St Mary the Virgin · Runcton Holme · Marham
Deeping St Nicholas · Aswick Grange · Whaplode Drove · Sutton St Edmund · Fitton End · Gorefield · West Walton Highway · St John's Fen End · Wiggenhall St Mary Magdalen · Watlington · Shouldham · Shouldham Thorpe
South Holland · Holbeach Drove · Gedney Hill · Church End · Leverington · Walsoken · Marshland Fen · Thorpland · South Runcton · Fincham
Crowland · Crowland Abbey · Parson Drove · Wisbech St Mary · New Walsoken · Wisbech · Emneth · Stow Bardolph · Stowbridge · Stow Bardolph · Wimbotsham · Stradsett · 33
North Fen · Murrow · Tholomas Drove · Elm · Emneth Hungate · Wisbech · Bexwell · Crimplesham
Eye Green · Thorney · Wryde Croft · Guyhirn · Friday Bridge · Outwell · Middle Level Main · Downham Market · Boughton · Oxborough
Eye (North Level) · Ring's End · Coldham · Upwell · North District · Barroway Drove · Denver · West Dereham · Wereham
Priors Fen · Horse Lots Bridge · Laddus Fens · Three Holes · Nordelph · Fordham · Stoke Ferry · Whittington
Peterborough · Whittlesey · Elternell · Morton's Leam · White Moor · Westry · Euximoor Fen · Upwell Fen · Hilgay · Ten Mile Bank · 38 · Southery
Eastrea · Coates · West Fen · March · Binnimoor Fen · Christchurch · Lakesend · Hilgay Fen · Southery Fens · Methwold · 26
King's Delph · Town End · Welney · Gold Hill · Methwold Hythe · Thetford · Feltwell
Flag Fen · 15 · West Moor · Upwell Fen · Queen's Ground · B1386
Glass Moor · Ranson Moor · Wimblington · Bedford Level · Brandon Creek · Hockwold cum Wilton
Pondersbridge · White Fen · Benwick · Doddington · Manea · Wimblington Fen · Manea Sta. · Apes Hall · Brandon Bank · Hockwold Fens
Whittlesey Mere · The Herne · Middle Moor · Mere Side · Bedford Level (Middle Level) · Horseway · Purls Bridge · Pymore · Burnt Fen
Ramsey Mereside · Ramsey Forty Foot · West Moor · Welches Dam · Langwood Fen · Little Downham · Shippea Hill · Grime Fen · Wangford
Ramsey St Mary's · Ramsey Hollow · Ramsey Abbey · Chatteris · Horseley Fen · Ely · Chettisham · Padnal Fen · Prickwillow · Wangford Fen · 27
Ramsey Heights · Ramsey · Bury · Tick Fen · Somersham High North Fen · Pidley Fen · Coveney · Wardy Hill · Queen Adelaide · Lakenheath · The Delph
Wistow · CAMBRIDGESHIRE · Mepal · Witcham · Witchford · Kennyhill · Eriswell · Holywell
Upwood · Warboys · Fenton · Pidley · Somersham · Sutton · Wentworth · Stuntney · Mildenhall Fen · 28
Great Raveley · Little Raveley · 49 · 50 · 51 · 52
Wennington · Abbots Ripton · Broughton · Somersham · Chatteris Fen · 33 · B1381
48 · 17 · 48

Grid panel letters: A · B · C · D · E · F · G · K
Numbered tiles: 48 · 53 · 49 · 22 · 50 · 51 · 52 · 36 · 31 · 35 · 30 · 34 · 33 · 44 · 37 · 26 · 27 · 28 · 38 · 20 · 21 · 12 · 13 · 14 · 15 · 16 · 6 · 7

Road numbers: A16 · A52 · A1121 · A17 · A1391 · A1101 · A1073 · A151 · A1066 · A47 · A10 · A134 · A148 · A149 · A1078 · A141 · A142 · A605 · B1040 · B1050 · B1093 · B1098 · B1099 · B1165 · B1166 · B1357 · B1359 · B1411

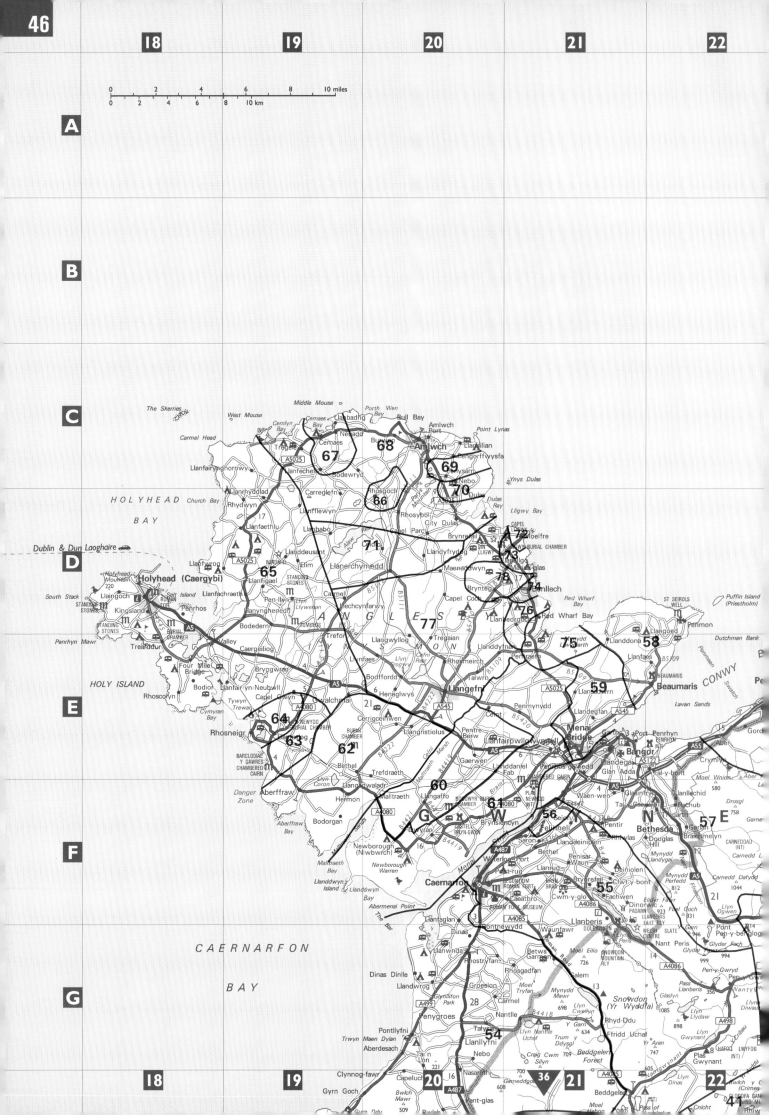

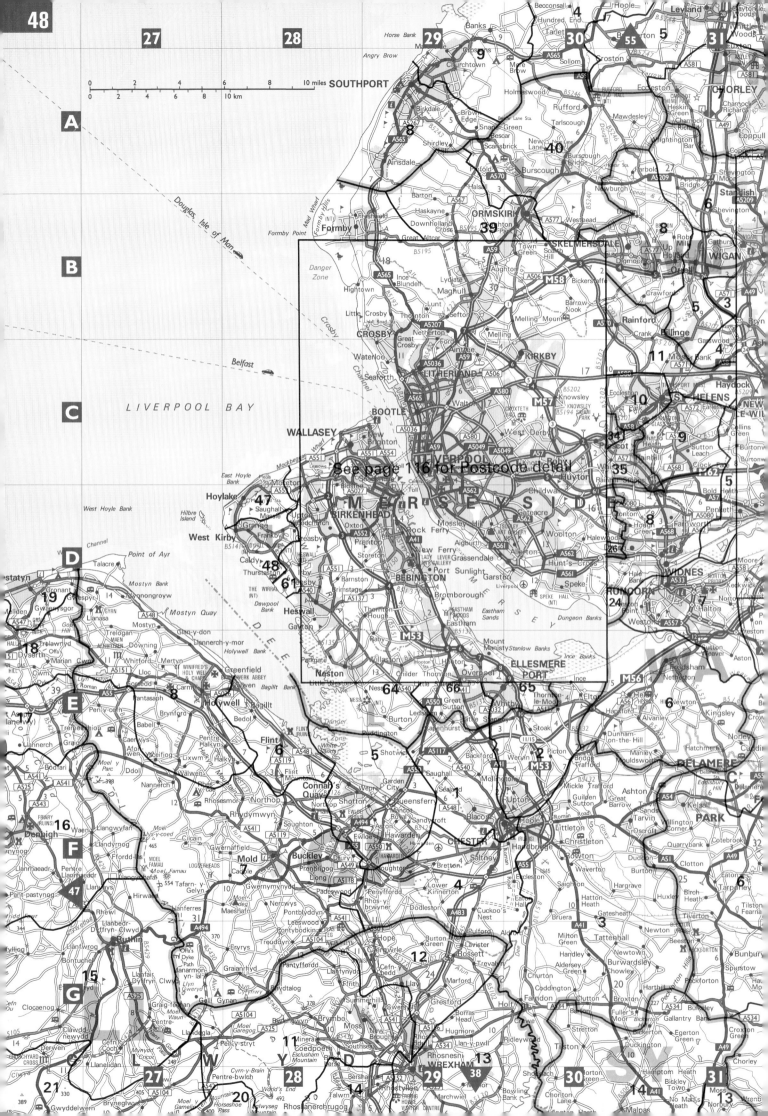

See pages 112 - 113 for Postcode detail

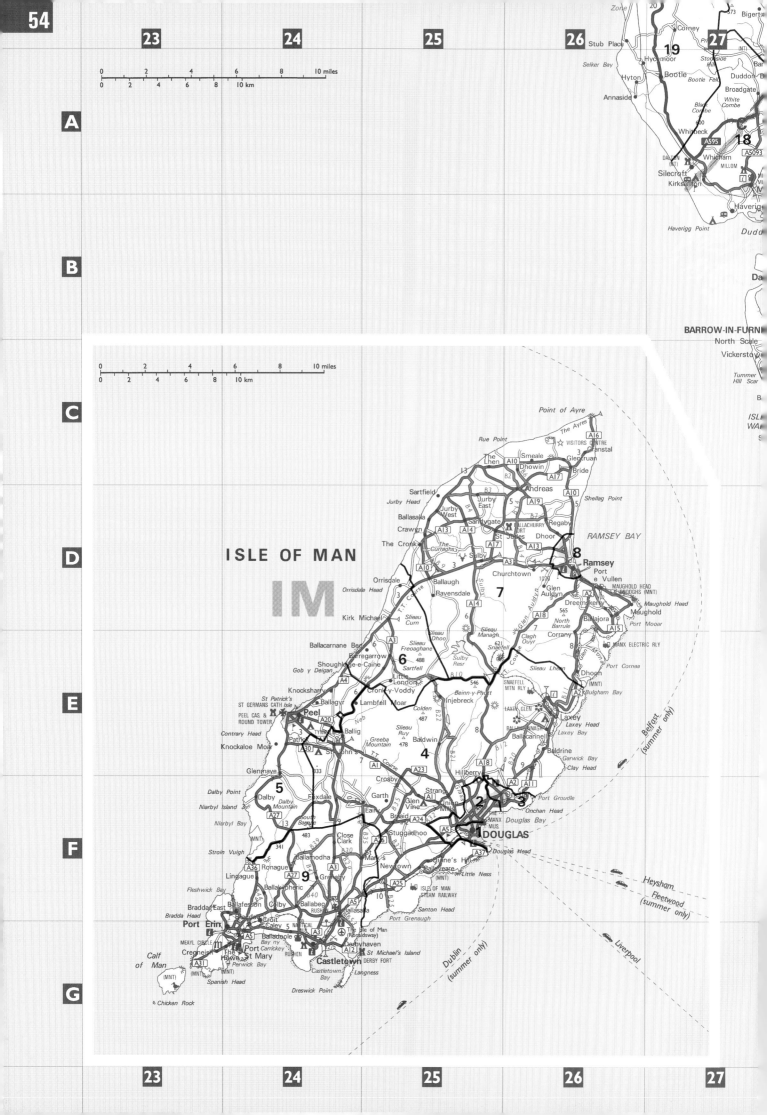

See pages 114 - 115 for Postcode detail

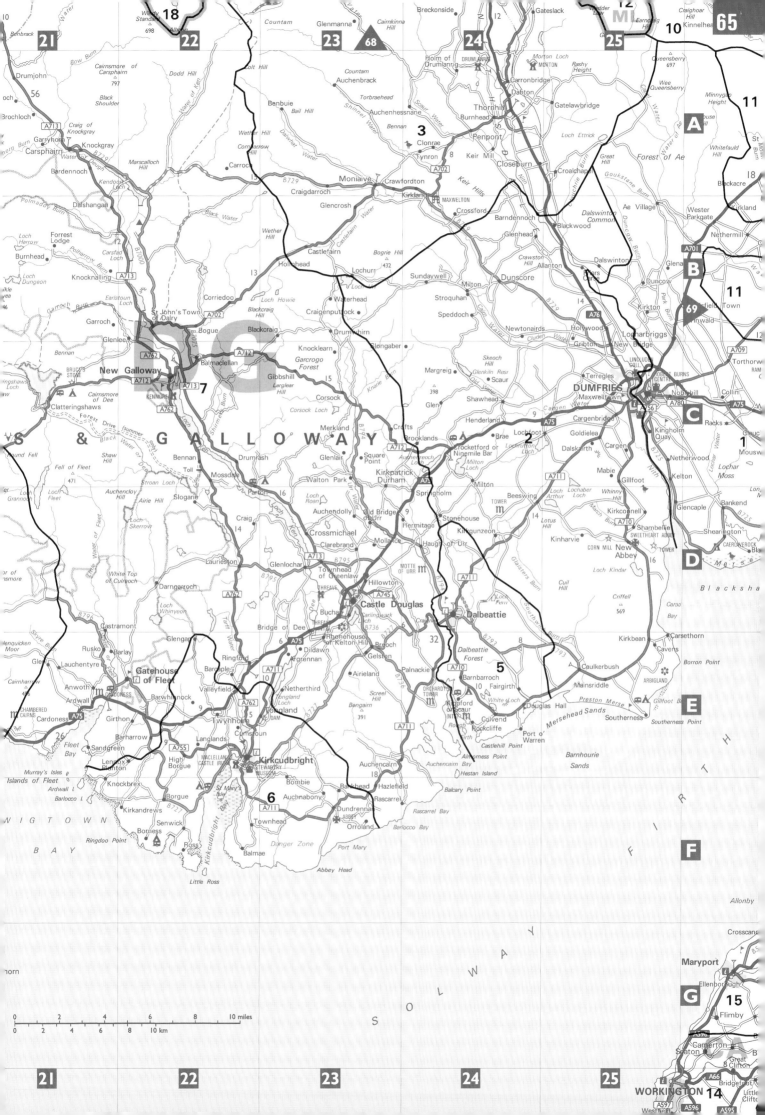

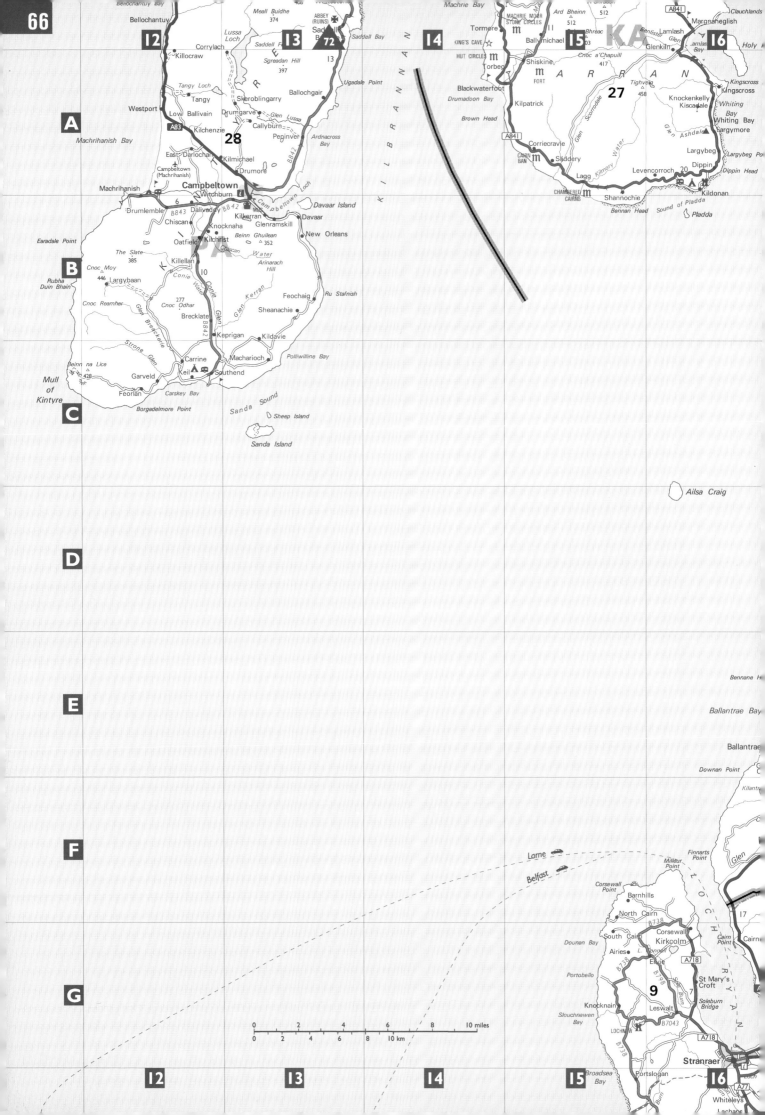

A

Bellochantuy Bay
Bellochantuy
Meall Buidhe 374
Machrie Bay
ABBEY (RUINS)
72
MACHRIE MOOR STONE CIRCLES
Ard Bheinn 512
512
Bhreac 03
A841
Clauchlands
Magnaheglish
Corrylach
Lussa Loch
Saddell Bay
Saddell Bay
Tormore
Ballymichael
Cnoc a'Chapuill 417
Lamlash
Larnlash Bay
Holy I
Killocraw
Saddell Fo
Sgreadan Hill 397
13
KING'S CAVE
Shiskine
MAARRAN
Glenkiln
Tangy
Ballochgair
HUT CIRCLES
Torbeg
FORT
Tighvein 458
Kingscross
Kingscross
Low Ballivain
Tangy Loch
Blackwaterfoot
27
Knockenkelly
Kiscadale
Whiting Bay
Westport
Skeroblingarry
Ugadale Point
Drumadoon Bay
Kilpatrick
Whiting Bay
A83
Drumgarve
Glen Lussa
Brown Head
Largymore
Kilchenzie
28
Callyburn
Pepinver
Ardnacross Bay
A841
Largybeg
Largybeg Head
East Darlochan
Kilmichael
Corriecravie
Sliddery
Glen Ashdale
Dippin
Campbeltown (Machrihanish)
Drumore
CAIRN BAN
Lagg
Levencorroch
20
Dippin Head
Machrihanish
Campbeltown
Witchburn
CHAMBERED CAIRNS
Shannochie
Kildonan
Machrihanish Bay
Drumlemble
Dalivaddy
Campbeltown Loch
Davaar Island
Bennan Head
Sound of Pladda
Pladda
Chiscan
Kilkerran
Davaar
New Orleans
Oatfield
Kilchrist
Beinn Ghuilean 352
Killellan
Chiscan Water
Arinarach Hill
Ailsa Craig

B

Cnoc Moy 446
Largybaan
The Slate 385
Conie Water
10
Glen Kerran
Feochaig
Ru Stafnish
Rubha Duin Bhain
Cnoc Reamhar
277 Cnoc Odhar
Brecklate
B842
Sheanachie
Earadale Point

C

Beinn na Lice 428
Carrine
Keil
Southend
Macharioch
Polliwilline Bay
Garveld
Feorlan
Mull of Kintyre
Carskey Bay
Borgadelmore Point
Sanda Sound
Sheep Island
Sanda Island

D

E

Bennane H
Ballantrae Bay
Ballantrae
Downan Point
Kilantr

F

Larne
Belfast
Finnarts Point
Milleur Point
Corsewall Point
Barnhills
North Cairn
South Cairn
Dounan Bay
Corsewall Point
Cairn Point
Cairn
17
Kirkcolm
Aires
Ervie
A718
Portobello
St Mary's Croft

G

9
Knocknain
Leswalt
Soleburn Bridge
Slouchnwen Bay
LOCHN
B7043
Broadsea Bay
Stranraer
Portslogan
A718
Whiteleys
Lechan

0   2   4   6   8   10 miles
0   2   4   6   8   10 km

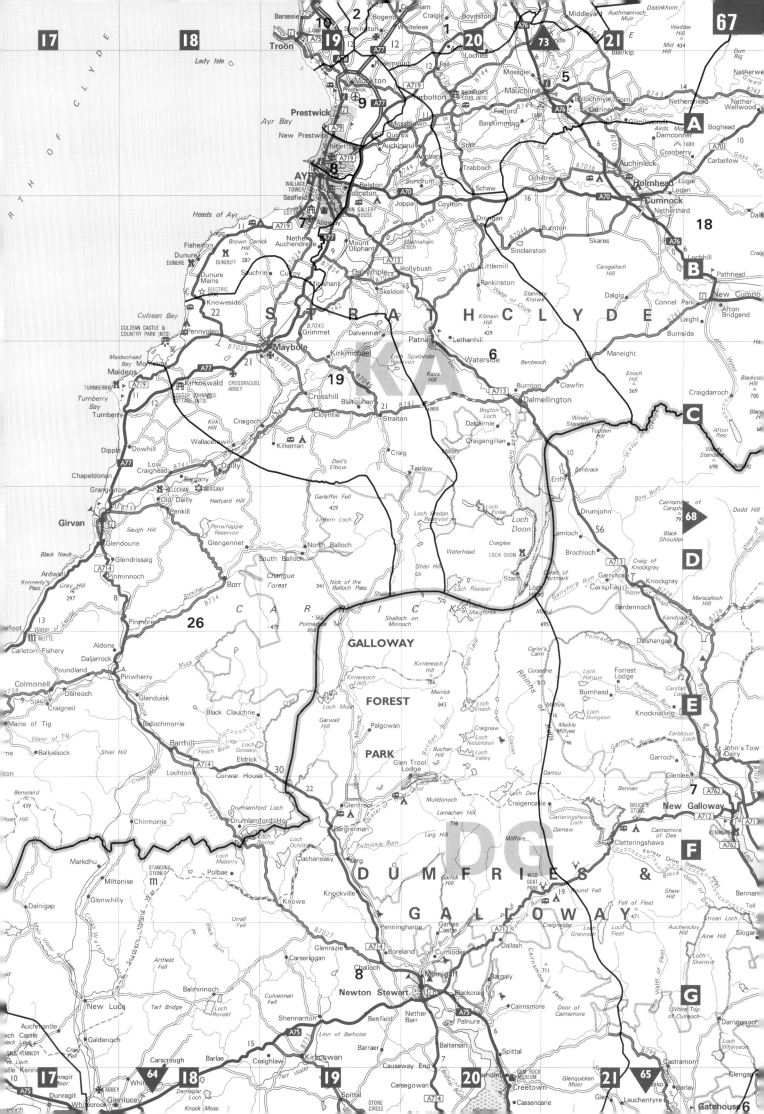

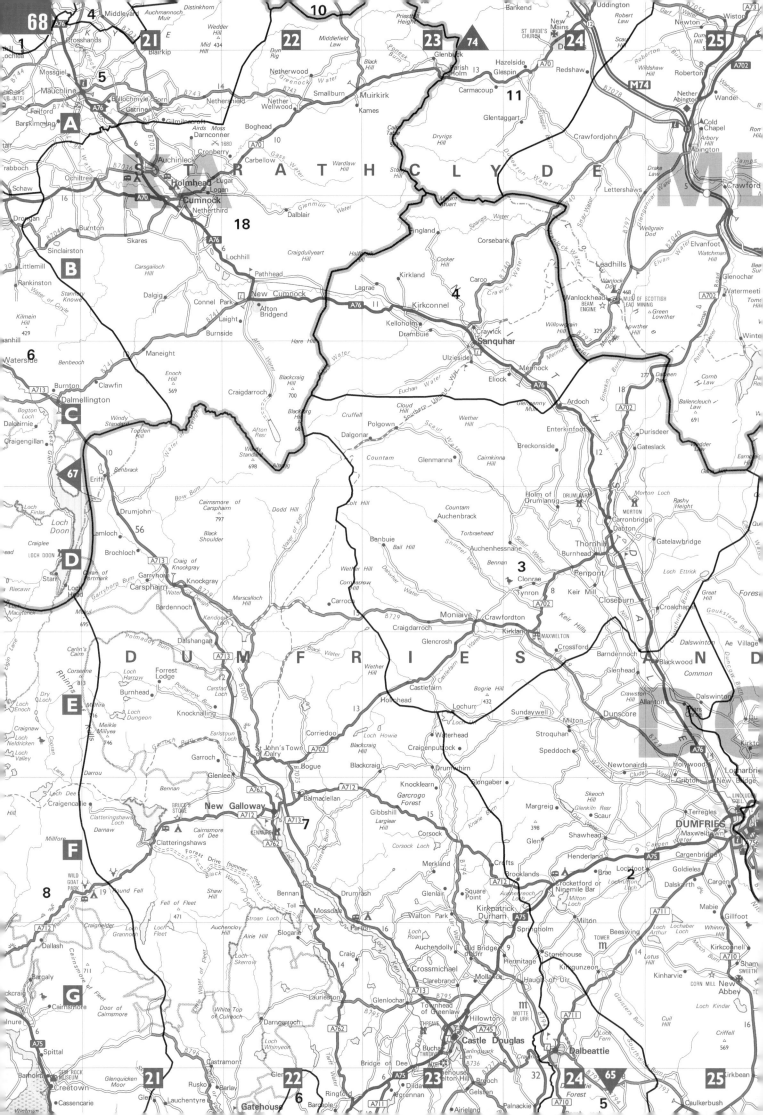

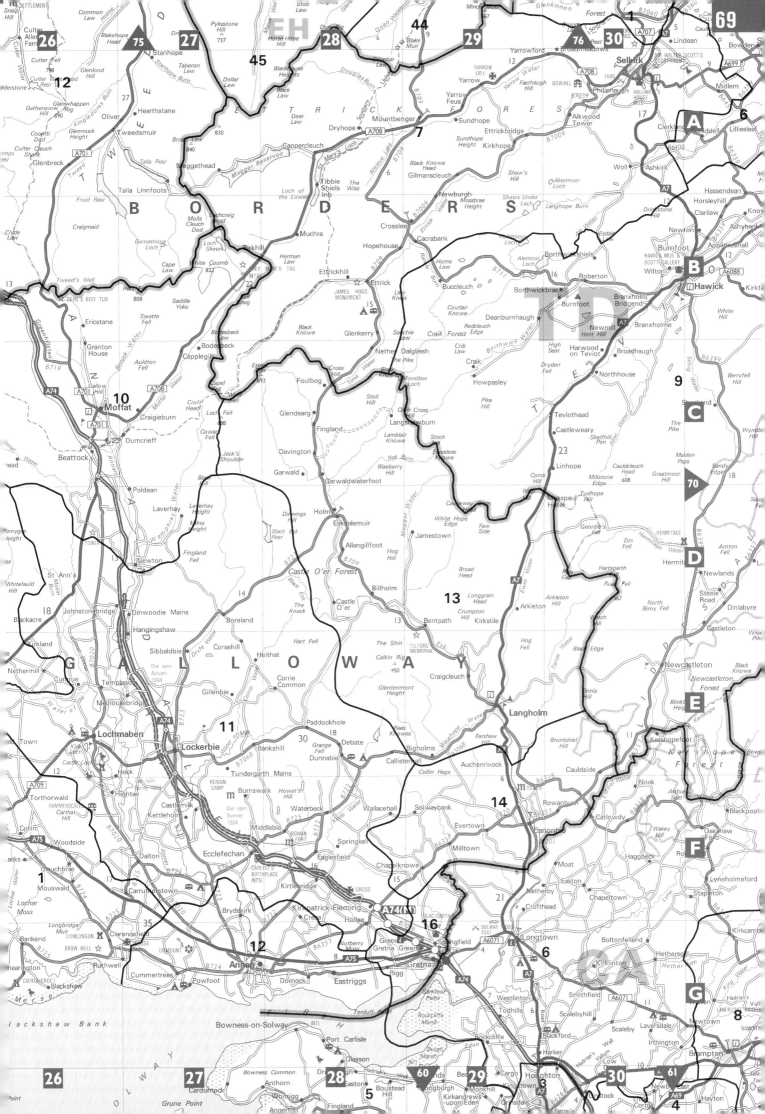

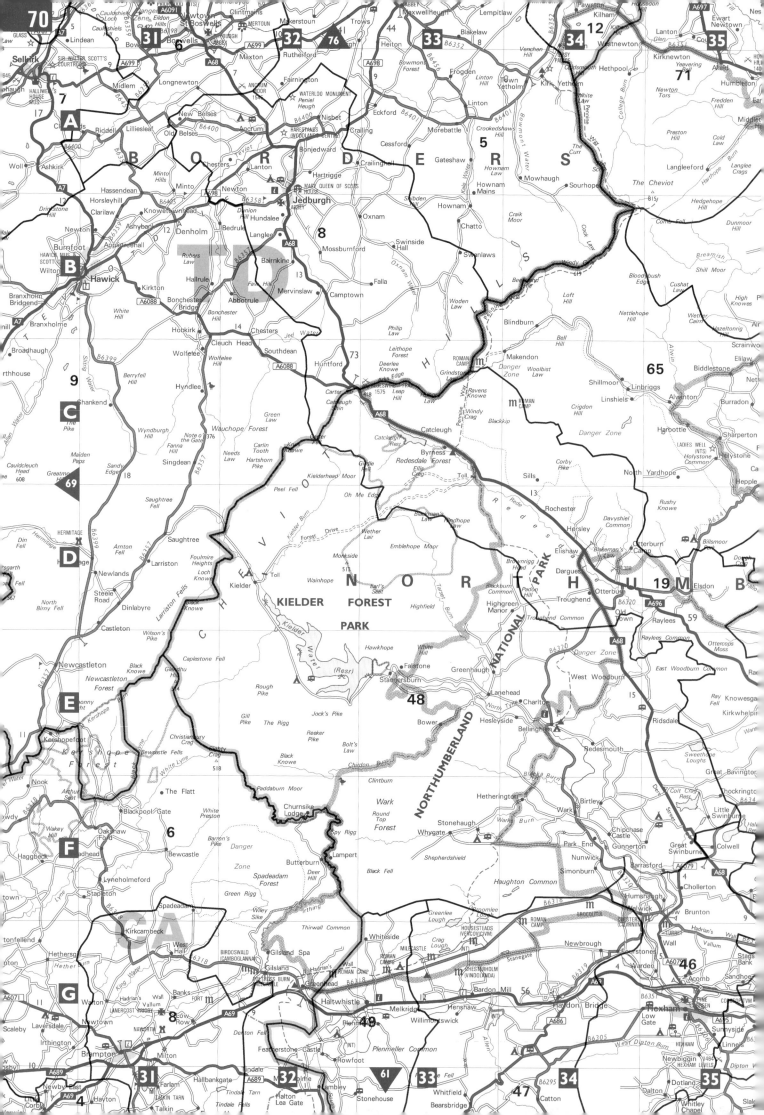

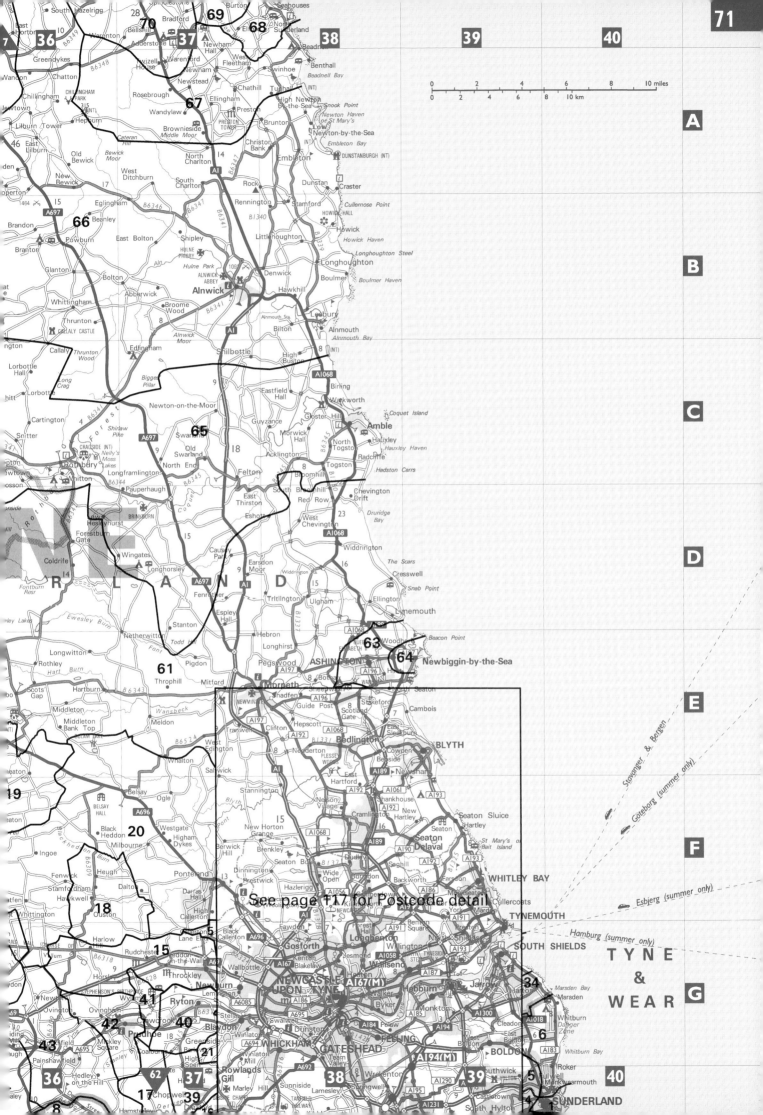

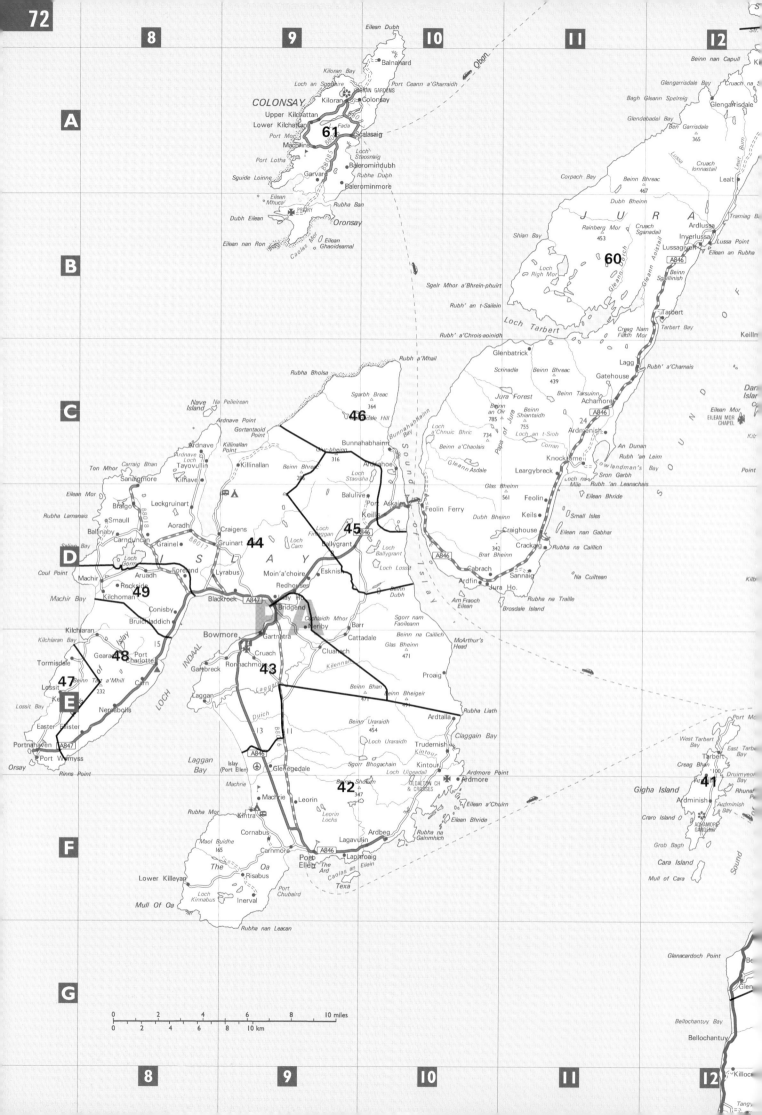

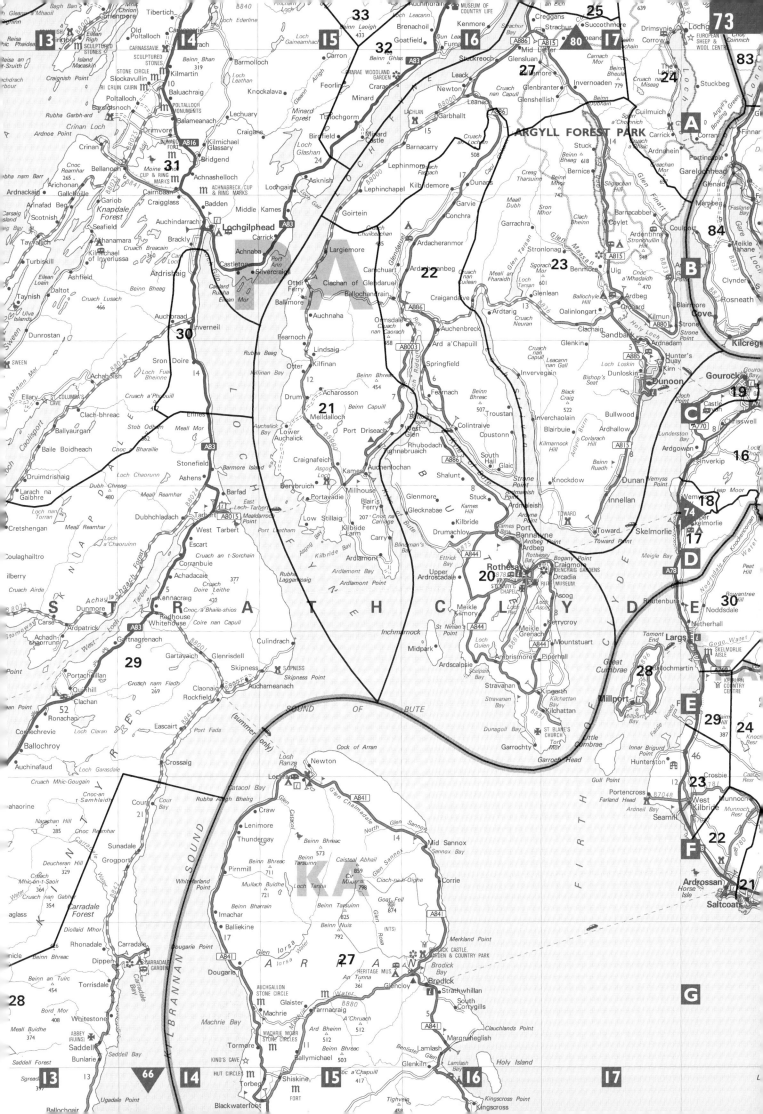

33   34   35   36   37

0   2   4   6   8   10 miles
0   2   4   6   8   10 km

A

B

C

Barns Ness
Skateraw   Skateraw Harbour
Thorntonloch
wick
Bilsdean   Reed Point
DOUGLASS   Pease
CHURCH   Bay
Cockburnspath   Siccar Point   FAST   Wheat Stack
amstocks
Telegraph
Hill
13   Lumsdaine
Ecclaw   A1   Meikle   Coldingham   St Abb's Head
Black Law   Loch   (NTS)
Ecclaw   A1107   Cross   Northfield
Hill   Law   Coldingham   St Abbs
Way   Blackburn Rig   Moor   12   Coldingham Bay
Laughing   Grantshouse   PRESS
Law   R   Houndwood   PRIORY
Southern   14   Coldingham   MUS
ABBEY &   U   Cairncross   Eyemouth
TROUT FARM   Eye   Ale Water
bey St Bathans   M   Horseley   20   B6438   Reston
nford   Hill   Auchencrow   Ayton   Ayton   Burnmouth
R   Drakemire   Ayton
Cockburn   Marygold   B64   Hilton Bay
Law   Whiteadder Water   Millerton   8   Lamberton
EDIN'S HALL   Hill   Beach
BROCH   A6112   Lintlaw   B6355   Lamberton
B6355   Preston   Chirnside   TITHE   Needles Eye
Chirnsidebridge   BARN   A1
DUNS   EDROM   Foulden   Mordington   Sharper's Head
NORMAN ARCH   9   Halidon   RAVENSDOWNE BARRACKS
Duns   Edrom   Clappers   Hill   Berwick-upon-Tweed
MANDERSTON   A6105   Allanton   A6105   BERWICK
A6105   Cheeklaw   Blackadder   Hutton   Paxton   Tweedmouth
Gavinton   Whitelaw   B6460   Spittal
Chornlee   A6105   East   East
A6112   Whitsome   B6437   Fisnwick   UNION   Ord   Redshin Cove
Polwarth   Sinclair's Hill   BRIDGE   A698   Scremerston
Moss   Fogo   Horncliffe   Longridge
Swinton   B64461   Towers   Myrton
Fogorig   Horndean   Thornton   Allerdeanmill
naw   B6470   NORHAM   Park   Cheswick
Swintonmill   Ladykirk   Norham   Thornton   Black Rocks
Purves   Simprim   Upsettlington   Shoreswood   West   Cheswick   Goswick
Hall   B64   13   Shoresdean   Allerdean   A1
Leitholm   6   Grindon   B6354   Ancroft
Easter   12   Orange   Felkington   Berrington   Emmanuel Head
Howlaws   Lane   Duddo   Bowsden   Holy Island or
A697   THE HIRSEL   A6112   West Mains   Lindisfarne
mehall   GROUNDS &   Castle   Beal   LINDISFARNE (NT)
S   Eccles   DUNDOCK   Lennel   Heaton   Holy Island Sands   Castle Point
egars   WOOD   A698   West Kyloe   PRIORY   Burrows
Coldstream   MUS   Cornhill   Pallinsburn   Barmoor Lane End   Guile Point   Hole
Ednam   Birgham   on Tweed   House   Fenwick   Fenham Flats   Longstone
A698   Wark   Crookham   Ford   Lowick   (NT)
KELSO   Carham   Branxton   ETAL   Buckton   Staple Sound   Farne
Hendersyde   12   East   FLODDEN FIELD   Detchant   Elwick   Islands
Park   Learmouth   1513   Ross   Budle Point   Farne Island
Hadden   Pressen   Holburn   Middleton   Budle   DARLING   Bamburgh
Kelso   Sprouston   Downham   Howtel   Flodden   70 A1   Easington   MUSEUM   Rocks
Maxwellheugh   B4296   Milfield   Fenton   North Hazelrigg   Belford   Waren Mill   Spindlestone   G   House
Lempitlaw   Mindrum   Pawston   A697   Doddington   South Hazelrigg   B1342   Bradford   69   Burton
5   Blakelaw   Kilham   Lanton   Nesbit   West   East   10   NE   Ballshill   Adderstone   68
B6352   8   Shotton   Glen   Newtown   Horton   Horton   Warenton   Lucker   Newham
33   70   34   Venchen   Wistnewton   Coupland   66   Spindlestone   37   71
Froggen   Hill   Kirknewton   HOMILDON   Chatton   Dykes   Newham
Linton   Kirk Yetholm   Yeavering   HILL   Wooler   B6348   Twizell   67
Yetholm   71   Bell   1402   House   Newstead
Bowmont   Town   Hethpool   Humbleton   Chattton   Swinhoe
Forest   Yetholm   Newton   Haugh   B6348   CHILLINGHAM   Chathill   (NT)

NORTHUMBERLAND

NT

A   D   E   F   G

5   **6**   **7**   **8**   **9**

Lochboisdale

Castlebay

Point of A

A

Eag na Maoille

Eilean Mor

Rubha Mor

Rubh' a'Bhinnein

Beusd

Rubha Sgor-Innis

Rubha Sgor-Innis

Loch Fada

Sorisdale

Torastan

Bagh na Coille

Cliad Bay

Arnabost

Grishipoll Bay

Grishipoll

73

Clabhach

2

Ballyhaugh

Ben Hogh

2

Hogh Bay

104

78

Loch Cliad

Totamore

Arinagour

Totronald

Loch Eatharna

Caliach Point

Port na

B

Uig

Sunipol

COLL

Langan

Port Mine

Acha

5

Eilean Ornsay

Mornish

Feall Bay

Gorton

Port na Eatha

Cruach Sleibhe

166

Calgary Point

Crossapol

Friesland Bay

Rubha nan Oirean

Crossapol Bay

Caolas Bay

Rubha Fasachd

Calgary

Bay

Gunna

Loch Breachacha

Soa

Ensay

Urvaig

Port a'Mhurain

Treshnish Point

Miodar

Treshnish

Sgeir Bharrach

Rubha Dubh

C

The Green

Balephetrish Bay

Vaul

Caolas

Beinn Dubh

Rubh' a'Chaoil

191

Balephetrish Hill

Ruaig

Port Ban

Rubh' an t-Suibhein

T I R E E

4

Hough Bay

77

Brock

Rubha Liath

Cairn na Burgh More

Cairn na Burgh Beg

Kilkenneth

3

Scarinish

Gott Bay

Soa

Sgeir a Chaisteil

Loch Tu

Moss

Tiree

5

Fladda

Eilean Dioghlum

Saundaig

Heylipoll

Crossapol

Heanish

Lunga

Rubha Maol

Gometra

2

Hynish Bay

Balephuil

B8065

Bay

na Mine

Ho

Gometra

Barrapoll

Baugh

Sgeir a Chaisteil

Maisgeir

B8067

Balemartine

Treshnish Isles

Rinn Thorbhais

3

Mannel

Bac Mor or

Little

B8066

Hynish

Dutchman's Cap

Colonsay

SKERRYVORE

Bac Beag

MUSEUM

Staffa

Eilean Dubh

D

Fingal's

STAFFA (NTS)

Cave

Erisge

Aird na

Reidh Eilean

Eilean Chalbha

MACLEAN'S CROSS

Rubha nan Caarc

E

Dun

IONA ABBEY

Kintra

Port an Duine Mhairbh

Beinn Chladan

Eorabu

76

IONA

Sound of Iona

Bunessan

Ruanaich

Fionnphort

Loch na

Lathaich

Stac an Aoineidh

Aridhglas

66 A849

Iona

Fidden

Soa Island

R O S S

Knockvologan

Ardalanish

Erraid

Torr Fada

Ardchia

Eilean Dubh

Aird Mor

Por

Mo

Eilean a'Chalmain

Eilean Mor

Rubh' Ard

F

Torran Rocks

Dearg Sgeir

West Reef

Na Torrain

Ruadh Sgeir

McPhail's Anvil

Torran Sgoilte

Sgeir Ghobhlach

Otter Rock

G

0   2   4   6   8   10 miles

0 2 4 6 8 10 km

Dubh Artach

COLO

5   **6**   **7**   **8**   **72**   **9**

Kilor

Loch an Sgoile

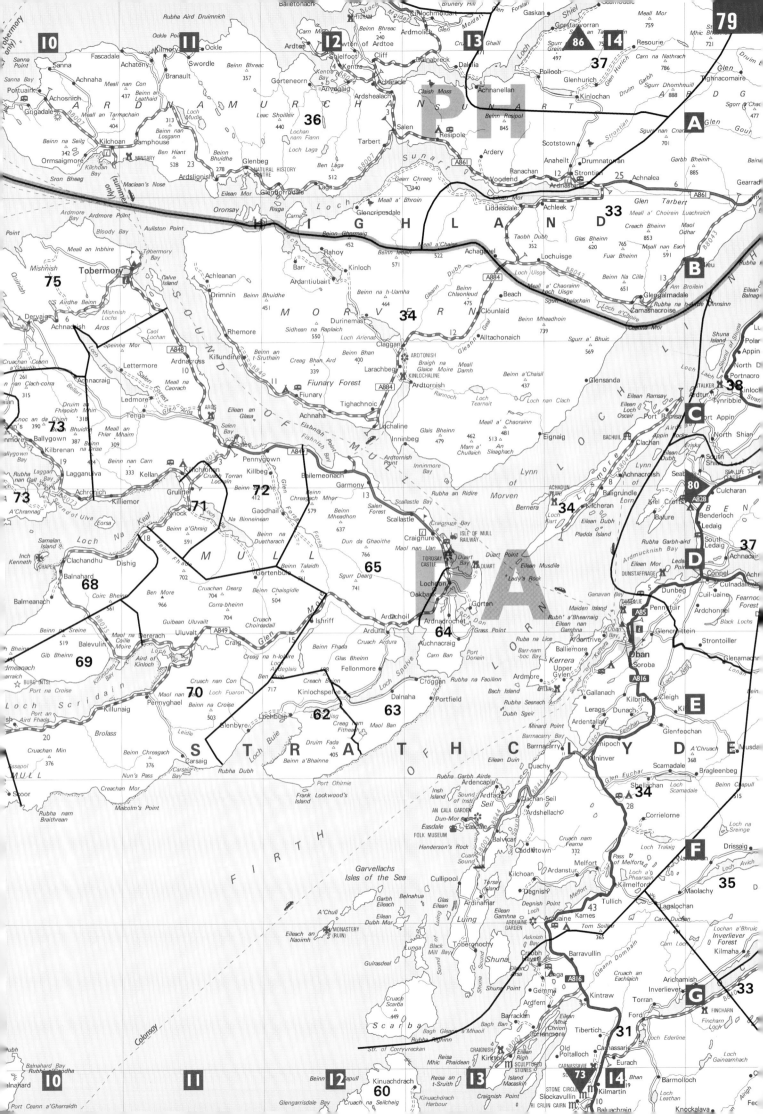

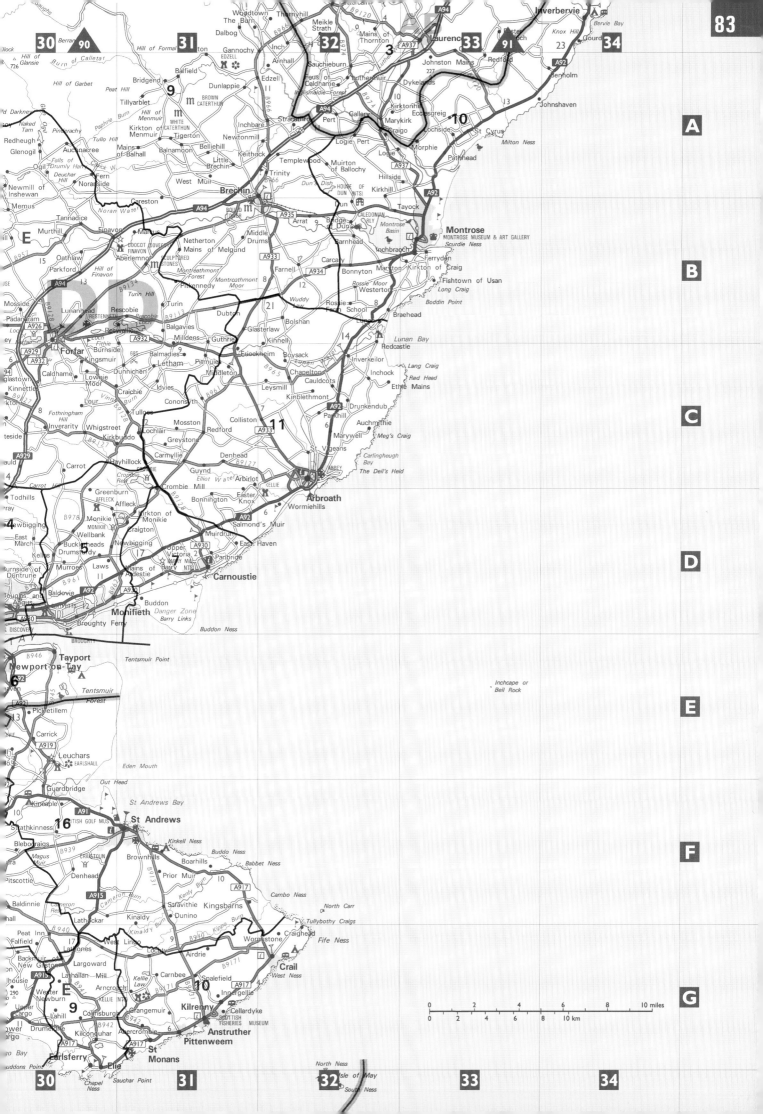

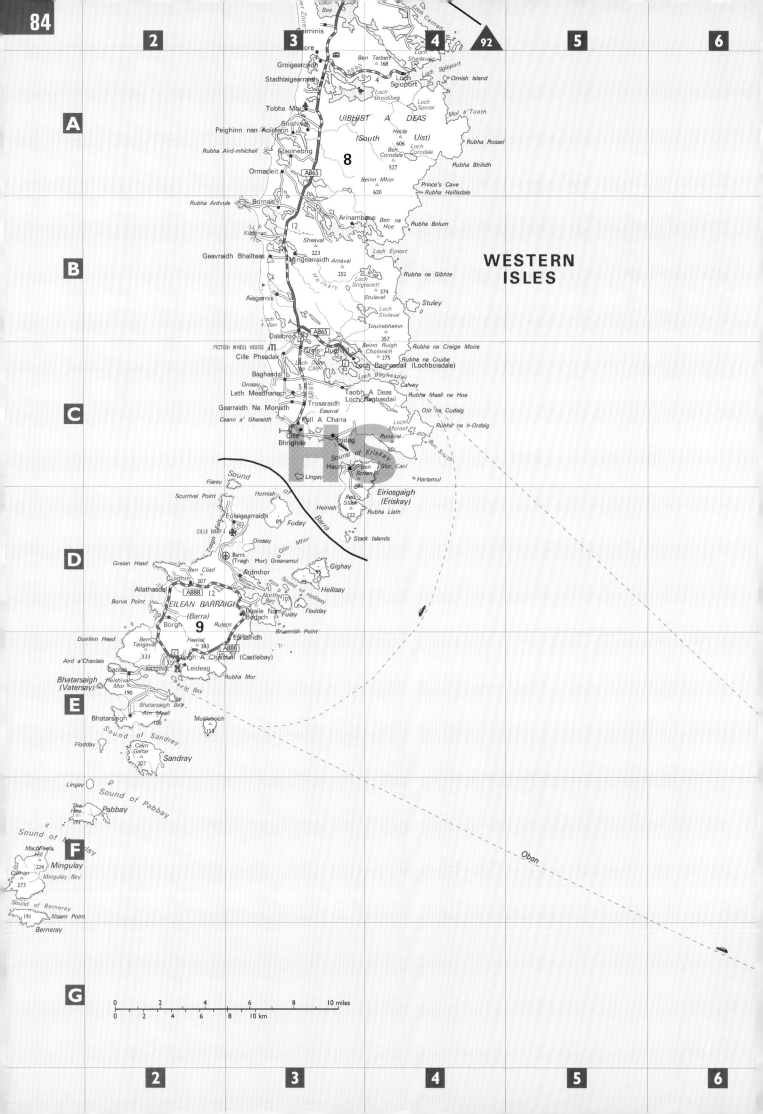

WESTERN
ISLES

UIBHIST A DEAS
(South Uist)

8

EILEAN BARRAIGH
(Barra)

9

Eiriosgaigh
(Eriskay)

Bhatarsaigh
(Vatersay)

Sandray

Pabbay

Mingulay

Berneray

Oban

0   2   4   6   8   10 miles
0   2   4   6   8   10 km

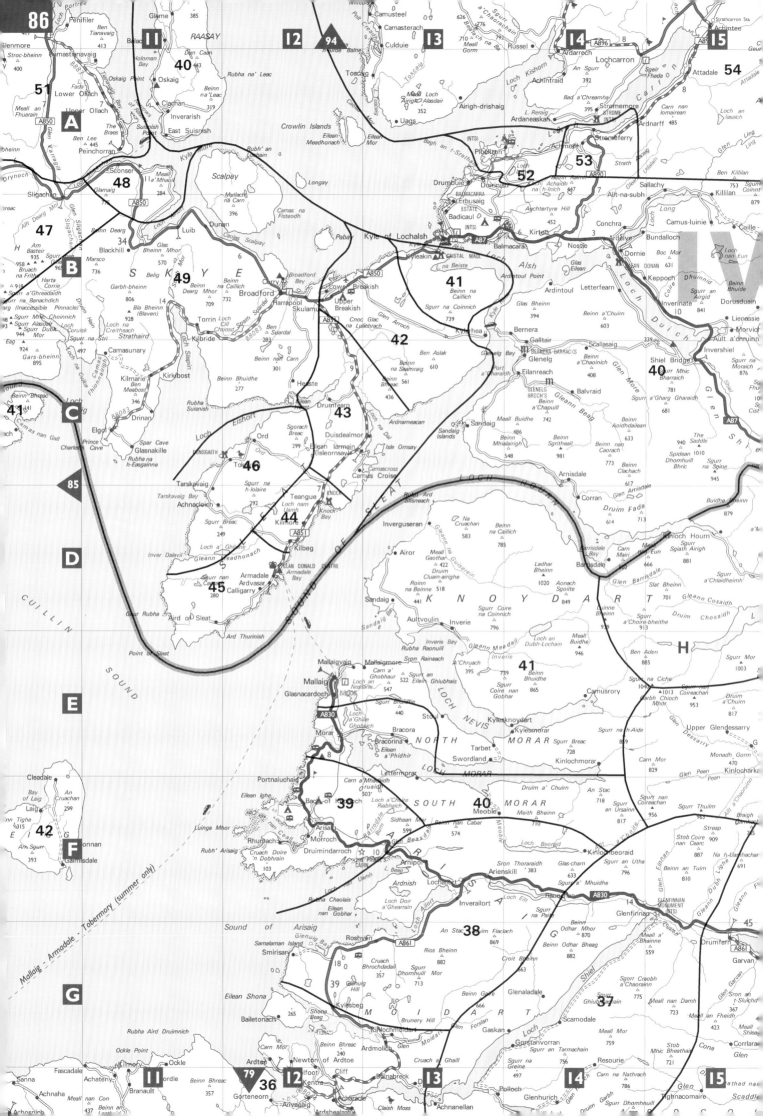

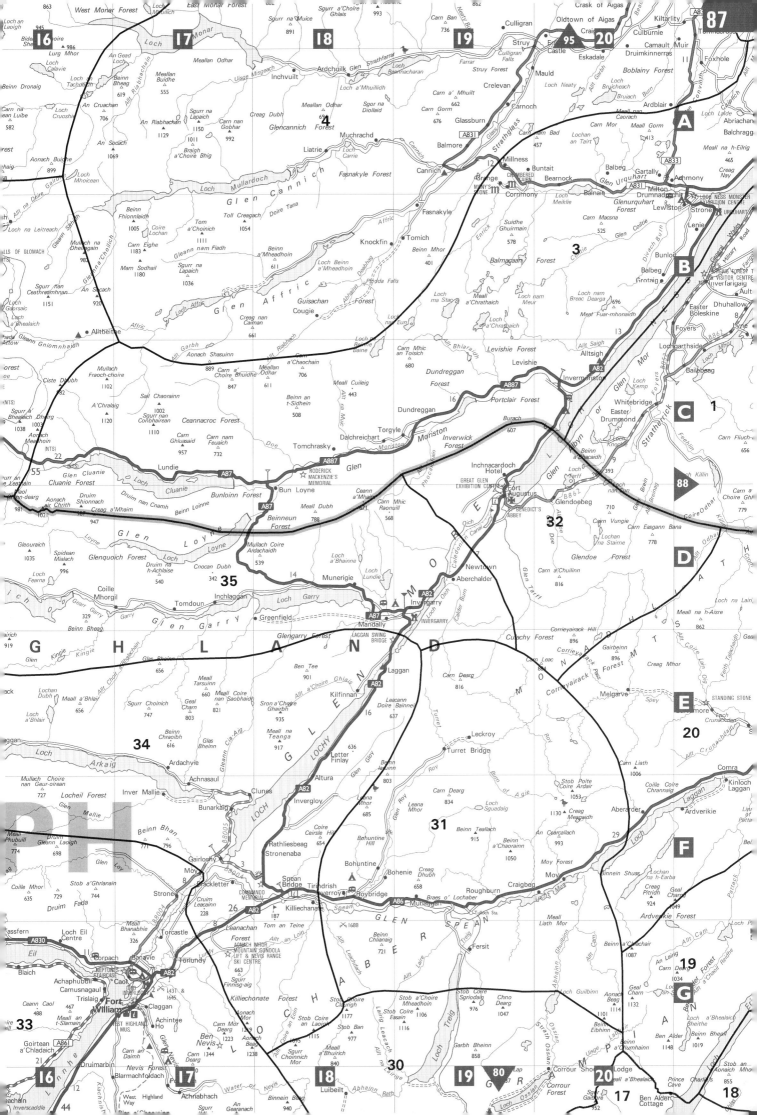

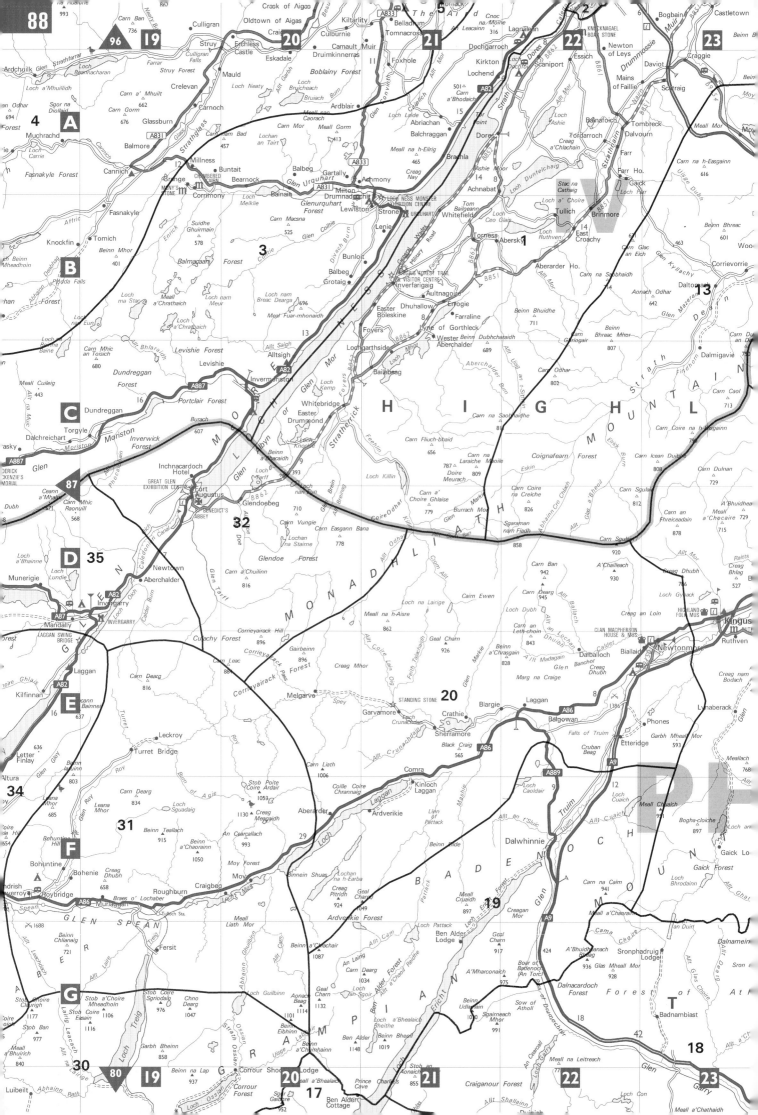

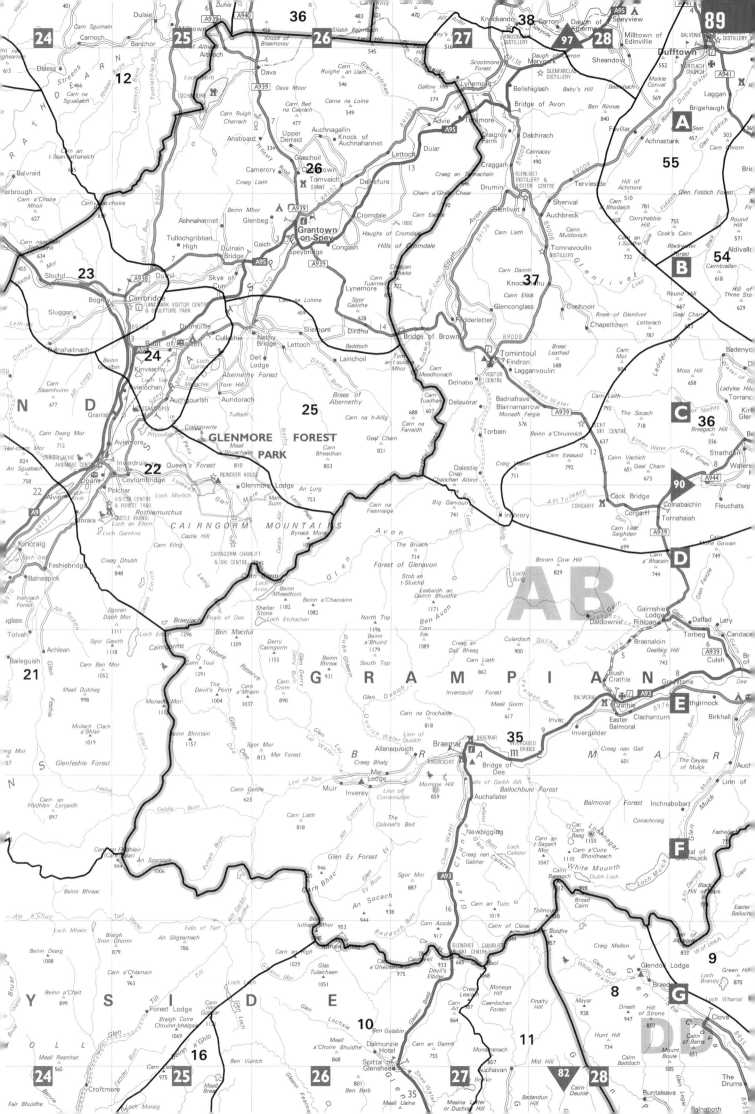

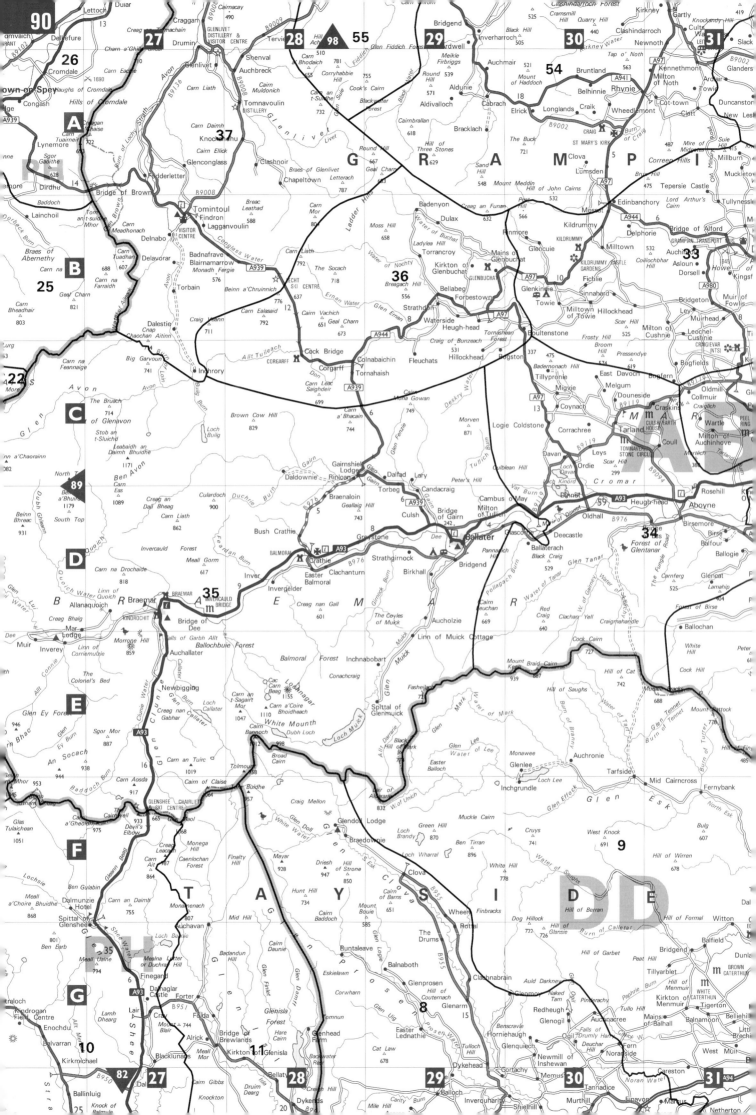

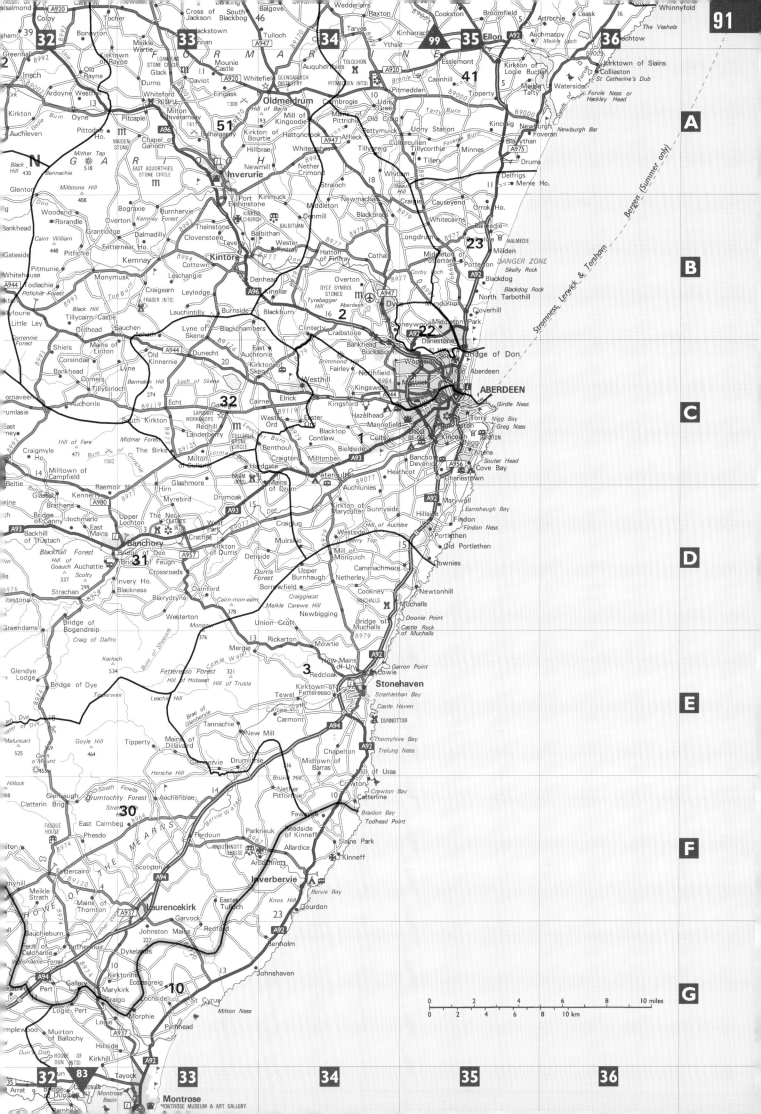

WESTERN

ISLES

2　3　4　5　6

A

B

C

D

E

F

G

2　3　4　5　6

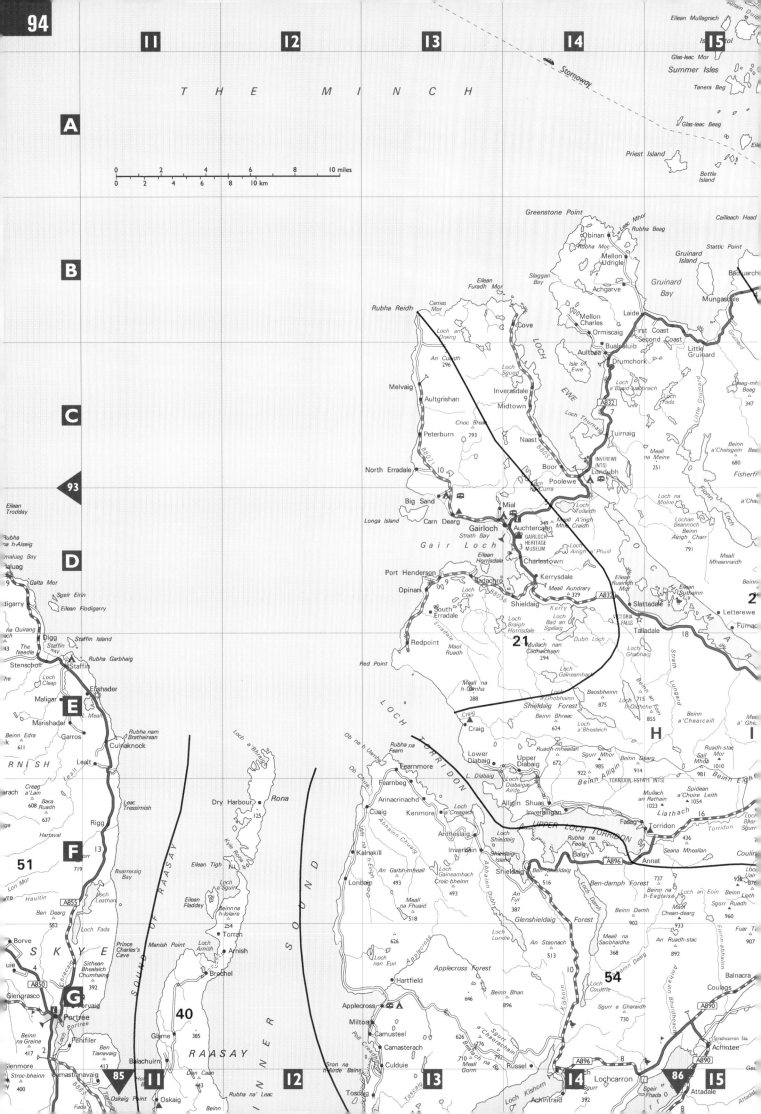

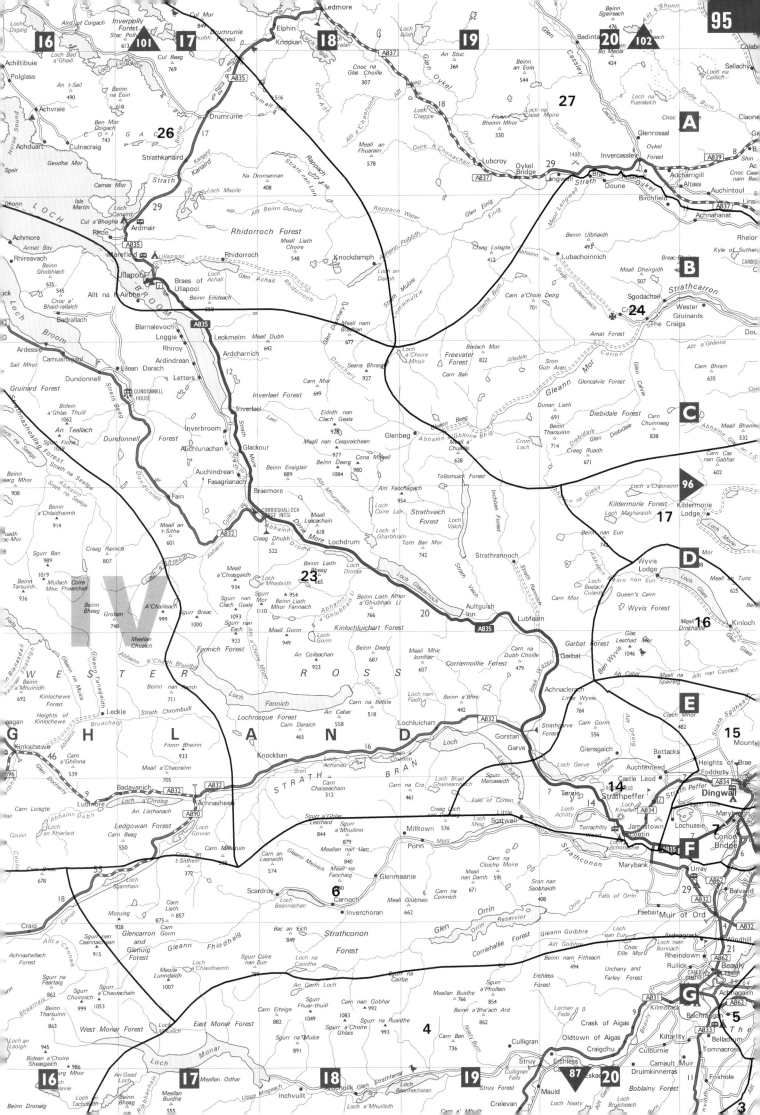

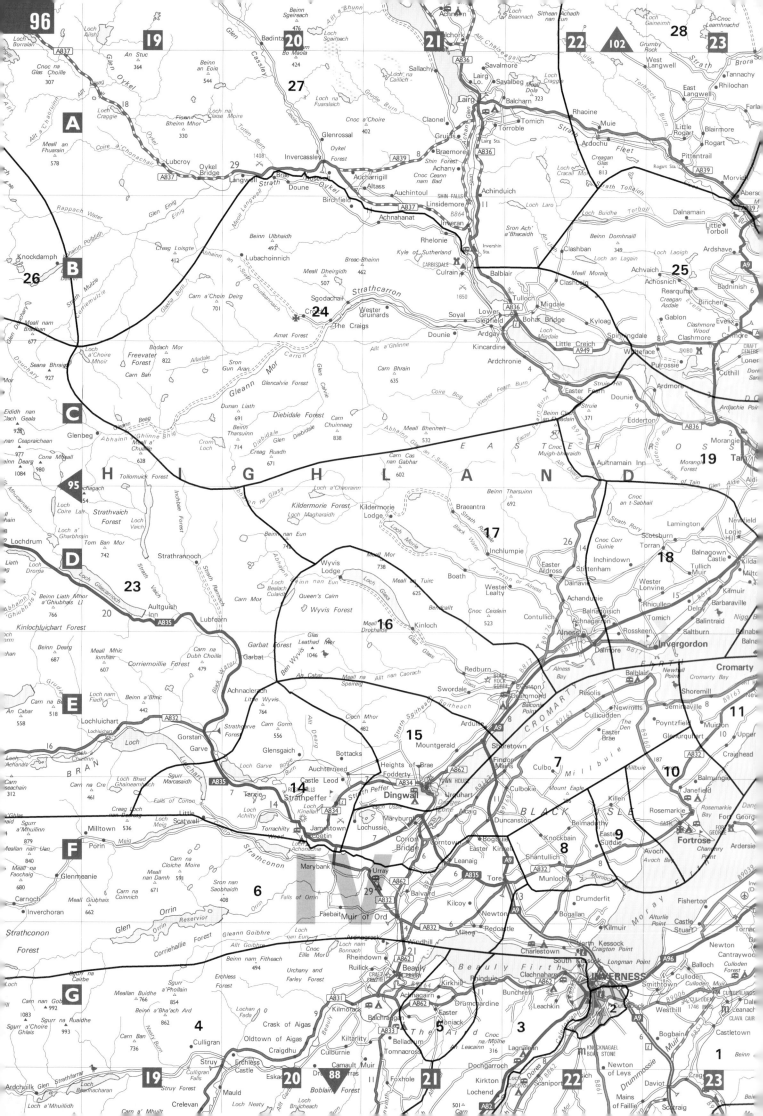

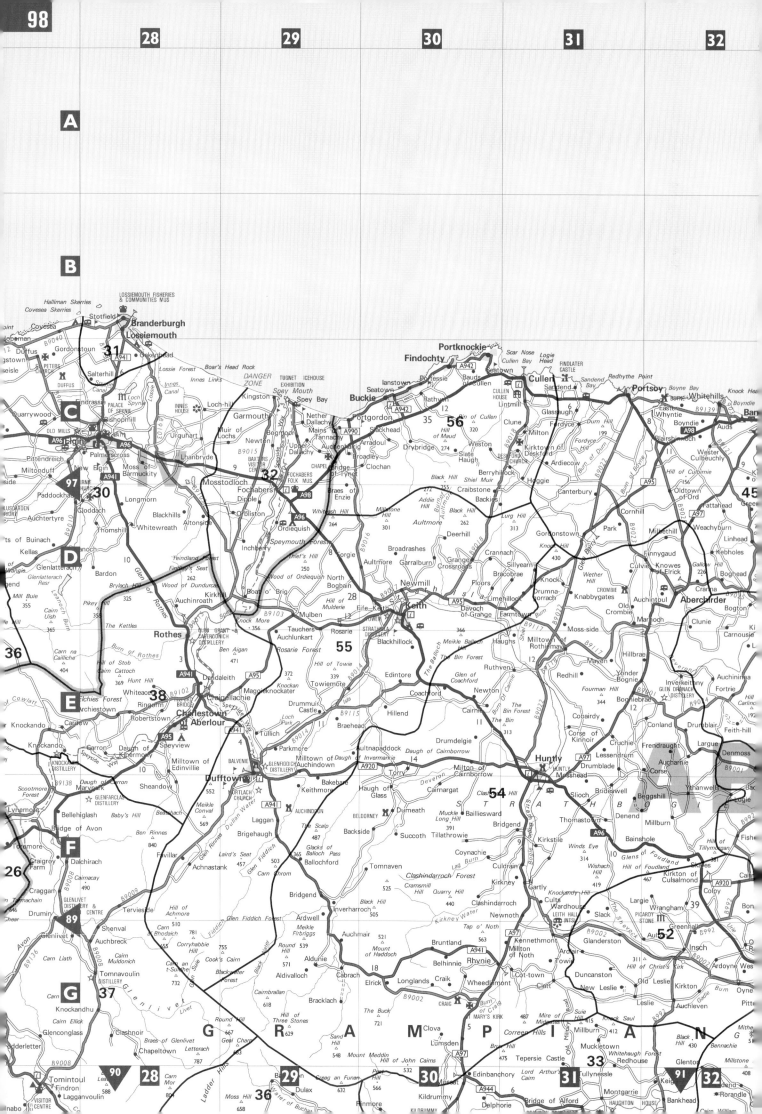

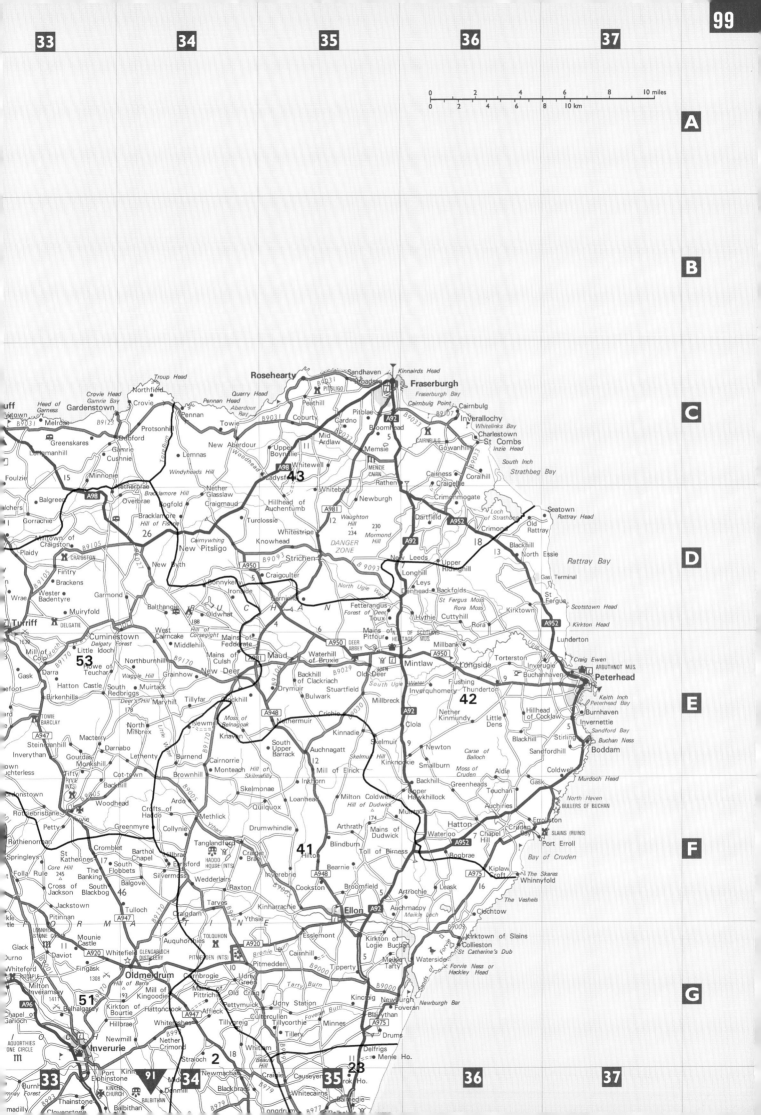

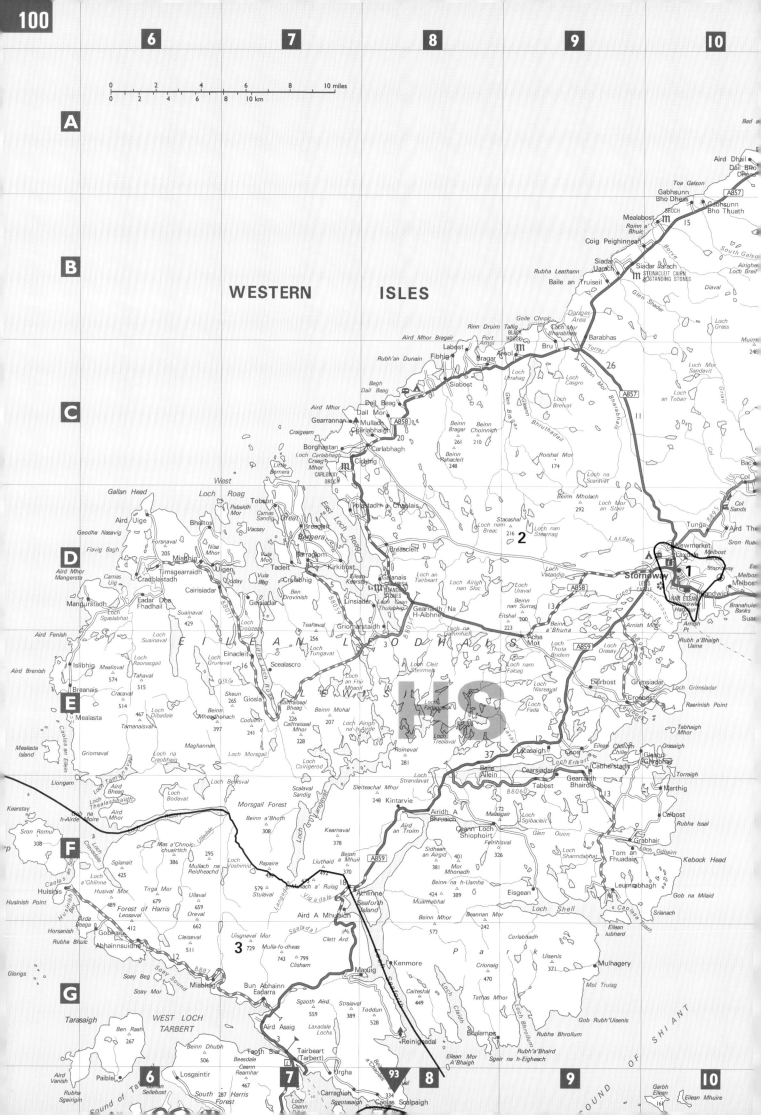

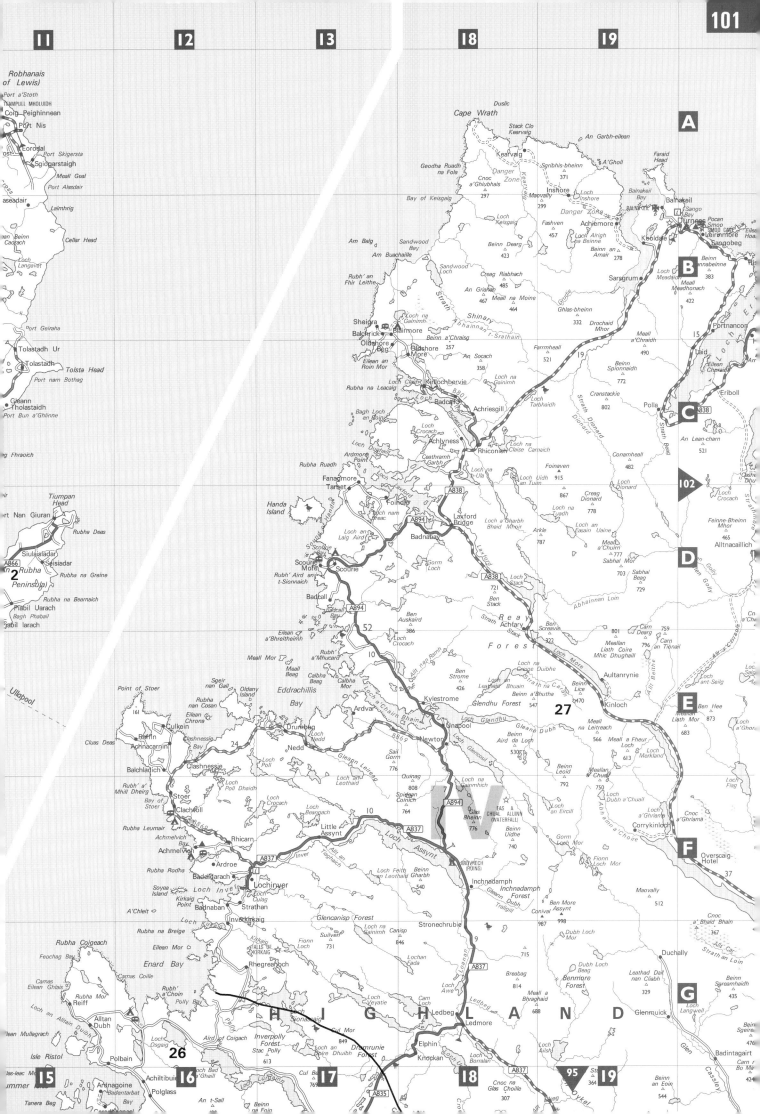

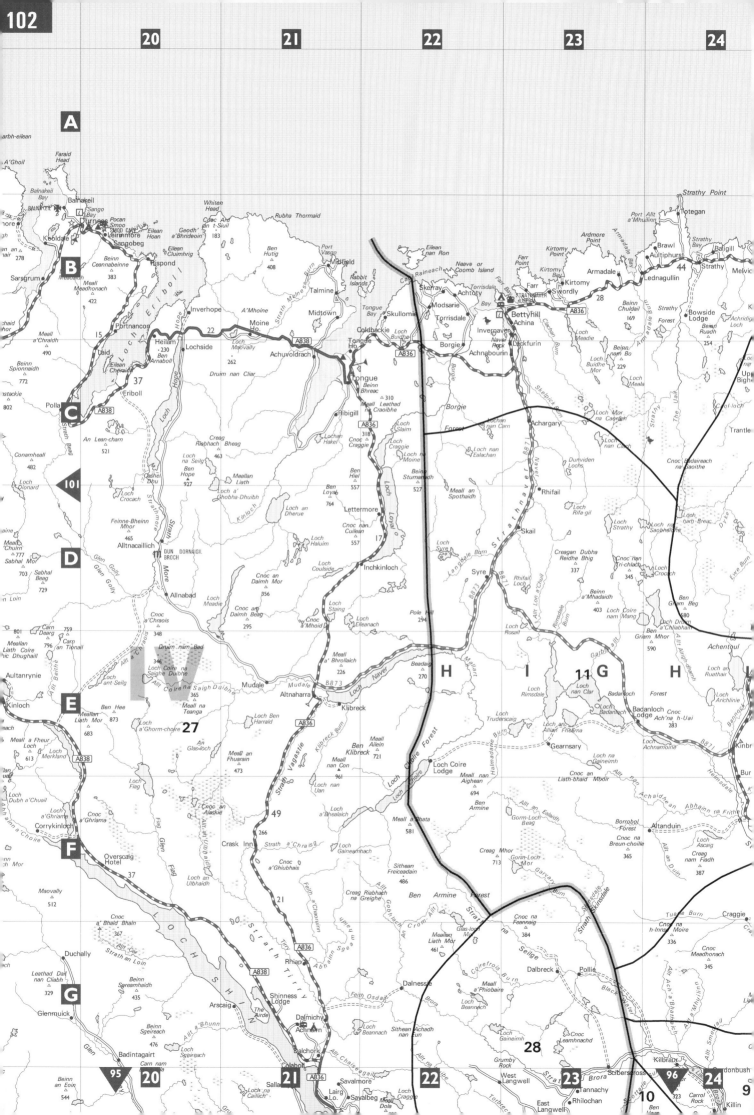

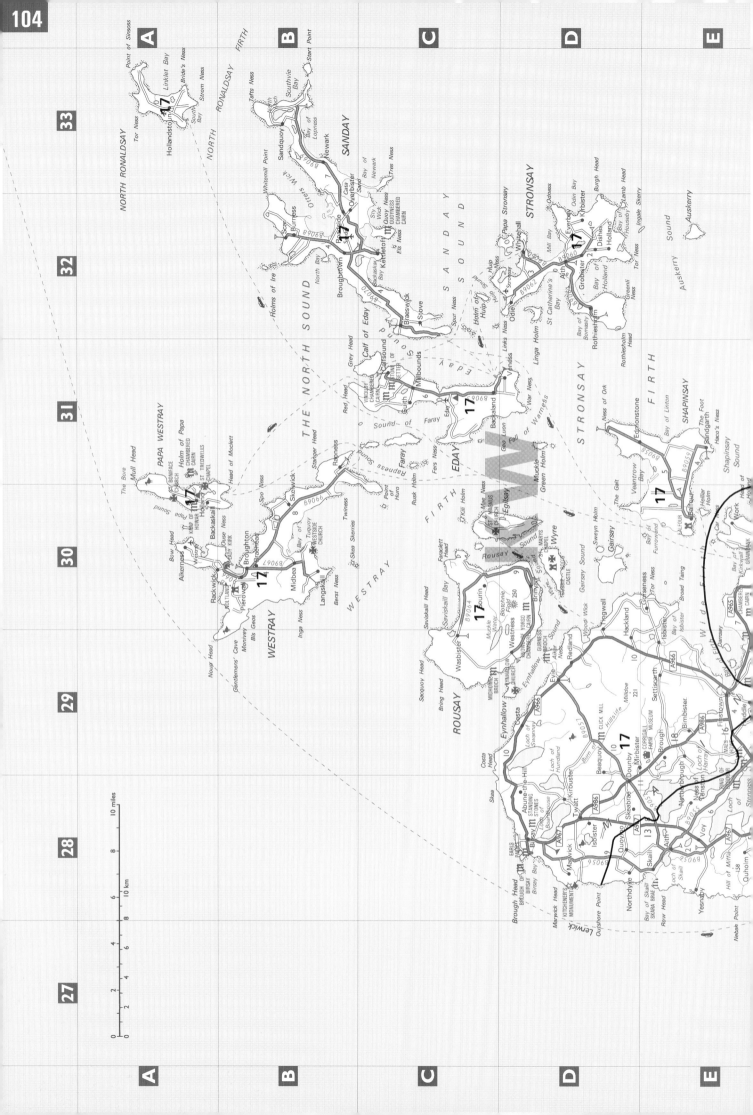

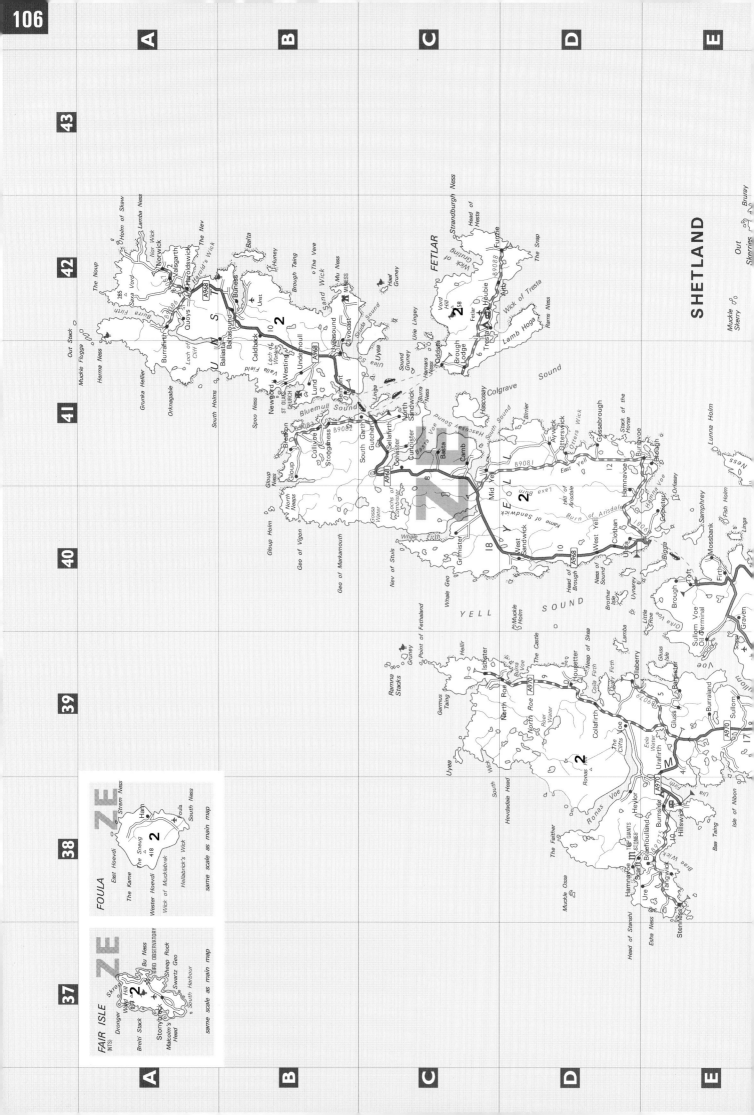

SHETLAND

FETLAR

UNST

YELL

FOULA

FAIR ISLE
(NTS)

YELL SOUND

Out Skerries

Bruray

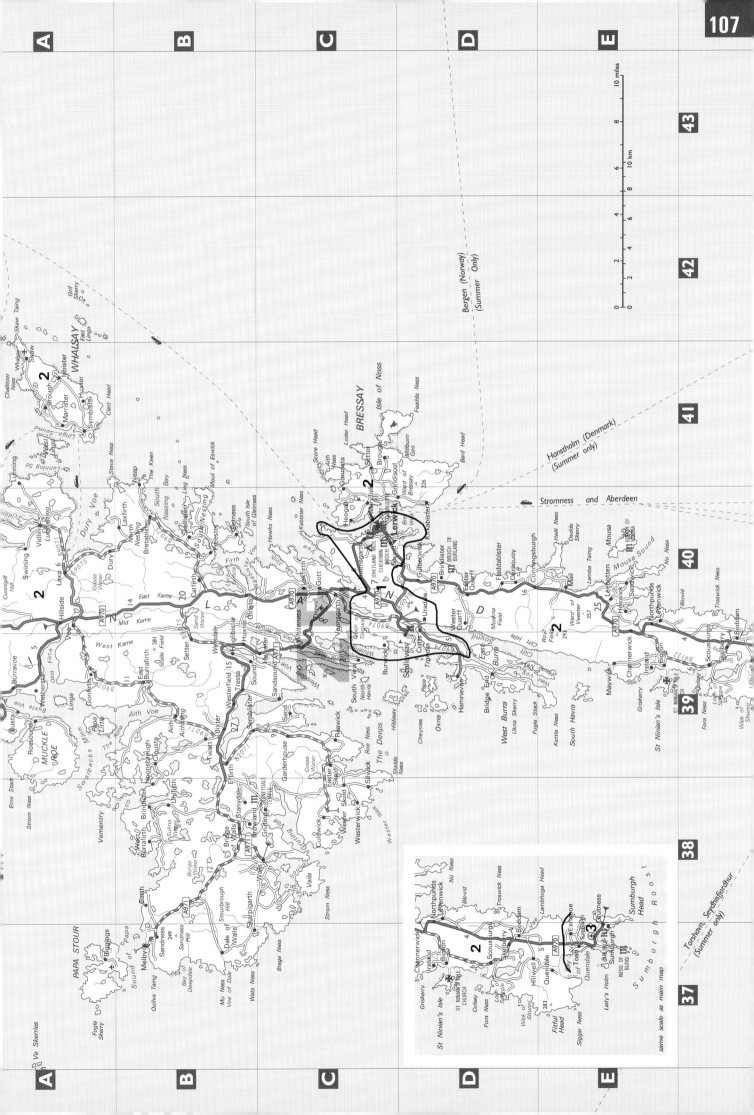

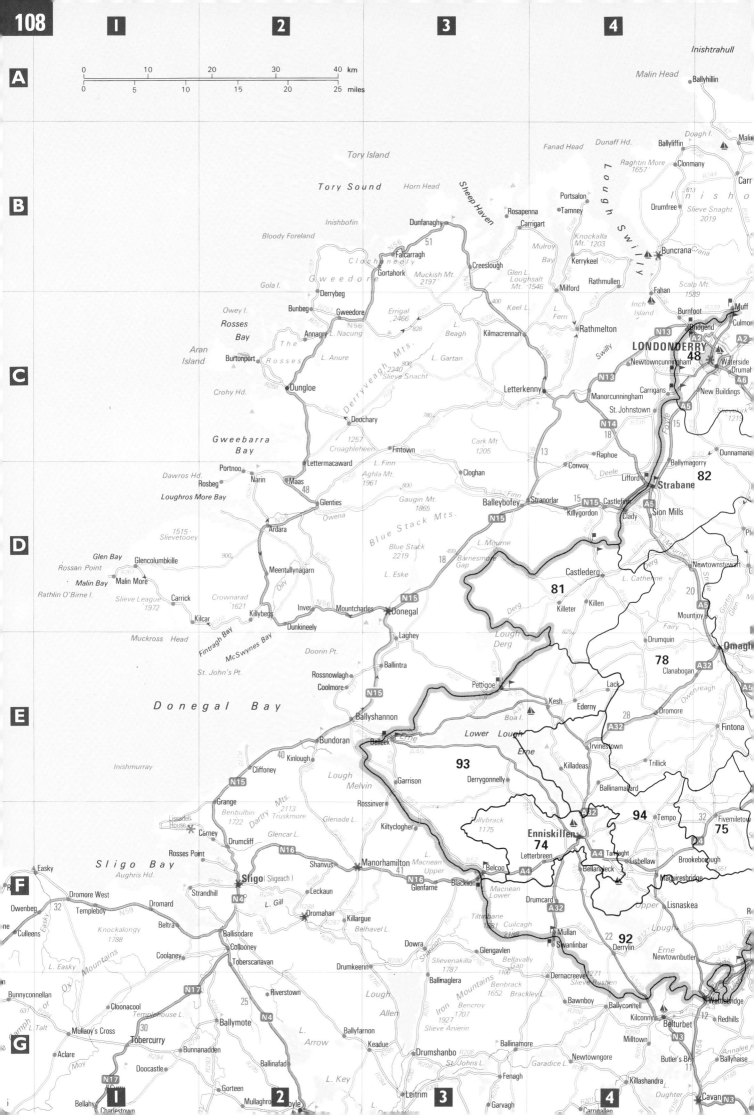

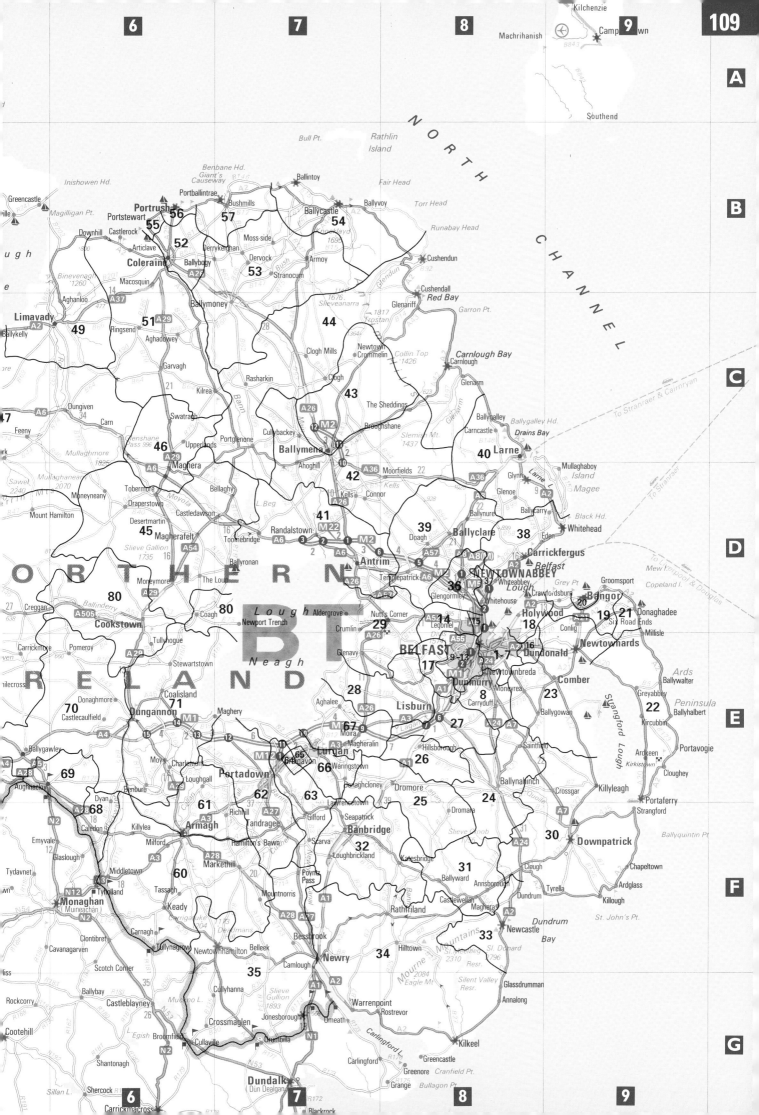

Conurbation Map Section

111	Birmingham
112-113	Greater Manchester
114-115	Bradford / Leeds
116	Liverpool
117	Newcastle upon Tyne
118	Glasgow

KEY TO MAPS

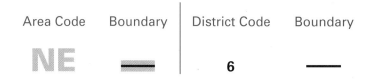

Area Code	Boundary	District Code	Boundary
NE	▬▬	6	▬▬

Scale 1:100 000 (1.6 miles to 1 inch)

NEWMINSTER ABBEY
High Ho. CAS
Park Ho.
Shadfen
Shadfen Park
North Choppington
Guide Post
Stakeford
63
Seaton Colliery
L.C.
W. Sleekburn
Cambois
Mitford Steads
High Church
Stobhill
Hepscott Red Ho.
Healeywood
Choppington
62
Bomarsund
Scotland Gate
E. Sleekburn
The Rockers

High Common Ho.
Catchburn Fm.
Coalburn Fm.
Hepscott Manor Fm.
Netherton Colliery
Blue House Fm.
Nedderton
Mine
North Blyth
North Blyth Ferry

Tranwell
Catch Burn
Clifton
Glororum
Well Hill
Hosp.
61
Duddo Hill
Dovecote Fm.
High Clifton Fm.
BEDLINGTON
22
Bebside
Bebside Hall
Cowpen
L.C.
BLYTH
Seaton Sea Rocks

N. Saltwick Hosp.
Lough Ho.
East Moor
52m
Stannington
Plessey Hall
Hartford Br.
Acorn Bank
East Hartford
New Delaval
South Newsham
Gloucester Lo. Fm.
Seaton Sluice

Mid Duddo
Catraw
West House Fm.
Stannington Bridge
Industrial Estate
Plessey New Houses
Shankhouse
Verock Hall
New Delaval
Newsham
Link Ho.

Bellasis Fm.
R. Blyth
Shotton
Nelson Village
Cramlington
Hartley
Seaton Delaval Hall
Seaton Starlight Cas.

Berwick Hill Low Ho.
Blagdon Hall
Blagdon Park
White Hall Fm.
East Cramlington
Wks.
45m
New Hartley
Seaton Delaval
26
Hartley

Make me Rich Ewe Hill
Milkhope
Plessey South Manor Fm.
SEATON VALLEY
23
High Barnes
Armitsford
Seghill
Seaton Terrace
Holywell
St. Mary's or Bates' Island

Old Horton Grange
New Horton Grange
Carr Ho.
Brenkley
Seven Mile Ho.
Seaton Burn
Dudley
Mine (disused)
Seghill Hall
Seaton Burn
Bank Top
Brier Dene
Dene Burn
Whitley Sands

Berwick Hill
Park Ho.
20
Dinnington
N.E. Mason Fm.
Six Mile Bridge
13
Arcot Hall
Mine
Burradon Ho. TOWER
East Holywell
West Holywell
Earsdon
25
Crow Hall Fm.
Whitley Sands

Prestwick Carr
Mason
Mill Hill
Brunswick Village
Seaton Burn Ho.
Burradon
West Holywell
27
WHITLEY BAY

Prestwick
Street Houses
Hack Hall
Morley Hill Fm.
Wide Open
High Westside
Camperdown
Backworth
Shiremoor
Monkseaton
Cullercoats

Woolsington Hall
Sunnyside
Hazlerigg
Nth. Brunton
Mid Brunton
High Gosforth Park
Killingworth
East House Fm.
Palmersville
West Allotment
NE
New York
Marden
Long San.

Black Callerton
Woolsington
Bullock Steads
East Brunton
Gosforth Lake
Forest Hall
12
West Allotment
Hosp.
Murton
Preston
TYN

Whorlton Hall
Whorlton Grange
Kenton Bank Foot
Fawdon
STA
Coxlodge
3
LONGBENTON
Rising Sun Fm.
Chirton
29
North Shields
ROMAN FORT

5
N. Walbottle
Blakelaw
Nuns Moor
GOSFORTH
7
Little Benton
Howdon
Percy Main
30

Hill Head
Westerhope
Kenton
Jesmond
Heaton
WALLSEND
28
Rosehill
Willington Quay
33

NEWCASTLE UPON TYNE
Town Moor
Hosp.
Hosp.
Hosp.
JARROW
West Park

NEWBURN
15
Denton
Fenham
2
Walker
6
Byker
HEBBURN
32
West Harton
34

Bell's Close
Scotswood
4
Elswick
1
St. Anthony's
31
Monkton
Primrose Hill
Hedworth
Simonside

Path Head
Delaval Haugh
Low Team
Felling Shore
Bill Quay
FELLING
Felgate
Boldon Colliery
35
BOLDON
East Boldon

AYDON
Winlaton
Axwell Park
Dunston
Whickham Thorns
8
Mount Pleasant
Heworth
Wardley
West Boldon
36
Belle Vue Villa
Field Ho.

21
Winlaton Mill
Swalwell
Dunston Hill
GATESHEAD
Whickham Hill
High Felling
Windy Nook
Scot's Ho.
38m
Strother House Fm.
Hylton Grove
Downhill Fm.

WHICKHAM
Team Valley
Low Fell
10
Eighton Banks
9
Springwell
37
East Ho.
HYLTON CAS.
Southwi
Castletown

9
Sunniside
Street Gate
11
Lady Park
Lamesley
Wrekenton
The Leam
WASHINGTON
38
5
South Hylton

Cut Thorn
Hill Head Wood
216m
High Park Wood
16
Kibblesworth
Old Ravensworth
Long Acre Fm.
Blackfell
Usworth
Sulgrave Ho.
Wildfowl
R. Don
Mundles

Byermoor
Ravensworth Grange
Andrew's Ho.
Gibsider
Hillhead

Central London Map Section

KEY TO CENTRAL LONDON POSTCODES

Area

Code	Boundary
E	▬▬▬
EC (Central)	

District		Sector	
Code	Boundary	Code	Boundary
1	———	6	———
1A (Central)			

KEY TO CENTRAL LONDON MAPS

Scale 1:19 650 (3.25 inches to 1 mile)

0   0.25   0.50   0.75   1 kilometre
0   ¼   ½ mile

| 120 | | 121 | 122 | | 123 |
| 124 | | 125 | 126 | | 127 |

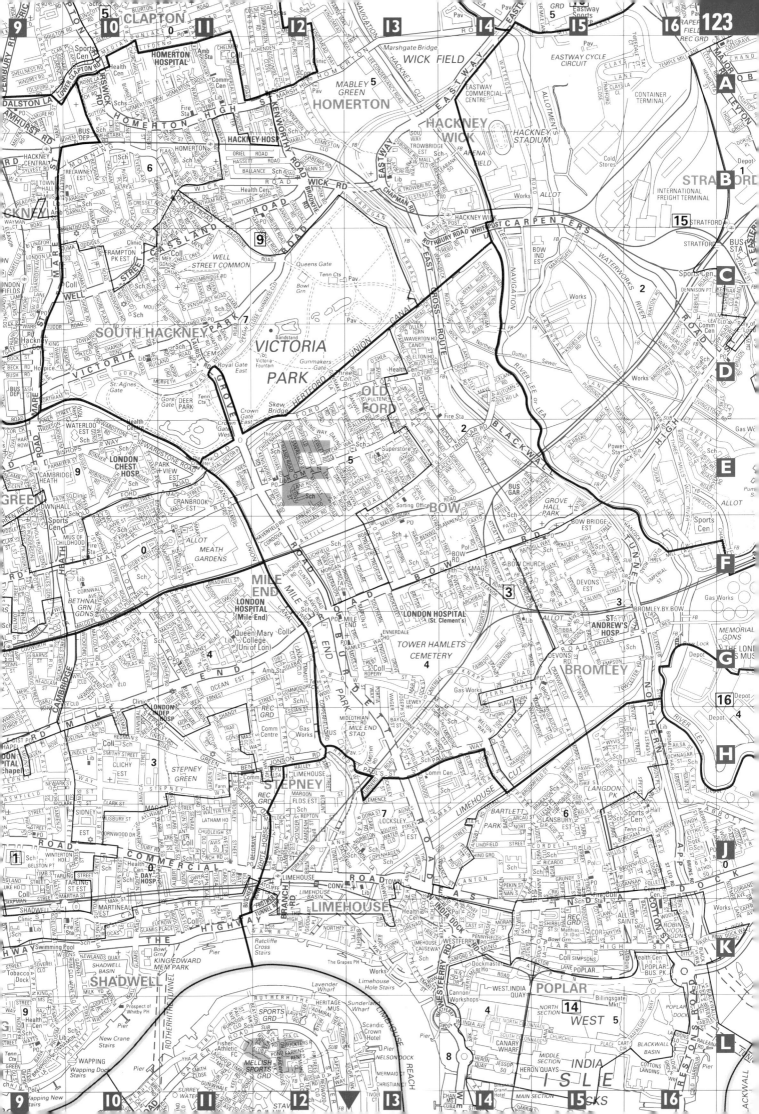

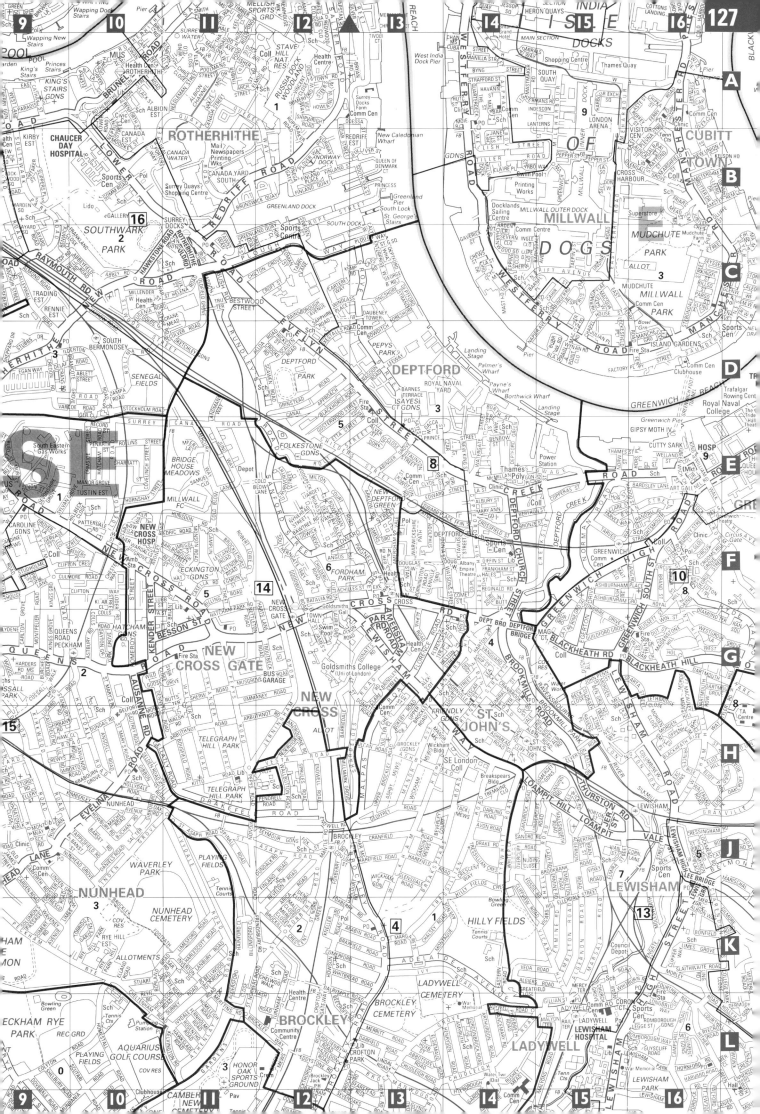

INDEX TO GREAT BRITAIN AND NORTHERN IRELAND

Abbreviations

Ant.	Antrim	*Cum.*	Cumbria	*G.M.*	Greater Manchester	*Lan.*	Lancashire	*Ork.*	Orkney	*Tay.*	Tayside
Arm.	Armagh	*Dby.*	Derbyshire	*Grm.*	Grampian	*Lcn.*	Lincolnshire	*Oxf.*	Oxfordshire	*T.&W.*	Tyne & Wear
Bfd.	Bedfordshire	*Dev.*	Devon	*Gwe.*	Gwent	*Ldy*	Londonderry	*Pow.*	Powys	*Tyr.*	Tyrone
Bkh.	Buckinghamshire	*D.&G.*	Dumfries & Galloway	*Gwy.*	Gwynedd	*Lei.*	Leicestershire	*Sfk*	Suffolk	*War.*	Warwickshire
Bor.	Borders	*Dor.*	Dorset	*Ham.*	Hampshire	*Ltn*	Lothian	*S.G.*	South Glamorgan	*W.G.*	West Glamorgan
Brk.	Berkshire	*Drm*	Durham	*Hfs.*	Hertfordshire	*Mer.*	Merseyside	*She.*	Shetland	*W.I.*	Western Isles
Cbs.	Cambridgeshire	*Dyf.*	Dyfed	*Hgh.*	Highland	*M.G.*	Mid Glamorgan	*Shr.*	Shropshire	*W.M.*	West Midlands
Cen.	Central	*E.S.*	East Sussex	*Hum.*	Humberside	*Nfk*	Norfolk	*Som.*	Somerset	*W.S.*	West Sussex
Che.	Cheshire	*Esx*	Essex	*H.&W.*	Hereford & Worcester	*Nmp.*	Northamptonshire	*Sry*	Surrey	*Wts.*	Wiltshire
Cle.	Cleveland	*Fer.*	Fermanagh	*I.o.M.*	Isle of Man	*Nor.*	Northumberland	*Stf.*	Staffordshire	*W.Y.*	West Yorkshire
Clw.	Clwyd	*G.L.*	Greater London	*I.o.S.*	Isles of Scilly	*Not.*	Nottinghamshire	*Str.*	Strathclyde		
Cnw.	Cornwall	*Glo.*	Gloucestershire	*I.o.W.*	Isle of Wight	*N.Y.*	North Yorkshire	*S.Y.*	South Yorkshire		

A

9 B32 Abbas Combe BA8
29 B33 Abberley WR6
34 G56 Abberton *Esx* CO5
29 C35 Abberton *H.&W.* WR10
71 B37 Abberwick NE66
33 G51 Abbess Roding CM5
27 A26 Abbeycwmhir LD1
28 E29 Abbey Dore HR2
40 A35 Abbey Hulton ST2
77 D33 Abbey St Bathans TD11
55 D31 Abbeystead LA2
60 A27 Abbeytown CA5
23 D50 Abbey Wood SE2
70 B31 Abbotrule TD9
6 D19 Abbots Bickington EX22
40 C36 Abbots Bromley WS15
8 F31 Abbotsbury DT3
6 C19 Abbotsham EX39
5 D24 Abbotskerswell TQ12
22 A46 Abbots Langley WD2
19 D31 Abbots Leigh BS8
33 C48 Abbotsley PE19
30 C36 Abbots Morton WR7
32 A47 Abbots Ripton PE17
30 C36 Abbot's Salford WR11
21 G39 Abbotts Ann SP11
10 B39 Abbottswood SO51
38 G31 Abdon SY7
26 D20 Aber *Dyf.* SA40
46 E22 Aber *Gwy.* LL33
36 B18 Aber *Gwy.* LL53
18 B25 Aber *M.G.* CF32
26 B20 Aberaeron SA46
18 A25 Aberaman CF44
37 E24 Aberangell SY20
17 A18 Aberarad SA38
88 F20 Aberarder PH20
88 B22 Aberarder Ho. IV1
82 F27 Aberargie PH2
26 B20 Aberarth SA46
18 B23 Aberavon SA12
26 D19 Aber-banc SA44
18 A27 Aber Bargoed CF8
18 A27 Aberbeeg NP3
17 A22 Aber Bowlan SA19
18 A26 Abercanaid CF48
18 B27 Abercarn NP1
16 A14 Abercastle SA62
37 E23 Abercegir SY20
88 D19 Aberchalder PH35
98 D31 Aberchirder AB54
75 C26 Abercorn EH30
27 G24 Abercraf SA9
83 G30 Abercrombie KY10
27 E23 Abercrychan SA20
18 A25 Abercwmboi CF44
26 D18 Abercych SA37
27 G26 Abercynafon LD3
18 B26 Abercynon CF45
37 D24 Aber-cywarch SY20
82 E26 Aberdalgie PH2
18 A25 Aberdare CF44
36 C17 Aberdaron LL53
91 C35 Aberdeen AB
46 G20 Aberdesach LL54
75 B27 Aberdour KY3
27 C26 Aberduhonw LD2
18 B23 Aberdulais SA10
36 F21 Aberdyfi LL35
27 D26 Aberedw LD2
16 A13 Abereiddy SA62
36 B19 Abererch LL53
18 A26 Aberfan CF48
81 C24 Aberfeldy PH15
46 F19 Aberffraw LL62
27 A22 Aberffrwd SY23
57 F40 Aberford LS25
81 G21 Aberfoyle FK8
18 C25 Abergarw CF32
28 G28 Abergavenny NP7
47 E25 Abergele LL22
26 D20 Abergiar SA40
17 A21 Abergorlech SA32
27 C24 Abergwesyn LD5
17 B20 Abergwili SA31
37 E23 Abergwydol SY20
37 D22 Abergwynant LL40
18 B24 Abergwynfi SA13
37 E22 Abergynolwyn LL36
37 F26 Aberhafesp SY16
37 F23 Aberhosan SY20
18 C24 Aberkenfig CF32
76 B30 Aberlady EH32
83 B30 Aberlemno DD8
37 E23 Aberllefenni SY20
27 G25 Aber-Ilia CF44
26 A21 Abermad SY23
26 C21 Abermeurig SA48
38 F27 Abermule SY15
38 C27 Aber-Naint SY22
18 A25 Aber-nant CF44
17 B19 Abernant SA33
82 F27 Abernethy PH2
82 D28 Abernyte PH14
18 A24 Aber-pergwm SA11
26 C18 Aberporth SA43
38 E27 Aberriw (Berriew) SY21
96 A23 Aberscross KW10
88 B21 Abersky IV1
36 C18 Abersoch LL53
19 A28 Abersychan NP4
18 D26 Aberthin CF7
18 A27 Abertillery NP3
18 C26 Abertridwr *M.G.* CF8
37 D26 Abertridwr *Pow.* SY10
18 A27 Abertysswg NP2
82 F25 Aberuthven PH3
27 F25 Aberyscir LD3
36 G21 Aberystwyth SY23
100 G6 Abhainnsuidhe HS3
21 B40 Abingdon OX14
22 G47 Abinger Common RH5
22 G46 Abinger Hammer RH5
68 A25 Abington ML12
33 D48 Abington Pigotts SG8
12 E47 Abingworth RH20
41 C42 Ab Kettleby LE14
20 A36 Ablington GL7
50 E37 Abney S30
90 D31 Aboyne AB34
49 B32 Abram WN2
88 A21 Abriachan IV3
23 B50 Abridge RM4
19 D32 Abson BS15
31 D42 Abthorpe NN12
104 D28 Abune-the-Hill KW17
53 E50 Aby LN13
58 E41 Acaster Malbis YO2
58 E41 Acaster Selby YO5
56 G33 Accrington BB5
80 E16 Accurrach PA33
78 B7 Acha PA78
80 C15 Achacha PA37
73 D14 Achadacaie PA29
73 E13 Achadh-chaorrunn PA29
80 F17 Achadunan PA26
79 B13 Achagavel PH33
72 F12 Achaglass PA29
73 C13 Achahoish PA31
82 C27 Achalader PH10
80 C19 Achallader PA36
100 E9 Acha Mor HS2
72 C11 Achamore PA60
73 B13 Achanamara PA31
96 D22 Achandunie IV17
96 A21 Achany IV27
87 G16 Achaphubuil PH33
79 A12 Acharacle PH36
102 C22 Achargary KW11
80 D17 Acharn *Str.* PA35
81 C23 Acharn *Tay.* PH15
73 C15 Acharosson PA21
79 A11 Achateny PH36
91 B33 Achath AB32
103 D27 Achavanich KW5
95 A16 Achduart IV26
102 E24 Achentoul KW11
101 D18 Achfary IV27
94 B14 Achgarve IV22
101 B19 Achiemore *Hgh.* IV27
102 C24 Achiemore *Hgh.* KW13
103 C27 Achies KW12
85 D8 A'Chill PH44
94 A15 Achiltibuie IV26
102 B22 Achina KW14
97 G24 Achindown IV12
96 A21 Achinduich IV27
103 B27 Achingills KW12
94 G15 Achintee IV54
87 G17 Achintee Ho PH33
86 A14 Achintraid IV54
89 E24 Achlean PH21
79 B11 Achleanan PA34
79 B13 Achleek PH33
80 E17 Achlian PA33
101 C18 Achlyness IV27
101 F16 Achmelvich IV27
88 A20 Achmony IV3
81 D21 Achmore *Cen.* FK21
95 B16 Achmore *Hgh.* IV23
86 A14 Achmore *Hgh.* IV53
73 B14 Achnaba PA31
88 A21 Achnabat IV1
102 C22 Achnabourin KW14
80 D15 Achnacairn PA37
101 E16 Achnacarnin IV27
96 E19 Achnaclerach IV23
80 D15 Achnacloich PA37
86 D11 Achnacloich IV46
103 E26 Achnaclyth KW6
79 C10 Achnacraig PA73
79 C14 Achnacroish PA34
79 B10 Achnadrish PA75
80 E17 Achnafalnich PA33
81 D24 Achnafauld PH8
96 G21 Achnagairn IV5
96 D22 Achnagarron IV18
79 C12 Achnaha *Hgh.* PA34
79 A10 Achnaha *Hgh.* PH36
96 B20 Achnahanat IV24
89 B25 Achnahannet PH26
102 G21 Achnairn IV27
79 A14 Achnalea PH33
79 A13 Achnanellan PH37
87 F17 Achnasaul PH34
95 F17 Achnasheen IV22
73 A14 Achnashelloch PA31
98 F28 Achnastank AB55
103 E27 Achorn KW6
96 B22 Achosnich *Hgh.* IV25
79 A10 Achosnich *Hgh.* PH36
103 B25 Achreamie KW14
80 A17 Achriabhach PH33
101 C18 Achriesgill IV27
97 A24 Achrimsdale KW9
79 D10 Achronich PA72
102 B22 Achtoty KW14
42 G46 Achurch PE8
102 C21 Achuvoldrach IV27
96 B22 Achvaich IV25
103 B25 Achvarasdal KW14
80 B15 Achvlair PA38
95 A16 Achvraie IV26
103 C29 Ackergill KW1
62 E40 Acklam *Cle.* TS5
58 C43 Acklam *N.Y.* YO17
39 F33 Ackleton WV6
71 C38 Acklington NE65
57 G40 Ackton WF7
51 A40 Ackworth Moor Top WF7
45 D59 Acle NR13
40 G36 Acock's Green B27
25 E58 Acol CT7
58 D41 Acomb *N.Y.* YO2
70 G35 Acomb *Nor.* NE46
28 E30 Aconbury HR2
56 G33 Acre BB5
38 A28 Acrefair LL14
15 C57 Acrise Place CT18
49 G32 Acton *Che.* CW5
22 C47 Acton *G.L.* W3
29 B34 Acton *H.&W.* DY13
34 D54 Acton *Sfk* CO10
38 G28 Acton *Shr.* SY9
29 C32 Acton Beauchamp WR6
48 E31 Acton Bridge CW8
38 E31 Acton Burnell SY5
29 D32 Acton Green WR6
38 E31 Acton Pigott SY5
39 F32 Acton Round WV16
38 G30 Acton Scott SY6
40 D35 Acton Trussell ST18
20 C34 Acton Turville GL9
74 G20 Adamhill KA1
39 C33 Adbaston ST20
8 B31 Adber DT9
31 E40 Adderbury OX17
39 B32 Adderley TF9
77 G37 Adderstone NE70
75 D25 Addiewell EH55
57 E36 Addingham LS29
31 F43 Addington *Bkh.* MK18
23 E49 Addington *G.L.* CR0
23 F52 Addington *Kent* ME19
22 E46 Addlestone KT15
53 F51 Addlethorpe PE24
57 F38 Adel LS16
39 D32 Adeney TF10
37 E26 Adfa SY16
28 A29 Adforton SY7
15 B57 Adisham CT3
30 F38 Adlestrop GL56
58 G44 Adlingfleet DN14
49 D35 Adlington *Che.* SK10
48 A31 Adlington *Lan.* BL6
39 D32 Admaston *Shr.* TF5
40 C36 Admaston *Stf.* WS15
30 D37 Admington CV36
8 B28 Adsborough TA2
31 E43 Adstock MK18
31 C41 Adstone NN12
12 D46 Adversane RH14
57 G38 Adwalton BD11
21 B42 Adwell OX9
51 B41 Adwick le Street DN6
51 B40 Adwick upon Dearne S64
68 E25 Ae Village DG1
91 A34 Affleck *Grm.* AB2
83 D30 Affleck *Tay.* DD5
9 E33 Affpuddle DT2
47 E27 Afon-wen CH7
68 B22 Afton Bridgend KA18
57 A36 Agglethorpe DL8
109 C6 Aghadowey BT51
109 E7 Aghalee BT67
109 C6 Aghanloo BT49
109 D7 Ahoghill BT42
48 D29 Aigburth L17
100 D10 Aignis HS2
59 E46 Aike YO25
104 A30 Aikerness KW17
105 B30 Aikers KW17
61 B30 Aiketgate CA4
60 B27 Aikshaw CA5
60 A28 Aikton CA7
69 A30 Aikwood Tower TD7
28 D29 Ailey HR3
42 F47 Ailsworth PE5
103 B27 Aimster KW14
57 A39 Ainderby Quernhow YO7
62 G39 Ainderby Steeple DL7
35 G57 Aingers Green CO7
48 A29 Ainsdale PR8
61 B31 Ainstable CA4
49 A33 Ainsworth BL2
63 F42 Ainthorpe YO21
48 C29 Aintree L10
92 F3 Aird HS7
92 G3 Aird A Mhachair HS8
100 F7 Aird A Mhulaidh HS3
100 G7 Aird Asaig HS3
100 A10 Aird Dhail HS2
92 C6 Aird Leimhe HS3
92 B6 Aird Mhige HS3
92 C6 Aird Mhighe HS3
86 D11 Aird of Sleat IV45
83 G31 Airdrie *Fife* KY10
75 D23 Airdrie *Str.* ML6
100 D10 Aird Thunga HS2
100 D6 Aird Uige HS2
100 F8 Airidh A Bhruaich HS2
65 E23 Airieland DG7
86 A13 Airigh-drishaig IV54
58 G43 Airmyn DN14
82 D26 Airntully PH1
86 D13 Airor PH41
75 B24 Airth FK2
56 D35 Airton BD23
64 F19 Airyhassen DG8
52 C44 Aisby *Lcn.* DN21
42 B46 Aisby *Lcn.* NG32
84 B3 Aisgernis HS8
57 A38 Aiskew DL8
62 E39 Aislaby *Cle.* TS16
58 A43 Aislaby *N.Y.* YO18
63 F44 Aislaby *N.Y.* YO21
52 D45 Aisthorpe LN1
104 E28 Aith *Ork.* KW16
104 D32 Aith *Ork.* KW17
106 D42 Aith *She.* ZE2
107 B39 Aith *She.* ZE2
89 A25 Aitnoch PH26
70 A35 Akeld NE71
31 E42 Akeley MK18
35 D57 Akenham IP1
4 C20 Albaston PL18
38 D29 Alberbury SY5
13 E48 Albourne BN6
38 D30 Albrighton *Shr.* SY4
39 E33 Albrighton *Shr.* WV7
45 G58 Alburgh IP20
33 F50 Albury *Hfs.* SG11
22 G46 Albury *Sry* GU5
22 G46 Albury Heath GU5
45 B57 Alby Hill NR11
96 F21 Alcaig IV7
38 G30 Alcaston SY6
30 C36 Alcester B49
13 F50 Alciston BN26
7 A25 Alcombe TA24
32 A47 Alconbury PE17
32 A47 Alconbury Hill PE17
32 A47 Alconbury Weston PE17
57 C40 Aldborough *N.Y.* YO5
45 B57 Aldborough *Nfk* NR11
21 D38 Aldbourne SN8
59 F48 Aldbrough HU11
62 E37 Aldbrough St John DL11
57 B38 Aldburgh HG4
32 G45 Aldbury HP23
81 A24 Aldclune PH16
35 C60 Aldeburgh IP15
45 F60 Aldeby NR34
22 B47 Aldenham WD2
10 B37 Alderbury SP5
45 D57 Alderford NR9
109 D7 Aldergrove BT29
10 C37 Alderholt SP6
20 B33 Alderley GL12
49 E34 Alderley Edge SK9
41 G39 Alderman's Green CV2
21 E41 Aldermaston RG7
21 E41 Aldermaston Soke RG7
21 E42 Aldermaston Wharf RG7
30 D38 Alderminster CV37
48 G30 Aldersey Green CH3
22 F43 Aldershot GU12
29 E35 Alderton *Glo.* GL20
31 D43 Alderton *Nmp.* NN12
35 D59 Alderton *Sfk* IP12
38 C30 Alderton *Shr.* SY4
20 C34 Alderton *Wts.* SN14
50 G38 Alderwasley DE56
57 C38 Aldfield HG4
48 G29 Aldford CH3
34 F55 Aldham *Esx* CO6
34 D56 Aldham *Sfk* IP7
99 E36 Aldie *Grm.* AB42
96 C23 Aldie *Hgh.* IV19
12 F44 Aldingbourne PO20
55 B28 Aldingham LA12
30 D36 Aldington *H.&W.* WR11
15 D56 Aldington *Kent* TN25
90 A29 Aldivalloch AB54
74 A19 Aldochlay G83
67 E17 Aldons KA26
33 A50 Aldreth CB6
40 E36 Aldridge WS9
35 B60 Aldringham IP16
58 C44 Aldro YO17
20 A37 Aldsworth GL54
90 A29 Aldunie AB54
82 D25 Aldville PH8
50 G38 Aldwark *Dby.* DE4
57 C40 Aldwark *N.Y.* YO6
12 G45 Aldwick PO21
42 G45 Aldwincle NN14
21 D41 Aldworth RG8
74 C19 Alexandria G83
6 D18 Alfardisworthy EX22
7 F27 Alfington EX11
12 C46 Alfold GU6
12 C46 Alfold Crossways GU6
90 B31 Alford *Grm.* AB33
53 E50 Alford *Lcn.* LN13
9 A32 Alford *Som.* BA7
51 G39 Alfreton DE55
29 C33 Alfrick WR6
13 F50 Alfriston BN26
43 B48 Algarkirk PE20
9 A32 Alhampton BA4
58 G44 Alkborough DN15
30 D39 Alkerton OX15
15 C58 Alkham CT15
38 B31 Alkington SY13
40 B37 Alkmonton DE6
5 E24 Allaleigh TQ9
89 E26 Allanaquoich AB35
90 D31 Allancreich AB34
69 D28 Allangillfoot DG13
77 E34 Allanton *Bor.* TD11
68 E24 Allanton *D.&G.* DG2
75 E23 Allanton *Str.* ML3
75 E24 Allanton *Str.* ML7
91 F33 Allardice DD10
84 D2 Allathasdal HS9
20 E36 All Cannings SN10
61 A34 Allendale Town NE47
61 B34 Allenheads NE47
62 A36 Allensford DH8
33 G50 Allen's Green CM21
28 E30 Allensmore HR2

Ashurstwood

8 B29 Aller TA10
60 C26 Allerby CA5
6 G20 Allerford *Dev.* EX20
7 A25 Allerford *Som.* TA24
58 A44 Allerston YO18
58 E43 Allerthorpe YO4
48 D30 Allerton *Mer.* L18
57 F37 Allerton *W.Y.* BD15
57 G39 Allerton Bywater WF10
40 G38 Allesley CV5
41 B39 Allestree DE22
42 E44 Allexton LE15
49 F35 Allgreave SK11
24 D54 Allhallows ME3
94 F13 Alligin Shuas IV22
40 D34 Allimore Green ST18
42 A44 Allington *Lcn.* NG32
20 E36 Allington *Wts.* SN10
10 A38 Allington *Wts.* SP4
55 B29 Allithwaite LA11
102 D20 Allnabad IV27
75 A24 Alloa FK10
60 B26 Allonby CA15
67 B19 Alloway KA7
45 G59 All Saints South Elmham IP19
39 F33 Allscot WV15
38 F30 All Stretton SY6
79 B13 Alltachonaich PA34
101 G15 Alltan Dubh IV26
87 B16 Alltbeithe IV40
37 C25 Alltforgan SY10
27 D26 Alltmawr LD2
102 D20 Alltnacaillich IV27
95 B16 Allt na h-Airbhe IV26
86 B14 Allt-na-subh IV40
88 C20 Alltsigh IV3
17 A20 Alltwalis SA33
18 A23 Alltwen SA8
26 D21 Alltyblaca SA40
9 C32 Allweston DT9
28 C29 Almeley HR3
9 E34 Almer DT11
39 B33 Almington TF9
6 C19 Almiston Cross EX39
82 E26 Almondbank PH1
50 A37 Almondbury HD4
19 C31 Almondsbury BS12
57 C40 Alne YO6
96 E22 Alness IV17
70 B35 Alnham NE65
71 B38 Alnmouth NE66
71 B37 Alnwick NE66
34 E54 Alphamstone CO8
34 C54 Alpheton CO10
7 G25 Alphington EX2
45 E58 Alpington NR14
50 F38 Alport DE45
48 G31 Alpraham CW6
34 F56 Alresford CO7
40 D37 Alrewas DE13
82 A27 Alrick PH11
49 G33 Alsager ST7
40 A34 Alsagers Bank ST7
50 G37 Alsop en le Dale DE6
61 B33 Alston *Cum.* CA9
8 D29 Alston *Dev.* EX13
29 E35 Alstone GL20
50 G36 Alstonefield DE6
6 C22 Alswear EX36
102 F23 Altanduin KW11
4 B18 Altarnun PL15
96 A20 Altass IV27
91 C35 Altens AB1
103 B28 Alterwall KW1
56 F33 Altham BB5
25 B55 Althorne CM3
52 B44 Althorpe DN17
64 E18 Alticry DG8
80 B17 Altnafeadh PA39
102 E21 Altnaharra IV27
57 G39 Altofts WF6
51 F39 Alton *Dby.* S42
22 G43 Alton *Ham.* GU34
40 A36 Alton *Stf.* ST10
20 E37 Alton Barnes SN9
9 D32 Alton Pancras DT2
20 E37 Alton Priors SN8
98 D28 Altonside IV30
49 D33 Altrincham WA14
87 E18 Altura PH34
75 A24 Alva FK12
48 E30 Alvanley WA6
41 B39 Alvaston DE24
30 A36 Alvechurch B48
40 E38 Alvecote B79
9 B35 Alvediston SP5
39 G33 Alveley WV15
6 C21 Alverdiscott EX31
11 E42 Alverstoke PO12
11 F41 Alverstone PO36
42 A43 Alverton NG13
97 E27 Alves IV30
21 A38 Alvescot OX18
19 C32 Alveston *Avon* BS12
30 C38 Alveston *War.* CV37
89 D24 Alvie PH21
53 C49 Alvingham LN11
19 A31 Alvington GL15
42 F47 Alwalton PE2
70 C34 Alwinton NE65
57 E39 Alwoodley Gates LS17
82 C28 Alyth PH11
2 E10 Amalebra TR20
51 G39 Ambergate DE56
43 A48 Amber Hill PE20
20 A34 Amberley *Glo.* GL5
12 E46 Amberley *W.S.* BN18
71 C38 Amble NE65
40 G34 Amblecote DY8
60 F29 Ambleside LA22
16 B15 Ambleston SA62
73 E16 Ambrismore PA20
31 G41 Ambrosden OX6
52 A44 Amcotts DN17
22 B45 Amersham HP7
20 G37 Amesbury SP4
40 E38 Amington B77
68 E25 Amisfield Town DG1
46 C20 Amlwch LL68
46 C20 Amlwch Port LL68
17 C21 Ammanford SA18
58 B43 Amotherby YO17
10 B39 Ampfield SO51
58 B41 Ampleforth YO6
58 B41 Ampleforth College YO6
20 A36 Ampney Crucis GL7
20 A36 Ampney St Mary GL7
20 A36 Ampney St Peter GL7
21 G38 Amport SP11
32 E46 Ampthill MK45
34 A54 Ampton IP31
16 D17 Amroth SA67
81 D24 Amulree PH8
89 A25 Anaboard PH26
79 A14 Anaheilt PH36
42 A45 Ancaster NG32
38 G27 Anchor SY7
77 F35 Ancroft TD15
70 A32 Ancrum TD8
12 F45 Ancton PO22
53 E51 Anderby PE24
9 E34 Anderson DT11
49 E32 Anderton CW8
21 G38 Andover SP10
21 G39 Andover Down SP11
29 G35 Andoversford GL54
54 D25 Andreas IM7
36 C17 Anelog LL53
2 E11 Angarrack TR27
7 D27 Angersleigh TA3
60 A28 Angerton CA5
16 D14 Angle SA71
37 F23 Angler's Retreat SY20
12 F46 Angmering BN16
57 E40 Angram YO2
81 F21 Anie FK17
96 D23 Ankerville IV19
59 G46 Anlaby HU10
44 C53 Anmer PE31
109 G8 Annalong BT34
69 G27 Annan DG12
54 A26 Annaside LA19
94 F14 Annat *Hgh.* IV22
80 E16 Annat *Str.* PA35
21 G39 Anna Valley SP11
67 A20 Annbank KA6
51 G40 Annesley NG15
51 G40 Annesley Woodhouse NG15
62 A37 Annfield Plain DH9
109 F8 Annsborough BT31
38 E30 Annscroft SY5
55 G29 Ansdell FY8
9 A32 Ansford BA7
40 F38 Ansley CV10
40 C37 Anslow DE13
40 C37 Anslow Gate DE13
33 E50 Anstey *Hfs.* SG9
41 E41 Anstey *Lei.* LE7
83 G31 Anstruther KY10
13 D48 Ansty *W.S.* RH17
41 G39 Ansty *War.* CV7
9 B35 Ansty *Wts.* SP3
11 C42 Anthill Common PO7
60 A27 Anthorn CA5
45 B58 Antingham NR28
92 C5 An T-ob HS5
4 E20 Antony PL11
109 D7 Antrim BT41
49 E32 Antrobus CW9
6 E19 Anvil Corner EX22
52 G47 Anwick NG34
65 E21 Anwoth DG7
72 D8 Aoradh PA44
43 G51 Apes Hall CB6
42 F46 Apethorpe PE8
52 E46 Apley LN3
51 E39 Apperknowle S18
29 F34 Apperley GL19
80 C15 Appin Ho. PA38
52 A45 Appleby DN15
41 D39 Appleby Magna DE12
41 E39 Appleby Parva DE12
94 G12 Applecross IV54
7 D26 Appledore *Dev.* EX15
6 B20 Appledore *Dev.* EX39
14 E55 Appledore *Kent* TN26
14 D55 Appledore Heath TN26
21 B41 Appleford OX14
21 G39 Appleshaw SP11
60 D28 Applethwaite CA12
21 A40 Appleton OX13
58 A43 Appleton-le-Moors YO6
58 B43 Appleton-le-Street YO17
58 E41 Appleton Roebuck YO5
49 D32 Appleton Thorn WA4
62 F39 Appleton Wiske DL6
69 B30 Appletreehall TD9
57 C36 Appletreewick BD23
7 C26 Appley TA21
48 A31 Appley Bridge WN6
11 F41 Apse Heath PO36
22 A46 Apsley HP3
32 E47 Apsley End SG5
12 F44 Apuldram PO20
83 C31 Arbirlot DD11
22 E43 Arborfield RG2
22 E43 Arborfield Cross RG2
22 E43 Arborfield Garrison RG11
83 D32 Arbroath DD11
91 F33 Arbuthnott AB30
62 E38 Archdeacon Newton DL2
97 G27 Archiestown AB38
49 F33 Arclid CW11
73 C16 Ard a'Chapuill PA22
73 B16 Ardacheranbeg PA22
73 B16 Ardacheranmor PA22
79 D12 Ardachoil PA65
87 E17 Ardachvie PH34
72 F12 Ardailly PA41
78 F9 Ardalanish PA67
80 E16 Ardanaiseig PA35
86 A14 Ardaneaskan IV54
79 F14 Ardanstur PA34
79 B12 Ardantiobairt PA34
79 E14 Ardantrive PA34
86 A14 Ardarroch IV54
73 D16 Ardbeg *Str.* PA20
73 B17 Ardbeg *Str.* PA23
72 F10 Ardbeg *Str.* PA42
88 A20 Ardblair IV4
80 E16 Ardbrecknish PA33
95 C17 Ardcharnich IV23
78 F9 Ardchiavaig PA67
79 D14 Ardchonnel PA37
80 F15 Ardchonnell PA33
78 E9 Ardchrishnish PA70
96 C21 Ardchronie IV24
87 A18 Ardchuilk IV4
81 F21 Ardchullarie More FK18
81 E21 Ardchyle FK20
38 D28 Arddlin SY22
33 F48 Ardeley SG2
86 B14 Ardelve IV40
74 B19 Arden G83
79 F13 Ardencaple PA34
30 C37 Ardens Grafton B49
79 E14 Ardentallan PA34
73 B17 Ardentinny PA23
81 D22 Ardeonaig FK21
96 F23 Ardersier IV1
79 A13 Ardery PH36
95 C16 Ardessie IV23
79 F13 Ardfad PA34
79 G13 Ardfern PA31
72 D10 Ardfin PA60
80 G18 Ardgartan G83
96 B21 Ardgay IV24
80 F17 Ardgenavan PA26
109 F9 Ardglass BT30
73 C17 Ardgowan PA16
90 B31 Ardgowse AB33
97 E27 Ardgye IV30
73 C17 Ardhallow PA23
94 F13 Ardheslaig IV54
98 C31 Ardiecow AB45
79 F13 Ardinamar PA34
95 C17 Ardindrean IV23
13 D49 Ardingly RH17
21 C40 Ardington OX12
86 B14 Ardintoul IV40
109 E9 Ardkeen BT22
80 G17 Ardkinglas Ho PA26
90 A31 Ardlair AB52
73 D15 Ardlamont PA21
34 F56 Ardleigh CO7
80 F19 Ardleish G83
82 C28 Ardler PH12
31 F41 Ardley OX6
80 F19 Ardlui G83
72 B12 Ardlussa PA60
80 D16 Ardmaddy PA35
95 B16 Ardmair IV26
73 D16 Ardmaleish PA20
80 G18 Ardmay G83
72 C11 Ardmenish PA60
84 D3 Ardmhor HS9
72 F12 Ardminish PA41
86 G13 Ardmolich PH36
96 C23 Ardmore *Hgh.* IV19
74 C19 Ardmore *Str.* G82
79 E13 Ardmore *Str.* PA34
72 F10 Ardmore *Str.* PA42
73 A13 Ardnackaig PA31
79 C11 Ardnacross PA72
73 C17 Ardnadam PA23
79 D12 Ardnadrochet PA64
94 A15 Ardnagoine IV26
80 G16 Ardnagowan PA25
96 G20 Ardnagrask IV4
73 A17 Ardnahein PA24
72 C10 Ardnahoe PA46
86 A14 Ardnarff IV54
79 A13 Ardnastang PH36
72 C8 Ardnave PA44
80 G17 Ardno PA26
99 F34 Ardo AB41
68 C24 Ardoch *D.&G.* DG3
97 F27 Ardoch *Grm.* IV36
82 D26 Ardoch *Tay.* PH1
74 F22 Ardochrig G75
96 A22 Ardochu IV28
91 A32 Ardoyne AB52
73 D13 Ardpatrick PA29
73 B17 Ardpeaton G84
81 C22 Ardradnaig PH15
73 B14 Ardrishaig PA30
101 F16 Ardroe IV27
73 F17 Ardrossan KA22
73 E16 Ardscalpsie PA20
96 B23 Ardshave IV25
79 A12 Ardshealach PH36
79 F13 Ardshellach PA34
51 B39 Ardsley S71
79 A11 Ardslignish PH36
72 E10 Ardtalla PA42
81 D22 Ardtalnaig PH15
73 B16 Ardtarig PA23
80 E17 Ardteatle PA33
86 G12 Ardtoe PH36
79 C12 Ardtornish PA34
81 E22 Ardtrostan PH6
80 C15 Ardtur PA38
79 F13 Arduaine PA34
96 E21 Ardullie IV16
79 D12 Ardura PA65
101 E17 Ardvar IV27
86 D12 Ardvasar IV45
81 E22 Ardveich FK19
88 F20 Ardverikie PH20
80 F19 Ardvorlich *Str.* G83
81 E22 Ardvorlich *Tay.* FK19
65 E21 Ardwall DG7
64 F17 Ardwell *D.&G.* DG9
98 F29 Ardwell *Grm.* AB54
67 D17 Ardwell *Str.* KA26
29 A33 Areley Kings DY13
12 C44 Arford GU35
81 G23 Argaty FK16
18 B27 Argoed NP2
27 B25 Argoed Mill LD1
65 E22 Argrennan DG7
79 G14 Arichamish PA31
80 D18 Arichastlich PA36
73 A13 Arichonan PA31
78 E9 Aridhglas PA66
86 F13 Arienskill PH38
78 B7 Arileod PA78
94 F13 Arinacrinachd IV54
73 B13 Arinafad Beg PA31
78 B8 Arinagour PA78
84 B3 Arinambane HS8
86 F12 Arisaig PH39
79 A12 Arivegaig PH36
57 C39 Arkendale HG5
33 E50 Arkesden CB11
55 B31 Arkholme LA6
60 B27 Arkleby CA5
57 A36 Arkleside DL8
69 D29 Arkleton DG13
23 B48 Arkley EN5
51 B41 Arksey DN5
51 F40 Arkwright Town S44
82 G27 Arlary KY13
60 E26 Arlecdon CA26
32 E47 Arlesey SG15
39 D32 Arleston TF1
49 D32 Arley CW9
29 G32 Arlingham GL2
6 A22 Arlington *Dev.* EX31
13 F51 Arlington *E.S.* BN26
20 A36 Arlington *Glo.* GL7
6 A22 Arlington Beccott EX31
86 D12 Armadale *Hgh.* IV45
102 B23 Armadale *Hgh.* KW14
75 D25 Armadale *Ltn* EH48
109 F6 Armagh BT61
61 B30 Armathwaite CA4
45 E58 Arminghall NR14
40 D36 Armitage WS15
109 B7 Armoy BT53
30 D38 Armscote CV37
42 G46 Armston PE8
51 B42 Armthorpe DN3
78 B7 Arnabost PA78
56 B35 Arncliffe BD23
56 B35 Arncliffe Cote BD23
83 G30 Arncroach KY10
9 F35 Arne BH20
41 F42 Arnesby LE8
82 F27 Arngask PH2
74 A22 Arngibbon FK8
74 A22 Arngomery FK8
83 A31 Arnhall DD9
73 G13 Arnicle PA29
86 F13 Arnipol PH38
86 C14 Arnisdale IV40
94 G12 Arnish IV40
76 D29 Arniston Engine EH23
100 C8 Arnol HS2
41 A41 Arnold NG5
74 F22 Arnprior FK8
55 B30 Arnside LA5
38 B30 Arowry SY13
55 A29 Arrad Foot LA12
98 C30 Arradoul AB56
59 E46 Arram HU17
83 B32 Arrat DD9
62 G37 Arrathorne DL8
11 F41 Arreton PO30
33 C49 Arrington SG8
80 D18 Arrivain PA33
80 G18 Arrochar G83
30 C36 Arrow B49
102 G20 Arscaig IV27
57 E38 Arthington LS21
42 G43 Arthingworth LE16
37 D22 Arthog LL39
99 F35 Arthrath AB41
82 C28 Arthurstone PH13
109 B6 Articlave BT51
99 F35 Artrochie AB41
72 D8 Aruadh PA49
12 F46 Arundel BN18
80 A15 Aryhoulan PH33
60 D26 Asby CA14
73 D17 Ascog PA20
22 E45 Ascot SL5
30 E39 Ascott CV36
30 G39 Ascott-under-Wychwood OX7
82 B29 Ascreavie DD8
57 B39 Asenby YO7
41 D42 Asfordby LE14
42 D43 Asfordby Hill LE14
42 A47 Asgarby *Lcn.* NG34
53 F49 Asgarby *Lcn.* PE23
6 E21 Ash *Dev.* EX20
15 B58 Ash *Kent* CT3
23 E51 Ash *Kent* TN15
8 B30 Ash *Som.* TA12
22 F44 Ash *Sry* GU12
21 D41 Ashampstead RG8
35 C57 Ashbocking IP6
40 A37 Ashbourne DE6
7 C26 Ashbrittle TA21
7 E23 Ash Bullayne EX17
13 E52 Ashburnham Place TN33
5 C23 Ashburton TQ13
6 F21 Ashbury *Dev.* EX20
21 C38 Ashbury *Oxf.* SN6
52 B45 Ashby DN16
53 F50 Ashby by Partney PE23
53 B48 Ashby cum Fenby DN37
52 G46 Ashby de la Launde LN4
41 D39 Ashby de la Zouch LE65
42 D43 Ashby Folville LE14
41 F41 Ashby Magna LE17
41 G41 Ashby Parva LE17
53 E49 Ashby Puerorum LN9
31 B41 Ashby St Ledgers CV23
45 E59 Ashby St Mary NR14
29 E35 Ashchurch GL20
5 C25 Ashcombe EX7
8 A30 Ashcott TA7
33 D51 Ashdon CB10
21 G41 Ashe RG25
25 A55 Asheldham CM0
34 D53 Ashen CO10
14 D54 Ashenden TN30
31 G42 Ashendon HP18
73 C14 Ashens PA29
81 G23 Ashfield *Cen.* FK15
35 B57 Ashfield *Sfk* IP14
73 B13 Ashfield *Str.* PA31
35 A58 Ashfield Green IP21
13 D48 Ashfold Crossways RH13
6 B21 Ashford *Dev.* EX31
5 F22 Ashford *Dev.* TQ7
10 C37 Ashford *Ham.* SP6
14 C55 Ashford *Kent* TN24
22 D46 Ashford *Sry* TW15
28 A30 Ashford Bowdler SY8
28 A31 Ashford Carbonel SY8
21 E41 Ashford Hill RG19
50 E37 Ashford in the Water DE45
75 E23 Ashgill ML9
76 G30 Ashiestiel TD1
7 D26 Ashill *Dev.* EX15
44 E54 Ashill *Nfk* IP25
8 C29 Ashill *Som.* TA19
24 B54 Ashingdon SS4
71 E38 Ashington *Nor.* NE63
8 B31 Ashington *Som.* BA22
12 E47 Ashington *W.S.* RH20
69 A30 Ashkirk TD7
29 F33 Ashleworth GL19
33 B52 Ashley *Cbs.* CB8
49 D33 Ashley *Che.* WA15
6 D22 Ashley *Dev.* EX18
20 B35 Ashley *Glo.* GL8
10 E38 Ashley *Ham.* BH25
10 A39 Ashley *Ham.* SO20
15 C58 Ashley *Kent* CT15
42 F43 Ashley *Nmp.* LE16
39 B33 Ashley *Stf.* TF9
20 E33 Ashley *Wts.* SN13
22 A45 Ashley Green HP5
10 D37 Ashley Heath BH24
38 B31 Ash Magna SY13
45 C59 Ashmanhaugh NR12
21 F40 Ashmansworth RG20
6 D18 Ashmansworthy EX39
7 C23 Ash Mill EX36
9 C35 Ashmore *Dor.* SP5
82 B27 Ashmore *Tay.* PH10
30 C38 Ashorne CV35
51 F39 Ashover S45
30 A38 Ashow CV8
29 D32 Ashperton HR8
5 E23 Ashprington TQ9
7 C27 Ash Priors TA4
6 D21 Ashreigney EX18
22 F47 Ashtead KT21
7 D26 Ash Thomas EX16
48 F30 Ashton *Che.* CH3
4 D19 Ashton *Cnw.* PL17
2 F11 Ashton *Cnw.* TR13
28 B31 Ashton *H.&W.* HR6
31 C43 Ashton *Nmp.* NN7
42 G46 Ashton *Nmp.* PE8
20 F34 Ashton Common BA14
48 C31 Ashton-in-Makerfield WN4
20 B36 Ashton Keynes SN6
29 E35 Ashton under Hill WR11
49 C35 Ashton-under-Lyne OL7
49 C33 Ashton upon Mersey M33
13 C50 Ashurst *E.S.* TN3
10 C39 Ashurst *Ham.* SO40
12 E47 Ashurst *W.S.* BN44
13 C50 Ashurstwood RH18

Ash Vale

130

Belmesthorpe

83 C31 Balmadies DD8
65 F22 Balmae DG6
74 A20 Balmaha G63
82 G28 Balmalcolm KY15
79 D10 Balmeanach PA68
91 B35 Balmedie AB23
82 E29 Balmerino DD6
10 D39 Balmerlawn SO42
64 D18 Balminnoch DG8
97 G24 Balmore *Hgh.* IV12
88 A19 Balmore *Hgh.* IV4
93 G8 Balmore *Hgh.* IV55
74 C22 Balmore *Str.* G64
83 E30 Balmullo KY16
96 F23 Balmungie IV10
82 B26 Balmyle PH10
82 A28 Balnaboth DD8
96 D23 Balnabruaich IV19
94 G16 Balnacra IV54
88 A22 Balnafoich IV1
97 C24 Balnagall IV20
96 D23 Balnagown Castle IV18
82 B25 Balnaguard PH9
96 D22 Balnaguisich IV18
72 A10 Balnahard *Str.* PA61
79 D10 Balnahard *Str.* PA68
88 A20 Balnain IV3
101 B19 Balnakeil IV27
93 E10 Balnaknock IV51
83 A31 Balnamoon DD9
96 E23 Balnapaling IV19
89 D24 Balnespick PH21
81 E21 Balquhidder FK19
30 A38 Balsall CV7
30 A38 Balsall Common CV7
30 D39 Balscote OX15
33 C51 Balsham CB1
106 B41 Baltasound ZE2
39 A33 Balterley CW2
64 D20 Baltersan DG8
99 D34 Balthangie AB53
82 E27 Balthayock PH2
8 A31 Baltonsborough BA6
73 A14 Baluachraig PA31
72 D9 Balulive PA45
80 D16 Balure *Str.* PA35
79 D14 Balure *Str.* PA37
96 F21 Balvaird IV6
82 A26 Balvarran PH10
79 F13 Balvicar PA34
89 A24 Balvraid *Hgh.* IV13
86 C14 Balvraid *Hgh.* IV40
55 G31 Bamber Bridge PR5
33 F51 Bamber's Green CM22
77 G37 Bamburgh NE69
82 B28 Bamff PH11
50 D37 Bamford S30
61 E30 Bampton *Cum.* CA10
7 C25 Bampton *Dev.* EX16
21 A38 Bampton *Oxf.* OX18
87 G16 Banavie PH33
109 F7 Banbridge BT32
31 D40 Banbury OX16
17 C20 Bancffosfelen SA15
97 G24 Banchor IV12
91 D32 Banchory AB31
91 C35 Banchory-Devenick AB1
17 C18 Bancyfelin SA33
17 A19 Banc-y-ffordd SA44
82 G28 Bandon KY7
98 C32 Banff AB45
109 D9 Bangor *Down* BT20
46 E21 Bangor *Gwy.* LL57
38 A29 Bangor-is-y-coed LL13
26 D19 Bangor Teifi SA44
44 G56 Banham NR16
10 D38 Bank SO43
69 G26 Bankend *D.&G.* DG1
75 G24 Bankend *Str.* ML11
54 A27 Bank End LA20
82 D26 Bankfoot PH1
65 F23 Bankhead *D.&G.* DG6
91 C34 Bankhead *Grm.* AB2
91 B32 Bankhead *Grm.* AB33
91 C32 Bankhead *Grm.* AB51
56 D35 Bank Newton BD23
75 C23 Banknock FK4
70 G31 Banks *Cum.* CA8
55 G29 Banks *Lan.* PR9
69 E27 Bankshill DG11
29 B32 Bank Street WR15
45 C58 Banningham NR11
33 F52 Bannister Green CM6
75 A24 Bannockburn FK7
23 F48 Banstead SM7
5 F22 Bantham TQ7
75 C23 Banton G65
19 F29 Banwell BS24
25 E55 Bapchild ME9
74 B21 Baptiston G63
100 B9 Barabhas HS2
80 E16 Barachander PA35
74 G18 Barassie KA10
96 D23 Barbaraville IV18
50 D37 Barber Booth S30
56 A32 Barbon LA6
7 A23 Barbrook EX35
31 A41 Barby CV23
80 C15 Barcaldine PA37
65 E22 Barcaple DG7
30 D38 Barcheston CV36
13 E50 Barcombe BN8
13 E50 Barcombe Cross BN8
62 G37 Barden DL8
67 D21 Bardennoch DG7
33 E52 Bardfield End Green CM6
33 F52 Bardfield Saling CM7
106 E39 Bardister ZE2
52 F45 Bardney LN3
97 F28 Bardon *Grm.* IV30
41 D40 Bardon *Lei.* LE67
70 G33 Bardon Mill NE47
55 B28 Bardsea LA12
57 E39 Bardsey LS17
49 B35 Bardsley OL8
34 A55 Bardwell IP31
28 C29 Barewood HR6
73 D14 Barfad PA29
45 E57 Barford *Nfk* NR9
30 B38 Barford *War.* CV35
31 E40 Barford St John OX15
10 A36 Barford St Martin SP3
30 E39 Barford St Michael OX15
15 B58 Barfreston CT15
64 D20 Bargaly DG8
67 C18 Bargany KA26
18 B27 Bargoed CF8
64 C19 Bargrennan DG8
32 A47 Barham *Cbs.* PE18
15 B57 Barham *Kent* CT4
35 C57 Barham *Sfk* IP6
65 E21 Barharrow DG7
33 B49 Bar Hill CB3
64 E20 Barholm *D.&G.* DG8
42 D46 Barholm *Lcn.* PE9
41 E42 Barkby LE7
41 E42 Barkby Thorpe LE7
42 B43 Barkestone-le-Vale NG13
22 E43 Barkham RG41
23 C50 Barking *G.L.* IG
34 C56 Barking *Sfk* IP6
23 C50 Barking & Dagenham RM
23 C50 Barkingside IG6
50 A36 Barkisland HX4
42 A45 Barkston *Lcn.* NG32
57 F40 Barkston *N.Y.* LS24
33 E49 Barkway SG8
64 D18 Barlae DG8
40 B34 Barlaston ST12
12 E45 Barlavington GU28
65 E21 Barlay DG7
51 E40 Barlborough S43
58 F42 Barlby YO8
41 E40 Barlestone CV13
33 E49 Barley *Hfs.* SG8
56 E34 Barley *Lan.* BB12
33 F49 Barleycroft End SG9
62 A36 Barleyhill NE44
42 E44 Barleythorpe LE15
25 C55 Barling SS3
52 E46 Barlings LN3
51 E39 Barlow *Dby.* S18
58 G42 Barlow *N.Y.* YO8
71 G37 Barlow *T.&W.* NE21
58 E43 Barmby Moor YO4
58 G42 Barmby on the Marsh DN14
73 A14 Barmolloch PA31
77 F35 Barmoor Lane End TD15
36 D21 Barmouth LL42
62 E38 Barmpton DL1
59 D47 Barmston YO25
73 B17 Barnacabber PA23
73 A16 Barnacarry PA27
42 E46 Barnack PE9
41 G39 Barnacle CV7
80 C16 Barnamuc PA38
62 E36 Barnard Castle DL12
31 G40 Barnard Gate OX8
33 D52 Barnardiston CB9
29 D33 Barnard's Green WR14
65 E24 Barnbarroch *D.&G.* DG5
64 E19 Barnbarroch *D.&G.* DG8
51 B40 Barnburgh DN5
45 F60 Barnby NR34
51 B41 Barnby Dun DN3
52 G44 Barnby in the Willows NG24
51 D42 Barnby Moor DN22
68 E24 Barndennoch DG3
23 D48 Barnes SW13
23 B48 Barnet NW
52 B46 Barnetby le Wold DN38
44 B55 Barney NR21
34 A54 Barnham *Sfk* IP24
12 F45 Barnham *W.S.* PO22
44 E56 Barnham Broom NR9
83 B32 Barnhead DD10
97 F27 Barnhill IV30
62 E36 Barningham *Drm* DL11
34 A55 Barningham *Sfk* IP31
53 B48 Barnoldby le Beck DN37
56 E34 Barnoldswick BB8
12 D47 Barns Green RH13
20 A36 Barnsley *Glo.* GL7
51 B39 Barnsley *S.Y.* S70
6 B21 Barnstaple EX31
33 G52 Barnston *Esx* CM6
48 D28 Barnston *Mer.* L61
42 B43 Barnstone NG13
30 A36 Barnt Green B45
49 E32 Barnton CW8
42 G46 Barnwell All Saints PE8
42 G46 Barnwell St Andrew PE8
29 G34 Barnwood GL4
79 B12 Barr *Hgh.* PA34
67 D18 Barr *Str.* KA26
72 D9 Barr *Str.* PA44
79 G13 Barrackan PA31
64 D19 Barraer DG8
100 D7 Barraglom HS2
72 B12 Barrahormid PA31
80 E17 Barran PA33
78 C5 Barrapoll PA77
70 F34 Barrasford NE48
84 D3 Barra (Traigh Mor) Airport HS9
79 G13 Barravullin PA31
54 E24 Barregarrow IM6
34 E53 Barr Hall CO9
74 E21 Barrhead G78
67 E18 Barrhill KA26
33 D49 Barrington *Cbs.* CB2
8 C29 Barrington *Som.* TA19
2 E12 Barripper TR14
86 D14 Barrisdale IV40
74 E19 Barrmill KA15
79 E13 Barrnacarry PA34
103 A28 Barrock KW14
56 F33 Barrow *Lan.* BB7
42 D44 Barrow *Lei.* LE15
34 B53 Barrow *Sfk* IP29
39 E32 Barrow *Shr.* TF12
9 A33 Barrow *Som.* BA9
42 B44 Barrowby NG32
42 E45 Barrowden LE15
56 F34 Barrowford BB9
19 E31 Barrow Gurney BS19
59 G46 Barrow Haven DN19
54 B27 Barrow-in-Furness LA14
48 B30 Barrow Nook L39
9 A34 Barrow Street BA12
59 G46 Barrow upon Humber DN19
41 D41 Barrow upon Soar LE12
41 C39 Barrow upon Trent DE73
18 E27 Barry *S.G.* CF62
83 D31 Barry *Tay.* DD7
41 D42 Barsby LE7
45 F59 Barsham NR34
67 A20 Barskimming KA5
73 A13 Barsloisnoch PA31
30 A37 Barston B93
28 D31 Bartestree HR1
99 F34 Barthol Chapel AB51
49 G33 Barthomley CW2
10 C39 Bartley SO40
33 D51 Bartlow CB1
33 C49 Barton *Cbs.* CB3
48 G30 Barton *Che.* SY14
5 D25 Barton *Dev.* TQ2
30 F36 Barton *Glo.* GL54
48 B29 Barton *Lan.* L39
55 F30 Barton *Lan.* PR3
62 F38 Barton *N.Y.* DL10
30 C37 Barton *War.* B50
44 E53 Barton Bendish PE33
45 C59 Barton Common NR12
20 B34 Barton End GL6
31 E42 Barton Hartshorn MK18
41 B41 Barton in Fabis NG11
41 E40 Barton in the Beans CV13
32 E46 Barton-le-Clay MK45
58 B43 Barton-le-Street YO17
58 C43 Barton-le-Willows YO6
34 A53 Barton Mills IP28
10 E38 Barton on Sea BH25
30 E38 Barton-on-the-Heath GL56
32 A44 Barton Seagrave NN15
21 G40 Barton Stacey SO21
21 G40 Barton Stacey Camp SO21
8 A31 Barton St David TA11
45 C59 Barton Turf NR12
40 D37 Barton-under-Needwood DE13
59 G45 Barton-upon-Humber DN18
33 A51 Barway CB7
41 F40 Barwell LE9
65 E22 Barwhinnock DG6
8 C31 Barwick BA22
57 F39 Barwick in Elmet LS15
64 F19 Barwinnock DG8
38 C29 Baschurch SY4
30 B39 Bascote CV23
49 G35 Basford Green ST13
56 E32 Bashall Eaves BB7
56 E32 Bashall Town BB7
10 E38 Bashley BH25
21 D42 Basildon *Brk.* RG8
24 C53 Basildon *Esx* SS14
21 F41 Basingstoke RG21
50 E38 Baslow DE45
19 G29 Bason Bridge TA9
19 C28 Bassaleg NP1
60 C27 Bassenthwaite CA12
11 C40 Bassett SO16
6 E21 Bassett's Cross EX20
33 D48 Bassingbourn SG8
41 B42 Bassingfield NG12
52 F44 Bassingham LN5
42 C45 Bassingthorpe NG33
106 C41 Basta ZE2
42 D47 Baston PE6
45 D60 Bastwick NR29
81 D20 Batavaime FK21
22 B46 Batchworth WD3
22 B46 Batchworth Heath WD3
9 D32 Batcombe *Dor.* DT2
9 A32 Batcombe *Som.* BA4
49 E32 Bate Heath CW9
20 E33 Bath BA
20 E33 Bathampton BA2
7 C26 Bathealton TA4
20 E33 Batheaston BA1
20 E33 Bathford BA1
75 D25 Bathgate EH48
51 G43 Bathley NG23
4 C18 Bathpool *Cnw.* PL15
8 B28 Bathpool *Som.* TA1
57 G38 Batley WF17
30 E37 Batsford GL56
63 F41 Battersby TS9
23 D48 Battersea SW11
5 F22 Battisborough Cross PL8
34 C56 Battisford IP14
34 C56 Battisford Tye IP14
14 F53 Battle *E.S.* TN33
27 E25 Battle *Pow.* LD3
38 D31 Battlefield SY1
24 B53 Battlesbridge SS11
32 F45 Battlesden MK17
7 C24 Battleton TA22
10 E38 Battramsley SO41
22 G44 Batt's Corner GU10
98 C30 Bauds of Cullen AB56
78 C6 Baugh PA77
29 D34 Baughton WR8
21 F41 Baughurst RG26
90 D31 Baulds AB31
21 B39 Baulking SN7
53 E48 Baumber LN9
20 A36 Baunton GL7
29 A32 Baveney Wood DY14
10 A36 Baverstock SP3
45 E57 Bawburgh NR9
44 C56 Bawdeswell NR20
8 A29 Bawdrip TA7
35 D59 Bawdsey IP12
51 C42 Bawtry DN10
56 G33 Baxenden BB5
40 F38 Baxterley CV9
55 B28 Baycliff LA12
21 D38 Baydon SN8
23 A48 Bayford *Bfd.* SG13
9 B33 Bayford *Som.* BA9
33 G48 Bayfordbury SG13
13 C52 Bayham Abbey TN3
61 B32 Bayles CA9
34 C56 Baylham IP6
31 F41 Baynards Green OX6
28 F31 Baysham HR9
38 E30 Bayston Hill SY3
34 D53 Baythorn End CB9
29 A32 Bayton DY14
79 B13 Beach PA34
31 E43 Beachampton MK19
72 F12 Beacharr PA29
15 D57 Beachborough CT18
19 B31 Beachley NP6
7 E27 Beacon EX14
34 F55 Beacon End CO3
12 C44 Beacon Hill GU26
22 B43 Beacon's Bottom HP14
22 B45 Beaconsfield HP9
58 A42 Beadlam YO6
71 A38 Beadnell NE67
6 D21 Beaford EX19
58 G41 Beal *N.Y.* DN14
77 F36 Beal *Nor.* TD15
80 B15 Bealach PA38
49 G32 Beambridge CW5
40 B36 Beamhurst ST14
8 D30 Beaminster DT8
62 A38 Beamish DH9
57 D36 Beamsley BD23
23 D51 Bean DA2
20 E34 Beanacre SN12
71 B36 Beanley NE66
104 D28 Beaquoy KW17
6 G21 Beardon EX20
22 G47 Beare Green RH5
30 B37 Bearley CV37
99 F35 Bearnie AB41
88 A19 Bearnock IV3
78 C9 Bearnus PA73
62 B38 Bearpark DH7
61 A33 Bearsbridge NE47
74 C21 Bearsden G61
14 B53 Bearsted ME14
10 E36 Bearwood BH11
69 C26 Beattock DG10
33 G51 Beauchamp Roding CM5
51 D39 Beauchief S8
30 B37 Beaudesert B95
28 G27 Beaufort NP3
10 D39 Beaulieu SO42
96 G21 Beauly IV4
46 E21 Beaumaris LL58
60 A29 Beaumont *Cum.* CA5
35 F57 Beaumont *Esx* CO16
30 A38 Beausale CV35
11 B41 Beauworth SO24
6 F20 Beaworthy EX21
34 F53 Beazley End CM7
48 D29 Bebington L63
71 E38 Bebside NE24
45 F60 Beccles NR34
55 G30 Becconsall PR4
39 E33 Beckbury TF11
23 E49 Beckenham BR3
60 F25 Beckermet CA21
60 F27 Beckfoot *Cum.* CA19
60 B26 Beckfoot *Cum.* CA5
61 G32 Beck Foot LA8
29 E35 Beckford GL20
20 E36 Beckhampton SN8
63 F44 Beck Hole YO22
52 G44 Beckingham *Lcn.* LN5
51 C43 Beckingham *Not.* DN10
20 F33 Beckington BA3
14 E54 Beckley *E.S.* TN31
31 G41 Beckley *Oxf.* OX3
33 A52 Beck Row IP28
55 A28 Beck Side LA17
23 C50 Beckton E6
57 D38 Beckwithshaw HG3
23 C50 Becontree RM9
57 A38 Bedale DL8
62 C36 Bedburn DL13
9 C34 Bedchester SP7
18 C26 Beddau CF38
36 A21 Beddgelert LL55
13 F50 Beddingham BN8
23 E48 Beddington SM6
23 E48 Beddington Corner CR4
35 B57 Bedfield IP13
32 C46 Bedford MK40
13 C52 Bedgebury Cross TN17
11 D43 Bedhampton PO9
35 B57 Bedingfield IP23
71 E38 Bedlington NE22
18 A26 Bedlinog CF46
22 A46 Bedmond WD5
40 D35 Bednall ST17
48 E28 Bedol CH6
70 B31 Bedrule TD9
28 A29 Bedstone SY7
18 C27 Bedwas NP1
18 A27 Bedwellty NP2
41 G39 Bedworth CV12
41 E42 Beeby LE7
11 A42 Beech *Ham.* GU34
40 B34 Beech *Stf.* ST4
44 E53 Beechamwell PE37
21 E42 Beech Hill RG7
20 F36 Beechingstoke SN9
21 D40 Beedon RG20
59 D47 Beeford YO25
50 F38 Beeley DE4
53 B48 Beelsby DN37
21 E41 Beenham RG7
8 F28 Beer EX12
8 B29 Beercrocombe TA3
9 C32 Beer Hackett DT9
5 F24 Beesands TQ7
53 D50 Beesby LN13
5 F23 Beeson TQ7
32 D47 Beeston *Bfd.* SG19
48 G31 Beeston *Che.* CW6
44 D55 Beeston *Nfk* PE32
41 B41 Beeston *Not.* NG9
57 F38 Beeston *W.Y.* LS11
45 A57 Beeston Regis NR26
45 C59 Beeston St Lawrence NR12
65 D24 Beeswing DG2
55 B30 Beetham LA7
44 D55 Beetley NR20
19 C28 Began CF3
31 G40 Begbroke OX5
16 D17 Begelly SA68
98 F31 Beggshill AB54
28 A27 Beguildy LD7
51 D40 Beighton *Dby.* S19
45 E59 Beighton *Nfk* NR13
74 E19 Beith KA15
15 B57 Bekesbourne CT4
45 D58 Belaugh NR12
29 A34 Belbroughton DY9
34 D54 Belchamp Otten CO10
34 D53 Belchamp St Paul CO10
34 D54 Belchamp Walter CO10
53 E48 Belchford LN9
108 F3 Belcoo BT93
109 E8 Belfast BT
77 G36 Belford NE70
41 E41 Belgrave LE4
76 C32 Belhaven EH42
91 B35 Belhelvie AB23
90 A30 Belhinnie AB54
90 B29 Bellabeg AB36
96 G21 Belladrum IV4
109 D7 Bellaghy BT45
108 F4 Bellanaleck BT92
73 A13 Bellanoch PA31
58 G44 Bellasize DN14
82 B28 Bellaty PH11
23 A48 Bell Bar AL9
56 D35 Bell Busk BD23
53 E49 Belleau LN13
109 F7 Belleek *Arm.* BT35
108 E3 Belleek *Fer.* BT93
29 A35 Bell End DY9
62 G37 Bellerby DL8
5 C22 Bellever PL20
83 A31 Belliehill DD9
22 A45 Bellingdon HP5
70 E34 Bellingham NE48
72 G12 Belloch PA29
72 G12 Bellochantuy PA28
75 B25 Bellsdyke FK2
77 G37 Bellshill *Nor.* NE70
75 E23 Bellshill *Str.* ML4
75 E24 Bellside ML1
75 G27 Bellspool EH45
75 D26 Bellsquarry EH54
13 C52 Bells Yew Green TN3
19 E31 Belluton BS18
96 F22 Belmaduthy IV8
42 D46 Belmesthorpe PE9

Belmont

23 E48 Belmont *G.L.* SM2
49 A32 Belmont *Lan.* BL7
106 B41 Belmont *She.* ZE2
3 B15 Belowda PL26
41 A39 Belper DE56
51 G39 Belper Lane End DE56
71 F36 Belsay NE20
5 E23 Belsford TQ9
35 D57 Belstead IP8
67 A19 Belston KA6
6 F21 Belstone EX20
6 F22 Belstone Corner EX20
75 C25 Belsyde EH49
56 G33 Belthorn BB1
25 E57 Beltinge CT6
52 B44 Beltoft DN9
51 B43 Belton *Hum.* DN9
42 B45 Belton *Lcn.* NG32
41 C40 Belton *Lei.* LE12
42 E44 Belton *Lei.* LE15
45 E60 Belton *Nfk* NR31
23 G52 Beltring TN12
23 D50 Belvedere DA17
42 B44 Belvoir NG32
11 F42 Bembridge PO35
76 G31 Bemersyde TD6
59 B47 Bempton YO15
45 G61 Benacre NR34
81 A20 Ben Alder Cottage PH17
88 G21 Ben Alder Lodge PH19
92 F3 Benbecula (Bhaile A Mhanaich) Airport HS7
68 D22 Benbuie DG3
109 E6 Benburb BT71
79 D14 Benderloch PA37
32 F47 Bendish SG4
14 D54 Benenden TN17
64 D19 Benfield DG8
45 C58 Bengate NR28
33 G49 Bengeo SG14
91 G34 Benholm DD10
58 D41 Beningbrough YO6
33 F48 Benington *Hfs.* SG2
43 A49 Benington *Lcn.* PE22
43 A50 Benington Sea End PE22
46 D20 Benllech LL74
81 E20 Benmore *Cen.* FK20
73 B17 Benmore *Str.* PA23
4 A18 Bennacott PL15
65 C22 Bennan DG7
53 D48 Benniworth LN3
14 C53 Benover ME18
21 B42 Benson OX10
71 A38 Benthall *Nor.* NE67
39 E32 Benthall *Shr.* TF12
29 G35 Bentham GL51
91 C33 Benthoul AB1
22 G43 Bentley *Ham.* GU10
59 F46 Bentley *Hum.* HU17
51 B41 Bentley *S.Y.* DN5
40 F38 Bentley *War.* CV9
30 A37 Bentley Heath B93
6 B22 Benton EX32
71 G39 Benton Square NE12
69 D28 Bentpath DG13
21 G42 Bentworth GU34
82 D29 Benvie DD2
8 D31 Benville Lane DT2
43 G49 Benwick PE15
30 B36 Beoley B98
12 E44 Bepton GU29
108 E5 Beragh BT79
33 F50 Berden CM23
16 B13 Berea SA62
4 D20 Bere Alston PL20
4 D20 Bere Ferrers PL20
2 F12 Berepper TR12
9 E34 Bere Regis BH20
45 E59 Bergh Apton NR15
21 B41 Berinsfield OX10
19 B32 Berkeley GL13
22 A45 Berkhamsted HP4
20 G33 Berkley BA11
30 A38 Berkswell CV7
23 D49 Bermondsey SE16
86 B14 Bernera IV40
24 A52 Berners Roding CM5
73 A17 Bernice PA23
93 F9 Bernisdale IV51
21 B42 Berrick Salome OX10
103 F26 Berriedale KW7
38 E27 Berriew (Aberriw) SY21
77 F35 Berrington *Nor.* TD15
38 E31 Berrington *Shr.* SY5
19 F28 Berrow TA8
29 C33 Berrow Green WR6
6 A21 Berry Down Cross EX34
16 A16 Berry Hill *Dyf.* SA42
28 G31 Berry Hill *Glo.* GL16
98 C30 Berryhillock AB56
6 A21 Berrynarbor EX34
5 D24 Berry Pomeroy TQ9
38 A28 Bersham LL14
104 E30 Berstane KW15
13 F50 Berwick BN26
20 D36 Berwick Bassett SN4
71 F37 Berwick Hill NE20
10 A36 Berwick St James SP3
9 B35 Berwick St John SP7
9 A35 Berwick St Leonard SP3
77 E35 Berwick-upon-Tweed TD15
48 A29 Bescar L40
29 D35 Besford *H.&W.* WR8
38 C31 Besford *Shr.* SY4
51 B41 Bessacarr DN4
109 F7 Bessbrook BT35
21 A40 Bessels Leigh OX13
59 C47 Bessingby YO16
45 B57 Bessingham NR11
13 C52 Best Beech Hill TN5
44 F56 Besthorpe *Nfk* NR17
52 F44 Besthorpe *Not.* NG23
59 E46 Beswick YO25
23 F48 Betchworth RH3
26 B21 Bethania *Dyf.* SY23
37 A22 Bethania *Gwy.* LL41
37 A25 Bethel *Gwy.* LL21
46 F21 Bethel *Gwy.* LL55
46 E19 Bethel *Gwy.* LL62
14 D55 Bethersden TN26
16 C16 Bethesda *Dyf.* SA67
46 F21 Bethesda *Gwy.* LL57
17 B22 Bethlehem SA19
23 C49 Bethnal Green E2
39 A33 Betley CW3
24 D52 Betsham DA13
15 B58 Betteshanger CT14
8 E29 Bettiscombe DT6
38 B30 Bettisfield SY13
38 E29 Betton *Shr.* SY5
39 B32 Betton *Shr.* TF9
19 B28 Bettws NP9
26 C21 Bettws Bledrws SA48
38 F27 Bettws Cedewain SY16
26 D18 Bettws Evan SA38
37 A26 Bettws Gwerfil Goch LL21
19 A29 Bettws-Newydd NP5
38 G27 Bettws-y-crwyn SY7
102 B22 Bettyhill KW14
17 C22 Betws *Dyf.* SA18
18 C24 Betws *M.G.* CF32
27 C26 Betws Disserth LD1
46 G21 Betws Garmon LL54
47 G23 Betws-y-coed LL24
47 E24 Betws-yn-Rhos LL22
26 D18 Beulah *Dyf.* SA38
27 C25 Beulah *Pow.* LD5
13 F49 Bevendean BN2
51 E42 Bevercotes NG22
59 F46 Beverley HU17
20 B34 Beverstone GL8
19 B32 Bevington GL13
60 C27 Bewaldeth CA13
70 F31 Bewcastle CA6
29 A33 Bewdley DY12
57 C37 Bewerley HG3
59 E47 Bewholme YO25
20 E35 Bewley Common SN15
14 G53 Bexhill TN40
23 D50 Bexley DA
23 D50 Bexleyheath DA6
44 E52 Bexwell PE38
34 B55 Beyton IP30
34 B55 Beyton Green IP30
100 B8 Bhalamus HS2
100 D6 Bhaltos HS2
84 E2 Bhatarsaigh HS9
88 E22 Biallaid PH20
20 A37 Bibury GL7
31 F41 Bicester OX6
8 C28 Bickenhall TA3
40 G37 Bickenhill B92
43 B48 Bicker PE20
48 B30 Bickerstaffe L39
48 G30 Bickerton *Che.* SY14
57 D40 Bickerton *N.Y.* LS22
40 D34 Bickford ST19
5 E23 Bickham Bridge TQ9
7 G25 Bickham House EX6
6 B21 Bickington *Dev.* EX31
5 C23 Bickington *Dev.* TQ12
7 E25 Bickleigh *Dev.* EX16
5 D21 Bickleigh *Dev.* PL6
6 B21 Bickleton EX31
23 E50 Bickley BR1
38 A31 Bickley Moss SY14
38 A31 Bickley Town SY14
24 A53 Bicknacre CM3
7 B26 Bicknoller TA4
14 B54 Bicknor ME9
10 C37 Bickton SP6
38 D30 Bicton *Shr.* SY3
38 G28 Bicton *Shr.* SY7
38 D30 Bicton Heath SY3
23 G51 Bidborough TN4
14 D54 Biddenden TN27
32 D46 Biddenham MK40
20 D34 Biddestone SN14
19 F29 Biddisham BS26
31 D42 Biddlesden NN13
70 C35 Biddlestone NE65
49 G34 Biddulph ST8
49 G35 Biddulph Moor ST8
6 C20 Bideford EX39
30 C36 Bidford-on-Avon B50
48 C28 Bidston L43
58 E43 Bielby YO4
91 C34 Bieldside AB1
11 G40 Bierley *I.o.W.* PO38
57 G37 Bierley *W.Y.* BD4
32 G44 Bierton HP22
5 F22 Bigbury TQ7
5 F21 Bigbury-on-Sea TQ7
52 B46 Bigby DN38
60 G27 Bigert Mire LA20
54 C27 Biggar *Cum.* LA14
75 G26 Biggar *Str.* ML12
40 A38 Biggin *Dby.* DE6
50 G37 Biggin *Dby.* SK17
58 F41 Biggin *N.Y.* LS25
107 A37 Biggings ZE2
23 F50 Biggin Hill TN16
32 D47 Biggleswade SG18
69 E29 Bigholms DG13
102 B24 Bighouse KW14
11 A42 Bighton SO24
60 A28 Biglands CA7
12 E45 Bignor RH20
60 E25 Bigrigg CA24
94 D13 Big Sand IV21
107 E39 Bigton ZE2
4 E16 Bilberry PL26
41 A41 Bilborough NG8
7 A26 Bilbrook *Som.* TA24
40 E34 Bilbrook *Stf.* WV8
58 E41 Bilbrough YO2
103 C28 Bilbster KW1
62 D37 Bildershaw DL14
34 D55 Bildeston IP7
24 B52 Billericay CM12
42 E43 Billesdon LE7
30 C37 Billesley B49
69 D28 Billholm DG13
42 B47 Billingborough NG34
48 B31 Billinge WN5
35 A57 Billingford *Nfk* IP21
44 C55 Billingford *Nfk* NR20
62 D40 Billingham TS23
52 G47 Billinghay LN4
51 B40 Billingley S72
12 D46 Billingshurst RH14
39 G32 Billingsley WV16
32 F45 Billington *Bfd.* LU7
56 F32 Billington *Lan.* BB7
45 D60 Billockby NR29
62 C37 Billy Row DL15
55 E30 Bilsborrow PR3
53 E50 Bilsby LN13
77 C33 Bilsdean TD13
12 F45 Bilsham BN18
15 D56 Bilsington TN25
51 F42 Bilsthorpe NG22
76 D28 Bilston *Ltn* EH25
40 F35 Bilston *W.M.* WV14
41 E39 Bilstone CV13
15 C56 Bilting TN25
59 F47 Bilton *Hum.* HU11
57 D39 Bilton *N.Y.* HG1
57 D40 Bilton *N.Y.* YO5
71 B38 Bilton *Nor.* NE66
31 A40 Bilton *War.* CV22
104 E29 Bimbister KW17
53 C48 Binbrook LN3
9 F32 Bincombe DT3
97 C25 Bindal IV20
19 G31 Binegar BA3
12 E47 Bines Green RH13
22 D44 Binfield RG42
22 D43 Binfield Heath RG9
70 F35 Bingfield NE19
41 B42 Bingham NG13
9 D33 Bingham`s Melcombe DT2
57 F37 Bingley BD16
44 B55 Binham NR21
21 F40 Binley *Ham.* SP11
30 A39 Binley *War.* CV3
75 C24 Binniehill FK1
57 A38 Binsoe HG4
11 E41 Binstead PO33
22 G43 Binsted *Ham.* GU34
12 F45 Binsted *W.S.* BN18
30 C37 Binton CV37
44 C56 Bintree NR20
38 E28 Binweston SY5
34 G55 Birch *Esx* CO2
49 B34 Birch *G.M.* M24
33 F50 Birchanger CM23
28 B30 Bircher HR6
96 B20 Birchfield IV24
18 C27 Birchgrove *S.G.* CF4
18 B23 Birchgrove *W.G.* SA7
48 F31 Birch Heath CW6
25 E58 Birchington CT7
50 F38 Birchover DE4
50 D36 Birch Vale SK12
51 C42 Bircotes DN11
33 D52 Birdbrook CO9
40 F36 Bird End B71
73 A15 Birdfield PA32
12 G44 Birdham PO20
31 B40 Birdingbury CV23
29 G35 Birdlip GL4
58 C44 Birdsall YO17
39 G33 Birdsgreen WV15
8 D29 Birdsmoor Gate DT6
51 B39 Birdwell S70
29 G33 Birdwood GL19
77 G33 Birgham TD12
96 B23 Birichen IV25
62 F39 Birkby DL7
48 A29 Birkdale *Mer.* PR8
61 F34 Birkdale *N.Y.* DL11
48 D28 Birkenhead L41
99 E33 Birkenhills AB53
57 G37 Birkenshaw BD11
90 D29 Birkhall AB35
76 F31 Birkhill *Bor.* TD4
69 B27 Birkhill *Bor.* TD7
82 D29 Birkhill *Tay.* DD2
58 G41 Birkin WF11
75 G23 Birkwood ML11
28 C30 Birley HR4
51 C39 Birley Carr S6
24 E52 Birling *Kent* ME19
71 C38 Birling *Nor.* NE65
13 G51 Birling Gap BN20
29 D35 Birlingham WR10
40 G36 Birmingham B
40 G37 Birmingham Airport B37
82 C26 Birnam PH8
104 D28 Birsay KW17
90 D31 Birse AB34
90 D31 Birsemore AB34
41 E41 Birstall LE4
57 G38 Birstall Smithies WF17
57 D38 Birstwith HG3
42 B46 Birthorpe NG34
62 A38 Birtley *Drm* DH3
28 B29 Birtley *H.&W.* SY7
70 F34 Birtley *Nor.* NE48
29 E33 Birts Street WR13
42 F44 Bisbrooke LE15
22 C44 Bisham SL7
29 C35 Bishampton WR10
7 C23 Bish Mill EX36
62 D38 Bishop Auckland DL14
52 C46 Bishopbridge LN2
74 C21 Bishopbriggs G64
59 F45 Bishop Burton HU17
62 C39 Bishop Middleham DL17
97 E27 Bishopmill IV30
57 C39 Bishop Monkton HG3
52 C45 Bishop Norton LN2
15 B57 Bishopsbourne CT4
20 E36 Bishops Cannings SN10
38 G28 Bishop`s Castle SY9
9 C32 Bishop`s Caundle DT9
29 F35 Bishop`s Cleeve GL52
29 D32 Bishop`s Frome WR6
33 G52 Bishop`s Green CM6
7 C27 Bishop`s Hull TA1
30 C39 Bishop`s Itchington CV33
7 C27 Bishop`s Lydeard TA4
7 C23 Bishop`s Nympton EX36
39 C33 Bishop`s Offley ST21
33 F50 Bishop`s Stortford CM23
11 A42 Bishop`s Sutton SO24
30 B39 Bishop`s Tachbrook CV33
6 B21 Bishop`s Tawton EX32
5 C25 Bishopsteignton TQ14
11 C40 Bishopstoke SO50
17 F21 Bishopston SA3
31 G43 Bishopstone *Bkh.* HP17
13 F50 Bishopstone *E.S.* BN25
28 D29 Bishopstone *H.&W.* HR4
21 C38 Bishopstone *Wts.* SN6
10 B36 Bishopstone *Wts.* SP5
20 G34 Bishopstrow BA12
19 F31 Bishop Sutton BS18
11 C41 Bishop`s Waltham SO32
40 E34 Bishop`s Wood ST19
8 C28 Bishopswood TA20
19 E31 Bishopsworth BS13
57 C38 Bishop Thornton HG3
58 E41 Bishopthorpe YO2
62 D39 Bishopton *Drm* TS21
74 C20 Bishopton *Str.* PA7
58 D43 Bishop Wilton YO4
19 C29 Bishton NP6
20 A35 Bisley *Glo.* GL6
22 F45 Bisley *Sry* GU24
55 E28 Bispham FY2
2 D13 Bissoe TR4
10 D37 Bisterne BH24
10 D38 Bisterne Close BH24
42 C45 Bitchfield NG33
6 A21 Bittadon EX31
5 E22 Bittaford PL21
44 D55 Bittering NR19
28 A31 Bitterley SY8
11 C40 Bitterne SO18
41 G41 Bitteswell LE17
19 E32 Bitton BS15
22 C43 Bix RG9
107 B39 Bixter ZE2
41 F41 Blaby LE8
69 D26 Blackacre DG11
77 E34 Blackadder TD11
5 E23 Blackawton TQ9
7 E26 Blackborough EX15
44 D52 Blackborough End PE32
21 A38 Black Bourton OX18
13 D51 Blackboys TN22
75 C24 Blackbraes *Cen.* FK1
91 B34 Blackbraes *Grm.* AB2
39 B33 Blackbrook ST5
91 B34 Blackburn *Grm.* AB2
56 G32 Blackburn *Lan.* BB
75 D25 Blackburn *Ltn* EH47
71 G37 Black Callerton NE5
97 F24 Blackcastle IV1
91 B33 Blackchambers AB32
67 E18 Black Clauchrie KA26
80 B18 Black Corries Lodge PA39
68 E22 Blackcraig *D.&G.* DG7
64 D20 Blackcraig *D.&G.* DG8
3 B14 Black Cross TR8
49 E33 Blackden Heath CW4
91 B35 Blackdog AB23
7 E24 Black Dog EX17
5 C21 Blackdown *Dev.* PL19
8 D29 Blackdown *Dor.* DT8
11 D40 Blackfield SO45
69 G29 Blackford *Cum.* CA6
98 F32 Blackford *Grm.* AB51
9 B32 Blackford *Som.* BA22
19 G29 Blackford *Som.* BS28
81 G24 Blackford *Tay.* PH4
41 D39 Blackfordby DE11
11 G40 Blackgang PO38
76 C28 Blackhall EH4
62 B40 Blackhall Colliery TS27
62 C40 Blackhall Rocks TS27
13 C51 Blackham TN3
34 F55 Blackheath *Esx* CO2
35 A59 Blackheath *Sfk* IP19
22 G46 Blackheath *Sry* GU4
40 G35 Blackheath *W.M.* B65
71 F36 Black Heddon NE20
99 D36 Blackhill *Grm.* AB42
99 E36 Blackhill *Grm.* AB42
86 B11 Blackhill *Hgh.* IV49
98 E30 Blackhillock AB55
98 D28 Blackhills IV30
20 E35 Blackland SN11
82 A27 Blacklunans PH10
38 F29 Black Marsh SY5
18 C25 Blackmill CF35
11 A43 Blackmoor *Ham.* GU33
7 D27 Blackmoor *Som.* TA21
6 A22 Blackmoor Gate EX31
23 A51 Blackmore CM4
34 E53 Blackmore End *Esx* CM7
32 G47 Blackmore End *Hfs.* AL4
80 C18 Black Mount PA36
75 C26 Blackness *Cen.* EH49
91 D32 Blackness *Grm.* AB31
103 E28 Blackness *Hgh.* KW3
22 G43 Blacknest GU34
34 F53 Black Notley CM7
56 E34 Blacko BB9
17 E22 Black Pill SA3
55 F28 Blackpool FY
55 F29 Blackpool Airport TY4
69 F30 Blackpool Gate CA6
75 D24 Blackridge EH48
28 G27 Blackrock *Gwe.* NP7
72 D8 Blackrock *Str.* PA44
48 A31 Blackrod BL6
69 G26 Blackshaw DG1
56 G35 Blackshaw Head HX7
34 E56 Blacksmith`s Corner CO4
13 E48 Blackstone BN5
31 G41 Blackthorn OX6
34 B54 Blackthorpe IP30
58 G44 Blacktoft DN14
91 C34 Blacktop AB1
6 E20 Black Torrington EX21
19 C28 Blacktown CF3
2 D12 Blackwater *Cnw.* TR4
22 F44 Blackwater *Ham.* GU17
11 F41 Blackwater *I.o.W.* PO30
35 A60 Blackwater *Sfk* IP18
66 A14 Blackwaterfoot KA27
51 G40 Blackwell *Dby.* DE55
50 E37 Blackwell *Dby.* SK17
62 E38 Blackwell *Drm* DL2
29 A35 Blackwell *H.&W.* B60
30 D38 Blackwell *War.* CV36
29 F33 Blackwells End GL19
68 E24 Blackwood *D.&G.* DG2
18 B27 Blackwood *Gwe.* NP2
75 F23 Blackwood *Str.* ML11
49 G35 Blackwood Hill ST9
48 F29 Blacon CH1
15 C57 Bladbean CT4
62 G35 Blades DL11
64 E20 Bladnoch DG8
31 G40 Bladon OX20
26 D18 Blaenannerch SA43
46 G22 Blaenau Dolwyddelan LL25
37 A23 Blaenau Ffestiniog LL41
19 A28 Blaenavon NP4
28 G28 Blaenawey NP7
18 A24 Blaencwm CF42
27 E25 Blaen Dyryn LD3
16 A17 Blaenffos SA37
18 B24 Blaengarw CF32
17 C22 Blaengweche SA18
18 A24 Blaengwrach SA11

Bradmore

18 **B24** Blaengwynfi SA13
27 **E23** Blaenos SA20
27 **B22** Blaenpennal SY23
26 **A21** Blaenplwyf SY23
26 **D18** Blaenporth SA43
18 **A25** Blaenrhondda CF42
17 **B18** Blaenwaun SA34
17 **B19** Blaen-y-coed SA33
19 **F30** Blagdon *Avon* BS18
5 **D24** Blagdon *Dev.* TQ3
8 **C28** Blagdon Hill TA3
87 **G16** Blaich PH33
18 **A27** Blaina NP3
74 **F18** Blair KA24
80 **G18** Blairannaich G83
81 **A24** Blair Atholl PH18
73 **C16** Blairbuie PA23
75 **A23** Blair Drummond FK9
82 **C27** Blairgowrie PH10
75 **B25** Blairhall KY12
81 **C21** Blairhoyle FK8
81 **G20** Blairhullichan FK8
75 **A25** Blairingone FK14
74 **G21** Blairkip KA5
75 **A24** Blairlogie FK9
101 **B17** Blairmore *Hgh.* IV27
96 **A23** Blairmore *Hgh.* IV28
73 **B17** Blairmore *Str.* PA23
74 **B19** Blairnairn G84
90 **B27** Blairnamarrow AB37
74 **E18** Blairpark KA24
67 **C19** Blairquhan KA19
74 **B21** Blairquhosh G63
73 **D15** Blair's Ferry PA21
98 **C32** Blairshinnoch AB45
81 **G20** Blairuskinmore FK8
74 **B18** Blairvadach G84
91 **D33** Blairydryne AB31
91 **A35** Blairythan AB41
29 **G32** Blaisdon GL17
29 **A33** Blakebrook DY11
29 **A34** Blakedown DY10
33 **F52** Blake End CM7
77 **G33** Blakelaw *Bor.* TD5
71 **G38** Blakelaw *T.&W.* NE4
28 **D29** Blakemere HR2
19 **A32** Blakeney *Glo.* GL15
44 **A56** Blakeney *Nfk* NR25
39 **A33** Blakenhall *Che.* CW5
40 **F34** Blakenhall *Stf.* WV2
40 **G34** Blakeshall DY11
31 **C42** Blakesley NN12
61 **A35** Blanchland DH8
9 **D35** Blandford Camp DT11
9 **D34** Blandford Forum DT11
9 **D34** Blandford St Mary DT11
57 **D38** Bland Hill HG3
74 **C21** Blanefield G63
52 **F46** Blankney LN4
80 **A16** Blar a'Chaorainn PH33
88 **E21** Blargie PH20
74 **B19** Blarglas G83
80 **A16** Blarmachfoldach PH33
95 **B17** Blarnalevoch IV23
10 **D37** Blashford BH24
42 **F43** Blaston LE16
92 **D4** Blathaisbhal HS6
42 **F45** Blatherwycke PE8
55 **A28** Blawith LA12
35 **C59** Blaxhall IP12
51 **B42** Blaxton DN9
71 **G37** Blaydon NE21
19 **G30** Bleadney BA5
19 **F29** Bleadon BS24
49 **B35** Bleak Hey Nook OL3
25 **E57** Blean CT2
42 **A43** Bleasby NG14
61 **E33** Bleatarn CA16
83 **F30** Blebocraigs KY15
28 **B27** Bleddfa LD7
30 **F38** Bledington OX7
22 **A43** Bledlow HP27
22 **B43** Bledlow Ridge HP14
61 **C32** Blencarn CA10
60 **B27** Blencogo CA7
60 **C30** Blencow CA11
11 **C43** Blendworth PO8
60 **B27** Blennerhasset CA5
97 **F26** Blervie Castle IV36
31 **G40** Bletchingdon OX5
23 **F49** Bletchingley RH1
32 **E44** Bletchley *Bkh.* MK3
39 **B32** Bletchley *Shr.* TF9
16 **B16** Bletherston SA66
32 **C46** Bletsoe MK44
21 **C41** Blewbury OX11
45 **C57** Blickling NR11
51 **G41** Blidworth NG21
99 **F35** Blindburn *Grm.* AB41
70 **B34** Blindburn *Nor.* NE65
60 **C27** Blindcrake CA13
23 **G49** Blindley Heath RH7
4 **C17** Blisland PL30
10 **C37** Blissford SP6
29 **A33** Bliss Gate DY14
31 **C43** Blisworth NN7
40 **C36** Blithbury WS15
60 **A26** Blitterlees CA5
30 **E37** Blockley GL56
45 **E59** Blofield NR13
34 **A56** Blo Norton IP22
40 **A37** Blore DE6
30 **A37** Blossomfield B90
40 **B36** Blount's Green ST14
31 **E40** Bloxham OX15
52 **G46** Bloxholm LN4
40 **E36** Bloxwich WS3
9 **E34** Bloxworth BH20
57 **D37** Blubberhouses LS21
3 **C15** Blue Anchor *Cnw.* TR8
7 **A26** Blue Anchor *Som.* TA24
24 **E53** Blue Bell Hill ME5
45 **F60** Blundeston NR32
32 **C47** Blunham MK44
20 **B37** Blunsdon St Andrew SN2
33 **A49** Bluntisham PE17
4 **D19** Blunts PL12
52 **C45** Blyborough DN21
35 **A60** Blyford IP19
40 **D34** Blymhill TF11
71 **E39** Blyth *Nor.* NE24
51 **D42** Blyth *Not.* S81
75 **F27** Blyth Bridge EH46
35 **A60** Blythburgh IP19
40 **A35** Blythe Bridge ST11
40 **A35** Blythe Marsh ST11
52 **C44** Blyton DN21
83 **F31** Boarhills KY16
11 **D41** Boarhunt PO17
13 **C25** Boarshead TN6
21 **A40** Boars Hill OX1
31 **G42** Boarstall HP18
14 **E53** Boarzell TN19
6 **F20** Boasley Cross EX20
96 **D21** Boath IV17
98 **D28** Boat o' Brig IV32
89 **C25** Boat of Garten PH24
24 **E54** Bobbing ME9
39 **F33** Bobbington DY7
23 **A51** Bobbingworth CM5
4 **E17** Bocaddon PL13
81 **G21** Bochastle FK17
21 **D39** Bockhampton RG17
34 **F53** Bocking CM7
34 **F53** Bocking Churchstreet CM7
4 **D17** Boconnoc PL22
99 **E37** Boddam *Grm.* AB42
107 **D37** Boddam *She.* ZE2
29 **F34** Boddington GL51
46 **D19** Bodedern LL65
47 **E26** Bodelwyddan LL18
28 **C31** Bodenham *H.&W.* HR1
10 **B37** Bodenham *Wts.* SP5
28 **C31** Bodenham Moor HR1
69 **C27** Bodesbeck DG10
46 **C19** Bodewryd LL68
47 **E26** Bodfari LL16
46 **E20** Bodffordd LL77
36 **B19** Bodfuan LL53
45 **A57** Bodham Street NR25
14 **E53** Bodiam TN32
31 **E40** Bodicote OX15
3 **A15** Bodieve PL27
4 **E17** Bodinnick PL23
46 **E18** Bodior LL65
13 **E52** Bodle Street Green BN27
4 **D16** Bodmin PL31
44 **F54** Bodney IP26
46 **F19** Bodorgan LL62
15 **C56** Bodsham Green TN25
4 **D16** Bodwen PL26
96 **F22** Bogallan IV1
96 **G22** Bogbain IV1
99 **F36** Bogbrae AB42
96 **F21** Bogbuie IV6
74 **G19** Bogend KA1
90 **C31** Bogfern AB33
90 **C31** Bogfields AB33
99 **D34** Bogfold AB43
98 **D32** Boghead *Grm.* AB45
68 **A22** Boghead *Str.* KA18
75 **F23** Boghead *Str.* ML11
97 **F25** Boghole Fm IV12
98 **C29** Bogmoor IV32
98 **E31** Bogniebrae AB54
12 **G45** Bognor Regis PO21
91 **B32** Bograxie AB51
89 **B24** Bogroy PH23
75 **A25** Bogside FK10
90 **C29** Bogston AB36
98 **D32** Bogton AB53
68 **E22** Bogue DG7
87 **F18** Bohenie PH31
3 **E14** Bohortha TR2
87 **F18** Bohuntine PH31
92 **C6** Boirseam HS3
2 **E9** Bojewyan TR19
62 **D37** Bolam DL2
5 **G22** Bolberry TQ7
10 **D38** Bolderwood SO43
48 **D31** Bold Heath WA8
71 **G39** Boldon NE36
10 **E38** Boldre SO41
62 **E36** Boldron DL12
51 **D43** Bole DN22
50 **G38** Bolehill DE4
2 **F10** Boleigh TR19
76 **G30** Boleside TD6
81 **C23** Bolfracks PH15
17 **D21** Bolgoed SA4
7 **D25** Bolham EX16
7 **D27** Bolham Water EX15
2 **C13** Bolingey TR6
49 **E35** Bollington *Che.* SK10
49 **D33** Bollington *Che.* WA14
13 **D48** Bolney RH17
32 **C46** Bolnhurst MK44
83 **B32** Bolshan DD11
51 **E40** Bolsover S44
50 **C38** Bolsterstone S30
28 **E31** Bolstone HR2
57 **A40** Boltby YO7
22 **B43** Bolter End HP14
61 **D32** Bolton *Cum.* CA16
49 **B32** Bolton *G.M.* BL
58 **D43** Bolton *Hum.* YO4
76 **C31** Bolton *Ltn* EH41
71 **B36** Bolton *Nor.* NE66
57 **D36** Bolton Abbey BD23
57 **D36** Bolton Bridge BD23
56 **E33** Bolton by Bowland BB7
69 **G30** Boltonfellend CA6
60 **B28** Boltongate CA5
55 **C30** Bolton-le-Sands LA5
60 **B28** Bolton Low Houses CA7
62 **G38** Bolton-on-Swale DL10
58 **E41** Bolton Percy YO5
51 **B40** Bolton upon Dearne S63
4 **C17** Bolventor PL15
65 **F23** Bombie DG6
38 **D30** Bomere Heath SY4
96 **B21** Bonar Bridge IV24
80 **D15** Bonawe PA35
80 **D16** Bonawe Quarries PA37
52 **A46** Bonby DN20
16 **A17** Boncath SA37
70 **B31** Bonchester Bridge TD9
11 **G41** Bonchurch PO38
6 **E22** Bondleigh EX20
40 **E37** Bonehill B78
75 **B25** Bo'ness EH51
74 **C19** Bonhill G83
39 **E33** Boningale WV7
70 **A32** Bonjedward TD8
75 **E24** Bonkle ML2
15 **D56** Bonnington *Kent* TN25
83 **D31** Bonnington *Tay.* DD11
82 **G29** Bonnybank KY8
75 **B24** Bonnybridge FK4
99 **D34** Bonnykelly AB53
76 **D28** Bonnyrigg EH19
98 **F32** Bonnyton *Grm.* AB52
83 **B32** Bonnyton *Tay.* DD10
82 **D29** Bonnyton *Tay.* DD3
50 **G38** Bonsall DE4
28 **G29** Bont NP7
37 **D22** Bontddu LL40
37 **F24** Bont dolgadfan SY19
37 **G22** Bont-goch (Elerch) SY24
37 **C23** Bont Newydd LL40
46 **F20** Bontnewydd LL55
47 **G26** Bontuchel LL15
18 **D26** Bonvilston CF5
17 **E22** Bon-y-maen SA1
5 **E25** Boohay TQ6
22 **B44** Booker HP12
38 **C31** Booley SY4
94 **C14** Boor IV22
63 **E42** Boosbeck TS12
60 **F27** Boot CA19
52 **G45** Boothby Graffoe LN5
42 **B45** Boothby Pagnell NG33
49 **B33** Boothstown M28
57 **G36** Boothtown HX3
31 **B43** Boothville NN3
50 **A36** Booth Wood HX6
54 **A27** Bootle *Cum.* LA19
48 **C29** Bootle *Mer.* L20
45 **C57** Booton NR10
74 **B21** Boquhan G63
28 **A31** Boraston WR15
24 **E54** Borden ME9
56 **C35** Bordley BD23
11 **A43** Bordon GU35
24 **A53** Boreham *Esx* CM3
20 **G34** Boreham *Wts.* BA12
13 **E52** Boreham Street BN27
22 **B47** Borehamwood WD6
81 **D21** Boreland *Cen.* FK21
69 **D27** Boreland *D.&G.* DG11
64 **D19** Boreland *D.&G.* DG8
93 **F7** Boreraig IV55
92 **C4** Borgh *W.I.* HS6
84 **D2** Borgh *W.I.* HS9
100 **C7** Borghastan HS2
102 **C22** Borgie KW14
65 **F22** Borgue *D.&G.* DG6
103 **F27** Borgue *Hgh.* KW7
34 **D54** Borley CO10
84 **B3** Bornais HS8
65 **F22** Borness DG6
57 **C39** Boroughbridge YO5
23 **F51** Borough Green TN15
48 **G29** Borras Head LL13
41 **B39** Borrowash DE72
63 **E43** Borrowby *N.Y.* TS13
57 **A40** Borrowby *N.Y.* YO7
62 **B28** Borrowdale CA12
91 **D34** Borrowfield AB3
24 **E53** Borstal ME1
36 **G21** Borth SY24
76 **E29** Borthwick EH23
69 **B29** Borthwickbrae TD9
69 **B30** Borthwickshiels TD9
36 **B21** Borth-y-Gest LL49
93 **G10** Borve IV51
55 **B31** Borwick LA6
2 **E9** Bosavern TR19
29 **D32** Bosbury HR8
4 **A16** Boscastle PL35
10 **E37** Boscombe *Dor.* BH5
10 **A37** Boscombe *Wts.* SP4
4 **E16** Boscoppa PL25
12 **F44** Bosham PO18
16 **E15** Bosherston SA71
49 **F35** Bosley SK11
58 **C43** Bossall YO6
4 **B16** Bossiney PL34
15 **C57** Bossingham CT4
10 **A39** Bossington *Ham.* SO20
7 **A24** Bossington *Som.* TA24
49 **F32** Bostock Green CW10
43 **A48** Boston PE21
57 **E40** Boston Spa LS23
3 **D15** Boswinger PL26
2 **E9** Botallack TR19
23 **B49** Botany Bay EN2
92 **D3** Botarua HS6
41 **E40** Botcheston LE9
34 **A56** Botesdale IP22
71 **E38** Bothal NE61
51 **E42** Bothamsall DN22
60 **C27** Bothel CA5
8 **E30** Bothenhampton DT6
75 **E23** Bothwell G71
22 **A45** Botley *Bkh.* HP5
11 **C41** Botley *Ham.* SO30
21 **A40** Botley *Oxf.* OX2
29 **F32** Botloe's Green GL18
44 **E56** Botolph NR18
31 **F43** Botolph Claydon MK18
12 **F47** Botolphs BN44
96 **E20** Bottacks IV14
52 **B45** Bottesford *Hum.* DN16
42 **B43** Bottesford *Lei.* NG13
33 **B51** Bottisham CB5
82 **E29** Bottomcraig DD6
56 **C32** Bottom Head LA2
4 **D19** Botusfleming PL12
36 **B18** Botwnnog LL53
23 **G50** Bough Beech TN8
28 **E27** Boughrood LD3
19 **B31** Boughspring NP6
44 **E52** Boughton *Nfk* PE33
31 **B43** Boughton *Nmp.* NN2
51 **F42** Boughton *Not.* NG22
14 **C55** Boughton Aluph TN25
14 **B53** Boughton Green ME17
15 **C56** Boughton Lees TN25
14 **C54** Boughton Malherbe ME17
15 **B56** Boughton Street ME13
63 **E43** Boulby TS13
38 **G31** Bouldon SY7
71 **B38** Boulmer NE66
16 **C15** Boulston SA62
90 **B29** Boultenstone AB36
52 **F45** Boultham LN6
33 **C49** Bourn CB3
40 **G36** Bournbrook B29
42 **C47** Bourne PE10
23 **B51** Bournebridge RM4
32 **D45** Bourne End *Bfd.* MK43
22 **C44** Bourne End *Bkh.* SL8
22 **A46** Bourne End *Hfs.* HP1
10 **F36** Bournemouth BH
10 **E37** Bournemouth (Hurn) Airport BH23
20 **A35** Bournes Green GL6
29 **A35** Bournheath B61
62 **A38** Bournmoor DH4
40 **G36** Bournville B30
19 **E29** Bourton *Avon* BS22
9 **A33** Bourton *Dor.* SP8
21 **C38** Bourton *Oxf.* SN6
38 **F31** Bourton *Shr.* TF13
31 **A40** Bourton on Dunsmore CV23
30 **E37** Bourton-on-the-Hill GL56
30 **F37** Bourton-on-the-Water GL54
78 **A8** Bousd PA78
60 **A28** Boustead Hill CA5
55 **A29** Bouth LA12
57 **B37** Bouthwaite HG3
81 **D21** Bovain FK20
22 **D45** Boveney SL4
10 **C36** Boveridge BH21
18 **E25** Boverton CF61
5 **C24** Bovey Tracey TQ13
22 **A45** Bovingdon HP3
23 **A51** Bovinger CM5
9 **F34** Bovington Camp BH20
7 **E23** Bow *Dev.* EX17
105 **B29** Bow *Ork.* KW16
61 **D35** Bowbank DL12
32 **E45** Bow Brickhill MK17
62 **C38** Bowburn DH6
11 **F40** Bowcombe PO30
7 **G27** Bowd EX10
76 **G31** Bowden *Bor.* TD6
5 **F24** Bowden *Dev.* TQ6
20 **E35** Bowden Hill SN15
49 **D33** Bowdon WA14
70 **E33** Bower NE48
10 **B36** Bowerchalke SP5
8 **C30** Bower Hinton TA12
103 **B28** Bowermadden KW1
24 **C53** Bowers Gifford SS13
75 **A26** Bowershall KY12
103 **B28** Bowertower KW1
62 **E35** Bowes DL12
55 **E30** Bowgreave PR3
55 **A30** Bowland Bridge LA11
28 **C31** Bowley HR1
12 **C45** Bowlhead Green GU8
74 **C20** Bowling G60
38 **A29** Bowling Bank LL13
19 **G31** Bowlish BA4
60 **G29** Bowmanstead LA21
72 **E8** Bowmore PA43
69 **G27** Bowness-on-Solway CA5
60 **G30** Bowness-on-Windermere LA23
82 **F29** Bow of Fife KY15
77 **F35** Bowsden TD15
102 **B24** Bowside Lodge KW14
37 **G22** Bow Street SY24
45 **E57** Bowthorpe NR5
75 **B24** Bowtrees FK2
20 **A34** Box *Glo.* GL6
20 **E34** Box *Wts.* SN13
29 **G33** Boxbush GL14
32 **D45** Box End MK43
21 **D40** Boxford *Brk.* RG20
34 **D55** Boxford *Sfk* CO10
12 **F45** Boxgrove PO18
14 **B53** Boxley ME14
22 **A46** Boxmoor HP1
34 **E55** Boxted *Esx* CO4
34 **C54** Boxted *Sfk* IP29
34 **E55** Boxted Cross CO4
33 **B49** Boxworth CB3
33 **B49** Boxworth End CB4
25 **E58** Boyden Gate CT3
74 **G20** Boydston KA1
40 **B37** Boylestone DE6
98 **C32** Boyndie AB45
59 **C47** Boynton YO16
83 **C31** Boysack DD11
6 **F19** Boyton *Cnw.* PL15
35 **D59** Boyton *Sfk* IP12
9 **A35** Boyton *Wts.* BA12
24 **A52** Boyton Cross CM1
32 **C44** Bozeat NN29
54 **F25** Braaid IM4
103 **B27** Braal Castle KW12
35 **B58** Brabling Green IP13
15 **C56** Brabourne TN25
15 **C56** Brabourne Lees TN25
103 **B28** Brabster KW1
85 **A9** Bracadale IV56
42 **D46** Braceborough PE9
52 **F45** Bracebridge LN5
52 **F45** Bracebridge Heath LN4
42 **B46** Braceby NG34
56 **E34** Bracewell BD23
88 **A21** Brachla IV3
61 **D32** Brackenber CA16
51 **G39** Brackenfield DE55
99 **D33** Brackens AB53
90 **A29** Bracklach AB54
99 **D34** Bracklamore AB43
87 **F17** Brackletter PH34
97 **F24** Brackley *Hgh.* IV1
31 **E41** Brackley *Nmp.* NN13
73 **B14** Brackly PA31
22 **E44** Bracknell RG12
81 **G24** Braco FK15
98 **D30** Bracobrae AB55
45 **F57** Bracon Ash NR14
86 **E13** Bracora PH40
86 **E13** Bracorina PH40
50 **G37** Bradbourne DE6
62 **D38** Bradbury TS21
54 **F23** Bradda IM9
54 **F23** Bradda East IM9
31 **D42** Bradden NN12
22 **B44** Bradenham HP14
20 **D35** Bradenstoke SN15
21 **D42** Bradfield *Brk.* RG7
7 **E26** Bradfield *Dev.* EX15
35 **E57** Bradfield *Esx* CO11
45 **B58** Bradfield *Nfk* NR28
34 **C54** Bradfield Combust IP30
49 **G32** Bradfield Green CW1
35 **F57** Bradfield Heath CO11
34 **C55** Bradfield St Clare IP30
34 **C55** Bradfield St George IP30
6 **E20** Bradford *Dev.* EX22
77 **G37** Bradford *Nor.* NE70
57 **F37** Bradford *W.Y.* BD
8 **C31** Bradford Abbas DT9
20 **E34** Bradford Leigh BA15
20 **E33** Bradford-on-Avon BA15
7 **C27** Bradford-on-Tone TA4
9 **E32** Bradford Peverell DT2
11 **F42** Brading PO36
40 **A38** Bradley *Dby.* DE6
21 **G42** Bradley *Ham.* SO24
53 **B48** Bradley *Hum.* DN37
57 **A36** Bradley *N.Y.* DL8
40 **D34** Bradley *Stf.* ST18
40 **F35** Bradley *W.M.* WV14
29 **B35** Bradley Green B96
40 **A36** Bradley in the Moors ST10
19 **C32** Bradley Stoke BS12
41 **B41** Bradmore *Not.* NG11

17 C18 Bron-y-Gaer SA33
38 B28 Bronygarth LL14
17 D18 Brook Dyf. SA33
10 B39 Brook Ham. SO20
10 C38 Brook Ham. SO43
10 F39 Brook I.o.W. PO30
15 C56 Brook Kent TN25
12 C45 Brook Sry GU8
42 E44 Brooke Lei. LE15
45 F58 Brooke Nfk NR15
108 F4 Brookeborough BT94
19 B31 Brookend GL15
55 C31 Brookhouse LA2
49 F33 Brookhouse Green CW11
14 E55 Brookland TN29
65 C23 Brooklands DG2
23 A48 Brookmans Park AL9
38 F27 Brooks SY21
41 D42 Brooksby LE14
12 D47 Brooks Green RH13
23 B51 Brook Street Esx CM14
14 D55 Brook Street Kent TN30
34 D54 Brook Street Sfk CO10
13 D48 Brook Street W.S. RH17
29 G34 Brookthorpe GL4
22 F45 Brookwood GU24
32 D47 Broom Bfd. SG18
30 C36 Broom War. B50
38 E31 Broomcroft SY5
29 A34 Broome H.&W. DY9
45 F59 Broome Nfk NR35
38 G29 Broome Shr. SY7
49 D33 Broomedge WA13
12 D47 Broome's Corner RH13
71 B37 Broome Wood NE66
24 A52 Broomfield Esx CM1
99 F35 Broomfield Grm. AB41
25 E57 Broomfield Kent CT6
14 B54 Broomfield Kent ME17
7 B27 Broomfield Som. TA5
58 G44 Broomfleet HU15
71 G36 Broomhaugh NE44
99 C35 Broomhead AB43
10 D36 Broom Hill BH21
71 C38 Broomhill NE65
82 F25 Broom of Dalreach PH3
29 E32 Broom's Green GL18
97 A24 Brora KW9
39 E32 Broseley TF12
61 C35 Brotherlee DL13
43 A48 Brothertoft PE20
57 G40 Brotherton WF11
63 D42 Brotton TS12
103 B26 Broubster KW14
61 E33 Brough Cum. CA17
50 D37 Brough Dby. S30
59 G45 Brough Hum. HU15
52 G44 Brough Not. NG23
104 E29 Brough Ork. KW17
106 E40 Brough She. ZE2
106 E41 Brough She. ZE2
107 C41 Brough She. ZE2
107 A41 Brough She. ZE2
38 A31 Broughall SY13
61 D31 Brougham CA10
106 C41 Brough Lodge ZE2
109 C7 Broughshane BT42
61 E33 Brough Sowerby CA17
32 D44 Broughton Bkh. MK16
75 G26 Broughton Bor. ML12
33 A48 Broughton Cbs. PE17
48 F29 Broughton Clw. CH4
49 C34 Broughton G.M. M7
10 A39 Broughton Ham. SO20
55 F31 Broughton Lan. PR3
52 B45 Broughton Lcn. DN20
18 D24 Broughton M.G. CF7
56 D35 Broughton N.Y. BD23
58 B43 Broughton N.Y. YO17
32 A44 Broughton Nmp. NN14

104 B30 Broughton Ork. KW17
31 E40 Broughton Oxf. OX15
41 F41 Broughton Astley LE9
55 A28 Broughton Beck LA12
20 E34 Broughton Gifford SN12
29 C35 Broughton Hackett WR7
55 A28 Broughton in Furness LA20
60 G27 Broughton Mills LA20
60 C26 Broughton Moor CA15
21 A38 Broughton Poggs GL7
104 B32 Broughton KW17
83 D30 Broughty Ferry DD5
107 B38 Browland ZE2
11 A41 Brown Candover SO24
48 A29 Brown Edge Lan. PR8
49 G35 Brown Edge Stf. ST6
99 E34 Brownhill AB41
83 F31 Brownhills Fife KY16
40 E36 Brownhills W.M. WS8
71 A37 Brownieside NE67
49 G34 Brown Lees ST8
49 F34 Brownlow Heath CW12
40 G38 Brownshill Green CV5
5 E22 Brownston PL21
63 G45 Broxa YO13
23 A49 Broxbourne EN10
76 C32 Broxburn Ltn EH42
75 C26 Broxburn Ltn EH52
52 E44 Broxholme LN1
33 F51 Broxted CM6
48 G30 Broxton CH3
28 C29 Broxwood HR6
100 C9 Bru HS2
97 G24 Bruachmary IV12
103 E28 Bruan KW2
48 F30 Bruera CH3
72 D8 Bruichladdich PA49
35 B59 Bruisyard IP13
35 B59 Bruisyard Street IP13
50 F36 Brund SK17
45 E59 Brundall NR13
35 B58 Brundish IP13
35 A58 Brundish Street IP13
41 G41 Bruntingthorpe LE17
90 A30 Bruntland AB54
82 E29 Brunton Fife KY15
71 A37 Brunton Nor. NE66
7 C24 Brushford TA22
6 E22 Brushford Barton EX18
9 A32 Bruton BA10
9 D34 Bryanston DT11
69 F27 Brydekirk DG12
48 G28 Brymbo LL11
17 D21 Bryn Dyf. SA14
48 B31 Bryn G.M. WN4
38 G28 Bryn Shr. SY9
18 B24 Bryn W.G. SA13
17 C22 Brynamman SA18
16 A16 Brynberian SA41
18 C25 Bryncae CF7
18 C25 Bryncethin CF32
36 A20 Bryncir LL51
18 B23 Bryn-Coch SA10
36 B17 Bryncross LL53
36 E21 Bryncrug LL36
38 A27 Bryneglwys LL21
47 E27 Brynford CH8
48 B31 Bryn Gates WN2
46 E19 Bryngwran LL65
19 A29 Bryngwyn Gwe. NP5
28 D27 Bryngwyn Pow. NP5
16 A15 Bryn-henllan SA42
26 C19 Brynhoffnant SA44
28 G27 Brynmawr NP3
28 A27 Brynmelyn LD1
18 C25 Brynmenyn CF32
18 C25 Brynna CF7
26 C21 Brynog SA48
46 F21 Brynrefail Gwy. LL55
46 D20 Brynrefail Gwy. LL68
18 D25 Brynsadler CF7
46 F20 Brynsiencyn LL61

46 D20 Brynteg LL78
47 E24 Bryn-y-maen LL28
84 D3 Buaile Nam Bodach HS9
85 B9 Bualintur IV47
94 C14 Bualnaluib IV22
30 A39 Bubbenhall CV8
58 F42 Bubwith YO8
69 B29 Buccleuch TD9
65 D23 Buchan DG7
74 B20 Buchanan Castle G63
99 E36 Buchanhaven AB42
82 E25 Buchanty PH1
74 A21 Buchlyvie FK8
60 B29 Buckabank CA5
31 B41 Buckby Wharf NN11
32 B47 Buckden Cbs. PE18
56 B35 Buckden N.Y. BD23
45 E59 Buckenham NR13
7 E27 Buckerell EX14
5 D23 Buckfast TQ11
5 D22 Buckfastleigh TQ11
76 A29 Buckhaven KY8
76 G30 Buckholm TD1
9 B33 Buckhorn Weston SP8
23 B50 Buckhurst Hill IG9
98 C29 Buckie AB56
103 B26 Buckies KW14
31 E42 Buckingham MK18
32 G44 Buckland Bkh. HP22
5 F22 Buckland Dev. TQ7
30 E36 Buckland Glo. WR12
33 E49 Buckland Hfs. SG9
15 C58 Buckland Kent CT16
21 B39 Buckland Oxf. SN7
23 F48 Buckland Sry RH3
6 C20 Buckland Brewer EX39
22 A45 Buckland Common HP23
20 F33 Buckland Dinham BA11
6 E20 Buckland Filleigh EX21
5 C23 Buckland in the Moor TQ13
4 D20 Buckland Monachorum PL20
9 D32 Buckland Newton DT2
8 C28 Buckland St Mary TA20
5 F23 Buckland-tout-Saints TQ7
21 D41 Bucklebury RG7
83 D30 Bucklerheads DD5
10 D39 Bucklers Hard SO42
35 D58 Bucklesham IP10
48 F28 Buckley CH7
12 D46 Buckman Corner RH14
42 C44 Buckminster NG33
52 F47 Bucknall Lcn. LN3
40 A35 Bucknall Stf. ST2
31 F41 Bucknell Oxf. OX6
28 A29 Bucknell Shr. SY7
91 C34 Bucksburn AB2
6 C19 Buck's Cross EX39
12 C46 Bucks Green RH12
22 A46 Bucks Hill WD4
22 G44 Bucks Horn Oak GU10
6 C19 Buck's Mills EX39
16 E15 Buckspool SA71
28 A29 Buckton H.&W. SY7
59 B47 Buckton Hum. YO15
77 G36 Buckton Nor. NE70
32 A47 Buckworth PE18
30 B38 Budbrooke CV35
51 F42 Budby NG22
83 D31 Buddon DD7
6 E18 Bude EX23
7 E25 Budlake EX5
77 A37 Budle NE69
7 G26 Budleigh Salterton EX9
2 E13 Budock Water TR11
39 A32 Buerton CW3
31 C42 Bugbrooke NN7
3 C15 Bugle PL26
58 D43 Bugthorpe YO4
39 E32 Buildwas TF8
27 C26 Builth Road LD2
27 D26 Builth Wells LD2
92 B6 Buirgh HS3
42 C46 Bulby PE10
103 B25 Buldoo KW14
20 G37 Bulford SP4
20 G37 Bulford Camp SP4
48 G31 Bulkeley SY14
41 G39 Bulkington War. CV12
20 F35 Bulkington Wts. SN10
6 D19 Bulkworthy EX22

46 C20 Bull Bay LL68
29 F33 Bulley GL2
14 D55 Bull Green TN26
21 G40 Bullington SO21
56 A32 Bullpot Farm LA6
33 G48 Bull's Green SG3
73 C17 Bullwood PA23
34 D54 Bulmer Esx CO10
58 C42 Bulmer N.Y. YO6
34 E54 Bulmer Tye CO10
24 C52 Bulphan RM14
14 G53 Bulverhythe TN38
99 E35 Bulwark AB42
41 A41 Bulwell NG6
42 F45 Bulwick NN17
23 A50 Bumble's Green EN9
100 G7 Bun Abhainn Eadarra HS3
87 F17 Bunarkaig PH34
48 G31 Bunbury CW6
96 G22 Bunchrew IV3
86 B14 Bundalloch IV40
106 B42 Buness ZE2
78 E9 Bunessan PA67
45 G59 Bungay NR35
73 G13 Bunlarie PA28
88 B20 Bunloit IV3
87 D17 Bun Loyne IV3
72 C9 Bunnahabhainn PA46
41 C41 Bunny NG11
88 C19 Buntait IV3
33 F49 Buntingford SG9
45 F57 Bunwell NR16
45 F57 Bunwell Street NR16
50 E36 Burbage Dby. SK17
41 E40 Burbage Lei. LE10
21 E38 Burbage Wts. SN8
22 C44 Burchett's Green SL6
10 A36 Burcombe SP2
21 B41 Burcot OX14
32 F44 Burcott LU7
58 C44 Burdale YO17
12 D46 Burdocks RH14
34 E54 Bures CO8
34 E54 Bures Green CO8
30 G38 Burford OX18
34 A56 Burgate IP22
13 E49 Burgess Hill RH15
35 C58 Burgh IP13
60 A29 Burgh by Sands CA5
45 E60 Burgh Castle NR31
21 E40 Burghclere RG20
97 E26 Burghead IV30
21 E42 Burghfield RG31
21 E42 Burghfield Common RG7
21 E42 Burghfield Hill RG7
23 F48 Burgh Heath KT20
28 D30 Burghill HR4
53 F51 Burgh le Marsh PE24
45 C58 Burgh next Aylsham NR11
53 D48 Burgh on Bain LN3
45 D59 Burgh St Margaret NR29
45 F60 Burgh St Peter NR34
51 A41 Burghwallis DN6
24 E53 Burham ME1
11 B43 Buriton GU31
48 G31 Burland CW5
51 B47 Burlawn PL27
22 D45 Burleigh SL5
7 D26 Burlescombe EX16
9 E33 Burleston DT2
10 D37 Burley Ham. BH24
42 D44 Burley Lei. LE15
39 A32 Burleydam SY13
28 D31 Burley Gate HR1
57 E37 Burley in Wharfedale LS29
10 D38 Burley Street BH24
28 C28 Burlingjobb LD8
13 E51 Burlow TN21
38 C30 Burlton SY4
15 D56 Burmarsh TN29
30 E38 Burmington CV36
58 G41 Burn YO8
49 C34 Burnage M19
40 B38 Burnaston DE65
58 E44 Burnby YO4
12 F45 Burndell BN18
99 E34 Burnend AB41
61 G31 Burneside LA9
104 B32 Burness KW17
57 A39 Burneston DL8
19 E32 Burnett BS18
69 B30 Burnfoot Bor. TD9
102 E24 Burnfoot Hgh. KW11
82 G25 Burnfoot Tay. FK14

22 C45 Burnham Bkh. SL1
52 A46 Burnham Hum. DN18
44 A54 Burnham Deepdale PE31
33 G48 Burnham Green AL6
44 A53 Burnham Market PE31
44 A54 Burnham Norton PE31
25 B55 Burnham-on-Crouch CM0
19 G28 Burnham-on-Sea TA8
44 A54 Burnham Overy PE31
44 A54 Burnham Thorpe PE31
99 E37 Burnhaven AB42
68 D24 Burnhead D.&G. DG3
67 E21 Burnhead D.&G. DG7
91 B33 Burnhervie AB51
39 E33 Burnhill Green WV6
62 B37 Burnhope DH7
74 E19 Burnhouse KA15
63 G46 Burniston YO13
56 F34 Burnley BB11
77 D35 Burnmouth TD14
55 E29 Burn Naze FY5
81 G23 Burn of Cambus FK16
62 A37 Burnopfield NE16
57 C36 Burnsall BD23
49 F35 Burntcliff Top SK11
62 D37 Burnt Houses DL13
76 B28 Burntisland KY3
67 B20 Burnton Str. KA18
67 C20 Burnton Str. KA6
40 D36 Burntwood WS7
40 E36 Burntwood Green WS7
57 C38 Burnt Yates HG3
22 F46 Burpham Sry GU1
12 F46 Burpham W.S. BN18
70 C35 Burradon Nor. NE65
71 F38 Burradon T.&W. NE23
106 A41 Burrafirth ZE2
106 E39 Burraland ZE2
2 E12 Burras TR13
107 A39 Burravoe She. ZE2
106 D41 Burravoe She. ZE2
61 E32 Burrells CA16
82 D27 Burrelton PH13
11 C41 Burridge SO31
57 A38 Burrill DL8
52 B44 Burringham DN17
6 D21 Burrington Dev. EX37
28 A30 Burrington H.&W. SY8
19 F30 Burrington Som. BS18
33 C52 Burrough End CB8
33 C52 Burrough Green CB8
42 D43 Burrough on the Hill LE14
8 B29 Burrow Bridge TA7
22 E45 Burrowhill GU24
17 D20 Burry Port SA16
48 A30 Burscough L40
48 A30 Burscough Bridge L40
58 F44 Bursea YO4
59 E46 Burshill YO25
11 D40 Bursledon SO31
40 A34 Burslem ST6
34 D56 Burstall IP8
8 D30 Burstock DT8
45 G57 Burston Nfk IP22
40 B35 Burston Stf. ST18
23 G49 Burstow RH6
59 G48 Burstwick HU12
56 A34 Burtersett DL8
19 G29 Burtle TA7
48 F30 Burton Che. CW6
10 E37 Burton Dor. BH23
9 E32 Burton Dor. DT2
16 D15 Burton Dyf. SA73
52 E45 Burton Lcn. LN1
48 E29 Burton Mer. L64

77 G37 Burton Nor. NE69
7 A27 Burton Som. TA5
20 D34 Burton Wts. SN14
59 C47 Burton Agnes YO25
8 F30 Burton Bradstock DT6
42 C45 Burton Coggles NG33
48 G29 Burton Green Clw. LL12
30 A38 Burton Green W.M. CV8
41 F40 Burton Hastings CV11
55 B31 Burton-in-Kendal LA6
56 B32 Burton in Lonsdale LA6
41 A42 Burton Joyce NG14
32 A44 Burton Latimer NN15
42 D43 Burton Lazars LE14
57 C39 Burton Leonard HG3
41 C41 Burton on the Wolds LE12
41 F42 Burton Overy LE8
42 A47 Burton Pedwardine NG34
59 F48 Burton Pidsea HU12
57 G40 Burton Salmon LS25
52 A44 Burton upon Stather DN15
40 C38 Burton upon Trent DE14
48 C31 Burtonwood WA5
48 G30 Burwardsley CH3
38 G31 Burwarton WV16
13 D52 Burwash TN19
13 D52 Burwash Common TN19
13 D52 Burwash Weald TN19
33 B51 Burwell Cbs. CB5
53 E49 Burwell Lcn. LN11
46 C20 Burwen LL68
105 C30 Burwick Ork. KW17
107 A39 Burwick She. ZE1
43 G48 Bury Cbs. PE17
49 A33 Bury G.M. BL9
7 C25 Bury Som. TA22
12 E46 Bury W.S. RH20
2 F10 Buryas Bridge TR20
33 F50 Bury Green SG11
34 B54 Bury St Edmunds IP33
58 C43 Burythorpe YO17
22 G45 Busbridge GU7
74 E21 Busby Str. G76
82 E26 Busby Tay. PH1
21 B38 Buscot SN7
28 C30 Bush Bank HR4
40 E35 Bushbury WV10
41 E42 Bushby LE7
90 D28 Bush Crathie AB35
22 B46 Bushey WD1
22 B47 Bushey Heath WD2
45 G58 Bush Green IP21
29 E34 Bushley GL20
109 B7 Bushmills BT57
20 D36 Bushton SN4
20 A34 Bussage GL6
107 A39 Busta ZE2
13 D51 Butcher's Cross TN20
33 F52 Butcher's Pasture CM6
19 E30 Butcombe BS18
97 E27 Buthill IV30
8 A31 Butleigh BA6
8 A31 Butleigh Wootton BA6
22 A44 Butler's Cross HP17
41 A41 Butler's Hill NG15
30 C38 Butlers Marston CV35
35 C59 Butley IP12
62 B36 Butsfield DL13
70 F32 Butterburn CA6
58 D43 Buttercrambe YO4
62 D36 Butterknowle DL13
7 E25 Butterleigh EX15
51 G39 Butterley DE5
60 E27 Buttermere Cum. CA13
21 E39 Buttermere Wts. SN8
49 G34 Butters Green ST7
57 G37 Buttershaw BD6
82 C26 Butterstone PH8
50 G36 Butterton ST13
43 A49 Butterwick Lcn. PE22
59 B45 Butterwick N.Y. YO17

Butterwick

136

Craibstone

91 B34 Craibstone *Grm.* AB2
98 D30 Craibstone *Grm.* AB56
83 C30 Craichie DD8
65 D22 Craig *D.&G.* DG7
94 E13 Craig *Hgh.* IV22
95 G16 Craig *Hgh.* IV54
67 C19 Craig *Str.* KA19
80 D16 Craig *Str.* PA35
79 E11 Craig *Str.* PA70
73 B16 Craigandaive PA23
73 A14 Craigans PA31
109 E7 Craigavon BT65
88 F19 Craigbeg PH31
17 D22 Craigcefnparc SA6
69 E29 Craigcleuch DG13
99 D34 Craigculter AB43
82 E28 Craigdallie PH14
99 F34 Craigdam AB41
68 D23 Craigdarroch *D.&G.* DG3
68 C22 Craigdarroch *Str.* KA18
64 F19 Craigdhu *D.&G.* DG8
96 G20 Craigdhu *Hgh.* IV4
91 B32 Craigearn AB51
98 E28 Craigellachie AB38
99 C36 Craigellie AB43
64 C20 Craigencallie DG7
97 F27 Craigend *Grm.* IV36
82 F26 Craigend *Tay.* PH2
74 B19 Craigendoran G84
67 C20 Craigengillan KA6
68 E23 Craigenputtock DG2
72 D8 Craigens PA44
73 B14 Craigglass PA31
82 F29 Craighall KY15
74 B20 Craighat G63
83 G32 Craighead *Fife* KY10
96 E23 Craighead *Hgh.* IV11
64 D18 Craighlaw DG8
72 D11 Craighouse PA60
91 B35 Craigie *Grm.* AB23
74 G20 Craigie *Str.* KA1
82 C27 Craigie *Tay.* PH10
99 F34 Craigie Brae AB41
69 C26 Craigieburn DG10
82 D27 Craigieholm PH13
75 C27 Craiglockhart EH14
91 D33 Craiglug AB31
99 D34 Craigmaud AB43
76 C28 Craigmillar EH16
73 D17 Craigmore PA20
91 C32 Craigmyle Ho. AB31
73 C15 Craignafeich PA21
38 B28 Craignant SY10
81 D21 Craignavie FK21
67 E17 Craigneil KA26
79 D13 Craignure PA65
91 G32 Craigo DD10
67 C19 Craigoch KA19
82 G26 Craigow KY13
18 D25 Craig Penllyn CF7
82 F29 Craigrothie KY15
97 F27 Craigroy IV36
81 E20 Craigruie FK19
82 F29 Craigsanquhar KY15
74 B22 Craigton *Cen.* G63
91 C34 Craigton *Grm.* AB1
83 D31 Craigton *Tay.* DD5
82 B29 Craigton *Tay.* DD8
102 C24 Craigtown KW13
27 G24 Craig-y-nos SA9
69 C29 Craik *Bor.* TD9
90 A30 Craik *Grm.* AB54
83 G32 Crail KY10
70 A32 Crailing TD8
70 A32 Crailinghall TD8
51 C43 Craiselound DN9
57 B40 Crakehill YO7
58 C43 Crambe YO6
71 F38 Cramlington NE23
75 C27 Cramond EH4
49 F33 Cranage CW4
39 B33 Cranberry ST21
10 C36 Cranborne BH21
22 D45 Cranbourne SL4
14 D53 Cranbrook TN17
14 D53 Cranbrook Common TN17
32 D45 Cranfield MK43
6 C19 Cranford *Dev.* EX39
22 D47 Cranford *G.L.* TW5
32 A45 Cranford St Andrew NN14
32 A45 Cranford St John NN14
23 C51 Cranham *Esx* RM14
28 G34 Cranham *Glo.* GL4
48 B30 Crank WA11
12 C46 Cranleigh GU6
34 A56 Cranmer Green IP31
10 E39 Cranmore *I.o.W.* PO41
19 G32 Cranmore *Som.* BA4
98 D32 Cranna AB54
98 D30 Crannach AB55
42 F43 Cranoe LE16
35 B59 Cransford IP13
76 D32 Cranshaws TD11
54 C26 Cranstal IM7
2 B13 Crantock TR8
52 G46 Cranwell NG34
44 F53 Cranwich IP26
44 E55 Cranworth IP25
79 G13 Craobh Haven PA31
4 D20 Crapstone PL20
73 A15 Crarae PA32
102 F21 Crask Inn IV27
90 C30 Craskins AB34
96 G20 Crask of Aigas IV4
71 A38 Craster NE66
28 E28 Craswall HR2
35 A59 Cratfield IP19
91 D33 Crathes AB31
90 D28 Crathie *Grm.* AB35
88 E21 Crathie *Hgh.* PH20
62 F40 Crathorne TS15
38 G30 Craven Arms SY7
73 F14 Craw KA27
71 G37 Crawcrook NE40
48 B31 Crawford *Lan.* WN8
68 A25 Crawford *Str.* ML12
68 A24 Crawfordjohn ML12
109 D9 Crawfordsburn BT19
68 D23 Crawfordton DG3
68 B23 Crawick DG4
11 A40 Crawley *Ham.* SO21
30 G39 Crawley *Oxf.* OX8
13 C48 Crawley *W.S.* RH11
13 C49 Crawley Down RH10
62 B35 Crawleyside DL13
56 G33 Crawshawbooth BB4
91 F34 Crawton AB3
54 D25 Crawyn IM7
56 B35 Cray *N.Y.* BD23
27 F24 Cray *Pow.* LD3
82 A27 Cray *Tay.* PH10
23 D51 Crayford DA1
58 B41 Crayke YO6
24 B53 Crays Hill CM11
21 C42 Cray's Pond RG8
22 D43 Crazies Hill RG10
7 D24 Creacombe EX16
80 A15 Creagbheitheachain PH33
92 G3 Creag Ghoraidh HS7
31 A42 Creaton NN6
69 F28 Creca DG12
28 D30 Credenhill HR4
7 E24 Crediton EX17
8 B28 Creech St Michael TA3
3 D15 Creed TR2
7 E24 Creedy Park EX17
23 C50 Creekmouth IG11
34 C56 Creeting St Mary IP6
42 C46 Creeton NG33
64 E20 Creetown DG8
109 D5 Creggan BT79
80 G16 Creggans PA27
54 G23 Cregneish IM9
28 C27 Cregrina LD1
82 E29 Creich KY15
18 C26 Creigiau CF4
88 A19 Crelevan IV4
4 E20 Cremyll PL10
38 E31 Cressage SY5
16 D16 Cresselly SA68
34 F53 Cressing CM7
16 D16 Cresswell *Dyf.* SA68
71 D38 Cresswell *Nor.* NE61
40 B35 Cresswell *Stf.* ST11
51 E41 Creswell S80
35 B58 Cretingham IP13
72 D12 Cretshengan PA29
48 G30 Crewe *Che.* CH3
49 G33 Crewe *Che.* CW
38 D29 Crewgreen SY5
8 D30 Crewkerne TA18
41 B39 Crewton DE24
80 E19 Crianlarich FK20
26 C21 Cribyn SA48
36 B20 Criccieth LL52
51 G39 Crich DE4
51 G39 Crich Carr DE4
99 E35 Crichie AB42
76 D29 Crichton EH37
19 C30 Crick *Gwe.* NP6
31 A41 Crick *Nmp.* NN6
27 D26 Crickadarn LD2
8 C29 Cricket Malherbie TA19
8 D29 Cricket St Thomas TA20
38 C28 Crickheath SY10
28 G27 Crickhowell NP8
20 B36 Cricklade SN6
58 G41 Cridling Stubbs WF11
81 E24 Crieff PH7
38 D28 Criggion SY5
51 A39 Crigglestone WF4
62 C40 Crimdon Park TS27
99 D36 Crimond AB43
99 D36 Crimonmogate AB43
44 E52 Crimplesham PE33
73 A13 Crinan PA31
45 E57 Cringleford NR4
76 F28 Cringletie EH45
16 C17 Crinow SA67
2 E10 Cripplesease TR20
14 E53 Cripp's Corner TN32
34 G53 Crix CM3
68 D24 Croalchapel DG3
60 E26 Croasdale CA23
23 E50 Crockenhill BR8
7 F23 Crockernwell EX6
20 G34 Crockerton BA12
65 C24 Crocketford or Ninemile Bar DG2
58 E42 Crockey Hill YO1
23 F50 Crockham Hill TN8
23 G52 Crockhurst Street TN11
34 F56 Crockleford Heath CO7
8 C29 Crock Street TA19
38 C28 Croesau Bach SY10
18 B24 Croeserw SA13
16 B14 Croesgoch SA62
28 G29 Croes Hywel NP7
26 D19 Croes-lan SA44
37 A22 Croesor LL48
18 B27 Croespenmaen NP1
17 C20 Croesyceiliog *Dyf.* SA32
19 B29 Croesyceiliog *Gwe.* NP44
19 B28 Croes-y-mwyalch NP44
19 A28 Croes y pant NP4
49 C32 Croft *Che.* WA3
53 F51 Croft *Lcn.* PE24
41 F41 Croft *Lei.* LE9
69 F29 Crofthead CA6
81 A24 Croftmore PH18
51 A39 Crofton *W.Y.* WF4
21 E38 Crofton *Wts.* SN8
62 E38 Croft-on-Tees DL2
65 C23 Crofts DG7
103 E27 Crofts of Benachielt KW5
97 F27 Crofts of Buinach IV30
99 F34 Crofts of Haddo AB41
17 E21 Crofty SA4
37 B26 Crogen LL21
79 E12 Croggan PA63
61 B31 Croglin CA4
96 B20 Croick *Hgh.* IV24
102 C24 Croick *Hgh.* KW13
78 B9 Croig PA75
84 C3 Crois Dughaill HS8
54 G24 Croit e Caley IM9
96 E23 Cromarty IV11
83 C31 Crombie Mill DD7
99 F33 Cromblet AB51
89 B26 Cromdale PH26
33 F48 Cromer *Hfs.* SG2
45 A58 Cromer *Nfk* NR27
32 G47 Cromer Hyde AL8
50 G38 Cromford DE4
19 B32 Cromhall GL12
19 C32 Cromhall Common GL12
49 B35 Crompton Fold OL2
51 F43 Cromwell NG23
67 A21 Cronberry KA18
22 G43 Crondall GU10
54 E24 Cronk-y-Voddy IM6
48 D30 Cronton WA8
61 G30 Crook *Cum.* LA8
62 C37 Crook *Drm* DL15
74 G20 Crookedholm KA1
21 E41 Crookham *Brk.* RG19
77 G34 Crookham *Nor.* TD12
22 F43 Crookham Village GU13
55 A31 Crooklands LA7
82 G26 Crook of Devon KY13
31 D40 Cropredy OX17
41 D41 Cropston LE7
29 D35 Cropthorne WR10
58 A43 Cropton YO18
41 B42 Cropwell Bishop NG12
41 B42 Cropwell Butler NG12
101 A11 Cros HS2
74 F18 Crosbie KA23
100 E9 Crosbost HS2
60 C26 Crosby *Cum.* CA15
52 A44 Crosby *Hum.* DN15
54 F24 Crosby *I.o.M.* IM4
48 B28 Crosby *Mer.* L23
62 G39 Crosby Court DL6
61 F33 Crosby Garrett CA17
61 E32 Crosby Ravensworth CA10
19 G31 Croscombe BA5
19 F29 Cross BS26
73 E14 Crossaig PA29
78 B7 Crossapol PA78
78 C5 Crossapoll PA77
28 F29 Cross Ash NP7
14 C53 Cross-at-Hand TN12
12 F46 Cross Bush BN18
60 C26 Crosscanonby CA15
45 B58 Crossdale Street NR27
55 G29 Crossens PR9
68 E24 Crossford *D.&G.* DG3
75 B26 Crossford *Fife* KY12
75 F24 Crossford *Str.* ML8
37 D23 Cross Foxes Inn LL40
109 E9 Crossgar BT30
43 C48 Crossgate PE11
76 D29 Crossgatehall EH22
75 B27 Crossgates *Fife* KY4
27 B26 Crossgates *Pow.* LD1
82 E26 Crossgates *Tay.* PH1
57 F39 Cross Gates LS15
55 C31 Crossgill LA2
6 G19 Cross Green *Cnw.* PL15
34 C54 Cross Green *Sfk* IP30
34 C55 Cross Green *Sfk* IP7
17 C21 Cross Hands *Dyf.* SA14
16 C16 Cross Hands *Dyf.* SA67
74 G20 Crosshands KA5
75 A27 Crosshill *Fife* KY5
67 C19 Crosshill *Str.* KA19
41 A39 Cross Hill DE5
74 G19 Crosshouse KA2
38 E31 Cross Houses SY5
13 D51 Cross in Hand TN21
26 C19 Cross Inn *Dyf.* SA45
26 B21 Cross Inn *Dyf.* SY23
18 C26 Cross Inn *M.G.* CF7
18 B27 Crosskeys NP1
20 D34 Cross Keys SN13
103 A26 Crosskirk KW14
39 F32 Cross Lane Head WV16
2 F12 Crosslanes *Cnw.* TR12
2 D13 Cross Lanes *Cnw.* TR4
58 C41 Cross Lanes *N.Y.* YO6
38 D29 Crosslanes *Shr.* SY22
69 B28 Crosslee *Bor.* TD7
74 D20 Crosslee *Str.* PA6
74 C20 Crosslet G82
109 G6 Crossmaglen BT35
65 D23 Crossmichael DG7
55 F30 Crossmoor PR4
99 F33 Cross of Jackson AB51
40 A38 Cross o' the Hands DE56
91 D33 Crossroads *Grm.* AB31
74 G20 Crossroads *Str.* KA1
35 A57 Cross Street IP21
28 G30 Crossway *Gwe.* NP5
27 C26 Crossway *Pow.* LD1
29 B34 Crossway Green DY13
28 G31 Crossways GL16
16 A17 Crosswell SA41
60 G30 Crosthwaite LA8
48 A30 Croston PR5
45 D58 Crostwick NR12
45 C59 Crostwight NR28
23 F52 Crouch TN15
9 C32 Crouch Hill DT9
31 E41 Croughton NN13
99 C33 Crovie AB45
10 D37 Crow BH24
2 E12 Crowan TR14
13 C51 Crowborough TN6
7 B27 Crowcombe TA4
50 F36 Crowdecote SK17
11 B40 Crowdhill SO50
31 D41 Crowfield *Nmp.* NN13
35 C57 Crowfield *Sfk* IP6
29 F32 Crow Hill HR9
14 F53 Crowhurst *E.S.* TN33
23 G49 Crowhurst *Sry* RH7
23 G49 Crowhurst Lane End RH7
43 D48 Crowland *Lcn.* PE6
34 A56 Crowland *Sfk* IP31
2 E11 Crowlas TR20
29 C35 Crowle *H.&W.* WR7
51 A43 Crowle *Hum.* DN17
29 C34 Crowle Green WR7
21 C42 Crowmarsh Gifford OX10
4 E20 Crownhill PL6
44 E56 Crownthorpe NR18
2 E12 Crowntown TR13
2 F9 Crows-an-wra TR19
22 E44 Crowthorne RG45
48 E31 Crowton CW8
40 D37 Croxall WS13
62 C38 Croxdale DH6
40 B36 Croxden ST14
22 B46 Croxley Green WD3
33 C48 Croxton *Cbs.* PE19
52 A47 Croxton *Hum.* DN39
44 G54 Croxton *Nfk* IP24
39 B33 Croxton *Stf.* ST21
39 B33 Croxtonbank ST21
48 G31 Croxton Green SY14
42 C44 Croxton Kerrial NG32
96 G23 Croy *Hgh.* IV1
75 C23 Croy *Str.* G65
6 B20 Croyde EX33
33 D48 Croydon *Cbs.* SG8
23 E49 Croydon *Sry* CR
72 E9 Cruach PA43
98 E31 Cruchie AB54
38 E30 Cruckmeole SY5
38 D30 Cruckton SY5
99 F36 Cruden Bay AB42
39 D32 Crudgington TF6
20 B35 Crudwell SN16
28 A27 Crug LD1
3 A15 Crugmeer PL28
17 A22 Crugybar SA19
100 D7 Crulabhig HS2
109 D7 Crumlin *Ant.* BT29
18 B27 Crumlin *Gwe.* NP1
16 C15 Crundale *Dyf.* SA62
15 C56 Crundale *Kent* CT4
74 E22 Crutherland G75
7 D24 Cruwys Morchard EX16
21 F40 Crux Easton RG20
17 C20 Crwbin SA17
22 B44 Cryers Hill HP15
46 E22 Crymlyn LL57
16 A17 Crymych SA41
18 A23 Crynant SA10
23 D49 Crystal Palace SE26
94 F13 Cuaig IV54
30 B39 Cubbington CV32
2 C13 Cubert TR8
32 F44 Cublington LU7
13 D49 Cuckfield RH17
9 B33 Cucklington BA9
51 E41 Cuckney NG20
48 F29 Cuckoo's Nest CH4
21 A41 Cuddesdon OX44
31 G43 Cuddington *Bkh.* HP18
48 E31 Cuddington *Che.* CW8
38 A30 Cuddington Heath SY14
55 F30 Cuddy Hill PR4
23 F50 Cudham TN14
5 C21 Cudliptown PL19
51 B39 Cudworth *S.Y.* S72
8 C29 Cudworth *Som.* TA19
23 A48 Cuffley EN6
101 B11 Cuidhaseadair HS2
84 D2 Cuidhir HS9
92 C6 Cuidhtinis HS3
93 F9 Cuidrach IV51
73 A17 Cuilmuich PA24
79 D14 Cuil-uaine PA37
74 A19 Culag G83
96 E22 Culbo IV7
96 F21 Culbokie IV7
7 A24 Culbone TA24
96 G20 Culburnie IV4
96 G22 Culcabock IV2
79 D14 Culcharan PA37
97 F24 Culcharry IV12
49 C32 Culcheth WA3
98 F30 Culdrain AB54
94 G13 Culduie IV54
34 B54 Culford IP28
61 D31 Culgaith CA10
103 G25 Culgower KW8
21 B41 Culham OX14
73 E14 Culindrach PA29
101 E16 Culkein IV27
20 B35 Culkerton GL8
89 B25 Cullachie PH24
109 G6 Cullaville BT35
98 C31 Cullen AB56
71 F39 Cullercoats NE30
109 C7 Culleybackey BT42
96 E22 Cullicudden IV7
96 G19 Culligran IV4
57 F36 Cullingworth BD13
79 F13 Cullipool PA34
106 B41 Cullivoe ZE2
81 F23 Culloch PH6
96 G23 Culloden IV1
7 E25 Cullompton EX15
109 G7 Cullyhanna BT35
96 B23 Culmaily KW10
38 G30 Culmington SY8
108 C5 Culmore BT48
7 D26 Culmstock EX15
95 A16 Culnacraig IV26
80 D15 Culnadalloch PA37
94 E11 Culnaknock IV51
85 B10 Culnamean IV47
35 D57 Culpho IP6
64 E20 Culquhirk DG8
96 B21 Culrain IV24
75 B25 Culross KY12
67 B19 Culroy KA19
90 D29 Culsh AB35
64 E18 Culshabbin DG8
107 C38 Culswick ZE2
75 G26 Culter Allers Farm ML12
91 A34 Cultercullen AB41
64 F20 Cults *D.&G.* DG8
91 C34 Cults *Grm.* AB1
98 F31 Cults *Grm.* AB54
81 E23 Cultybraggan Camp PH6
24 E52 Culverstone Green DA13
42 A45 Culverthorpe NG32
98 D31 Culvie AB54
31 D41 Culworth OX17
75 G23 Cumberhead ML11
75 C23 Cumbernauld G67
53 E50 Cumberworth LN13
99 D33 Cuminestown AB53
64 D20 Cumloden DG8
60 A29 Cummersdale CA2
69 G27 Cummertrees DG12
97 E26 Cummingstown IV30
67 B21 Cumnock KA18
21 A40 Cumnor OX2
61 A31 Cumrew CA4
69 E26 Cumrue DG11
65 E22 Cumstoun DG6
60 A30 Cumwhinton CA4
61 A30 Cumwhitton CA4
57 B40 Cundall YO6
74 F19 Cunninghamhead KA3
107 E40 Cunningsburgh ZE2
106 C41 Cunnister ZE2
82 F28 Cunnoquhie KY15
82 F29 Cupar KY15
82 F29 Cupar Muir KY15
50 E38 Curbar S30
11 C41 Curbridge *Ham.* S030
21 A39 Curbridge *Oxf.* OX8
11 C41 Curdridge SO32
40 F37 Curdworth B76
8 C28 Curland TA3
8 B29 Curload TA3
21 D40 Curridge RG18
75 D27 Currie EH14
8 B29 Curry Mallet TA3
8 B29 Curry Rivel TA10
14 D54 Curteis' Corner TN27
14 C53 Curtisden Green TN17
2 F12 Cury TR12
109 B8 Cushendall BT44
109 B8 Cushendun BT44
99 C33 Cushnie AB45
7 B27 Cushuish TA2
28 D28 Cusop HR3
64 G20 Cutcloy DG8
7 B25 Cutcombe TA24
96 C23 Cuthill IV25
37 D22 Cutiau LL42
29 B34 Cutnall Green WR9
30 E36 Cutsdean GL54
51 E39 Cutthorpe S42
107 D39 Cutts ZE1

Douglas

99 D36 Cuttyhill AB42
21 B42 Cuxham OX9
24 E52 Cuxton ME2
52 B47 Cuxwold LN7
47 E26 Cwm *Clw.* LL18
18 A27 Cwm *Gwe.* NP3
17 E22 Cwm *W.G.* SA1
18 B23 Cwmafan SA12
18 B25 Cwmaman CF44
26 D21 Cwmann SA48
17 B18 Cwmbach *Dyf.* SA34
18 A25 Cwmbach *M.G.* CF44
28 D27 Cwmbach *Pow.* HR3
27 C26 Cwmbach *Pow.* LD2
37 G25 Cwmbelan SY18
19 B28 Cwmbran NP44
37 G22 Cwmbrwyno SY23
18 B27 Cwmcarn NP1
19 A30 Cwmcarvan NP5
37 D24 Cwm-Cewydd SY20
26 D18 Cwmcoy SA38
18 A25 Cwmdare CF44
17 A22 Cwmdu *Dyf.* SA19
28 F27 Cwmdu *Pow.* NP8
17 A19 Cwmduad SA33
16 C17 Cwmfelin Boeth SA34
18 B27 Cwmfelinfach NP1
16 B17 Cwmfelin Mynach SA34
17 C20 Cwmffrwd SA31
19 A28 Cwm Frrwd-oer NP4
27 G23 Cwmgiedd SA9
17 C22 Cwmgors SA18
18 A24 Cwmgwrach SA11
27 D24 Cwm Irfon LD5
17 C20 Cwmisfael SA32
37 E24 Cwm-Llinau SY20
37 C19 Cwmllyfri SA33
27 G23 Cwmllynfell SA9
17 A18 Cwm-Morgan SA35
27 D25 Cwm Owen LD2
18 B25 Cwm-parc CF42
17 A19 Cwmpengraig SA44
26 D20 Cwmsychbant SA40
37 G22 Cwmsymlog SY23
18 A27 Cwmtillery NP3
27 G23 Cwm-twrch Isaf SA9
46 F21 Cwm-y-glo LL55
28 F28 Cwmyoy NP7
27 A23 Cwmystwyth SY23
37 E22 Cwrt SY20
26 D20 Cwrt-newydd SA40
28 G28 Cwrt-y-gollen NP8
17 D20 Cydwelli (Kidwelly) SA17
47 G26 Cyffylliog LL15
18 B26 Cymmer *M.G.* CF39
18 B24 Cymmer *W.G.* SA13
27 E23 Cynghordy SA20
17 D20 Cynheidre SA15
37 A26 Cynwyd LL21
17 B19 Cynwyl Elfed SA33

D

68 D24 Dabton DG3
5 D24 Daccombe TQ12
60 D30 Dacre *Cum.* CA11
57 C37 Dacre *N.Y.* HG3
57 C37 Dacre Banks HG3
61 C34 Daddry Shield DL13
31 E42 Dadford MK18
41 F39 Dadlington CV13
17 D21 Dafen SA14
44 E55 Daffy Green IP25
23 C51 Dagenham RM10
10 C36 Daggons SP6
20 A35 Daglingworth GL7
32 G45 Dagnall HP4
80 D16 Dail PA35
00 C8 Dail Beag HS2
00 A10 Dail Bho Dheas HS2
00 A10 Dail Bho Thuath HS2
67 C18 Dailly KA26
00 C7 Dail Mor HS2
80 D15 Dailnamac PA35
82 F29 Dairsie or Osnaburgh KY15
84 B3 Dalabrog HS8
80 F15 Dalavich PA35
88 E22 Dalballoch PH20
65 D24 Dalbeattie DG5
68 B22 Dalblair KA18
90 F31 Dalbog DD9
02 G23 Dalbreck IV28
40 B38 Dalbury DE65
54 F24 Dalby IM5
67 C20 Dalcairnie KA6
81 A23 Dalchalloch PH18
97 A24 Dalchalm KW9
80 G16 Dalchenna PA32
02 G21 Dalchork IV27
87 C18 Dalchreichart IV3
81 F22 Dalchruin PH6
96 G23 Dalcross IV1
53 F48 Dalderby LN9
90 C28 Daldownie AB35
41 B40 Dale *Dby.* DE7
16 D14 Dale *Dyf.* SA62
107 B37 Dale *She.* ZE2
60 E30 Dale Head CA10
63 E43 Dalehouse TS13
79 A13 Dalelia PH36
12 F45 Dale Park BN18
89 A24 Daless IV12
90 B27 Dalestie AB37
90 C29 Dalfad AB35
103 D25 Dalganachan KW12
74 F18 Dalgarven KA13
75 B27 Dalgety Bay KY11
67 B21 Dalgig KA18
81 E23 Dalginross PH6
68 C22 Dalgonar DG3
82 C25 Dalguise PH8
102 C24 Dalhalvaig KW13
34 B53 Dalham CB8
74 B18 Daligan G84
66 B12 Dalivaddy PA28
67 E17 Daljarrock KA26
76 D29 Dalkeith EH22
97 F27 Dallas IV36
96 G23 Dallaschyle IV12
64 D20 Dallash DG8
35 C58 Dallinghoo IP13
13 E52 Dallington *E.S.* TN21
31 B43 Dallington *Nmp.* NN5
91 B33 Dalmadilly AB51
80 E17 Dalmally PA33
82 C25 Dalmarnock PH8
74 A21 Dalmary FK8
67 C20 Dalmellington KA6
75 C27 Dalmeny EH30
102 G21 Dalmichy IV27
88 C23 Dalmigavie IV13
96 E22 Dalmore IV17
89 G26 Dalmunzie Hotel PH10
79 A12 Dalnabreck PH36
82 A25 Dalnacarn PH10
82 A27 Dalnaglar Castle PH10
79 E12 Dalnaha PA63
89 C24 Dalnahaitnach PH23
96 B23 Dalnamain IV25
80 B15 Dalnatrat PA38
96 D22 Dalnavie IV17
80 B17 Dalness PA39
102 G22 Dalnessie IV27
64 C17 Dalnigap DG8
82 G26 Dalqueich KY13
67 E17 Dalreoch KA26
81 D23 Dalriech PH8
91 C31 Dalroy IV1
82 B27 Dalrulzian PH10
74 F18 Dalry KA24
67 B19 Dalrymple KA6
75 E24 Dalserf ML8
67 E21 Dalshangan DG7
65 C25 Dalskairth DG2
60 A29 Dalston CA5
68 E25 Dalswinton DG2
88 B23 Daltomach IV13
69 F26 Dalton *D.&G.* DG11
48 B30 Dalton *Lan.* WN8
62 F36 Dalton *N.Y.* DL11
57 B40 Dalton *N.Y.* YO7
71 F36 Dalton *Nor.* NE20
61 A35 Dalton *Nor.* NE46
51 C40 Dalton *S.Y.* S65
54 B27 Dalton-in-Furness LA15
62 B39 Dalton-le-Dale SR7
62 F38 Dalton-on-Tees DL2
62 C40 Dalton Piercy TS27
73 B13 Daltot PA31
97 G25 Daltra IV12
81 E22 Dalveich FK19
67 B19 Dalvennan KA19
88 A22 Dalvourn IV1
88 F22 Dalwhinnie PH19
8 D28 Dalwood EX13
10 C37 Damerham SP6
45 E60 Damgate NR13
64 G16 Damnaglaur DG9
82 F25 Damside PH3
24 A53 Danbury CM3
63 F42 Danby YO21
62 G39 Danby Wiske DL7
98 E28 Dandaleith AB38
76 D28 Danderhall EH22
49 F35 Danebridge SK11
33 F49 Dane End SG12
13 D50 Danehill RH17
41 E41 Dane Hills LE3
51 F39 Danesmoor S45
91 B34 Danestone AB22
76 D31 Danskine EH41
22 E44 Darby Green GU17
23 D51 Darenth DA2
48 D31 Daresbury WA4
51 B39 Darfield S73
25 E56 Dargate ME13
70 D34 Dargues NE19
4 D18 Darite PL14
40 F35 Darlaston WS10
57 D38 Darley HG3
50 F38 Darley Dale DE4
30 D38 Darlingscott CV36
62 E38 Darlington DL
38 B31 Darliston SY13
51 E43 Darlton NG22
99 E33 Darnabo AB53
51 D39 Darnall S9
67 A21 Darnconner KA18
91 D33 Darnford AB31
65 D22 Darngarroch DG7
76 G31 Darnick TD6
37 E24 Darowen SY20
99 E33 Darra AB53
71 F37 Darras Hall NE20
51 A40 Darrington WF8
35 B60 Darsham IP17
99 D36 Dartfield AB43
23 D51 Dartford DA
5 D23 Dartington TQ9
5 C22 Dartmeet TQ13
5 E24 Dartmouth TQ6
51 B39 Darton S75
74 G21 Darvel KA17
14 E53 Darwell TN32
56 G32 Darwen BB3
22 D45 Datchet SL3
33 G48 Datchworth SG3
33 G48 Datchworth Green SG3
49 B33 Daubhill BL3
98 E28 Daugh of Kinermony AB38
20 C35 Dauntsey SN15
89 A25 Dava PH26
66 B13 Davaar PA28
90 C30 Davan AB34
49 E32 Davenham CW9
31 B41 Daventry NN11
4 B17 Davidstow PL32
69 C28 Davington DG13
91 A33 Daviot *Hgh.* AB51
88 A23 Daviot *Hgh.* IV1
98 D30 Davoch of Grange AB55
39 E32 Dawley TF4
5 C25 Dawlish EX7
47 E24 Dawn LL22
24 C54 Daws Heath SS7
43 B50 Dawsmere PE12
30 F38 Daylesford GL56
47 E27 Ddol CH7
75 F23 Deadwaters ML11
15 B59 Deal CT14
25 B55 Deal Hall CM0
60 D26 Dean *Cum.* CA14
5 D23 Dean *Dev.* TQ11
9 C35 Dean *Dor.* SP5
11 C41 Dean *Ham.* SO32
30 F39 Dean *Oxf.* OX7
19 G32 Dean *Som.* BA4
62 C38 Dean Bank DL17
69 B29 Deanburnhaugh TD9
21 F41 Deane RG25
9 C35 Deanland SP5
5 D22 Dean Prior TQ11
49 D34 Dean Row SK9
60 D26 Deanscales CA13
31 D43 Deanshanger MK19
81 G22 Deanston FK16
14 B53 Dean Street ME15
60 C26 Dearham CA15
35 C58 Debach IP13
69 E28 Debate DG11
33 E51 Debden CB11
33 E51 Debden Green CB11
35 B57 Debenham IP14
75 C26 Dechmont EH52
31 E40 Deddington OX15
34 E56 Dedham CO7
90 D30 Deecastle AB34
42 F45 Deene NN17
42 F45 Deenethorpe NN17
50 C38 Deepcar S30
22 F45 Deepcut GU16
56 A33 Deepdale *Cum.* LA10
56 A34 Deepdale *N.Y.* BD23
42 E47 Deeping Gate PE6
42 D47 Deeping St James PE6
43 D48 Deeping St Nicholas PE11
98 D30 Deerhill AB55
29 E34 Deerhurst GL19
29 D35 Defford WR8
27 F25 Defynnog LD3
47 E23 Deganwy LL31
79 F13 Degnish PA34
62 F39 Deighton *N.Y.* DL6
58 E42 Deighton *N.Y.* YO4
46 F21 Deiniolen LL55
4 B16 Delabole PL33
48 F31 Delamere CW8
90 B27 Delavorar AB37
91 A35 Delfrigs AB23
89 A26 Delliefure PH26
89 C25 Dell Lodge PH25
90 B27 Delnabo AB37
96 D23 Delny IV18
49 B35 Delph OL3
90 B30 Delphorie AB33
62 A37 Delves DH8
82 C27 Delvine PH1
42 B46 Dembleby NG34
51 C40 Denaby DN12
51 C40 Denaby Main DN12
47 F26 Denbigh LL16
5 D23 Denbury TQ12
41 A39 Denby DE5
50 B38 Denby Dale HD8
21 B39 Denchworth OX12
55 B28 Dendron LA13
98 F31 Denend AB54
32 A45 Denford NN14
25 A55 Dengie CM0
22 C46 Denham *Bkh.* UB9
35 A57 Denham *Sfk* IP21
34 B53 Denham *Sfk* IP29
22 C46 Denham Green UB9
83 F30 Denhead *Fife* KY16
99 D36 Denhead *Grm.* AB42
91 B33 Denhead *Grm.* AB51
83 C31 Denhead *Tay.* DD11
82 D29 Denhead *Tay.* DD2
70 B31 Denholm TD9
57 F36 Denholme BD13
57 F36 Denholme Clough BD13
36 B19 Denio LL53
11 C42 Denmead PO7
91 B34 Denmill AB51
98 E32 Denmoss AB51
35 B58 Dennington IP13
75 B24 Denny FK6
75 B23 Dennyloanhead FK4
49 A35 Denshaw OL3
91 D33 Denside AB31
15 C57 Densole CT18
34 C53 Denston CB8
40 A36 Denstone ST14
56 A32 Dent LA10
42 G47 Denton *Cbs.* PE7
62 E37 Denton *Drm* DL2
13 F50 Denton *E.S.* BN9
49 C35 Denton *G.M.* M34
15 C57 Denton *Kent* CT4
42 B44 Denton *Lcn.* NG32
57 E37 Denton *N.Y.* LS29
45 G58 Denton *Nfk* IP20
32 C44 Denton *Nmp.* NN7
21 A41 Denton *Oxf.* OX44
43 E51 Denver PE38
11 D43 Denvilles PO9
71 B37 Denwick NE66
44 E56 Deopham NR18
44 F56 Deopham Green NR18
34 C53 Depden IP29
23 D49 Deptford *G.L.* SE8
10 A36 Deptford *Wts.* BA12
41 B39 Derby DE
54 G24 Derbyhaven IM9
79 E10 Dererach PA70
18 A27 Deri CF8
15 C57 Derringstone CT4
40 C34 Derrington ST18
81 E22 Derry FK19
108 E3 Derrygonnelly BT93
20 D35 Derry Hill SN11
109 B6 Derrykeighan BT53
108 F4 Derrylin BT92
52 B44 Derrythorpe DN17
79 B10 Dervaig PA75
109 B7 Dervock BT53
47 G26 Derwen LL21
37 F22 Derwenlas SY20
17 C21 Derwydd SA18
73 C15 Derybruich PA21
42 G43 Desborough NN14
109 D6 Desertmartin BT45
41 E40 Desford LE9
77 G36 Detchant NE70
14 B53 Detling ME14
38 D28 Deuddwr SY22
47 F25 Deunant LL16
39 G32 Deuxhill WV16
19 B30 Devauden NP6
27 A23 Devil's Bridge SY23
20 E36 Devizes SN10
4 E20 Devonport PL1
75 A25 Devonside FK13
2 E13 Devoran TR3
76 F29 Dewar EH38
9 E33 Dewlish DT2
28 E30 Dewsall Court HR2
57 G38 Dewsbury WF12
54 E26 Dhoon IM7
54 D26 Dhoor IM7
54 C25 Dhowin IM7
88 B21 Dhuhallow IV1
12 E47 Dial Post RH13
11 D40 Dibden SO45
10 D39 Dibden Purlieu SO45
45 G57 Dickleburgh IP21
30 E36 Didbrook GL54
21 C41 Didcot OX11
32 B47 Diddington PE18
38 G30 Diddlebury SY7
28 E30 Didley HR2
12 E44 Didling GU29
20 C33 Didmarton GL9
49 C34 Didsbury M20
5 D22 Didworthy TQ10
52 G46 Digby LN4
93 E10 Digg IV51
50 B36 Diggle OL3
48 B30 Digmoor WN8
33 G48 Digswell AL8
26 C20 Dihewyd SA48
65 E23 Dildawn DG7
45 C59 Dilham NR28
40 A35 Dilhorne ST10
70 G35 Dilston NE45
20 G34 Dilton Marsh BA13
28 C29 Dilwyn HR4
28 C30 Dilwyn Common HR4
17 B18 Dinas *Dyf.* SA33
16 A16 Dinas *Dyf.* SA42
36 B18 Dinas *Gwy.* LL53
46 G20 Dinas *Gwy.* LL54
37 D24 Dinas-Mawddwy SY20
18 D27 Dinas Powys CF64
19 G31 Dinder BA5
28 E31 Dinedor HR2
28 G30 Dingestow NP5
42 G43 Dingley LE16
96 F21 Dingwall IV15
70 D31 Dinlabyre TD9
90 D30 Dinnet AB34
51 D41 Dinnington *S.Y.* S31
8 C29 Dinnington *Som.* TA17
71 F37 Dinnington *T.&W.* NE13
46 F21 Dinorwic LL55
31 G43 Dinton *Bkh.* HP17
10 A36 Dinton *Wts.* SP3
69 D26 Dinwoodie Mains DG11
6 D19 Dinworthy EX22
73 G13 Dippen PA28
22 G43 Dippenhall GU10
66 A16 Dippin KA27
98 D29 Dipple *Grm.* IV32
67 C18 Dipple *Str.* KA26
5 E23 Diptford TQ9
62 A37 Dipton DH9
89 B26 Dirdhu PH26
76 B30 Dirleton EH39
28 B28 Discoed LD8
41 C40 Diseworth DE74
104 D32 Dishes KW17
57 B39 Dishforth YO7
79 D10 Dishig PA68
49 D35 Disley SK12
45 G57 Diss IP22
27 C26 Disserth LD1
60 D25 Distington CA14
9 A32 Ditcheat BA4
45 F59 Ditchingham NR35
30 F39 Ditchley OX8
13 E49 Ditchling BN6
20 E33 Ditteridge SN14
5 E24 Dittisham TQ6
48 D30 Ditton *Che.* WA8
23 F52 Ditton *Kent* ME20
33 C52 Ditton Green CB8
39 G32 Ditton Priors WV16
29 E35 Dixton *Glo.* GL20
28 G31 Dixton *H.&W.* NP5
109 D8 Doagh BT39
4 D18 Dobwalls PL14
7 G23 Doccombe TQ13
96 G21 Dochgarroch IV3
28 C31 Docklow HR6
60 D29 Dockray CA11
23 B51 Doddinghurst CM15
43 G49 Doddington *Cbs.* PE15
14 B55 Doddington *Kent* ME9
52 E44 Doddington *Lcn.* LN6
77 G35 Doddington *Nor.* NE71
28 A31 Doddington *Shr.* DY14
7 G24 Doddiscombsleigh EX6
29 A35 Dodford *H.&W.* B61
31 B42 Dodford *Nmp.* NN7
20 C33 Dodington *Avon* BS17
7 A27 Dodington *Som.* TA5
20 D33 Dodington Ash BS17
48 F29 Dodleston CH4
50 B38 Dodworth S75
51 F40 Doe Lea S44
52 G47 Dogdyke LN4
22 F43 Dogmersfield RG27
7 F25 Dog Village EX5
37 D26 Dolanog SY21
28 B27 Dolau LD1
27 D25 Dolau Honddu LD3
36 A20 Dolbenmaen LL49
27 A24 Dolfach SY18
37 E24 Dol Fawr SY19
37 G26 Dolfor SY16
27 E23 Dolgarreg SA20
47 F23 Dolgarrog LL32
37 D23 Dolgellau LL40
37 E22 Dolgoch LL36
17 A20 Dol-gran SA39
97 A24 Doll KW9
75 A25 Dollar FK14
75 A25 Dollarbeg FK14
28 D27 Dolleycanney HR5
55 D31 Dolphinholme LA2
75 F26 Dolphinton EH46
6 D21 Dolton EX19
47 E24 Dolwen *Clw.* LL22
37 E25 Dolwen *Pow.* SY21
47 G23 Dolwyddelan LL25
37 G22 Dolybont SY24
28 C28 Dolyhir LD8
38 B28 Dolywern LL20
38 D28 Domgay SY22
109 D9 Donaghadee BT21
109 E7 Donaghcloney BT66
109 E6 Donaghmore BT70
51 B41 Doncaster DN
9 B35 Donhead St Andrew SP7
9 B34 Donhead St Mary SP7
75 B27 Donibristle KY4
7 A26 Doniford TA23
43 B48 Donington PE11
41 D40 Donington le Heath LE67
53 D48 Donington on Bain LN11
40 D38 Donisthorpe DE12
22 E45 Donkey Town GU24
21 E40 Donnington *Brk.* RG14
30 F37 Donnington *Glo.* GL56
29 E33 Donnington *H.&W.* HR8
38 E31 Donnington *Shr.* SY5
39 D33 Donnington *Shr.* TF2
12 F44 Donnington *W.S.* PO20
8 C29 Donyatt TA19
9 E32 Dorchester *Dor.* DT1
21 B41 Dorchester *Oxf.* OX10
40 E38 Dordon B78
50 D38 Dore S17
88 A21 Dores IV1
41 A41 Dorket Head NG5
22 G47 Dorking RH4
23 G50 Dormansland RH7
23 G49 Dormans Park RH19
63 D41 Dormanstown TS10
28 D31 Dormington HR1
22 D45 Dorney SL4
86 B14 Dornie IV40
96 C23 Dornoch IV25
69 G28 Dornock DG12
103 C26 Dorrery KW12
30 A37 Dorridge B93
52 G46 Dorrington *Lcn.* LN4
38 E30 Dorrington *Shr.* SY5
90 B31 Dorsell AB33
30 C37 Dorsington CV37
28 D28 Dorstone HR3
31 G42 Dorton HP18
86 B15 Dorusduain IV40
40 F38 Dosthill B77
61 A35 Dotland NE46
8 E30 Dottery DT6
4 D17 Doublebois PL14
74 C21 Dougalston G62
73 G14 Dougarie KA27
20 B34 Doughton GL8
54 F25 Douglas *I.o.M.* IM1

Douglas

75 G24 Douglas *Str.* ML11
83 D30 Douglas and Angus DD5
65 E24 Douglas Hall DG5
46 F22 Douglas Hill LL57
82 C29 Douglastown DD8
75 G24 Douglas Water ML11
19 G32 Doulting BA4
104 D28 Dounby KW17
96 A20 Doune *Hgh.* IV24
89 C24 Doune *Hgh.* PH22
81 G23 Doune *Str.* FK16
80 F19 Doune *Str.* FK17
74 A18 Doune *Str.* G83
98 C32 Doune Park AB45
90 C30 Douneside AB34
96 C22 Dounie *Hgh.* IV19
96 B21 Dounie *Hgh.* IV24
103 B25 Dounreay KW14
5 D21 Dousland PL20
38 C29 Dovaston SY10
50 E36 Dove Holes SK17
60 C26 Dovenby CA13
15 C59 Dover CT16
29 B34 Doverdale WR9
40 B36 Doveridge DE6
23 G48 Doversgreen RH2
82 C25 Dowally PH9
29 F35 Dowdeswell GL54
67 C18 Dowhill KA26
6 D21 Dowland EX19
8 E28 Dowlands DT7
8 C29 Dowlish Wake TA19
20 B37 Down Ampney GL7
4 E18 Downderry PL11
23 E50 Downe BR6
19 D32 Downend *Avon* BS16
21 D40 Downend *Brk.* RG20
11 F41 Downend *I.o.W.* PO30
19 G28 Down End TA6
33 A51 Down Field CB7
82 D29 Downfield DD3
4 C19 Downgate PL17
24 B53 Downham *Esx* CM11
56 E33 Downham *Lan.* BB7
77 G34 Downham *Nor.* TD12
44 E52 Downham Market PE38
29 F34 Down Hatherley GL2
4 B18 Downhead *Cnw.* PL15
19 G32 Downhead *Som.* BA4
109 B6 Downhill BT51
48 B29 Downholland Cross L39
62 G37 Downholme DL11
91 D35 Downies AB1
47 E27 Downing CH8
22 B44 Downley HP13
109 F9 Downpatrick BT30
19 E30 Downside *Avon* BS19
19 G32 Downside *Som.* BA4
22 F47 Downside *Sry* KT11
7 E23 Down St Mary EX17
5 F21 Down Thomas PL9
6 G21 Downton *Dev.* EX20
5 E24 Downton *Dev.* TQ6
10 E38 Downton *Ham.* SO41
10 B37 Downton *Wts.* SP5
28 A30 Downton on the Rock SY8
42 B47 Dowsby PE10
60 D29 Dowthwaitehead CA11
19 D32 Doynton BS15
18 C27 Draethen NP1
75 F23 Draffan ML11
5 E21 Drakeland Corner PL7
29 D34 Drakes Broughton WR10
30 A36 Drakes Cross B47
68 B23 Drambuie DG4
109 D6 Draperstown BT45
57 D36 Draughton *N.Y.* BD23
31 A43 Draughton *Nmp.* NN6
58 G42 Drax YO8
31 A40 Draycote CV23
41 B40 Draycott *Dby.* DE72
30 E37 Draycott *Glo.* GL56
29 D34 Draycott *H.&W.* WR5
19 F30 Draycott *Som.* BS27
40 C37 Draycott in the Clay DE6
40 A35 Draycott in the Moors ST10
29 A35 Drayton *H.&W.* DY9
11 D42 Drayton *Ham.* PO6
43 B48 Drayton *Lcn.* PE20
42 F44 Drayton *Lei.* LE16
45 D57 Drayton *Nfk* NR8
21 B40 Drayton *Oxf.* OX14
31 D40 Drayton *Oxf.* OX15
8 B29 Drayton *Som.* TA10
40 E37 Drayton Bassett B78
32 G45 Drayton Beauchamp HP22
32 F44 Drayton Parslow MK17
21 B41 Drayton St Leonard OX10
57 D36 Drebley BD23
54 D26 Dreemskerry IM7
16 C14 Dreenhill SA62
17 C21 Drefach *Dyf.* SA14
17 A19 Drefach *Dyf.* SA44
26 D20 Dre-fach SA40
74 G19 Dreghorn KA11
15 C58 Drellingore CT18
76 B30 Drem EH39
7 F23 Drewsteignton EX6
53 E49 Driby LN13
20 B36 Driffield GL7
60 G26 Drigg CA19
57 G37 Drighlington BD11
80 F16 Drimfern PA32
80 F17 Drimlee PA32
79 B11 Drimnin PA34
92 G3 Drimore HS8
8 D29 Drimpton DT8
80 G17 Drimsynie PA24
73 A14 Drimvore PA31
86 C11 Drinan IV49
34 B55 Drinkstone IP30
34 C55 Drinkstone Green IP30
80 F17 Drishaig PA32
80 F15 Drissaig PA35
40 C36 Drointon ST18
29 B34 Droitwich WR9
109 F8 Dromara BT25
109 E8 Dromore *Down* BT25
108 E4 Dromore *Tyr.* BT78
82 F27 Dron PH2
51 E39 Dronfield S18
51 E39 Dronfield Woodhouse S18
67 B20 Drongan KA6
82 D29 Dronley DD2
22 C45 Dropmore SL1
11 C41 Droxford SO32
49 C34 Droylsden M43
37 A26 Druid LL21
16 C14 Druidston SA62
87 G16 Druimarbin PH33
80 C15 Druimavuic PA38
73 C13 Druimdrishaig PA31
86 F12 Druimindarroch PH39
88 A20 Druimkinnerras IV4
73 C15 Drum *Str.* PA21
82 G26 Drum *Tay.* KY13
73 D16 Drumachloy PA20
108 C5 Drumahoe BT48
101 E17 Drumbeg IV27
98 E31 Drumblade AB54
98 E32 Drumblair AB54
86 A13 Drumbuie IV40
60 A28 Drumburgh CA5
108 F4 Drumcard BT92
74 C21 Drumchapel G15
96 G21 Drumchardine IV5
94 C14 Drumchork IV22
74 G22 Drumclog ML10
98 E30 Drumdelgie AB54
96 F22 Drumderfit IV1
83 G30 Drumeldrie KY8
75 G27 Drumelzier ML12
86 C12 Drumfearn IV43
86 G15 Drumfern PH33
66 A13 Drumgarve PA28
82 B29 Drumgley DD8
88 E23 Drumguish PH21
90 D31 Drumhead AB31
96 F23 Drumine IV1
67 D21 Drumjohn DG7
64 C18 Drumlamford Ho. KA26
91 C32 Drumlasie AB31
66 B12 Drumlemble PA28
91 E33 Drumlithie AB3
81 G22 Drummond *Cen.* FK17
96 E22 Drummond *Hgh.* IV16
64 G17 Drummore DG9
98 E29 Drummuir Castle AB55
88 A20 Drumnadrochit IV3
98 D31 Drumna-gorrach AB55
79 A13 Drumnatorran PH36
91 D33 Drumoak AB31
66 A12 Drumore PA28
82 C25 Drumour PH8
108 E4 Drumquin BT78
65 C22 Drumrash DG7
95 A17 Drumrunie IV26
91 A35 Drums AB41
83 D30 Drumsturdy DD5
93 G10 Drumuie IV51
89 B25 Drumuillie PH24
81 G22 Drumvaich FK17
99 F34 Drumwhindle AB41
68 E23 Drumwhirn DG7
83 C32 Drunkendub DD11
48 F28 Drury CH7
61 E32 Drybeck CA16
98 C30 Drybridge *Grm.* AB56
74 G19 Drybridge *Str.* KA11
29 G32 Drybrook GL17
42 A44 Dry Doddington NG23
33 B49 Dry Drayton CB3
76 G31 Drygrange TD6
94 F11 Dry Harbour IV40
69 A28 Dryhope TD7
74 B20 Drymen G63
99 E34 Drymuir AB42
85 A9 Drynoch IV47
21 B40 Dry Sandford OX13
17 B21 Dryslwyn SA32
24 C52 Dry Street SS16
38 E31 Dryton SY5
79 E13 Duachy PA34
99 C33 Dubford AB45
73 D14 Dubhchladach PA29
82 E25 Dubheads PH7
83 B31 Dubton DD8
74 D19 Duchal PA13
101 G19 Duchally IV27
74 A20 Duchray FK8
33 F52 Duck End CM6
48 G30 Duckington SY14
21 A39 Ducklington OX8
32 C47 Duck`s Cross MK44
33 E50 Duddenhoe End CB11
76 C28 Duddingston EH15
42 E45 Duddington PE9
13 D50 Duddleswell TN22
77 F35 Duddo TD15
48 F30 Duddon CW6
54 A27 Duddon Bridge LA18
38 B29 Dudleston Heath SY12
71 F38 Dudley *T.&W.* NE13
40 F35 Dudley *W.M.* DY
57 F37 Dudley Hill BD4
40 F35 Dudley Port DY4
10 E36 Dudsbury BH22
41 A39 Duffield DE56
18 B24 Duffryn SA13
98 E28 Dufftown AB55
97 E27 Duffus IV30
61 D32 Dufton CA16
58 C44 Duggleby YO17
103 F25 Duible KW8
80 E17 Duiletter PA33
81 A21 Duinish PH18
86 A13 Duirinish IV40
86 C12 Duisdealmor IV43
86 G15 Duisky PH33
28 G27 Dukestown NP2
49 C35 Dukinfield SK16
46 D20 Dulas LL70
90 B29 Dulax AB36
19 G31 Dulcote BA5
7 E26 Dulford EX15
81 C23 Dull PH15
75 C23 Dullatur G68
33 C51 Dullingham CB8
89 B25 Dulnain Bridge PH26
32 B47 Duloe *Bfd.* PE19
4 E18 Duloe *Cnw.* PL14
97 G25 Dulsie IV12
7 C24 Dulverton TA22
23 D49 Dulwich SE21
74 C20 Dumbarton G82
29 E35 Dumbleton WR11
69 C26 Dumcrieff DG10
98 F30 Dumeath AB54
74 B19 Dumfin G84
65 C25 Dumfries DG
74 B21 Dumgoyne G63
21 G41 Dummer RG25
83 B32 Dun DD10
79 E14 Dunach PA34
81 B22 Dunalastair PH16
86 B11 Dunan *Hgh.* IV49
73 C17 Dunan *Str.* PA23
73 A16 Dunans PA22
19 G28 Dunball TA6
76 C32 Dunbar EH42
103 F27 Dunbeath KW6
79 D14 Dunbeg PA37
81 G23 Dunblane FK15
82 F28 Dunbog KY14
90 A31 Duncanston *Grm.* AB52
96 F21 Duncanston *Hgh.* IV7
7 G24 Dunchideock EX6
31 A40 Dunchurch CV22
31 C42 Duncote NN12
68 E25 Duncow DG1
81 G21 Duncraggan FK17
82 G27 Duncrievie PH2
81 D21 Duncroist FK21
82 F25 Duncrub PH2
74 B20 Duncryne G83
12 E45 Duncton GU28
82 D29 Dundee DD
82 E29 Dundee Airport DD2
8 A30 Dundon TA11
109 E8 Dundonald *Down* BT16
74 G19 Dundonald *Str.* KA2
95 C16 Dundonnell IV23
60 B27 Dundraw CA7
88 C19 Dundreggan IV3
65 F23 Dundrennan DG6
109 F8 Dundrum BT33
19 E31 Dundry BS18
75 B27 Dunearn KY3
91 C33 Dunecht AB32
75 B26 Dunfermline KY12
20 B37 Dunfield GL7
50 B37 Dunford Bridge S30
109 E6 Dungannon BT71
74 G22 Dungavel ML10
109 C6 Dungiven BT47
51 E43 Dunham NG22
48 E30 Dunham-on-the-Hill WA6
29 B34 Dunhampton DY13
49 D33 Dunham Town WA14
52 E46 Dunholme LN2
83 F31 Dunino KY16
75 B24 Dunipace FK6
81 E23 Dunira PH6
82 C26 Dunkeld PH8
19 F32 Dunkerton BA2
7 E27 Dunkeswell EX14
57 E39 Dunkeswick LS17
15 B56 Dunkirk ME13
23 F52 Dunk`s Green TN11
83 A31 Dunlappie DD9
29 B33 Dunley DY13
74 F19 Dunlop KA3
73 C17 Dunloskin PA23
4 D16 Dunmere PL31
75 B24 Dunmore *Cen.* FK2
73 D13 Dunmore *Str.* PA29
109 E8 Dunmurry BT17
103 C27 Dunn KW1
69 E28 Dunnabie DG11
108 C5 Dunnamanagh BT82
103 A28 Dunnet KW14
83 C30 Dunnichen DD8
82 F26 Dunning PH2
59 D47 Dunnington *Hum.* YO25
58 D42 Dunnington *N.Y.* YO1
30 C36 Dunnington *War.* B49
56 G33 Dunnockshaw BB4
73 C17 Dunoon PA23
64 E17 Dunragit DG9
73 B13 Dunrostan PA31
77 E33 Duns TD11
42 C47 Dunsby PE10
68 E24 Dunscore DG2
51 B42 Dunscroft DN7
63 E41 Dunsdale TS14
22 D43 Dunsden Green RG4
12 C46 Dunsfold GU8
7 G23 Dunsford EX6
82 F28 Dunshelt KY14
82 D27 Dunsinnan PH2
6 E20 Dunsland Cross EX22
63 E44 Dunsley YO21
22 A44 Dunsmore HP22
56 E32 Dunsop Bridge BB7
32 F45 Dunstable LU6
40 C37 Dunstall DE13
34 B53 Dunstall Green CB8
71 A38 Dunstan NE66
7 A25 Dunster TA24
31 F40 Duns Tew OX6
52 F46 Dunston *Lcn.* LN4
45 E58 Dunston *Nfk* NR14
40 D35 Dunston *Stf.* ST18
71 G38 Dunston *T.&W.* NE11
5 C23 Dunstone *Dev.* TQ13
5 F23 Dunstone *Dev.* TQ7
5 E21 Dunstone *Dev.* TQ7
51 B42 Dunsville DN7
59 F46 Dunswell HU6
75 F26 Dunsyre ML11
4 C19 Dunterton PL19
20 A35 Duntisbourne Abbots GL7
20 A35 Duntisbourne Leer GL7
20 A35 Duntisbourne Rouse GL7
9 D32 Duntish DT2
74 C20 Duntocher G81
33 D48 Dunton *Bfd.* SG18
32 F44 Dunton *Bkh.* MK18
41 F41 Dunton Bassett LE17
23 F51 Dunton Green TN13
24 B52 Dunton Wayletts CM13
93 D9 Duntulm IV51
67 B18 Dunure KA7
67 B18 Dunure Mains KA7
17 E21 Dunvant SA2
93 G8 Dunvegan IV55
35 A60 Dunwich IP17
83 F30 Dura KY15
60 A29 Durdar CA2
13 C52 Durgates TN5
62 B38 Durham DH1
79 B12 Durinemast PA34
68 C24 Durisdeer DG3
8 A28 Durleigh TA5
11 C41 Durley *Ham.* SO32
21 E38 Durley *Wts.* SN8
94 B15 Durnamuck IV23
101 B19 Durness IV27
91 A33 Durno AB51
80 B15 Duror PA38
103 B27 Durran *Hgh.* KW14
80 G15 Durran *Str.* PA33
12 F46 Durrington *W.S.* BN13
20 G37 Durrington *Wts.* SP4
20 B33 Dursley GL11
8 B28 Durston TA3
9 D34 Durweston DT11
107 A40 Dury ZE2
31 B43 Duston NN5
89 B25 Duthil PH23
28 A27 Dutlas LD7
33 F51 Duton Hill CM6
48 E31 Dutton WA4
33 D50 Duxford CB2
47 E23 Dwygyfylchi LL34
46 F20 Dwyran LL61
109 E6 Dyan BT68
91 B34 Dyce AB2
17 D20 Dyfatty SA16
16 A15 Dyffryn *Dyf.* SA64
18 B24 Dyffryn *M.G.* CF34
36 C21 Dyffryn Ardudwy LL44
37 G23 Dyffryn Castell SY23
17 B22 Dyffryn Ceidrych SA19
18 A24 Dyffryn Cellwen SA10
6 C19 Dyke *Dev.* EX39
97 F25 Dyke *Grm.* IV36
42 C47 Dyke *Lcn.* PE10
74 A22 Dykehead *Cen.* FK8
75 E24 Dykehead *Str.* ML7
82 A29 Dykehead *Tay.* DD8
91 G33 Dykelands AB30
82 B28 Dykends PH11
99 E33 Dykeside AB53
37 F24 Dylife SY19
15 E56 Dymchurch TN29
29 E32 Dymock GL18
20 D33 Dyrham SN14
76 A28 Dysart KY1
47 E26 Dyserth LL18

E

100 D6 Eadar Dha Fhadhail HS2
55 E30 Eagland Hill PR3
52 F44 Eagle LN6
62 E39 Eaglescliffe TS16
60 D26 Eaglesfield *Cum.* CA13
69 F28 Eaglesfield *D.&G.* DG11
74 E21 Eaglesham G76
42 F46 Eaglethorpe PE8
49 A33 Eagley BL1
54 F24 Eairy IM4
32 C44 Eakley MK16
51 F42 Eakring NG22
51 A43 Ealand DN17
22 C47 Ealing W
61 D30 Eamont Bridge CA10
56 E35 Earby BB8
56 G32 Earcroft BB3
39 F32 Eardington WV16
28 C29 Eardisland HR6
28 D28 Eardisley HR3
29 B32 Eardiston *H.&W.* WR15
38 C29 Eardiston *Shr.* SY1
33 A49 Earith PE17
70 A35 Earle NE71
48 C31 Earlestown WA12
45 E57 Earlham NR4
93 E9 Earlish IV51
32 B44 Earls Barton NN6
34 F54 Earls Colne CO6
29 B35 Earl`s Common WR9
29 D34 Earl`s Croome WR8
30 A38 Earlsdon CV5
83 G30 Earlsferry KY9
99 F34 Earlsford AB51
34 B56 Earl`s Green IP14
41 F40 Earl Shilton LE9
35 B58 Earl Soham IP13
50 F36 Earl Sterndale SK17
76 G31 Earlston TD4
35 C57 Earl Stonham IP14
19 B30 Earlswood *Gwe.* NP6
30 A36 Earlswood *War.* B94
12 G44 Earnley PO20
84 E3 Earsairidh HS9
71 F39 Earsdon NE25
71 D37 Earsdon Moor NE6
45 G59 Earsham NR35
58 D42 Earswick YO3
12 F45 Eartham PO18
19 C32 Earthcote Green BS12
63 F41 Easby TS9
73 E14 Eascairt PA29
79 F13 Easdale PA34
12 D44 Easebourne GU29
41 G40 Easenhall CV23
22 G45 Eashing GU7
21 A42 Easington *Bkh.* HP18
63 E43 Easington *Cle.* TS13
62 B39 Easington *Drm* SR8
53 A50 Easington *Hum.* HU12
77 G36 Easington *Nor.* NE70
21 B42 Easington *Oxf.* OX9
62 B39 Easington Colliery SR8
62 B39 Easington Lane DH
58 C41 Easingwold YO6
15 B58 Easole Street CT15
82 C29 Eassie and Nevay DD8
18 E26 East Aberthaw CF62
5 F23 East Allington TQ9
7 C24 East Anstey EX16
62 G38 East Appleton DL10
57 G38 East Ardsley WF3
11 F41 East Ashey PO33
12 F44 East Ashling PO18
91 C33 East Auchronie AB32
59 A45 East Ayton YO12
52 D47 East Barkwith LN3
14 B53 East Barming ME16
63 E44 East Barnby YO21
23 B48 East Barnet EN4
44 B55 East Barsham NR22
45 B57 East Beckham NR11
22 D46 East Bedfont TW14
34 E56 East Bergholt CO7
44 C55 East Bilney NR20
13 F50 East Blatchington BN25
71 G39 East Boldon NE36
10 D39 East Boldre SO42
71 B37 East Bolton NE66
62 E38 Eastbourne *Drm* DL1
13 G52 Eastbourne *E.S.* BN21
44 E55 East Bradenham IP25
19 F29 East Brent TA9
35 B60 East Bridge IP16
41 A42 East Bridgford NG13
97 A24 East Brora KW9
6 B22 East Buckland EX32
7 G26 East Budleigh EX9
59 D45 Eastburn YO25
107 B39 East Burrafirth ZE2
9 F34 East Burton BH20
21 D39 Eastbury *Brk.* RG17
22 B47 Eastbury *G.L.* HA6

Elton

57 D36 Eastby BD23
91 F32 East Cairnbeg AB30
75 D26 East Calder EH53
45 E57 East Carleton NR14
42 G44 East Carlton LE16
21 C39 East Challow OX12
5 F23 East Charleton TQ7
8 D31 East Chelborough DT2
13 E49 East Chiltington BN7
8 C30 East Chinnock BA22
20 F37 East Chisenbury SN9
25 D55 Eastchurch ME12
22 F46 East Clandon GU4
31 F43 East Claydon MK18
103 E28 East Clyth KW3
8 C31 East Coker BA22
20 A34 Eastcombe GL6
7 B27 East Combe TA4
5 E23 East Cornworthy TQ9
22 C47 Eastcote *G.L.* HA5
31 C42 Eastcote *Nmp.* NN12
30 A37 Eastcote *W.M.* B92
6 D18 Eastcott *Cnw.* EX23
20 F36 Eastcott *Wts.* SN10
58 E43 East Cottingwith YO4
20 B35 Eastcourt SN16
11 E41 East Cowes PO32
58 G42 East Cowick DN14
62 F39 East Cowton DL7
19 G32 East Cranmore BA4
9 F35 East Creech BH20
88 B22 East Croachy IV1
66 A12 East Darlochan PA28
90 C30 East Davoch AB34
13 G51 East Dean *E.S.* BN20
10 B38 East Dean *Ham.* SP5
12 E45 East Dean *W.S.* PO18
44 D55 East Dereham NR19
6 A21 East Down EX31
51 E43 East Drayton DN22
19 D30 East End *Avon* BS19
33 F50 East End *Cbs.* SG9
9 E35 East End *Dor.* BH21
21 E40 East End *Ham.* RG20
10 E39 East End *Ham.* SO41
14 D54 East End *Kent* TN17
30 G39 East End *Oxf.* OX8
35 E57 East End *Sfk* CO7
30 F39 Eastend OX7
96 D22 Easter Ardross IV17
90 D28 Easter Balmoral AB35
88 B21 Easter Boleskine IV1
81 G22 Easter Borland FK8
96 E22 Easter Brae IV7
75 B23 Easter Buckieburn FK6
19 C31 Easter Compton BS12
88 C20 Easter Drummond IV1
81 G21 Easter Dullater FK17
72 E8 Easter Ellister PA48
96 C22 Easter Fearn IV24
97 G24 Easter Galcantray IV12
12 F45 Eastergate PO20
77 F33 Easter Howlaws TD10
96 F21 Easter Kinkell IV6
83 D31 Easter Knox DD11
82 A29 Easter Lednathie DD8
96 G21 Easter Moniack IV5
91 C34 Easter Ord AB32
74 A22 Easter Poldar FK8
107 D40 Easter Quarff ZE2
107 C38 Easter Skeld ZE2
96 F22 Easter Suddie IV8
20 F35 Easterton SN10
19 F29 Eastertown BS24
91 F33 Easter Tulloch AB30
98 C32 Easter Whyntie AB45
14 B53 East Farleigh ME15
42 G43 East Farndon LE16
51 C43 East Ferry DN21
59 A46 Eastfield *N.Y.* YO11
75 D24 Eastfield *Str.* ML7
71 C38 Eastfield Hall NE65
76 B31 East Fortune EH39
21 D39 East Garston RG17
61 C35 Eastgate *Drm* DL13
42 D47 Eastgate *Lcn.* PE10
45 C57 Eastgate *Nfk* NR10
21 C40 East Ginge OX12
41 D42 East Goscote LE7
21 E38 East Grafton SN8
10 B38 East Grimstead SP5
13 C49 East Grinstead RH19
14 E55 East Guldeford TN31
31 B42 East Haddon NN6
21 C41 East Hagbourne OX11
52 A47 East Halton DN40
23 C50 East Ham E6
48 D29 Eastham L62
22 E44 Easthampstead RG12
21 B40 East Hanney OX12
24 A53 East Hanningfield CM3
51 A40 East Hardwick WF8
44 G55 East Harling NR16
62 F40 East Harlsey DL6
19 F31 East Harptree BS18
71 F38 East Hartford NE23
12 E44 East Harting GU31
9 B35 East Hatch SP3
33 C48 East Hatley SG19
62 G37 East Hauxwell DL8
83 D31 East Haven DD7
22 E44 Eastheath RG41
42 A47 East Heckington PE20
62 B37 East Hedleyhope DL13
103 G26 East Helmsdale KW8
21 C40 East Hendred OX12
59 B45 East Heslerton YO17
13 E51 East Hoathly BN8
38 F31 Easthope TF13
24 C52 East Horndon CM13
34 F55 Easthorpe *Esx* CO6
42 B43 Easthorpe *Lei.* NG13
51 G43 Easthorpe *Not.* NG25
19 G31 East Horrington BA5
22 F46 East Horsley KT24
77 G36 East Horton NE71
76 D29 Easthouses EH22
19 G29 East Huntspill TA9
32 G47 East Hyde LU1
21 C40 East Ilsley RG20
7 E23 Eastington *Dev.* EX17
20 A33 Eastington *Glo.* GL10
30 G37 Eastington *Glo.* GL54
53 F49 East Keal PE23
20 E37 East Kennett SN8
57 E39 East Keswick LS17
74 E22 East Kilbride G74
53 F49 East Kirkby PE23
58 B44 East Knapton YO17
9 F34 East Knighton DT2
9 A34 East Knoyle SP3
8 C30 East Lambrook TA13
15 C59 East Langdon CT15
42 F43 East Langton LE16
96 A23 East Langwell IV28
12 F44 East Lavant PO18
12 E45 East Lavington GU28
62 E37 East Layton DL11
21 A38 Eastleach Martin GL7
20 A37 Eastleach Turville GL7
41 C41 East Leake LE12
77 G34 East Learmouth TD12
91 C32 East Learney AB31
6 C20 Eastleigh *Dev.* EX39
11 C40 Eastleigh *Ham.* SO50
7 E23 East Leigh EX17
44 D54 East Lexham PE32
71 A36 East Lilburn NE66
14 B55 Eastling ME13
76 C31 East Linton EH40
11 B43 East Liss GU33
4 E18 East Looe PL13
51 C43 East Lound DN9
9 F34 East Lulworth BH20
59 C45 East Lutton YO17
8 A31 East Lydford TA11
91 D32 East Mains AB31
14 B53 East Malling ME19
83 D30 East March DD4
12 E44 East Marden PO18
51 E43 East Markham NG22
56 D34 East Marton BD23
11 B42 East Meon GU32
7 D25 East Mere EX16
34 G56 East Mersea CO5
103 A28 East Mey KW14
41 C40 East Midlands Airport DE74
22 E47 East Molesey KT8
9 E34 East Morden BH20
57 E36 East Morton BD20
58 B42 East Ness YO6
11 E42 Eastney PO4
29 E33 Eastnor HR8
42 E43 East Norton LE7
21 G41 East Oakley RG23
51 A43 Eastoft DN17
5 D24 East Ogwell TQ12
11 E43 Eastoke PO11
32 A47 Easton *Cbs.* PE18
60 A28 Easton *Cum.* CA5
69 F30 Easton *Cum.* CA6
9 G32 Easton *Dev.* DT5
7 G23 Easton *Dev.* TQ13
11 A41 Easton *Ham.* SO21
10 F39 Easton *I.o.W.* PO40
42 C45 Easton *Lcn.* NG33
45 D57 Easton *Nfk* NR9
35 C58 Easton *Sfk* IP13
19 G30 Easton *Som.* BA5
20 D34 Easton *Wts.* SN13
20 C34 Easton Grey SN16
19 D31 Easton-in -Gordano BS20
32 C44 Easton Maudit NN29
42 E46 Easton on the Hill PE9
21 E38 Easton Royal SN9
9 C34 East Orchard SP7
77 E35 East Ord TD15
6 F19 East Panson PL15
23 G52 East Peckham TN12
8 A31 East Pennard BA4
45 E58 East Poringland NR14
5 G23 East Portlemouth TQ8
5 G23 East Prawle TQ7
12 F46 East Preston BN16
6 D19 East Putford EX22
7 A27 East Quantoxhead TA5
62 B39 East Rainton DH5
53 C48 East Ravendale DN37
44 C54 East Raynham NR21
43 F48 Eastrea PE7
51 D42 East Retford (Retford) DN22
69 G28 Eastriggs DG12
57 E39 East Rigton LS17
58 F43 Eastrington DN14
19 E29 East Rolstone BS24
62 F40 East Rounton DL6
44 C54 East Rudham PE31
45 A57 East Runton NR27
45 C59 East Ruston NR12
15 B58 Eastry CT13
76 D30 East Saltoun EH34
21 D39 East Shefford RG17
105 B30 Eastside KW17
71 E38 East Sleekburn NE22
45 C60 East Somerton NR29
51 C43 East Stockwith DN21
9 F34 East Stoke *Dor.* BH20
42 A43 East Stoke *Not.* NG23
9 B33 East Stour SP8
25 E58 East Stourmouth CT3
11 A41 East Stratton SO21
15 B59 East Studdal CT15
86 A11 East Suisnish IV40
4 D17 East Taphouse PL14
6 C20 East-the-Water EX39
71 D37 East Thirston NE65
24 D52 East Tilbury RM18
11 A43 East Tisted GU34
52 D47 East Torrington LN3
44 D56 East Tuddenham NR20
10 B39 East Tytherley SP5
20 D35 East Tytherton SN15
7 E24 East Village EX17
53 G50 Eastville PE22
38 F31 East Wall TF13
44 D53 East Walton PE32
42 C43 Eastwell LE14
10 B39 East Wellow SO51
76 A29 East Wemyss KY1
75 D25 East Whitburn EH47
33 G50 Eastwick CM20
23 D50 East Wickham DA16
16 D16 East Williamston SA68
44 D52 East Winch PE32
11 E43 East Wittering PO20
57 A37 East Witton DL8
24 C54 Eastwood *Esx* SS9
41 A40 Eastwood *Not.* NG16
56 G35 Eastwood *W.Y.* HX7
21 E39 East Woodhay RG20
11 A43 East Worldham GU34
7 D23 East Worlington EX17
30 B39 Eathorpe CV33
49 F34 Eaton *Che.* CW12
48 F31 Eaton *Che.* CW6
42 C43 Eaton *Lei.* NG32
45 E58 Eaton *Nfk* NR2
51 E42 Eaton *Not.* DN22
21 A40 Eaton *Oxf.* OX13
38 F31 Eaton *Shr.* SY6
38 G29 Eaton *Shr.* SY9
28 E30 Eaton Bishop HR2
32 F45 Eaton Bray LU6
39 E32 Eaton Constantine SY5
32 C47 Eaton Ford PE19
32 F45 Eaton Green LU6
48 F30 Eaton Hall CH4
21 B38 Eaton Hastings SN7
32 C47 Eaton Socon PE19
39 C32 Eaton upon Tern TF9
57 C37 Eavestone HG4
58 A44 Ebberston YO13
9 B35 Ebbesborne Wake SP5
18 A27 Ebbw Vale NP3
62 A36 Ebchester DH8
7 G25 Ebford EX3
30 D37 Ebrington GL55
21 F40 Ecchinswell RG20
77 D33 Ecclaw TD13
69 F27 Ecclefechan DG11
77 F33 Eccles *Bor.* TD5
49 C33 Eccles *G.M.* M30
24 E53 Eccles *Kent* ME20
51 C39 Ecclesfield S30
83 A33 Ecclesgreig DD10
40 C34 Eccleshall ST21
75 C26 Ecclesmachan EH52
44 F56 Eccles Road NR16
48 F30 Eccleston *Che.* CH4
48 A30 Eccleston *Lan.* PR7
48 C30 Eccleston *Mer.* WA10
57 E38 Eccup LS16
91 C33 Echt AB32
70 A32 Eckford TD5
51 E40 Eckington *Dby.* S31
29 D35 Eckington *H.&W.* WR10
32 B44 Ecton *Nmp.* NN6
50 G37 Ecton *Stf.* SK17
50 D37 Edale S30
104 C31 Eday Airport KW17
13 E48 Edburton BN5
60 B26 Edderside CA15
96 C22 Edderton IV19
21 E39 Eddington RG17
76 F28 Eddleston EH45
75 E23 Eddlewood ML3
109 D8 Eden BT38
23 G50 Edenbridge TN8
80 E17 Edendonich PA33
49 A34 Edenfield BL0
61 C31 Edenhall CA11
42 C46 Edenham PE10
23 E49 Eden Park BR3
50 F38 Edensor DE45
74 A18 Edentaggart G83
51 B42 Edenthorpe DN3
36 B18 Edern LL53
108 E4 Ederny BT93
8 A30 Edgarley BA6
40 G36 Edgbaston B15
31 F42 Edgcott HP18
2 E13 Edgcumbe TR10
20 A34 Edge *Glo.* GL6
38 E29 Edge *Shr.* SY5
38 C31 Edgebolton SY4
28 G31 Edge End GL16
45 B57 Edgefield NR24
38 A31 Edgeley SY13
38 D29 Edgerley SY10
20 A34 Edgeworth GL6
5 D24 Edginswell TQ2
39 D32 Edgmond TF10
39 C33 Edgmond Marsh TF10
38 G29 Edgton SY7
22 B47 Edgware HA8
49 A33 Edgworth BL7
40 E36 Edial WS7
81 E21 Edinample FK19
93 F9 Edinbain IV51
90 B30 Edinbanchory AB33
74 C21 Edinbarnet G81
76 C28 Edinburgh EH
75 C27 Edinburgh (Turnhouse) Airport EH12
81 E21 Edinchip FK19
40 D37 Edingale B79
51 G42 Edingley NG22
45 B59 Edingthorpe NR28
8 A29 Edington *Som.* TA7
20 F35 Edington *Wts.* BA13
98 E30 Edintore AB55
97 F26 Edinvale IV36
6 C18 Edistone EX39
19 G29 Edithmead TA9
42 E45 Edith Weston LE15
40 A37 Edlaston DE6
32 G45 Edlesborough LU6
71 C36 Edlingham NE66
53 F48 Edlington LN9
10 C36 Edmondsham BH21
62 B38 Edmondsley DH2
42 D44 Edmondthorpe LE14
104 D31 Edmonstone KW17
23 B49 Edmonton N18
62 A36 Edmundbyres DH8
77 G33 Ednam TD5
40 A38 Ednaston DE6
24 A52 Edney Common CM1
81 F20 Edra FK17
81 B24 Edradynate PH9
77 E34 Edrom TD11
38 B31 Edstaston SY4
30 B37 Edstone B95
29 C32 Edvin Loach HR7
41 B41 Edwalton NG12
34 D55 Edwardstone CO10
17 A22 Edwinsford SA19
51 F41 Edwinstowe NG21
33 D48 Edworth SG18
29 C32 Edwyn Ralph HR7
83 A31 Edzell DD9
18 C26 Efail Isaf CF38
36 B19 Efailnewydd LL53
16 B17 Efailwen SA66
47 G26 Efenechtyd LL15
22 F46 Effingham KT24
107 B38 Effirth ZE2
7 E24 Efford EX17
21 F40 Egbury SP11
12 D45 Egdean RH20
49 A33 Egerton *G.M.* BL7
14 C55 Egerton *Kent* TN27
14 C54 Egerton Forstal TN27
48 G31 Egerton Green SY14
5 E21 Egg Buckland PL6
64 F20 Eggerness DG8
6 D22 Eggesford Barton EX18
32 F45 Eggington LU7
40 C38 Egginton DE65
62 E39 Egglescliffe TS16
62 D35 Eggleston DL12
22 D46 Egham TW20
42 E44 Egleton LE15
71 B36 Eglingham NE66
108 C5 Eglinton BT48
4 C16 Egloshayle PL27
4 B18 Egloskerry PL15
47 E23 Eglwysbach LL28
18 E25 Eglwys-Brewis CF62
38 A30 Eglwys Cross SY13
37 F22 Eglwys Fach SY20
16 A17 Eglwyswrw SA41
51 F43 Egmanton NG22
60 E25 Egremont CA22
63 F43 Egton YO21
63 F44 Egton Bridge YO21
21 G40 Egypt SO21
34 F55 Eight Ash Green CO6
79 C13 Eignaig PA34
89 C24 Eil PH22
86 C14 Eilanreach IV40
95 C16 Eilean Darach IV23
86 C12 Eilean Iarmain (Isleornsay) IV43
100 E7 Einacleit HS2
100 F9 Eisgean HS2
36 B21 Eisingrug LL46
37 G23 Eisteddfa Gurig SY23
27 B25 Elan Village LD1
19 C31 Elberton BS12
5 E21 Elburton PL9
82 E27 Elcho PH2
20 C36 Elcombe SN4
43 F48 Eldernell PE7
29 E33 Eldersfield GL19
74 D20 Elderslie PA5
67 E18 Eldrick KA26
56 C33 Eldroth LA2
57 E37 Eldwick BD16
37 G22 Elerch (Bont-goch) SY24
77 G37 Elford *Nor.* NE68
40 D37 Elford *Stf.* B79
97 E27 Elgin IV30
86 C11 Elgol IV49
15 C57 Elham CT4
83 G30 Elie KY9
70 C35 Elilaw NE65
46 D19 Elim LL65
10 C39 Eling SO40
68 C23 Eliock DG4
94 E11 Elishader IV51
70 D34 Elishaw NE19
51 E42 Elkesley DN22
29 G35 Elkstone GL53
57 G36 Elland HX5
73 C25 Ellary PA31
40 A36 Ellastone DE6
77 D33 Ellemford TD11
60 C26 Ellenborough CA15
40 C34 Ellenhall ST21
12 C47 Ellen's Green RH12
62 G40 Ellerbeck DL6
63 E43 Ellerby HU11
39 C32 Ellerdine Heath TF6
80 C16 Elleric PA38
59 G45 Ellerker HU15
58 E42 Ellerton *Hum.* YO4
62 G38 Ellerton *N.Y.* DL10
39 C33 Ellerton *Shr.* TF9
22 A44 Ellesborough HP17
38 B29 Ellesmere SY12
48 E30 Ellesmere Port L65
10 D36 Ellingham *Ham.* BH24
45 F59 Ellingham *Nfk* NR35
71 A37 Ellingham *Nor.* NE67
57 A37 Ellingstring HG4
32 A47 Ellington *Cbs.* PE18
71 D38 Ellington *Nor.* NE61
21 G42 Ellisfield RG25
41 D40 Ellistown LE67
99 F35 Ellon AB41
60 C30 Ellonby CA11
45 G60 Ellough NR34
59 G45 Elloughton HU15
19 A31 Ellwood GL16
43 E50 Elm PE14
29 B34 Elmbridge WR9
33 E50 Elmdon *Esx* CB11
40 G37 Elmdon *W.M.* B26
40 G37 Elmdon Heath B92
41 F40 Elmesthorpe LE9
40 D36 Elmhurst WS13
29 D35 Elmley Castle WR10
29 B34 Elmley Lovett WR9
29 G33 Elmore GL2
29 G33 Elmore Back GL2
23 C51 Elm Park RM12
6 C18 Elmscott EX39
34 D56 Elmsett IP7
34 F56 Elmstead Market CO7
25 E58 Elmstone CT3
29 F35 Elmstone Hardwicke GL51
59 D45 Elmswell *Hum.* YO25
34 B55 Elmswell *Sfk* IP30
51 E40 Elmton NG20
101 G18 Elphin IV27
76 C29 Elphinstone EH33
91 C34 Elrick *Grm.* AB32
90 A30 Elrick *Grm.* AB54
64 F19 Elrig DG8
80 F17 Elrigbeag PA32
70 D35 Elsdon NE19
51 C39 Elsecar S74
33 F51 Elsenham CM22
21 A41 Elsfield OX3
52 A46 Elsham DN20
44 D56 Elsing NR20
56 E35 Elslack BD23
38 B29 Elson SY12
75 F26 Elsrickle ML12
22 G44 Elstead GU8
12 E44 Elsted GU31
42 C46 Elsthorpe PE10
62 D39 Elstob TS21
55 F31 Elston *Lan.* PR2
42 A43 Elston *Not.* NG23
6 D22 Elstone EX37
32 D46 Elstow MK42
22 B47 Elstree WD6
59 F48 Elstronwick HU12
55 F30 Elswick PR4
33 B48 Elsworth CB3
60 F29 Elterwater LA22
23 D50 Eltham SE9
33 C48 Eltisley PE19
42 F46 Elton *Cbs.* PE8
48 E30 Elton *Che.* CH2
62 E39 Elton *Cle.* TS21
50 F38 Elton *Dby.* DE4

Garroch

11 E41 Fishbourne *I.o.W.* PO33
12 F44 Fishbourne *W.S.* PO18
62 C39 Fishburn TS21
98 F32 Fisherford AB51
11 B40 Fisher's Pond SO50
55 E30 Fisher's Row PR3
12 C45 Fisherstreet GU8
96 F23 Fisherton *Hgh.* IV1
67 B18 Fisherton *Str.* KA7
20 G35 Fisherton de la Mere BA12
16 A15 Fishguard SA65
51 A42 Fishlake DN7
6 C21 Fishley Barton EX37
8 E29 Fishpond Bottom DT6
19 D32 Fishponds BS16
49 B33 Fishpool BL9
43 A49 Fishtoft PE21
43 A48 Fishtoft Drove PE22
83 B32 Fishtown of Usan DD10
77 E34 Fishwick *Bor.* TD15
55 F31 Fishwick *Lan.* PR1
52 E46 Fiskerton *Lcn.* LN3
51 G43 Fiskerton *Not.* NG25
20 F37 Fittleton SP4
12 E46 Fittleworth RH20
43 D50 Fitton End PE13
38 D30 Fitz SY4
7 C27 Fitzhead TA4
51 A39 Fitzwilliam WF9
79 C12 Fiunary PA34
13 D50 Five Ash Down TN22
13 D51 Five Ashes TN20
29 D32 Five Bridges WR6
8 B29 Fivehead TA3
4 B17 Fivelanes PL15
108 F5 Fivemiletown BT75
23 G52 Five Oak Green TN12
12 D46 Five Oaks *W.S.* RH14
17 D20 Five Roads SA15
28 A28 Five Turnings LD7
14 B53 Five Wents ME17
22 C44 Flackwell Heath HP10
29 D35 Fladbury WR10
107 D40 Fladdabister ZE2
50 F37 Flagg SK17
59 B47 Flamborough YO15
32 G46 Flamstead AL3
23 A49 Flamstead End EN7
12 F45 Flansham PO22
56 D35 Flasby BD23
50 F36 Flash SK17
93 F9 Flashader IV51
63 F45 Flask Inn YO22
22 A46 Flaunden HP3
42 A43 Flawborough NG13
57 C40 Flawith YO6
19 E30 Flax Bourton BS19
57 D39 Flaxby HG5
29 G32 Flaxley GL14
7 B27 Flaxpool TA4
58 C42 Flaxton YO6
41 F42 Fleckney LE8
31 B40 Flecknoe CV23
22 F43 Fleet *Ham.* GU13
43 C49 Fleet *Lcn.* PE12
43 C49 Fleet Hargate PE12
55 E28 Fleetwood FY7
18 E25 Flemingston CF62
74 E22 Flemington G72
34 B53 Flempton IP28
92 C6 Fleoideabhagh HS3
60 B27 Fletchertown CA5
13 D50 Fletching TN22
5 E22 Flete PL21
90 C29 Fleuchats AB36
18 B27 Fleur-de-lis NP2
6 E18 Flexbury EX23
22 F45 Flexford GU3
60 C26 Flimby CA15
14 D53 Flimwell TN5
48 E28 Flint CH6
33 D49 Flint Cross SG8
42 A43 Flintham NG23
48 E28 Flint Mountain CH6
59 F48 Flinton HU11
14 D53 Flishinghurst TN17
44 C53 Flitcham PE31
32 E46 Flitton MK45
32 E46 Flitwick MK45
52 A44 Flixborough DN15
49 C33 Flixton *G.M.* M31
45 G59 Flixton *Sfk* NR35
50 A38 Flockton WF4
50 A38 Flockton Green WF4
77 G34 Flodden NE71
93 D10 Flodigarry IV51
55 B29 Flookburgh LA11
98 D30 Floors AB55
45 F57 Flordon NR15
31 B42 Flore NN7
70 C35 Flotterton NE65
34 D56 Flowton IP8
3 E14 Flushing *Cnw.* TR11
99 E36 Flushing *Grm.* AB42
29 C35 Flyford Flavell WR7
24 C53 Fobbing SS17
98 D29 Fochabers IV32
18 A26 Fochriw CF8
52 A44 Fockerby DN17
90 A27 Fodderletter AB37
96 E20 Fodderty IV15
37 D25 Foel SY21
82 C29 Foffarty DD8
58 F43 Foggathorpe YO8
77 F33 Fogo TD11
77 F33 Fogorig TD11
101 D17 Foindle IV27
82 A27 Folda PH11
40 B36 Fole ST14
41 G39 Foleshill CV6
9 C32 Folke DT9
15 D58 Folkestone CT19
42 B46 Folkingham NG34
13 F51 Folkington BN26
42 G47 Folksworth PE7
99 F33 Folla Rule AB51
57 D39 Follifoot HG3
9 D33 Folly *Dor.* DT2
16 B15 Folly *Dyf.* SA62
6 F21 Folly Gate EX20
9 A35 Fonthill Bishop SP3
9 A35 Fonthill Gifford SP3
9 C34 Fontmell Magna SP7
12 F45 Fontwell BN18
50 E37 Foolow S30
23 D50 Foots Cray DA14
90 B29 Forbestown AB36
60 G29 Force Forge LA12
62 E37 Forcett DL11
7 E23 Forches Cross EX17
22 A43 Ford *Bkh.* HP17
6 C20 Ford *Dev.* EX39
5 E22 Ford *Dev.* PL8
5 F23 Ford *Dev.* TQ7
16 B15 Ford *Dyf.* SA62
30 F36 Ford *Glo.* GL54
76 D29 Ford *Ltn* EH37
48 B29 Ford *Mer.* L30
77 G35 Ford *Nor.* TD15
38 D30 Ford *Shr.* SY5
7 C26 Ford *Som.* TA4
79 G14 Ford *Str.* PA31
12 F45 Ford *W.S.* BN18
20 D34 Ford *Wts.* SN14
23 G51 Fordcombe TN3
75 B27 Fordell KY4
38 E28 Forden SY21
33 G52 Ford End CM3
5 D23 Forder Green TQ13
33 A52 Fordham *Cbs.* CB7
34 F55 Fordham *Esx* CO6
43 F51 Fordham *Nfk* PE38
33 B52 Fordham Abbey CB7
10 C37 Fordingbridge SP6
91 F33 Fordoun AB30
34 F54 Fordstreet CO6
7 D27 Ford Street TA21
30 G38 Fordwells OX8
15 B57 Fordwich CT2
98 C31 Fordyce AB45
82 E25 Forebrae PH1
72 D8 Foreland PA49
71 D36 Forestburn Gate NE61
23 C50 Forest Gate E7
22 G46 Forest Green RH5
61 F31 Forest Hall *Cum.* LA8
71 G38 Forest Hall *T.&W.* NE12
61 A31 Forest Head CA8
21 A41 Forest Hill OX33
61 D34 Forest-in-Teesdale DL12
80 C18 Forest Lodge *Str.* PA36
89 G25 Forest Lodge *Tay.* PH18
75 A25 Forest Mill FK10
13 C50 Forest Row RH18
11 C43 Forestside PO9
51 F41 Forest Town NG19
83 C30 Forfar DD8
82 F26 Forgandenny PH2
98 D29 Forgie AB55
48 B28 Formby L37
45 F57 Forncett End NR16
45 F57 Forncett St Mary NR16
45 F57 Forncett St Peter NR16
82 C26 Forneth PH10
34 B53 Fornham All Saints IP28
34 B54 Fornham St Martin IP31
97 F25 Fornighty IV12
97 F26 Forres IV36
75 D24 Forrest ML6
67 E21 Forrest Lodge DG7
40 A35 Forsbrook ST11
103 E28 Forse KW5
103 B26 Forsie KW14
102 D24 Forsinain KW13
102 D24 Forsinard KW13
9 E32 Forston DT2
88 D19 Fort Augustus PH32
82 A27 Forter PH11
82 F26 Forteviot PH2
96 F23 Fort George IV1
75 E25 Forth ML11
29 E34 Forthampton GL19
81 C23 Fortingall PH15
21 G40 Forton *Ham.* SP11
55 D30 Forton *Lan.* PR3
38 D30 Forton *Shr.* SY4
8 D29 Forton *Som.* TA20
39 C33 Forton *Stf.* TF10
98 E32 Fortrie AB53
96 F23 Fortrose IV10
9 G32 Fortuneswell DT5
87 G16 Fort William PH33
22 B45 Forty Green HP9
23 B49 Forty Hill EN2
34 C56 Forward Green IP14
21 F39 Fosbury SN8
30 F38 Foscot OX7
43 B49 Fosdyke PE20
81 B23 Foss PH16
30 G36 Foss Cross GL54
61 G34 Fossdale DL8
30 G36 Fossebridge GL54
31 C42 Foster's Booth NN12
23 A50 Foster Street CM17
40 B37 Foston *Dby.* DE65
42 A44 Foston *Lcn.* NG32
58 C42 Foston *N.Y.* YO6
59 D47 Foston on the Wolds YO25
53 C48 Fotherby LN11
42 F46 Fotheringhay PE8
105 A31 Foubister KW17
69 C28 Foulbog DG13
77 E35 Foulden *Bor.* TD15
44 F53 Foulden *Nfk* IP26
13 E52 Foul Mile BN27
56 E34 Foulridge BB8
44 C56 Foulsham NR20
99 C33 Foulzie AB45
76 F30 Fountainhall TD1
34 A55 Four Ashes *Sfk* IP31
40 E35 Four Ashes *Stf.* WV10
37 A26 Four Crosses *Clw.* LL21
37 E26 Four Crosses *Pow.* SY21
38 D28 Four Crosses *Pow.* SY22
40 E35 Four Crosses *Stf.* WS11
23 G50 Four Elms TN8
8 A28 Four Forks TA5
43 D50 Four Gotes PE13
51 G39 Fourlane Ends DE55
2 E12 Four Lanes TR16
49 G34 Fourlanes End CW11
11 A42 Four Marks GU34
46 E18 Four Mile Bridge LL65
14 E54 Four Oaks *E.S.* TN31
40 F36 Four Oaks *W.M.* B74
40 G38 Four Oaks *W.M.* CV7
96 B23 Fourpenny IV25
17 D20 Four Roads SA17
70 G34 Fourstones NE47
14 E53 Four Throws TN18
10 B36 Fovant SP3
91 A35 Foveran AB41
4 E16 Fowey PL23
82 D29 Fowlis DD2
82 E25 Fowlis Wester PH7
33 D49 Fowlmere SG8
28 E31 Fownhope HR1
29 G35 Foxcote GL54
54 F24 Foxdale IM4
34 D54 Foxearth CO10
55 A28 Foxfield LA20
20 D35 Foxham SN15
3 C15 Foxhole *Cnw.* PL26
88 A21 Foxhole *Hgh.* IV4
13 E51 Foxhunt Green TN21
22 F44 Fox Lane GU14
28 D30 Foxley *H.&W.* HR4
44 C56 Foxley *Nfk* NR20
31 C42 Foxley *Nmp.* NN12
20 C34 Foxley *Wts.* SN16
34 F56 Fox Street CO7
40 A36 Foxt ST10
33 D49 Foxton *Cbs.* CB2
41 G43 Foxton *Lei.* LE16
62 D39 Foxton *N.Y.* TS21
56 B34 Foxup BD23
49 F32 Foxwist Green CW7
28 F31 Foy HR9
88 B20 Foyers IV1
78 B9 Frachadil PA75
2 E11 Fraddam TR27
3 C15 Fraddon TR9
40 D37 Fradley WS13
40 B35 Fradswell ST18
59 C47 Fraisthorpe YO15
13 D50 Framfield TN22
45 E58 Framingham Earl NR14
45 E58 Framingham Pigot NR14
35 B58 Framlingham IP13
9 E32 Frampton *Dor.* DT2
43 B49 Frampton *Lcn.* PE20
19 C32 Frampton Cotterell BS17
20 A34 Frampton Mansell GL6
20 A33 Frampton on Severn GL2
43 A49 Frampton West End PE20
35 C58 Framsden IP14
62 B38 Framwellgate Moor DH1
29 A34 Franche DY11
48 D28 Frankby L48
40 G35 Frankley B32
31 A40 Frankton CV23
13 C51 Frant TN3
99 C35 Fraserburgh AB43
34 F56 Frating Green CO7
11 D42 Fratton PO1
4 E19 Freathy PL10
33 A52 Freckenham IP28
55 G30 Freckleton PR4
42 C43 Freeby LE14
21 G40 Freefolk RG28
30 G39 Freeland OX8
11 C40 Freemantle SO15
107 B40 Freester ZE2
45 E60 Freethorpe NR13
45 E59 Freethorpe Common NR13
42 A45 Freiston *Lcn.* NG32
43 A49 Freiston *Lcn.* PE22
43 A50 Freiston Shore PE22
6 B21 Fremington *Dev.* EX31
62 G36 Fremington *N.Y.* DL11
19 D32 Frenchay BS16
6 G22 Frenchbeer TQ13
98 E31 Frendraught AB54
80 G19 Frenich FK8
22 G44 Frensham GU10
103 B25 Fresgoe KW14
48 B28 Freshfield L37
20 F33 Freshford BA3
10 F39 Freshwater PO40
16 E16 Freshwater East SA71
35 A58 Fressingfield IP21
35 E57 Freston IP9
103 B29 Freswick KW1
45 D58 Frettenham NR12
82 G28 Freuchie KY15
16 C15 Freystrop Cross SA62
68 E25 Friars Carse DG2
13 C50 Friar's Gate TN6
82 E26 Friarton PH2
43 E50 Friday Bridge PE14
13 F52 Friday Street *E.S.* BN23
22 G47 Friday Street *Sry* RH5
58 D44 Fridaythorpe YO25
23 B48 Friern Barnet N11
52 D46 Friesthorpe LN3
22 B43 Frieth RG9
21 B40 Frilford OX13
21 D41 Frilsham RG18
22 F44 Frimley GU16
22 F44 Frimley Green GU16
24 E53 Frindsbury ME2
31 F41 Fringford OX6
14 B54 Frinsted ME9
35 G58 Frinton-on-Sea CO13
83 C31 Friockheim DD11
37 D22 Friog LL38
41 D42 Frisby on the Wreake LE14
53 G50 Friskney PE22
53 G50 Friskney Eaudike PE22
13 G51 Friston *E.S.* BN20
35 C60 Friston *Sfk* IP17
51 G39 Fritchley DE56
14 B55 Frith ME13
10 C38 Fritham SO43
43 A49 Frith Bank PE22
29 A32 Frith Common WR15
6 D20 Frithelstock EX38
6 D20 Frithelstock Stone EX38
53 G49 Frithville PE22
14 C53 Frittenden TN17
45 F58 Fritton *Nfk* NR15
45 E60 Fritton *Nfk* NR31
31 F41 Fritwell OX6
60 E26 Frizington CA26
20 A33 Frocester GL10
38 E28 Frochas SY21
38 E30 Frodesley SY5
52 A44 Frodingham DN15
48 E31 Frodsham WA6
70 A33 Frogden TD5
33 C50 Frog End CB3
50 E38 Froggatt S30
40 A36 Froghall ST10
10 C37 Frogham SP6
5 F23 Frogmore *Dev.* TQ7
22 F44 Frogmore *Ham.* GU17
22 A47 Frogmore *Hfs.* AL2
29 B33 Frog Pool WR6
41 F40 Frolesworth LE17
20 G33 Frome BA11
29 D32 Fromes Hill HR8
8 D31 Frome St Quentin DT2
36 B19 Fron *Gwy.* LL53
27 B26 Fron *Pow.* LD1
38 E28 Fron *Pow.* SY21
38 A28 Froncysyllte LL20
37 B24 Fron-goch LL23
45 G60 Frostenden NR34
62 C36 Frosterley DL13
21 E38 Froxfield SN8
11 B43 Froxfield Green GU32
24 A52 Fryerning CM4
58 B42 Fryton YO6
10 A37 Fugglestone St Peter SP2
52 G45 Fulbeck NG32
33 C50 Fulbourn CB1
30 G38 Fulbrook OX18
58 E42 Fulford *N.Y.* YO1
7 C27 Fulford *Som.* TA2
40 B35 Fulford *Stf.* ST15
23 D48 Fulham SW6
13 E48 Fulking BN5
48 G30 Fuller's Moor CH3
34 G53 Fuller Street CM3
10 A39 Fullerton SP11
53 E48 Fulletby LN9
58 D43 Full Sutton YO4
74 F20 Fullwood KA3
22 C45 Fulmer SL3
44 B55 Fulmodeston NR21
52 E47 Fulnetby LN3
30 D38 Fulready CV37
53 C49 Fulstow LN11
30 F39 Fulwell *Oxf.* OX7
62 A39 Fulwell *T.&W.* SR5
55 F31 Fulwood *Lan.* PR2
51 D39 Fulwood *S.Y.* S10
45 F57 Fundenhall NR16
11 D43 Funtington PO18
11 D41 Funtley PO16
106 C42 Funzie ZE2
8 D28 Furley EX13
37 F22 Furnace *Dyf.* SY20
94 D15 Furnace *Hgh.* IV22
80 G16 Furnace *Str.* PA32
33 F50 Furneux Pelham SG9
7 A23 Furzehill EX35
22 C44 Furze Platt SL6
8 C28 Fyfett TA20
23 A51 Fyfield *Esx* CM5
21 A38 Fyfield *Glo.* GL7
21 G38 Fyfield *Ham.* SP11
21 B40 Fyfield *Oxf.* OX13
20 E37 Fyfield *Wts.* SN8
63 F45 Fylingthorpe YO22
99 F33 Fyvie AB53

G

100 A10 Gabhsunn Bho Dheas HS2
100 B10 Gabhsunn Bho Thuath HS2
96 B22 Gablon IV25
74 E20 Gabroc Hill KA3
41 D42 Gaddesby LE7
32 G46 Gaddesden Row HP2
28 F27 Gaer NP8
19 B30 Gaerllwyd NP6
46 E20 Gaerwen LL60
30 F39 Gagingwell OX7
89 B26 Gaich PH26
88 A22 Gaick IV1
88 F23 Gaick Lodge PH21
40 D34 Gailey ST19
62 E37 Gainford DL2
51 C43 Gainsborough DN21
94 D13 Gairloch IV21
87 F17 Gairlochy PH34
75 A27 Gairney Bank KY13
90 C28 Gairnshiel Lodge AB35
60 B29 Gaitsgill CA5
76 F30 Galabank TD1
76 G30 Galashiels TD1
41 E42 Galby LE7
64 D17 Galdenoch DG8
55 D30 Galgate LA2
9 B32 Galhampton BA22
79 E14 Gallanach PA34
48 G31 Gallantry Bank SY14
76 A28 Gallatown KY1
73 B13 Gallchoille PA31
91 G32 Gallery DD10
41 F39 Galley Common CV10
24 A52 Galleyend CM2
24 A52 Galleywood CM2
83 C30 Gallowfauld DD8
21 C42 Gallowstree Common RG4
39 G33 Gallowstree Elm DY7
86 C14 Galltair IV40
85 F10 Galmisdale PH42
5 E24 Galmpton *Dev.* TQ5
5 F22 Galmpton *Dev.* TQ7
57 B38 Galphay HG4
74 G21 Galston KA4
93 F7 Galtrigill IV55
61 C31 Gamblesby CA10
34 G53 Gamble's Green CM3
60 A28 Gamelsby CA7
33 C48 Gamlingay SG19
6 C20 Gammaton Moor EX39
57 A36 Gammersgill DL8
99 C33 Gamrie AB45
51 E42 Gamston *Not.* DN22
41 B41 Gamston *Not.* NG2
28 G31 Ganarew HR9
37 C23 Ganllwyd LL40
90 F31 Gannochy DD9
59 F47 Ganstead HU11
58 B42 Ganthorpe YO6
59 B45 Ganton YO12
79 D11 Gaodhail PA72
80 F18 Garabal G83
5 E23 Gara Bridge TQ9
94 A15 Garadheancal IV26
96 E20 Garbat IV23
73 A16 Garbhallt PA27
44 G56 Garboldisham IP22
74 A21 Garden FK8
48 F29 Garden City CH5
99 C33 Gardenstown AB45
107 C38 Garderhouse ZE2
59 E45 Gardham HU17
20 G33 Gare Hill BA11
73 A17 Garelochhead G84
21 B40 Garford OX13
57 F40 Garforth LS25
56 D35 Gargrave BD23
74 A22 Gargunnock FK8
73 B13 Gariob PA31
64 D20 Garlies Castle DG8
64 F20 Garlieston DG8
91 C33 Garlogie AB32
99 D33 Garmond AB53
79 C12 Garmony PA65
98 C28 Garmouth IV32
36 B18 Garn LL53
17 C22 Garnant SA18
36 A20 Garn-Dolbenmaen LL51
37 E23 Garneddwen SY20
61 G31 Garnett Bridge LA8
17 D22 Garnswllt SA18
100 D10 Garrabost HS2
73 B16 Garrachra PA23
98 D30 Garralburn AB55
2 F12 Garras TR12
36 A21 Garreg LL48
38 D28 Garreg Bank SY21
81 F24 Garrick FK15
61 B33 Garrigill CA9
108 E3 Garrison BT93
67 E21 Garroch DG7

Garrochty

146

Guisborough

49 **C34** Gorton *G.M.* M18
78 **B7** Gorton *Str.* PA78
35 **C57** Gosbeck IP6
43 **B48** Gosberton PE11
41 **C39** Goseley Dale DE11
34 **F53** Gosfield CO9
60 **F26** Gosforth *Cum.* CA20
71 **G38** Gosforth *T.&W.* NE3
32 **F47** Gosmore SG4
40 **F35** Gospel End DY3
11 **E41** Gosport PO12
106 **D41** Gossabrough ZE2
13 **C48** Gossops Green RH11
77 **F36** Goswick TD15
41 **B41** Gotham NG11
29 **F35** Gotherington GL52
107 **C40** Gott ZE2
13 **C52** Goudhurst TN17
53 **E48** Goulceby LN11
99 **E33** Gourdas AB53
91 **F34** Gourdon DD10
74 **C18** Gourock PA19
74 **D21** Govan G51
5 **F23** Goveton TQ7
28 **G28** Govilon NP7
99 **C36** Gowanhill AB43
58 **G42** Gowdall DN14
17 **E21** Gowerton SA4
75 **B26** Gowkhall KY12
58 **D43** Gowthorpe YO4
59 **G47** Goxhill *Hum.* DN19
59 **E47** Goxhill *Hum.* HU11
18 **C23** Goytre SA13
100 **F9** Grabhair HS2
49 **F35** Gradbach SK17
2 **G12** Grade TR12
12 **E45** Graffham GU28
32 **B47** Grafham *Cbs.* PE18
22 **G46** Grafham *Sry* GU5
28 **E30** Grafton *H.&W.* HR2
28 **B31** Grafton *H.&W.* HR6
57 **C39** Grafton *N.Y.* YO5
21 **A38** Grafton *Oxf.* OX18
38 **D30** Grafton *Shr.* SY4
29 **C35** Grafton Flyford WR7
31 **D43** Grafton Regis NN12
42 **G45** Grafton Underwood NN14
14 **C54** Grafty Green ME17
47 **G27** Graianrhyd CH7
47 **E26** Graig *Clw.* LL17
47 **E24** Graig *Gwy.* LL28
47 **G27** Graig-fechan LL15
24 **D54** Grain ME3
72 **D8** Grainel PA44
99 **E34** Grainhow AB53
53 **C48** Grainsby DN36
53 **C49** Grainthorpe LN11
3 **D15** Grampound TR2
3 **C15** Grampound Road TR2
92 **F4** Gramsdal HS7
31 **F43** Granborough MK18
42 **B43** Granby NG13
31 **B40** Grandborough CV23
81 **B24** Grandtully PH9
60 **E28** Grange *Cum.* CA12
88 **A19** Grange *Hgh.* IV3
24 **E53** Grange *Kent* ME7
48 **D28** Grange *Mer.* L48
63 **G41** Grange *N.Y.* TS9
82 **E28** Grange *Tay.* PH2
98 **D30** Grange Crossroads AB55
97 **E26** Grange Hall IV36
23 **B50** Grange Hill IG7
50 **G38** Grangemill DE4
50 **A38** Grange Moor WF4
75 **B25** Grangemouth FK3
83 **G31** Grangemuir KY10
82 **F28** Grange of Lindores KY14
55 **B30** Grange-over-Sands LA11
67 **D17** Grangeston KA26
63 **D41** Grangetown *Cle.* TS6
18 **D27** Grangetown *S.G.* CF1
62 **A38** Grange Villa DH2
89 **C24** Granish PH22
59 **D47** Gransmoor YO25
16 **A14** Granston SA62
33 **C49** Grantchester CB3
42 **B44** Grantham NG31
57 **B38** Grantley HG4
91 **B32** Grantlodge AB51
69 **C26** Granton House DG10
89 **B25** Grantown-on-Spey PH26
77 **D33** Grantshouse TD11
49 **D32** Grappenhall WA4
52 **B46** Grasby DN38
60 **F29** Grasmere LA22
49 **B35** Grasscroft OL4
48 **D29** Grassendale L19
61 **D34** Grassholme DL12
57 **C36** Grassington BD23
51 **F39** Grassmoor S42
51 **F43** Grassthorpe NG23
21 **G38** Grateley SP11
40 **B36** Gratwich ST14
33 **B48** Graveley *Cbs.* PE18
33 **F48** Graveley *Hfs.* SG4
40 **F37** Gravelly Hill B23
38 **F29** Gravels SY5
106 **E39** Graven ZE2
25 **E56** Graveney ME13
24 **D52** Gravesend DA12
52 **C45** Grayingham DN21
61 **G31** Grayrigg LA8
24 **D52** Grays RM17
12 **C44** Grayshott GU26
12 **C45** Grayswood GU27
21 **E42** Grazeley RG7
51 **C39** Greasbrough S61
48 **D28** Greasby L48
33 **D51** Great Abington CB1
32 **A45** Great Addington NN14
30 **C36** Great Alne B49
48 **B29** Great Altcar L37
33 **G49** Great Amwell SG12
61 **E32** Great Asby CA16
34 **B55** Great Ashfield IP31
63 **E41** Great Ayton TS9
24 **A53** Great Baddow CM2
33 **E52** Great Bardfield CM7
32 **C47** Great Barford MK44
40 **F36** Great Barr B43
30 **G38** Great Barrington OX18
48 **F30** Great Barrow CH3
34 **B54** Great Barton IP31
58 **B43** Great Barugh YO17
70 **E35** Great Bavington NE19
35 **D58** Great Bealings IP13
21 **E38** Great Bedwyn SN8
35 **F57** Great Bentley CO7
31 **B43** Great Billing NN3
34 **C56** Great Blakenham IP6
39 **C32** Great Bolas TF6
22 **F47** Great Bookham KT23
31 **D40** Great Bourton OX17
42 **G43** Great Bowden LE16
33 **C52** Great Bradley CB8
34 **G54** Great Braxted CM8
34 **C56** Great Bricett IP7
32 **E45** Great Brickhill MK17
40 **C34** Great Bridgeford ST18
31 **B42** Great Brington NN7
34 **F56** Great Bromley CO7
60 **C26** Great Broughton *Cum.* CA13
63 **F41** Great Broughton *N.Y.* TS9
49 **E32** Great Budworth CW9
62 **E39** Great Burdon DL1
24 **B52** Great Burstead CM11
63 **F41** Great Busby TS9
33 **G51** Great Canfield CM6
24 **A53** Great Canney CM3
53 **D50** Great Carlton LN11
42 **E46** Great Casterton PE9
14 **C55** Great Chart TN23
39 **D33** Great Chatwell TF10
33 **D50** Great Chesterford CB10
20 **F35** Great Cheverell SN10
33 **E50** Great Chishill SG8
35 **G57** Great Clacton CO15
60 **C26** Great Clifton CA14
53 **B48** Great Coates DN37
29 **D35** Great Comberton WR10
61 **A30** Great Corby CA4
34 **D54** Great Cornard CO10
59 **E48** Great Cowden HU11
21 **B38** Great Coxwell SN7
62 **G38** Great Crakehall DL8
32 **A44** Great Cransley NN14
44 **E54** Great Cressingham IP25
48 **C29** Great Crosby L23
40 **B37** Great Cubley DE6
42 **D43** Great Dalby LE14
32 **B44** Great Doddington NN29
59 **D46** Great Driffield YO25
44 **D54** Great Dunham PE32
33 **F52** Great Dunmow CM6
10 **A37** Great Durnford SP4
33 **F51** Great Easton *Esx* CM6
42 **F44** Great Easton *Lei.* LE16
55 **E29** Great Eccleston PR3
58 **A43** Great Edstone YO6
44 **F56** Great Ellingham NR17
20 **G33** Great Elm BA11
33 **C49** Great Eversden CB3
62 **G38** Great Fencote DL7
34 **C56** Great Finborough IP14
42 **D46** Greatford PE9
44 **D54** Great Fransham NR19
32 **G46** Great Gaddesden HP1
40 **A36** Greatgate ST10
42 **G47** Great Gidding PE17
58 **D44** Great Givendale YO4
35 **B58** Great Glemham IP17
41 **F42** Great Glen LE8
42 **B44** Great Gonerby NG31
33 **C48** Great Gransden SG19
45 **F58** Great Green *Nfk* IP20
34 **C55** Great Green *Sfk* IP30
58 **B43** Great Habton YO17
42 **A47** Great Hale NG34
33 **G51** Great Hallingbury CM22
62 **D40** Greatham *Cle.* TS25
11 **A43** Greatham *Ham.* GU33
12 **E46** Greatham *W.S.* RH20
38 **E30** Great Hanwood SY5
32 **A44** Great Harrowden NN9
56 **F33** Great Harwood BB6
21 **A42** Great Haseley OX44
59 **E47** Great Hatfield HU11
40 **C35** Great Haywood ST18
41 **G39** Great Heath CV6
58 **G41** Great Heck DN14
34 **E54** Great Henny CO9
20 **F35** Great Hinton BA14
44 **F55** Great Hockham IP24
35 **G58** Great Holland CO13
34 **E55** Great Horkesley CO6
33 **F49** Great Hormead SG9
31 **E43** Great Horwood MK17
31 **C43** Great Houghton *Nmp.* NN4
51 **B40** Great Houghton *S.Y.* S72
50 **E37** Great Hucklow SK17
59 **D47** Great Kelk YO25
22 **A43** Great Kimble HP17
22 **B44** Great Kingshill HP15
62 **G38** Great Langton DL7
34 **G53** Great Leighs CM3
52 **B47** Great Limber DN37
32 **D44** Great Linford MK14
34 **A54** Great Livermere IP31
50 **E38** Great Longstone DE45
62 **B38** Great Lumley DH3
38 **E30** Great Lyth SY3
29 **D33** Great Malvern WR14
34 **E54** Great Maplestead CO9
55 **F29** Great Marton FY4
44 **C54** Great Massingham PE32
45 **E57** Great Melton NR9
21 **A42** Great Milton OX44
22 **A44** Great Missenden HP16
56 **F33** Great Mitton BB7
15 **B59** Great Mongeham CT14
45 **F57** Great Moulton NR15
61 **E33** Great Musgrave CA17
38 **D29** Great Ness SY4
28 **G29** Great Oak NP5
35 **F57** Great Oakley *Esx* CO12
42 **G44** Great Oakley *Nmp.* NN14
32 **F47** Great Offley SG5
61 **E33** Great Ormside CA16
60 **A29** Great Orton CA5
57 **C40** Great Ouseburn YO5
42 **G43** Great Oxendon LE16
24 **A52** Great Oxney Green CM1
44 **D54** Great Palgrave PE32
23 **A50** Great Parndon CM19
33 **B48** Great Paxton PE19
55 **F29** Great Plumpton PR4
45 **D59** Great Plumstead NR13
42 **B44** Great Ponton NG33
57 **G40** Great Preston LS26
43 **G48** Great Raveley PE17
30 **G37** Great Rissington GL54
30 **E39** Great Rollright OX7
44 **C55** Great Ryburgh NR21
71 **B36** Great Ryle NE66
38 **E30** Great Ryton SY5
33 **F52** Great Saling CM7
61 **C31** Great Salkeld CA11
33 **E52** Great Sampford CB10
48 **D31** Great Sankey WA5
34 **B53** Great Saxham IP29
21 **D39** Great Shefford RG17
33 **C50** Great Shelford CB2
62 **F39** Great Smeaton DL6
44 **B55** Great Snoring NR21
20 **C35** Great Somerford SN15
62 **D39** Great Stainton TS21
24 **B54** Great Stambridge SS4
32 **B47** Great Staughton PE19
53 **F50** Great Steeping PE23
15 **B59** Great Stonar CT13
15 **E56** Greatstone-on-Sea TN28
61 **D31** Great Strickland CA10
33 **A48** Great Stukeley PE17
53 **E48** Great Sturton LN9
48 **E29** Great Sutton *Che.* L66
38 **G31** Great Sutton *Shr.* SY8
70 **F35** Great Swinburne NE48
30 **F39** Great Tew OX7
34 **F54** Great Tey CO6
33 **D52** Great Thurlow CB9
6 **D21** Great Torrington EX38
71 **C36** Great Tosson NE65
34 **G54** Great Totham *Esx* CM9
34 **G54** Great Totham *Esx* CM9
55 **B28** Great Urswick LA12
25 **C55** Great Wakering SS3
34 **D55** Great Waldingfield CO10
44 **B55** Great Walsingham NR22
33 **G52** Great Waltham CM3
23 **B51** Great Warley CM13
29 **E35** Great Washbourne GL20
34 **C54** Great Welnetham IP30
34 **E56** Great Wenham CO7
70 **F35** Great Whittington NE19
34 **G55** Great Wigborough CO5
33 **C51** Great Wilbraham CB1
10 **A36** Great Wishford SP2
29 **G35** Great Witcombe GL3
29 **B33** Great Witley WR6
30 **E38** Great Wolford CV36
32 **E44** Great Woolstone MK6
31 **D41** Greatworth OX17
33 **D52** Great Wratting CB9
33 **F48** Great Wymondley SG4
40 **E35** Great Wyrley WS6
38 **D31** Great Wytheford SY4
45 **E61** Great Yarmouth NR30
34 **E53** Great Yeldham CO9
83 **D30** Greenburn DD5
109 **G8** Greencastle BT34
62 **B37** Greencroft Hall DH7
91 **D32** Greendams AB31
71 **A36** Greendykes NE66
32 **C47** Green End *Bfd.* MK44
33 **F49** Green End *Hfs.* SG12
32 **E46** Greenfield *Bfd.* MK45
48 **E28** Greenfield *Clw.* CH8
50 **B36** Greenfield *G.M.* OL3
87 **D18** Greenfield *Hgh.* PH35
22 **B43** Greenfield *Oxf.* RG9
22 **C47** Greenford UB6
75 **C23** Greengairs ML6
55 **F30** Greenhalgh PR4
91 **A32** Greenhall AB52
21 **E40** Greenham *Brk.* RG14
7 **C26** Greenham *Som.* TA21
57 **D40** Green Hammerton YO5
70 **E33** Greenhaugh NE48
70 **G32** Greenhead CA6
99 **F36** Greenheads AB42
22 **C47** Greenhill *G.L.* HA1
97 **A25** Greenhill *Hgh.* KW9
51 **D39** Greenhill *S.Y.* S8
23 **D51** Greenhithe DA9
74 **G21** Greenholm KA16
61 **F31** Greenholme CA10
57 **C37** Greenhow Hill HG3
105 **A29** Greenigo KW15
103 **B28** Greenland KW14
22 **C43** Greenlands RG9
76 **F32** Greenlaw *Bor.* TD10
98 **D32** Greenlaw *Grm.* AB45
81 **G24** Greenloaning FK15
49 **A33** Greenmount BL8
99 **F33** Greenmyre AB53
74 **C18** Greenock PA16
55 **A29** Greenodd LA12
19 **F31** Green Ore BA5
81 **F23** Greenscares FK15
71 **G37** Greenside NE40
99 **C33** Greenskares AB45
31 **C42** Greens Norton NN12
34 **F54** Greenstead Green CO9
23 **A51** Greensted CM5
22 **B47** Green Street WD6
23 **E50** Green Street Green *G.L.* BR6
23 **D51** Green Street Green *Kent* DA2
33 **G50** Green Tye SG10
16 **A16** Greenway *Dyf.* SA62
8 **B29** Greenway *Som.* TA3
23 **D49** Greenwich SE10
30 **E36** Greet GL54
28 **A31** Greete SY8
53 **E49** Greetham *Lcn.* LN9
42 **D45** Greetham *Lei.* LE15
57 **G36** Greetland HX4
92 **D4** Greinetobht HS6
8 **A29** Greinton TA7
54 **F24** Grenaby IM9
32 **B44** Grendon *Nmp.* NN7
40 **E38** Grendon *War.* CV9
40 **F38** Grendon Common CV9
28 **C31** Grendon Green HR6
31 **F42** Grendon Underwood HP18
51 **C39** Grenoside S30
93 **B7** Greosabhagh HS3
48 **G29** Gresford LL12
45 **B57** Gresham NR11
93 **F9** Greshornish IV51
44 **D55** Gressenhall NR20
55 **B31** Gressingham LA2
62 **E36** Greta Bridge DL12
69 **G29** Gretna DG16
69 **G28** Gretna Green DG16
29 **E35** Gretton *Glo.* GL54
42 **F44** Gretton *Nmp.* NN17
38 **F31** Gretton *Shr.* SY6
57 **B37** Grewelthorpe HG4
109 **E9** Greyabbey BT22
57 **B37** Greygarth HG4
8 **A29** Greylake TA7
22 **C43** Greys Green RG9
60 **D26** Greysouthen CA13
60 **C30** Greystoke CA11
90 **D28** Greystone *Grm.* AB35
56 **E34** Greystone *Lan.* BB9
83 **C31** Greystone *Tay.* DD11
22 **F43** Greywell RG29
100 **C10** Griais HS2
58 **F43** Gribthorpe DN14
68 **E25** Gribton DG2
6 **F19** Gridley Corner PL15
41 **G39** Griff CV10
19 **B28** Griffithstown NP4
79 **A10** Grigadale PH36
60 **G30** Grigghall LA8
49 **A32** Grimeford Village PR6
51 **B40** Grimethorpe S72
92 **F3** Griminis HS7
106 **C40** Grimister ZE2
29 **B34** Grimley WR2
67 **B19** Grimmet KA19
105 **B30** Grimness KW17
53 **D49** Grimoldby LN11
38 **C29** Grimpo SY11
55 **F31** Grimsargh PR2
31 **D40** Grimsbury OX16
53 **B48** Grimsby DN32
31 **C42** Grimscote NN12
6 **E18** Grimscott EX23
100 **E9** Grimsiadar HS2
42 **C46** Grimsthorpe PE10
41 **C42** Grimston *Lei.* LE14
44 **C53** Grimston *Nfk* PE32
9 **E32** Grimstone DT2
59 **B47** Grindale YO16
107 **C40** Grindiscol ZE2
39 **E33** Grindle TF11
50 **E38** Grindleford S30
56 **E33** Grindleton BB7
40 **C36** Grindley ST14
50 **E37** Grindlow SK17
77 **F34** Grindon *Nor.* TD15
50 **G36** Grindon *Stf.* ST13
51 **C43** Gringley on the Hill DN10
60 **A29** Grinsdale CA5
38 **C31** Grinshill SY4
62 **G36** Grinton DL11
100 **D7** Griomarstaidh HS2
78 **B7** Grishipoll PA78
59 **A46** Gristhorpe YO14
44 **F55** Griston IP25
105 **A31** Gritley KW17
20 **C36** Grittenham SN15
20 **C34** Grittleton SN14
55 **A28** Grizebeck LA17
60 **G29** Grizedale LA22
104 **D32** Grobister KW17
41 **E41** Groby LE6
47 **F26** Groes LL16
18 **C26** Groes-faen CF7
36 **B18** Groesffordd LL53
47 **E26** Groesffordd Marli LL22
46 **G20** Groeslon LL54
38 **D27** Groes-lwyd SY21
73 **F13** Grogport PA28
84 **A3** Groigearraidh HS8
35 **C59** Gromford IP17
47 **D26** Gronant LL19
13 **C51** Groombridge TN3
109 **D9** Groomsport BT19
28 **F29** Grosmont *Gwe.* NP7
63 **F44** Grosmont *N.Y.* YO22
88 **B20** Grotaig IV3
34 **D55** Groton CO10
9 **G32** Grove *Dor.* DT5
25 **E58** Grove *Kent* CT3
51 **E43** Grove *Not.* DN22
21 **B39** Grove *Oxf.* OX12
23 **D50** Grove Park BR1
17 **D21** Grovesend SA4
96 **A21** Gruids IV27
72 **D8** Gruinart Flats PA44
79 **D11** Gruline PA71
82 **E26** Grundcruie PH1
35 **C57** Grundisburgh IP13
107 **C38** Gruting ZE2
107 **E38** Grutness ZE3
80 **C16** Gualachulain PA39
83 **F30** Guardbridge KY16
29 **D33** Guarlford WR13
82 **C25** Guay PH9
60 **G26** Gubbergill CA19
14 **F54** Guestling Green TN35
14 **F54** Guestling Thorn TN35
44 **C56** Guestwick NR20
71 **E38** Guide Post NE62
33 **D48** Guilden Morden SG8
48 **F30** Guilden Sutton CH3
22 **G46** Guildford GU
82 **D27** Guildtown PH2
31 **A42** Guilsborough NN6
38 **D28** Guilsfield SY21
63 **E41** Guisborough TS14

Guiseley

57 E37 Guiseley LS20
44 C55 Guist NR20
104 C31 Guith KW17
30 F36 Guiting Power GL54
107 D40 Gulberwick ZE2
76 B30 Gullane EH31
2 E10 Gulval TR18
4 C20 Gulworthy PL19
16 D16 Gumfreston SA70
41 F42 Gumley LE16
58 F43 Gunby *Hum.* YO8
42 C45 Gunby *Lcn.* NG33
11 A42 Gundleton SO24
6 B22 Gunn EX32
61 G35 Gunnerside DL11
70 F34 Gunnerton NE48
52 A44 Gunness DN15
4 C20 Gunnislake PL18
107 C40 Gunnista ZE2
12 D45 Gunter's Bridge GU28
44 B56 Gunthorpe *Nfk* NR24
41 A42 Gunthorpe *Not.* NG14
11 F40 Gunville PO30
2 F12 Gunwalloe TR12
11 E40 Gurnard PO31
19 G32 Gurney Slade BA3
18 A23 Gurnos SA9
9 C35 Gussage All Saints BH21
9 C35 Gussage St Michael BH21
15 C58 Guston CT15
106 C41 Gutcher ZE2
83 B31 Guthrie DD8
43 E50 Guyhirn PE13
83 C31 Guynd DD11
43 C50 Guy's Head PE12
9 B34 Guy's Marsh SP7
71 C37 Guyzance NE65
18 C26 Gwaelod-y-garth CF4
47 D26 Gwaenysgor LL18
28 C27 Gwaithla HR5
46 E19 Gwalchmai LL65
27 G23 Gwaun-Cae-Gurwen SA18
17 C22 Gwaun-leision SA18
47 F26 Gwaynynog LL16
26 C17 Gwbert SA43
2 F13 Gweek TR11
19 A29 Gwehelog NP5
27 D26 Gwenddwr LD2
2 D13 Gwennap TR16
2 G13 Gwenter TR12
47 F27 Gwernaffield CH7
19 A29 Gwernesney NP5
17 A21 Gwernogle SA32
48 F28 Gwernymynydd CH7
48 G29 Gwersyllt LL11
47 D26 Gwespyr CH8
2 E11 Gwinear TR27
2 D11 Gwithian TR27
37 A26 Gwyddelwern LL21
17 A20 Gwyddgrug SA39
27 B26 Gwystre LD1
47 F24 Gwytherin LL22
38 A29 Gyfelia LL13
47 E23 Gyffin LL32
105 A29 Gyre KW17
36 A19 Gyrn Goch LL54

H

38 E29 Habberley SY5
52 A47 Habrough DN40
5 D24 Haccombe TQ12
42 C47 Hacconby PE10
42 B46 Haceby NG34
35 C59 Hacheston IP13
51 D39 Hackenthorpe S12
44 E56 Hackford NR18
62 G38 Hackforth DL8
104 D29 Hackland KW17
31 C43 Hackleton NN7
15 B59 Hacklinge CT14
63 G45 Hackness *N.Y.* YO13
105 B29 Hackness *Ork.* KW16
23 C49 Hackney E
52 D45 Hackthorn LN2
61 D31 Hackthorpe CA10
77 G33 Hadden TD5
22 A43 Haddenham *Bkh.* HP17
33 A50 Haddenham *Cbs.* CB6
52 F44 Haddington *Lcn.* LN5
76 C30 Haddington *Ltn.* EH41
45 F60 Haddiscoe NR14
42 F47 Haddon PE7
40 E37 Hademore WS14
50 C36 Hadfield SK14
33 G50 Hadham Cross SG10
33 F50 Hadham Ford SG11
24 C50 Hadleigh *Esx* SS7
34 D56 Hadleigh *Sfk* IP7
39 D32 Hadley TF1
40 C37 Hadley End DE13
23 B48 Hadley Wood EN4
23 G52 Hadlow TN11
13 D51 Hadlow Down TN22
38 C31 Hadnall SY4
33 D51 Hadstock CB1
29 B35 Hadzor WR9
14 C54 Haffenden Quarter TN27
47 G24 Hafod-Dinbych LL24
47 F24 Hafodunos LL22
56 F34 Haggate BB10
69 F30 Haggbeck CA6
75 C23 Haggs FK4
40 G34 Hagley *H.&W.* DY9
28 D31 Hagley *H.&W.* HR1
53 F49 Hagnaby PE23
53 F49 Hagworthingham PE23
49 B32 Haigh WN2
55 F31 Haighton Green PR2
60 F26 Haile CA22
30 E36 Hailes GL54
23 A49 Hailey *Hfs.* EN11
21 C42 Hailey *Oxf.* OX10
30 G39 Hailey *Oxf.* OX8
13 F51 Hailsham BN27
32 B47 Hail Weston PE19
103 B27 Haimer KW14
23 B50 Hainault IG6
45 D58 Hainford NR10
52 D47 Hainton LN3
59 C47 Haisthorpe YO25
51 G42 Halam NG22
75 B27 Halbeath KY11
7 D25 Halberton EX16
103 B28 Halcro KW1
49 D33 Hale *G.M.* WA15
10 C37 Hale *Ham.* SP6
22 G44 Hale *Sry* GU9
48 D30 Hale Bank WA8
49 D33 Halebarns WA15
45 F59 Hales *Nfk* NR14
39 B33 Hales *Stf.* TF9
40 G35 Halesowen B63
15 B57 Hales Place CT2
23 G52 Hale Street TN12
35 A59 Halesworth IP19
48 D30 Halewood L26
38 G30 Halford *Shr.* SY7
30 D38 Halford *War.* CV36
40 F34 Halfpenny Green DY7
21 E39 Halfway *Brk.* RG20
27 E24 Halfway *Dyf.* LD3
17 A22 Halfway *Dyf.* SA19
51 D40 Halfway *S.Y.* S19
38 D29 Halfway House SY5
25 D55 Halfway Houses ME12
7 G26 Half Way Inn EX5
38 A29 Halghton Mill LL13
57 G36 Halifax HX
93 E8 Halistra IV55
103 C27 Halkirk KW12
47 E27 Halkyn CH8
74 E20 Hall G78
13 E51 Halland BN8
42 F43 Hallaton LE16
19 F32 Hallatrow BS18
61 A31 Hallbankgate CA8
60 G28 Hall Dunnerdale LA20
19 C31 Hallen BS10
40 G37 Hall Green B28
93 F8 Hallin IV55
24 E52 Halling ME2
53 D48 Hallington *Lcn.* LN11
70 F35 Hallington *Nor.* NE19
38 G28 Hall of the Forest SY7
51 G42 Halloughton NG25
29 C34 Hallow WR2
29 C34 Hallow Heath WR2
70 B31 Hallrule TD9
76 C32 Halls EH42
5 G24 Hallsands TQ7
33 F48 Hall's Green SG4
61 A31 Hall's Tenement CA4
43 A49 Halltoft End PE22
4 B17 Hallworthy PL32
39 A33 Halmer End ST7
19 A32 Halmore GL13
75 F27 Halmyre Mains EH46
12 F45 Halnaker PO18
48 A29 Halsall L39
31 D41 Halse *Nmp.* NN13
7 C27 Halse *Som.* TA4
2 E10 Halsetown TR26
59 G48 Halsham HU12
6 B21 Halsinger EX33
34 E53 Halstead *Esx* CO9
23 E50 Halstead *Kent* TN14
42 E43 Halstead *Lei.* LE7
8 D31 Halstock BA22
53 F48 Haltham LN9
32 G44 Halton *Bkh.* HP22
48 D31 Halton *Che.* WA7
38 B29 Halton *Clw.* LL14
55 C31 Halton *Lan.* LA2
70 G35 Halton *Nor.* NE45
57 D36 Halton East BD23
56 B34 Halton Gill BD23
53 F50 Halton Holegate PE23
61 A32 Halton Lea Gate CA6
56 D34 Halton West BD23
70 G32 Haltwhistle NE49
45 E60 Halvergate NR13
5 E23 Halwell TQ9
6 F19 Halwill EX21
6 F20 Halwill Junction EX21
22 D47 Ham *G.L.* TW10
19 B32 Ham *Glo.* GL13
103 A28 Ham *Hgh.* KW14
15 B59 Ham *Kent* CT14
106 A38 Ham *She.* ZE2
8 B28 Ham *Som.* TA3
21 E39 Ham *Wts.* SN8
11 D40 Hamble SO31
22 C43 Hambleden RG9
11 C42 Hambledon *Ham.* PO7
12 C45 Hambledon *Sry* GU8
55 E29 Hambleton *Lan.* FY6
58 F41 Hambleton *N.Y.* YO8
55 E29 Hambleton Moss Side FY6
8 B29 Hambridge TA10
19 D32 Hambrook *Avon* BS16
11 D43 Hambrook *W.S.* PO18
53 F49 Hameringham LN9
32 A47 Hamerton PE17
19 D31 Ham Green *Avon* BS20
29 B35 Ham Green *H.&W.* B97
24 E52 Ham Hill ME6
74 E22 Hamilton ML3
109 F7 Hamilton's Bawn BT60/61
7 F27 Hamlet EX14
12 C44 Hammer GU27
12 F46 Hammerpot BN16
22 D47 Hammersmith & Fulham W
40 E36 Hammerwich WS7
13 C50 Hammerwood RH19
23 A49 Hammond Street EN7
9 C33 Hammoon DT10
106 D38 Hamnavoe *She.* ZE2
107 D39 Hamnavoe *She.* ZE2
106 D40 Hamnavoe *She.* ZE2
106 E40 Hamnavoe *She.* ZE2
13 F52 Hampden Park BN22
30 G36 Hampnett GL54
51 B40 Hampole DN6
10 E36 Hampreston BH21
23 C48 Hampstead NW3
21 D41 Hampstead Norreys RG18
57 D38 Hampsthwaite HG3
38 A30 Hampton Heath SY14
22 E47 Hampton *G.L.* TW12
30 D36 Hampton *H.&W.* WR11
39 G33 Hampton *Shr.* WV16
28 E31 Hampton Bishop HR1
40 G38 Hampton in Arden B92
29 B34 Hampton Lovett WR9
30 C38 Hampton Lucy CV35
30 B38 Hampton on the Hill CV35
31 G40 Hampton Poyle OX5
10 B38 Hamptworth SP5
13 E50 Hamsey BN8
40 D36 Hamstall Ridware WS15
10 E39 Hamstead *I.o.W.* PO41
40 F36 Hamstead *W.M.* B43
21 E39 Hamstead Marshall RG20
62 C37 Hamsterley *Drm* DL13
62 A36 Hamsterley *Drm* NE17
8 A31 Ham Street BA6
14 D55 Hamstreet TN26
9 E35 Hamworthy BH15
29 B35 Hanbury *H.&.W.* B60
40 C37 Hanbury *Stf.* DE13
40 C37 Hanbury Woodend DE13
40 A34 Hanchurch ST4
48 F30 Handbridge CH4
13 D48 Handcross RH17
49 D34 Handforth SK9
48 G30 Handley CH3
40 D36 Handsacre WS15
51 D39 Handsworth *S.Y.* S13
40 F36 Handsworth *W.M.* B21
22 B44 Handy Cross SL7
40 A34 Hanford ST4
40 A37 Hanging Bridge DE6
9 A35 Hanging Langford SP3
69 E26 Hangingshaw DG11
13 F48 Hangleton BN3
19 D32 Hanham BS15
39 A32 Hankelow CW3
20 B35 Hankerton SN16
13 F52 Hankham BN24
40 A34 Hanley ST1
29 D34 Hanley Castle WR8
29 B32 Hanley Child WR15
29 D34 Hanley Swan WR8
29 B32 Hanley William WR15
56 C35 Hanlith BD23
38 B30 Hanmer SY13
53 E51 Hannah LN13
21 F41 Hannington *Ham.* RG26
31 A43 Hannington *Nmp.* NN6
20 B37 Hannington *Wts.* SN6
20 B37 Hannington Wick SN6
31 D43 Hanslope MK19
42 C46 Hanthorpe PE10
22 D47 Hanwell *G.L.* W7
31 D40 Hanwell *Oxf.* OX17
22 D47 Hanworth *G.L.* TW13
45 B57 Hanworth *Nfk.* NR11
45 B59 Happisburgh NR12
45 C59 Happisburgh Common NR12
48 E30 Hapsford WA6
56 F34 Hapton *Lan.* BB11
45 F57 Hapton *Nfk.* NR15
5 E23 Harberton TQ9
5 E23 Harbertonford TQ9
15 B56 Harbledown CT2
40 G36 Harborne B17
31 A40 Harborough Magna CV23
70 C35 Harbottle NE65
5 D22 Harbourneford TQ10
10 C37 Harbridge BH24
30 C39 Harbury CV33
42 B43 Harby *Lei.* LE14
52 E44 Harby *Not.* NG23
7 F27 Harcombe EX10
57 F36 Harden BD16
20 D34 Hardenhuish SN14
91 C33 Hardgate AB31
12 E46 Hardham RH20
44 E56 Hardingham NR9
31 C43 Hardingstone NN4
49 G33 Hardings Wood ST7
20 F33 Hardington BA11
8 C31 Hardington Mandeville BA22
8 D31 Hardington Marsh BA22
11 D40 Hardley SO45
45 E59 Hardley Street NR14
32 D45 Hardmead MK16
61 G34 Hardraw DL8
51 F40 Hardstoft S45
11 D41 Hardway *Ham.* PO12
9 A33 Hardway *Som.* BA10
31 G44 Hardwick *Bkh.* HP22
33 C49 Hardwick *Cbs.* CB3
45 F58 Hardwick *Nfk.* NR15
32 B44 Hardwick *Nmp.* NN9
31 F41 Hardwick *Oxf.* OX6
21 A39 Hardwick *Oxf.* OX8
29 G33 Hardwicke *Glo.* GL2
29 F34 Hardwicke *Glo.* GL51
28 D28 Hardwicke *H.&W.* HR3
34 G55 Hardy's Green CO2
53 F49 Hareby PE23
56 D32 Hareden BB7
22 B46 Harefield UB9
34 F56 Hare Green CO7
22 D44 Hare Hatch RG10
57 F39 Harehills LS9
75 F25 Harelaw ML11
61 B31 Haresceugh CA10
29 G34 Harescombe GL4
29 G33 Haresfield GL10
74 F22 Hareshaw ML10
33 F49 Hare Street *Hfs.* SG2
33 F49 Hare Street *Hfs.* SG9
57 E39 Harewood LS17
28 F31 Harewood End HR2
5 E22 Harford PL21
45 F57 Hargate NR16
48 F30 Hargrave *Che.* CH3
32 A46 Hargrave *Nmp.* NN9
34 C53 Hargrave *Sfk* IP29
23 C49 Haringey N
69 G29 Harker CA6
35 E57 Harkstead IP9
40 D37 Harlaston B79
42 B44 Harlaxton NG32
36 B21 Harlech LL46
23 C48 Harlesden NW10
45 G58 Harleston *Nfk* IP20
34 C56 Harleston *Sfk* IP14
31 B42 Harlestone NN7
56 F34 Harle Syke BB10
38 E31 Harley SY5
75 G25 Harleyholm ML12
32 E46 Harlington LU5
93 G8 Harlosh IV55
33 G50 Harlow CM17
71 G36 Harlow Hill NE15
58 F43 Harlthorpe YO8
33 C49 Harlton CB3
9 F35 Harman's Cross BH19
62 G37 Harmby DL8
33 G48 Harmer Green AL6
38 C30 Harmer Hill SY4
22 D46 Harmondsworth UB7
52 F45 Harmston LN5
10 B37 Harnham SP2
20 A36 Harnhill GL7
23 B51 Harold Hill RM3
16 C14 Haroldston West SA62
106 A42 Haroldswick ZE2
23 C51 Harold Wood RM3
58 A42 Harome YO6
32 G47 Harpenden AL5
7 F26 Harpford EX10
59 C47 Harpham YO25
29 B32 Harpley *H.&W.* WR6
44 C53 Harpley *Nfk* PE31
31 B42 Harpole NN7
55 A31 Harprigg LA6
103 C27 Harpsdale KW12
22 C43 Harpsden RG9
52 D45 Harpswell DN21
49 B34 Harpurhey M9
50 E36 Harpur Hill SK17
86 B12 Harrapool IV49
82 D25 Harrietfield PH1
14 B54 Harrietsham ME17
53 E49 Harrington *Lcn.* PE23
31 A43 Harrington *Nmp.* NN6
42 F44 Harringworth NN17
85 E9 Harris PH43
49 G34 Harriseahead ST7
57 D38 Harrogate HG
32 C45 Harrold MK43
22 C47 Harrow *G.L.* HA
103 A28 Harrow *Hgh.* KW14
4 C19 Harrowbarrow PL17
32 D46 Harrowden MK42
22 C47 Harrow on the Hill HA1
22 B47 Harrow Weald HA3
33 C50 Harston *Cbs.* CB2
42 B44 Harston *Lei.* NG32
62 C40 Hart TS27
71 E36 Hartburn *Cle.* NE61
62 E40 Hartburn *Nor.* TS18
34 C54 Hartest IP29
13 C50 Hartfield *E.S.* TN7
94 G13 Hartfield *Hgh.* IV54
33 A48 Hartford *Cbs* PE18
49 E32 Hartford *Che.* CW8
22 F43 Hartfordbridge RG27
33 G52 Hartford End CM6
48 G30 Harthill *Che.* CH3
75 D25 Harthill *Ltn* ML7
51 D40 Harthill *S.Y.* S31
50 F37 Hartington SK17
6 C18 Hartland EX39
29 A34 Hartlebury DY11
62 C40 Hartlepool TS24
61 F33 Hartley *Cum.* CA17
23 E51 Hartley *Kent* DA3
14 D53 Hartley *Kent* TN17
71 F39 Hartley *T.&W.* NE26
21 F42 Hartley Wespall RG27
22 F43 Hartley Wintney RG27
24 E54 Hartlip ME9
58 C43 Harton *N.Y.* YO6
38 G30 Harton *Shr.* SY6
71 G39 Harton *T.&W.* NE34
29 F33 Hartpury GL19
70 A32 Hartrigge TD8
41 F39 Hartshill CV10
40 C38 Hartshorne DE11
60 E29 Hartsop CA10
31 G43 Hartwell *Bkh.* HP17
13 C50 Hartwell *E.S.* TN7
31 D43 Hartwell *Nmp.* NN7
75 E24 Hartwood ML7
24 E52 Harvel DA13
29 A34 Harvington *H.&W.* DY10
30 D36 Harvington *H.&W.* WR11
21 C40 Harwell OX11
35 E58 Harwich CO12
61 C34 Harwood *Drm* DL12
49 A33 Harwood *G.M.* BL2
63 G45 Harwood Dale YO13
69 C30 Harwood on Teviot TD9
51 C41 Harworth DN11
40 G35 Hasbury B63
12 C46 Hascombe GU8
31 A42 Haselbech NN6
8 C30 Haselbury Plucknett TA18
30 B38 Haseley CV35
30 C37 Haselor B49
29 F34 Hasfield GL19
16 D14 Hasguard SA62
48 B29 Haskayne L39
35 C58 Hasketon IP13
51 F39 Hasland S41
12 C44 Haslemere GU27
56 G33 Haslingden BB4
56 G33 Haslingden Grane BB4
33 C49 Haslingfield CB3
49 G33 Haslington CW1
49 G33 Hassall CW11
49 G33 Hassall Green CW11
15 C56 Hassell Street TN25
70 A31 Hassendean TD9
45 E59 Hassingham NR13
13 E48 Hassocks BN6
50 E38 Hassop DE45
103 C29 Haster KW1
103 B28 Hastigrow KW1
15 C56 Hastingleigh TN25
14 G54 Hastings TN34
23 A50 Hastingwood CM17
22 A45 Hastoe HP23
62 B39 Haswell DH6
32 D47 Hatch *Bfd.* SG19
21 F42 Hatch *Ham.* RG24
8 B28 Hatch Beauchamp TA3
22 B47 Hatch End HA5
8 C28 Hatch Green TA3
32 G47 Hatching Green AL5
48 E31 Hatchmere WA6
53 B48 Hatcliffe DN37
28 C31 Hatfield *H.&W.* HR6
23 A48 Hatfield *Hfs.* AL10
51 B42 Hatfield *S.Y.* DN7
33 G51 Hatfield Broad Oak CM22
33 G50 Hatfield Heath CM22
33 G48 Hatfield Hyde AL7
34 G53 Hatfield Peverel CM3
51 B42 Hatfield Woodhouse DN7
21 B39 Hatford SN7
21 F39 Hatherden SP11
6 E21 Hatherleigh EX20
41 C40 Hathern LE12
20 A37 Hatherop GL7
50 D38 Hathersage S30
39 A32 Hatherton *Che.* CW5
40 D35 Hatherton *Stf.* WS11

149

High Kilburn

57 **A40** High Kilburn YO6
49 **F34** Highlane *Che.* SK11
41 **A40** High Lane *Dby* DE7
51 **D39** Highlane *Dby* S12
29 **B32** High Lane *H.&W.* WR6
23 **A51** High Laver CM5
60 **B27** Highlaws CA5
29 **F33** Highleadon GL18
49 **D33** High Legh WA16
12 **G44** Highleigh PO20
62 **E40** High Leven TS17
39 **G33** Highley WV16
19 **F32** High Littleton BS18
60 **D27** High Lorton CA13
26 **D20** Highmead SA40
51 **B41** High Melton DN5
21 **C42** Highmoor Cross RG9
19 **C30** Highmoor Hill NP6
29 **G33** Highnam GL2
55 **A30** High Newton LA11
71 **A38** High Newton by-the-Sea NE66
60 **G28** High Nibthwaite LA12
39 **C33** High Offley ST20
23 **A51** High Ongar CM5
40 **D34** High Onn ST20
52 **A45** High Risby DN15
33 **G51** High Roding CM6
12 **F47** High Salvington BN14
61 **G34** High Shaw DL8
71 **G37** High Spen NE39
25 **E57** Highstead CT3
24 **E54** Highsted ME9
3 **C15** High Street *Cnw.* PL26
14 **D53** High Street *Kent* TN18
35 **C60** High Street *Sfk* IP12
34 **E53** Highstreet Green CO9
34 **C56** High Street Green IP14
69 **F26** Hightae DG11
62 **C40** High Throston TS26
49 **F34** Hightown *Che.* CW12
48 **B28** Hightown *Mer.* L38
53 **F48** High Toynton LN9
71 **C36** High Trewhitt NE65
20 **D36** Highway SN11
5 **C24** Highweek TQ12
19 **B31** High Wollaston GL15
20 **B37** Highworth SN6
60 **G29** High Wray LA22
33 **G50** High Wych CM21
22 **B43** High Wycombe HP11
44 **E53** Hilborough IP26
20 **F37** Hilcott SN9
23 **G51** Hildenborough TN11
23 **G51** Hilden Park TN11
33 **D51** Hildersham CB1
40 **B35** Hilderstone ST15
59 **C47** Hilderthorpe YO15
9 **D32** Hilfield DT2
44 **F52** Hilgay PE38
19 **B32** Hill GL13
58 **G41** Hillam LS25
61 **E33** Hillbeck CA17
54 **E25** Hillberry IM4
25 **E57** Hillborough CT6
91 **A33** Hillbrae *Grm.* AB51
99 **F34** Hillbrae *Grm.* AB51
98 **E31** Hillbrae *Grm.* AB54
11 **B43** Hill Brow GU33
39 **B33** Hill Chorlton ST5
43 **A49** Hill Dyke PE22
62 **C36** Hill End *Drm* DL13
75 **B27** Hillend *Fife* KY11
75 **A26** Hill End *Fife* KY12
98 **E30** Hillend *Grm.* AB55
76 **D28** Hillend *Ltn.* EH10
57 **D36** Hill End *N.Y.* BD23
31 **F42** Hillesden MK18
20 **C33** Hillesley GL12
7 **C27** Hillfarrance TA4
11 **D41** Hill Head PO14
5 **E25** Hillhead TQ5
99 **D35** Hillhead of Auchentumb AB43
99 **E36** Hillhead of Cocklaw AB42
40 **D37** Hilliard's Cross WS13
103 **B27** Hilliclay KW14
22 **C46** Hillingdon UB
44 **C53** Hillington PE31
31 **A41** Hillmorton CV22
90 **B30** Hillockhead *Grm.* AB33
90 **C29** Hillockhead *Grm.* AB36
75 **A27** Hill of Beath KY4
97 **D24** Hill of Fearn IV20
65 **D23** Hillowton DG7
11 **C41** Hillpound SO32
40 **D36** Hill Ridware WS15
109 **E8** Hillsborough BT26
7 **A23** Hillsford Bridge EX35
91 **D35** Hillside *Grm.* AB1
97 **E27** Hillside *Grm.* IV30
107 **A39** Hillside *She.* ZE2
91 **G32** Hillside *Tay.* DD10
51 **F40** Hills Town S44
106 **E38** Hillswick ZE2
11 **D40** Hill Top *Ham.* SO42
51 **A39** Hill Top *W.Y.* WF2
109 **F8** Hilltown BT34
9 **E35** Hill View BH21
11 **F42** Hillway PO35
107 **D37** Hillwell ZE2
20 **D36** Hilmarton SN11
20 **F34** Hilperton BA14
11 **D42** Hilsea PO2
33 **B48** Hilton *Cbs.* PE18
62 **E40** Hilton *Cle.* TS15
61 **D33** Hilton *Cum.* CA16
40 **B38** Hilton *Dby.* DE65
9 **D33** Hilton *Dor.* DT11
62 **D37** Hilton *Drm* DL2
99 **F35** Hilton *Grm.* AB41
97 **C25** Hilton *Hgh.* IV20
39 **F33** Hilton *Shr.* WV15
97 **D24** Hilton of Cadboll IV20
97 **F24** Hilton of Delnies IV12
29 **C35** Himbleton WR9
40 **F34** Himley DY3
55 **A31** Hincaster LA7
41 **F40** Hinckley LE10
34 **A56** Hinderclay IP22
63 **E43** Hinderwell TS13
38 **B29** Hindford SY11
12 **C44** Hindhead GU26
49 **B32** Hindley WN2
49 **B32** Hindley Green WN2
29 **C34** Hindlip WR3
44 **C56** Hindolveston NR20
9 **A34** Hindon SP3
44 **B55** Hindringham NR21
44 **E56** Hingham NR9
39 **C32** Hinstock TF9
34 **D56** Hintlesham IP8
20 **D33** Hinton *Avon* SN14
28 **E29** Hinton *H.&W.* HR2
10 **E38** Hinton *Ham.* BH23
31 **C41** Hinton *Nmp.* NN11
38 **E30** Hinton *Shr.* SY5
10 **E37** Hinton Admiral BH23
11 **B42** Hinton Ampner SO24
19 **F31** Hinton Blewett BS18
20 **F33** Hinton Charterhouse BA3
31 **E41** Hinton-in-the-Hedges NN13
9 **D35** Hinton Martell BH21
29 **D35** Hinton on the Green WR11
21 **C38** Hinton Parva SN4
8 **C30** Hinton St George TA17
9 **C33** Hinton St Mary DT10
21 **B39** Hinton Waldrist SN7
29 **A32** Hints *Shr.* SY8
40 **E37** Hints *Stf.* B78
32 **B45** Hinwick NN29
15 **C56** Hinxhill TN24
33 **D50** Hinxton CB10
33 **D48** Hinxworth SG7
57 **G37** Hipperholme HX3
91 **D33** Hirn AB31
37 **C26** Hirnant SY10
71 **E38** Hirst NE63
58 **G42** Hirst Courtney YO8
47 **F27** Hirwaen LL15
18 **A25** Hirwaun CF44
6 **C21** Hiscott EX31
33 **B50** Histon CB4
22 **C45** Hitcham *Bkh.* SL6
34 **C55** Hitcham *Sfk* IP7
32 **E47** Hitchin SG5
23 **D49** Hither Green SE13
7 **F23** Hittisleigh EX6
40 **C35** Hixon ST18
15 **B58** Hoaden CT3
28 **F29** Hoaldalbert NP7
40 **C37** Hoar Cross DE13
28 **F31** Hoarwithy HR2
25 **E57** Hoath CT3
28 **A28** Hobarris SY7
105 **A29** Hobbister KW17
43 **E49** Hobbs Lots Bridge PE15
70 **B31** Hobkirk TD9
45 **E61** Hobland Hall NR31
62 **A37** Hobson NE16
41 **D42** Hoby LE14
44 **D56** Hockering NR20
51 **G42** Hockerton NG25
24 **B54** Hockley SS5
30 **A37** Hockley Heath B94
32 **F45** Hockliffe LU7
44 **G53** Hockwold cum Wilton IP26
7 **D26** Hockworthy TA21
23 **A49** Hoddesdon EN11
56 **G33** Hoddlesden BB3
16 **E16** Hodgeston SA71
39 **C32** Hodnet TF9
51 **E41** Hodthorpe S80
44 **D55** Hoe NR20
11 **C42** Hoe Gate PO7
61 **E32** Hoff CA16
43 **B48** Hoffleet Stow PE20
31 **F43** Hoggeston MK18
98 **C31** Hoggie AB56
92 **D2** Hogha Gearraidh HS6
55 **G31** Hoghton PR5
50 **G38** Hognaston DE6
53 **E51** Hogsthorpe PE24
43 **C49** Holbeach PE12
43 **C49** Holbeach Bank PE12
43 **C49** Holbeach Clough PE12
43 **D49** Holbeach Drove PE12
43 **C49** Holbeach Hurn PE12
43 **D49** Holbeach St Johns PE12
43 **B49** Holbeach St Marks PE12
43 **B50** Holbeach St Matthew PE12
51 **E41** Holbeck S80
29 **B35** Holberrow Green B96
5 **F22** Holbeton PL8
23 **C49** Holborn WC
24 **E53** Holborough ME2
41 **A39** Holbrook *Dby.* DE56
35 **E57** Holbrook *Sfk* IP9
77 **G36** Holburn TD15
11 **D40** Holbury SO45
5 **C25** Holcombe *Dev.* EX7
19 **G32** Holcombe *Som.* BA3
7 **D26** Holcombe Rogus TA21
31 **B43** Holcot NN6
56 **E33** Holden BB7
31 **B42** Holdenby NN6
10 **E37** Holdenhurst BH8
38 **G31** Holdgate TF13
42 **A46** Holdingham NG34
35 **D29** Holditch TA20
28 **F31** Hole-in-the-Wall HR9
14 **D54** Hole Park TN17
12 **E47** Hole Street BN44
7 **A27** Holford TA5
55 **B29** Holker LA11
44 **A54** Holkham NR23
6 **E19** Hollacombe EX22
104 **A30** Holland *Ork.* KW17
104 **D32** Holland *Ork.* KW17
23 **F50** Holland *Sry* RH8
35 **G58** Holland-on-Sea CO15
104 **A33** Hollandstoun KW17
69 **G28** Hollee DG11
35 **D59** Hollesley IP12
14 **B54** Hollingbourne ME17
13 **F49** Hollingbury BN1
40 **B38** Hollington *Dby.* DE6
14 **F53** Hollington *E.S.* TN37
40 **B36** Hollington *Stf.* ST10
49 **C35** Hollingworth SK14
49 **B33** Hollins BL9
50 **F36** Hollinsclough SK17
49 **C32** Hollins Green WA3
39 **E33** Hollinswood TF3
38 **B31** Hollinwood SY13
6 **D21** Hollocombe EX18
51 **G39** Holloway DE4
31 **A42** Hollowell NN6
18 **A27** Hollybush *Gwe.* NP2
29 **E33** Hollybush *H.&W.* HR8
67 **B19** Hollybush *Str.* KA6
43 **E51** Holly End PE14
29 **D34** Holly Green WR8
59 **G49** Hollym HU19
69 **D28** Holm DG13
22 **G47** Holmbury St Mary RH5
4 **E16** Holmbush *Cnw.* PL25
13 **C48** Holmbush *W.S.* RH12
42 **G47** Holme *Cbs.* PE7
55 **B31** Holme *Cum.* LA6
52 **G44** Holme *Not.* NG23
50 **B36** Holme *W.Y.* HD7
9 **F34** Holmebridge BH20
56 **G34** Holme Chapel BB10
44 **E54** Holme Hale IP25
28 **E31** Holme Lacy HR2
28 **C29** Holme Marsh HR5
44 **A52** Holme next the Sea PE36
58 **F43** Holme-on-Spalding-Moor YO4
59 **E45** Holme on the Wolds HU17
41 **B42** Holme Pierrepont NG12
28 **D30** Holmer HR1
22 **B45** Holmer Green HP15
49 **F33** Holmes Chapel CW4
50 **E38** Holmesfield S18
13 **E51** Holme's Hill BN8
48 **A29** Holmeswood L40
51 **F40** Holmewood S42
57 **G36** Holmfield HX2
50 **B37** Holmfirth HD7
68 **E23** Holmhead *D.&G.* DG7
67 **A21** Holmhead *Str.* KA18
68 **D24** Holm of Drumlanrig DG3
59 **G49** Holmpton HU19
60 **F26** Holmrook CA19
107 **C40** Holmsgarth ZE1
62 **B37** Holmside DH7
67 **A19** Holmston KA7
61 **B30** Holmwrangle CA4
5 **D23** Holne TQ13
9 **D32** Holnest DT9
6 **E19** Holsworthy EX22
6 **E19** Holsworthy Beacon EX22
48 **G29** Holt *Clw.* LL13
10 **D36** Holt *Dor.* BH21
29 **B34** Holt *H.&W.* WR6
44 **B56** Holt *Nfk* NR25
20 **E34** Holt *Wts.* BA14
58 **D42** Holtby YO1
30 **B36** Holt End *H.&W.* B98
11 **A42** Holt End *Ham.* GU34
29 **B34** Holt Fleet WR9
10 **D36** Holt Heath *Dor.* BH21
29 **B34** Holt Heath *H.&W.* WR6
52 **D47** Holton *Lcn.* LN3
21 **A41** Holton *Oxf.* OX33
35 **A59** Holton *Sfk* IP19
9 **B32** Holton *Som.* BA9
9 **E35** Holton Heath BH16
53 **B48** Holton le Clay DN36
52 **C46** Holton le Moor LN7
34 **E56** Holton St Mary CO7
22 **B45** Holtspur HP9
13 **C50** Holtye Common TN8
9 **C32** Holwell *Dor.* DT10
32 **E47** Holwell *Hfs.* SG5
42 **C43** Holwell *Lei.* LE14
21 **A38** Holwell *Oxf.* OX18
20 **G33** Holwell *Som.* BA11
61 **D34** Holwick DL12
9 **F33** Holworth DT2
22 **G43** Holybourne GU34
29 **A34** Holy Cross DY9
51 **F39** Holymoorside S42
22 **D44** Holyport SL6
70 **C35** Holystone NE65
75 **D23** Holytown ML1
33 **A49** Holywell *Cbs.* PE17
47 **E27** Holywell *Clw.* CH8
2 **C13** Holywell *Cnw.* TR8
8 **D31** Holywell *Dor.* DT2
13 **G52** Holywell *E.S.* BN20
50 **A36** Holywell Green HX4
7 **D27** Holywell Lake TA21
34 **A53** Holywell Row IP28
68 **E25** Holywood *D.&G.* DG2
109 **D8** Holywood *Down* BT18
39 **E32** Homer TF13
45 **G58** Homersfield IP20
28 **F31** Hom Green HR9
10 **B37** Homington SP5
16 **D15** Honeyborough SA73
30 **D36** Honeybourne WR11
6 **E22** Honeychurch EX20
25 **E57** Honey Hill CT2
34 **E55** Honey Tye CO6
30 **A38** Honiley CV8
45 **C59** Honing NR28
45 **D57** Honingham NR9
42 **A45** Honington *Lcn.* NG32
34 **A54** Honington *Sfk* IP31
30 **D38** Honington *War.* CV36
7 **E27** Honiton EX14
50 **A37** Honley HD7
24 **D53** Hoo *Kent* ME3
35 **C58** Hoo *Sfk* IP13
4 **E20** Hooe *Dev.* PL9
13 **F52** Hooe *E.S.* TN33
13 **E52** Hooe Common TN33
16 **C15** Hook *Dyf.* SA62
22 **E47** Hook *G.L.* KT9
22 **F43** Hook *Ham.* RG27
58 **G43** Hook *Hum.* DN14
20 **C36** Hook *Wts.* SN4
38 **E30** Hook-a-Gate SY5
8 **D31** Hooke DT8
39 **B33** Hookgate TF9
24 **E52** Hook Green *Kent* DA13
24 **D52** Hook Green *Kent* DA13
13 **C52** Hook Green *Kent* TN3
30 **E39** Hook Norton OX15
7 **F24** Hookway EX17
23 **G48** Hookwood RH6
48 **F30** Hoole CH3
23 **F48** Hooley CR5
48 **E29** Hooton L66
51 **C41** Hooton Levitt S66
51 **B40** Hooton Pagnell DN5
51 **C40** Hooton Roberts S65
31 **F40** Hopcrofts Holt OX6
48 **G29** Hope *Clw.* LL12
50 **D37** Hope *Dby.* S30
5 **G22** Hope *Dev.* TQ7
38 **E28** Hope *Pow.* SY21
38 **E29** Hope *Shr.* SY5
28 **A31** Hope Bagot SY8
38 **F30** Hope Bowdler SY6
33 **G51** Hope End Green CM22
69 **B28** Hopehouse TD7
97 **E27** Hopeman IV30
29 **G32** Hope Mansell HR9
38 **G29** Hopesay SY7
24 **C53** Hope's Green SS7
28 **C30** Hope under Dinmore HR6
18 **B26** Hopkinstown CF37
50 **G38** Hopton *Dby.* DE4
45 **E61** Hopton *Nfk* NR31
34 **A55** Hopton *Sfk* IP22
38 **C31** Hopton *Shr.* TF9
40 **C35** Hopton *Stf.* ST18
38 **G31** Hopton Cangeford SY8
28 **A29** Hopton Castle SY7
28 **A29** Hoptonheath SY7
29 **A32** Hopton Wafers DY14
40 **E37** Hopwas B78
30 **A36** Hopwood B48
13 **E51** Horam TN21
42 **B47** Horbling NG34
50 **A38** Horbury WF4
62 **B40** Horden SR8
38 **G29** Horderley SY7
10 **E38** Hordle SO41
38 **B29** Hordley SY12
17 **D21** Horeb *Dyf.* SA15
26 **D19** Horeb *Dyf.* SA44
19 **D31** Horfield BS7
35 **A58** Horham IP21
34 **F55** Horkesley Heath CO6
52 **A45** Horkstow DN18
31 **D40** Horley *Oxf.* OX15
23 **G48** Horley *W.S.* RH6
8 **A31** Hornblotton Green BA4
55 **C31** Hornby *Lan.* LA2
62 **F39** Hornby *N.Y.* DL6
62 **G38** Hornby *N.Y.* DL8
53 **F48** Horncastle LN9
23 **C51** Hornchurch RM12
77 **E35** Horncliffe TD15
77 **F34** Horndean *Bor.* TD15
11 **C42** Horndean *Ham.* PO8
6 **G21** Horndon PL19
24 **C52** Horndon on the Hill SS17
23 **G49** Horne RH6
22 **B46** Horn Hill SL9
82 **A29** Horniehaugh DD8
45 **D59** Horning NR12
42 **F43** Horninghold LE16
40 **C38** Horninglow DE13
33 **B50** Horningsea CB5
20 **G33** Horningsham BA12
44 **C55** Horningtoft NR20
4 **D18** Horningtops PL14
61 **B30** Hornsby CA4
61 **A31** Hornsby Gate CA4
6 **C19** Horns Cross *Dev.* EX39
14 **E54** Horns Cross *E.S.* TN31
59 **E48** Hornsea HU18
23 **C48** Hornsey N8
30 **D39** Hornton OX15
4 **D20** Horrabridge PL20
5 **C23** Horridge TQ13
34 **B54** Horringer IP29
4 **C20** Horsebridge *Dev.* PL19
10 **A39** Horsebridge *Ham.* SO20
49 **G35** Horse Bridge ST9
40 **D34** Horsebrook ST19
39 **E32** Horsehay TF4
33 **D51** Horseheath CB1
57 **A36** Horsehouse DL8
22 **F45** Horsell GU21
38 **A30** Horseman's Green SY13
43 **G50** Horseway PE16
45 **C60** Horsey NR29
45 **D57** Horsford NR10
57 **F38** Horsforth LS18
29 **C33** Horsham *H.&W.* WR6
12 **C47** Horsham *W.S.* RH12
45 **D58** Horsham St Faith NR10
52 **F47** Horsington *Lcn.* LN3
9 **B32** Horsington *Som.* BA8
41 **A39** Horsley *Dby.* DE21
20 **B34** Horsley *Glo.* GL6
71 **G36** Horsley *Nor.* NE15
70 **D34** Horsley *Nor.* NE19
35 **F57** Horsley Cross CO11
35 **F57** Horsleycross Street CO11
70 **B31** Horsleyhill TD9
41 **A39** Horsley Woodhouse DE7
23 **G52** Horsmonden TN12
21 **A41** Horspath OX33
45 **D58** Horstead NR12
13 **D49** Horsted Keynes RH17
20 **C33** Horton *Avon* BS17
32 **G45** Horton *Bkh.* LU7
22 **D46** Horton *Bkh.* SL3
10 **D36** Horton *Dor.* BH21
56 **D34** Horton *Lan.* BD23
32 **C44** Horton *Nmp.* NN7
8 **C29** Horton *Som.* TA19
49 **G35** Horton *Stf.* ST13
17 **F20** Horton *W.G.* SA3
20 **E36** Horton *Wts.* SN10
8 **C29** Horton Cross TA19
31 **G41** Horton-cum-Studley OX33
38 **A30** Horton Green SY14
11 **C40** Horton Heath SO50
10 **D36** Horton Inn BH21
56 **B34** Horton in Ribblesdale BD24
23 **E51** Horton Kirby DA4
49 **A32** Horwich BL6
6 **C21** Horwood EX39
42 **C43** Hose LE14
60 **G28** Hoses LA20
81 **E24** Hosh PH7
92 **D3** Hosta HS6
107 **E40** Hoswick ZE2
58 **F44** Hotham YO4
14 **C55** Hothfield TN26
41 **C41** Hoton LE12
106 **C42** Houbie ZE2
49 **G33** Hough CW2
42 **A44** Hougham NG32
48 **D30** Hough Green WA8
42 **A44** Hough-on-the-Hill NG32
33 **A48** Houghton *Cbs.* PE17
60 **A29** Houghton *Cum.* CA3
5 **F22** Houghton *Dev.* TQ7
16 **D15** Houghton *Dyf.* SA73
10 **A39** Houghton *Ham.* SO20
12 **E45** Houghton *W.S.* BN18
62 **D38** Houghton Bank DL2

Johnstone

32 D46 Houghton Conquest MK45
62 D38 Houghton-le-Side DL2
62 A39 Houghton le Spring DH4
41 E42 Houghton on the Hill LE7
32 F46 Houghton Regis LU5
44 B55 Houghton St Giles NR22
63 F43 Houlsyke YO21
11 D40 Hound SO31
22 F43 Hound Green RG27
76 F32 Houndslow TD3
77 D34 Houndwood TD14
10 C39 Hounsdown SO40
22 D47 Hounslow TW
33 G52 Hounslow Green CM6
97 F24 Househill IV12
106 D39 Housetter ZE2
74 D19 Houston PA6
103 E27 Houstry KW6
103 C27 Houstry of Dunn KW1
105 A29 Houton KW17
13 F48 Hove BN3
41 A42 Hoveringham NG14
45 D59 Hoveton NR12
58 B42 Hovingham YO6
61 A31 How CA4
28 E31 How Caple HR1
58 G43 Howden DN14
62 C37 Howden-le-Wear DL15
55 A30 Howe *Cum.* LA8
103 B29 Howe *Hgh.* KW1
57 A39 Howe *N.Y.* YO7
45 E58 Howe *Nfk* NR15
24 A53 Howe Green CM2
42 A47 Howell NG34
32 D46 How End MK45
99 E33 Howe of Teuchar AB53
33 G52 Howe Street *Esx* CM3
33 E52 Howe Street *Esx* CM7
27 C26 Howey LD1
76 E28 Howgate EH26
57 D36 Howgill BD23
71 B38 Howick NE66
39 C32 Howle TF10
33 E51 Howlett End CB10
8 D28 Howley TA20
60 F25 How Man CA22
70 B33 Hownam TD5
70 A33 Hownam Mains TD5
69 C29 Howpasley TD9
52 B46 Howsham *Hum.* LN7
58 C43 Howsham *N.Y.* YO6
77 G34 Howtel TD12
28 F29 Howton HR2
74 D20 Howwood PA9
105 B30 Hoxa KW17
35 A57 Hoxne IP21
103 B28 Hoy KW14
47 D27 Hoylake L47
51 B39 Hoyland S74
50 B38 Hoyland Swaine S30
56 B34 Hubberholme BD23
43 A48 Hubbert's Bridge PE20
57 E38 Huby *N.Y.* LS17
58 C41 Huby *N.Y.* YO6
29 G34 Hucclecote GL3
14 B54 Hucking ME17
41 A41 Hucknall NG15
50 A37 Huddersfield HD
29 C35 Huddington WR9
6 C22 Hudscott EX37
62 F37 Hudswell DL11
58 D44 Huggate YO4
41 D40 Hugglescote LE67
22 B44 Hughenden Valley HP15
38 F31 Hughley SY5
2 A10 Hugh Town TR21
48 G29 Hugmore LL13
6 D21 Huish *Dev.* EX20
20 E37 Huish *Wts.* SN8
7 C26 Huish Champflower TA4
8 B29 Huish Episcopi TA10
100 F6 Huisinis HS3
32 G44 Hulcott HP22
40 A38 Hulland DE6
20 C34 Hullavington SN14
24 B54 Hullbridge SS5
50 G37 Hulme End SK17
49 F34 Hulme Walfield CW12
45 G60 Hulver Street NR34
28 C31 Humber Court HR6
52 B46 Humberside Airport DN39
53 B49 Humberston DN36
41 E42 Humberstone LE5
76 D30 Humbie EH36
59 F48 Humbleton *Hum.* HU11
70 A35 Humbleton *Nor.* NE71
42 B46 Humby NG33
76 F32 Hume TD5
76 F32 Humehall TD5
70 F34 Humshaugh NE46
103 A29 Huna KW1
56 F33 Huncoat BB5
41 F41 Huncote LE9
70 B32 Hundalee TD8
62 D35 Hunderthwaite DL12
53 F49 Hundleby PE23
16 D15 Hundleton SA71
34 D53 Hundon CO10
11 C41 Hundred Acres PO17
55 G30 Hundred End PR4
28 C27 Hundred House LD1
41 E42 Hungarton LE7
21 E39 Hungerford *Bkh.* RG17
10 C37 Hungerford *Ham.* SP6
21 D39 Hungerford Newtown RG17
93 D9 Hunglader IV51
30 B39 Hunningham CV33
11 F40 Hunny Hill PO30
33 G49 Hunsdon SG12
57 D40 Hunsingore LS22
61 C31 Hunsonby CA10
103 A27 Hunspow KW14
44 A52 Hunstanton PE36
61 B35 Hunstanworth DH8
34 B55 Hunston *Sfk* IP31
12 F44 Hunston *W.S.* PO20
19 E32 Hunstrete BS18
30 B36 Hunt End B97
21 C42 Huntercombe End RG9
25 E57 Hunters Forstal CT6
73 C17 Hunter's Quay PA23
73 E17 Hunterston KA23
70 C32 Huntford TD8
63 G44 Hunt House YO22
33 A48 Huntingdon PE18
35 A59 Huntingfield IP19
9 B33 Huntingford SP8
28 C28 Huntington *H.&W.* HR5
58 D42 Huntington *N.Y.* YO3
40 D35 Huntington *Stf.* WS12
82 E26 Huntingtower PH1
29 G33 Huntley GL19
98 E31 Huntly AB54
76 F31 Huntlywood TD4
11 A40 Hunton *Ham.* SO21
14 C53 Hunton *Kent* ME15
62 G37 Hunton *N.Y.* DL8
22 A46 Huntonbridge WD4
48 D30 Hunt's Cross L25
7 C25 Huntsham EX16
6 C21 Huntshaw Cross EX31
19 G28 Huntspill TA9
8 A28 Huntworth TA7
62 C37 Hunwick DL15
44 B56 Hunworth NR24
49 E35 Hurdsfield SK10
22 C44 Hurley *Brk.* SL6
40 F38 Hurley *War.* CV9
22 C44 Hurley Bottom SL6
74 G20 Hurlford KA1
105 C28 Hurliness KW16
10 E37 Hurn BH23
11 B40 Hursley SO21
22 D43 Hurst *Brk.* RG10
49 B35 Hurst *G.M.* OL6
62 F36 Hurst *N.Y.* DL11
21 G40 Hurstbourne Priors RG28
21 F39 Hurstbourne Tarrant SP11
14 E53 Hurst Green *E.S.* TN19
56 F32 Hurst Green *Lan.* BB7
13 E48 Hurstpierpoint BN6
28 D28 Hurstway Common HR3
56 F34 Hurstwood BB10
22 G45 Hurtmore GU7
62 E38 Hurworth-on-Tees DL2
61 D35 Hury DL12
93 F7 Husabost IV55
41 G42 Husbands Bosworth LE17
32 E45 Husborne Crawley MK43
58 B41 Husthwaite YO6
51 G40 Huthwaite NG17
53 E51 Huttoft LN13
19 F29 Hutton *Avon* BS24
77 E34 Hutton *Bor.* TD15
60 D30 Hutton *Cum.* CA11
24 B52 Hutton *Esx* CM13
55 G30 Hutton *Lan.* PR4
62 F39 Hutton Bonville DL7
59 A45 Hutton Buscel YO13
57 B39 Hutton Conyers HG4
59 D46 Hutton Cranswick YO25
60 C30 Hutton End CA11
62 C40 Hutton Henry TS27
63 G42 Hutton-le-Hole YO6
62 E37 Hutton Magna DL11
60 C29 Hutton Roof *Cum.* CA11
55 B31 Hutton Roof *Cum.* LA6
62 F40 Hutton Rudby TS15
57 B40 Hutton Sessay YO7
58 D41 Hutton Wandesley YO5
48 F31 Huxley CH3
107 B39 Huxter *She.* ZE2
107 A41 Huxter *She.* ZE2
48 C30 Huyton L36
54 A26 Hycemoor LA19
49 C35 Hyde *G.M.* SK14
20 A34 Hyde *Glo.* GL6
22 B45 Hyde Heath HP6
40 D34 Hyde Lea ST18
22 G45 Hydestile GU8
75 F25 Hyndford Bridge ML11
70 C31 Hyndlee TD9
78 D5 Hynish PA77
38 F28 Hyssington SY15
11 D40 Hythe *Ham.* SO45
15 D57 Hythe *Kent* CT21
22 D46 Hythe End TW19
99 D36 Hythie AB42
54 A26 Hyton LA19

I

98 C30 Ianstown AB56
9 D33 Ibberton DT11
50 G38 Ible DE4
10 D37 Ibsley BH24
41 D39 Ibstock LE67
22 B43 Ibstone HP14
21 F39 Ibthorpe SP11
21 F41 Ibworth RG26
19 E29 Icelton BS22
44 F53 Ickburgh IP26
22 C46 Ickenham UB10
21 A42 Ickford HP18
15 B57 Ickham CT3
32 E47 Ickleford SG5
14 F54 Icklesham TN36
33 D50 Ickleton CB10
34 A53 Icklingham IP28
32 D47 Ickwell Green SG18
30 F37 Icomb GL54
30 F38 Idbury OX7
6 E21 Iddesleigh EX19
7 F24 Ide EX2
5 C24 Ideford TQ13
23 F50 Ide Hill TN14
14 E55 Iden TN31
14 D53 Iden Green *Kent* TN17
14 D54 Iden Green *Kent* TN17
30 D38 Idlicote CV36
10 A38 Idmiston SP4
40 A38 Idridgehay DE56
93 E9 Idrigil IV51
21 C38 Idstone SN6
83 C31 Idvies DD8
21 A41 Iffley OX4
13 C48 Ifield RH11
13 C48 Ifieldwood RH11
12 C46 Ifold RH14
13 F50 Iford BN7
38 B29 Ifton Heath SY11
38 C31 Ightfield SY13
23 F51 Ightham TN15
35 C60 Iken IP12
50 G37 Ilam DE6
8 B31 Ilchester BA22
70 A35 Ilderton NE66
23 C50 Ilford IG
6 A20 Ilfracombe EX34
41 A40 Ilkeston DE7
45 G59 Ilketshall St Andrew NR34
45 G59 Ilketshall St Lawrence NR34
45 G59 Ilketshall St Margaret NR35
57 E36 Ilkley LS29
40 G35 Illey B62
44 G55 Illington IP24
57 G36 Illingworth HX2
2 D12 Illogan TR16
42 F43 Illston on the Hill LE7
22 A43 Ilmer HP27
30 D37 Ilmington CV36
8 C29 Ilminster TA19
5 C23 Ilsington TQ13
17 E21 Ilston SA2
57 B37 Ilton *N.Y.* HG4
8 C29 Ilton *Som.* TA19
73 F14 Imachar KA27
81 F21 Immeroin FK19
52 A47 Immingham DN40
53 A48 Immingham Dock DN40
33 B50 Impington CB4
48 E30 Ince CH2
48 B29 Ince Blundell L38
48 B31 Ince-in-Makerfield WN3
91 F32 Inch DD9
83 A31 Inchbare DD9
98 D28 Inchberry IV32
83 B32 Inchbraoch DD10
90 F29 Inchgrundle DD9
96 D22 Inchindown IV18
74 D20 Inchinnan PA4
102 D21 Inchkinloch IV27
87 D17 Inchlaggan PH35
96 D21 Inchlumpie IV17
91 D32 Inchmarlo AB31
90 E28 Inchnabobart AB35
88 C19 Inchnacardoch Hotel PH32
101 F18 Inchnadamph IV27
83 C32 Inchock DD11
90 C27 Inchrory AB37
82 E28 Inchture PH14
87 A18 Inchvuilt IV4
82 E27 Inchyra PH2
3 C15 Indian Queens TR9
72 F9 Inerval PA42
24 A52 Ingatestone CM4
50 B38 Ingbirchworth S30
57 C38 Ingerthorpe HG3
40 C33 Ingestre ST18
52 D45 Ingham *Lcn.* LN1
45 C59 Ingham *Nfk* NR12
34 A54 Ingham *Sfk* IP31
41 C39 Ingleby DE73
62 F40 Ingleby Arncliffe DL6
62 E40 Ingleby Barwick TS17
62 F40 Ingleby Cross DL6
63 F41 Ingleby Greenhow TS9
19 E32 Inglesbatch BA2
20 B37 Inglesham SN6
62 D37 Ingleton *Drm.* DL2
56 B32 Ingleton *N.Y.* LA6
55 E31 Inglewhite PR3
61 G32 Ingmire Hall LA10
71 F36 Ingoe NE20
53 F51 Ingoldmells PE25
42 B45 Ingoldsby NG33
30 C38 Ingon CV37
70 B35 Ingram NE66
24 B52 Ingrave CM13
57 F36 Ingrow BD21
60 G30 Ings LA8
19 C31 Ingst BS12
45 B57 Ingworth NR11
80 E16 Inistrynich PA33
54 E25 Injebreck IM4
29 C35 Inkberrow WR7
99 F35 Inkhorn AB41
21 E39 Inkpen RG17
103 A28 Inkstack KW14
73 D17 Innellan PA23
83 G31 Innergellie KY10
76 G29 Innerleithen EH44
82 G29 Innerleven KY8
64 D16 Innermessan DG9
76 C32 Innerwick *Ltn.* EH42
81 C21 Innerwick *Tay.* PH15
79 C12 Inninbeg PA34
29 F34 Innsworth GL2
91 A32 Insch AB52
89 D24 Insh PH21
101 A19 Inshore IV27
55 F30 Inskip PR4
6 B20 Instow EX39
51 D39 Intake S12
45 E57 Intwood NR4
90 D28 Inver *Grm.* AB35
97 C24 Inver *Hgh.* IV20
103 F27 Inver *Hgh.* KW6
80 C15 Inver *Str.* PA38
82 C26 Inver *Tay.* PH8
86 F13 Inverailort PH38
94 F14 Inveralligan IV22
99 C36 Inverallochy AB43
96 B21 Inveran IV27
80 G16 Inveraray PA32
81 G23 Inverardoch Mains FK15
80 E19 Inverardran FK20
86 A11 Inverarish IV40
83 C30 Inverarity DD8
80 F18 Inverarnan G83
94 C13 Inverasdale IV22
94 F13 Inverbain IV54
74 A19 Inverbeg G83
91 F34 Inverbervie DD10
95 C17 Inverbroom IV23
88 B23 Inverbrough IV13
96 A20 Invercassley IV27
73 C16 Inverchaolain PA23
80 C17 Invercharnan PA39
80 F17 Inverchorachan PA26
95 F18 Inverchoran IV6
80 C15 Invercreran PA38
89 C24 Inverdruie PH22
99 F35 Inverebrie AB41
88 A23 Invereen IV13
97 E26 Inverernie IV36
76 C29 Inveresk EH21
89 E35 Inverey AB35
88 B20 Inverfarigaig IV1
87 D18 Invergarry PH35
90 D28 Invergelder AB35
81 E23 Invergeldie PH6
87 F18 Invergloy PH34
96 E22 Invergordon IV18
82 D29 Invergowrie DD2
86 D13 Inverguseran PH41
81 B22 Inverhadden PH16
98 F29 Inverharroch AB54
80 E19 Inverherive FK20
102 B20 Inverhope IV27
86 D13 Inverie PH41
80 F15 Inverinan PA35
86 B15 Inverinate IV40
83 C32 Inverkeilor DD11
75 B26 Inverkeithing KY11
98 E32 Inverkeithny AB54
74 C18 Inverkip PA16
101 F16 Inverkirkaig IV27
95 C17 Inverlael IV23
74 B18 Inverlauren G84
79 G14 Inverliever PA31
80 D16 Inverliver PA35
81 F20 Inverlochlarig FK19
80 E17 Inverlochy PA33
72 B12 Inverlussa PA60
87 F17 Inver Mallie PH34
82 F26 Invermay PH2
88 C19 Invermoriston IV3
102 B22 Invernaver KW14
73 B14 Inverneil PA30
96 G22 Inverness IV
96 F22 Inverness (Dalcross) Airport IV1
99 E37 Invernettie AB42
73 A17 Invernoaden PA27
80 C18 Inveroran Hotel PA36
82 B29 Inverquharity DD8
99 E36 Inverquhomery AB42
87 F18 Inverroy PH31
80 B15 Inversanda PH33
86 C15 Invershiel IV40
80 G19 Inversnaid Hotel FK8
81 G21 Invertrossachs FK17
99 E36 Inverugie AB42
80 G18 Inveruglas G83
88 D23 Inveruglass PH21
91 A33 Inverurie AB51
81 C22 Invervar PH15
73 C16 Invervegain PA23
91 D32 Invery Ho. AB31
99 E33 Inveryhan AB53
6 F21 Inwardleigh EX20
34 G54 Inworth CO5
92 G3 Iochda HS8
12 D44 Iping GU29
5 D24 Ipplepen TQ12
21 C42 Ipsden OX10
50 G36 Ipstones ST10
35 D57 Ipswich IP
48 D28 Irby L61
53 F50 Irby in the Marsh PE24
52 B47 Irby upon Humber DN37
32 B45 Irchester NN29
60 C28 Ireby *Cum.* CA5
56 B32 Ireby *Lan.* LA6
105 A29 Ireland *Ork.* KW16
107 E39 Ireland *She.* ZE2
55 B28 Ireleth LA16
61 C34 Ireshopeburn DL13
49 C33 Irlam M44
42 C46 Irnham NG33
19 C32 Iron Acton BS17
39 E32 Ironbridge TF8
30 C36 Iron Cross WR11
99 D34 Ironside AB53
51 G40 Ironville DE55
45 C59 Irstead NR12
69 G30 Irthington CA6
32 B45 Irthlingborough NN9
59 A46 Irton YO12
74 G18 Irvine KA12
108 E4 Irvinestown BT94
103 B25 Isauld KW14
104 D28 Isbister *Ork.* KW17
104 E29 Isbister *Ork.* KW17
106 C39 Isbister *She.* ZE2
107 A41 Isbister *She.* ZE2
13 E50 Isfield TN22
32 A44 Isham NN14
79 D12 Ishriff PA65
72 D9 Islay Ho. PA44
8 B29 Isle Abbotts TA3
8 B29 Isle Brewers TA3
33 A52 Isleham CB7
23 D49 Isle of Dogs E
64 G20 Isle of Whithorn DG8
86 C12 Isleornsay (Eilean Iarmain) IV43
107 A39 Islesburgh ZE2
22 D47 Isleworth TW7
41 C40 Isley Walton DE74
100 E6 Islibhig HS2
23 C48 Islington N
32 A45 Islip *Nmp.* NN14
31 G41 Islip *Oxf.* OX5
38 D31 Isombridge TF6
24 E52 Istead Rise DA13
11 C40 Itchen SO19
11 A41 Itchen Abbas SO21
11 A41 Itchen Stoke SO24
12 D47 Itchingfield RH13
19 C32 Itchington BS12
45 B57 Itteringham NR11
6 F22 Itton EX20
19 B30 Itton Common NP6
60 B29 Ivegill CA4
61 G35 Ivelet DL11
22 C46 Iver SL0
22 C45 Iver Heath SL0
62 A37 Iveston DH8
32 G45 Ivinghoe LU7
32 G45 Ivinghoe Aston LU7
28 C30 Ivington HR6
28 C30 Ivington Green HR6
5 E21 Ivybridge PL21
15 E56 Ivychurch TN29
23 F51 Ivy Hatch TN15
44 E54 Ivy Todd PE37
25 E55 Iwade ME9
9 C34 Iwerne Courtney or Shroton DT11
9 C34 Iwerne Minster DT11
34 B55 Ixworth IP31
34 A54 Ixworth Thorpe IP31

J

57 D37 Jack Hill LS21
99 F33 Jackstown AB51
74 E21 Jackton G75
4 A18 Jacobstow EX23
6 E21 Jacobstowe EX20
16 E16 Jameston SA70
69 D29 Jamestown *D.&G.* DG13
96 F20 Jamestown *Hgh.* IV14
74 B19 Jamestown *Str.* G83
96 F23 Janefield IV10
103 B26 Janetstown KW14
71 G39 Jarrow NE32
13 D51 Jarvis Brook TN6
33 F52 Jasper's Green CM7
75 C24 Jawcraig FK1
22 G47 Jayes Park RH5
35 G57 Jaywick CO15
70 B32 Jedburgh TD8
16 D16 Jeffreyston SA68
96 E22 Jemimaville IV7
75 D24 Jersay ML7
75 F24 Jerviswood ML11
71 G38 Jesmond NE2
13 F51 Jevington BN26
49 E33 Jodrell Bank SK11
60 C30 Johnby CA11
103 A29 John 'o' Groats KW1
14 E53 John's Cross TN32
91 G33 Johnshaven DD10
16 C15 Johnston SA62
74 D20 Johnstone PA5

Johnstonebridge

69 D26 Johnstonebridge DG11
74 D20 Johnstone Castle PA5
91 G33 Johnston Mains AB30
38 A29 Johnstown *Clw.* LL14
17 C19 Johnstown *Dyf.* SA31
109 G7 Jonesborough BT35
76 C29 Joppa *Ltn.* EH15
67 B19 Joppa *Str.* KA6
22 B45 Jordans HP9
16 A14 Jordanston SA62
82 C28 Jordanstone PH11
51 B39 Jump S74
75 D27 Juniper Green EH14
72 D10 Jura Ho. PA60
54 D25 Jurby East IM7
54 D25 Jurby West IM7

K

61 E33 Kaber CA17
76 D28 Kaimes EH17
94 F12 Kalnakill IV54
68 A22 Kames *Str.* KA18
73 C15 Kames *Str.* PA21
79 F14 Kames *Str.* PA34
109 F8 Katesbridge BT32
2 D13 Kea TR3
52 A44 Keadby DN17
109 F6 Keady BT60
53 F49 Keal Cotes PE23
49 B33 Kearsley BL4
55 A31 Kearstwick LA6
62 G35 Kearton DL11
101 A18 Kearvaig IV27
56 C33 Keasden LA2
98 D32 Kebholes AB45
48 D31 Keckwick WA4
53 D49 Keddington LN11
33 D52 Kedington CB9
40 A38 Kedleston DE22
52 B47 Keelby DN37
40 A34 Keele ST5
32 D46 Keeley Green MK43
33 G51 Keeres Green CM6
16 C15 Keeston SA62
20 F35 Keevil BA14
41 C40 Kegworth DE74
2 D11 Kehelland TR14
91 B32 Keig AB33
57 E36 Keighley BD21
80 B15 Keil *Hgh.* PA38
66 C12 Keil *Str.* PA28
98 D32 Keilhill AB45
72 B12 Keillmore PA31
82 C28 Keillor PH13
82 E25 Keillour PH1
72 D10 Keills PA46
72 D11 Keils PA60
8 A31 Keinton Mandeville TA11
75 A23 Keir FK15
68 D24 Keir Mill DG3
42 C46 Keisby PE10
61 D32 Keisley CA16
103 B29 Keiss KW1
98 D30 Keith AB55
82 D27 Keithick PH13
98 F29 Keithmore AB55
83 A31 Keithock DD9
56 E35 Kelbrook BB8
42 A45 Kelby NG32
61 E31 Keld *Cum.* CA10
61 F34 Keld *N.Y.* DL11
58 A43 Keldholme YO6
63 G43 Keldy Castle YO18
52 B44 Kelfield *Hum.* DN9
58 F41 Kelfield *N.Y.* YO4
51 G43 Kelham NG23
79 C11 Kellan PA72
97 F27 Kellas *Grm.* IV30
83 D30 Kellas *Tay.* DD5
5 G24 Kellaton TQ7
61 F32 Kelleth CA10
59 D46 Kelleythorpe YO25
44 A56 Kelling NR25
58 G41 Kellington DN14
62 C39 Kelloe DH6
68 B23 Kelloholm DG4
109 D7 Kells BT42
4 C16 Kelly *Cnw.* PL27
6 G19 Kelly *Dev.* PL16
4 C19 Kelly Bray PL17
31 A43 Kelmarsh NN6
21 B38 Kelmscott GL7
35 B59 Kelsale IP17
48 F31 Kelsall CW6
72 E8 Kelsay PA47
33 E49 Kelshall SG8
60 A27 Kelsick CA5
77 G33 Kelso TD5
51 F39 Kelstedge S45
53 C48 Kelstern LN11
19 E32 Kelston BA1
81 C23 Keltneyburn PH15
65 C25 Kelton DG1
75 A27 Kelty KY4
34 G54 Kelvedon CO5
23 B51 Kelvedon Hatch CM15
2 E9 Kelynack TR19
83 F30 Kemback KY15
39 E33 Kemberton TF11
20 B35 Kemble GL7
29 E35 Kemerton GL20
19 A29 Kemeys Commander NP5
19 B29 Kemeys Inferior NP6
91 B33 Kemnay AB51
29 F32 Kempley GL18
29 F32 Kempley Green GL18
29 D34 Kempsey WR5
20 B37 Kempsford GL7
21 G41 Kempshott RG22
32 D46 Kempston MK42
32 D46 Kempston Church End MK43
32 D46 Kempston Hardwick MK45
38 G29 Kempton SY7
13 F49 Kemp Town BN2
23 F51 Kemsing TN15
24 E54 Kemsley ME10
14 D55 Kenardington TN26
28 D30 Kenchester HR4
21 A38 Kencott GL7
61 G30 Kendal LA9
28 F29 Kenderchurch HR2
18 C23 Kenfig CF33
18 C24 Kenfig Hill CF33
30 A38 Kenilworth CV8
81 D20 Kenknock *Cen.* FK21
81 C21 Kenknock *Tay.* PH15
23 F49 Kenley *G.L.* CR8
38 E31 Kenley *Shr.* SY5
94 F13 Kenmore *Hgh.* IV54
80 G16 Kenmore *Str.* PA32
81 C23 Kenmore *Tay.* PH15
100 G8 Kenmore *W.I.* HS2
19 E30 Kenn *Avon* BS21
7 G25 Kenn *Dev.* EX6
73 D14 Kennacraig PA29
4 B18 Kennards House PL15
93 B8 Kennavay HS4
7 E23 Kennerleigh EX17
91 D32 Kennerty AB31
75 A25 Kennet FK10
90 A31 Kennethmont AB54
33 B52 Kennett CB8
7 G25 Kennford EX6
44 G56 Kenninghall NR16
14 C55 Kennington *Kent* TN24
21 A40 Kennington *Oxf.* OX1
82 G29 Kennoway KY8
33 A52 Kennyhill IP28
58 C43 Kennythorpe YO17
93 F10 Kensaleyre IV51
23 D48 Kensington & Chelsea W,SW
32 G46 Kensworth LU6
32 G46 Kensworth Common LU6
80 B15 Kentallen PA38
28 F29 Kentchurch HR2
33 B52 Kentford CB8
7 E26 Kentisbeare EX15
6 A22 Kentisbury EX31
6 A22 Kentisbury Ford EX31
60 F30 Kentmere LA8
7 G25 Kenton *Dev.* EX6
35 B57 Kenton *Sfk* IP14
71 G38 Kenton *T.&W.* NE3
79 A12 Kentra PH36
55 B30 Kents Bank LA11
29 F33 Kent`s Green GL18
10 B39 Kent`s Oak SO51
14 F53 Kent Street *E.S.* TN33
23 F52 Kent Street *Kent* ME18
38 B29 Kenwick SY12
3 D14 Kenwyn TR1
49 C32 Kenyon WA3
101 B19 Keoldale IV27
80 A16 Keppanach PH33
86 B15 Keppoch *Hgh.* IV40
74 C19 Keppoch *Str.* G82
66 B12 Keprigan PA28
62 G40 Kepwick YO7
40 G38 Keresley CV6
28 G31 Kerne Bridge HR9
49 E35 Kerridge SK10
2 F10 Kerris TR19
38 G27 Kerry SY16
73 D17 Kerrycroy PA20
94 D14 Kerrysdale IV21
28 E29 Kerry`s Gate HR2
51 F43 Kersall NG22
34 D55 Kersey IP7
69 E30 Kershopefoot CA6
7 E26 Kerswell EX15
29 D34 Kerswell Green WR5
35 D58 Kesgrave IP5
108 E4 Kesh BT93
45 G61 Kessingland NR33
45 G61 Kessingland Beach NR33
3 C14 Kestle Mill TR8
23 E49 Keston BR2
60 D28 Keswick *Cum.* CA12
45 B59 Keswick *Nfk* NR12
45 E58 Keswick *Nfk* NR4
53 E49 Ketsby LN11
32 A44 Kettering NN15
45 E57 Ketteringham NR18
82 D28 Kettins PH13
34 D55 Kettlebaston IP7
82 G28 Kettlebridge KY15
40 E37 Kettlebrook B77
35 C58 Kettleburgh IP13
69 F27 Kettleholm DG11
63 E44 Kettleness YO21
49 E35 Kettleshulme SK12
57 D38 Kettlesing HG3
57 D38 Kettlesing Bottom HG3
44 B55 Kettlestone NR21
52 E44 Kettlethorpe LN1
104 C32 Kettletoft KW17
56 B35 Kettlewell BD23
42 E45 Ketton PE9
22 D47 Kew TW9
19 E29 Kewstoke BS22
50 B38 Kexbrough S75
52 D44 Kexby *Lcn.* DN21
58 D43 Kexby *N.Y.* YO4
49 F34 Key Green CW12
41 E42 Keyham LE7
10 E39 Keyhaven SO41
59 G48 Keyingham HU12
13 E49 Keymer BN6
19 E32 Keynsham BS18
32 B46 Keysoe MK44
32 B46 Keysoe Row MK44
53 G50 Key`s Toft PE24
32 A46 Keyston PE18
41 B41 Keyworth NG12
62 A38 Kibblesworth NE11
41 F42 Kibworth Beauchamp LE8
41 F42 Kibworth Harcourt LE8
23 D50 Kidbrooke SE3
57 F40 Kiddal Lane End LS15
40 E34 Kiddemore Green ST19
29 A33 Kidderminster DY10
30 F39 Kiddington OX20
31 G40 Kidlington OX5
21 D42 Kidmore End RG4
64 G20 Kidsdale DG8
49 G34 Kidsgrove ST7
56 A35 Kidstones DL8
17 D20 Kidwelly (Cydweli) SA17
79 D14 Kiel Crofts PA37
70 D32 Kielder NE48
74 D19 Kilbarchan PA10
86 D12 Kilbeg IV44
73 D13 Kilberry PA29
74 E18 Kilbirnie KA25
80 F17 Kilblaan PA32
102 G24 Kilbraur KW9
79 C10 Kilbrenan PA73
86 B11 Kilbride *Hgh.* IV49
73 D16 Kilbride *Str.* PA20
79 E14 Kilbride *Str.* PA34
73 D15 Kilbride Farm PA21
73 A15 Kilbridemore PA22
41 A39 Kilburn *Dby.* DE56
57 B40 Kilburn *N.Y.* YO6
41 F42 Kilby LE18
75 F24 Kilcadzow ML8
73 E17 Kilchattan PA20
66 A12 Kilchenzie PA28
79 D14 Kilcheran PA34
72 E8 Kilchlaren PA48
79 F13 Kilchoan *Hgh.* PA34
79 A10 Kilchoan *Str.* PH36
80 E16 Kilchrenan PA35
66 B12 Kilchrist PA28
83 G30 Kilconquhar KY9
29 F32 Kilcot GL18
96 F21 Kilcoy IV6
74 B18 Kilcreggan G84
63 F41 Kildale YO21
96 D23 Kildary IV18
66 B13 Kildavie PA28
96 D20 Kildermorie Lodge IV17
66 A16 Kildonan KA27
103 F25 Kildonan Lodge KW8
85 F10 Kildonnan PH42
64 E16 Kildrochet DG9
90 B30 Kildrummy AB33
57 E36 Kildwick BD20
73 C15 Kilfinan PA21
87 E18 Kilfinnan PH34
16 D17 Kilgetty SA68
19 B30 Kilgwrrwg Common NP6
59 C46 Kilham *Hum.* YO25
77 G34 Kilham *Nor.* TD12
109 G8 Kilkeel BT34
78 C5 Kilkenneth PA77
29 G35 Kilkenny GL54
67 C19 Kilkerran *Str.* KA19
66 B13 Kilkerran *Str.* PA28
6 D18 Kilkhampton EX23
108 E4 Killadeas BT94
51 D40 Killamarsh S31
17 E22 Killay SA2
79 C11 Killbeg PA72
72 F12 Killean *Str.* PA29
80 G16 Killean *Str.* PA32
74 B21 Killearn G63
66 B12 Killellan PA28
96 F22 Killen *Hgh.* IV9
108 D4 Killen *Tyr.* BT81
62 D37 Killerby DL2
108 D4 Killeter BT81
81 B21 Killichonan PH17
79 C11 Killichronan PA72
87 F18 Killiechanate PH34
81 A24 Killiecrankie PH16
88 E23 Killiehuntly PH21
79 D10 Killiemor PA72
86 A15 Killilan IV40
103 C28 Killimster KW1
81 D21 Killin *Cen.* FK21
97 A24 Killin *Hgh.* KW9
72 C8 Killinallan PA44
57 D38 Killinghall HG3
56 A32 Killington LA6
71 F38 Killingworth NE12
76 F30 Killochyett TD1
66 A12 Killocraw PA28
109 F9 Killough BT30
79 E10 Killunaig PA70
79 C11 Killundine PA34
109 F6 Killylea BT60
109 E9 Killyleagh BT30
74 D19 Kilmacolm PA13
80 G15 Kilmaha PA35
81 G21 Kilmahog FK17
79 B14 Kilmalieu PH33
93 D10 Kilmaluag IV51
82 E29 Kilmany KY15
86 C11 Kilmarie IV49
74 G20 Kilmarnock KA
73 A14 Kilmartin PA31
74 F20 Kilmaurs KA3
79 F14 Kilmelford PA34
19 F32 Kilmersdon BA3
11 B41 Kilmeston SO24
66 A12 Kilmichael PA28
73 A14 Kilmichael Glassary PA31
73 B13 Kilmichael of Inverlussa PA31
8 E28 Kilmington *Dev.* EX13
9 A33 Kilmington *Wts.* BA12
9 A33 Kilmington Street BA12
96 G20 Kilmorack IV4
86 D12 Kilmore *Hgh.* IV44
79 E14 Kilmore *Str.* PA34
86 G11 Kilmory *Hgh.* PH36
85 D9 Kilmory *Hgh.* PH43
73 B13 Kilmory *Str.* PA31
72 C12 Kilmory *Str.* PA31
103 G25 Kilmote KW8
96 G22 Kilmuir *Hgh.* IV1
96 D23 Kilmuir *Hgh.* IV18
93 D9 Kilmuir *Hgh.* IV51
93 G8 Kilmuir *Hgh.* IV55
73 B17 Kilmun PA23
82 G29 Kilmux KY8
72 C8 Kilnave PA44
14 D53 Kilndown TN17
22 D44 Kiln Green RG10
51 C40 Kilnhurst S64
78 C9 Kilninian PA74
79 E14 Kilninver PA34
62 A36 Kiln Pit Hill DH8
53 A50 Kilnsea HU12
56 C35 Kilnsey BD23
59 E46 Kilnwick YO25
72 A9 Kiloran PA61
66 A14 Kilpatrick KA27
28 E30 Kilpeck HR2
103 G25 Kilphedir KW8
58 G43 Kilpin DN14
109 C6 Kilrea BT51
83 G31 Kilrenny KY10
31 A41 Kilsby CV23
82 E28 Kilspindie PH2
64 G17 Kilstay DG9
74 C22 Kilsyth G65
96 G20 Kiltarlity IV4
63 E42 Kilton *Cle.* TS13
7 A27 Kilton *Som.* TA5
81 D22 Kiltyre FK21
93 E9 Kilvaxter IV51
7 A27 Kilve TA5
44 G54 Kilverstone IP24
42 A43 Kilvington NG13
74 F18 Kilwinning KA13
44 E56 Kimberley *Nfk* NR18
41 A40 Kimberley *Not.* NG16
62 B38 Kimblesworth DH2
22 A43 Kimble Wick HP17
32 B46 Kimbolton *Cbs.* PE18
28 B31 Kimbolton *H.&W.* HR6
41 G41 Kimcote LE17
9 F34 Kimmeridge BH20
77 G35 Kimmerston NE71
21 G38 Kimpton *Ham.* SP11
32 G47 Kimpton *Hfs.* SG4
83 F30 Kinaldy KY16
83 C32 Kinblethmont DD11
102 E24 Kinbrace KW11
86 E15 Kinbreack PH34
81 G23 Kinbuck FK15
82 C29 Kincaldrum DD8
83 F30 Kincaple KY16
75 B25 Kincardine *Fife* FK10
96 C21 Kincardine *Hgh.* IV24
90 D31 Kincardine O`Neil AB34
82 D27 Kinclaven PH1
91 C35 Kincorth AB1
91 A35 Kincraig *Grm.* AB41
89 D24 Kincraig *Hgh.* PH21
82 C25 Kincraigie PH8
82 C25 Kindallachan PH9
82 A26 Kindrogan Field Centre PH10
91 B33 Kinellar AB2
30 F36 Kineton *Glo.* GL54
30 C39 Kineton *War.* CV35
40 G36 Kineton Green B92
82 E27 Kinfauns PH2
73 E16 Kingarth PA20
19 A30 Kingcoed NP5
52 C46 Kingerby LN8
30 F38 Kingham OX7
65 C25 Kingholm Quay DG1
76 B28 Kinghorn KY3
76 A28 Kinglassie KY5
82 E29 Kingoodie DD2
4 E20 Kingsand PL10
83 F31 Kingsbarns KY16
5 F23 Kingsbridge *Dev.* TQ7
7 B25 Kingsbridge *Som.* TA23
40 D37 King`s Bromley DE13
93 F9 Kingsburgh IV51
22 C47 Kingsbury *G.L.* HA3
40 F38 Kingsbury *War.* B78
8 B30 Kingsbury Episcopi TA12
28 F31 Kings Caple HR1
75 C26 Kingscavil EH49
21 F41 Kingsclere RG20
42 F45 King`s Cliffe PE8
20 B33 Kingscote GL8
6 D21 Kingscott EX38
30 C36 King`s Coughton B49
66 A16 Kingscross KA27
82 G29 Kingsdale KY8
8 B30 Kingsdon TA11
15 C59 Kingsdown CT14
75 A27 Kingseat KY12
22 A43 Kingsey HP27
16 E15 Kingsfold *Dyf.* SA71
12 C47 Kingsfold *W.S.* RH12
91 C34 Kingsford *Grm.* AB1
90 B31 Kingsford *Grm.* AB33
99 E33 Kingsford *Grm.* AB53
39 G33 Kingsford *H.&W.* DY11
74 F20 Kingsford *Str.* KA3
52 A46 Kingsforth DN18
25 D59 Kingsgate CT10
29 E33 King`s Green WR13
6 B21 Kingsheanton EX31
40 G36 King`s Heath B14
40 F35 King`s Hill WS10
81 E21 Kingshouse FK19
80 B18 Kingshouse Hotel PA39
5 D24 Kingskerswell TQ12
82 G28 Kingskettle KY15
46 D18 Kingsland *Gwy.* LL65
28 B30 Kingsland *H.&W.* HR6
22 A46 Kings Langley WD4
48 E31 Kingsley *Che.* WA6
11 A43 Kingsley *Ham.* GU35
40 A35 Kingsley *Stf.* ST10
12 C44 Kingsley Green GU27
43 C51 King`s Lynn PE30
61 D32 Kings Meaburn CA10
83 C30 Kingsmuir DD8
76 G28 Kings Muir EH45
41 C39 King`s Newton DE73
14 D55 Kingsnorth TN23
24 D54 Kingsnorth Power Station ME3
41 E42 King`s Norton *Lei.* LE7
30 A36 King`s Norton *W.M.* B38
6 D22 King`s Nympton EX37
28 C30 King`s Pyon HR4
33 A48 Kings Ripton PE17
10 A39 King`s Somborne SO20
9 C32 King`s Stag DT10
20 A34 King`s Stanley GL10
31 E41 King`s Sutton OX17
40 F36 Kingstanding B44
5 C24 Kingsteignton TQ12
97 F24 Kingsteps IV12
50 E36 King Sterndale SK17
28 E30 Kingsthorne HR2
31 B43 Kingsthorpe NN2
33 C49 Kingston *Cbs.* CB3
5 F22 Kingston *Dev.* TQ7
9 G35 Kingston *Dor.* BH20
9 D33 Kingston *Dor.* DT10
98 C29 Kingston *Grm.* IV32
10 D37 Kingston *Ham.* BH24
11 F40 Kingston *I.o.W.* PO38
15 B57 Kingston *Kent* CT4
76 B31 Kingston *Ltn.* EH39
12 F46 Kingston *W.S.* BN16
21 B39 Kingston Bagpuize OX13
22 B43 Kingston Blount OX9
13 F48 Kingston by Sea BN43
9 A34 Kingston Deverill BA12
28 E30 Kingstone *H.&W.* HR2
8 C29 Kingstone *Som.* TA19
40 C36 Kingstone *Stf.* ST14
21 C39 Kingston Lisle OX12
13 F49 Kingston near Lewes BN7
41 C40 Kingston on Soar NG11
8 E31 Kingston Russell DT2
19 E29 Kingston Seymour BS21
8 B28 Kingston St Mary TA2
59 G47 Kingston Upon Hull HU
22 D47 Kingston upon Thames KT
21 C39 Kingston Warren OX12
60 A29 Kingstown CA3
32 F47 King`s Walden SG4
5 E24 Kingswear TQ6
74 F21 Kingswell KA3
91 C34 Kingswells AB1
40 G34 Kingswinford DY6
19 D32 Kingswood *Avon* BS15
31 G42 Kingswood *Bkh.* HP18
20 B33 Kingswood *Glo.* GL12
14 B54 Kingswood *Kent* ME17
38 E28 Kingswood *Pow.* SY21

Langford End

23 F48 Kingswood *Sry* KT20
30 A37 Kingswood *War.* B94
28 C28 Kingswood Common HR5
11 A40 King's Worthy SO23
52 E47 Kingthorpe LN3
28 C28 Kington *H.&W.* HR5
29 C35 Kington *H.&W.* WR7
20 D35 Kington Langley SN15
9 B33 Kington Magna SP8
20 D34 Kington St Michael SN14
88 D23 Kingussie PH21
8 A31 Kingweston TA11
99 F34 Kinharrachie AB41
65 D25 Kinharvie DG2
74 C22 Kinkell G65
82 F25 Kinkell Bridge PH3
99 E35 Kinknockie AB42
39 G33 Kinlet DY12
82 F28 Kinloch *Fife* KY15
96 D21 Kinloch *Hgh.* IV16
101 E19 Kinloch *Hgh.* IV27
79 B12 Kinloch *Hgh.* PA34
85 E10 Kinloch *Hgh.* PH43
82 C27 Kinloch *Tay.* PH10
82 C28 Kinloch *Tay.* PH12
79 A14 Kinlochan PH37
81 G20 Kinlochard FK8
86 E15 Kinlocharkaig PH34
86 F14 Kinlochbeoraid PH38
101 C17 Kinlochbervie IV27
86 G15 Kinlocheil PH33
80 C16 Kinlochetive PA39
95 E16 Kinlochewe IV22
86 D15 Kinloch Hourn PH35
88 F21 Kinloch Laggan PH20
80 C15 Kinlochlaich PA38
80 A17 Kinlochleven PA40
86 G12 Kinlochmoidart PH36
86 E14 Kinlochmorar PH41
80 A17 Kinlochmore PA40
81 B22 Kinloch Rannoch PH16
79 E12 Kinlochspelve PA63
97 E26 Kinloss IV36
47 D25 Kinmel Bay LL22
91 B34 Kinmuck AB51
99 E35 Kinnadie AB41
82 E28 Kinnaird PH14
91 F34 Kinneff DD10
69 C26 Kinnelhead DG10
81 D21 Kinnell *Cen.* FK21
83 B32 Kinnell *Tay.* DD11
38 C29 Kinnerley SY10
28 D29 Kinnersley *H.&W.* HR3
29 D34 Kinnersley *H.&W.* WR8
28 B28 Kinnerton LD8
82 G27 Kinnesswood KY13
83 C30 Kinnettles DD8
62 D36 Kinninvie DL12
82 B29 Kinnordy DD8
41 B42 Kinoulton NG12
89 D24 Kinrara PH22
82 G26 Kinross KY13
82 D27 Kinrossie PH2
32 G47 Kinsbourne Green AL5
28 B29 Kinsham LD8
51 A39 Kinsley WF9
10 E36 Kinson BH11
100 F8 Kintarvie HS2
21 E39 Kintbury RG17
97 E25 Kintessack IV36
82 F27 Kintillo PH2
90 C31 Kintocher AB33
28 A30 Kinton *H.&W.* SY7
38 D29 Kinton *Shr.* SY4
91 B33 Kintore AB51
72 E10 Kintour PA42
72 F9 Kintra *Str.* PA42
78 E9 Kintra *Str.* PA66
97 A24 Kintradwell KW9
79 G14 Kintraw PA31
72 A12 Kinuachdrach PA60
89 C24 Kinveachy PH24
40 G34 Kinver DY7
99 F36 Kiplaw Croft AB42
62 G38 Kiplin DL10
81 F21 Kipp FK18
57 F39 Kippax LS25
74 A22 Kippen *Cen.* FK8
82 F26 Kippen *Tay.* PH2
81 G23 Kippenross Ho FK15
65 E24 Kippford or Scaur DG5
23 G52 Kipping's Cross TN12
105 A29 Kirbister *Ork.* KW16
104 D32 Kirbister *Ork.* KW17
104 D28 Kirbuster KW17
45 E58 Kirby Bedon NR14
45 F59 Kirby Cane NR35
30 A38 Kirby Corner CV4
35 F57 Kirby Cross CO13
59 C45 Kirby Grindalythe YO17
62 F37 Kirby Hill *N.Y.* DL11
57 C39 Kirby Hill *N.Y.* HG4
57 A40 Kirby Knowle YO7
35 F58 Kirby le Soken CO13
58 B43 Kirby Misperton YO17
41 E41 Kirby Muxloe LE9
45 F59 Kirby Row NR35
62 G39 Kirby Sigston DL6
58 D44 Kirby Underdale YO4
57 A39 Kirby Wiske YO7
109 E9 Kircubbin BT22
12 D46 Kirdford RH14
103 C28 Kirk KW1
107 D40 Kirkabister ZE2
65 F21 Kirkandrews DG6
60 A29 Kirkandrews-upon-Eden CA5
60 A28 Kirkbampton CA5
65 E25 Kirkbean DG2
51 A42 Kirk Bramwith DN7
60 A28 Kirkbride CA5
62 G38 Kirkbridge DL8
83 C30 Kirkbuddo DD8
76 G28 Kirkburn *Bor.* EH45
59 D45 Kirkburn *Hum.* YO25
50 A38 Kirkburton HD8
52 C46 Kirkby *Lcn.* LN8
48 C30 Kirkby *Mer.* L32
63 F41 Kirkby *N.Y.* TS9
41 D42 Kirkby Bellars LE14
62 G38 Kirkby Fleetham DL7
52 G46 Kirkby Green LN4
51 G40 Kirkby in Ashfield NG17
42 A47 Kirkby la Thorpe NG34
55 B31 Kirkby Lonsdale LA6
56 C34 Kirkby Malham BD23
41 E40 Kirkby Mallory LE9
57 B38 Kirkby Malzeard HG4
58 A43 Kirkby Mills YO6
58 A42 Kirkbymoorside YO6
53 F48 Kirkby on Bain LN10
57 E39 Kirkby Overblow HG3
61 F33 Kirkby Stephen CA17
61 D32 Kirkby Thore CA10
42 C46 Kirkby Underwood PE10
58 E41 Kirkby Wharfe LS24
76 A28 Kirkcaldy KY
70 G31 Kirkcambeck CA8
64 D16 Kirkcolm DG9
68 B23 Kirkconnel DG4
65 D25 Kirkconnell DG2
64 D19 Kirkcowan DG8
65 F22 Kirkcudbright DG6
65 E21 Kirkdale DG8
75 F27 Kirkdean EH46
57 D39 Kirk Deighton LS22
59 G46 Kirk Ella HU10
75 F24 Kirkfieldbank ML11
65 D24 Kirkgunzeon DG2
41 B40 Kirk Hallam DE7
55 F30 Kirkham *Lan.* PR4
58 C43 Kirkham *N.Y.* YO6
57 G38 Kirkhamgate WF2
57 D40 Kirk Hammerton YO5
70 E35 Kirkharle NE19
61 A32 Kirkhaugh CA9
71 F36 Kirkheaton *Nor.* NE19
50 A37 Kirkheaton *W.Y.* HD5
98 D28 Kirkhill *Grm.* AB38
96 G21 Kirkhill *Hgh.* IV5
91 G32 Kirkhill *Tay.* DD10
69 A29 Kirkhope TD7
86 C11 Kirkibost *Hgh.* IV49
100 D7 Kirkibost *W.I.* HS2
82 C28 Kirkinch PH12
64 E20 Kirkinner DG8
74 C22 Kirkintilloch G66
50 G38 Kirk Ireton DE6
61 C32 Kirkland *Cum.* CA10
60 E26 Kirkland *Cum.* CA26
69 E26 Kirkland *D.&G.* DG11
68 D23 Kirkland *D.&G.* DG3
68 B23 Kirkland *D.&G.* DG4
64 F19 Kirkland of Longcastle DG8
40 B38 Kirk Langley DE6
63 D41 Kirkleatham TS10
62 E39 Kirklevington TS15
45 F61 Kirkley NR33
57 A38 Kirklington *N.Y.* DL8
51 G42 Kirklington *Not.* NG22
69 G30 Kirklinton CA6
75 C27 Kirkliston EH29
64 G16 Kirkmaiden DG9
62 C38 Kirk Merrington DL16
67 C19 Kirkmichael *Str.* KA19
82 A26 Kirkmichael *Tay.* PH10
54 D24 Kirk Michael IM6
75 F23 Kirkmuirhill ML11
75 D26 Kirknewton *Ltn.* EH27
70 A34 Kirknewton *Nor.* NE71
98 F30 Kirkney AB54
75 D24 Kirk of Shotts ML7
61 B31 Kirkoswald *Cum.* CA10
67 C18 Kirkoswald *Str.* KA19
65 C23 Kirkpatrick Durham DG7
69 F28 Kirkpatrick-Fleming DG11
51 B42 Kirk Sandall DN3
54 A27 Kirksanton LA18
51 A41 Kirk Smeaton WF8
57 F38 Kirkstall LS5
52 F47 Kirkstead LN10
69 D29 Kirkstile *D.&G.* DG13
98 F31 Kirkstile *Grm.* AB54
70 B31 Kirkton *Bor.* TD9
68 E25 Kirkton *D.&G.* DG1
82 E29 Kirkton *Fife* DD6
91 B32 Kirkton *Grm.* AB33
91 A32 Kirkton *Grm.* AB52
98 D32 Kirkton *Grm.* AB53
96 F23 Kirkton *Hgh.* IV1
88 A21 Kirkton *Hgh.* IV3
96 B23 Kirkton *Hgh.* KW10
102 B24 Kirkton *Hgh.* KW13
79 G13 Kirkton *Str.* PA31
83 C30 Kirkton *Tay.* DD8
82 F25 Kirkton *Tay.* PH3
91 G32 Kirktonhill AB30
76 G28 Kirkton Manor EH45
82 B29 Kirkton of Airlie DD8
82 D29 Kirkton of Auchterhouse DD3
97 G24 Kirkton of Barevan IV12
91 A33 Kirkton of Bourtie AB51
82 D27 Kirkton of Collace PH2
83 B32 Kirkton of Craig DD10
98 F32 Kirkton of Culsalmond AB52
91 D33 Kirkton of Durris AB31
90 B29 Kirkton of Glenbuchat AB36
82 A28 Kirkton of Glenisla PH11
82 B29 Kirkton of Kingoldrum DD8
82 C27 Kirkton of Lethendy PH1
91 A35 Kirkton of Logie Buchan AB41
91 D34 Kirkton of Maryculter AB1
83 A31 Kirkton of Menmuir DD9
83 D31 Kirkton of Monikie DD5
91 C33 Kirkton of Skene AB32
82 D29 Kirkton of Strathmartine DD3
82 D29 Kirkton of Tealing DD4
99 D36 Kirktown AB42
98 C32 Kirktown of Alvah AB45
99 E33 Kirktown of Auchterless AB53
98 C31 Kirktown of Deskford AB56
91 E34 Kirktown of Fetteresso AB3
91 A32 Kirktown of Rayne AB51
91 A36 Kirktown of Slains AB41
104 E30 Kirkwall KW15
105 A30 Kirkwall Airport KW17
70 E35 Kirkwhelpington NE19
70 A33 Kirk Yetholm TD5
52 A47 Kirmington DN39
52 C47 Kirmond le Mire LN3
73 C17 Kirn PA23
82 B29 Kirriemuir DD8
45 F58 Kirstead Green NR15
69 F28 Kirtlebridge DG11
33 C52 Kirtling CB8
33 C52 Kirtling Green CB8
31 G40 Kirtlington OX5
102 B23 Kirtomy KW14
86 B14 Kirton *Hgh.* IV40
43 B48 Kirton *Lcn.* PE20
51 F42 Kirton *Not.* NG22
35 E58 Kirton *Sfk* IP10
43 B48 Kirton End PE20
43 A48 Kirton Holme PE20
52 C45 Kirton in Lindsey DN21
66 A16 Kiscadale KA27
31 C42 Kislingbury NN7
6 D19 Kismeblon Bridge EX22
31 B40 Kites Hardwick CV23
5 E21 Kitley PL8
7 C26 Kittisford TA21
11 A42 Kitwood SO24
51 D40 Kiveton Park S31
102 E21 Klibreck IV27
98 D31 Knabbygates AB54
52 D44 Knaith DN21
9 B33 Knap Corner SP8
22 F45 Knaphill GU21
8 B28 Knapp *Som.* TA3
82 D28 Knapp *Tay.* PH14
58 D41 Knapton *N.Y.* YO2
45 B58 Knapton *Nfk* NR28
28 C30 Knapton Green HR4
33 B49 Knapwell CB3
57 D39 Knaresborough HG5
61 A32 Knarsdale CA6
99 E34 Knaven AB42
57 A40 Knayton YO7
33 F48 Knebworth SG3
58 G43 Knedlington DN14
51 F42 Kneesall NG22
33 D49 Kneesworth SG8
41 A42 Kneeton NG13
17 F20 Knelston SA3
44 G55 Knettishall IP22
6 B22 Knightacott EX31
30 C39 Knightcote CV33
5 F21 Knighton *Dev.* PL9
41 E41 Knighton *Lei.* LE2
28 A28 Knighton *Pow.* LD7
7 A27 Knighton *Som.* TA5
39 C33 Knighton *Stf.* ST20
39 B33 Knighton *Stf.* TF9
21 D38 Knighton *Wts.* SN8
29 C33 Knightwick WR6
28 B28 Knill LD8
79 E14 Knipoch PA34
42 B44 Knipton NG32
62 B36 Knitsley DH8
50 G37 Kniveton DE6
61 D32 Knock *Cum.* CA16
98 D31 Knock *Grm.* AB54
79 D11 Knock *Str.* PA71
73 A14 Knockalava PA31
103 F27 Knockally KW6
54 E24 Knockaloe Moar IM5
101 G17 Knockan IV27
90 A27 Knockandhu AB37
97 G27 Knockando AB38
96 F22 Knockbain IV8
95 E17 Knockban IV23
96 C23 Knockbreck IV19
65 F21 Knockbrex DG6
95 B18 Knockdamph IV26
103 B27 Knockdee KW12
73 C17 Knockdow PA23
20 C34 Knockdown GL8
66 A15 Knockenkelly KA27
74 G19 Knockentiber KA2
87 B18 Knockfin IV4
67 D21 Knockgray DG7
23 F50 Knockholt TN14
23 F50 Knockholt Pound TN14
38 C29 Knockin SY10
65 C23 Knocklearn DG7
66 B12 Knocknaha PA28
67 E21 Knocknalling DG7
89 A26 Knock of Auchnahannet PH26
72 C11 Knockrome PA60
54 E24 Knocksharry IM5
64 C19 Knockville DG8
78 F8 Knockvologan PA66
35 B60 Knodishall IP17
49 E34 Knolls Green WA16
38 B29 Knolton LL13
20 G35 Knook BA12
42 E43 Knossington LE15
55 E29 Knott End-on-Sea FY6
32 B45 Knotting MK44
32 B46 Knotting Green MK44
57 G40 Knottingley WF11
48 C30 Knotty Ash L14
22 B45 Knotty Green HP9
28 A31 Knowbury SY8
64 C19 Knowe DG8
70 E35 Knowesgate NE19
67 B18 Knoweside KA19
98 D32 Knowes of Elrick AB54
70 B31 Knowetownhead TD9
99 D34 Knowhead AB43
19 D31 Knowle *Avon* BS4
7 E23 Knowle *Dev.* EX17
6 B20 Knowle *Dev.* EX33
7 G26 Knowle *Dev.* EX9
28 A31 Knowle *Shr.* SY8
30 A37 Knowle *W.M.* B93
56 F32 Knowle Green PR3
19 G29 Knowle Hall TA7
34 D53 Knowl Green CO10
22 D44 Knowl Hill RG10
10 C36 Knowlton *Dor.* BH21
15 B58 Knowlton *Kent* CT3
40 B34 Knowl Wall ST4
48 C30 Knowsley L34
7 C24 Knowstone EX36
28 A28 Knucklas LD7
49 E33 Knutsford WA16
49 G34 Knypersley ST8
2 G13 Kuggar TR12
86 B13 Kyleakin IV41
86 B13 Kyle of Lochalsh IV40
86 B13 Kylerhea IV40
86 G12 Kylesbeg PH36
86 E13 Kylesknoydart PH41
86 E13 Kylesmorar PH41
101 E17 Kylestrome IV27
96 B22 Kyloag IV24
39 D32 Kynnersley TF6
29 B32 Kyre Park WR15

L

100 C8 Labost HS2
100 E9 Lacasaigh HS2
53 B48 Laceby DN37
22 B44 Lacey Green HP27
49 E33 Lach Dennis CW9
108 E4 Lack BT93
34 A53 Lackford IP28
20 E34 Lacock SN15
31 C40 Ladbroke CV33
23 G52 Laddingford ME18
53 G50 Lade Bank PE22
3 C14 Ladock TR2
82 F28 Ladybank KY15
6 G19 Ladycross PL15
80 F16 Ladyfield PA32
54 A27 Lady Hall LA18
77 F34 Ladykirk TD15
99 C34 Ladysford AB43
34 C53 Lady's Green CB8
79 A12 Laga PH36
79 F14 Lagalochan PA35
72 F9 Lagavulin PA42
66 A15 Lagg *Str.* KA27
67 B18 Lagg *Str.* KA7
72 C11 Lagg *Str.* PA60
81 F21 Laggan *Cen.* FK18
98 F29 Laggan *Grm.* AB55
88 E22 Laggan *Hgh.* PH20
87 E18 Laggan *Hgh.* PH34
72 E8 Laggan *Str.* PA43
79 C10 Lagganulva PA73
90 B27 Lagganvoulin AB37
80 G17 Laglingarten PA25
96 G21 Lagnalean IV3
68 B22 Lagrae DG4
82 D26 Laguna PH1
83 G30 Lahill KY9
102 C20 Laid IV27
94 B14 Laide IV22
85 F10 Laig PH42
67 B21 Laight KA18
89 C26 Lainchoil PH25
24 C52 Laindon SS15
82 A27 Lair PH10
96 A21 Lairg IV27
96 A21 Lairg Lo. IV27
80 A16 Lairigmor PH33
98 E32 Laithers AB53
60 C30 Laithes CA11
10 A37 Lake SP4
45 E58 Lakenham NR1
44 G52 Lakenheath IP27
43 F50 Lakesend PE14
55 A29 Lakeside LA12
22 E46 Laleham TW18
18 D24 Laleston CF32
34 E54 Lamarsh CO8
45 C58 Lamas NR10
34 E56 Lamb Corner CO7
13 C52 Lamberhurst TN3
13 C52 Lamberhurst Quarter TN3
77 E35 Lamberton TD15
23 D48 Lambeth SE,SW
54 E24 Lambfell Moar IM4
61 A32 Lambley *Nor.* CA6
41 A42 Lambley *Not.* NG4
21 D38 Lambourn RG17
23 B50 Lambourne End RM4
21 D39 Lambourn Woodlands RG17
13 C48 Lambs Green RH12
16 C14 Lambston SA62
4 D18 Lamellion PL14
4 C20 Lamerton PL19
62 A38 Lamesley NE11
96 D23 Lamington *Hgh.* IV18
75 G25 Lamington *Str.* ML12
73 G15 Lamlash KA27
67 D21 Lamloch DG7
60 C29 Lamonby CA11
3 D14 Lamorran TR2
70 F32 Lampert NE48
26 D21 Lampeter SA48
16 C17 Lampeter Velfrey SA67
16 D15 Lamphey SA71
60 D26 Lamplugh CA14
31 A43 Lamport NN6
9 A32 Lamyatt BA4
6 F19 Lana EX22
75 F24 Lanark ML11
55 C30 Lancaster LA1
62 B37 Lanchester DH7
33 B50 Landbeach CB4
6 C20 Landcross EX39
91 C33 Landerberry AB32
2 G13 Landewednack TR12
10 C38 Landford SP5
17 E20 Landimore SA3
6 B21 Landkey EX32
17 E22 Landore SA1
4 D19 Landrake PL12
5 D23 Landscove TQ13
16 C15 Landshipping SA67
4 D20 Landulph PL12
33 B51 Landwade CB8
40 E35 Landywood WS6
4 B18 Laneast PL15
22 B44 Lane End *Bkh.* HP14
60 G27 Lane End *Cum.* LA19
51 F40 Lane End *Dby.* DE55
9 E34 Lane End *Dor.* BH20
23 D51 Lane End *Kent* DA2
4 D16 Lane-end PL30
40 E34 Lane Green WV8
51 E43 Laneham DN22
50 B37 Lane Head *Dby.* HD8
62 E36 Lane Head *Drm.* DL11
49 C32 Lane Head *G.M.* WA3
70 E33 Lanehead NE48
56 E35 Laneshaw Bridge BB8
92 E4 Langais HS6
78 B9 Langamull PA75
42 B43 Langar NG13
74 C19 Langbank PA14
57 D36 Langbar LS29
56 C34 Langcliffe BD24
63 G45 Langdale End YO13
4 A18 Langdon EX23
61 C34 Langdon Beck DL12
24 C52 Langdon Hills SS16
5 C25 Langdon House EX7
82 G29 Langdyke KY8
34 G56 Langenhoe CO5
32 D47 Langford *Bfd.* SG18
7 E25 Langford *Dev.* EX15
24 A54 Langford *Esx* CM9
52 G44 Langford *Not.* NG23
21 A38 Langford *Oxf.* GL7
7 C26 Langford Budville TA21
32 C47 Langford End SG19

Langham

Llangynog

Marrel

85 A10 Lower Ollach IV51
18 D27 Lower Penarth CF64
40 F34 Lower Penn WV4
10 E39 Lower Pennington SO41
49 E33 Lower Peover WA16
30 D37 Lower Quinton CV37
20 C35 Lower Seagry SN15
32 D45 Lower Shelton MK43
22 D43 Lower Shiplake RG9
31 B40 Lower Shuckburgh NN11
30 F37 Lower Slaughter GL54
20 C35 Lower Stanton St Quintin SN14
24 D54 Lower Stoke ME3
32 E47 Lower Stondon SG16
13 E52 Lower Street TN33
32 F46 Lower Sundon LU5
11 D40 Lower Swanwick SO31
30 F37 Lower Swell GL54
40 B35 Lower Tean ST10
45 F60 Lower Thurlton NR14
55 D30 Lower Thurnham LA2
16 A15 Lower Town *Dyf.* SA65
2 A11 Lower Town *I.o.S.* TR25
30 D39 Lower Tysoe CV35
11 C41 Lower Upham SO32
7 B27 Lower Vexford TA4
38 E29 Lower Wallop SY5
48 D31 Lower Walton WA4
19 F30 Lower Weare BS26
28 C28 Lower Welson HR3
49 E32 Lower Whitley WA4
21 G42 Lower Wield SO24
31 G43 Lower Winchendon HP18
49 F34 Lower Withington SK11
22 C44 Lower Woodend SL7
10 A37 Lower Woodford SP4
8 D31 Lower Wraxall DT2
29 D33 Lower Wyche WR14
42 E43 Lowesby LE7
45 F61 Lowestoft NR32
45 F61 Lowestoft End NR32
60 D27 Loweswater CA13
62 D37 Low Etherley DL14
13 C48 Lowfield Heath RH11
70 G35 Low Gate NE46
61 G32 Lowgill *Cum.* LA8
56 C32 Lowgill *Lan.* LA2
29 A33 Low Habberley DY11
8 B30 Low Ham TA10
63 F45 Low Hawkser YO22
61 G32 Low Haygarth LA10
60 B30 Low Hesket CA4
71 D36 Low Hesleyhurst NE65
58 C43 Low Hutton YO6
55 A28 Lowick *Cum.* LA12
42 G45 Lowick *Nmp.* NN14
77 G35 Lowick *Nor.* TD15
57 C37 Low Laithe HG3
49 D35 Low Leighton SK12
58 B44 Low Marishes YO17
63 G42 Low Mill YO6
56 E32 Low Moor BB7
71 A38 Low Newton-by-the-Sea NE66
83 C30 Lownie Moor DD8
62 C36 Low Redford DL13
52 A45 Low Risby DN15
70 G31 Low Row *Cum.* CA8
62 G35 Low Row *N.Y.* DL11
52 A45 Low Santon DN15
30 B37 Lowsonford B95
73 D15 Low Stillaig PA21
45 C59 Low Street NR12
61 D31 Lowther CA10
61 D31 Lowther Castle CA10
59 D46 Lowthorpe YO25
48 C31 Lowton WA3
49 C32 Lowton Common WA3
75 B26 Low Torry KY12
53 E48 Low Toynton LN9
75 E23 Low Waters ML3
55 A29 Low Wood LA12
62 E39 Low Worsall TS15
7 D24 Loxbeare EX16
12 C46 Loxhill GU8
6 B22 Loxhore EX31
30 C38 Loxley CV35
19 F29 Loxton BS26
12 C46 Loxwood RH14
96 B19 Lubachoinnich IV24
96 A19 Lubcroy IV27
42 G43 Lubenham LE16
96 D19 Lubfearn IV23
95 F16 Lubmore IV22
81 C20 Lubreoch PH15
7 A25 Luccombe TA24
11 G41 Luccombe Village PO37
77 G37 Lucker NE70
4 C19 Luckett PL17
20 C34 Luckington SN14
82 E29 Lucklawhill KY16
7 B24 Luckwell Bridge TA24
28 B30 Lucton HR6
84 C3 Ludag HS8
53 C48 Ludborough DN36
16 C17 Ludchurch SA67
57 G36 Luddenden HX2
25 E55 Luddenham Court ME13
24 E52 Luddesdown DA13
52 A44 Luddington *Hum.* DN17
30 C37 Luddington *War.* CV37
42 G46 Luddington in the Brook PE8
28 A31 Ludford SY8
53 D48 Ludford Magna LN3
52 D47 Ludford Parva LN3
31 G42 Ludgershall *Bkh.* HP18
21 F38 Ludgershall *Wts.* SP11
2 E10 Ludgvan TR20
45 D59 Ludham NR29
28 A30 Ludlow SY8
53 C49 Ludney LN11
29 E32 Ludstock HR8
9 B34 Ludwell SP7
62 B39 Ludworth DH6
4 A18 Luffincott EX22
76 B30 Luffness EH32
67 A21 Lugar KA18
75 C23 Luggiebank G67
74 E20 Lugton KA3
28 D31 Lugwardine HR1
86 B11 Luib IV49
80 A18 Luibeilt PH30
28 D29 Lulham HR2
40 D38 Lullington *Dby.* DE12
20 F33 Lullington *Som.* BA11
19 E30 Lulsgate Bottom BS18
29 C33 Lulsley WR6
9 F34 Lulworth Camp BH20
57 G36 Lumb HX6
56 G35 Lumbutts OL14
57 F40 Lumby LS25
90 C31 Lumphanan AB31
75 A27 Lumphinnans KY4
77 D34 Lumsdaine TD14
90 A30 Lumsden AB54
83 B32 Lunan DD11
83 B30 Lunanhead DD8
82 E26 Luncarty PH1
59 E45 Lund *Hum.* YO25
58 F42 Lund *N.Y.* YO8
106 B41 Lund *She.* ZE2
80 A16 Lundavra PH33
99 E37 Lunderton AB42
87 C17 Lundie *Hgh.* IV3
82 D28 Lundie *Tay.* DD2
82 G29 Lundin Links KY8
79 G13 Lunga PA31
107 A40 Lunna ZE2
107 A41 Lunning ZE2
14 F53 Lunsford's Cross TN39
48 B29 Lunt L29
28 C29 Luntley HR6
7 E27 Luppitt EX14
55 A31 Lupton LA6
109 E7 Lurgan BT66
12 D45 Lurgashall GU28
80 B15 Lurignich PA38
53 F49 Lusby PE23
74 A19 Luss G83
72 B12 Lussagiven PA60
93 F8 Lusta IV55
7 G23 Lustleigh TQ13
28 B30 Luston HR6
91 G32 Luthermuir AB30
82 F29 Luthrie KY15
32 F46 Luton *Bfd.* LU
7 E26 Luton *Dev.* EX14
5 C24 Luton *Dev.* TQ13
24 E53 Luton *Kent* ME5
32 F47 Luton Airport LU2
41 G41 Lutterworth LE17
5 E21 Lutton *Dev.* PL21
43 C50 Lutton *Lcn.* PE12
42 G47 Lutton *Nmp.* PE8
7 B25 Luxborough TA23
4 E16 Luxulyan PL30
103 B26 Lybster *Hgh.* KW14
103 E28 Lybster *Hgh.* KW3
6 E20 Lydacott EX21
38 G29 Lydbury North SY7
6 B22 Lydcott EX32
15 E56 Lydd TN29
15 E56 Lydd Airport TN29
15 C58 Lydden CT15
42 F44 Lyddington LE15
15 E56 Lydd-on-Sea TN29
7 B27 Lydeard St Lawrence TA4
6 G20 Lydford EX20
8 A31 Lydford-on-Fosse TA11
56 G35 Lydgate OL14
38 F29 Lydham SY9
20 C36 Lydiard Millicent SN5
48 B29 Lydiate L31
9 C33 Lydlinch DT10
19 A32 Lydney GL15
16 E16 Lydstep SA70
40 G35 Lye DY9
22 A45 Lye Green HP5
21 B39 Lyford OX12
15 C56 Lymbridge Green TN25
74 E22 Lymekilns G74
8 E29 Lyme Regis DT7
15 C57 Lyminge CT18
10 E38 Lymington SO41
12 F45 Lyminster BN17
49 D32 Lymm WA13
10 E39 Lymore SO41
15 D57 Lympne CT21
19 F29 Lympsham BS24
7 G25 Lympstone EX8
88 E23 Lynaberack PH21
88 D23 Lynchat PH21
10 D39 Lyndhurst SO43
42 E44 Lyndon LE15
91 C33 Lyne *Grm.* AB51
22 E45 Lyne *Sry* KT16
38 B30 Lyneal SY12
93 F9 Lynedale Ho IV51
103 C28 Lynegar KW1
30 F38 Lyneham *Oxf.* OX7
20 C36 Lyneham *Wts.* SN15
69 F30 Lyneholmeford CA6
89 B26 Lynemore PH26
71 D38 Lynemouth NE61
88 B20 Lyne of Gorthleck IV1
91 B33 Lyne of Skene AB32
105 B28 Lyness KW16
44 F54 Lynford IP26
44 D56 Lyng *Nfk* NR9
8 B29 Lyng *Som.* TA3
7 A23 Lynmouth EX35
25 E55 Lynsted ME9
7 A23 Lynton EX35
9 D32 Lyon's Gate DT2
28 C29 Lyonshall HR5
72 D8 Lyrabus PA44
9 E35 Lytchett Matravers BH16
9 E35 Lytchett Minster BH16
103 B28 Lyth KW1
55 G29 Lytham FY8
55 G28 Lytham St Anne's FY8
63 E44 Lythe YO21
12 C45 Lythe Hill GU27
105 C30 Lythes KW17
103 B26 Lythmore KW14

M

2 E13 Mabe Burnthouse TR10
65 C25 Mabie DG2
53 D51 Mablethorpe LN12
49 E35 Macclesfield SK11
49 E35 Macclesfield Forest SK11
98 C32 Macduff AB44
75 E23 Machan ML9
81 F24 Machany PH3
66 C13 Macharioch PA28
18 C27 Machen NP1
73 G14 Machrie *Str.* KA27
72 F9 Machrie *Str.* PA42
66 A12 Machrihanish PA28
72 A9 Machrins PA61
37 E23 Machynlleth SY20
40 B38 Mackworth DE22
76 C30 Macmerry EH33
109 B6 Macosquin BT51
99 E33 Macterry AB53
82 E25 Madderty PH7
75 C25 Maddiston FK2
12 E45 Madehurst BN18
39 E33 Madeley *Shr.* TF7
39 A33 Madeley *Stf.* CW3
39 A33 Madeley Heath CW3
7 D27 Madford EX15
33 C49 Madingley CB3
9 B34 Madjeston SP8
28 E30 Madley HR2
29 D33 Madresfield WR13
2 E10 Madron TR20
46 D20 Maenaddwyn LL77
16 B16 Maenclochog SA66
18 D25 Maendy CF7
37 A22 Maentwrog LL41
39 B33 Maer ST5
37 A26 Maerdy *Clw.* LL21
17 B22 Maerdy *Dyf.* SA19
19 A29 Maerdy *Gwe.* NP7
18 B25 Maerdy *M.G.* CF43
38 C28 Maesbrook SY22
38 C28 Maesbury Marsh SY10
19 C28 Maes-glas NP9
16 B17 Maesgwynne SA34
47 F27 Maeshafn CH7
26 D19 Maesllyn SA44
27 D25 Maesmynis LD2
18 B24 Maesteg CF34
28 B28 Maes-Treylow LD8
17 C21 Maesybont SA14
26 D20 Maesycrugiau SA39
18 B27 Maes-y-cwmmer CF8
23 A51 Magdalen Laver CM5
98 E28 Maggieknockater AB38
13 E51 Magham Down BN27
109 F8 Maghera *Down* BT31
109 D6 Maghera *Ldy* BT46
109 D6 Magherafelt BT45
109 E7 Magheralin BT67
109 E7 Maghery BT71
48 B29 Maghull L31
19 C30 Magor NP6
108 F4 Maguiresbridge BT94
9 A34 Maiden Bradley BA12
5 D25 Maidencombe TQ1
22 C44 Maidenhead SL6
62 A37 Maiden Law DH7
8 E31 Maiden Newton DT2
67 C17 Maidens KA26
22 D45 Maiden's Green RG12
4 C17 Maidenwell *Cnw.* PL30
53 E49 Maidenwell *Lcn.* LN11
16 E15 Maiden Wells SA71
31 C41 Maidford NN12
31 E43 Maids' Moreton MK18
14 B53 Maidstone ME14
31 A43 Maidwell NN6
107 E40 Mail ZE2
83 D31 Mains of Ardestie DD5
83 A30 Mains of Balhall DD9
82 B29 Mains of Ballindarg DD8
97 F26 Mains of Burgie IV36
99 E34 Mains of Culsh AB53
91 E33 Mains of Dillavaird AB30
91 C34 Mains of Drum AB31
99 F35 Mains of Dudwick AB41
88 A22 Mains of Faillie IV1
99 E34 Mains of Fedderate AB42
90 B29 Mains of Glenbuchat AB36
91 C32 Mains of Linton AB51
83 B31 Mains of Melgund DD9
99 E35 Mains of Pitfour AB42
91 A34 Mains of Pittrichie AB2
97 F25 Mains of Sluie IV36
98 C29 Mains of Tannachy AB56
91 F32 Mains of Thornton AB30
66 E16 Mains of Tig KA26
103 C28 Mains of Watten KW1
65 E25 Mainsriddle DG2
38 G28 Mainstone SY9
29 F33 Maisemore GL2
70 C33 Makendon NE65
76 G32 Makerstoun TD5
92 D3 Malacleit HS6
5 G23 Malborough TQ7
23 E48 Malden KT4
22 E47 Malden Rushett KT9
24 A54 Maldon CM9
56 C34 Malham BD23
93 E10 Maligar IV51
86 E12 Mallaig PH41
86 E12 Mallaigmore PH41
86 E12 Mallaigvaig PH41
75 D27 Malleny Mills EH14
74 E20 Malletsheugh G77
81 G21 Malling FK8
46 F19 Malltraeth LL62
37 D24 Mallwyd SY20
20 C35 Malmesbury SN16
7 A23 Malmsmead EX35
38 A30 Malpas *Che.* SY14
3 D14 Malpas *Cnw.* TR1
19 B28 Malpas *Gwe.* NP9
62 E40 Maltby *Cle.* TS8
51 C41 Maltby *S.Y.* S66
53 D50 Maltby le Marsh LN13
14 C54 Maltman's Hill TN27
58 B43 Malton YO17
29 D33 Malvern Link WR14
29 D33 Malvern Wells WR14
74 B18 Mambeg G84
29 A32 Mamble DY14
7 G25 Mamhead EX6
2 F13 Manaccan TR12
38 E27 Manafon SY21
92 C6 Manais HS3
7 G23 Manaton TQ13
53 D50 Manby LN11
40 F38 Mancetter CV9
49 C34 Manchester M
48 F29 Mancot Royal CH5
87 D18 Mandally PH35
43 G50 Manea PE15
67 C21 Maneight KA18
62 E37 Manfield DL2
106 E39 Mangaster ZE2
19 D32 Mangotsfield BS16
100 D6 Mangurstadh HS2
56 G35 Mankinholes OL14
48 E30 Manley WA6
18 A27 Manmoel NP2
78 C5 Mannel PA77
20 F37 Manningford Abbots SN9
20 F37 Manningford Bohune SN9
20 E37 Manningford Bruce SN9
13 D48 Mannings Heath RH13
10 D36 Mannington BH21
34 E56 Manningtree CO11
91 C34 Mannofield AB1
16 E16 Manorbier SA70
26 D18 Manordeifi SA43
17 B22 Manordeilo SA19
16 A14 Manorowen SA65
28 D29 Mansell Gamage HR4
28 D30 Mansell Lacy HR4
55 A31 Mansergh LA6
51 F41 Mansfield NG18
51 F41 Mansfield Woodhouse NG19
55 A28 Mansriggs LA12
9 C33 Manston *Dor.* DT10
25 E59 Manston *Kent* CT12
25 E59 Manston Airport CT12
9 D35 Manswood BH21
42 B45 Manthorpe *Lcn.* NG31
42 D46 Manthorpe *Lcn.* PE10
52 B45 Manton *Hum.* DN21
42 E44 Manton *Lei.* LE15
20 E37 Manton *Wts.* SN8
33 F50 Manuden CM23
79 F14 Maolachy PA35
9 B32 Maperton BA9
51 F42 Maplebeck NG22
22 B46 Maple Cross WD3
21 D42 Mapledurham RG4
21 F42 Mapledurwell RG25
12 D47 Maplehurst RH13
40 A37 Mapleton DE6
41 A40 Mapperley DE7
8 E30 Mapperton DT8
30 B36 Mappleborough Green B80
59 E48 Mappleton HU18
51 B39 Mapplewell S75
9 D33 Mappowder DT10
2 E11 Marazion TR17
38 A31 Marbury SY13
43 F50 March PE15
21 B40 Marcham OX13
38 C31 Marchamley SY4
40 B37 Marchington ST14
40 C37 Marchington Woodlands ST14
38 A29 Marchwiel LL13
10 C39 Marchwood S040
18 E24 Marcross CF61
83 B30 Marcus DD8
28 D31 Marden *H.&W.* HR1
14 C53 Marden *Kent* TN12
71 F39 Marden *T.&W.* NE30
20 F36 Marden *Wts.* SN10
14 C53 Marden Beech TN12
14 C53 Marden Thorn TN12
28 G28 Mardy NP7
42 E43 Marefield LE15
8 B29 Mare Green TA3
53 F48 Mareham le Fen PE22
53 F48 Mareham on the Hill LN9
13 D50 Maresfield TN22
59 G47 Marfleet HU9
48 G29 Marford LL12
18 C23 Margam SA13
9 C34 Margaret Marsh SP7
33 G51 Margaret Roding CM6
24 A52 Margaretting CM4
25 D59 Margate CT9
73 G16 Margnaheglish KA27
65 C24 Margreig DG2
63 E42 Margrove Park TS12
44 E53 Marham PE33
6 E18 Marhamchurch EX23
42 E47 Marholm PE6
47 E26 Marian Cwm LL18
46 D20 Marian-glas LL78
7 C23 Mariansleigh EX36
93 E10 Marishader IV51
4 D20 Maristow PL6
19 G29 Mark TA9
23 G50 Markbeech TN8
53 E50 Markby LN13
19 G29 Mark Causeway TA9
13 C51 Mark Cross TN6
64 C17 Markdhu DG8
41 E39 Market Bosworth CV13
42 D47 Market Deeping PE6
39 B32 Market Drayton TF9
42 G43 Market Harborough LE16
109 F7 Markethill *Arm.* BT61
82 D28 Markethill *Tay.* PH13
20 F36 Market Lavington SN10
42 D44 Market Overton LE15
52 D47 Market Rasen LN8
53 D48 Market Stainton LN3
45 C58 Market Street NR12
58 E44 Market Weighton YO4
34 A55 Market Weston IP22
41 D40 Markfield LE67
18 A27 Markham NP2
51 E42 Markham Moor DN22
82 G28 Markinch KY7
57 C38 Markington HG3
19 E32 Marksbury BA2
23 B50 Marks Gate RM6
34 F54 Marks Tey CO6
4 E19 Markwell PL12
32 G46 Markyate AL3
20 D37 Marlborough SN8
5 D24 Marldon TQ3
35 C59 Marlesford IP13
38 A31 Marley Green SY13
62 A37 Marley Hill NE16
45 E57 Marlingford NR9
89 E26 Mar Lodge AB35
16 D13 Marloes SA62
22 C44 Marlow SL7
23 G50 Marlpit Hill TN8
41 A40 Marlpool DE75
9 C33 Marnhull DT10
98 D31 Marnoch AB54
49 D35 Marple SK6
51 B41 Marr DN5
103 G26 Marrel KW8

Marrick

62 G36 Marrick DL11
107 A41 Marrister ZE2
16 D17 Marros SA33
71 G39 Marsden *T.&W.* SR6
50 A36 Marsden *W.Y.* HD7
56 A34 Marsett DL8
8 C28 Marsh EX14
32 G47 Marshall's Heath AL4
8 D29 Marshalsea DT6
45 C57 Marsham NR10
55 D31 Marshaw LA2
21 B41 Marsh Baldon OX44
15 B58 Marshborough CT13
38 G30 Marshbrook SY6
53 C49 Marsh Chapel DN36
20 D33 Marshfield *Avon* SN14
19 C28 Marshfield *Gwe.* CF3
4 A17 Marshgate PL32
31 F42 Marsh Gibbon OX6
7 F26 Marsh Green *Dev.* EX5
23 G50 Marsh Green *Kent* TN8
39 D32 Marsh Green *Shr.* TF6
51 E39 Marsh Lane S31
48 A29 Marshside PR9
7 A25 Marsh Street TA24
8 E29 Marshwood DT6
62 F36 Marske DL11
63 D41 Marske-by-the-Sea TS11
49 E32 Marston *Che.* CW9
28 C29 Marston *H.&W.* HR6
42 A44 Marston *Lcn.* NG32
21 A41 Marston *Oxf.* OX3
40 C35 Marston *Stf.* ST18
40 D34 Marston *Stf.* ST20
40 F38 Marston *War.* B76
20 F35 Marston *Wts.* SN10
40 G37 Marston Green B37
8 B31 Marston Magna BA22
20 B37 Marston Meysey SN6
40 B37 Marston Montgomery DE6
32 D45 Marston Moretaine MK43
40 B38 Marston on Dove DE65
28 C31 Marston Stannett HR6
31 D41 Marston St Lawrence OX17
41 G42 Marston Trussell LE16
28 G31 Marstow HR9
32 G44 Marsworth HP23
21 E38 Marten SN8
49 E34 Marthall WA16
45 D60 Martham NR29
100 F10 Marthig HS2
10 C36 Martin *Ham.* SP6
52 F47 Martin *Lcn.* LN4
10 B36 Martin Drove End SP6
6 A22 Martinhoe EX31
29 B34 Martin Hussingtree WR3
49 D32 Martinscroft WA1
9 F32 Martinstown DT2
35 D58 Martlesham IP12
35 D58 Martlesham Heath IP5
16 C16 Martletwy SA67
29 B33 Martley WR6
8 C30 Martock TA12
49 F34 Marton *Che.* SK11
63 E41 Marton *Cle.* TS7
55 B28 Marton *Cum.* LA12
59 F47 Marton *Hum.* HU11
52 D44 Marton *Lcn.* DN21
57 C40 Marton *N.Y.* YO5
58 A43 Marton *N.Y.* YO6
38 E28 Marton *Shr.* SY21
31 B40 Marton *War.* CV23
58 C41 Marton Abbey YO6
57 B39 Marton-le-Moor HG4
22 F46 Martyr's Green KT11
11 A41 Martyr Worthy SO21
100 G7 Maruig HS3
104 D28 Marwick KW17
6 B21 Marwood EX31
96 F20 Marybank IV6
96 F21 Maryburgh IV7
107 C40 Maryfield ZE2
77 D33 Marygold TD11
99 E34 Maryhill *Grm.* AB53
74 D21 Maryhill *Str.* G20
91 G32 Marykirk AB30
23 C48 Marylebone *G.L.* W1M
48 B31 Marylebone *G.M.* WN1
60 C26 Maryport *Cum.* CA15
64 G17 Maryport *D.&G.* DG9
6 G20 Marystow PL16
4 C20 Mary Tavy PL19
83 B32 Maryton DD10
91 D35 Marywell *Grm.* AB1
90 D31 Marywell *Grm.* AB34
83 C32 Marywell *Tay.* DD11
57 A38 Masham HG4
33 G52 Mashbury CM1
91 C34 Mastrick AB2
33 G51 Matching CM17
33 G51 Matching Green CM17
33 G51 Matching Tye CM17
71 F36 Matfen NE20
23 G52 Matfield TN12
19 B31 Mathern NP6
29 D33 Mathon WR13
16 A14 Mathry SA62
45 B57 Matlaske NR11
50 F38 Matlock DE4
50 F38 Matlock Bank DE4
50 G38 Matlock Bath DE4
29 G34 Matson GL4
60 D29 Matterdale End CA11
51 D42 Mattersey DN10
22 F43 Mattingley RG27
44 D56 Mattishall NR20
44 D56 Mattishall Burgh NR20
67 A20 Mauchline KA5
99 E35 Maud AB42
30 F37 Maugersbury GL54
54 D26 Maughold IM7
88 A19 Mauld IV4
32 E46 Maulden MK45
61 E32 Maulds Meaburn CA16
57 A39 Maunby YO7
28 C31 Maund Bryan HR1
7 C26 Maundown TA4
45 D60 Mautby NR29
40 D36 Mavesyn Ridware WS15
53 F49 Mavis Enderby PE23
60 B26 Mawbray CA15
48 A30 Mawdesley L40
18 C23 Mawdlam CF33
2 F12 Mawgan TR12
40 F36 Maw Green WS1
2 D12 Mawla TR16
2 F13 Mawnan TR11
2 F13 Mawnan Smith TR11
42 E47 Maxey PE6
40 G38 Maxstoke B46
70 A31 Maxton *Bor.* TD6
15 C58 Maxton *Kent* CT17
76 G32 Maxwellheugh TD5
65 C25 Maxwelltown DG2
4 A18 Maxworthy PL15
67 C19 Maybole KA19
98 E31 Mayen AB54
13 D51 Mayfield *E.S.* TN20
76 D29 Mayfield *Ltn* EH22
40 A37 Mayfield *Stf.* DE6
22 F45 Mayford GU22
24 A54 Mayland CM3
24 A54 Maylandsea CM3
13 E51 Maynard's Green TN21
2 A11 Maypole *I.o.S.* TR21
25 E57 Maypole *Kent* CT3
45 F60 Maypole Green NR14
107 E39 Maywick ZE2
93 B7 Meabhag HS3
10 B36 Mead End SP5
22 A43 Meadle HP17
76 C29 Meadowmill EH33
38 E28 Meadowtown SY5
100 B9 Mealabost HS2
100 E6 Mealasta HS2
61 G31 Meal Bank LA9
53 C50 Meals LN11
60 B27 Mealsgate CA5
56 D33 Meanley BB7
56 C34 Mearbeck BD23
19 G30 Meare BA6
74 E21 Mearns G77
32 B44 Mears Ashby NN6
41 D39 Measham DE12
55 A30 Meathop LA11
5 D21 Meavy PL20
42 F43 Medbourne LE16
6 D18 Meddon EX39
51 F41 Meden Vale NG20
22 C44 Medmenham SL7
62 A37 Medomsley DH8
11 A42 Medstead GU34
49 F35 Meerbrook ST13
30 A38 Meer End CV8
33 E50 Meesden SG9
6 E21 Meeth EX20
69 A27 Meggethead TD7
17 B18 Meidrim SA33
47 G26 Meifod *Clw.* LL16
38 D27 Meifod *Pow.* SY22
82 C28 Meigle PH12
74 E22 Meikle Earnock ML3
73 D16 Meikle Grenach PA20
73 D16 Meikle Kilmory PA20
82 D27 Meikleour PH2
74 B18 Meikle Rahane G84
91 F32 Meikle Strath AB30
91 A35 Meikle Tarty AB41
99 F33 Meikle Wartle AB51
17 C20 Meinciau SA17
40 A35 Meir ST3
40 B35 Meirheath ST3
100 D10 Melbost HS2
33 D49 Melbourn SG8
41 C39 Melbourne *Dby.* DE73
58 E43 Melbourne *Hum.* YO4
6 D19 Melbury EX39
9 C34 Melbury Abbas SP7
8 D31 Melbury Bubb DT2
8 D31 Melbury Osmond DT2
8 D31 Melbury Sampford DT2
107 B37 Melby ZE2
32 B46 Melchbourne MK44
10 B38 Melchet Court SO51
9 D33 Melcombe Bingham DT2
9 F32 Melcombe Regis DT4
6 F21 Meldon *Dev.* EX20
71 E37 Meldon *Nor.* NE61
33 D49 Meldreth SG8
79 F14 Melfort PA34
88 E20 Melgarve PH20
90 C30 Melgum AB34
47 D26 Meliden LL19
18 A23 Melincourt SA11
18 B23 Melincryddan SA11
47 F23 Melin-y-coed LL26
37 E26 Melin-y-ddol SY21
37 E26 Melin-y-grug SY21
37 A26 Melin-y-Wig LL21
61 D31 Melkinthorpe CA10
70 G33 Melkridge NE49
20 E34 Melksham SN12
20 E35 Melksham Forest SN12
73 C15 Melldalloch PA21
55 B31 Melling *Lan.* LA6
48 B29 Melling *Mer.* L31
48 B30 Melling Mount L31
34 A56 Mellis IP23
94 B14 Mellon Charles IV22
94 B14 Mellon Udrigle IV22
49 D35 Mellor *G.M.* SK6
56 F32 Mellor *Lan.* BB2
56 F32 Mellor Brook BB2
20 G33 Mells BA11
61 C32 Melmerby *Cum.* CA10
57 A36 Melmerby *N.Y.* DL8
57 B39 Melmerby *N.Y.* HG4
8 E30 Melplash DT6
76 G31 Melrose *Bor.* TD6
99 C33 Melrose *Grm.* AB45
105 C28 Melsetter KW16
62 F37 Melsonby DL10
50 A37 Meltham HD7
35 C58 Melton IP12
58 D43 Meltonby YO4
44 B56 Melton Constable NR24
42 D43 Melton Mowbray LE13
52 B46 Melton Ross DN38
94 C13 Melvaig IV21
38 D29 Melverley SY22
38 D29 Melverley Green SY22
102 B24 Melvich KW14
8 D28 Membury EX13
99 C35 Memsie AB43
83 B30 Memus DD8
4 E16 Menabilly PL24
46 E21 Menai Bridge LL59
45 G58 Mendham IP20
34 B56 Mendlesham IP14
34 B56 Mendlesham Green IP14
58 C43 Menethorpe YO17
4 D18 Menheniot PL14
91 A35 Menie Ho. AB23
68 C24 Mennock DG4
57 E37 Menston LS29
75 A24 Menstrie FK11
32 G44 Mentmore LU7
86 F13 Meoble PH40
38 D30 Meole Brace SY3
11 D41 Meon PO14
11 C42 Meonstoke SO32
24 E52 Meopham DA13
24 E52 Meopham Green DA13
43 G50 Mepal CB6
32 E47 Meppershall SG17
28 D28 Merbach HR3
40 A38 Mercaston DE6
49 D33 Mere *Che.* WA16
9 A34 Mere *Wts.* BA12
48 A30 Mere Brow PR9
40 F36 Mere Green B75
23 F52 Mereworth ME18
91 E33 Mergie AB3
40 G38 Meriden CV7
65 C23 Merkland DG7
16 C15 Merlin's Bridge SA61
7 B27 Merridge TA5
5 F24 Merrifield TQ7
38 C30 Merrington SY4
16 E15 Merrion SA71
8 C30 Merriott TA16
5 C21 Merrivale PL19
22 F46 Merrow GU1
22 B47 Merry Hill WD2
4 D18 Merrymeet PL14
15 D56 Mersham TN25
23 F48 Merstham RH1
12 F44 Merston PO20
11 F40 Merstone PO30
3 D14 Merther TR2
17 B19 Merthyr SA33
27 E25 Merthyr Cynog LD3
18 E26 Merthyr Dyfan CF62
18 D24 Merthyr Mawr CF32
18 A26 Merthyr Tydfil CF47
18 B26 Merthyr Vale CF48
6 D21 Merton *Dev.* EX20
23 E48 Merton *G.L.* SW
44 F54 Merton *Nfk* IP25
31 G41 Merton *Oxf.* OX6
47 E27 Mertyn CH8
70 B32 Mervinslaw TD8
7 D23 Meshaw EX36
34 G54 Messing CO5
52 B44 Messingham DN17
45 G58 Metfield IP20
52 F46 Metheringham LN4
76 A29 Methil KY8
36 B17 Methlem LL53
57 G39 Methley LS26
99 F34 Methlick AB41
82 E26 Methven PH1
44 F53 Methwold IP26
44 F53 Methwold Hythe IP26
45 G59 Mettingham NR35
45 B57 Metton NR11
4 F16 Mevagissey PL26
51 C40 Mexborough S64
103 A28 Mey KW14
20 B36 Meysey Hampton GL7
100 G6 Miabhag HS3
100 D6 Miabhig HS2
94 D13 Mial IV21
28 F31 Michaelchurch HR2
28 E28 Michaelchurch Escley HR2
28 C28 Michaelchurch-on-Arrow HR5
18 D27 Michaelston-le-Pit CF64
19 C28 Michaelston-y-Fedw CF3
4 C16 Michaelstow PL30
11 A41 Micheldever SO21
10 B39 Michelmersh SO51
35 B57 Mickfield IP14
63 E43 Mickleby TS13
22 F47 Mickleham RH5
49 B35 Micklehurst OL5
40 B38 Mickleover DE3
60 A28 Micklethwaite CA7
61 D35 Mickleton *Drm* DL12
30 D37 Mickleton *Glo.* GL55
57 G39 Mickletown LS26
48 F30 Mickle Trafford CH3
57 B38 Mickley HG4
71 G36 Mickley Square NE43
99 C35 Mid Ardlaw AB43
104 B30 Midbea KW17
90 C31 Mid Beltie AB31
90 F30 Mid Cairncross DD9
75 D26 Mid Calder EH53
103 E28 Mid Clyth KW3
22 C43 Middle Assendon RG9
31 F40 Middle Aston OX6
31 F40 Middle Barton OX7
69 F27 Middlebie DG11
31 F43 Middle Claydon MK18
83 B31 Middle Drums DD9
57 A36 Middleham DL8
51 E40 Middle Handley S31
44 G55 Middle Harling NR16
4 D18 Middlehill *Cnw.* PL14
99 E34 Middlehill *Grm.* AB53
38 G30 Middlehope SY7
73 B14 Middle Kames PA31
30 D36 Middle Littleton WR11
28 E29 Middle Maes-coed HR2
9 D32 Middlemarsh DT9
16 B14 Middle Mill SA62
52 D46 Middle Rasen LN8
82 G26 Middle Rigg PH2
56 C32 Middle Salter LA2
62 D40 Middlesbrough TS1
55 A31 Middleshaw LA8
57 B36 Middlesmoor HG3
62 C38 Middlestone Moor DL16
50 A38 Middlestown WF4
63 C41 Middleton *Cle.* TS24
56 A32 Middleton *Cum.* LA6
50 G38 Middleton *Dby.* DE4
50 F38 Middleton *Dby.* DE45
34 E54 Middleton *Esx* CO10
49 B34 Middleton *G.M.* M24
91 B34 Middleton *Grm.* AB2
21 G40 Middleton *Ham.* SP11
55 D30 Middleton *Lan.* LA3
76 E29 Middleton *Ltn* EH23
58 A43 Middleton *N.Y.* YO18
44 D52 Middleton *Nfk* PE32
42 G44 Middleton *Nmp.* LE16
71 E36 Middleton *Nor.* NE61
77 G36 Middleton *Nor.* NE70
35 B60 Middleton *Sfk* IP17
38 C29 Middleton *Shr.* SY11
38 F28 Middleton *Shr.* SY15
28 A31 Middleton *Shr.* SY8
83 C31 Middleton *Tay.* DD11
82 G27 Middleton *Tay.* KY13
82 C27 Middleton *Tay.* PH10
17 F20 Middleton *W.G.* SA3
57 G39 Middleton *W.Y.* LS10
57 E37 Middleton *W.Y.* LS29
40 F37 Middleton *War.* B78
71 E36 Middleton Bank Top NE61
31 D40 Middleton Cheney OX17
40 B35 Middleton Green ST10
70 A35 Middleton Hall NE71
61 D34 Middleton-in-Teesdale DL12
91 B35 Middleton of Potterton AB23
62 E39 Middleton One Row DL2
62 E40 Middleton-on-Leven TS15
12 G45 Middleton-on-Sea PO22
28 B31 Middleton on the Hill SY8
59 D45 Middleton-on -the-Wolds YO25
91 B34 Middleton Park AB22
39 F32 Middleton Priors WV16
57 B39 Middleton Quernhow HG4
39 G32 Middleton Scriven WV16
62 E39 Middleton St George DL2
31 F41 Middleton Stoney OX6
62 F37 Middleton Tyas DL10
109 F6 Middletown *Arm.* BT60
60 F25 Middletown *Cum.* CA22
38 D28 Middletown *Pow.* SY21
2 A11 Middle Town TR25
30 D39 Middle Tysoe CV35
10 A38 Middle Wallop SO20
49 F33 Middlewich CW10
10 A38 Middle Winterslow SP5
49 D35 Middlewood SK12
10 A37 Middle Woodford SP4
34 B56 Middlewood Green IP14
74 G21 Middleyard KA4
8 A29 Middlezoy TA7
62 D38 Middridge DL4
102 B21 Midfield IV27
20 E33 Midford BA2
55 G31 Midge Hall PR5
61 A32 Midgeholme CA6
21 E41 Midgham RG7
57 G36 Midgley *W.Y.* HX7
50 A38 Midgley *W.Y.* WF4
50 C38 Midhopestones S30
12 D44 Midhurst GU29
12 F44 Mid Lavant PO18
70 A31 Midlem TD7
80 G16 Mid Letter PA27
81 E21 Mid Lix FK20
61 G34 Mid Mossdale DL8
73 E15 Midpark PA20
73 F16 Mid Sannox KA27
19 F32 Midsomer Norton BA3
94 C13 Midtown *Hgh.* IV22
102 B21 Midtown *Hgh.* IV27
91 E34 Midtown of Barras AB3
53 G49 Midville PE22
106 C40 Mid Yell ZE2
96 B22 Migdale IV24
90 C30 Migvie AB34
74 A20 Milarrochy G63
5 C24 Milber TQ12
98 D31 Milbethill AB54
9 C32 Milborne Port DT9
9 E34 Milborne St Andrew DT11
9 B32 Milborne Wick DT9
71 F36 Milbourne NE20
61 D32 Milburn CA10
19 C32 Milbury Heath GL12
30 E39 Milcombe OX15
34 D55 Milden IP7
34 A52 Mildenhall *Sfk* IP28
21 D38 Mildenhall *Wts.* SN8
28 A28 Milebrook LD7
14 C53 Milebush TN12
20 E35 Mile Elm SN11
34 F55 Mile End *Esx* CO4
28 G31 Mile End *Glo.* GL16
44 D55 Mileham PE32
75 B26 Milesmark KY12
77 G35 Milfield NE71
109 F6 Milford *Arm.* BT60
41 A39 Milford *Dby.* DE56
6 C18 Milford *Dev.* EX39
38 C30 Milford *Shr.* SY4
22 G45 Milford *Sry* GU8
40 C35 Milford *Stf.* ST17
16 D15 Milford Haven SA73
10 E38 Milford on Sea SO41
19 A31 Milkwall GL16
12 D44 Milland Marsh GU30
99 E36 Millbank AB42
57 G36 Mill Bank HX6
60 D28 Millbeck CA12
104 C31 Millbounds KW17
99 E35 Millbreck AB42
22 G44 Millbridge GU10
32 E45 Millbrook *Bfd.* MK45
4 E19 Millbrook *Cnw.* PL10
10 C39 Millbrook *Ham.* SO15
90 A31 Millburn *Grm.* AB33
98 F32 Millburn *Grm.* AB54
5 F24 Millcombe TQ9
14 E54 Millcorner TN31
91 B35 Millden AB23
83 B31 Milldens DD8
82 F25 Millearn PH3

Mungrisdale

22 C43 Mill End *Bkh.* RG9
33 E49 Mill End *Hfs.* SG9
33 F52 Mill End Green CM6
38 B31 Millenheath SY13
76 D29 Millerhill EH22
50 E37 Miller's Dale SK17
24 A52 Mill Green *Esx* CM4
39 C32 Mill Green *Shr.* TF9
23 B48 Mill Hill NW7
61 G31 Millholme LA8
60 C29 Millhouse *Cum.* CA7
73 D15 Millhouse *Str.* PA21
69 E26 Millhousebridge DG11
56 C32 Mill Houses LA2
74 D19 Millikenpark PA10
58 D44 Millington YO4
09 E9 Millisle BT22
22 F43 Mill Lane GU10
40 B34 Millmeece ST21
88 A19 Millness IV3
99 E33 Mill of Colp AB53
99 E35 Mill of Elrick AB41
81 F23 Mill of Fortune PH6
91 A34 Mill of Kingoodie AB51
91 D34 Mill of Monquich AB3
91 E34 Mill of Uras AB3
54 A27 Millom LA18
73 E17 Millport KA28
44 D56 Mill Street NR20
61 G32 Millthrop LA10
91 C34 Milltimber AB1
90 A31 Millton of Noth AB54
69 F29 Milltown *D.&G.* DG14
51 F39 Milltown *Dby.* S45
6 B21 Milltown *Dev.* EX31
90 B30 Milltown *Grm.* AB33
97 G25 Milltown *Hgh.* IV12
95 F19 Milltown *Hgh.* IV6
82 E26 Milltown of Aberdalgie PH2
98 E29 Milltown of Auchindown AB55
91 C32 Milltown of Campfield AB31
99 D33 Milltown of Craigston AB53
98 E28 Milltown of Edinvillie AB38
98 E31 Milltown of Rothiemay AB54
90 B30 Milltown of Towie AB33
82 G26 Milnathort KY13
74 C21 Milngavie G62
49 A35 Milnrow OL16
50 A37 Milnsbridge HD4
55 A30 Milnthorpe LA7
93 F7 Milovaig IV55
74 G21 Milrig KA4
29 A32 Milson DY14
14 B54 Milstead ME9
20 G37 Milston SP4
19 E29 Milton *Avon* BS22
33 B50 Milton *Cbs.* CB4
81 G21 Milton *Cen.* FK17
81 G20 Milton *Cen.* FK8
74 A20 Milton *Cen.* G63
70 G31 Milton *Cum.* CA8
65 C24 Milton *D.&G.* DG2
68 E24 Milton *D.&G.* DG2
41 C39 Milton *Dby.* DE65
16 D16 Milton *Dyf.* SA70
98 C31 Milton *Grm.* AB56
19 C29 Milton *Gwe.* NP9
97 F25 Milton *Hgh.* IV12
96 D23 Milton *Hgh.* IV18
88 A20 Milton *Hgh.* IV3
94 G12 Milton *Hgh.* IV54
96 G21 Milton *Hgh.* IV6
03 C29 Milton *Hgh.* KW1
51 E42 Milton *Not.* NG22
21 B40 Milton *Oxf.* OX14
31 E40 Milton *Oxf.* OX15
49 G35 Milton *Stf.* ST2
74 C20 Milton *Str.* G82
82 C29 Milton *Tay.* DD8
82 D25 Milton *Tay.* PH8
9 D34 Milton Abbas DT11
4 C19 Milton Abbot PL19
76 D28 Milton Bridge EH26
32 E45 Milton Bryan MK17
9 A32 Milton Clevedon BA4
99 F35 Milton Coldwells AB41
4 D20 Milton Combe PL20
6 D19 Milton Damerel EX22
97 E27 Miltonduff IV30
32 C46 Milton Ernest MK44
48 G30 Milton Green CH3
97 E26 Miltonhill IV36
21 B40 Milton Hill OX13
91 A33 Milton Inveramsay AB51
64 C17 Miltonise DG8
32 E44 Milton Keynes MK
32 E44 Milton Keynes Village MK10
20 E37 Milton Lilbourne SN9
75 F24 Milton Lockhart ML8
31 C43 Milton Malsor NN7
81 D21 Milton Morenish FK21
90 C31 Milton of Auchinhove AB31
82 G29 Milton of Balgonie KY7
98 E30 Milton of Cairnborrow AB54
74 C22 Milton of Campsie G65
91 C33 Milton of Cullerlie AB32
90 B30 Milton of Cushnie AB33
82 B25 Milton of Dalcapon PH16
90 D29 Milton of Tullich AB35
9 B33 Milton on Stour SP8
24 E54 Milton Regis ME10
30 G38 Milton-under-Wychwood OX7
7 C27 Milverton TA4
40 B35 Milwich ST18
73 A15 Minard PA32
73 A15 Minard Castle PA32
9 C35 Minchington DT11
20 A34 Minchinhampton GL6
77 G34 Mindrum TD12
7 A25 Minehead TA24
48 G28 Minera LL11
20 B36 Minety SN16
37 D23 Minffordd *Gwy.* LL40
36 B21 Minffordd *Gwy.* LL48
84 B3 Mingearraidh HS8
53 F49 Miningsby PE23
4 C18 Minions PL14
67 B19 Minishant KA7
22 F43 Minley Manor GU17
37 D24 Minllyn SY20
91 A35 Minnes AB41
64 D19 Minnigaff DG8
99 C33 Minnonie AB45
57 C39 Minskip YO5
10 C38 Minstead SO43
25 E58 Minster *Kent* CT12
25 D55 Minster *Kent* ME12
38 E29 Minsterley SY5
30 G38 Minster Lovell OX8
29 G33 Minsterworth GL2
9 D32 Minterne Magna DT2
52 E47 Minting LN9
99 E36 Mintlaw AB42
70 A31 Minto TD9
38 F30 Minton SY6
16 C16 Minwear SA67
40 F37 Minworth B76
78 C6 Miodar PA77
104 D28 Mirbister KW17
103 B28 Mireland KW1
57 G38 Mirfield WF14
20 A35 Miserden GL6
18 B26 Miskin *M.G.* CF45
18 C26 Miskin *M.G.* CF7
51 C42 Misson DN10
41 G41 Misterton *Lei.* LE17
51 C43 Misterton *Not.* DN10
8 D30 Misterton *Som.* TA18
23 E48 Mitcham CR4
29 G32 Mitcheldean GL17
3 C14 Mitchell TR8
60 G30 Mitchelland LA8
19 A30 Mitchel Troy NP5
19 A30 Mitcheltroy Common NP5
71 E37 Mitford NE61
2 C13 Mithian TR5
40 D34 Mitton ST19
31 E41 Mixbury NN13
81 C21 Moar PH15
69 F29 Moat CA6
49 E33 Mobberley WA16
28 D29 Moccas HR2
47 E24 Mochdre *Clw.* LL28
37 G26 Mochdre *Pow.* SY16
64 F19 Mochrum DG8
14 C53 Mockbeggar TN12
60 D26 Mockerkin CA13
5 E22 Modbury PL21
40 B35 Moddershall ST15
102 B22 Modsarie KW14
38 C27 Moelfre *Clw.* SY10
46 D20 Moelfre *Gwy.* LL72
69 C26 Moffat DG10
32 D47 Mogerhanger MK44
72 D9 Moin'a'choire PA44
102 B21 Moine Ho. IV27
109 E7 Moira *Arm.* BT67
41 D39 Moira *Lei.* DE12
15 B56 Molash CT4
85 C10 Mol-chlach PH41
48 F28 Mold CH7
33 F51 Molehill Green CM6
59 E46 Molescroft HU17
32 A46 Molesworth PE18
6 A21 Mollacott Cross EX34
65 D23 Mollance DG7
7 C24 Molland EX36
48 F29 Mollington *Che.* CH1
31 D40 Mollington *Oxf.* OX17
75 C23 Mollinsburn G67
26 B20 Monachty SY23
81 F20 Monachylemore FK19
82 F27 Moncreiffe PH2
80 G17 Monevechadan PA24
35 C58 Monewden IP13
82 E26 Moneydie PH1
109 D6 Moneymore BT45
109 D6 Moneyneany BT45
109 E8 Moneyrea BT23
68 D23 Moniaive DG3
83 D30 Monifieth DD5
83 D30 Monikie DD5
82 F28 Monimail KY15
26 D17 Monington SA43
23 B48 Monken Hadley EN5
58 F41 Monk Fryston LS25
60 A29 Monkhill CA5
39 F32 Monkhopton WV16
28 C30 Monkland HR6
6 C20 Monkleigh EX39
18 D24 Monknash CF7
6 E21 Monkokehampton EX19
71 F39 Monkseaton NE25
34 D55 Monks Eleigh IP7
12 D47 Monk's Gate RH13
49 E34 Monks' Heath SK10
21 F41 Monk Sherborne RG26
99 E33 Monkshill AB53
7 B26 Monksilver TA4
41 G40 Monks Kirby CV23
35 B58 Monk Soham IP13
22 A43 Monks Risborough HP27
93 E9 Monkstadt IV51
33 F51 Monk Street CM6
19 A29 Monkswood NP5
7 E27 Monkton *Dev.* EX14
25 E58 Monkton *Kent* CT12
67 A19 Monkton *Str.* KA9
71 G39 Monkton *T.&W.* NE32
20 E33 Monkton Combe BA2
9 A34 Monkton Deverill BA12
20 E33 Monkton Farleigh BA15
8 B28 Monkton Heathfield TA2
10 C36 Monkton Up Wimborne BH21
62 A39 Monkwearmouth SR6
11 A42 Monkwood SO24
40 F35 Monmore Green WV1
28 G30 Monmouth (Trefynwy) NP5
28 D29 Monnington on Wye HR4
64 F19 Monreith DG8
25 B55 Monsale CM0
8 C30 Montacute TA15
99 E34 Monteach AB41
38 D29 Montford SY4
38 D30 Montford Bridge SY4
90 B31 Montgarrie AB33
38 F28 Montgomery (Trefaldwyn) SY15
74 F19 Montgreenan KA13
82 G29 Montrave KY8
83 B33 Montrose DD10
21 G39 Monxton SP11
50 F37 Monyash DE45
91 B32 Monymusk AB51
81 E24 Monzie PH7
74 C22 Moodiesburn G69
82 F29 Moonzie KY15
57 F39 Moor Allerton LS17
53 F48 Moorby PE22
56 C32 Moor Cock LA2
28 C29 Moorcot HR5
9 D35 Moor Crichel BH21
10 E36 Moordown BH9
48 D31 Moore WA4
55 B31 Moor End *Cum.* LA6
58 F44 Moor End *Hum.* YO4
51 A42 Moorends DN8
109 D8 Moorfields BT42
55 C31 Moorgate LA2
41 A40 Moorgreen NG16
50 E38 Moorhall S30
28 D29 Moorhampton HR4
60 A29 Moorhouse *Cum.* CA5
51 F43 Moorhouse *Not.* NG23
8 A29 Moorlinch TA7
58 D41 Moor Monkton YO5
56 F32 Moor Nook PR3
63 E42 Moorsholm TS12
49 B35 Moorside OL4
53 G48 Moor Side PE22
11 F40 Moortown *I.o.W.* PO30
52 C46 Moortown *Lcn.* LN7
96 C23 Morangie IV19
86 E12 Morar PH40
42 F47 Morborne PE7
7 E23 Morchard Bishop EX17
8 E30 Morcombelake DT6
42 E45 Morcott LE15
38 C28 Morda SY10
9 E34 Morden *Dor.* BH20
23 E48 Morden *G.L.* SM4
28 E31 Mordiford HR1
77 E35 Mordington TD15
62 D39 Mordon TS21
38 F29 More SY9
7 C25 Morebath EX16
70 A33 Morebattle TD5
55 C29 Morecambe LA4
95 B16 Morefield IV26
5 E23 Moreleigh TQ9
81 D21 Morenish FK21
60 D25 Moresby CA28
11 B41 Morestead SO21
9 F34 Moreton *Dor.* DT2
23 A51 Moreton *Esx* CM5
28 B30 Moreton *H.&W.* HR6
48 D28 Moreton *Mer.* L46
21 A42 Moreton *Oxf.* OX9
38 C31 Moreton Corbet SY4
6 G22 Moretonhampstead TQ13
30 E38 Moreton-in-Marsh GL56
29 D32 Moreton Jeffries HR1
30 C38 Moreton Morrell CV35
28 D31 Moreton on Lugg HR4
31 D41 Moreton Pinkney NN11
39 B32 Moreton Say TF9
29 G33 Moreton Valence GL2
4 D20 Morewellham PL19
36 B21 Morfa Bychan LL49
18 A24 Morfa Glas SA11
36 A18 Morfa Nefyn LL53
10 B37 Morgan's Vale SP5
19 A31 Mork GL15
61 D31 Morland CA10
41 A39 Morley *Dby.* DE7
62 D37 Morley *Drm* DL14
57 G38 Morley *W.Y.* LS27
49 D34 Morley Green SK9
44 E56 Morley St NR18
76 C28 Morningside *Ltn* EH10
75 E24 Morningside *Str.* ML2
45 F58 Morningthorpe NR15
71 E37 Morpeth NE61
91 G33 Morphie DD10
40 D37 Morrey DE13
67 C18 Morriston *Str.* KA19
17 E22 Morriston *W.G.* SA6
86 F12 Morroch PH39
44 A55 Morston NR25
6 A20 Mortehoe EX34
21 E42 Mortimer RG7
28 B29 Mortimer's Cross HR6
21 E42 Mortimer West End RG7
22 D47 Mortlake SW14
19 B32 Morton *Avon* BS12
51 G39 Morton *Dby.* DE55
51 C43 Morton *Lcn.* DN21
42 C47 Morton *Lcn.* PE10
45 D57 Morton *Nfk* NR9
51 G43 Morton *Not.* NG25
38 C28 Morton *Shr.* SY10
30 B37 Morton Bagot B80
62 G39 Morton-on-Swale DL7
2 E9 Morvah TR20
4 E18 Morval PL13
96 A23 Morvich *Hgh.* IV28
86 B15 Morvich *Hgh.* IV40
16 A16 Morvil SA62
39 F32 Morville WV16
6 D18 Morwenstow EX23
71 C38 Morwick Hall NE65
51 D40 Mosborough S19
74 F20 Moscow KA4
60 C29 Mosedale CA11
50 A36 Moselden Height HD3
29 C34 Moseley *H.&W.* WR2
40 G36 Moseley *W.M.* B13
48 G28 Moss *Clw.* LL11
51 A41 Moss *S.Y.* DN6
78 C5 Moss *Str.* PA77
90 B30 Mossat AB33
48 C31 Moss Bank WA11
106 E40 Mossbank ZE2
67 A19 Mossblown KA6
70 B32 Mossburnford TD8
65 C22 Mossdale DG7
75 E23 Mossend ML4
67 A20 Mossgiel KA5
98 F31 Mosshead AB54
83 B30 Mosside DD8
49 B35 Mossley OL5
48 D29 Mossley Hill L18
49 D34 Moss Nook M22
98 C28 Moss of Barmuckity IV30
69 D30 Mosspaul Hotel DG13
109 B7 Moss-side *Ant.* BT53
98 D31 Moss-side *Grm.* AB54
97 F24 Moss-side *Hgh.* IV12
55 F29 Moss Side PR4
98 D28 Mosstodloch IV32
83 C31 Mosston DD11
8 D30 Mosterton DT8
47 D27 Mostyn CH8
9 B34 Motcombe SP7
60 D30 Motherby CA11
75 E23 Motherwell ML1
23 D50 Mottingham SE9
10 B39 Mottisfont SO51
11 F40 Mottistone PO30
49 C35 Mottram in Longdendale SK14
49 E34 Mottram St Andrew SK10
48 E30 Mouldsworth WA6
82 B25 Moulin PH16
13 F49 Moulsecoomb BN2
21 C41 Moulsford OX10
24 A52 Moulsham CM2
32 D44 Moulsoe MK16
49 F32 Moulton *Che.* CW9
43 C48 Moulton *Lcn.* PE12
62 F38 Moulton *N.Y.* DL10
31 B43 Moulton *Nmp.* NN3
33 B52 Moulton *Sfk* CB8
43 D48 Moulton Chapel PE12
43 C49 Moulton Seas End PE12
45 E59 Moulton St Mary NR13
91 A33 Mounie Castle AB51
4 D17 Mount *Cnw.* PL30
2 C13 Mount *Cnw.* TR8
97 G25 Mount *Hgh.* IV12
18 B26 Mountain Ash CF45
75 F27 Mountain Cross EH46
16 B14 Mountain Water SA62
69 A28 Mountbenger TD7
98 D32 Mountblairy AB45
34 E54 Mount Bures CO8
4 E20 Mount Edgcumbe PL10
14 E53 Mountfield TN32
96 E21 Mountgerald IV15
109 D5 Mount Hamilton BT79
2 D12 Mount Hawke TR4
3 B14 Mountjoy *Cnw.* TR8
108 D5 Mountjoy *Tyr.* BT78
48 E29 Mount Manisty L65
23 B51 Mountnessing CM15
109 F7 Mountnorris BT60
67 B19 Mount Oliphant KA6
19 B30 Mounton NP6
41 A39 Mount Pleasant *Dby.* DE56
35 A60 Mount Pleasant *Sfk* IP18
41 D41 Mountsorrel LE12
73 E17 Mountstuart PA20
57 G36 Mount Tabor HX2
2 F10 Mousehole TR19
69 F26 Mouswald DG1
49 G34 Mow Cop ST7
62 E38 Mowden DL3
70 A33 Mowhaugh TD5
41 G42 Mowsley LE17
91 E34 Mowtie AB3
40 F35 Moxley WS10
88 A23 Moy *Hgh.* IV13
88 F20 Moy *Hgh.* PH31
87 F17 Moy *Hgh.* PH33
109 E6 Moy *Tyr.* BT71
97 E25 Moy House IV36
10 D37 Moyles Court BH24
16 A17 Moylgrove SA43
72 F12 Muasdale PA29
91 D34 Muchalls AB3
28 E30 Much Birch HR2
29 D32 Much Cowarne HR7
28 E30 Much Dewchurch HR2
8 B30 Muchelney TA10
33 G50 Much Hadham SG10
55 G30 Much Hoole PR4
4 E17 Muchlarnick PL13
29 E32 Much Marcle HR8
69 B28 Muchra TD7
87 A18 Muchrachd IV4
39 F32 Much Wenlock TF13
24 C52 Mucking SS17
39 B33 Mucklestone TF9
38 C31 Muckleton TF6
90 A31 Muckletown AB33
53 D49 Muckton LN11
102 E21 Mudale IV27
6 B21 Muddiford EX31
13 E51 Muddles Green BN8
13 E48 Muddleswood BN6
10 E37 Mudeford BH23
8 C31 Mudford BA21
19 G30 Mudgley BS28
85 A10 Mugeary IV51
40 A38 Mugginton DE6
62 A36 Muggleswick DH8
96 A22 Muie IV28
89 F26 Muir AB35
98 D32 Muirden AB53
83 D31 Muirdrum DD7
82 G28 Muirhead *Fife* KY15
90 B31 Muirhead *Grm.* AB33
97 E26 Muirhead *Grm.* IV36
74 D22 Muirhead *Str.* G69
82 D29 Muirhead *Tay.* DD2
75 B25 Muirhouses EH51
68 A22 Muirkirk KA18
75 B23 Muirmill FK6
90 B31 Muir of Fowlis AB33
98 C28 Muir of Lochs IV32
96 F20 Muir of Ord IV6
91 D34 Muirskie AB1
99 F35 Muirtack *Grm.* AB41
99 E34 Muirtack *Grm.* AB53
96 E23 Muirton IV11
82 C27 Muirton of Ardblair PH10
91 G32 Muirton of Ballochy DD10
82 F25 Muirtown PH3
99 D33 Muiryfold AB53
61 G34 Muker DL11
45 E57 Mulbarton NR14
98 D29 Mulben AB55
100 G9 Mulhagery HS2
100 C7 Mullach Charlabhaigh HS2
109 D9 Mullaghaboy BT40
108 F4 Mullan BT92
2 G12 Mullion TR12
53 E51 Mumby LN13
29 C32 Munderfield Row HR7
29 C32 Munderfield Stocks HR7
45 B59 Mundesley NR11
44 F53 Mundford IP26
45 F59 Mundham NR14
24 A54 Mundon CM9
91 B35 Mundurno AB23
87 D18 Munerigie PH35
94 B15 Mungasdale IV22
76 C30 Mungoswells EH39
60 C29 Mungrisdale CA11

Munlochy

19 C29 Newport *Gwe.* NP9
103 F27 Newport *Hgh.* KW7
58 F44 Newport *Hum.* HU15
11 F41 Newport *I.o.W.* PO30
45 D61 Newport *Nfk* NR29
39 D33 Newport *Shr.* TF10
83 E30 Newport-on-Tay DD6
32 D44 Newport Pagnell MK16
109 D7 Newport Trench BT80
12 D46 Newpound Common RH14
67 A18 New Prestwick KA8
26 C19 New Quay SA45
2 B13 Newquay TR7
3 B14 Newquay (St Mawgan) Airport TR8
45 D58 New Rackheath NR13
28 B27 New Radnor LD8
61 C30 New Rent CA11
15 E56 New Romney TN28
51 C42 New Rossington DN11
56 F32 New Row PR3
109 F7 Newry BT34/35
75 A24 New Sauchie FK10
41 B40 New Sawley NG10
82 E27 New Scone PH2
98 F32 Newseat AB51
55 F31 Newsham *Lan.* PR3
62 E37 Newsham *N.Y.* DL11
57 A39 Newsham *N.Y.* YO7
71 E38 Newsham *Nor.* NE24
58 G43 Newsholme *Hum.* DN14
56 D34 Newsholme *Lan.* BB7
62 A39 New Silksworth SR3
76 G31 Newstead *Bor.* TD6
71 A37 Newstead *Nor.* NE67
51 G40 Newstead *Not.* NG15
57 F40 Newthorpe LS25
69 B30 Newton *Bor.* DG7
70 A31 Newton *Bor.* TD8
33 D50 Newton *Cbs.* CB2
48 G30 Newton *Che.* CH3
48 E31 Newton *Che.* WA6
55 B28 Newton *Cum.* LA13
69 D27 Newton *D.&G.* DG10
16 B14 Newton *Dyf.* SA62
16 D15 Newton *Dyf.* SA71
49 C35 Newton *G.M.* SK14
99 E36 Newton *Grm.* AB42
98 E30 Newton *Grm.* AB54
98 C29 Newton *Grm.* IV32
28 B29 Newton *H.&W.* SY7
10 B38 Newton *Ham.* SP5
96 G23 Newton *Hgh.* IV1
96 E23 Newton *Hgh.* IV11
101 E18 Newton *Hgh.* IV27
96 F21 Newton *Hgh.* IV6
103 C28 Newton *Hgh.* KW1
103 D29 Newton *Hgh.* KW1
56 D32 Newton *Lan.* BB7
55 B31 Newton *Lan.* LA6
42 B46 Newton *Lcn.* NG34
75 C26 Newton *Ltn* EH52
18 D24 Newton *M.G.* CF36
43 D50 Newton *Nfk* PE13
44 D54 Newton *Nfk* PE32
42 G44 Newton *Nmp.* NN14
71 G36 Newton *Nor.* NE43
41 A42 Newton *Not.* NG13
34 D55 Newton *Sfk* CO10
40 C36 Newton *Stf.* WS15
73 E15 Newton *Str.* KA27
75 G25 Newton *Str.* ML12
73 A16 Newton *Str.* PA27
81 D24 Newton *Tay.* PH8
17 F21 Newton *W.G.* SA3
92 D4 Newton *W.I.* HS6
57 G40 Newton *W.Y.* WF10
31 A41 Newton *War.* CV23
5 C24 Newton Abbot TQ12
68 E24 Newtonairds DG2
60 A27 Newton Arlosh CA5
62 D38 Newton Aycliffe DL5
62 D40 Newton Bewley TS22
32 C45 Newton Blossomville MK43
32 B46 Newton Bromswold MK44

41 E39 Newton Burgoland LE67
52 D46 Newton by Toft LN8
5 F21 Newton Ferrers PL8
45 F57 Newton Flotman NR15
76 D29 Newtongrange EH22
41 F42 Newton Harcourt LE8
91 D34 Newtonhill AB3
57 E40 Newton Kyme LS24
48 C31 Newton-le-Willows *Mer.* WA12
62 G37 Newton-le-Willows *N.Y.* DL8
32 E44 Newton Longville MK17
74 E21 Newton Mearns G77
83 A31 Newtonmill DD9
88 E22 Newtonmore PH20
62 F38 Newton Morrell DL10
16 D15 Newton Mountain SA73
63 E43 Newton Mulgrave TS13
86 G12 Newton of Ardtoe PH36
82 F27 Newton of Balcanquhal PH2
97 F25 Newton of Dalvey IV36
82 G28 Newton of Falkland KY15
96 G22 Newton of Leys IV1
58 C41 Newton-on-Ouse YO6
63 G43 Newton-on-Rawcliffe YO18
71 C37 Newton-on-the-Moor NE65
51 E43 Newton on Trent LN1
7 G26 Newton Poppleford EX10
31 E42 Newton Purcell MK18
40 E38 Newton Regis B79
61 C30 Newton Reigny CA11
40 C38 Newton Solney DE15
21 G40 Newton Stacey SO20
7 F24 Newton St Cyres EX5
64 D19 Newton Stewart DG8
45 D58 Newton St Faith NR10
19 E32 Newton St Loe BA2
6 D20 Newton St Petrock EX22
21 G38 Newton Tony SP4
6 C21 Newton Tracey EX31
63 E41 Newton under Roseberry TS9
58 E42 Newton upon Derwent YO4
11 A43 Newton Valence GU34
22 A45 Newtown *Bkh.* HP5
21 E40 Newtown *Brk.* RG20
48 G30 Newtown *Che.* CH3
49 D35 Newtown *Che.* SK12
69 G30 Newtown *Cum.* CA6
10 E36 Newtown *Dor.* BH12
13 D50 New Town *E.S.* TN22
30 E36 New Town *Glo.* GL54
99 C33 Newtown *Grm.* AB44
28 A27 Newtown *Gwe.* NP3
29 E32 Newtown *H.&W.* HR8
29 D32 Newtown *H.&W.* HR8
11 C41 Newtown *Ham.* PO17
11 C41 Newtown *Ham.* SO32
10 C38 Newtown *Ham.* SO43
88 D19 Newtown *Hgh.* PH35
54 F25 Newtown *I.o.M.* IM4
11 E40 Newtown *I.o.W.* PO30
76 C30 New Town *Ltn* EH34
71 C36 Newtown *Nor.* NE65

71 A36 Newtown *Nor.* NE66
38 B30 Newtown *Shr.* SY4
50 F36 Newtown *Stf.* SK17
49 F35 Newtown *Stf.* ST8
10 B38 Newtown *Wts.* SO51
9 B34 Newtown *Wts.* SP3
38 F27 Newtown (Y Drenewydd) SY16
109 D8 Newtownabbey BT37
109 E9 Newtownards BT23
109 E8 Newtownbreda BT8
108 F5 Newtownbutler BT92
109 C7 Newtown Crommelin BT43
109 F7 Newtownhamilton BT35
2 F13 Newtown in St Martin TR12
41 E41 Newtown Linford LE6
76 G31 Newtown St Boswells TD6
108 D4 Newtownstewart BT78
41 E40 Newtown Unthank LE9
18 A27 New Tredegar NP2
82 C28 Newtyle PH12
73 B13 New Ulva PA31
43 E50 New Walsoken PE13
53 B48 New Waltham DN36
33 D49 New Wimpole SG8
76 C30 New Winton *Ltn* EH33
30 G39 New Yatt OX8
53 G48 New York *Lcn.* LN4
71 F39 New York *T.&W.* NE27
16 D15 Neyland SA73
19 C32 Nibley *Avon* BS17
19 A32 Nibley *Glo.* GL15
7 D26 Nicholashayne TA21
17 F21 Nicholaston SA3
57 C39 Nidd HG3
76 C28 Niddrie EH16
91 C35 Nigg *Grm.* AB1
97 D24 Nigg *Hgh.* IV19
7 C24 Nightcott TA22
47 G26 Nilig LL15
23 A51 Nine Ashes CM4
61 A33 Ninebanks NE47
20 C37 Nine Elms SN5
75 E27 Nine Mile Burn EH26
14 F53 Ninfield TN33
11 F40 Ningwood PO30
70 A32 Nisbet TD8
11 G40 Niton PO38
74 D20 Nitshill G53
46 F19 Niwbwrch (Newborough) LL60
23 F51 Nizels TN11
23 B51 Noak Hill RM4
65 C25 Noblehill DG1
31 B42 Nobottle NN7
52 F46 Nocton LN4
74 D18 Noddsdale KA30
31 G41 Noke OX3
16 C14 Nolton SA62
38 A31 No Man`s Heath *Che.* SY14
40 E38 No Man`s Heath *War.* B79
7 D24 Nomansland *Dev.* EX16
10 C38 Nomansland *Ham.* SP5
38 C30 Noneley SY4
15 B58 Nonington CT15
69 F30 Nook *Cum.* CA6
55 A31 Nook *Cum.* LA6
107 B38 Noonsbrough ZE2
83 A30 Noranside DD8
22 E47 Norbiton KT2
55 E28 Norbreck FY5
38 A31 Norbury *Che.* SY13
40 A37 Norbury *Dby.* DE6
38 F29 Norbury *Shr.* SY9
39 C33 Norbury *Stf.* ST20
29 B34 Norchard DY13
43 E51 Nordelph PE38
9 F35 Norden BH20
39 F32 Nordley WV16
77 F34 Norham TD15
57 G36 Norland Town HX6
48 E31 Norley WA6
10 E39 Norleywood SO41
63 E41 Normanby *Cle.* TS7
52 A44 Normanby *Hum.* DN15
58 A43 Normanby *N.Y.* YO6

52 D46 Normanby by Spital LN2
52 C47 Normanby le Wold LN7
42 F47 Norman Cross PE7
22 F45 Normandy GU3
79 C10 Norman`s Ruh PA74
13 F52 Norman`s Bay BN24
7 E26 Norman`s Green EX15
41 B39 Normanton *Dby.* DE23
42 A45 Normanton *Lcn.* NG32
42 E45 Normanton *Lei.* LE15
42 A44 Normanton *Lei.* NG13
51 G43 Normanton *Not.* NG25
57 G39 Normanton *W.Y.* WF6
41 D39 Normanton le Heath LE67
41 C41 Normanton on Soar LE12
41 B42 Normanton on the Wolds NG12
51 F43 Normanton on Trent NG23
55 F29 Normoss FY3
20 E34 Norrington Common SN12
41 D39 Norris Hill DE12
44 F55 Northacre NR17
62 G39 Northallerton DL6
44 D56 Northall Green NR20
6 C20 Northam *Dev.* EX39
11 C40 Northam *Ham.* SO14
31 B43 Northampton NN
51 D41 North Anston S31
22 E44 North Ascot SL5
31 F40 North Aston OX6
23 A48 Northaw EN6
8 C28 Northay TA20
10 B39 North Baddesley SO52
80 A16 North Ballachulish PH33
67 D19 North Balloch KA26
9 B32 North Barrow BA22
24 C53 North Benfleet SS12
12 F45 North Bersted PO22
76 B31 North Berwick EH39
11 D41 North Boarhunt PO17
98 D29 North Bogbain AB55
42 E47 Northborough PE6
15 B58 Northbourne CT14
7 G23 North Bovey TQ13
20 F34 North Bradley BA14
6 G20 North Brentor PL19
9 A33 North Brewham BA10
31 F40 Northbrook OX6
6 A20 North Buckland EX33
45 D59 North Burlingham NR13
99 E33 Northburnhill AB53
9 B32 North Cadbury BA22
52 E45 North Carlton LN1
58 F44 North Cave HU15
20 A36 North Cerney GL7
13 D49 North Chailey BN8
12 D45 Northchapel GU28
10 B38 North Charford SP5
71 A37 North Charlton NE66
9 B32 North Cheriton BA8
22 A45 Northchurch HP4
58 F44 North Cliffe YO4
52 E44 North Clifton NG23
53 C49 North Cockerington LN11
8 C31 North Coker BA22
18 C24 North Cornelly CF33
6 D22 Northcote Manor EX37
53 B49 North Cotes DN36
6 F19 Northcott PL15
45 G60 North Cove NR34
62 F38 North Cowton DL7
32 D45 North Crawley MK16
23 D50 North Cray DA14
8 B29 North Curry TA3
80 C15 North Dallens PA38
59 D45 North Dalton YO25
105 A30 North Dawn KW17
57 D39 North Deighton LS22

58 F42 North Duffield YO8
104 D28 Northdyke KW16
53 C48 North Elkington LN11
44 C55 North Elmham NR20
51 A40 North Elmsall WF9
20 E33 Northend *Avon* BA1
19 E30 North End *Avon* BS19
22 B43 Northend *Bkh.* HP14
32 F44 North End *Bkh.* LU7
33 G52 North End *Esx* CM6
11 D42 North End *Ham.* PO2
21 E40 North End *Ham.* RG20
44 F56 North End *Nfk* NR16
71 C37 North End *Nor.* NE65
12 E47 North End *W.S.* BN14
30 C39 Northend *War.* CV33
94 C12 North Erradale IV21
99 D36 North Essie AB42
59 G45 North Ferriby HU14
77 D34 Northfield *Bor.* TD14
91 C34 Northfield *Grm.* AB2
99 C34 Northfield *Grm.* AB45
103 D29 Northfield *Hgh.* KW1
30 A36 Northfield *W.M.* B31
24 D52 Northfleet DA10
59 D47 North Frodingham YO25
10 C37 North Gorley SP6
45 G58 North Green IP21
58 C44 North Grimston YO17
11 D43 North Hayling PO11
77 G36 North Hazelrigg NE66
7 B23 North Heasley EX36
12 D46 North Heath RH20
4 C18 North Hill PL15
21 A40 North Hinksey OX2
22 G47 North Holmwood RH5
69 C30 Northhouse TD9
5 E23 North Huish TQ10
52 F45 North Hykeham LN6
14 E54 Northiam TN31
32 D47 Northill SG18
11 A41 Northington SO24
16 C15 North Johnston SA62
52 B46 North Kelsey LN7
96 G22 North Kessock IV1
52 A47 North Killingholme DN40
57 A40 North Kilvington YO7
41 G42 North Kilworth LE17
52 G47 North Kyme LN4
12 F47 North Lancing BN15
53 G49 Northlands PE22
30 G36 Northleach GL54
22 A44 North Lee HP22
7 F27 Northleigh *Dev.* EX13
6 B22 Northleigh *Dev.* EX32
30 G39 North Leigh OX8
51 D43 North Leverton with Habblesthorpe DN22
6 F21 Northlew EX20
30 D36 North Littleton WR11
44 G56 North Lopham IP22
42 E45 North Luffenham LE15
12 E44 North Marden PO18
31 F43 North Marston MK18
76 E29 North Middleton EH23
99 E34 North Millbrex AB53
7 C23 North Molton EX36
21 A40 Northmoor OX8
8 A28 Northmoor Green or Moorland TA7
21 C41 North Moreton OX11
82 B29 Northmuir DD8
12 F44 North Mundham PO20
51 G43 North Muskham NG23
59 F45 North Newbald YO4
30 E39 North Newington OX15

20 F37 North Newton SN9
8 A28 North Newton TA7
11 D43 Northney PO11
20 B33 North Nibley GL11
21 F41 North Oakley RG26
23 C51 North Ockendon RM14
22 C47 Northolt UB5
48 F28 Northop CH7
48 F28 Northop Hall CH7
63 E41 North Ormesby TS3
53 C48 North Ormsby LN11
52 C44 Northorpe *Lcn.* DN21
42 D46 Northorpe *Lcn.* PE10
42 B47 Northorpe *Lcn.* PE11
62 G39 North Otterington DL7
8 B30 Northover BA22
52 C46 North Owersby LN8
57 G37 Northowram HX3
8 D30 North Perrott TA18
8 A28 North Petherton TA6
4 B18 North Petherwin PL15
44 E54 North Pickenham PE37
29 C35 North Piddle WR7
8 E31 North Poorton DT6
80 E16 North Port PA35
107 A40 Northpunds ZE2
75 B27 North Queensferry KY11
7 B23 North Radworthy EX36
42 A46 North Rauceby NG34
45 B58 Northrepps NR27
53 D49 North Reston LN11
57 E38 North Rigton LS17
49 F34 North Rode CW12
106 D39 North Roe ZE2
44 D52 North Runcton PE33
106 C41 North Sandwick ZE2
54 C27 North Scale LA14
52 F44 North Scarle LN6
71 E38 North Seaton NE63
79 C14 North Shian PA38
71 G39 North Shields NE30
25 C55 North Shoebury SS3
43 F48 North Side PE6
63 E42 North Skelton TS12
53 C50 North Somercotes LN11
57 B38 North Stainley HG4
61 E34 North Stainmore CA17
23 C51 North Stifford RM16
19 E32 North Stoke *Avon* BA1
21 C42 North Stoke *Oxf.* OX10
12 E46 North Stoke *W.S.* BN18
11 C40 North Stoneham SO50
21 D42 North Street *Brk.* RG7
11 A42 North Street *Ham.* SO24
15 B56 North Street *Kent* ME13
77 G37 North Sunderland NE68
4 A18 North Tamerton EX22
91 B35 North Tarbothill AB23
6 E22 North Tawton EX20
75 A23 North Third FK7
53 C48 North Thoresby DN36
21 G38 North Tidworth SP9
71 C38 North Togston NE65
6 E20 North Town *Dev.* EX20
22 F44 North Town *Ham.* GU12
105 B30 Northtown KW17
44 D56 North Tuddenham NR20
45 B58 North Walsham NR28
21 G41 North Waltham RG25
22 F43 North Warnborough RG29
103 C28 North Watten KW1
29 E34 Northway GL20
23 A50 North Weald Bassett CM16

North Wheatley

51 D43 North Wheatley DN22
5 D24 North Whilborough TQ12
49 E32 Northwich CW8
19 C31 Northwick BS12
19 E31 North Wick BS18
19 F31 North Widcombe BS18
52 D47 North Willingham LN8
51 F39 North Wingfield S42
42 C44 North Witham NG33
44 F53 Northwold IP26
22 B46 Northwood *G.L.* HA6
11 E40 Northwood *I.o.W.* PO31
38 B30 Northwood *Shr.* SY4
29 G33 Northwood Green GL14
9 C32 North Wootton *Dor.* DT9
44 C52 North Wootton *Nfk* PE30
19 G31 North Wootton *Som.* BA4
20 D34 North Wraxall SN14
20 C37 North Wroughton SN4
70 C34 North Yardhope NE65
48 D31 Norton *Che.* WA7
62 D40 Norton *Cle.* TS20
29 F34 Norton *Glo.* GL2
30 D36 Norton *H.&W.* WR11
29 C34 Norton *H.&W.* WR5
33 E48 Norton *Hfs.* SG6
10 F39 Norton *I.o.W.* PO41
58 B43 Norton *N.Y.* YO17
31 B41 Norton *Nmp.* NN11
51 E41 Norton *Not.* NG20
28 B28 Norton *Pow.* LD8
51 A41 Norton *S.Y.* DN6
51 D39 Norton *S.Y.* S8
34 B55 Norton *Sfk* IP31
38 E31 Norton *Shr.* SY4
38 G30 Norton *Shr.* SY7
39 E33 Norton *Shr.* TF11
40 G34 Norton *W.M.* DY8
12 G44 Norton *W.S.* PO20
12 F45 Norton *W.S.* PO20
20 C34 Norton *Wts.* SN16
20 G35 Norton Bavant BA12
40 B34 Norton Bridge ST15
40 E36 Norton Canes WS11
28 D29 Norton Canon HR4
52 G44 Norton Disney LN6
9 A33 Norton Ferris BA12
7 C27 Norton Fitzwarren TA2
10 F39 Norton Green PO40
19 E31 Norton Hawkfield BS18
24 A52 Norton Heath CM4
39 B32 Norton in Hales TF9
49 G34 Norton in the Moors ST6
40 E38 Norton-Juxta-Twycross CV9
57 B39 Norton-le-Clay YO6
30 B38 Norton Lindsey CV35
19 E32 Norton Malreward BS18
23 A51 Norton Mandeville CM5
20 F33 Norton St Philip BA3
45 F59 Norton Subcourse NR14
8 C30 Norton sub Hamdon TA14
28 D29 Norton Wood HR4
51 F43 Norwell NG23
51 F43 Norwell Woodhouse NG23
45 E58 Norwich NR
45 D58 Norwich Airport NR6
106 A42 Norwick ZE2
22 D47 Norwood Green UB2
23 G48 Norwood Hill RH6
42 F43 Noseley LE7
5 F21 Noss Mayo PL8
57 A38 Nosterfield DL8
86 B14 Nostie IV40
30 F36 Notgrove GL54
18 D23 Nottage CF36
103 E27 Nottingham *Hgh.* KW5
41 A41 Nottingham *Not.* NG
51 A39 Notton *W.Y.* WF4
20 E34 Notton *Wts.* SN15
24 A53 Nounsley CM3
29 B33 Noutard's Green WR6
34 B54 Nowton IP29
38 D30 Nox SY5
26 D18 Noyadd Trefawr SA43
21 C42 Nuffield RG9
58 E44 Nunburnholme YO4
41 F39 Nuneaton CV11
21 B41 Nuneham Courtenay OX44
57 D40 Nun Monkton YO5
20 G33 Nunney BA11
58 B42 Nunnington YO6
7 C26 Nunnington Park TA4
63 E41 Nunthorpe TS7
10 B37 Nunton SP5
57 B39 Nunwick *N.Y.* HG4
70 F34 Nunwick *Nor.* NE48
32 G44 Nup End *Bkh.* HP22
29 F33 Nup End *Glo.* GL19
10 C39 Nursling S016
11 B43 Nursted GU31
40 F34 Nurton WV6
11 D43 Nutbourne *W.S.* PO18
12 E46 Nutbourne *W.S.* RH20
23 F48 Nutfield RH1
41 A41 Nuthall NG16
33 E49 Nuthampstead SG8
12 D47 Nuthurst *W.S.* RH13
30 A37 Nuthurst *War.* B94
13 D50 Nutley *E.S.* TN22
21 G42 Nutley *Ham.* RG25
109 D8 Nutt's Corner BT29
51 B42 Nutwell DN3
75 A23 Nyadd FK9
103 B29 Nybster KW1
12 G44 Nyetimber PO21
12 D44 Nyewood GU31
6 E22 Nymet Rowland EX17
7 E23 Nymet Tracey EX17
20 A33 Nympsfield GL10
7 C27 Nynehead TA21
8 A30 Nythe TA7
12 F45 Nyton PO20

O

41 E42 Oadby LE2
24 E54 Oad Street ME9
40 A36 Oakamoor ST10
75 D26 Oakbank *Ltn* EH53
79 D13 Oakbank *Str.* PA64
6 F21 Oak Cross EX20
18 B27 Oakdale NP2
7 C27 Oake TA4
40 E34 Oaken WV8
55 E31 Oakenclough PR3
39 D32 Oakengates TF2
98 C28 Oakenhead IV31
62 C37 Oakenshaw *Drm* DL15
57 G37 Oakenshaw *W.Y.* BD12
7 C24 Oakford *Dev.* EX16
26 C20 Oakford *Dyf.* SA47
7 C25 Oakfordbridge EX16
49 F35 Oakgrove SK11
42 E44 Oakham LE15
11 A43 Oakhanger GU35
19 G32 Oakhill BA3
33 B49 Oakington CB4
47 G24 Oaklands *Clw.* LL26
33 G48 Oaklands *Hfs.* AL3
29 G33 Oakle Street GL2
32 C46 Oakley *Bfd.* MK43
31 G42 Oakley *Bkh.* HP18
75 B26 Oakley *Fife* KY12
21 F41 Oakley *Ham.* RG23
35 A57 Oakley *Sfk* IP21
22 D45 Oakley Green SL4
37 G25 Oakley Park SY17
20 A34 Oakridge GL6
38 E30 Oaks SY5
20 B35 Oaksey SN16
70 F31 Oakshaw Ford CA6
41 D39 Oakthorpe DE12
62 G39 Oaktree Hill DL6
12 C47 Oakwoodhill RH5
57 F36 Oakworth BD22
73 B17 Oalinlongart PA23
25 E55 Oare *Kent* ME13
7 A24 Oare *Som.* EX35
20 E37 Oare *Wts.* SN8
42 B45 Oasby NG32
66 B12 Oatfield PA28
83 B30 Oathlaw DD8
79 E14 Oban PA34
94 B14 Obinan IV22
28 A29 Obley SY7
9 C32 Oborne DT9
49 F32 Occlestone Green CW10
35 A57 Occold IP23
103 E28 Occumster KW3
67 A20 Ochiltree KA18
18 A25 Ochr-y-Mynydd CF48
81 F24 Ochtermuthill PH5
75 A23 Ochtertyre *Cen.* FK9
81 E24 Ochtertyre *Tay.* PH7
41 B40 Ockbrook DE72
22 F46 Ockham GU23
86 G11 Ockle PH36
12 C47 Ockley RH5
28 D31 Ocle Pychard HR1
59 C46 Octon YO25
8 C30 Odcombe BA22
20 E33 Odd Down BA2
29 C34 Oddingley WR9
31 G41 Oddington OX5
106 C41 Oddsta ZE2
32 C45 Odell MK43
104 D32 Odie KW17
22 F43 Odiham RG29
10 B37 Odstock SP5
41 E39 Odstone CV13
30 B39 Offchurch CV33
30 D36 Offenham WR11
49 D35 Offerton SK2
13 E49 Offham *E.S.* BN8
23 F52 Offham *Kent* ME19
32 B47 Offord Cluny PE18
32 B47 Offord D'Arcy PE18
34 D56 Offton IP8
7 F27 Offwell EX14
20 D37 Ogbourne Maizey SN8
20 D37 Ogbourne St Andrew SN8
20 D37 Ogbourne St George SN8
57 F36 Ogden HX2
83 A30 Ogil DD8
71 F37 Ogle NE20
18 D24 Ogmore CF32
18 D24 Ogmore-by-Sea CF32
18 B25 Ogmore Vale CF32
105 B29 Oil Terminal KW16
9 C34 Okeford Fitzpaine DT11
6 F21 Okehampton EX20
6 F21 Okehampton Camp EX20
107 D40 Okraquoy ZE2
31 A43 Old NN6
91 C35 Old Aberdeen AB2
11 A41 Old Alresford SO24
40 F38 Old Arley CV7
41 A41 Old Basford NG6
21 F42 Old Basing RG24
70 A31 Old Belses TD6
30 B36 Oldberrow B95
71 A36 Old Bewick NE66
53 F49 Old Bolingbroke PE23
7 E23 Oldborough EX17
51 E39 Old Brampton S42
65 D23 Old Bridge of Urr DG7
44 F56 Old Buckenham NR17
21 F40 Old Burghclere RG20
23 F51 Oldbury *Kent* TN15
39 F32 Oldbury *Shr.* WV16
40 F35 Oldbury *W.M.* B69
41 F39 Oldbury *War.* CV10
19 B32 Oldbury Naite BS12
19 B32 Oldbury -on-Severn BS12
20 C33 Oldbury on the Hill GL9
58 A41 Old Byland YO6
28 F29 Oldcastle NP7
38 A30 Oldcastle Heath SY14
7 A26 Old Cleeve TA24
47 E24 Old Colwyn LL29
51 D41 Oldcotes S81
91 A34 Old Craig AB41
76 C29 Old Craighall EH22
98 D31 Old Crombie AB54
67 D18 Old Dailly KA26
41 C42 Old Dalby LE14
99 E35 Old Deer AB42
59 F47 Old Ellerby HU11
35 E59 Old Felixstowe IP11
29 B34 Oldfield *H.&W.* WR9
56 F35 Oldfield *W.Y.* BD22
42 F47 Old Fletton PE2
20 F33 Oldford BA11
50 C36 Old Glossop SK13
37 G22 Old Goginan SY23
58 G43 Old Goole DN14
29 F32 Old Gore HR9
2 A10 Old Grimsby TR24
90 D30 Oldhall *Grm.* AB34
103 C27 Oldhall *Hgh.* KW1
53 A48 Old Hall HU12
49 B35 Oldham OL
77 C33 Oldhamstocks TD13
34 F56 Old Heath CO2
40 G35 Old Hill B64
33 A48 Oldhurst PE17
55 A31 Old Hutton LA8
3 D14 Old Kea TR3
74 C20 Old Kilpatrick G60
91 C33 Old Kinnernie AB32
33 G48 Old Knebworth SG3
19 D32 Oldland BS15
43 A49 Old Leake PE22
90 A31 Old Leslie AB52
58 B44 Old Malton YO17
91 A33 Oldmeldrum AB51
57 F40 Old Micklefield LS25
90 C31 Oldmill AB31
30 B38 Old Milverton CV32
11 C40 Old Netley SO31
34 B56 Old Newton IP14
39 E32 Oldpark TF3
75 C26 Old Philpstoun EH52
79 G14 Old Poltalloch PA31
91 D35 Old Portlethen AB1
28 C28 Old Radnor LD8
99 D36 Old Rattray AB42
91 A32 Old Rayne AB52
7 F24 Oldridge EX6
15 E56 Old Romney TN29
82 E26 Old Scone PH2
75 C24 Old Shields G67
101 C17 Oldshore Beg IV27
101 C18 Oldshore More IV27
20 C33 Old Sodbury BS17
42 B45 Old Somerby NG33
58 A41 Oldstead YO6
31 D43 Old Stratford MK19
59 D46 Old Sunderlandwick YO25
71 C37 Old Swarland NE65
40 G34 Old Swinford DY8
55 A31 Old Town *Cum.* LA6
2 A11 Old Town *I.o.S.* TR21
70 D34 Old Town *Nor.* NE19
96 G20 Oldtown of Aigas IV4
98 D32 Oldtown of Ord AB45
17 E20 Oldwalls SA3
32 D47 Old Warden SG18
7 C24 Oldways End EX16
32 A46 Old Weston PE17
99 D34 Oldwhat AB53
22 D45 Old Windsor SL4
15 B56 Old Wives Lees CT4
22 F46 Old Woking GU22
32 D44 Old Wolverton MK12
38 C30 Old Woods SY4
103 C26 Olgrinmore KW12
69 A26 Oliver ML12
11 B40 Oliver's Battery SO22
106 D39 Ollaberry ZE2
49 E33 Ollerton *Che.* WA16
51 F42 Ollerton *Not.* NG22
39 C32 Ollerton *Shr.* TF9
33 D52 Olmstead Green CB1
32 C44 Olney *Bkh.* MK46
31 D42 Olney *Nmp.* NN12
103 B27 Olrig House KW14
40 G37 Olton B92
19 C31 Olveston BS12
108 E5 Omagh BT78
29 B34 Ombersley WR9
51 F42 Ompton NG22
54 F25 Onchan IM3
50 G36 Onecote ST13
43 C51 Ongar Hill PE34
28 B29 Ongar Street HR6
28 A30 Onibury SY7
80 A16 Onich PH33
27 G24 Onllwyn SA10
39 A33 Onneley CW3
22 G45 Onslow Village GU2
94 D13 Opinan IV21
77 F33 Orange Lane TD12
98 D28 Orbliston IV32
93 G8 Orbost IV55
53 F50 Orby PE24
73 D17 Orcadia PA20
73 B17 Orchard PA23
8 B28 Orchard Portman TA3
7 B26 Orchard Wyndham TA4
20 G36 Orcheston SP3
28 F30 Orcop HR2
28 F30 Orcop Hill HR2
86 C18 Ord IV46
91 B32 Ordhead AB51
90 C30 Ordie AB34
98 D29 Ordiequish IV32
51 E42 Ordsall DN22
14 F54 Ore TN35
12 E47 Oreham Common BN5
5 E21 Oreston PL9
39 G32 Oreton DY14
49 C32 Orford *Che.* WA2
35 D60 Orford *Sfk* IP12
40 D37 Orgreave DE13
28 B30 Orleton *H.&W.* SY8
29 B32 Orleton *H.&W.* WR6
28 B30 Orleton Common SY8
32 A44 Orlingbury NN14
84 A3 Ormacleit HS8
63 E41 Ormesby TS3
45 D60 Ormesby St Margaret NR29
45 D60 Ormesby St Michael NR29
94 B14 Ormiscaig IV22
76 D29 Ormiston EH35
79 A10 Ormsaigmore PH36
73 B16 Ormsdale PA22
48 B29 Ormskirk L39
103 B26 Ormwe KW14
23 E50 Orpington BR6
48 B31 Orrell WN5
54 D25 Orrisdale IM6
91 B35 Orrok Ho. AB23
65 F23 Orroland DG6
24 C52 Orsett RM16
40 D34 Orslow TF10
42 A43 Orston NG13
61 F32 Orton *Cum.* CA10
31 A44 Orton *Nmp.* NN14
42 F47 Orton Longueville PE2
40 E38 Orton-on-the-Hill CV9
42 F47 Orton Waterville PE2
33 C49 Orwell SG8
56 F32 Osbaldeston BB2
58 D42 Osbaldwick YO1
41 E40 Osbaston *Lei.* CV13
38 D31 Osbaston *Shr.* TF6
11 E40 Osborne PO32
42 B46 Osbournby NG34
48 F30 Oscroft CH3
93 G9 Ose IV56
41 D40 Osgathorpe LE12
52 C46 Osgodby *Lcn.* LN8
59 A46 Osgodby *N.Y.* YO11
58 F42 Osgodby *N.Y.* YO8
86 A11 Oskaig IV40
41 B39 Osmaston *Dby.* DE24
40 A37 Osmaston *Dby.* DE6
9 F33 Osmington DT3
9 F33 Osmington Mills DT3
62 G40 Osmotherley DL6
21 A40 Osney OX2
57 G38 Ossett WF5
51 F43 Ossington NG23
25 B55 Ostend CM0
22 D47 Osterley TW7
58 B42 Oswaldkirk YO6
56 G32 Oswaldtwistle BB5
38 C28 Oswestry SY11
23 F51 Otford TN14
14 B53 Otham ME15
8 A29 Othery TA7
35 C58 Otley *Sfk* IP6
57 E37 Otley *W.Y.* LS21
73 C15 Otter PA21
11 B40 Otterbourne SO21
56 D34 Otterburn *N.Y.* BD23
70 D34 Otterburn *Nor.* NE19
70 D34 Otterburn Camp NE19
14 B55 Otterden Place ME13
73 B15 Otter Ferry PA21
4 A17 Otterham PL32
19 G28 Otterhampton TA5
22 E45 Ottershaw KT16
106 D41 Otterswick ZE2
7 G26 Otterton EX9
7 F27 Ottery St Mary EX11
15 C57 Ottinge CT4
59 G48 Ottringham HU12
60 A28 Oughterby CA5
56 A34 Oughtershaw BD23
50 C38 Oughtibridge S30
58 B41 Oulston YO6
60 A28 Oulton *Cum.* CA7
45 C57 Oulton *Nfk* NR11
45 F61 Oulton *Sfk* NR32
40 B34 Oulton *Stf.* ST15
57 G39 Oulton *W.Y.* LS26
45 F60 Oulton Broad NR33
45 C57 Oulton Street NR11
42 G46 Oundle PE8
61 C32 Ousby CA10
103 F26 Ousdale KW7
34 C53 Ousden CB8
58 G44 Ousefleet DN14
62 A38 Ouston *Drm* DH2
71 F36 Ouston *Nor.* NE18
104 E28 Outertown KW16
60 G29 Outgate LA22
61 F33 Outhgill CA17
39 C33 Outlands ST20
50 A36 Outlane HD3
59 G49 Out Newton HU19
55 E30 Out Rawcliffe PR3
43 E50 Outwell PE14
23 G49 Outwood *Sry* RH1
57 G39 Outwood *W.Y.* WF1
20 E33 Oval The BA2
57 G36 Ovenden HX3
19 C31 Over *Avon* BS12
33 B49 Over *Cbs.* CB4
49 F32 Over *Che.* CW7
104 B32 Overbister KW17
99 D33 Overbrae AB53
29 E35 Overbury GL20
9 F32 Overcombe DT3
8 C31 Over Compton DT9
50 E38 Over End DE45
50 F38 Over Haddon DE45
55 B31 Over Kellet LA6
30 F39 Over Kiddington OX20
8 A30 Overleigh BA16
30 F39 Over Norton OX7
49 E33 Over Peover WA16
48 E29 Overpool L65
82 F29 Over Rankeilour KY15
102 F20 Overscaig Hotel IV27
40 D38 Overseal DE12
62 G40 Over Silton YO7
15 B56 Oversland ME13
30 C36 Oversley Green B49
31 B43 Overstone NN6
7 B27 Over Stowey TA5
45 A58 Overstrand NR27
8 C30 Over Stratton TA13
49 D33 Over Tabley WA16
38 A29 Overton *Clw.* LL13
91 B34 Overton *Grm.* AB2
91 B32 Overton *Grm.* AB51
21 G41 Overton *Ham.* RG25
55 D30 Overton *Lan.* LA3
58 D41 Overton *N.Y.* YO3
28 A30 Overton *Shr.* SY8
17 F20 Overton *W.G.* SA3
75 E24 Overtown ML2
10 A38 Over Wallop SO20
40 F38 Over Whitacre B46
31 F40 Over Worton OX7
44 A54 Overy Staithe PE31
31 F43 Oving *Bkh.* HP22
12 F44 Oving *W.S.* PO20
13 F49 Ovingdean BN2
71 G36 Ovingham NE42
62 E37 Ovington *Drm* DL11
34 D53 Ovington *Esx* CO10
11 A41 Ovington *Ham.* SO24
44 E55 Ovington *Nfk* IP25
71 G36 Ovington *Nor.* NE42
10 C39 Ower SO51
9 F33 Owermoigne DT2
22 A43 Owlswick HP27
52 B46 Owmby DN38
52 D46 Owmby by Spital LN2
11 B41 Owslebury SO21
42 E43 Owston LE15
51 B43 Owston Ferry DN9
59 F48 Owstwick HU12
41 B42 Owthorpe NG12
44 E53 Oxborough PE33
55 C30 Oxcliffe Hill LA3
53 E49 Oxcombe LN9
33 F52 Oxen End CM7
61 G31 Oxenholme LA9
57 F36 Oxenhope BD22
55 A28 Oxen Park LA12
29 E35 Oxenton GL52
21 F39 Oxenwood SN8
21 A41 Oxford OX
30 D39 Oxhill CV35
40 E34 Oxley WV10
34 G55 Oxley Green CM9
13 D52 Oxley's Green TN32
70 B32 Oxnam TD8

Pinchbeck

43 C48 Pinchbeck PE11
42 C47 Pinchbeck Bars PE11
43 C48 Pinchbeck West PE11
63 E41 Pinchinthorpe TS14
48 A29 Pinfold L40
8 E29 Pinhay DT7
7 F25 Pinhoe EX1
22 C44 Pinkneys Green SL6
30 B37 Pinley Green CV35
67 D17 Pinminnoch KA26
67 D17 Pinmore KA26
7 G26 Pinn EX10
22 C47 Pinner HA5
22 B47 Pinner Green HA5
29 D35 Pinvin WR10
67 E17 Pinwherry KA26
51 G40 Pinxton NG16
28 D30 Pipe and Lyde HR1
39 A33 Pipe Gate TF9
73 E17 Piperhall PA20
97 F24 Piperhill IV12
40 D36 Pipe Ridware WS15
4 B18 Piper's Pool PL15
42 G44 Pipewell NN14
6 B20 Pippacott EX31
28 E27 Pipton LD3
22 F45 Pirbright GU24
73 F14 Pirnmill KA27
29 D34 Pirton *H.&W.* WR8
32 E47 Pirton *Hfs.* SG5
81 G23 Pisgah FK15
22 C43 Pishill RG9
36 A19 Pistyll LL53
81 A24 Pitagowan PH18
99 C35 Pitblae AB43
82 E26 Pitcairngreen PH1
82 F26 Pitcairns PH2
91 A33 Pitcaple AB51
20 A34 Pitchcombe GL6
31 G43 Pitchcott HP22
38 E31 Pitchford SY5
22 A43 Pitch Green HP27
22 F45 Pitch Place GU3
9 A32 Pitcombe BA10
18 D25 Pitcot CF32
76 C32 Pitcox EH42
82 D28 Pitcur PH13
91 B32 Pitfichie AB51
96 B23 Pitgrudy IV25
99 F33 Pitinnan AB51
83 B31 Pitkennedy DD8
82 G28 Pitkevy KY6
82 G29 Pitlessie KY15
82 B25 Pitlochry PH16
91 A34 Pitmedden AB41
7 D27 Pitminster TA3
83 C31 Pitmuies DD8
91 B32 Pitmunie AB51
82 B25 Pitnacree PH9
8 B30 Pitney TA10
82 E27 Pitroddie PH2
83 F30 Pitscottie KY15
24 C53 Pitsea SS13
31 B43 Pitsford NN6
7 B26 Pitsford Hill TA4
32 G45 Pitstone LU7
32 G45 Pitstone Green LU7
7 D26 Pitt *Dev.* EX16
11 B40 Pitt *Ham.* SO22
97 E27 Pittendreich IV30
96 A23 Pittentrail IV28
83 G31 Pittenweem KY10
62 B39 Pittington DH6
91 A32 Pittodrie Ho. AB51
10 A37 Pitton SP5
62 B38 Pity Me DH1
3 A15 Pityme PL27
35 A58 Pixey Green IP21
58 B44 Place Newton YO17
99 D33 Plaidy AB53
75 D23 Plains ML6
38 F31 Plaish SY6
12 C45 Plaistow RH14
10 C38 Plaitford SP5
17 B20 Plas SA32
37 G22 Plas Gogerddan SY23
46 G22 Plas Gwynant LL55
47 F25 Plasisaf LL16
37 A26 Plas Isaf LL21
47 E25 Plas Llwyd LL18
37 E23 Plas Llwyngwern SY20
37 F25 Plas Llysyn SY17
38 B27 Plas Nantyr LL20
37 E24 Plas-rhiw-Saeson SY19
21 E41 Plastow Green RG19
47 E25 Plas-yn-Cefn LL17
23 F52 Platt TN15
38 B31 Platt Lane SY13
62 B38 Plawsworth DH2
23 F51 Plaxtol TN15
14 E55 Playden TN31
35 D57 Playford IP6
22 D43 Play Hatch RG4
3 D14 Playing Place TR3
38 E30 Plealey SY5
75 B24 Plean FK7
82 F28 Pleasance KY14
56 G32 Pleasington BB2
51 F40 Pleasley NG19
70 G32 Plenmeller NE49
33 G52 Pleshey CM3
86 A13 Plockton IV52
28 D29 Ploughfield HR2
38 G29 Plowden SY7
38 E29 Ploxgreen SY5
14 C55 Pluckley TN27
14 C55 Pluckley Thorne TN27
60 C27 Plumbland CA5
108 D5 Plumbridge BT79
49 E33 Plumley WA16
61 C30 Plumpton *Cum.* CA11
13 E49 Plumpton *E.S.* BN7
31 D42 Plumpton End NN12
13 E49 Plumpton Green BN7
61 C31 Plumpton Head CA11
23 D50 Plumstead *G.L.* SE18
45 B57 Plumstead *Nfk* NR11
41 B41 Plumtree NG12
42 B43 Plungar NG13
9 D33 Plush DT2
26 C19 Plwmp SA44
5 E21 Plym Bridge PL7
5 E21 Plymouth PL
5 E21 Plympton PL7
5 E21 Plymstock PL9
7 E26 Plymtree EX15
58 A42 Pockley YO6
58 E44 Pocklington YO4
7 F24 Pocombe Bridge EX2
43 C48 Pode Hole PE11
8 B31 Podimore BA22
32 B45 Podington NN29
39 B33 Podmore ST21
30 G39 Poffley End OX8
42 B47 Pointon NG34
10 E37 Pokesdown BH5
80 B15 Polanach PA38
4 B18 Polapit Tamar PL15
64 C18 Polbae DG8
101 G15 Polbain IV26
4 E19 Polbathic PL11
75 D26 Polbeth EH55
89 D24 Polchar PH22
69 D26 Poldean DG10
42 G46 Polebrook PE8
13 F51 Polegate BN26
50 A36 Pole Moor HD3
96 B23 Poles IV25
40 E38 Polesworth B78
95 A16 Polglass IV26
3 C15 Polgooth PL26
68 C22 Polgown DG3
12 F46 Poling BN18
12 F46 Poling Corner BN18
4 E16 Polkerris PL24
101 C19 Polla IV27
84 C3 Poll A Charra HS8
80 A17 Polldubh PH33
102 G23 Pollie IV28
51 A42 Pollington DN14
79 A13 Polloch PH37
74 D21 Pollokshaws G43
3 D15 Polmassick PL26
75 C25 Polmont FK2
74 E21 Polnoon G76
4 E18 Polperro PL13
4 E17 Polruan PL23
19 G30 Polsham BA5
34 E55 Polstead CO6
73 A13 Poltalloch PA31
7 F25 Poltimore EX4
76 D28 Polton EH18
77 E33 Polwarth TD10
4 B18 Polyphant PL15
3 A15 Polzeath PL27
109 E6 Pomeroy BT70
43 F48 Pondersbridge PE17
23 B49 Ponders End EN3
33 E50 Pond Street CB11
2 E13 Ponsanooth TR3
60 F26 Ponsonby CA20
5 C23 Ponsworthy TQ13
27 F23 Pont Aber SA19
36 A21 Pont Aber Glaslyn LL55
17 C22 Pontamman SA18
17 C20 Pontantwn SA17
17 D22 Pontardawe SA8
17 D21 Pontardulais SA4
17 B20 Pontargothi SA32
17 B20 Pontarsais SA33
48 F28 Pontblyddyn CH7
18 A25 Pontbren llwyd CF44
26 D18 Pont Ceri SA38
37 F24 Pont Crugnant SY19
47 G23 Pont Cyfyng LL24
47 F23 Pont Dolgarrog LL32
57 G40 Pontefract WF8
71 F37 Ponteland NE20
37 G23 Ponterwyd SY23
38 E29 Pontesbury SY5
38 E29 Pontesford SY5
38 B28 Pontfadog LL20
27 E25 Pont-faen LD3
16 A16 Pontfaen SA65
17 D20 Pont-Henri SA15
19 B29 Ponthir NP6
26 D18 Ponthirwaun SA43
18 B27 Pontllanfraith NP2
17 D21 Pontlliw SA4
46 G20 Pontllyfni LL54
18 A26 Pontlottyn CF8
18 A24 Pont Nedd Fechan SA11
19 B28 Pontnewydd NP44
19 A28 Pontnewynydd NP4
46 G22 Pont Pen-y-benglog LL57
27 B22 Pontrhydfendigaid SY25
37 C24 Pont Rhyd-sarn LL40
18 C24 Pont Rhyd-y-cyff CF34
18 B23 Pont-rhyd-y-fen SA12
27 A23 Pont-rhyd-y-groes SY25
19 B28 Pontrhydyrun NP44
28 F29 Pontrilas HR2
38 D27 Pontrobert SY22
46 F20 Pont-rug LL55
13 E52 Ponts Green TN33
26 D20 Pontshaen SA44
29 F32 Pontshill HR9
27 G24 Pontsticill CF48
18 A24 Pont Walby SA11
17 A19 Pontwelly SA44
17 D20 Pontyates SA15
17 C20 Pontyberem SA15
48 G28 Pontybodkin CH7
18 C26 Pontyclun CF7
18 B24 Pontycymer CF32
18 B25 Pont y gwaith CF43
19 B28 Pontymister NP1
47 G23 Pont-y-pant LL25
19 A28 Pontypool NP4
18 B26 Pontypridd CF37
47 G25 Pont yr Alwen LL21
18 B27 Pontywaun NP1
10 C39 Pooksgreen S040
2 D12 Pool *Cnw.* TR15
57 E38 Pool *W.Y.* LS21
55 A30 Pool Bank LA11
9 E35 Poole BH15
20 B35 Poole Keynes GL7
94 C14 Poolewe IV22
61 D30 Pooley Bridge CA10
29 F33 Poolhill GL18
82 G26 Pool of Muckhart FK14
38 D28 Pool Quay SY21
34 E53 Pool Street CO9
16 C15 Pope Hill SA62
22 E44 Popeswood RG12
21 G41 Popham SO21
23 C49 Poplar E14
11 E40 Porchfield PO30
96 F19 Porin IV6
2 E12 Porkellis TR13
7 A24 Porlock TA24
7 A24 Porlock Weir TA24
73 E13 Portachoillan PA29
109 E7 Portadown BT62
109 E8 Portaferry BT22
82 E28 Port Allen PH2
79 C14 Port Appin PA38
72 D10 Port Askaig PA46
73 D15 Portavadie PA21
109 E9 Portavogie BT22
109 B6 Portballintrae BT57
73 D16 Port Bannatyne PA20
19 D30 Portbury BS20
69 G28 Port Carlisle CA5
72 E8 Port Charlotte PA48
11 D41 Portchester PO16
62 D40 Port Clarence TS2
73 C15 Port Driseach PA21
72 F9 Port Ellen PA42
91 B33 Port Elphinstone AB51
73 F17 Portencross KA23
54 G23 Port Erin IM9
99 F37 Port Erroll AB42
9 F32 Portesham DT3
98 C30 Portessie AB56
54 D26 Port e Vullen IM7
17 F20 Port Eynon SA3
79 E13 Portfield PA63
16 C15 Portfield Gate SA62
6 G19 Portgate EX20
4 B16 Port Gaverne PL29
74 C19 Port Glasgow PA14
109 C7 Portglenone BT44
98 C29 Portgordon AB56
103 G25 Portgower KW8
3 B14 Porth *Cnw.* TR7
18 B26 Porth *M.G.* CF39
4 E18 Porthallow *Cnw.* PL13
2 F13 Porthallow *Cnw.* TR12
18 D23 Porthcawl CF36
36 B17 Porth Colmon LL53
3 A14 Porthcothan PL28
2 F9 Porthcurno TR19
94 D13 Port Henderson IV21
16 A13 Porthgain SA62
18 E26 Porthkerry CF62
2 F11 Porthleven TR13
36 B21 Porthmadog LL49
2 G12 Porth Mellin TR12
2 E9 Porthmeor TR20
2 F13 Porth Navas TR11
3 D15 Portholland PL26
3 F14 Porthoustock TR12
4 E16 Porthpean PL26
2 D12 Porthtowan TR4
17 A22 Porthyrhyd *Dyf.* SA19
17 C21 Porthyrhyd *Dyf.* SA32
38 C28 Porth-y-waen SY10
73 A17 Portincaple G84
58 F43 Portington DN14
80 F15 Portinnisherrich PA33
60 D28 Portinscale CA12
3 A15 Port Isaac PL29
19 D30 Portishead BS20
98 C30 Portknockie AB56
91 D35 Portlethen AB1
3 E15 Portloe TR2
64 F16 Port Logan DG9
97 C24 Portmahomack IV20
36 B21 Portmeirion LL48
85 G10 Port Mor PH42
10 E39 Portmore SO41
63 E43 Port Mulgrave TS13
82 B25 Port na Craig PH16
80 C15 Portnacroish PA38
72 E8 Portnahaven PA47
85 A9 Portnalong IV47
86 F12 Portnaluchaig PH39
102 B20 Portnancon IV27
101 D11 Port Nan Giuran HS2
92 D4 Port Nan Long HS6
101 A11 Port Nis HS2
76 C28 Portobello EH15
81 G21 Port of Menteith FK8
10 A37 Porton SP4
65 E24 Port o' Warren DG5
46 E21 Port Penrhyn LL57
3 A15 Portquin PL29
79 C14 Port Ramsay PA34
2 D12 Portreath TR16
93 G10 Portree IV51
109 B6 Portrush BT56
3 E14 Portscatho TR2
11 D42 Portsea PO1
102 B24 Portskerra KW14
19 C30 Portskewett NP6
13 F48 Portslade BN41
13 F48 Portslade-by-Sea BN3
11 E42 Portsmouth PO
98 C31 Portsoy AB45
109 B6 Portstewart BT55
54 G24 Port St Mary IM9
48 D29 Port Sunlight L62
11 C40 Portswood SO17
18 C23 Port Talbot SA12
79 A10 Portuairk PH36
28 D29 Portway *H.&W.* HR4
30 A36 Portway *War.* B48
72 E8 Port Wemyss PA47
64 F19 Port William DG8
15 E19 Portwrinkle PL11
64 G20 Portyerrock DG8
34 D53 Poslingford CO10
5 C22 Postbridge PL20
22 B43 Postcombe OX9
15 D57 Postling CT21
45 E58 Postwick NR13
90 D31 Potarch AB31
32 F45 Potsgrove MK17
22 A46 Potten End HP4
52 F46 Potterhanworth LN4
52 F46 Potterhanworth Booths LN4
45 C60 Potter Heigham NR29
20 F35 Potterne SN10
20 F35 Potterne Wick SN10
23 A48 Potters Bar EN6
40 G34 Potter's Cross DY7
22 A47 Potters Crouch AL2
31 D43 Potterspury NN12
23 A50 Potter Street CM17
91 B35 Potterton AB23
62 F40 Potto DL6
33 D48 Potton SG19
44 C53 Pott Row PE32
49 E35 Pott Shrigley SK10
6 E18 Poughill *Cnw.* EX23
7 E24 Poughill *Dev.* EX17
10 D37 Poulner BH24
20 E35 Poulshot SN10
20 A36 Poulton GL7
55 F29 Poulton-le-Fylde FY6
29 A33 Pound Bank DY14
17 E21 Poundffald SA4
13 D50 Poundgate TN6
13 D51 Pound Green TN22
13 C48 Pound Hill RH10
67 E17 Poundland KA26
31 F42 Poundon OX6
23 G51 Poundsbridge TN11
5 C23 Poundsgate TQ13
4 A17 Poundstock EX23
23 G48 Povey Cross RH6
71 B36 Powburn NE66
7 G25 Powderham EX6
8 E31 Powerstock DT6
69 G27 Powfoot DG12
29 D32 Pow Green HR8
29 C34 Powick WR2
6 D19 Powler's Piece EX39
75 A26 Powmill FK14
9 F33 Poxwell DT2
22 D46 Poyle SL3
13 E48 Poynings BN45
9 C32 Poyntington DT9
49 D35 Poynton *Che.* SK12
38 D31 Poynton *Shr.* TF6
38 D31 Poynton Green SY4
96 E22 Poyntzfield IV7
109 F7 Poyntz Pass BT35
35 A59 Poys Street IP17
16 C15 Poyston Cross SA62
34 C55 Poystreet Green IP30
2 F11 Praa Sands TR13
82 G29 Pratis KY8
23 E50 Pratt's Bottom BR6
2 E12 Praze-an-Beeble TR14
2 G11 Predannack Wollas TR12
38 B31 Prees SY13
55 E29 Preesall FY6
38 B31 Prees Green SY13
38 B28 Preesgweene SY10
38 B31 Prees Higher Heath SY13
48 F28 Prenbrigog CH7
16 C15 Prendergast SA61
70 B35 Prendwick NE66
26 D20 Pren-gwyn SA44
36 A21 Prenteg LL49
48 D28 Prenton L42
48 C30 Prescot L34
38 C30 Prescott SY4
97 F25 Presley IV36
77 G34 Pressen TD12
47 D26 Prestatyn LL19
49 E35 Prestbury *Che.* SK10
29 F35 Prestbury *Glo.* GL52
28 B28 Presteigne LD8
38 F31 Presthope TF13
19 G32 Prestleigh BA4
49 B33 Prestolee M26
77 E33 Preston *Bor.* TD11
9 F33 Preston *Dev.* DT3
5 C24 Preston *Dev.* TQ12
13 F49 Preston *E.S.* BN1
20 A36 Preston *Glo.* GL7
29 E32 Preston *H.&W.* HR8
32 F47 Preston *Hfs.* SG4
59 F47 Preston *Hum.* HU12
25 E58 Preston *Kent* CT3
25 E56 Preston *Kent* ME13
55 G31 Preston *Lan.* PR
42 E44 Preston *Lei.* LE15
76 C31 Preston *Ltn* EH40
71 A37 Preston *Nor.* NE67
34 C55 Preston *Sfk* CO10
71 G39 Preston *T.&W.* NE30
20 D36 Preston *Wts.* SN15
30 B37 Preston Bagot B95
31 F42 Preston Bissett MK18
38 C31 Preston Brockhurst SY4
48 D31 Preston Brook WA7
21 G41 Preston Candover RG25
31 C41 Preston Capes NN11
31 C43 Preston Deanery NN7
38 D30 Preston Gubbals SY4
30 D37 Preston on Stour CV37
48 D31 Preston on the Hill WA4
28 D29 Preston on Wye HR2
76 C29 Prestonpans EH32
8 C31 Preston Plucknett BA20
62 G36 Preston-under-Scar DL8
39 D32 Preston upon the Weald Moors TF6
28 D31 Preston Wynne HR1
49 B33 Prestwich M25
67 A19 Prestwick *Str.* KA9
71 F37 Prestwick *T.&W.* NE20
67 A19 Prestwick Airport KA9
41 C41 Prestwold LE12
22 A44 Prestwood HP16
18 B25 Price Town CF32
43 G51 Prickwillow CB7
19 F31 Priddy BA5
55 F31 Priest Hill PR3
55 B31 Priest Hutton LA6
74 G21 Priestland KA17
38 F28 Priestweston SY15
41 F40 Primethorpe LE9
44 D56 Primrose Green NR9
40 F35 Princes End DY4
16 C17 Princes Gate SA67
22 A43 Princes Risborough HP27
30 A39 Princethorpe CV23
5 C21 Princetown *Dev.* PL20
27 G26 Princetown *M.G.* NP2
83 F31 Prior Muir KY16
28 E31 Prior's Frome HR1
31 C40 Priors Hardwick CV23
31 C40 Priors Marston CV23
28 D28 Priory Wood HR3
19 E32 Priston BA2
24 C54 Prittlewell SS0
11 B42 Privett GU34
6 B21 Prixford EX31
72 E10 Proaig PA44
3 D14 Probus TR2
99 C33 Protsonhill AB45
71 G36 Prudhoe NE42
81 C20 Pubil PH15
19 E32 Publow BS18
33 F49 Puckeridge SG11
8 C29 Puckington TA19
19 D32 Pucklechurch BS17
49 E32 Puddinglake CW10
48 E28 Puddington *Che.* L64
7 D23 Puddington *Dev.* EX16
29 G32 Puddlebrook GL17
44 F56 Puddledock NR17
9 E33 Puddletown DT2
28 C31 Pudleston HR6
57 F38 Pudsey LS28
12 E46 Pulborough RH20
103 D28 Puldagon KW1
39 C33 Puleston TF10
48 G29 Pulford CH4
9 D32 Pulham DT2
45 G57 Pulham Market IP21
45 G58 Pulham St Mary IP21
32 E46 Pulloxhill MK45
96 C23 Pulrossie IV25
38 E30 Pulverbatch SY5
75 D26 Pumpherston EH53
27 D22 Pumsaint SA19
16 B15 Puncheston SA62
8 F31 Puncknowle DT2
13 D52 Punnett's Town TN21
11 D42 Purbrook PO7
23 D51 Purfleet RM19
19 G29 Puriton TA7
24 A54 Purleigh CM3
23 E49 Purley CR8
21 D42 Purley on Thames RG8

Shadforth

29 C33 Smith End Green WR6
69 G30 Smithfield CA6
7 D26 Smithincott EX15
33 F51 Smith`s Green CM22
96 G22 Smithtown IV1
49 E33 Smithy Green WA16
22 A47 Smug Oak AL2
66 E16 Smyrton KA26
34 G54 Smythe`s Green CO5
38 E29 Snailbeach SY5
33 B52 Snailwell CB8
59 A45 Snainton YO13
58 G42 Snaith DN14
57 A38 Snape N.Y. DL8
35 C59 Snape Sfk IP17
48 A29 Snape Green PR8
41 E39 Snarestone DE12
52 D46 Snarford LN8
14 E55 Snargate TN29
15 D56 Snave TN29
29 C34 Sneachill WR7
38 F28 Snead SY15
63 F44 Sneaton YO22
63 F44 Sneatonthorpe YO22
52 D46 Snelland LN3
60 F25 Snellings CA22
40 A37 Snelston DE6
44 F55 Snetterton NR16
41 D39 Snibston LE67
29 F33 Snig`s End GL19
84 A3 Snishival HS8
71 C36 Snitter NE65
52 C45 Snitterby DN21
30 C37 Snitterfield CV37
28 A31 Snitton SY8
28 D29 Snodhill HR3
24 E52 Snodland ME6
30 E36 Snowshill WR12
5 G22 Soar Dev. TQ7
17 B22 Soar Dyf. SA19
11 C42 Soberton SO32
11 C42 Soberton Heath SO32
62 F39 Sockburn DL2
38 A29 Sodylt Bank SY12
33 A51 Soham CB7
92 D4 Solas HS6
6 D19 Soldon Cross EX22
11 A42 Soldridge GU34
15 C56 Sole Street Kent CT4
24 E52 Sole Street Kent DA12
30 A37 Solihull B91
30 A36 Solihull Lodge B90
28 C30 Sollers Dilwyn HR4
29 E32 Sollers Hope HR1
48 A30 Sollom PR4
75 A25 Solsgirth FK14
16 B13 Solva SA62
69 F28 Solwaybank DG14
42 D43 Somerby LE14
51 G39 Somercotes DE55
20 B36 Somerford Keynes GL7
11 E43 Somerley PO20
45 F60 Somerleyton NR32
40 B37 Somersal Herbert DE6
53 E49 Somersby PE23
33 A49 Somersham Cbs. PE17
34 D56 Somersham Sfk IP8
31 F40 Somerton Oxf. OX6
34 C53 Somerton Sfk IP29
8 B30 Somerton Som. TA11
12 F47 Sompting BN15
22 D43 Sonning RG4
22 D43 Sonning Common RG4
22 D43 Sonning Eye RG4
10 E37 Sopley BH23
20 C33 Sopworth SN14
64 F20 Sorbie DG8
103 B27 Sordale KW12
78 A8 Sorisdale PA78
67 A21 Sorn KA5
74 G21 Sornhill KA4
79 E14 Soroba PA34
103 B28 Sortat KW1
53 E48 Sotby LN3
52 F47 Sots Hole LN4
45 G60 Sotterly NR34
39 C33 Soudley TF9
48 F28 Soughton CH7
32 F44 Soulbury LU7
61 E33 Soulby LA17
31 E41 Souldern OX6
32 B45 Souldrop MK44
39 A32 Sound Che. CW5
107 C40 Sound She. ZE1

107 B39 Sound She. ZE2
19 D32 Soundwell BS16
70 A34 Sourhope TD5
104 C30 Sourin KW17
6 G21 Sourton EX20
55 A28 Soutergate LA17
44 D53 South Acre PE32
22 C47 Southall UB
5 G23 South Allington TQ7
75 A24 South Alloa FK7
29 F35 Southam Glo. GL52
31 B40 Southam War. CV33
12 E45 South Ambersham GU29
10 C39 Southampton So
11 C40 Southampton Airport SO50
51 D41 South Anston S31
22 E45 South Ascot SL5
80 B16 South Ballachulish PA39
67 D18 South Balloch KA26
63 D41 South Bank TS6
74 D20 Southbar PA4
8 B31 South Barrow BA22
23 E48 South Beddington SM6
24 C53 South Benfleet SS7
12 G45 South Bersted PO22
99 F33 South Blackbog AB51
23 G51 Southborough TN4
10 E37 Southbourne Dor. BH6
11 D43 Southbourne W.S. PO10
8 E30 South Bowood DT6
5 D22 South Brent TQ10
6 G20 South Brentor PL19
9 A33 South Brewham BA10
71 D38 South Broomhill NE61
44 E56 Southburgh IP25
45 E59 South Burlingham NR13
59 D45 Southburn YO25
9 B32 South Cadbury BA22
52 E45 South Carlton LN1
59 F45 South Cave HU15
20 B36 South Cerney GL7
8 D28 South Chard TA20
71 A37 South Charlton NE66
9 B32 South Cheriton BA8
24 C54 Southchurch SS1
58 F44 South Cliffe YO4
52 E44 South Clifton NG23
53 D49 South Cockerington LN11
13 E49 South Common BN8
18 D23 South Cornelly CF33
73 G16 South Corrigills KA27
6 F21 Southcott EX20
45 G60 South Cove NR34
80 C15 South Creagan PA35
41 D42 South Croxton LE7
59 E45 South Dalton HU17
23 E51 South Darenth DA4
70 C32 Southdean TD9
58 F42 South Duffield YO8
13 F50 Southease BN7
53 D48 South Elkington LN11
51 A40 South Elmsall WF9
32 F44 South End Bkh. LU7
21 D42 Southend Brk. RG7
54 C27 South End Cum. LA14
99 E33 Southend Grm. AB53
52 A47 South End Hum. DN19
66 C12 Southend Str. PA28
24 C54 Southend Airport SS2
24 C54 Southend-on-Sea SS
18 D24 Southerndown CF32
65 E25 Southerness DG2
94 D13 South Erradale IV21
43 F51 Southery PE38
24 B54 South Fambridge SS4
21 C39 South Fawley OX12
59 G45 South Ferriby DN18
24 D52 Southfleet DA13
99 F33 South Flobbets AB51
22 A46 South Garth ZE2

23 B48 Southgate G.L. N14
45 C57 Southgate Nfk NR10
23 G49 South Godstone RH9
10 C37 South Gorley SP6
24 B52 South Green Esx CM11
44 D56 South Green Nfk NR20
73 C16 South Hall PA22
24 B53 South Hanningfield CM3
11 C43 South Harting GU31
11 E43 South Hayling PO11
77 G36 South Hazelrigg NE66
22 A45 South Heath HP16
13 F50 South Heighton BN9
62 B39 South Hetton DH6
51 A39 South Hiendley S72
4 C19 South Hill PL17
6 D18 South Hole EX39
22 G47 South Holmwood RH5
23 C51 South Hornchurch RM13
74 E18 South Hourat KA24
5 F22 South Huish TQ7
52 F45 South Hykeham LN6
62 A39 South Hylton SR4
32 D47 Southill SG18
21 G40 Southington RG25
52 C46 South Kelsey LN7
96 G22 South Kessock IV3
52 A47 South Killingholme DN40
57 A40 South Kilvington YO7
41 G41 South Kilworth LE17
51 B40 South Kirkby WF9
91 C33 South Kirkton AB32
52 G47 South Kyme LN4
12 F47 South Lancing BN15
80 D15 South Ledaig PA37
8 E28 Southleigh EX13
21 A39 South Leigh OX8
51 D43 South Leverton DN22
30 D36 South Littleton WR11
44 G56 South Lopham IP22
42 E45 South Luffenham LE15
13 E50 South Malling BN7
20 C37 South Marston SN3
58 F41 South Milford LS25
5 F23 South Milton TQ7
23 A48 South Mimms EN6
25 B55 Southminster CM0
7 C23 South Molton EX36
62 A37 South Moor DH9
21 C41 South Moreton OX11
82 B29 Southmuir DD8
12 G44 South Mundham PO20
51 G43 South Muskham NG23
59 F45 South Newbald YO4
31 E40 South Newington OX15
10 A36 South Newton SP2
51 G40 South Normanton DE55
23 E49 South Norwood SE25
23 G48 South Nutfield RH1
23 C51 South Ockendon RM15
32 B47 Southoe PE18
35 B57 Southolt IP23
53 E49 South Ormsby LN11
42 E46 Southorpe PE9
57 A39 South Otterington DL7
57 G36 Southowram HX3
22 B46 South Oxhey WD1
23 G48 South Park RH2
8 D30 South Perrott DT8
8 C30 South Petherton TA13
6 G19 South Petherwin PL15
44 E54 South Pickenham PE37
5 F23 South Pool TQ7
48 A28 Southport PR8
75 C27 South Queensferry EH30
7 B23 South Radworthy EX36
42 A46 South Rauceby NG34

44 C54 South Raynham NR21
99 E33 South Redbriggs AB53
45 B58 Southrepps NR11
53 D50 South Reston LN11
52 F47 Southrey LN3
20 A37 Southrop GL7
21 G42 Southrope RG25
44 E52 South Runcton PE33
52 F44 South Scarle NG23
48 G28 Southsea Clw. LL11
11 E42 Southsea Ham. PO4
80 C15 South Shian PA37
71 G39 South Shields NE33
59 F47 South Skirlaugh HU11
53 C50 South Somercotes LN11
57 C39 South Stainley HG3
21 C42 South Stoke Oxf. RG8
12 F46 South Stoke W.S. BN18
20 E33 Southstoke BA2
13 E49 South Street E.S. BN8
24 E52 South Street Kent DA13
6 F22 South Tawton EX20
53 E50 South Thoresby LN13
21 G38 South Tidworth SP9
45 E61 Southtown Nfk NR31
105 B30 Southtown Ork. KW17
11 A42 South Town GU34
99 E35 South Upper Barrack AB41
107 C39 South View ZE2
61 F33 Southwaite Cum. CA17
60 B30 Southwaite Cum. CA4
45 D59 South Walsham NR13
23 D49 Southwark SE
22 G43 South Warnborough RG25
12 D47 Southwater RH13
19 G30 Southway BA5
23 B51 South Weald CM14
9 G32 Southwell Dor. DT5
51 G42 Southwell Not. NG25
21 B42 South Weston OX9
4 A18 South Wheatley Cnw. PL15
51 D43 South Wheatley Not. DN22
11 D42 Southwick Ham. PO17
42 F46 Southwick Nmp. PE8
62 A39 Southwick T.&W. SR5
13 F48 Southwick W.S. BN42
20 F34 Southwick Wts. BA14
19 F31 South Widcombe BS18
41 F41 South Wigston LE18
14 C55 South Willesborough TN24
52 D47 South Willingham LN3
62 C40 South Wingate TS27
51 G39 South Wingfield DE55
42 D44 South Witham NG33
35 A61 Southwold IP18
11 A40 South Wonston SO21
45 E59 Southwood Nfk NR13
8 A31 Southwood Som. BA6
24 B54 South Woodham Ferrers CM3
44 C52 South Wootton PE30
20 E34 South Wraxall BA15
40 G37 South Yardley B26
6 F22 South Zeal EX20
57 A40 Sowerby N.Y. YO7
57 G36 Sowerby W.Y. HX6
57 G36 Sowerby Bridge HX6
60 B29 Sowerby Row CA4
7 F25 Sowton EX5
96 B21 Soyal IV24

45 B58 Spa Common NR28
70 F31 Spadeadam CA8
43 C48 Spalding PE11
58 F43 Spaldington DN14
32 A46 Spaldwick PE18
83 G31 Spalefield KY10
52 F44 Spalford NG23
42 B46 Spanby NG34
44 C56 Sparham NR9
55 A29 Spark Bridge LA12
8 B31 Sparkford BA22
5 E21 Sparkwell PL7
50 D36 Sparrowpit SK17
13 C52 Sparrow`s Green TN5
11 A40 Sparsholt Ham. SO21
21 C39 Sparsholt Oxf. OX12
61 B34 Spartylea NE47
63 G43 Spaunton YO6
8 A28 Spaxton TA5
87 F18 Spean Bridge PH34
68 E24 Speddoch DG2
22 A44 Speen Bkh. HP27
21 E40 Speen Brk. RG14
59 B47 Speeton YO14
48 D30 Speke L24
23 G51 Speldhurst TN3
33 G50 Spellbrook CM23
30 F39 Spelsbury OX7
22 E43 Spencers Wood RG7
49 F34 Spen Green CW11
57 A37 Spennithorne DL8
62 C38 Spennymoor DL16
29 C34 Spetchley WR5
9 D34 Spetisbury DT11
45 G59 Spexhall IP19
98 C29 Spey Bay IV32
89 B26 Speybridge PH26
98 E28 Speyview AB38
53 F50 Spilsby PE23
77 G37 Spindlestone NE70
51 E40 Spinkhill S31
96 B22 Spinningdale IV24
20 D35 Spirthill SN11
22 D45 Spital Brk. SL4
103 C27 Spital Hgh. KW1
23 A49 Spitalbrook EN11
52 C45 Spital in the Street LN2
13 E50 Spithurst BN8
64 D20 Spittal D.&G. DG8
64 E19 Spittal D.&G. DG8
16 B15 Spittal Dyf. SA62
76 C30 Spittal Ltn EH32
77 E36 Spittal Nor. TD15
82 C26 Spittalfield PH1
90 E29 Spittal of Glenmuick AB35
89 G26 Spittal of Glenshee PH10
45 D58 Spixworth NR10
57 D39 Spofforth HG3
41 B39 Spondon DE21
44 F56 Spooner Row NR18
39 B32 Spoonley TF9
44 D54 Sporle PE32
47 F25 Sportsman`s Arms LL22
76 C32 Spott EH42
31 B43 Spratton NN6
22 G44 Spreakley GU10
6 F22 Spreyton EX17
52 D46 Spridlington LN2
74 D22 Springburn G21
69 G28 Springfield D.&G. DG16
82 F29 Springfield Fife KY15
97 E26 Springfield Grm. IV36
40 G36 Springfield W.M. B13
65 D23 Springholm DG7
69 F28 Springkell DG11
99 F33 Springleys AB51
74 G19 Springside KA11
62 A38 Springwell NE9
59 F48 Sproatley HU11
49 F33 Sproston Green CW4
51 B41 Sprotbrough DN5
35 D57 Sproughton IP8
77 G33 Sprouston TD5
45 D58 Sprowston NR7
57 G36 Sproxton Lei. LE14
58 A42 Sproxton N.Y. YO6
48 G31 Spurstow CW6
65 C23 Square Point DG7
55 F28 Squires Gate FY4

73 C14 Sron Doire PA30
88 G22 Sronphadruig Lodge PH18
39 B33 Stableford ST5
56 C33 Stackhouse BD24
16 E15 Stackpole SA71
56 G34 Stacksteads OL13
5 E21 Staddiscombe PL9
58 G44 Staddlethorpe HU15
21 B42 Stadhampton OX44
84 A3 Stadhlaigearraidh HS8
61 B31 Staffield CA10
93 E10 Staffin IV51
40 C35 Stafford ST16
33 G52 Stagden Cross CM1
32 D45 Stagsden MK43
70 G35 Stagshaw Bank NE45
103 B29 Stain KW1
57 E38 Stainburn LS21
42 C44 Stainby NG33
51 B39 Staincross S75
62 D37 Staindrop DL2
22 D46 Staines TW18
52 E46 Stainfield Lcn. LN3
42 C46 Stainfield Lcn. PE10
56 C34 Stainforth N.Y. BD24
51 A42 Stainforth S.Y. DN7
55 F29 Staining FY3
50 A36 Stainland HX4
63 F44 Stainsacre YO22
62 E40 Stainton Cle. TS8
61 D30 Stainton Cum. CA11
55 A31 Stainton Cum. LA8
62 E36 Stainton Drm DL12
62 G36 Stainton N.Y. DL11
51 C41 Stainton S.Y. S66
52 E46 Stainton by Langworth LN3
63 G45 Staintondale YO13
52 C47 Stainton le Vale LN3
55 B28 Stainton with Adgarley LA13
60 D28 Stair Cum. CA12
67 A20 Stair Str. KA5
63 E43 Staithes TS13
71 E38 Stakeford NE62
55 E30 Stake Pool PR3
9 C33 Stalbridge DT10
9 C33 Stalbridge Weston DT10
45 C59 Stalham NR12
45 C59 Stalham Green NR12
14 B55 Stalisfield Green ME13
53 A48 Stallingborough DN37
56 A35 Stalling Busk DL8
55 E29 Stalmine FY6
49 C35 Stalybridge SK15
33 E52 Stambourne CO9
42 E45 Stamford Lcn. PE9
71 B38 Stamford Nor. NE66
58 D43 Stamford Bridge YO4
71 F36 Stamfordham NE18
32 G47 Stanborough AL8
32 F45 Stanbridge Bfd. LU7
9 D35 Stanbridge Dor. BH21
10 B39 Stanbridge Earls SO51
56 F35 Stanbury BD22
75 D23 Stand ML6
75 C25 Standburn FK1
40 E34 Standeford WV10
14 C54 Standen TN27
12 C44 Standford GU35
48 A31 Standish WN6
21 A39 Standlake OX8
11 B40 Standon Ham. SO21
33 F49 Standon Hfs. SG11
39 B33 Standon Stf. ST21
75 E24 Stane ML7
44 C55 Stanfield NR20
32 D47 Stanford Bfd. SG18
15 D57 Stanford Kent TN25
29 C32 Stanford Bishop WR6
29 B33 Stanford Bridge WR6
21 D41 Stanford Dingley RG7
21 B39 Stanford in the Vale SN7
24 C52 Stanford-le-Hope SS17
31 A41 Stanford on Avon NN6
41 C41 Stanford on Soar LE12
29 B32 Stanford on Teme WR6

Stanford Rivers

170

Templand

69 E26 Templand DG11
4 C17 Temple *Cnw.* PL30
76 E29 Temple *Ltn* EH23
26 C21 Temple Bar SA48
19 F32 Temple Cloud BS18
9 B32 Templecombe BA8
15 C58 Temple Ewell CT16
30 C36 Temple Grafton B49
30 F36 Temple Guiting GL54
58 G42 Temple Hirst YO8
51 F40 Temple Normanton S42
109 D8 Templepatrick BT39
61 D31 Temple Sowerby CA10
7 D24 Templeton *Dev.* EX16
16 C16 Templeton *Dyf.* SA67
7 D24 Templeton Bridge EX16
83 A31 Templewood DD9
108 F4 Tempo BT94
32 C47 Tempsford SG19
28 B31 Tenbury Wells WR15
16 D17 Tenby SA70
35 F57 Tendring CO16
79 C11 Tenga PA72
43 F51 Ten Mile Bank PE38
14 D54 Tenterden TN30
90 A31 Tepersie Castle AB33
64 F17 Terally DG9
34 G53 Terling CM3
39 B32 Ternhill TF9
65 C25 Terregles DG2
58 B42 Terrington YO6
43 C51 Terrington St Clement PE34
43 D51 Terrington St John PE34
98 F28 Tervieside AB37
14 B53 Teston ME18
10 C39 Testwood SO40
20 B34 Tetbury GL8
20 B34 Tetbury Upton GL8
38 B29 Tetchill SY12
6 F19 Tetcott EX22
53 E49 Tetford LN9
53 B49 Tetney DN36
53 B49 Tetney Lock DN36
21 A42 Tetsworth OX9
40 E34 Tettenhall WV6
40 F34 Tettenhall Wood WV6
33 C48 Tetworth SG19
99 F36 Teuchan AB42
51 F40 Teversal NG17
33 C50 Teversham CB1
69 C29 Teviothead TD9
91 E34 Tewel AB3
33 G48 Tewin AL6
29 E34 Tewkesbury GL20
25 E55 Teynham ME9
91 F32 Thainston AB30
91 B33 Thainstone AB51
12 E47 Thakeham RH20
21 A42 Thame OX9
22 E47 Thames Ditton KT7
24 C53 Thames Haven SS17
23 C50 Thamesmead SE28
15 B57 Thanington CT1
75 G25 Thankerton ML12
45 F57 Tharston NR15
21 E41 Thatcham RG18
48 C30 Thatto Heath WA9
33 E51 Thaxted CM6
57 A38 Theakston DL8
52 A45 Thealby DN15
21 D42 Theale *Brk.* RG7
19 G30 Theale *Som.* BS28
59 F46 Thearne HU17
28 D28 The Bage HR3
99 F33 The Banking AB51
12 D47 The Bar RH13
35 B60 Theberton IP16
91 C33 The Birks AB32
38 F29 The Bog SY5
22 G44 The Bourne GU9
40 F34 The Bratch WV5
19 A29 The Bryn NP7
29 B34 The Burf DY13
90 F31 The Burn DD9
20 A35 The Camp GL6
38 A30 The Chequer SY13
22 B43 The City HP14
10 A38 The Common SP5
96 B20 The Craigs IV24
54 D25 The Cronk IM7
11 A42 Thedden Grange GU34
41 G42 Theddingworth LE17
53 D50 Theddlethorpe All Saints LN12
53 D50 Theddlethorpe St Helen LN12
74 E19 The Den KA24
13 F51 The Dicker BN27
82 A29 The Drums DD8
19 A31 The Eaves GL15
70 F31 The Flatt CA6
32 G47 The Folly AL4
38 B29 The Grange *Shr.* SY12
23 G49 The Grange *Sry* RH9
78 C5 The Green *Str.* PA77
9 A34 The Green *Wts.* SP3
12 C46 The Haven RH14
23 F48 The Hermitage KT20
54 G24 The Howe IM9
38 D30 The Isle SY4
23 G52 The Knowle TN12
45 F59 The Laurels NR14
7 D23 Thelbridge Barton EX17
14 D55 The Leacon TN26
22 A44 The Lee HP16
54 C25 The Lhen IM7
34 A56 Thelnetham IP22
73 A17 The Lodge PA24
45 G57 Thelveton IP21
49 D32 Thelwall WA4
38 F28 The Marsh SY5
44 C56 Themelthorpe NR20
14 F53 The Moor TN18
17 F22 The Mumbles SA3
29 E34 The Mythe GL20
91 D33 The Neuk AB31
31 D41 Thenford OX17
32 G47 The Node SG4
33 E49 Therfield SG8
16 C15 The Rhos SA62
40 B34 The Rowe ST5
22 G44 The Sands GU10
20 D34 The Shoe SN14
39 F32 The Smithies WV16
14 E55 The Stocks TN30
44 G54 Thetford IP24
28 D31 The Vauld HR1
23 E48 The Wrythe SM5
39 E33 The Wyke TF11
23 B50 Theydon Bois CM16
20 D34 Thickwood SN14
53 E48 Thimbleby *Lcn.* LN9
62 G40 Thimbleby *N.Y.* DL6
57 B40 Thirkleby YO7
57 A40 Thirlby YO7
76 F31 Thirlestane TD2
57 A38 Thirn HG4
57 A40 Thirsk YO7
55 F30 Thistleton *Lan.* PR4
42 D44 Thistleton *Lei.* LE15
33 A52 Thistley Green IP28
58 C34 Thixendale YO17
70 F35 Thockrington NE48
43 E50 Tholomas Drove PE13
57 C40 Tholthorpe YO6
16 D16 Thomas Chapel SA68
98 F31 Thomastown AB54
44 F54 Thompson IP24
97 F27 Thomshill IV30
24 D52 Thong DA12
56 A35 Thoralby DL8
51 E42 Thoresby NG22
52 C47 Thoresway LN8
52 C47 Thorganby *Lcn.* DN37
58 E42 Thorganby *N.Y.* YO4
63 G42 Thorgill YO18
35 A60 Thorington IP19
34 E56 Thorington Street CO6
56 D35 Thorlby BD23
33 G50 Thorley CM23
10 F39 Thorley Street *Ham.* PO41
33 G50 Thorley Street *Hfs.* CM23
57 B40 Thormanby YO6
62 E40 Thornaby-on-Tees TS17
44 B56 Thornage NR25
31 E43 Thornborough *Bkh.* MK18
57 B38 Thornborough *N.Y.* DL8
19 B32 Thornbury *Avon* BS12
6 E19 Thornbury *Dev.* EX22
29 C32 Thornbury *H.&W.* HR7
31 A42 Thornby NN6
49 G35 Thorncliff ST13
8 D29 Thorncombe TA20
22 G46 Thorncombe Street GU8
32 D47 Thorncote Green SG19
35 B57 Thorndon IP23
51 A42 Thorne DN8
57 E39 Thorner LS14
40 E36 Thornes WS9
7 C26 Thorne St Margaret TA21
22 D46 Thorney *Bkh.* SL0
43 E48 Thorney *Cbs.* PE6
52 E44 Thorney *Not.* NG23
8 B30 Thorney *Som.* TA10
10 D38 Thorney Hill BH23
8 B28 Thorn Falcon TA3
8 C31 Thornford DT9
8 A29 Thorngrove TA7
59 G48 Thorngumbald HU12
44 A53 Thornham PE36
34 A56 Thornham Magna IP23
35 A57 Thornham Parva IP23
42 E46 Thornhaugh PE8
81 G22 Thornhill *Cen.* FK8
68 D24 Thornhill *D.&G.* DG3
50 D37 Thornhill *Dby.* S30
11 C40 Thornhill *Ham.* SO19
18 C27 Thornhill *M.G.* CF8
50 A38 Thornhill *W.Y.* WF12
59 C47 Thornholme YO25
9 D34 Thornicombe DT11
62 B39 Thornley *Drm* DH6
62 C37 Thornley *Drm.* DL13
74 E21 Thornliebank G46
34 C53 Thorns CB8
49 D35 Thornsett SK12
60 D27 Thornthwaite *Cum.* CA12
57 D37 Thornthwaite *N.Y.* HG3
31 E43 Thornton *Bkh.* MK17
62 E40 Thornton *Cle.* TS8
16 D15 Thornton *Dyf.* SA73
76 A28 Thornton *Fife* KY1
58 E43 Thornton *Hum.* YO4
55 E29 Thornton *Lan.* FY5
53 F48 Thornton *Lcn.* LN9
41 E40 Thornton *Lei.* LE67
48 B29 Thornton *Mer.* L23
77 F35 Thornton *Nor.* TD15
82 C29 Thornton *Tay.* DD8
82 C26 Thornton *Tay.* PH1
57 F36 Thornton *W.Y.* BD13
6 F21 Thornton Cross EX20
52 A46 Thornton Curtis DN39
58 A44 Thornton Dale YO18
74 E21 Thorntonhall G74
48 D29 Thornton Hough L63
56 E35 Thornton-in-Craven BD23
62 G40 Thornton-le-Beans DL6
58 C42 Thornton-le-Clay YO6
57 A39 Thornton-le-Moor DL7
52 C46 Thornton le Moor LN7
48 E30 Thornton-le-Moors CH2
57 A39 Thornton-le -Street YO7
77 C33 Thorntonloch EH42
77 F35 Thornton Park TD15
56 A35 Thornton Rust DL8
57 A37 Thornton Steward HG4
57 A38 Thornton Watlass HG4
23 A50 Thornwood Common CM16
91 F32 Thornyhill AB30
76 G29 Thornylee TD1
42 A43 Thoroton NG13
57 E40 Thorp Arch LS23
50 G37 Thorpe *Dby.* DE6
59 E46 Thorpe *Hum.* YO25
53 D50 Thorpe *Lcn.* LN12
57 C36 Thorpe *N.Y.* BD23
45 F60 Thorpe *Nfk* NR14
51 G43 Thorpe *Not.* NG23
22 E46 Thorpe *Sry* TW20
45 G57 Thorpe Abbotts IP21
41 D40 Thorpe Acre LE11
42 C43 Thorpe Arnold LE14
51 A40 Thorpe Audlin WF8
58 B44 Thorpe Bassett YO17
25 C55 Thorpe Bay SS1
42 F44 Thorpe by Water LE15
40 E38 Thorpe Constantine B79
53 F50 Thorpe Culvert PE24
45 D58 Thorpe End Garden Village NR13
34 C55 Thorpe Green IP30
58 B41 Thorpe Hall YO6
51 C39 Thorpe Hesley S61
51 A41 Thorpe in Balne DN6
52 D45 Thorpe in the Fallows LN1
42 F43 Thorpe Langton LE16
62 D39 Thorpe Larches TS21
35 F57 Thorpe-le-Soken CO16
58 E44 Thorpe le Street YO4
32 A44 Thorpe Malsor NN14
31 D40 Thorpe Mandeville OX17
45 B58 Thorpe Market NR11
34 C55 Thorpe Morieux IP30
35 C60 Thorpeness IP16
52 F44 Thorpe on the Hill *Lcn.* LN6
57 G38 Thorpe on the Hill *W.Y.* WF3
51 D41 Thorpe Salvin S80
42 D43 Thorpe Satchville LE14
45 E58 Thorpe St Andrew NR7
53 F50 Thorpe St Peter PE24
62 D39 Thorpe Thewles TS21
52 G47 Thorpe Tilney Dales LN4
57 D40 Thorpe Underwood YO5
42 G46 Thorpe Waterville NN14
58 F41 Thorpe Willoughby YO8
43 E51 Thorpland PE33
34 G56 Thorrington CO7
7 E24 Thorverton EX5
34 A56 Thrandeston IP21
32 A45 Thrapston NN14
56 C35 Threapland BD23
38 A30 Threapwood SY14
13 C48 Three Bridges RH10
2 D13 Three Burrows TR4
14 D54 Three Chimneys TN27
28 E27 Three Cocks LD3
17 E21 Three Crosses SA4
13 D52 Three Cups Corner TN21
43 E51 Three Holes PE14
42 B46 Threekingham NG34
13 C52 Three Leg Cross TN5
10 D36 Three Legged Cross BH21
22 E43 Three Mile Cross RG7
2 D13 Threemilestone TR3
60 D28 Threlkeld CA12
23 A50 Threshers Bush CM17
56 C35 Threshfield BD23
44 E54 Threxton Hill IP25
82 D28 Thriepley DD2
45 D60 Thrigby NR29
61 D35 Thringarth DL12
41 D40 Thringstone LE67
62 G39 Thrintoft DL7
33 D50 Thriplow SG8
33 E49 Throcking SG9
71 G37 Throckley NE15
29 C35 Throckmorton WR10
71 E37 Throphill NE61
71 C36 Thropton NE65
6 F22 Throwleigh EX20
14 B55 Throwley ME13
33 F52 Throws CM6
41 B40 Thrumpton NG11
103 D29 Thrumster KW1
71 B36 Thrunton NE66
20 A34 Thrupp *Glo.* GL5
31 G40 Thrupp *Oxf.* OX5
6 G20 Thrushelton EX20
41 D42 Thrussington LE7
28 E30 Thruxton *H.&W.* HR2
21 G38 Thruxton *Ham.* SP11
51 C40 Thrybergh S65
41 B39 Thulston DE72
73 F14 Thundergay KA27
24 C53 Thundersley SS7
99 E36 Thunderton AB42
33 G49 Thundridge SG12
41 D41 Thurcaston LE7
51 D40 Thurcroft S66
103 B27 Thurdistoft KW14
45 B57 Thurgarton *Nfk* NR11
41 A42 Thurgarton *Not.* NG14
50 B38 Thurgoland S30
41 F40 Thurlaston *Lei.* LE9
31 A40 Thurlaston *War.* CV23
8 B28 Thurlbear TA3
52 F44 Thurlby *Lcn.* LN5
42 D47 Thurlby *Lcn.* PE10
32 C46 Thurleigh MK44
5 F22 Thurlestone TQ7
8 A28 Thurloxton TA2
50 B38 Thurlstone S30
45 F60 Thurlton NR14
41 E41 Thurmaston LE4
41 E42 Thurnby LE7
45 D59 Thurne NR29
14 B54 Thurnham ME14
44 C56 Thurning *Nfk* NR20
42 G46 Thurning *Nmp.* PE8
51 B40 Thurnscoe S63
60 A29 Thursby CA5
44 B55 Thursford NR21
12 C44 Thursley GU8
103 B26 Thurso KW14
48 D28 Thurstaston L48
34 B55 Thurston IP31
60 A28 Thurstonfield CA5
50 B37 Thurstonland HD7
45 E59 Thurton NR14
40 B38 Thurvaston DE6
103 C28 Thuster KW1
44 E56 Thuxton NR9
61 G34 Thwaite *N.Y.* DL11
34 B56 Thwaite *Sfk* IP23
55 A29 Thwaite Head LA12
45 F59 Thwaite St Mary NR35
59 C46 Thwing YO25
82 E26 Tibbermore PH1
29 F33 Tibberton *Glo.* GL19
29 C35 Tibberton *H.&W.* WR9
39 C32 Tibberton *Shr.* TF10
69 A28 Tibbie Shiels Inn TD7
45 F57 Tibenham NR16
79 G14 Tibertich PA31
51 F40 Tibshelf DE55
59 D45 Tibthorpe YO25
13 C52 Ticehurst TN5
11 A41 Tichborne SO24
42 E45 Tickencote PE9
19 D30 Tickenham BS21
51 C41 Tickhill DN11
38 F30 Ticklerton SY6
41 C39 Ticknall DE73
59 E46 Tickton HU17
21 F38 Tidcombe SN8
21 A42 Tiddington *Oxf.* OX9
30 C37 Tiddington *War.* CV37
13 D52 Tidebrook TN5
4 E19 Tideford PL12
19 B31 Tidenham NP6
19 B31 Tidenham Chase NP6
50 E37 Tideswell SK17
21 D42 Tidmarsh RG8
30 E38 Tidmington CV36
10 C36 Tidpit SP6
16 C15 Tiers Cross SA62
31 C42 Tiffield NN12
99 E33 Tifty AB53
83 A31 Tigerton DD9
79 C12 Tighachnoic PA34
92 D2 Tigh A Ghearraidh HS6
81 F23 Tighnablair PH6
73 C15 Tighnabruaich PA21
80 A15 Tighnacomaire PH33
5 D23 Tigley TQ9
32 B46 Tilbrook PE18
24 D52 Tilbury RM18
40 G37 Tile Cross B33
30 A38 Tile Hill CV4
21 D42 Tilehurst RG31
22 G44 Tilford GU10
98 F30 Tillathrowie AB54
29 E32 Tillers' Green GL18
91 A35 Tillery AB41
38 C30 Tilley SY4
75 A24 Tillicoultry FK13
25 A55 Tillingham CM0
28 D30 Tillington *H.&W.* HR4
12 D45 Tillington *W.S.* GU28
28 D30 Tillington Common HR4
83 A30 Tillyarblet DD9
91 C32 Tillybirloch AB51
91 B32 Tillycairn Castle AB51
91 A34 Tillycorthie AB41
90 D31 Tillydrine AB31
99 E34 Tillyfar AB53
90 B31 Tillyfour AB33
91 B32 Tillyfourie AB51
91 A34 Tillygreig AB41
90 C30 Tillypronie AB34
15 B58 Tilmanstone CT14
43 D51 Tilney All Saints PE34
43 D51 Tilney High End PE34
43 D51 Tilney St Lawrence PE34
20 G36 Tilshead SP3
38 B31 Tilstock SY13
48 G30 Tilston SY14
48 F31 Tilstone Fearnall CW6
32 F45 Tilsworth LU7
42 E43 Tilton on the Hill LE7
20 B34 Tiltups End GL6
52 G47 Timberland LN4
52 F47 Timberland Dales LN10
49 F34 Timbersbrook CW12
7 A25 Timberscombe TA24
57 D37 Timble LS21
49 D33 Timperley WA15
19 F32 Timsbury *Avon* BA3
10 B39 Timsbury *Ham.* SO51
100 D6 Timsgearraidh HS2
34 B54 Timworth Green IP31
9 E33 Tincleton DT2
61 A32 Tindale CA8
31 E46 Tingewick MK18
57 G38 Tingley WF3
32 E45 Tingrith MK17
104 D29 Tingwall KW17
6 G20 Tinhay PL16
4 A18 Tinney EX22
57 E38 Tinshill LS16
51 C39 Tinsley S9
13 C48 Tinsley Green RH10
4 B16 Tintagel PL34
19 A31 Tintern Parva NP6
8 C30 Tintinhull BA22
50 C36 Tintwistle SK14
68 E25 Tinwald DG1
42 E45 Tinwell PE9
91 E33 Tipperty *Grm.* AB30
91 A35 Tipperty *Grm.* AB41
10 E38 Tiptoe SO41
40 F35 Tipton DY4
7 F26 Tipton St John EX10
34 G54 Tiptree CO5
34 G54 Tiptree Heath CO5
27 D34 Tirabad LD4
17 E22 Tirdeunaw SA5
78 C5 Tiree Airport PA77
87 F18 Tirindrish PH34
29 F34 Tirley GL19
18 A27 Tirphil NP2
61 D30 Tirril CA10
17 C22 Tir-y-dail SA18
9 B35 Tisbury SP3
50 G37 Tissington DE6
103 B27 Tister KW12
6 C18 Titchberry EX39
11 D41 Titchfield PO14
32 A46 Titchmarsh NN14
44 A53 Titchwell PE31
41 B42 Tithby NG13
28 B29 Titley HR5
23 F50 Titsey RH8
6 E18 Titson EX23
40 B34 Tittensor ST12
44 C54 Tittleshall PE32
48 F31 Tiverton *Che.* CW6
7 D25 Tiverton *Dev.* EX16
45 G57 Tivetshall St Margaret NR15
45 G57 Tivetshall St Mary NR15

Tyldesley

40 C35 Tixall ST18
42 E45 Tixover PE9
105 A31 Toab *Ork.* KW17
107 E37 Toab *She.* ZE3
109 D6 Tobermore BT45
79 B10 Tobermory PA75
79 G13 Toberonochy PA34
84 A3 Tobha Mor HS8
100 D7 Tobson HS2
98 F32 Tocher AB51
20 D36 Tockenham SN4
20 C36 Tockenham Wick SN4
56 G32 Tockholes BB3
19 C31 Tockington BS12
57 D40 Tockwith YO5
9 C33 Todber DT10
32 F45 Toddington *Bfd.* LU5
30 E36 Toddington *Glo.* GL54
12 F46 Toddington *W.S.* BN17
30 E38 Todenham GL56
69 G29 Todhills *Cum.* CA6
83 D30 Todhills *Tay.* DD4
91 B32 Todlachie AB51
56 G35 Todmorden OL14
51 D40 Todwick S31
33 C49 Toft *Cbs.* CB3
42 D46 Toft *Lcn.* PE10
106 E40 Toft *She.* ZE2
103 D29 Toftcarl KW1
62 D37 Toft Hill DL14
45 F60 Toft Monks NR34
52 D46 Toft next Newton LN8
44 C54 Toftrees NR21
103 B29 Tofts KW1
44 D55 Toftwood NR19
71 C38 Togston NE65
86 C12 Tokavaig IV46
22 D43 Tokers Green RG4
101 C11 Tolastadh HS2
100 D7 Tolastadh a Chaolais HS2
101 C11 Tolastadh Ur HS2
7 B26 Tolland TA4
9 C35 Tollard Royal SP5
74 D22 Tollcross G32
8 D31 Toller Down Gate DT2
8 E31 Toller Fratrum DT2
8 E31 Toller Porcorum DT2
57 C40 Tollerton *N.Y.* YO6
41 B41 Tollerton *Not.* NG12
8 D31 Toller Whelme DT8
25 A55 Tollesbury CM9
62 E40 Tollesby TS7
34 G55 Tolleshunt D`Arcy CM9
34 G55 Tolleshunt Knights CM9
34 G54 Tolleshunt Major CM9
99 F35 Toll of Birness AB41
9 E33 Tolpuddle DT2
89 E24 Tolvah PH21
22 E47 Tolworth KT6
100 F9 Tom an Fhuadain HS2
88 B23 Tomatin IV13
88 A22 Tombreck IV1
87 C18 Tomchrasky IV3
87 D17 Tomdoun PH35
97 G25 Tomdow IV36
96 D22 Tomich *Hgh.* IV18
96 A22 Tomich *Hgh.* IV27
87 B19 Tomich *Hgh.* IV4
90 B27 Tomintoul AB37
96 G20 Tomnacross IV4
97 F26 Tomnamoon IV36
98 F29 Tomnaven AB54
90 A27 Tomnavoulin AB37
89 A26 Tomvaich PH26
23 G51 Tonbridge TN
18 C24 Tondu CF32
36 E21 Tonfanau LL36
39 E33 Tong TF11
41 C40 Tonge DE73
22 G44 Tongham GU10
65 E22 Tongland DG6
39 E33 Tong Norton TF11
57 F37 Tong Street BD4
102 C21 Tongue IV27
102 C21 Tongue Ho. IV27
18 C27 Tongwynlais CF4
18 B23 Tonna SA11
18 B25 Ton-Pentre CF41
18 C26 Ton-teg CF38
33 G49 Tonwell SG12
18 B25 Tonypandy CF40
18 C25 Tonyrefail CF39
109 D7 Toomebridge BT41
21 A41 Toot Baldon OX44
23 A50 Toot Hill CM5
10 C39 Toothill SO51
57 B39 Topcliffe YO7
45 F58 Topcroft NR35
45 F58 Topcroft Street NR35
32 B46 Top End MK44
34 E53 Toppesfield CO9
49 A33 Toppings BL7
7 G25 Topsham EX3
5 E23 Topsham Bridge TQ7
78 A8 Torastan PA78
90 B27 Torbain AB37
90 D29 Torbeg *Grm.* AB35
66 A14 Torbeg *Str.* KA27
5 D24 Torbryan TQ12
87 G17 Torcastle PH33
5 F24 Torcross TQ7
88 A22 Tordarroch IV1
96 F21 Tore IV6
97 E26 Toreduff IV36
103 E27 Toremore KW6
87 C18 Torgyle IV3
52 E44 Torksey LN1
92 F3 Torlum HS7
87 G17 Torlundy PH33
20 D33 Tormarton GL9
72 E8 Tormisdale PA47
73 G14 Tormore KA27
103 C27 Tormsdale KW12
96 G23 Tornagrain IV1
90 C28 Tornahaish AB36
90 C31 Tornaveen AB31
88 B21 Torness IV1
60 C27 Torpenhow CA5
75 C25 Torphichen EH48
90 C31 Torphins AB31
4 E20 Torpoint PL11
5 D25 Torquay TQ
76 F30 Torquhan TD1
5 E21 Torr PL8
96 D22 Torran *Hgh.* IV18
94 G11 Torran *Hgh.* IV40
79 G14 Torran *Str.* PA31
74 C22 Torrance *Str.* G64
74 E22 Torrance *Str.* G75
90 B29 Torrancroy AB36
97 F24 Torrich IV12
94 F15 Torridon IV22
86 B11 Torrin IV49
102 B22 Torrisdale *Hgh.* KW14
73 G13 Torrisdale *Str.* PA28
103 G25 Torrish KW8
55 C30 Torrisholme LA4
96 A21 Torroble IV27
91 C35 Torry *Grm.* AB1
98 E30 Torry *Grm.* AB54
75 B26 Torryburn KY12
76 F30 Torsonce TD1
99 E36 Torterston AB42
69 F26 Torthorwald DG1
12 F45 Tortington BN18
19 B32 Tortworth GL12
93 G10 Torvaig IV51
60 G28 Torver LA21
75 B24 Torwood FK5
51 D42 Torworth DN22
6 C18 Tosberry EX39
86 A12 Toscaig IV54
33 B48 Toseland PE19
56 D33 Tosside BD23
78 C9 Tostarie PA74
34 B55 Tostock IP30
93 F8 Totaig IV55
78 B7 Totamore PA78
93 G10 Tote IV51
102 B24 Totegan KW14
11 A41 Totford SO24
53 D50 Tothill LN13
10 F39 Totland PO39
51 D39 Totley S17
5 D23 Totnes TQ9
41 B40 Toton NG9
78 B7 Totronald PA78
23 B49 Tottenham N17
44 D52 Tottenhill PE33
23 B48 Totteridge N20
32 F45 Totternhoe LU6
49 A33 Tottington *G.M.* BL8
44 F54 Tottington *Nfk* IP24
10 C39 Totton SO40
22 D44 Touchen-End SL6
7 B27 Toulton TA4
99 D35 Toux AB42
14 B53 Tovil ME15
73 D17 Toward PA23
31 D42 Towcester NN12
2 E10 Towednack TR26
23 C49 Tower Hamlets E
22 A43 Towersey OX9
90 B30 Towie *Grm.* AB33
99 C34 Towie *Grm.* AB43
90 A31 Towie *Grm.* AB54
98 E29 Towiemore AB55
62 C37 Tow Law DL13
43 F49 Town End *Cbs.* PE15
55 A30 Town End *Cum.* LA11
74 C20 Townend G82
48 B30 Town Green L39
65 F22 Townhead DG6
65 D23 Townhead of Greenlaw DG7
75 B26 Townhill KY12
13 C51 Town Row TN6
2 E11 Townshend TR27
44 G53 Town Street IP27
70 A33 Town Yetholm TD5
58 C44 Towthorpe *Hum.* YO25
58 D42 Towthorpe *N.Y.* YO3
57 F40 Towton LS24
47 E25 Towyn LL22
53 F49 Toynton All Saints PE23
53 F49 Toynton Fen Side PE23
53 F50 Toynton St Peter PE23
23 F50 Toy`s Hill TN16
67 A20 Trabboch KA5
2 F13 Traboe TR12
97 F24 Tradespark *Hgh.* IV12
105 A30 Tradespark *Ork.* KW15
49 C33 Trafford Park M17
27 F25 Trallong LD3
19 A28 Tranch NP4
76 C29 Tranent EH33
102 C24 Trantlebeg KW13
102 C24 Trantlemore KW13
71 E37 Tranwell NE61
17 C22 Trapp SA19
76 C31 Traprain EH41
76 G29 Traquair EH44
56 F35 Trawden BB8
37 B22 Trawsfynydd LL41
18 B25 Trealaw CF40
55 F30 Treales PR4
46 E18 Trearddur LL65
93 F9 Treaslane IV51
18 C26 Trebanog CF39
17 D22 Trebanos SA8
4 A18 Trebarrow EX22
4 C18 Trebartha PL15
4 B16 Trebarwith PL33
3 A15 Trebetherick PL27
7 B25 Treborough TA23
3 B15 Trebudannon TR8
4 C18 Trebullett PL15
4 C19 Treburley PL15
4 D16 Trebyan PL30
27 F24 Trecastle LD3
16 A15 Trecwn SA62
18 A25 Trecynon CF44
2 F10 Tredavoe TR20
16 B14 Tre-ddiog SA62
18 A27 Tredegar NP2
29 F34 Tredington *Glo.* GL20
30 D38 Tredington *War.* CV36
4 E18 Tredinnick *Cnw.* PL14
3 A15 Tredinnick *Cnw.* PL27
16 A16 Tredissi SA42
27 E26 Tredomen LD3
19 B29 Tredunnock NP5
2 F9 Treen TR19
51 D40 Treeton S60
38 F28 Trefaldwyn (Montgomery) SY15
16 A14 Trefasser SA64
46 E19 Trefdraeth LL62
28 E27 Trefecca LD3
37 F25 Trefeglwys SY17
26 B21 Trefenter SY23
16 B15 Treffgarne SA62
16 B14 Treffynnon SA62
16 B14 Trefgarn Owen SA62
28 G27 Trefil NP2
26 C21 Trefilan SA48
38 C28 Treflach SY10
38 D27 Trefnanney SY22
47 E26 Trefnant LL16
38 C28 Trefonen SY10
36 A19 Trefor *Gwy.* LL54
46 D19 Trefor *Gwy.* LL65
18 C26 Treforest CF37
18 C26 Treforest Ind. Est. CF37
47 F23 Trefriw LL27
28 G30 Trefynwy (Monmouth) NP5
4 B18 Tregadillett PL15
46 E20 Tregaian LL77
28 G30 Tregare NP5
27 C22 Tregaron SY25
46 F21 Tregarth LL57
2 D13 Tregavethan TR4
3 C14 Tregear TR2
4 B18 Tregeare PL15
38 B27 Tregeiriog LL20
46 C19 Tregele LL68
2 F13 Tregidden TR12
16 B13 Treglemais SA62
3 A14 Tregolds PL28
4 A17 Tregole EX23
3 B15 Tregonetha TR9
3 D15 Tregony TR2
28 E27 Tregoyd LD3
26 D20 Tre-groes *Dyf.* SA44
18 C25 Tre-groes *M.G.* CF35
18 D26 Treguff CF62
3 B14 Tregurrian TR8
37 F26 Tregynon SY16
18 B26 Trehafod CF37
18 B26 Treharris CF46
18 B25 Treherbert CF42
4 C19 Trekenner PL15
4 A17 Trelash PL15
3 C14 Trelassick TR2
47 E26 Trelawnyd LL18
17 A18 Trelech SA33
17 B18 Trelech a`r Betws SA33
18 B26 Trelewis CF46
3 A15 Treligths PL29
4 C16 Trelill PL30
3 E14 Trelissick TR3
19 A30 Trelleck NP5
19 A30 Trelleck Grange NP6
47 D27 Trelogan CH8
38 E28 Trelystan SY21
36 A21 Tremadog LL49
4 B17 Tremail PL32
26 D18 Tremain SA43
4 B18 Tremaine PL15
4 D18 Tremar PL14
4 E19 Trematon PL12
47 E26 Tremeirchion LL17
2 E9 Tremethick Cross TR20
3 B14 Trenance TR8
4 F16 Trenarren PL26
38 B29 Trench *Clw.* LL13
39 D32 Trench *Shr.* TF2
4 B18 Treneglos PL15
4 E17 Trenewan PL13
8 C31 Trent DT9
40 A34 Trentham ST4
6 A22 Trentishoe EX31
18 D25 Treoes CF35
18 B25 Treorchy CF42
37 F22 Tre`r-ddol SY20
26 D17 Tre-Rhys SA43
4 E19 Trerule Foot PL12
26 C18 Tresaith SA43
40 F34 Trescott WV6
2 E11 Trescowe TR20
20 B33 Tresham GL12
78 C9 Treshnish PA75
3 D14 Tresillian TR2
4 B17 Tresinney PL32
16 A14 Tresinwen SA64
4 A18 Treskinnick Cross EX23
4 B18 Tresmeer PL15
4 A17 Tresparrett PL32
4 A16 Tresparrett Posts PL32
81 A24 Tressait PH16
107 B39 Tresta *She.* ZE2
106 C42 Tresta *She.* ZE2
51 E43 Treswell DN22
4 E16 Trethurgy PL26
16 B13 Tretio SA62
28 F31 Tretire HR2
28 F27 Tretower NP8
48 G28 Treuddyn CH7
4 A16 Trevalga PL35
48 G29 Trevalyn LL12
3 A15 Trevanson PL27
3 B15 Trevarren TR9
3 D15 Trevarrick PL26
17 B19 Tre-vaughan SA31
16 C17 Trevaughan SA34
2 C13 Trevellas TR5
4 D18 Trevelmond PL14
2 E13 Treverva TR11
2 F9 Trevescan TR19
19 A28 Trevethin NP4
4 D19 Trevigro PL17
16 A14 Trevine *Dyf.* SA62
80 E16 Trevine *Str.* PA35
3 C15 Treviscoe PL26
3 A14 Trevone PL28
38 A28 Trevor LL20
4 B16 Trewalder PL33
4 B16 Trewarmett PL34
3 D14 Trewarthenick TR2
4 B17 Trewassa PL32
2 E9 Trewellard TR19
4 B18 Trewen PL15
38 D28 Trewern SY21
4 E18 Trewidland PL14
26 D17 Trewilym SA41
4 A17 Trewint EX23
3 E14 Trewithian TR2
3 C15 Trewoon PL25
3 A15 Treworнan PL27
3 A14 Treyarnon PL28
12 E44 Treyford GU29
57 G36 Triangle HX6
10 D36 Trickett`s Cross BH22
108 E4 Trillick BT78
62 C39 Trimdon TS29
62 C39 Trimdon Colliery TS29
62 C39 Trimdon Grange TS29
45 B58 Trimingham NR27
35 E58 Trimley St Martin IP10
35 E58 Trimley St Mary IP10
29 A33 Trimpley DY12
17 D20 Trimsaran SA17
6 A21 Trimstone EX34
81 A23 Trinafour PH18
18 B27 Trinant NP1
32 G45 Tring HP23
83 A31 Trinity DD9
87 G16 Trislaig PH33
3 C14 Trispen TR4
71 D37 Tritlington NE61
82 C25 Trochry PH8
26 D19 Troedyraur SA38
18 A26 Troedyrhiw CF48
106 E39 Trondavoe ZE2
2 E12 Troon *Cnw.* TR14
74 G19 Troon *Str.* KA10
84 C3 Trosaraidh HS8
34 A54 Troston IP31
4 A18 Troswell PL15
24 E52 Trottiscliffe ME19
12 D44 Trotton GU31
70 D34 Troughend NE19
73 C16 Troustan PA22
60 F29 Troutbeck LA23
60 F29 Troutbeck Bridge LA23
20 F34 Trowbridge BA14
19 A31 Trow Green GL15
20 F34 Trowle Common BA14
32 G46 Trowley Bottom AL3
76 G32 Trows TD5
45 E58 Trowse Newton NR14
72 E10 Trudernish PA42
20 G33 Trudoxhill BA11
8 B28 Trull TA3
92 D4 Trumaisge Arraidh HS6
93 E8 Trumpan IV55
29 E32 Trumpet HR8
33 C50 Trumpington CB2
45 B58 Trunch NR28
55 E29 Trunnah FY5
3 D14 Truro TR1
7 G24 Trusham TQ13
40 B38 Trusley DE6
53 D51 Trusthorpe LN12
3 C14 Truthan TR4
40 F34 Trysull WV5
21 B40 Tubney OX13
5 E23 Tuckenhay TQ9
2 D12 Tuckingmill TR14
34 A53 Tuddenham *Sfk* IP28
35 D57 Tuddenham *Sfk* IP6
23 G52 Tudeley TN11
62 C38 Tudhoe DL16
36 B18 Tudweiloig LL53
29 G34 Tuffley GL4
16 B16 Tufton *Dyf.* SA63
21 G40 Tufton *Ham.* RG28
42 E43 Tugby LE7
38 G31 Tugford SY7
71 A37 Tughall NE67
94 C14 Tuirnaig IV22
82 E25 Tulchan PH1
75 A24 Tullibody FK10
81 D21 Tullich *Cen.* FK21
98 E29 Tullich *Grm.* AB55
88 B22 Tullich *Hgh.* IV1
97 D24 Tullich *Hgh.* IV20
80 F16 Tullich *Str.* PA32
79 F14 Tullich *Str.* PA34
96 D23 Tullich Muir IV18
82 B25 Tulliemet PH9
99 F34 Tulloch *Grm.* AB51
97 F26 Tulloch *Grm.* IV36
96 B22 Tulloch *Hgh.* IV24
73 A15 Tullochgorm PA32
89 B25 Tullochgribban High PH26
90 C31 Tullochvenus AB31
83 C30 Tulloes DD8
81 E23 Tullybannocher PH6
82 D26 Tullybelton PH1
82 C27 Tullyfergus PH11
109 E6 Tullyhogue BT80
82 B27 Tullymurdoch PH11
109 F6 Tullynagrow BT60
90 B31 Tullynessle AB33
17 C21 Tumble SA14
53 G48 Tumby PE22
53 G48 Tumby Woodside PE22
81 B23 Tummel Bridge PH16
69 E27 Tundergarth Mains DG11
100 D10 Tunga HS2
59 F49 Tunstall *Hum.* HU12
24 E54 Tunstall *Kent* ME9
55 B31 Tunstall *Lan.* LA6
62 G37 Tunstall *N.Y.* DL10
45 E60 Tunstall *Nfk* NR13
35 C59 Tunstall *Sfk* IP12
49 G34 Tunstall *Stf.* ST6
45 C58 Tunstead NR12
21 G42 Tunworth RG25
28 E31 Tupsley HR1
73 B13 Turbiskill PA31
99 D34 Turclossie AB43
21 F42 Turgis Green RG27
83 B31 Turin DD8
30 G36 Turkdean GL54
42 F43 Tur Langton LE8
28 E29 Turnastone HR2
67 C17 Turnberry KA26
4 E20 Turnchapel PL9
40 A38 Turnditch DE56
30 A37 Turner`s Green CV35
13 C49 Turners Hill RH10
9 E34 Turners Puddle DT2
23 A49 Turnford EN10
9 D33 Turnworth DT11
88 E19 Turret Bridge PH31
99 D33 Turriff AB53
49 A33 Turton Bottoms BL7
32 C45 Turvey MK43
22 B43 Turville RG9
22 B43 Turville Heath RG9
31 E41 Turweston NN13
40 C37 Tutbury DE13
29 A35 Tutnall B60
19 B31 Tutshill NP6
45 C58 Tuttington NR11
51 E43 Tuxford NG22
104 D28 Twatt *Ork.* KW17
107 B39 Twatt *She.* ZE2
74 C22 Twechar G65
77 E35 Tweedmouth TD15
69 A26 Tweedsmuir ML12
2 D13 Twelveheads TR4
42 C47 Twenty PE10
19 E32 Twerton BA2
22 D47 Twickenham TW
29 F34 Twigworth GL2
13 D48 Twineham RH17
20 F33 Twinhoe BA2
34 E54 Twinstead CO10
49 C32 Twiss Green WA3
7 B23 Twitchen *Dev.* EX36
28 A29 Twitchen *Shr.* SY7
71 A37 Twizell House NE70
5 C22 Two Bridges PL20
50 F38 Two Dales DE4
40 E38 Two Gates B77
41 E39 Twycross CV9
31 F42 Twyford *Bkh.* MK18
22 D43 Twyford *Brk.* RG10
41 C39 Twyford *Dby.* DE73
9 C34 Twyford *Dor.* SP7
11 B40 Twyford *Ham.* SO21
42 D43 Twyford *Lei.* LE14
44 C56 Twyford *Nfk* NR20
28 E31 Twyford Common HR2
65 E22 Twynholm DG6
29 E34 Twyning GL20
29 E34 Twyning Green GL20
27 F23 Twynllanan SA19
18 D26 Twyn-yr-odyn CF5
19 A29 Twyn-y-Sheriff NP5
32 A45 Twywell NN14
28 D29 Tyberton HR2
40 F37 Tyburn B24
17 C21 Tycroes SA18
37 D26 Tycrwyn SY22
43 D50 Tydd Gote PE13
43 D49 Tydd St Giles PE13
43 D50 Tydd St Mary PE13
24 B52 Tye Common CM12
34 F53 Tye Green CM7
36 B17 Ty-hen LL53
49 B32 Tyldesley M29

Tyle-garw

18 C26 Tyle-garw CF7
25 E57 Tyler Hill CT2
22 B44 Tylers Green *Bkh.* HP10
23 A51 Tylers Green *Esx* CM16
18 B25 Tylorstown CF43
27 A25 Tylwch LD6
38 A27 Ty-mawr *Clw.* LL21
37 A25 Ty-mawr *Clw.* LL21
37 A25 Ty-nant *Clw.* LL21
37 C25 Ty-nant *Gwy.* LL23
80 D19 Tyndrum FK20
9 F34 Tyneham BH20
76 E29 Tynehead EH37
71 F39 Tynemouth NE30
18 B24 Tynewydd CF42
76 C31 Tyninghame EH42
80 C15 Tynribbie PA38
68 D23 Tynron DG3
37 A26 Tyn-y-cefn LL21
37 G24 Tyn-y-Cwm SY18
37 B26 Tyn-y-ffridd SY10
27 D25 Tyn-y-graig LD2
27 B22 Tynygraig SY25
47 E23 Ty'n-y-groes LL32
109 F9 Tyrella BT30
32 D44 Tyringham MK16
18 D24 Tythegston CF32
19 C32 Tytherington *Avon* GL12
49 E34 Tytherington *Che.* SK10
20 G33 Tytherington *Som.* BA11
20 G34 Tytherington *Wts.* BA12
8 D28 Tytherleigh EX13
37 C25 Ty-uchaf SY10
4 E16 Tywardreath PL24
4 E16 Tywardreath Highway PL24
47 E23 Tywyn *Gwy.* LL31
36 E21 Tywyn *Gwy.* LL36

U

92 F3 Uachdar HS7
86 A13 Uags IV54
35 A59 Ubbeston Green IP19
19 F31 Ubley BS18
62 F38 Uckerby DL10
13 D50 Uckfield TN22
29 E34 Uckinghall GL20
29 F34 Uckington GL51
74 D22 Uddingston G71
75 G24 Uddington ML11
14 F54 Udimore TN31
91 A34 Udny Green AB41
91 A34 Udny Station AB41
75 F23 Udstonhead ML10
20 D37 Uffcott SN4
7 D26 Uffculme EX15
42 E46 Uffington *Lcn.* PE9
21 C39 Uffington *Oxf.* SN7
38 D31 Uffington *Shr.* SY4
42 E46 Ufford *Cbs.* PE9
35 C58 Ufford *Sfk* IP13
30 B39 Ufton CV33
21 E42 Ufton Nervet RG7
5 E22 Ugborough PL21
35 A60 Uggeshall NR34
63 F44 Ugglebarnby YO22
33 F51 Ugley CM22
33 F50 Ugley Green CM22
63 E43 Ugthorpe YO21
93 E9 Uig *Hgh.* IV51
93 F7 Uig *Hgh.* IV55
73 B17 Uig *Str.* PA23
78 B7 Uig *Str.* PA78
100 D6 Uigen HS2
93 G8 Uiginish IV55
93 G10 Uigshader IV51
92 G4 Uisgebhagh HS7
78 F9 Uisken PA67
103 D29 Ulbster KW2
60 D29 Ulcat row CA11
52 A47 Ulceby *Hum.* DN39
53 E50 Ulceby *Lcn.* LN13
53 E50 Ulceby Cross LN13
14 C54 Ulcombe ME17
60 C28 Uldale CA5
61 G33 Uldale House CA17
20 B33 Uley GL11
71 D38 Ulgham NE61
95 B17 Ullapool IV26
30 B37 Ullenhall B95
29 G35 Ullenwood GL53
58 E41 Ulleskelf LS24
41 G40 Ullesthorpe LE17
51 D40 Ulley S31
28 D31 Ullingswick HR1
85 A9 Ullinish IV56
60 D26 Ullock CA14
60 G27 Ulpha LA20
59 D47 Ulrome YO25
106 D40 Ulsta ZE2
24 A53 Ulting CM9
79 E11 Uluvalt PA70
55 B28 Ulverston LA12
10 F36 Ulwell BH19
68 C23 Ulzieside DG4
6 C22 Umberleigh EX37
101 E18 Unapool IV27
60 G30 Underbarrow LA8
106 B41 Underhoull ZE2
23 F51 Underriver TN15
19 C29 Underwood *Gwe.* NP6
51 G40 Underwood *Not.* NG16
19 C30 Undy NP6
107 B38 Unifirth ZE2
91 D34 Union Croft AB3
54 F25 Union Mills IM4
51 E39 Unstone S18
60 C30 Unthank CA11
20 F37 Upavon SN9
9 D32 Up Cerne DT2
24 E54 Upchurch ME9
6 F20 Upcott *Dev.* EX21
28 C29 Upcott *H.&W.* HR3
33 C52 Upend CB8
7 E25 Up Exe EX5
8 D31 Uphall *Dor.* DT2
75 C26 Uphall *Ltn* EH52
75 C26 Uphall Station EH54
7 E24 Upham *Dev.* EX17
11 B41 Upham *Ham.* SO32
29 B34 Uphampton WR9
29 F34 Up Hatherley GL51
19 F29 Uphill BS23
48 B31 Up Holland WN8
29 F33 Upleadon GL18
63 D42 Upleatham TS11
25 E55 Uplees ME13
8 E31 Uploders DT6
7 D25 Uplowman EX16
8 E29 Uplyme DT7
11 C43 Up Marden PO18
23 C51 Upminster RM14
21 F42 Up Nately RG27
7 E27 Upottery EX14
38 G30 Upper Affcot SY6
73 D16 Upper Ardroscadale PA20
39 G33 Upper Arley DY12
31 G42 Upper Arncott OX6
40 F34 Upper Aston WV5
31 E41 Upper Astrop OX17
21 D41 Upper Basildon RG8
12 E47 Upper Beeding BN44
42 G45 Upper Benefield PE8
102 C24 Upper Bighouse KW13
18 C26 Upper Boat CF37
31 C40 Upper Boddington NN11
36 G21 Upper Borth SY24
99 C35 Upper Boyndlie AB43
30 D38 Upper Brailes OX15
86 B12 Upper Breakish IV42
28 D30 Upper Breinton HR4
41 C42 Upper Broughton LE14
21 E41 Upper Bucklebury RG7
10 C37 Upper Burgate SP6
91 D34 Upper Burnhaugh AB3
32 D47 Upper Caldecote SG18
103 D28 Upper Camster KW3
29 A35 Upper Catshill B61
27 D26 Upper Chapel LD3
21 F38 Upper Chute SP11
21 G39 Upper Clatford SP11
29 G35 Upper Coberley GL53
38 E31 Upper Cound SY5
19 B28 Upper Cwmbran NP44
98 C29 Upper Dallachy IV32
32 B46 Upper Dean PE18
50 B38 Upper Denby HD8
89 A26 Upper Derraid PH26
94 E14 Upper Diabaig IV22
13 E51 Upper Dicker BN27
35 F58 Upper Dovercourt CO12
57 C40 Upper Dunsforth YO5
40 G38 Upper Eastern Green CV5
96 E23 Upper Eathie IV11
50 G36 Upper Elkstone SK17
50 E36 Upper End SK17
11 A43 Upper Farringdon GU34
29 G33 Upper Framilode GL2
22 G43 Upper Froyle GU34
103 A29 Upper Gills KW1
86 E15 Upper Glendessarry PH34
19 G30 Upper Godney BA5
40 F35 Upper Gornal DY3
32 E47 Upper Gravenhurst MK45
21 E39 Upper Green *Brk.* RG20
33 E50 Upper Green *Esx* CB11
28 G29 Upper Green *Gwe.* NP7
79 E14 Upper Gylen PA34
50 F38 Upper Hackney DE4
22 E46 Upper Halliford TW17
24 E52 Upper Halling ME2
42 E45 Upper Hambleton LE15
15 B57 Upper Hardres Court CT4
13 C50 Upper Hartfield TN7
99 F36 Upper Hawkhillock AB42
38 G31 Upper Hayton SY8
38 G31 Upper Heath SY7
58 D42 Upper Helmsley YO4
28 C28 Upper Hergest HR5
31 F40 Upper Heyford OX6
28 C30 Upper Hill HR6
50 A37 Upper Hopton WF14
13 E51 Upper Horsebridge BN27
49 F35 Upper Hulme ST13
20 B37 Upper Inglesham SN6
72 A9 Upper Kilchattan PA61
17 E21 Upper Killay SA2
97 G27 Upper Knockando AB38
21 C38 Upper Lambourn RG17
109 C6 Upperlands BT46
51 E41 Upper Langwith NG20
83 G30 Upper Largo KY8
91 D33 Upper Lochton AB31
40 D36 Upper Longdon WS15
40 F34 Upper Ludstone WV5
103 E28 Upper Lybster KW3
29 G32 Upper Lydbrook GL17
28 E29 Upper Maes-coed HR2
50 C37 Upper Midhope S30
49 B35 Uppermill OL3
20 B36 Upper Minety SN16
29 A33 Upper Mitton DY13
22 B44 Upper North Dean HP14
23 D49 Upper Norwood SE19
82 D26 Upper Obney PH1
30 F37 Upper Oddington GL56
85 A10 Upper Ollach IV51
58 D41 Upper Poppleton YO2
30 D37 Upper Quinton CV37
99 D36 Upper Ridinghill AB43
29 B32 Upper Rochford WR15
105 A31 Upper Sanday KW17
29 B32 Upper Sapey WR6
20 C35 Upper Seagry SN15
32 D45 Upper Shelton MK43
45 A57 Upper Sheringham NR26
74 D18 Upper Skelmorlie PA17
30 F37 Upper Slaughter GL54
80 E16 Upper Sonachan PA33
29 G32 Upper Soudley GL14
41 G39 Upper Stoke CV2
32 E47 Upper Stondon SG16
31 C42 Upper Stowe NN7
10 C37 Upper Street *Ham.* SP6
45 D59 Upper Street *Nfk* NR12
35 E57 Upper Street *Sfk* IP9
32 F46 Upper Sundon LU5
30 F37 Upper Swell GL54
40 B35 Upper Tean ST10
50 B36 Upperthong HD7
55 D30 Upper Thurnham LA2
82 G26 Upper Tillyrie KY13
12 D45 Upperton GU28
23 D48 Upper Tooting SW17
19 E30 Upper Town BS18
103 A29 Uppertown KW1
30 D39 Upper Tysoe CV35
21 D38 Upper Upham SN8
24 D53 Upper Upnor ME2
83 D31 Upper Victoria DD7
31 D40 Upper Wardington OX17
31 E43 Upper Weald MK19
31 C42 Upper Weedon NN7
28 C28 Upper Welson HR3
11 A42 Upper Wield SO24
31 G43 Upper Winchendon HP18
10 A37 Upper Woodford SP4
21 F41 Upper Wootton RG26
20 D33 Upper Wraxall SN14
29 D33 Upper Wyche WR14
42 F44 Uppingham LE15
10 D36 Uppington *Dor.* BH21
38 E31 Uppington *Shr.* TF6
57 A40 Upsall YO7
77 F34 Upsettlington TD15
23 A49 Upshire EN9
11 A40 Up Somborne SO20
25 E57 Upstreet CT3
9 D32 Up Sydling DT2
31 G43 Upton *Bkh.* HP17
22 D45 Upton *Brk.* SL1
32 A47 Upton *Cbs.* PE17
42 E47 Upton *Cbs.* PE5
48 F30 Upton *Che.* CH2
4 C18 Upton *Cnw.* PL14
7 E26 Upton *Dev.* EX14
5 F23 Upton *Dev.* TQ7
9 E35 Upton *Dor.* BH16
10 C39 Upton *Ham.* S016
21 F39 Upton *Ham.* SP11
52 D44 Upton *Lcn.* DN21
48 D28 Upton *Mer.* L49
45 D59 Upton *Nfk* NR13
31 B43 Upton *Nmp.* NN5
51 E43 Upton *Not.* DN22
51 G43 Upton *Not.* NG23
21 C40 Upton *Oxf.* OX11
7 C25 Upton *Som.* TA4
51 A40 Upton *W.Y.* WF9
29 F32 Upton Bishop HR9
19 D32 Upton Cheyney BS15
39 F32 Upton Cressett WV16
4 C18 Upton Cross PL14
32 E47 Upton End SG5
45 D59 Upton Green NR13
22 G43 Upton Grey RG25
7 E24 Upton Hellions EX17
20 G35 Upton Lovell BA12
38 D31 Upton Magna SY4
9 A33 Upton Noble BA4
7 F25 Upton Pyne EX5
20 G34 Upton Scudamore BA12
29 C35 Upton Snodsbury WR7
29 G34 Upton St Leonards GL4
29 D34 Upton upon Severn WR8
29 B35 Upton Warren B61
12 E45 Upwaltham GU28
33 B51 Upware CB7
43 E51 Upwell PE14
9 F32 Upwey DT3
43 G48 Upwood PE17
107 D39 Uradale ZE1
106 E38 Urafirth ZE2
97 G24 Urchany IV12
20 F36 Urchfont SN10
28 D31 Urdimarsh HR1
106 E33 Ure ZE2
93 B7 Urgha HS3
62 E39 Urlay Nook TS16
49 C33 Urmston M31
98 C28 Urquhart *Grm.* IV30
96 F21 Urquhart *Hgh.* IV7
63 F41 Urra TS9
96 F20 Urray IV6
62 B38 Ushaw Moor DH7
19 A29 Usk NP5
52 C46 Usselby LN8
57 E36 Utley BD20
7 F24 Uton EX17
53 C48 Utterby LN11
40 B36 Uttoxeter ST14
36 C17 Uwchmynydd LL53
22 C46 Uxbridge UB8
106 B41 Uyeasound ZE2
16 C15 Uzmaston SA62

V

46 E18 Valley LL65
65 E22 Valleyfield *D.&G.* DG6
75 B25 Valleyfield *Fife* KY12
4 B17 Valley Trudde PL32
106 A42 Valsgarth ZE2
24 C53 Vange SS16
17 D22 Vardre SA6
19 A28 Varteg NP4
93 G8 Vatten IV55
78 C6 Vaul PA77
27 G26 Vaynor CF48
38 E27 Vaynor Park SY21
28 C27 Veaullt HR5
107 C39 Veensgarth ZE2
16 A16 Velindre *Dyf.* SA41
28 E27 Velindre *Pow.* LD3
7 B26 Vellow TA4
104 D31 Veness KW17
5 F23 Venn TQ7
38 E29 Vennington SY5
7 F26 Venn Ottery EX11
11 G41 Ventnor PO38
21 F39 Vernham Dean SP11
21 F39 Vernham Street SP11
38 G30 Vernolds Common SY7
26 D17 Verwig SA43
10 D36 Verwood BH31
3 E15 Veryan TR2
8 F28 Vicarage EX12
54 C27 Vickerstown LA14
3 B15 Victoria PL26
107 A40 Vidlin ZE2
103 B26 Viewfield KW14
75 D23 Viewpark G71
40 E36 Vigo WS9
24 E52 Vigo Village DA13
6 D21 Villavin EX19
14 E53 Vinehall Street TN32
13 E51 Vine's Cross TN21
19 A32 Viney Hill GL15
22 E45 Virginia Water GU25
6 F19 Virginstow EX21
34 G55 Virley CM9
19 G32 Vobster BA3
106 D39 Voe *She.* ZE2
107 A40 Voe *She.* ZE2
28 E29 Vowchurch HR2
104 E28 Voy KW16

W

62 D37 Wackerfield DL2
45 F57 Wacton NR15
29 D34 Wadborough WR8
31 G43 Waddesdon HP18
52 C45 Waddingham DN21
56 E33 Waddington *Lan.* BB7
52 F45 Waddington *Lcn.* LN5
52 E47 Waddingworth LN3
3 A15 Wadebridge PL27
8 C28 Wadeford TA20
42 G45 Wadenhoe PE8
33 G49 Wadesmill SG12
13 C52 Wadhurst TN5
50 E38 Wadshelf S42
51 C39 Wadsley Bridge S5
51 C41 Wadworth DN11
59 G48 Wadworth Hill HU12
47 F26 Waen LL16
38 D28 Waen-fach SY22
46 F21 Waen-wen LL57
103 F26 Wag KW7
53 G51 Wainfleet All Saints PE24
53 G50 Wainfleet Bank PE24
4 A17 Wainhouse Corner EX23
24 D53 Wainscott ME3
57 G36 Wainstalls HX2
61 F33 Waitby CA17
57 G39 Wakefield WF
42 F45 Wakerley LE15
34 F54 Wakes Colne CO6
35 A60 Walberswick IP17
12 F45 Walberton BN18
58 G44 Walcot *Hum.* DN15
52 G47 Walcot *Lcn.* LN4
42 B46 Walcot *Lcn.* NG34
38 G29 Walcot *Shr.* SY7
38 D31 Walcot *Shr.* TF6
52 G47 Walcot Dales LN4
41 G41 Walcote *Lei.* LE17
30 C37 Walcote *War.* B49
45 G57 Walcot Green IP22
45 B59 Walcott NR12
57 A36 Walden DL8
56 A35 Walden Head DL8
51 A41 Walden Stubbs DN6
24 E53 Walderslade ME5
11 C43 Walderton PO18
8 E30 Walditch DT6
40 B37 Waldley DE6
62 A38 Waldridge DH2
35 D58 Waldringfield IP12
13 E51 Waldron TN21
51 D40 Wales S31
52 C47 Walesby *Lcn.* LN8
51 E42 Walesby *Not.* NG22
28 F31 Walford *H.&W.* HR9
28 A29 Walford *H.&W.* SY7
38 C30 Walford *Shr.* SY4
39 A32 Walgherton CW5
31 A43 Walgrave NN6
10 E39 Walhampton SO41
49 B33 Walkden M28
71 G38 Walker NE6
76 G29 Walkerburn EH43
56 E32 Walker Fold BB7
51 C43 Walkeringham DN10
51 C43 Walkerith DN21
33 F48 Walkern SG2
28 D30 Walker's Green HR1
82 G28 Walkerton KY6
5 D21 Walkhampton PL20
56 F34 Walk Mill BB10
30 B36 Walkwood B97
70 G35 Wall *Nor.* NE46
40 E36 Wall *Stf.* WS14
69 F28 Wallacehall DG11
67 C18 Wallacetown KA19
48 C28 Wallasey L45
38 F30 Wall Bank SY6
71 G37 Wallbottle NE5
24 D54 Wallend ME3
29 E32 Waller's Green HR8
40 G34 Wall Heath DY6
21 C41 Wallingford OX10
23 E48 Wallington *G.L.* SM6
11 D41 Wallington *Ham.* PO16
33 E48 Wallington *Hfs.* SG7
16 B16 Wallis SA62
10 E36 Wallisdown BH12
12 C47 Walliswood RH5
107 C38 Walls ZE2
71 G38 Wallsend NE28
38 F31 Wall under Heywood SY6
76 C29 Wallyford EH21
15 B59 Walmer CT14
55 G30 Walmer Bridge PR4
49 A33 Walmersley BL9
40 F37 Walmley B76
35 A59 Walpole IP19
43 C51 Walpole Cross Keys PE34
43 D51 Walpole Highway PE14
43 D51 Walpole St Andrew PE14
43 D51 Walpole St Peter PE14
40 F35 Walsall WS
40 E36 Walsall Wood WS9
56 G35 Walsden OL14
41 G39 Walsgrave on Sowe CV2
34 A55 Walsham le Willows IP31
43 D50 Walsoken PE13
75 F26 Walston ML11
32 E47 Walsworth SG4
28 F29 Walterstone HR2
53 B48 Waltham *Hum.* DN37
15 C56 Waltham *Kent* CT4
23 A49 Waltham Abbey EN9
11 C41 Waltham Chase SO32
23 B49 Waltham Forest E
42 C44 Waltham on the Wolds LE14

West Farleigh

INDEX TO CENTRAL LONDON

General Abbreviations

All	Alley
Allot	Allotments
Amb	Ambulance
App	Approach
Arc	Arcade
Ave	Avenue
Bdy	Broadway
Bks	Barracks
Bldgs	Buildings
Boul	Boulevard
Bowl	Bowling
Bri	Bridge
Cath	Cathedral
Cem	Cemetery
Cen	Central, Centre
Cft	Croft
Ch	Church
Chyd	Churchyard
Cin	Cinema
Circ	Circus
Clo	Close
Coll	College
Comm	Community
Conv	Convent
Cor	Corner
Coron	Coroners
Cotts	Cottages
Cov	Covered
Crem	Crematorium
Cres	Crescent
Ct	Court
Cts	Courts
Ctyd	Courtyard
Dep	Depot
Dev	Development
Dr	Drive
Dws	Dwellings
E	East
Elec	Electricity
Embk	Embankment
Est	Estate
Ex	Exchange
FB	Footbridge
Fld	Field
Flds	Fields
Fm	Farm
Gall	Gallery
Gar	Garage
Gdn	Garden
Gdns	Gardens
Govt	Government
Gra	Grange
Grd	Ground
Grds	Grounds
Grn	Green
Gro	Grove
Ho	House
Hos	Houses
Hosp	Hospital
Ind	Industrial
Junct	Junction
La	Lane
Las	Lanes
Lo	Lodge
Lwr	Lower
Mag	Magistrates
Mans	Mansions
Meml	Memorial
Mkt	Market
Mkts	Markets
Ms	Mews
Mt	Mount
Mus	Museum
N	North
Off	Office
PH	Public House
Par	Parade
Pas	Passage
Pav	Pavilion
Pk	Park
Pl	Place
Pow	Power
Prec	Precinct
Prom	Promenade
Pt	Point
Rd	Road
Rec	Recreation
Res	Reservoir
Ri	Rise
Rvr	River
S	South
Sch	School
Shop	Shopping
Sq	Square
St	Street
St.	Saint
Sta	Station
Sub	Subway
Swim	Swimming
TA	Territorial Army
Tenn	Tennis
Ter	Terrace
Thea	Theatre
Trd	Trading
Twr	Tower
Und	Underpass
Vill	Villas
Vw	View
W	West
WC	Toilet
Wd	Wood
Wf	Wharf
Wk	Walk
Wks	Works
Yd	Yard

NOTES

The figures and letters preceding a street name indicate the page and map square where the name can be found.

A

120 E8 Abbey Gdns. NW8
124 E4 Abbey Gdns. W6
123 E16 Abbey La. E15
125 B15 Abbey Orchard St. SW1
120 C7 Abbey Rd. NW6
120 D7 Abbey Rd. NW8
120 D7 Abbey Rd. Est. NW8
126 B7 Abbey St. SE1
127 C10 Abbeyfield Rd. SE16
122 B7 Abbot St. E8
120 D7 Abbot's Pl. NW6
123 E16 Abbotsbury Clo. E15
124 A4 Abbotsbury Rd. W14
124 J2 Abbotstone Rd. SW15
127 L13 Abbotswell Rd. SE4
123 J16 Abbott Rd. E14
122 K5 Abchurch La. EC4
120 L1 Abdale Rd. W12
123 F12 Aberavon Rd. E3
120 F8 Abercorn Clo. NW8
120 F8 Abercorn Pl. NW8
126 D8 Abercorn Way SE1
125 H10 Abercrombie St. SW11
120 C7 Aberdare Gdns. NW6
122 A4 Aberdeen La. N5
122 A4 Aberdeen Pk. N5
121 G9 Aberdeen Pl. NW8
126 C6 Aberdour St. SE1
123 J16 Aberfeldy St. E14
122 A7 Abersham Rd. E8
124 B6 Abingdon Rd. W8
125 B16 Abingdon St. SW1
124 B6 Abingdon Vill. W8
127 E13 Abinger Gro. SE8
127 D10 Ablett St. SE16
121 E9 Acacia Pl. NW8
121 E9 Acacia Rd. NW8
126 D8 Acanthus Dr. SE1
125 J12 Acanthus Rd. SW11
124 G7 Acfold Rd. SW6
126 D8 Achilles Clo. SE1
120 A6 Achilles Rd. NW6
127 F12 Achilles St. SE14
124 G6 Ackmar Rd. SW6
123 H13 Ackroyd Dr. E3
126 K5 Acland Cres. SE5
120 B1 Acland Rd. NW2
120 C6 Acol Rd. NW6
123 L12 Acorn Wk. SE16
125 K16 Acre La. SW2
124 L8 Acris St. SW18
122 D7 Acton Ms. E8
122 F1 Acton St. WC1
122 D8 Ada Pl. E2
126 F6 Ada Rd. SE5
123 D9 Ada St. E8
120 G4 Adair Rd. W10
124 B6 Adam & Eve Ms. W8
121 K16 Adam St. WC2
124 F2 Adam Wk. SW6
121 K12 Adams Row W1
121 C9 Adamson Rd. NW3
123 J16 Adderley St. E14
123 F14 Addington Rd. E3
126 E5 Addington Sq. SE5
120 L4 Addison Ave. W11
124 C5 Addison Bri. Pl. W14
124 B4 Addison Cres. W14
124 B3 Addison Gdns. W14
120 L4 Addison Pl. W11
124 B4 Addison Rd. W14
127 K13 Adelaide Ave. SE4
121 C9 Adelaide Rd. NW3
123 H10 Adelina Gro. E1
121 H15 Adeline Pl. WC1
121 K16 Adelphi Ter. WC2
124 E3 Adeney Clo. W6
124 B2 Adie Rd. W6
122 J8 Adler St. E1
123 L16 Admiral Pl. SE16
124 G8 Admiral Sq. SW10
127 G14 Admiral St. SE8
127 A14 Admirals Way E14
127 F13 Adolphus St. SE8
121 H9 Adpar St. W2
124 E7 Adrian Ms. SW10
126 J7 Adys Rd. SE15
125 H10 Afghan Rd. SW11
120 A5 Agamemnon Rd. NW6
121 C14 Agar Gro. NW1
121 C14 Agar Gro. Est. NW1
121 C14 Agar Pl. NW1
121 K16 Agar St. WC2
124 B2 Agate Rd. W6
122 G3 Agdon St. EC1
123 J13 Agnes St. E14
123 H16 Ailsa St. E14
121 C11 Ainger Rd. NW3
123 F9 Ainsley St. E2
123 C10 Ainsworth Rd. E9
120 D8 Ainsworth Way NW8
124 F4 Aintree St. SW6
121 K14 Air St. W1
122 C1 Airdrie Clo. N1
124 D5 Aisgill Ave. W14
120 A5 Ajax Rd. NW6
121 A9 Akenside Rd. NW3
126 H3 Akerman Rd. SW9
126 E5 Albany Rd. SE5
121 E13 Albany St. NW1
121 K13 Albemarle St. W1
126 F1 Albert Ave. SW8
125 E10 Albert Bri. SW3
125 F10 Albert Bri. SW11
125 F10 Albert Bri. Rd. SW11
125 A9 Albert Ct. SW7
125 D16 Albert Embk. SE1
123 J11 Albert Gdns. E1
124 A7 Albert Pl. W8
120 E5 Albert Rd. NW6
126 F1 Albert Sq. SW8
121 D13 Albert St. NW1
121 D12 Albert Ter. NW1
126 D3 Alberta Est. SE17
126 D3 Alberta St. SE17
125 H15 Albion Ave. SW8
122 C7 Albion Dr. E8
127 A10 Albion Est. SE16
124 C1 Albion Gdns. W6
122 C2 Albion Ms. N1
121 J10 Albion Ms. W2
122 H3 Albion Pl. EC1
122 C7 Albion Sq. E8
127 A10 Albion St. SE16
121 J10 Albion St. W2
122 C7 Albion Ter. E8
127 K16 Albion Way SE13
126 J6 Albrighton Rd. SE22
127 E14 Albury St. SE8
127 G14 Albyn Rd. SE8
126 D6 Aldbridge St. SE17
125 F16 Aldebert Ter. SW8
121 E14 Aldenham St. NW1
124 B1 Aldensley Rd. W6
126 E7 Alder Clo. SE15
122 J4 Aldermanbury EC2
120 J3 Aldermaston St. W10
123 G11 Alderney Rd. E1
125 C13 Alderney St. SW1
127 L11 Aldersford Clo. SE4
122 H4 Aldersgate St. EC1
120 D5 Aldershot Rd. NW6
126 J4 Alderton Rd. SE24
124 H5 Alderville Rd. SW6
121 L12 Aldford St. W1
122 J6 Aldgate EC3
122 J7 Aldgate High St. EC3
120 L2 Aldine St. W12
120 A6 Aldred Rd. NW6
120 H5 Aldridge Rd. Vill. W11
120 G7 Aldsworth Clo. W9
122 K1 Aldwych WC2
120 C1 Alexander Ave. NW10
125 C10 Alexander Pl. SW7
125 C10 Alexander Sq. SW3
120 J6 Alexander St. W2
125 G12 Alexandra Ave. SW11
127 G13 Alexandra Cotts. SE14
120 D7 Alexandra Est. NW8
120 D8 Alexandra Pl. NW8
120 C8 Alexandra Rd. NW8
127 F12 Alexandra St. SE14
126 C8 Alexis St. SE16
125 G15 Alford Rd. SW8
121 H15 Alfred Ms. W1
121 H15 Alfred Pl. WC1
120 H6 Alfred Rd. W2
123 F13 Alfred St. E3
125 G13 Alfreda St. SW11
125 L11 Alfriston Rd. SW11
120 D6 Algernon Rd. NW6
127 J15 Algernon Rd. SE13
127 K14 Algiers Rd. SE13
124 D5 Alice Gilliatt Ct. W14
126 B6 Alice St. SE1
122 J7 Alie St. E1
125 K10 Aliwal Rd. SW11
120 J5 All Saints Rd. W11
122 E1 All Saints St. N1
120 E1 All Souls Ave. NW10
126 K1 Allardyce St. SW4
121 A12 Allcroft Rd. NW5
125 G16 Allen Edwards Dr. SW8
123 E13 Allen Rd. E3
124 B6 Allen St. W8
121 C15 Allensbury Pl. NW1
124 F4 Allestree Rd. SW6
122 E7 Allgood St. E2
122 E4 Allingham St. N1
120 E4 Allington Rd. W10
125 B13 Allington St. SW1
121 E10 Allitsen Rd. NW8
125 L15 Allnutt Way SW4
127 D12 Alloa Rd. SE8
123 F12 Alloway Rd. E3
121 G11 Allsop Pl. NW1
126 C7 Alma Gro. SE1
124 K8 Alma Rd. SW18
120 F8 Alma Sq. NW8
121 B13 Alma St. NW5
122 C3 Almeida St. N1
125 K11 Almeric Rd. SW11
126 H8 Almond Clo. SE15
127 C9 Almond Rd. SE16
122 C5 Almorah Rd. N1
120 G4 Alperton St. W10
127 A14 Alpha Gro. E14
120 E6 Alpha Pl. NW6
125 E10 Alpha Pl. SW3
127 G13 Alpha Rd. SE14
126 H8 Alpha St. SE15
127 C10 Alpine Rd. SE16
126 C7 Alscot Rd. SE1
126 C7 Alscot Way SE1
125 K11 Altenburg Gdns. SW11
124 H7 Althea St. SW6
123 H15 Alton St. E14
120 A7 Alvanley Gdns. NW6
120 C2 Alverstone Rd. NW2
127 D13 Alverton St. SE8
126 D6 Alvey St. SE17
122 A7 Alvington Cres. E8
122 B4 Alwyne Pl. N1
122 C4 Alwyne Rd. N1
122 B4 Alwyne Sq. N1
122 C3 Alwyne Vill. N1
126 D3 Ambergate St. SE17
120 H6 Amberley Rd. W9
125 B14 Ambrosden Ave. SW1
127 C9 Ambrose St. SE16
126 D3 Amelia St. SE17
124 L5 Amerland Rd. SW18
127 F13 Amersham Gro. SE14
127 G13 Amersham Rd. SE14
127 F13 Amersham Vale SE14
120 D1 Amery Gdns. NW10
122 A8 Amhurst Pas. E8
123 A9 Amhurst Rd. E8
123 G10 Amiel St. E1
125 J11 Amies St. SW11
124 B2 Amor Rd. W6
126 J8 Amott Rd. SE15
123 J14 Amoy Pl. E14
122 F1 Ampton Pl. WC1
122 F1 Ampton St. WC1
127 B16 Amsterdam Rd. E14
122 F2 Amwell St. EC1
127 L14 Amyruth Rd. SE4
127 C9 Anchor St. SE16
124 E4 Ancill Clo. W6
125 J16 Andalus Rd. SW9
123 B11 Anderson Rd. E9
125 D11 Anderson St. SW3
126 J5 Anderton Clo. SE5
120 E7 Andover Pl. NW6
122 A8 Andre St. E8
123 J16 Andrew St. E14
123 D9 Andrew's Rd. E8
125 H11 Anerley St. SW11
122 E2 Angel Ms. N1
122 J4 Angel St. EC1
124 D2 Angel Wk. W6
126 J2 Angell Pk. Gdns. SW9
126 J2 Angell Rd. SW9
121 B13 Angler's La. NW5
123 J12 Anglia Ho. E14
123 E13 Anglo Rd. E3
122 D7 Angrave Ct. E8
127 F12 Angus St. SE14
124 A3 Anley Rd. W14
125 F9 Ann La. SW10
122 D7 Anna Clo. E8
123 J15 Annabel Clo. E14
123 D13 Annie Besant Clo. E3
123 B12 Annis Rd. E9
127 H10 Ansdell Rd. SE15
124 B7 Ansdell St. W8
124 E6 Anselm Rd. SW6
120 K3 Ansleigh Pl. W11
120 A1 Anson Rd. NW2
126 J8 Anstey Rd. SE15
123 J9 Anthony St. E1
123 F12 Antill Rd. E3
123 J11 Antill Ter. E1
122 A8 Anton St. E8
121 B11 Antrim Gro. NW3
121 B11 Antrim Rd. NW3
126 L2 Appach Rd. SW2
122 C8 Appleby Rd. E8
122 E7 Appleby St. E2
120 G4 Appleford Rd. W10
124 B3 Applegarth Rd. W14
122 H6 Appold St. EC2
123 E10 Approach Rd. E2
121 E9 Aquila St. NW8
127 K12 Arabin Rd. SE4
123 F12 Arbery Rd. E3
123 J11 Arbour Sq. E1
127 H11 Arbuthnot Rd. SE14
122 D7 Arbutus St. E8
123 J14 Arcadia St. E14
126 B4 Arch St. SE1
127 A11 Archangel St. SE16
126 L7 Archdale Rd. SE22
124 E5 Archel Rd. W14
121 J10 Archery Clo. W2
121 K12 Archibald Ms. W1
123 F14 Archibald St. E3
122 A7 Arcola St. E8
126 L5 Ardbeg Rd. SE24
127 C14 Arden Cres. E14
122 E6 Arden Est. N1
122 B6 Ardleigh Rd. N1
124 F6 Argon Ms. SW6
124 C1 Argyle Pl. W6
123 G11 Argyle Rd. E1
121 F16 Argyle Sq. WC1
121 F16 Argyle St. WC1
124 A6 Argyll Rd. W8
121 J14 Argyll St. W1
127 K12 Arica Rd. SE4
120 B6 Ariel Rd. NW6
120 L2 Ariel Way W12
125 J15 Aristotle Rd. SW4
127 E13 Arklow Rd. SE14
120 A8 Arkwright Rd. NW3
125 J16 Arlesford Rd. SW9
126 L2 Arlingford Rd. SW2
122 D4 Arlington Ave. N1
126 K1 Arlington Lo. SW2
121 D13 Arlington Rd. NW1
122 D4 Arlington Sq. N1
121 L14 Arlington St. SW1
122 F2 Arlington Way EC1
127 E14 Armada St. SE8
124 F6 Armadale Rd. SW6
123 D13 Armagh Rd. E3
120 L1 Arminger Rd. W12
124 L6 Armoury Way SW18
125 B9 Armstrong Rd. SW7
121 J16 Arne St. WC2
122 F7 Arnold Circ. E2
126 A7 Arnold Est. SE1
123 F14 Arnold Rd. E3
126 K5 Arnould Ave. SE5
126 E4 Arnside St. SE17
122 C4 Arran Wk. N1
123 F15 Arrow Rd. E3
120 J6 Artesian Rd. W2
124 H5 Arthur Henderson Ho. SW6
127 L14 Arthurdon Rd. SE4
126 G5 Artichoke Pl. SE5
122 H6 Artillery La. E1
125 B15 Artillery Row SW1
120 K5 Arundel Gdns. W11
122 A6 Arundel Gro. N16
122 B2 Arundel Pl. N1
122 B2 Arundel Sq. N7
122 K1 Arundel St. WC2
124 E1 Arundel Ter. SW13
122 A2 Arvon Rd. N5
125 F14 Ascalon St. SW8
121 A14 Ascham St. NW5
123 D9 Ash Gro. E8
126 L7 Ashbourne Gro. SE22
121 G10 Ashbridge St. NW8
124 C8 Ashburn Gdns. SW7
124 C8 Ashburn Pl. SW7
127 F15 Ashburnham Gro. SE10
127 F15 Ashburnham Pl. SE10
127 F15 Ashburnham Retreat SE10
120 F2 Ashburnham Rd. NW10
124 F8 Ashburnham Rd. SW10
125 J11 Ashbury Rd. SW11
122 C4 Ashby Gro. N1
127 H13 Ashby Ms. SE4
127 H13 Ashby Rd. SE4
124 H7 Ashcombe St. SW6
123 F12 Ashcroft Rd. E3
123 A12 Ashenden Rd. E5
122 L8 Asher Way E1
123 H9 Ashfield St. E1
124 H5 Ashington Rd. SW6
121 H12 Ashland Pl. W1
125 J12 Ashley Cres. SW11
125 B14 Ashley Pl. SW1
124 J2 Ashlone Rd. SW15
127 H14 Ashmead Rd. SE8
125 K16 Ashmere Gro. SW2
121 H10 Ashmill St. NW1
126 E1 Ashmole Pl. SW8
126 E1 Ashmole St. SW8
120 E5 Ashmore Rd. W9
125 L11 Ashness Rd. SW11
123 K16 Ashton St. E14
122 B7 Ashwin St. E8
120 F7 Ashworth Rd. W9
120 A4 Asmara Rd. NW2
124 D1 Aspen Gdns. W6
123 K16 Aspen Way E14
124 E3 Aspenlea Rd. W6
121 A10 Aspern Rd. NW3
127 J11 Aspinall Rd. SE4
127 C9 Aspinden Rd. SE16
124 L7 Aspley Rd. SW18
123 H10 Assembly Pas. E1
127 G10 Astbury Rd. SE15
127 A16 Aste St. E14
125 D10 Astell St. SW3
125 H12 Astle St. SW11
120 A2 Astley Ave. NW2
123 J12 Aston St. E14
126 J2 Astoria Wk. SW9
124 B2 Astrop Ms. W6
124 A2 Astrop Ter. W6
124 C7 Astwood Ms. SW7
127 F9 Asylum Rd. SE15
124 G3 Atalanta St. SW6
123 E13 Athelstane Gro. E3
127 L11 Athenlay Rd. SE15
125 J16 Atherfold Rd. SW9
124 C8 Atherstone Ms. SW7
125 H10 Atherton St. SW11
121 B12 Athlone St. NW5
123 J16 Athol Sq. E14
126 K2 Atlantic Rd. SW9
122 B1 Atlas Ms. N7
123 D14 Atley Rd. E3
124 K4 Atney Rd. SW15
125 C16 Atterbury St. SW1
124 C1 Atwood Rd. W6
120 L5 Aubrey Rd. W8
120 L5 Aubrey Wk. W8
125 K10 Auckland Rd. SW11
121 D12 Auden Pl. NW1
125 J12 Audley Clo. SW11
122 E8 Audrey St. E2
123 J15 Augusta St. E14
124 B3 Augustine Rd. W14
121 E13 Augustus St. NW1
122 A5 Auriga Ms. N16
124 C4 Auriol Rd. W14
120 F6 Austen Ho. NW6
122 J5 Austin Friars EC2
125 G12 Austin Rd. SW11
122 F7 Austin St. E2
126 C3 Austral St. SE11
120 K1 Australia Rd. W12
123 D14 Autumn St. E3
124 G7 Avalon Rd. SW6
122 J3 Ave Maria La. EC4
126 D2 Aveline St. SE11
120 D3 Avenue, The NW6
125 L12 Avenue, The SW4
121 D10 Avenue Clo. NW8
121 C9 Avenue Rd. NW3
121 C9 Avenue Rd. NW8
124 E3 Averill St. W6
121 K13 Avery Row W1
127 J11 Avignon Rd. SE4
123 J11 Avis Sq. E1
127 J14 Avon Rd. SE4
120 K4 Avondale Pk. Gdns. W11
120 K4 Avondale Pk. Rd. W11
126 J7 Avondale Ri. SE15
126 D8 Avondale Sq. SE1
127 F10 Avonley Rd. SE14
124 C4 Avonmore Rd. W14
126 B4 Avonmouth St. SE1
121 H12 Aybrook St. W1
126 D5 Aylesbury Rd. SE17
122 G3 Aylesbury St. EC1
125 D15 Aylesford St. SW1
120 C3 Aylestone Ave. NW6
123 J10 Aylward St. E1
126 B6 Aylwyn Est. SE1
124 C3 Aynhoe Rd. W14
126 A4 Ayres St. SE1
126 H1 Aytoun Pl. SW9
126 H1 Aytoun Rd. SW9
126 H7 Azenby Rd. SE15

B

122 A3 Baalbec Rd. N5
122 F5 Baches St. N1
122 K8 Back Ch. La. E1
122 G2 Back Hill EC1
126 B7 Bacon Gro. SE1
122 G7 Bacon St. E1
122 G7 Bacon St. E2
121 A12 Bacton NW5
126 G4 Badsworth Rd. SE5
124 G7 Bagley's La. SW6
126 D6 Bagshot St. SE17
121 J15 Bainbridge St. WC1
121 G11 Baker St. NW1
121 H11 Baker St. W1
122 G2 Baker's Row EC1
126 C7 Balaclava Rd. SE1
121 G11 Balcombe St. NW1
123 C10 Balcorne St. E9
121 J12 Balderton St. W1
123 E15 Baldock St. E3
126 G4 Baldwin Cres. SE5
122 E4 Baldwin Ter. N1
122 H2 Baldwin's Gdns. EC1
121 E16 Balfe St. N1
125 H10 Balfern St. SW11
124 K1 Balfour Pl. SW15
126 C5 Balfour St. SE17
123 B11 Ballance Rd. E9
124 K8 Ballantine St. SW18
125 K16 Ballater Rd. SW2
120 J3 Balliol Rd. W10
122 B5 Balls Pond Rd. N1
123 E13 Balmer Rd. E3
122 D5 Balmes Rd. N1
122 B1 Balmoral Gro. N7
120 B1 Balmoral Rd. NW2
124 K2 Balmuir Gdns. SW15
125 D15 Balniel Gate SW1
122 G4 Baltic St. EC1
124 A2 Bamborough Gdns. W12
123 C11 Banbury Rd. E9
125 H10 Banbury St. SW11
123 F11 Bancroft Rd. E1
124 J2 Bangalore St. SW15
124 C1 Banim St. W6
120 F3 Banister Rd. W10
122 L4 Bank End SE1

Bankside

122 K4 Bankside SE1
126 K2 Bankton Rd. SW2
122 G4 Banner St. EC1
126 E1 Bannerman Ho. SW8
127 J10 Banstead St. SE15
126 F5 Bantry St. SE5
124 B2 Barb Ms. W6
123 E15 Barbers Rd. E15
122 H4 Barbican, The EC2
124 L7 Barchard St. SW18
123 H15 Barchester St. E14
124 F6 Barclay Clo. SW6
124 F6 Barclay Rd. SW6
120 K3 Bard Rd. W10
123 H10 Bardsey Pl. E1
127 E16 Bardsley La. SE10
120 G5 Barfett St. W10
122 D2 Barford St. N1
127 J9 Barforth Rd. SE15
122 D5 Baring St. N1
120 K7 Bark Pl. W2
121 C14 Barker Dr. NW1
124 E8 Barker St. SW10
124 C7 Barkston Gdns. SW5
127 F11 Barlborough St. SE14
120 G3 Barlby Gdns. W10
120 H2 Barlby Rd. W10
123 K13 Barleycorn Way E14
120 B5 Barlow Rd. NW6
124 H2 Barn Elms Pk. SW15
123 A11 Barnabas Rd. E9
125 C9 Barnaby Pl. SW7
125 K10 Barnard Ms. SW11
125 K10 Barnard Rd. SW11
121 F14 Barnby St. NW1
123 J12 Barnes St. E14
127 D13 Barnes Ter. SE8
122 F8 Barnet Gro. E2
127 C14 Barnfield Pl. E14
126 A6 Barnham St. SE1
122 B1 Barnsbury Gro. N7
122 C2 Barnsbury Pk. N1
122 E2 Barnsbury Rd. N1
122 C2 Barnsbury Sq. N1
122 C2 Barnsbury St. N1
122 C1 Barnsbury Ter. N1
127 C15 Barnsdale Ave. E14
120 G5 Barnsdale Rd. W9
123 G9 Barnsley St. E1
126 L2 Barnwell Rd. SW2
120 G7 Barnwood Clo. W9
122 E2 Baron St. N1
124 D4 Barons Ct. Rd. W14
124 D4 Barons Keep W14
126 A2 Barons Pl. SE1
121 J12 Barrett St. W1
122 A6 Barretts Gro. N16
127 H12 Barriedale SE14
126 J3 Barrington Rd. SW9
121 E10 Barrow Hill Rd. NW8
127 J10 Barset Rd. SE15
121 H16 Barter St. WC1
122 H4 Bartholomew Clo. EC1
124 K8 Bartholomew Clo. SW18
121 B14 Bartholomew Rd. NW5
122 G4 Bartholomew Sq. EC1
126 B5 Bartholomew St. SE1
121 B14 Bartholomew Vill. NW5
120 J4 Bartle Rd. W11
123 J14 Bartlett Clo. E14
124 D4 Barton Rd. W14
127 L12 Bartram Rd. SE4
125 B11 Basil St. SW3
126 G7 Basing Ct. SE15
120 J5 Basing St. W11
126 K5 Basingdon Way SE5
122 H5 Basinghall Ave. EC2
122 H4 Basinghall St. EC2
122 D4 Basire St. N1
125 J12 Basnett Rd. SW11
126 L7 Bassano St. SE22
120 J3 Bassett Rd. W10
121 B12 Bassett St. NW5
122 G4 Bastwick St. EC1
124 G6 Basuto Rd. SW6
127 F12 Batavia Rd. SE14
122 E2 Batchelor St. N1
122 G6 Bateman's Row EC2
122 F4 Bath St. EC1
126 B4 Bath Ter. SE1
120 E1 Bathurst Gdns. NW10
121 K9 Bathurst St. W2
120 L1 Batman Clo. W12
124 B2 Batoum Gdns. W6
125 J10 Batten St. SW11
125 F9 Battersea Bri. SW3
125 F10 Battersea Bri. SW11
125 F10 Battersea Bri. Rd. SW11
125 G9 Battersea Ch. Rd. SW11
125 G9 Battersea High St. SW11
125 F11 Battersea Pk. SW11
125 G13 Battersea Pk. Rd. SW8
125 H10 Battersea Pk. Rd. SW11
125 L9 Battersea Ri. SW11
122 L6 Battle Bri. La. SE1
121 E16 Battle Bri. Rd. NW1
122 A3 Battledean Rd. N5
122 J8 Batty St. E1
126 H4 Bavent Rd. SE5
126 L7 Bawdale Rd. SE22
127 F12 Bawtree Rd. SE14
122 F8 Baxendale St. E2
122 B5 Baxter Rd. N1
120 F3 Bayford Rd. NW10
123 C9 Bayford St. E8
121 D14 Bayham Pl. NW1
121 D14 Bayham St. NW1
121 H15 Bayley St. WC1
126 A2 Baylis Rd. SE1
121 C14 Baynes St. NW1
124 E4 Bayonne Rd. W6
120 K7 Bayswater Rd. W2
123 H13 Baythorne St. E3
126 K1 Baytree Rd. SW2
123 K16 Bazely St. E14
123 C14 Beachy Rd. E3
121 A16 Beacon Hill N7
126 E5 Beaconsfield Rd. SE17
124 B4 Beaconsfield Ter. Rd. W14
124 C2 Beadon Rd. W6
121 K14 Beak St. W1
123 E13 Beale Pl. E3
123 D13 Beale Rd. E3
123 B13 Beanacre Clo. E9
122 L4 Bear Gdns. SE1
122 L3 Bear La. SE1
127 L13 Bearstead Ri. SE4
124 B7 Beatrice Pl. W8
126 C8 Beatrice Rd. SE1
123 L12 Beatson Wk. SE16
121 E14 Beatty St. NW1
125 B10 Beauchamp Pl. SW3
125 K10 Beauchamp Rd. SW11
124 B1 Beauclerc Rd. W6
125 B10 Beaufort Gdns. SW3
125 E9 Beaufort St. SW3
126 C1 Beaufoy Wk. SE11
126 J5 Beaulieu Clo. SE5
124 D5 Beaumont Ave. W14
124 D5 Beaumont Cres. W14
123 G11 Beaumont Gro. E1
121 G14 Beaumont Pl. W1
123 G11 Beaumont Sq. E1
121 H12 Beaumont St. W1
121 C11 Beaumont Wk. NW3
123 K13 Beccles St. E14
127 G15 Beck Clo. SE13
123 D9 Beck Rd. E8
126 C5 Beckway St. SE17
124 K4 Bective Rd. SW15
122 L5 Bedale St. SE1
121 H15 Bedford Ave. WC1
120 L6 Bedford Gdns. W8
125 K16 Bedford Ho. SW4
121 H16 Bedford Pl. WC1
125 J16 Bedford Rd. SW4
122 H1 Bedford Row WC1
121 H15 Bedford Sq. WC1
121 K16 Bedford St. WC2
121 G15 Bedford Way WC1
122 H4 Beech St. EC2
125 G11 Beechmore Rd. SW11
122 B7 Beechwood Rd. E8
127 L12 Beecroft Rd. SE4
126 J2 Beehive Pl. SW9
125 B13 Beeston Pl. SW1
120 F4 Beethoven St. W10
127 H10 Belfort Rd. SE15
120 D7 Belgrave Gdns. NW8
125 B12 Belgrave Ms. N. SW1
125 B12 Belgrave Ms. S. SW1
125 B12 Belgrave Ms. W. SW1
125 B12 Belgrave Pl. SW1
125 C13 Belgrave Rd. SW1
125 B12 Belgrave Sq. SW1
123 H11 Belgrave St. E1
121 F16 Belgrove St. WC1
126 J3 Belinda Rd. SW9
122 C1 Belitha Vill. N1
122 H7 Bell La. E1
121 H10 Bell St. NW1
122 J2 Bell Yd. WC2
126 J1 Bellefields Rd. SW9
126 J7 Bellenden Rd. SE15
125 L10 Belleville Rd. SW11
124 H6 Bells All. SW6
127 K11 Bellwood Rd. SE15
125 J14 Belmont Clo. SW4
127 J16 Belmont Hill SE13
125 J14 Belmont Rd. SW4
121 C12 Belmont St. NW1
121 A15 Belmore La. N7
125 G15 Belmore St. SW8
123 B10 Belsham St. E9
121 B9 Belsize Ave. NW3
121 A9 Belsize Cres. NW3
121 B10 Belsize Gro. NW3
121 B9 Belsize La. NW3
121 B9 Belsize Pk. NW3
121 B10 Belsize Pk. Gdns. NW3
120 D7 Belsize Rd. NW6
121 B9 Belsize Sq. NW3
121 B9 Belsize Ter. NW3
123 H14 Belton Way E3
124 H7 Beltran Rd. SW6
126 A1 Belvedere Rd. SE1
120 C4 Bembridge Clo. NW6
121 C16 Bemerton Est. N1
122 D1 Bemerton St. N1
124 J3 Bemish Rd. SW15
123 H11 Ben Jonson Rd. E1
124 B1 Benbow Rd. W6
127 E14 Benbow St. SE8
124 J3 Bendemeer Rd. SW15
126 J1 Benedict Rd. SW9
126 J4 Bengeworth Rd. SE5
125 J9 Benham Clo. SW11
126 F5 Benhill Rd. SE5
122 D8 Benjamin Clo. E8
122 H3 Benjamin St. EC1
123 B12 Benn St. E9
125 L10 Bennerley Rd. SW11
127 G15 Bennett Gro. SE13
123 B11 Bentham Rd. E9
121 J12 Bentinck St. W1
120 J1 Bentworth Rd. W12
127 C9 Benwick Clo. SE16
123 F13 Benworth St. E3
125 L11 Berber Rd. SW11
120 F3 Berens Rd. NW10
122 A5 Beresford Rd. N5
122 A4 Beresford Ter. N5
123 B11 Berger Rd. E9
121 K13 Berkeley Sq. W1
121 L13 Berkeley St. W1
121 C11 Berkley Rd. NW1
123 B13 Berkshire Rd. E9
126 A6 Bermondsey St. SE1
126 A8 Bermondsey Wall E. SE16
126 A8 Bermondsey Wall W. SE16
121 G16 Bernard St. WC1
126 K1 Bernays Gro. SW9
121 H14 Berners Ms. W1
121 J14 Berners Pl. W1
122 D2 Berners Rd. N1
121 H14 Berners St. W1
122 G3 Berry St. EC1
126 D3 Berryfield Rd. SE17
127 F14 Berthon St. SE8
127 J15 Bertrand St. SE13
121 J14 Berwick St. W1
124 D3 Beryl Rd. W6
125 D15 Bessborough Gdns. SW1
125 D15 Bessborough Pl. SW1
125 D15 Bessborough St. SW1
126 H4 Bessemer Rd. SE5
127 G10 Besson St. SE14
127 C11 Bestwood St. SE8
122 G7 Bethnal Grn. Rd. E1
122 G7 Bethnal Grn. Rd. E2
126 F3 Bethwin Rd. SE5
121 J16 Betterton St. WC2
124 H5 Bettridge Rd. SW6
122 D4 Bevan St. N1
122 F5 Bevenden St. N1
127 J13 Beverley Ct. SE4
126 L1 Beverstone Rd. SW2
123 L12 Bevin Clo. SE16
120 H4 Bevington Rd. W10
126 A8 Bevington St. SE16
122 J6 Bevis Marks EC3
122 C2 Bewdley St. N1
125 H13 Bewick St. SW8
123 K9 Bewley St. E1
126 E7 Bianca Rd. SE15
126 E6 Bibury Clo. SE15
121 H11 Bickenhall St. W1
126 J4 Bicknell Rd. SE5
121 F16 Bidborough St. WC1
120 F7 Biddulph Rd. W9
127 G9 Bidwell St. SE15
123 D16 Biggerstaff Rd. E15
123 J9 Bigland St. E1
124 F7 Billing Pl. SW10
124 F7 Billing Rd. SW10
124 F7 Billing St. SW10
127 K11 Billingford Clo. SE4
127 F11 Billington Rd. SE14
122 J6 Billiter St. EC3
127 C16 Billson St. E14
124 C8 Bina Gdns. SW5
125 G16 Binfield Rd. SW4
121 D16 Bingfield St. N1
122 B5 Bingham St. N1
121 J12 Binney St. W1
126 H8 Birch Clo. SE15
123 K14 Birchfield St. E14
122 J5 Birchin La. EC3
120 D6 Birchington Rd. NW6
126 F8 Bird in Bush Rd. SE15
125 A14 Birdcage Wk. SW1
124 K8 Birdhurst Rd. SW18
126 E6 Birdlip Clo. SE15
123 D13 Birdsfield La. E3
122 A7 Birkbeck Rd. E8
121 F16 Birkenhead St. WC1
125 H12 Birley St. SW11
124 D3 Biscay Rd. W6
124 C4 Bishop Kings Rd. W14
122 D4 Bishop St. N1
124 H3 Bishops Ave. SW6
120 H8 Bishops Bri. W2
120 J7 Bishops Bri. Rd. W2
124 H3 Bishop's Pk. Rd. SW6
124 G4 Bishops Rd. SW6
126 C2 Bishops Ter. SE11
123 E9 Bishops Way E2
122 J6 Bishopsgate EC2
123 E16 Bisson Rd. E15
122 J3 Black Friars La. EC4
126 C1 Black Prince Rd. SE1
126 C1 Black Prince Rd. SE11
120 B7 Blackburn Rd. NW6
121 K12 Blackburne's Ms. W1
124 J3 Blackett St. SW15
122 K3 Blackfriars Bri. EC4
122 K3 Blackfriars Bri. SE1
122 L3 Blackfriars Rd. SE1
127 G16 Blackheath Hill SE10
127 H16 Blackheath Ri. SE13
127 G15 Blackheath Rd. SE10
127 D12 Blackhorse Rd. SE8
125 C11 Blackland Ter. SW3
127 H9 Blackpool Rd. SE15
122 C8 Blackstone Est. E8
120 A2 Blackstone Rd. NW2
123 G14 Blackthorn St. E3
126 J2 Blacktree Ms. SW9
123 E14 Blackwall Tunnel Northern App. E3
123 G16 Blackwall Tunnel Northern App. E14
123 K16 Blackwall Way E14
126 L7 Blackwater St. SE22
126 D5 Blackwood St. SE17
120 H4 Blagrove Rd. W10
122 B4 Blair Clo. N1
123 J16 Blair St. E14
120 H2 Blake Clo. W10
124 G7 Blake Gdns. SW6
123 D16 Blaker Rd. E15
126 F6 Blakes Rd. SE15
122 B8 Blanchard Way E8
126 K5 Blanchedowne SE5
121 G10 Blandford Sq. NW1
121 J11 Blandford St. W1
125 F9 Blantyre St. SW10
121 C11 Blashford NW3
127 D14 Blasker Wk. E14
120 K4 Blenheim Cres. W11
120 B2 Blenheim Gdns. NW2
126 H8 Blenheim Gro. SE15
120 E8 Blenheim Rd. NW8
120 E8 Blenheim Ter. NW8
122 E4 Bletchley St. N1
127 G16 Blissett St. SE10
124 B7 Blithfield St. W8
120 L1 Bloemfontein Ave. W12
120 K1 Bloemfontein Rd. W12
120 H7 Blomfield Rd. W9
122 H5 Blomfield St. EC2
120 H7 Blomfield Vill. W2
125 H12 Blondel St. SW11
123 E14 Blondin St. E3
124 F5 Bloom Pk. Rd. SW6
125 D12 Bloomfield Ter. SW1
121 H16 Bloomsbury Sq. WC1
121 H15 Bloomsbury St. WC1
121 H16 Bloomsbury Way WC1
122 G6 Blossom St. E1
123 H12 Blount St. E14
126 F4 Blucher Rd. SE5
126 C8 Blue Anchor La. SE16
122 K8 Blue Anchor Yd. E1
121 C16 Blundell St. N7
124 B3 Blythe Rd. W14
123 F9 Blythe St. E2
126 F7 Boathouse Wk. SE15
125 J14 Bobbin Clo. SW4
123 D9 Bocking St. E8
123 A9 Bodney Rd. E8
123 B10 Bohemia Pl. E8
127 H15 Bolden St. SE8
122 A6 Boleyn Rd. N16
127 D10 Bolina Rd. SE16
124 B3 Bolingbroke Rd. W14
125 G9 Bolingbroke Wk. SW11
126 F1 Bolney St. SW8
121 G13 Bolsover St. W1
126 E3 Bolton Cres. SE5
120 E3 Bolton Gdns. NW10
124 D7 Bolton Gdns. SW5
124 D7 Bolton Gdns. Ms. SW10
120 D7 Bolton Rd. NW8
121 L13 Bolton St. W1
124 D8 Boltons, The SW10
127 C9 Bombay St. SE16
120 K4 Bomore Rd. W11
126 F8 Bonar Rd. SE15
120 H4 Bonchurch Rd. W10
125 E16 Bondway SW8
127 K16 Bonfield Rd. SE13
126 L1 Bonham Rd. SW2
122 G5 Bonhill St. EC2
123 E10 Bonner Rd. E2
123 E10 Bonner St. E2
126 E1 Bonnington Sq. SW8
121 C14 Bonny St. NW1
126 F6 Bonsor St. SE5
122 F6 Boot St. N1
127 K10 Borland Rd. SE15
124 J2 Borneo St. SW15
126 A4 Borough High St. SE1
126 B3 Borough Rd. SE1
127 D14 Borthwick St. SE8
125 C12 Boscobel Pl. SW1
121 G9 Boscobel St. NW8
123 A12 Boscombe Clo. E5
121 G11 Boston Pl. NW1
121 H16 Boswell St. WC1
120 G4 Bosworth Rd. W10
123 J11 Boulcott St. E1
126 E4 Boundary La. SE17
120 D7 Boundary Rd. NW8
122 G7 Boundary St. E2
121 K13 Bourdon St. W1
122 H2 Bourne Est. EC1
125 C12 Bourne St. SW1
120 H7 Bourne Ter. W2
126 H8 Bournemouth Rd. SE15
127 H11 Bousfield Rd. SE14
125 K10 Boutflower Rd. SW11
121 J9 Bouverie Pl. W2
122 J2 Bouverie St. EC4
124 G7 Bovingdon Rd. SW6
123 E15 Bow Bri. Est. E3
123 G12 Bow Common La. E3
123 C15 Bow Ind. Est. E15
122 J4 Bow La. EC4
123 F13 Bow Rd. E3
121 J16 Bow St. WC2
126 D2 Bowden St. SE11
127 D13 Bowditch SE8
123 J15 Bowen St. E14
123 J11 Bower St. E1
124 G7 Bowerdean St. SW6
127 E12 Bowerman Ave. SE14
124 E2 Bowfell Rd. W6
126 F2 Bowhill Clo. SW9
125 K15 Bowland Rd. SW4
122 G6 Bowling Grn. Ct. EC2
122 G2 Bowling Grn. La. EC1
126 A5 Bowling Grn. Pl. SE1
126 E2 Bowling Grn. St. SE11
125 L12 Bowood Rd. SW11
126 F4 Bowyer Pl. SE5
126 F4 Bowyer St. SE5
122 J8 Boyd St. E1
126 A3 Boyfield St. SE1
127 J16 Boyne Rd. SE13
120 L5 Boyne Ter. Ms. W11
126 E5 Boyson Rd. SE17
123 J15 Brabazon St. E14
127 H10 Brabourn Gro. SE15
120 H2 Bracewell Rd. W10
124 B1 Brackenbury Gdns. W6
124 B1 Brackenbury Rd. W6
122 E5 Bracklyn St. N1
120 A7 Bracknell Gate NW3
124 H6 Bradbourne St. SW6
122 A6 Bradbury St. N16
126 E5 Bradenham Clo. SE17
120 F5 Bradiston Rd. W9
125 F13 Bradmead SW8
124 C1 Bradmore Pk. Rd. W6
123 B11 Bradstock Rd. E9
123 F11 Bradwell St. E1
123 G9 Brady St. E1
122 C3 Braes St. N1
126 D3 Braganza St. SE17
122 J7 Braham St. E1
126 L2 Brailsford Rd. SW2
123 G10 Braintree St. E2
126 G2 Bramah Grn. SW9
124 E5 Bramber Rd. W14
127 D10 Bramcote Gro. SE16
124 K1 Bramcote Rd. SW15
125 E10 Bramerton St. SW3
124 K8 Bramford Rd. SW18
124 D7 Bramham Gdns. SW5
125 J10 Bramlands Clo. SW11
120 K3 Bramley Rd. W10
120 J3 Bramley St. W10
123 B11 Bramshaw Rd. E9
122 D5 Branch Pl. N1
123 K12 Branch Rd. E14
127 F16 Brand St. SE10
124 K5 Brandlehow Rd. SW15
126 E3 Brandon Est. SE17
121 C16 Brandon Rd. N7
126 C4 Brandon St. SE17
126 D1 Brangton Rd. SE11
124 F4 Branksea St. SW6
125 K16 Branksome Rd. SW2
127 J15 Branscombe St. SE13
126 L4 Brantwood Rd. SE24
120 B5 Brassey Rd. NW6
125 J12 Brassey Sq. SW11
120 F5 Bravington Rd. W9
127 K12 Braxfield Rd. SE4
121 C10 Bray NW3
125 C11 Bray Pl. SW3
127 H9 Brayards Rd. SE15
125 H14 Brayburne Ave. SW4
122 K4 Bread St. EC4
127 J13 Breakspears Rd. SE4
123 C14 Bream St. E3
122 J2 Bream's Bldgs. EC4
124 K1 Breasley Clo. SW15
121 A15 Brecknock Rd. N7
124 E4 Brecon Rd. W6
126 J4 Bredon Rd. SE5
124 J7 Breer St. SW6
121 J10 Brendon St. W1
123 B10 Brenthouse Rd. E9
123 J12 Brenton St. E14
125 B13 Bressenden Pl. SW1
123 A9 Brett Rd. E8
121 K14 Brewer St. W1
121 C16 Brewery Rd. N7
123 L9 Brewhouse La. E1
124 J4 Brewhouse St. SW15
123 L12 Brewhouse Wk. SE16
120 H2 Brewster Gdns. W10
123 K13 Brewster Ho. E14
127 G11 Briant St. SE14
124 K1 Briar Wk. SW15
125 L15 Briarwood Rd. SW4
122 G7 Brick La. E1
122 F7 Brick La. E2
121 L13 Brick St. W1
123 G15 Brickfield Rd. E3
122 B1 Bride St. N7
121 C12 Bridge App. NW1
124 D1 Bridge Ave. W6
125 G10 Bridge La. SW11
124 L6 Bridge Pk. SW18
125 C13 Bridge Pl. SW1
125 A16 Bridge St. SW1
124 D2 Bridge Vw. W6
125 D16 Bridgefoot SE1
122 C1 Bridgeman Rd. N1
121 E10 Bridgeman St. NW8
124 K8 Bridgend Rd. SW18
125 J9 Bridges Ct. SW11
124 G5 Bridges Pl. SW6
121 E14 Bridgeway St. NW1
123 D16 Bridgwater Rd. E15
122 D5 Bridport Pl. N1
126 G3 Brief St. SE5
123 J15 Bright St. E14
123 K13 Brightlingsea Pl. E14
126 K1 Brighton Ter. SW9
121 E15 Brill Pl. NW1
127 G13 Brindley St. SE14
120 H7 Brinklow Ho. W2
123 B13 Brinkworth Way E9
123 H16 Brion Pl. E14
126 F5 Brisbane St. SE5
120 G7 Bristol Gdns. W9
127 C14 Britannia Rd. E14
124 F7 Britannia Rd. SW6
122 D3 Britannia Row N1
122 F1 Britannia St. WC1
123 F13 British St. E3
125 D10 Britten St. SW3
122 G3 Britton St. EC1
126 K2 Brixton Oval SW2
126 J2 Brixton Rd. SW9
126 J2 Brixton Sta. Rd. SW9
126 L2 Brixton Water La. SW2
122 H6 Broad La. EC2
125 A15 Broad Sanctuary SW1
121 L12 Broad Wk. W1
120 L8 Broad Wk., The W8
121 C16 Broadfield La. NW1
125 J13 Broadhinton Rd. SW4
120 B7 Broadhurst Gdns. NW6
121 H9 Bradley St. NW8
121 G10 Broadley Ter. NW1
122 L2 Broadwall SE1
125 B15 Broadway SW1
123 D9 Broadway Mkt. E8
121 J14 Broadwick St. W1
123 G15 Brock Pl. E3
126 B4 Brockham St. SE1
127 K13 Brockill Cres. SE4
127 F11 Brocklehurst St. SE14
127 K10 Brockley Footpath SE15
127 H13 Brockley Gdns. SE4
127 L13 Brockley Gro. SE4
127 L12 Brockley Hall Rd. SE4
127 L12 Brockley Ms. SE4
127 J13 Brockley Rd. SE4
127 L11 Brockley Way SE4
126 E6 Brockworth Clo. SE15
123 K11 Brodlove La. E1
123 F13 Brokesley St. E3
126 J6 Bromar Rd. SE5
125 K14 Bromell's Rd. SW4
125 J15 Bromfelde Rd. SW4
125 H16 Bromfelde Wk. SW4
122 E2 Bromfield St. N1
123 H16 Bromley Hall Rd. E14
123 F15 Bromley High St. E3
123 H11 Bromley St. E1
124 E7 Brompton Pk. Cres. SW6
125 B10 Brompton Pl. SW3
125 A11 Brompton Rd. SW1
125 C10 Brompton Rd. SW3
125 B10 Brompton Rd. SW7
125 B10 Brompton Sq. SW3
120 B3 Brondesbury Ct. NW2
120 C2 Brondesbury Pk. NW2
120 C3 Brondesbury Pk. NW6
120 E5 Brondesbury Rd. NW6
120 E5 Brondesbury Vill. NW6
124 F4 Bronsart Rd. SW6
120 F6 Bronte Ho. NW6
126 D4 Bronti Clo. SE17
127 F14 Bronze St. SE8
126 B2 Brook Dr. SE11
124 B2 Brook Grn. W6
121 K12 Brook St. W1
121 K9 Brook St. W2
127 J14 Brookbank Rd. SE13
122 H2 Brooke St. EC1
123 B12 Brookfield Rd. E9
125 G15 Brooklands St. SW8
127 G14 Brookmill Rd. SE8
121 K13 Brook's Ms. W1
123 B10 Brooksbank St. E9
122 C2 Brooksby St. N1
123 A11 Brooksby's Wk. E9
120 D4 Brooksville Ave. NW6
124 F5 Brookville Rd. SW6
126 F4 Broome Way SE5
123 H14 Broomfield St. E14
126 H1 Broomgrove Rd. SW9
124 L6 Broomhill Rd. SW18
124 H6 Broomhouse La. SW6
124 H6 Broomhouse Rd. SW6
120 A5 Broomsleigh St. NW6
122 D8 Brougham Rd. E8
126 K2 Broughton Dr. SW9
124 H7 Broughton Rd. SW6
125 H12 Broughton St. SW8
121 K12 Brown Hart Gdns. W1
121 J11 Brown St. W1
123 J15 Brownfield St. E14
126 D4 Browning Est. SE17
126 D4 Browning St. SE17
122 G1 Brownlow Ms. WC1
122 D7 Brownlow Rd. E8
121 A13 Browns La. NW5
121 D10 Broxwood Way NW8
123 F15 Bruce Rd. E3
120 F5 Bruckner St. W10
122 H7 Brune St. E1
120 H6 Brunel Est. W2
127 A10 Brunel Rd. SE16
126 A6 Brunswick Ct. SE1
120 L6 Brunswick Gdns. W8
126 G5 Brunswick Pk. SE5
122 F5 Brunswick Pl. N1
127 B11 Brunswick Quay SE16
123 J16 Brunswick Rd. E14
121 G16 Brunswick Sq. WC1
126 G6 Brunswick Vill. SE5
123 J12 Brunton Pl. E14
122 H6 Brushfield St. E1
125 K9 Brussels Rd. SW11
121 K13 Bruton La. W1
121 K13 Bruton Pl. W1
121 K13 Bruton St. W1
120 C1 Bryan Ave. NW10
127 A13 Bryan Rd. SE16
121 H11 Bryanston Pl. W1
121 H11 Bryanston Sq. W1
121 J11 Bryanston St. W1
122 A2 Bryantwood Rd. N7
123 E14 Brymay Clo. E3
125 G11 Brynmaer Rd. SW11
127 J10 Buchan Rd. SE15
120 E1 Buchanan Gdns. NW10
121 C13 Buck St. NW1
122 F8 Buckfast St. E2
123 G9 Buckhurst St. E1
125 B13 Buckingham Gate SW1
125 C13 Buckingham Palace Rd. SW1
122 B6 Buckingham Rd. N1
121 C9 Buckland Cres. NW3
122 E5 Buckland St. N1
122 J5 Bucklersbury EC4
120 C5 Buckley Rd. NW6
125 K10 Buckmaster Rd. SW11
121 J15 Bucknall St. WC2
126 K1 Bucknell Clo. SW2
126 K1 Buckner Rd. SW2
123 L12 Buckters Rents SE16
121 K9 Budge's Wk. W2
124 H4 Buer Rd. SW6
125 C15 Bulinga St. SW1
123 F11 Bullards Pl. E2
125 H10 Bullen St. SW11
126 F8 Buller Clo. SE15
123 J16 Bullivant St. E14

181

College Rd.

120 E2 College Rd. NW10
123 F13 College Ter. E3
123 B10 Collent St. E9
126 B8 Collett Rd. SE16
122 E1 Collier St. N1
120 L1 Collingbourne Rd. W12
124 C7 Collingham Gdns. SW5
124 C7 Collingham Pl. SW5
124 C7 Collingham Rd. SW5
123 G9 Collingwood St. E1
127 G10 Colls Rd. SE15
127 G9 Colmore Ms. SE15
126 B3 Colnbrook St. SE1
125 K9 Cologne Rd. SW11
122 L3 Colombo St. SE1
121 G16 Colonnade WC1
122 F7 Columbia Rd. E2
127 H16 Columbine Way SE13
122 A7 Colvestone Cres. E8
122 D6 Colville Est. N1
120 J5 Colville Gdns. W11
120 J5 Colville Hos. W11
120 J5 Colville Rd. W11
120 J5 Colville Sq. W11
120 J5 Colville Ter. W11
126 L7 Colwell Rd. SE22
124 E2 Colwith Rd. W6
127 L9 Colyton Rd. SE22
126 F4 Comber Gro. SE5
126 J1 Combermere Rd. SW9
124 D4 Comeragh Rd. W14
127 K12 Comerford Rd. SE4
127 F14 Comet Pl. SE8
127 F14 Comet St. SE8
122 J8 Commercial Rd. E1
123 J12 Commercial Rd. E14
122 G7 Commercial St. E1
126 F7 Commercial Way SE15
124 G8 Commodore Sq. SW10
123 G12 Commodore St. E1
124 J2 Commondale SW15
120 K1 Commonwealth Ave. W12
120 C7 Compayne Gdns. NW6
122 B3 Compton Ave. N1
122 B3 Compton Rd. N1
120 F3 Compton Rd. NW10
122 G3 Compton St. EC1
122 B3 Compton Ter. N1
126 C6 Comus Pl. SE17
125 K10 Comyn Rd. SW11
126 K1 Concanon Rd. SW2
122 L1 Concert Hall App. SE1
125 G14 Condell Rd. SW8
123 J12 Conder St. E14
126 J4 Conderton Rd. SE5
125 F10 Condray Pl. SW11
121 J9 Conduit Ms. W2
121 J9 Conduit Pl. W2
121 K13 Conduit St. W1
126 E13 Coney Way SW8
126 C6 Congreve St. SE17
124 H6 Conigar Rd. SW6
120 L1 Coningham Rd. W12
127 H15 Conington Rd. SE13
121 C16 Conistone Way N7
120 G4 Conlan St. W10
121 K11 Connaught Pl. W2
121 J11 Connaught Sq. W2
121 J10 Connaught St. W2
122 A6 Conrad Ho. N16
127 G9 Consort Rd. SE15
125 A13 Constitution Hill SW1
126 C4 Content St. SE17
121 G14 Conway St. W1
123 E12 Conyer St. E3
123 E15 Cook's Rd. E15
126 E3 Cooks Rd. SE17
122 E3 Coombs St. N1
124 E5 Coomer Pl. SW6
123 G10 Coopers Clo. E1
121 E15 Coopers La. NW1
126 D7 Coopers Rd. SE1
123 A11 Coopersale Rd. E9
124 B6 Cope Pl. W8
127 C11 Cope St. SE16
127 C14 Copeland Dr. E14
126 H8 Copeland Rd. SE15
123 J13 Copenhagen Pl. E14
121 D16 Copenhagen St. N1
126 H7 Copleston Ms. SE15
126 H7 Copleston Pas. SE15
126 J7 Copleston Rd. SE15
127 E15 Copperas St. SE8
123 G12 Copperfield Rd. E3
126 A3 Copperfield St. SE1
125 H10 Coppock Clo. SW11
122 J5 Copthall Ave. EC2
122 J5 Copthall Ct. EC2
121 H16 Coptic St. WC1
126 A2 Coral St. SE1
121 G16 Coram St. WC1
122 D6 Corbiere Ho. N1
123 E9 Corbridge Cres. E2
123 J15 Cordelia St. E14
123 F12 Cordova Rd. E3
123 F9 Corfield St. E2
121 K14 Cork St. W1
126 G3 Cormont Rd. SE5
122 B1 Cornelia St. N7
122 J5 Cornhill EC3
127 J16 Cornmill La. SE13
123 F10 Cornwall Ave. E2
120 J4 Cornwall Cres. W11
120 B1 Cornwall Gdns. NW10
124 B7 Cornwall Gdns. SW7
124 B8 Cornwall Ms. S. SW7
122 L2 Cornwall Rd. SE1
123 J10 Cornwood Dr. E1
122 F6 Coronet St. N1
122 G2 Corporation Row EC1
121 A16 Corporation St. N7
125 K16 Corrance Rd. SW2
122 F5 Corsham St. N1
122 B3 Corsica St. N5
124 H5 Cortayne Rd. SW6
125 G14 Corunna Rd. SW8
125 G14 Corunna Ter. SW8
126 L4 Cosbycote Ave. SE24
127 G9 Cossall Wk. SE15
126 B2 Cosser St. SE1
126 H8 Costa St. SE15
121 H10 Cosway St. NW1
123 J14 Cotall St. E14
120 C6 Cotleigh Rd. NW6
126 F5 Cottage Grn. SE5
125 J16 Cottage Gro. SW9
125 B10 Cottage Pl. SW3
123 K15 Cottage St. E14
124 B7 Cottesmore Gdns. W8
126 F1 Cottingham Rd. SW8
126 C3 Cottington Clo. SE11
125 J9 Cotton Row SW11
123 K16 Cotton St. E14
127 J12 Coulgate St. SE4
125 D11 Coulson St. SW3
124 B1 Coulter Rd. W6
126 F4 Councillor St. SE5
121 A14 Countess Rd. NW5
126 G4 County Gro. SE5
126 B4 County St. SE1
125 H15 Courland Gro. SW8
125 G15 Courland St. SW8
126 E3 Courtenay St. SE11
124 C7 Courtfield Gdns. SW5
124 C8 Courtfield Rd. SW7
127 K16 Courthill Rd. SE13
120 J6 Courtnell St. W2
123 K9 Courtyard, The E1
121 K16 Covent Gdn. WC2
123 G9 Coventry Rd. E1
123 G9 Coventry Rd. E2
121 K15 Coventry St. W1
120 C3 Coverdale Rd. NW2
124 A1 Coverdale Rd. W12
122 H8 Coverley Clo. E1
122 H3 Cowcross St. EC1
126 G2 Cowley Rd. SW9
122 A6 Cowper Rd. N16
122 G5 Cowper St. EC2
125 G15 Cowthorpe Rd. SW8
123 F9 Crabtree La. SW6
124 E4 Cramond Clo. W6
126 C4 Crampton St. SE17
121 K15 Cranbourn St. WC2
123 E11 Cranbrook Est. E2
127 G14 Cranbrook Rd. SE8
124 H7 Cranbury Rd. SW6
122 B1 Crane Gro. N7
127 C11 Crane Mead SE16
127 J13 Cranfield Rd. SE4
123 K11 Cranford St. E1
120 A2 Cranhurst Rd. NW2
125 H10 Cranleigh Ms. SW11
121 E14 Cranleigh St. NW1
124 D8 Cranley Gdns. SW7
124 D8 Cranley Ms. SW7
125 C9 Cranley Pl. SW7
125 J15 Cranmer Ct. SW4
126 F2 Cranmer Rd. SW9
122 E5 Cranston Est. N1
127 D9 Cranswick Rd. SE16
123 G15 Cranwell Clo. E3
122 F5 Cranwood St. EC1
126 G2 Cranworth Gdns. SW9
120 K8 Craven Hill W2
120 K8 Craven Hill Gdns. W2
120 K8 Craven Hill Ms. W2
120 J8 Craven Rd. W2
121 L16 Craven St. WC2
120 K8 Craven Ter. W2
126 H4 Crawford Est. SE5
121 H10 Crawford Pl. W1
121 G4 Crawford Rd. SE5
121 H11 Crawford St. W1
126 K7 Crawthew Gro. SE22
120 A7 Crediton Hill NW6
120 D3 Crediton Rd. NW10
127 D9 Credon Rd. SE16
122 J6 Creechurch La. EC3
127 E14 Creek Rd. SE8
127 E15 Creek Rd. SE10
127 F15 Creekside SE8
124 E3 Crefeld Clo. W6
120 E3 Creighton Rd. NW6
122 E7 Cremer St. E2
124 F8 Cremorne Rd. SW10
125 K14 Crescent Gro. SW4
125 K14 Crescent La. SW4
125 C10 Crescent Pl. SW3
122 C1 Crescent St. N1
127 J14 Crescent Way SE4
124 G7 Cresford Rd. SW6
123 B10 Cresset Rd. E9
125 J15 Cresset St. SW4
121 A12 Cressfield Clo. NW5
127 J16 Cressingham Rd. SE13
124 D8 Cresswell Gdns. SW5
124 D8 Cresswell Pl. SW10
124 B1 Cressy Ct. W6
123 H10 Cressy Pl. E1
121 A11 Cressy Rd. NW3
121 F16 Crestfield St. WC1
126 F2 Crewdson Rd. SW9
127 C14 Crews St. E14
127 H9 Crewys Rd. SE15
126 B6 Crimscott St. SE1
127 F13 Crimsworth Rd. SW8
121 E16 Crinan St. N1
125 F14 Cringle St. SW8
124 D2 Crisp Rd. W6
123 J9 Crispin St. E1
124 H2 Cristowe Rd. SW6
127 C12 Croft St. SE8
121 D15 Crofters Way NW1
126 G6 Crofton Rd. SE5
127 L12 Croftongate Way SE4
122 K8 Crofts St. E1
121 C12 Crogsland Rd. NW1
121 F16 Cromer St. WC1
124 L6 Cromford Rd. SW18
121 G9 Crompton St. W2
124 C1 Cromwell Ave. W6
124 C6 Cromwell Cres. SW5
125 B9 Cromwell Gdns. SW7
124 B2 Cromwell Gro. W6
125 C9 Cromwell Ms. SW7
125 C9 Cromwell Pl. SW7
124 C7 Cromwell Rd. SW5
124 C7 Cromwell Rd. SW7
126 G3 Cromwell Rd. SW9
124 G6 Crondace Rd. SW6
122 E5 Crondall St. N1
127 D12 Crooke Rd. SE8
124 G5 Crookham Rd. SW6
127 F16 Crooms Hill SE10
127 F16 Crooms Hill Gro. SE10
122 E5 Cropley St. N1
126 A5 Crosby Row SE1
126 H6 Cross Rd. SE5
122 D3 Cross St. N1
122 B9 Crossfield Rd. NW3
127 F14 Crossfield St. SE8
125 H16 Crossford St. SW9
122 B2 Crossley St. N7
126 K5 Crossthwaite Ave. SE5
122 K7 Crosswall EC3
122 A6 Crossway N16
122 D8 Croston St. E8
123 K9 Crowder St. E1
126 H2 Crowhurst Clo. SW9
122 C5 Crowland Ter. N1
123 D14 Crown Clo. E3
126 F4 Crown St. SE5
121 E14 Crowndale Rd. NW1
126 L2 Crownstone Rd. SW2
120 J3 Crowthorne Rd. W10
120 F5 Croxley Rd. W9
123 A11 Crozier Ter. E9
126 A6 Crucifix La. SE1
122 D3 Cruden St. N1
122 F2 Cruikshank St. WC1
126 K6 Crutched Friars EC3
127 A14 Cuba St. E14
122 F1 Cubitt St. WC1
125 J14 Cubitt Ter. SW4
123 G9 Cudworth St. E1
125 C11 Culford Gdns. SW3
122 B6 Culford Gro. N1
122 C6 Culford Rd. N1
123 J16 Culloden St. E14
127 F9 Culmore Rd. SE15
125 L12 Culmstock Rd. SW11
121 K12 Culross St. W1
125 H12 Culvert Pl. SW11
125 G11 Culvert Rd. SW11
122 B7 Cumberland Clo. E8
124 C4 Cumberland Cres. W14
121 K11 Cumberland Gate W1
121 F13 Cumberland Mkt. NW1
125 D13 Cumberland St. SW1
122 E1 Cumming St. N1
125 C12 Cundy St. SW1
121 G9 Cunningham Pl. NW8
125 G13 Cupar Rd. SW11
125 C15 Cureton St. SW1
126 A7 Curlew St. SE1
122 J2 Cursitor St. EC4
122 F6 Curtain Rd. EC2
126 C7 Curtis St. SE1
126 C7 Curtis Way SE1
121 L12 Curzon St. W1
126 A2 Cut, The SE1
126 H4 Cutcombe Rd. SE5
121 G9 Cuthbert St. W2
122 J6 Cutler St. E1
127 C14 Cyclops Ms. E14
122 E1 Cynthia St. N1
123 E10 Cyprus Pl. E2
123 E10 Cyprus St. E2
125 G11 Cyril Mans. SW11
122 G3 Cyrus St. EC1
127 E14 Czar St. SE8

D

127 G16 Dabin Cres. SE10
127 E13 Dacca St. SE8
123 D14 Dace Rd. E3
125 B15 Dacre St. SW1
120 E3 Dagmar Gdns. NW10
126 G6 Dagmar Rd. SE5
122 D3 Dagmar Ter. N1
125 H11 Dagnall St. SW11
125 J16 Dairy Ms. SW9
124 J6 Daisy La. SW6
126 L2 Dalberg Rd. SW2
124 K8 Dalby Rd. SW18
121 B13 Dalby St. NW5
126 E3 Dale Rd. SE17
121 A9 Daleham Gdns. NW3
121 B9 Daleham Ms. NW3
121 E14 Dalehead NW1
123 B11 Daley St. E9
125 J13 Daley Thompson Way SW8
120 H2 Dalgarno Gdns. W10
120 G2 Dalgarno Gdns. Est. W10
120 G2 Dalgarno Way W10
123 J13 Dalgleish St. E14
123 E12 Daling Way E3
124 C1 Dalling Rd. W6
122 G3 Dallington St. EC1
127 K12 Dalrymple Rd. SE4
122 B7 Dalston La. E8
126 G6 Dalwood St. SE5
126 J1 Dalyell Rd. SW9
122 E4 Dame St. N1
123 J9 Damien St. E1
122 E3 Danbury St. N1
126 J7 Danby St. SE15
124 G5 Dancer Rd. SW6
126 L4 Danecroft Rd. SE24
124 G4 Danehurst St. SW6
124 J2 Danemere St. SW15
123 B12 Danesdale Rd. E9
126 G5 Daneville Rd. SE5
126 F7 Daniel Gdns. SE15
127 J10 Daniels Rd. SE15
126 C3 Dante Rd. SE11
125 E9 Danvers St. SW3
121 J14 D'Arblay St. W1
127 L13 Darfield Rd. SE4
120 J3 Darfield Way W10
124 J3 Darfur St. SW15
125 J9 Darien Rd. SW11
124 F5 Darlan Rd. SW6
127 J14 Darling Rd. SE4
123 G9 Darling Row E1
123 B10 Darnley Rd. E9
126 L8 Darrell Rd. SE22
125 G16 Darsley Dr. SW8
120 F4 Dart St. W10
126 E4 Dartford St. SE17
120 J6 Dartmouth Clo. W11
127 G16 Dartmouth Gro. SE10
127 G16 Dartmouth Hill SE10
120 B3 Dartmouth Rd. NW2
127 G16 Dartmouth Row SE10
125 A15 Dartmouth St. SW1
126 C5 Darwin St. SE17
126 G5 Datchelor Pl. SE5
126 D4 Date St. SE17
127 C13 Daubeney Twr. SE8
122 H8 Davenant St. E1
121 H10 Daventry St. NW1
122 B1 Davey Clo. N7
126 E7 Davey St. SE15
126 A3 Davidge St. SE1
125 F16 Davidson Gdns. SW8
121 K13 Davies St. W1
124 F4 Dawes Rd. SW6
126 D5 Dawes St. SE17
120 B3 Dawlish Rd. NW2
120 K6 Dawson Pl. W2
120 A2 Dawson Rd. NW2
122 E7 Dawson St. E2
127 G10 Dayton Gro. SE15
122 D6 De Beauvoir Cres. N1
122 D5 De Beauvoir Est. N1
122 D6 De Beauvoir Rd. N1
122 C6 De Beauvoir Sq. N1
126 H5 De Crespigny Pk. SE5
126 D3 De Laune St. SE17
124 J7 De Morgan Rd. SW6
124 A8 De Vere Gdns. W8
126 C4 Deacon Way SE17
127 B10 Deal Porters Way SE16
122 H8 Deal St. E1
124 K2 Dealtry Rd. SW15
125 B16 Dean Bradley St. SW1
125 B15 Dean Farrar St. SW1
120 B2 Dean Rd. NW2
125 C16 Dean Ryle St. SW1
125 B16 Dean Stanley St. SW1
121 J15 Dean St. W1
123 J10 Deancross St. E1
121 L12 Deanery St. W1
126 C5 Deans Bldgs. SE17
125 D15 Dean's Pl. SW1
126 B6 Decima St. SE1
123 J16 Dee St. E14
125 G15 Deeley Rd. SW8
126 K5 Deepdene Rd. SE5
126 K4 Deerdale Rd. SE24
120 B3 Deerhurst Rd. NW2
127 D9 Delaford Rd. SE16
124 F4 Delaford St. SW6
120 H7 Delamere Ter. W2
121 D13 Delancey St. NW1
120 G7 Delaware Rd. W9
121 D16 Delhi St. N1
123 K9 Dellow St. E1
127 G14 Deloraine St. SE8
124 E3 Delorme St. W6
126 D3 Delverton Rd. SE17
124 G6 Delvino Rd. SW6
124 L8 Dempster Rd. SW18
120 K5 Denbigh Clo. W11
125 D14 Denbigh Pl. SW1
120 K5 Denbigh Rd. W11
125 C14 Denbigh St. SW1
120 K5 Denbigh Ter. W11
127 J12 Dene Clo. SE4
120 F5 Denholme Rd. W9
126 G7 Denman Rd. SE15
122 E2 Denmark Gro. N1
126 G5 Denmark Hill SE5
126 K5 Denmark Hill Est. SE5
120 E5 Denmark Rd. NW6
126 G4 Denmark Rd. SE5
121 J15 Denmark St. WC2
122 D7 Denne Ter. E8
127 G10 Dennetts Rd. SE14
120 F8 Denning Clo. NW8
120 B6 Dennington Pk. Rd. NW6
123 C16 Dennison Pt. E15
126 D2 Denny St. SE11
125 C10 Denyer St. SW3
124 K4 Deodar Rd. SW15
127 G14 Deptford Bri. SE8
127 G14 Deptford Bdy. SE8
127 E14 Deptford Ch. St. SE8
127 C14 Deptford Ferry Rd. E14
127 E14 Deptford Grn. SE8
127 E14 Deptford High St. SE8
127 C13 Deptford Strand SE8
127 C13 Deptford Wf. SE8
123 D11 Derby Rd. E9
122 F8 Derbyshire St. E2
122 D8 Dericote St. E8
121 J13 Dering St. W1
124 A7 Derry St. W8
126 K7 Derwent Gro. SE22
127 E12 Desmond St. SE14
123 G15 Devas St. E3
126 B5 Deverell St. SE1
127 E9 Devon St. SE15
122 E3 Devonia Rd. N1
124 A1 Devonport Rd. W12
123 J11 Devonport St. E1
123 F15 Devons Est. E3
123 H14 Devons Rd. E3
121 H13 Devonshire Clo. W1
127 F15 Devonshire Dr. SE10
127 E9 Devonshire Gro. SE15
121 H13 Devonshire Ms. S. W1
121 G13 Devonshire Ms. W. W1
121 G12 Devonshire Pl. W1
121 H13 Devonshire St. W1
120 J8 Devonshire Ter. W2
126 J8 Dewar St. SE15
123 H16 Dewberry St. E14
122 E2 Dewey Rd. N1
124 B3 Dewhurst Rd. W14
126 G5 D'Eynsford Rd. SE5
126 F6 Diamond St. SE15
127 G16 Diamond Ter. SE10
121 G13 Diana Pl. NW1
122 D4 Dibden St. N1
126 A7 Dickens Est. SE1
126 A7 Dickens Est. SE16
126 B4 Dickens Sq. SE1
125 H13 Dickens St. SW8
123 A11 Digby Rd. E9
123 F10 Digby St. E2
124 L8 Dighton Rd. SW18
125 E11 Dilke St. SW3
123 K14 Dingle Gdns. E14
122 F4 Dingley Pl. EC1
122 F4 Dingley Rd. EC1
124 E4 Disbrowe Rd. W6
124 K3 Disraeli Rd. SW15
122 F7 Diss St. E2
122 K4 Distaff La. EC4
124 D2 Distillery Rd. W6
127 G15 Ditch All. SE10
123 K16 Ditchburn St. E14
127 G12 Dixon Rd. SE14
120 C1 Dobree Ave. NW10
121 C9 Dobson Clo. NW6
127 A11 Dock Hill Ave. SE16
122 K8 Dock St. E1
127 C14 Dockers Tanner Rd. E14
126 A7 Dockhead SE1
126 B8 Dockley Rd. SE16
122 B6 Docwra's Bldgs. N1
123 J14 Dod St. E14
126 E3 Doddington Gro. SE17
126 E3 Doddington Pl. SE17
126 A2 Dodson St. SE1
126 J6 Dog Kennel Hill SE22
126 J6 Dog Kennel Hill Est. SE22
122 L3 Dolben St. SE1
124 H5 Dolby Rd. SW6
126 D1 Dolland St. SE11
126 K1 Dolman St. SW4
123 K15 Dolphin La. E14
125 D14 Dolphin Sq. SW1
122 H1 Dombey St. WC1
126 K5 Domett Clo. SE5
126 G5 Don Phelan Clo. SE5
120 D5 Donaldson Rd. NW6
122 E1 Donegal St. N1
124 H3 Doneraile St. SW6
125 C10 Donne Pl. SW3
120 C1 Donnington Rd. NW10
123 J13 Dora St. E14
123 C16 Doran Wk. E15
126 L4 Dorchester Ct. SE24
126 L4 Dorchester Dr. SE24
124 H5 Doria Rd. SW6
121 F15 Doric Way NW1
127 E13 Dorking Clo. SE8
121 D9 Dorman Way NW8
124 L7 Dormay St. SW18
124 H4 Dorncliffe Rd. SW6
121 C10 Dorney NW3
120 A5 Dornfell St. NW6
125 J11 Dorothy Rd. SW11
122 H2 Dorrington St. EC1
122 F7 Dorset Est. E2
122 J3 Dorset Ri. EC4
125 F16 Dorset Rd. SW8
121 G11 Dorset Sq. NW1
121 H11 Dorset St. W1
124 B1 Dorville Cres. W6
122 G1 Doughty Ms. WC1
122 G1 Doughty St. WC1
122 C4 Douglas Rd. N1
120 D5 Douglas Rd. NW6
125 C15 Douglas St. SW1
127 F13 Douglas Way SE8
124 B7 Douro Pl. W8
123 E14 Douro St. E3
124 C8 Dove Ms. SW5
122 B5 Dove Rd. N1
122 D8 Dove Row E2
127 L9 Dovedale Rd. SE22
125 D9 Dovehouse St. SW3
121 K13 Dover St. W1
122 K5 Dowgate Hill EC4
120 F4 Dowland St. W10
126 F6 Dowlas St. SE5
124 D1 Down Pl. W6
121 L13 Down St. W1
120 G7 Downfield Clo. W9
122 C5 Downham Rd. N1
125 A16 Downing St. SW1
122 A8 Downs Pk. Rd. E5
122 A7 Downs Pk. Rd. E8
121 A10 Downside Cres. NW3
127 A12 Downtown Rd. SE16
126 K5 Dowson Clo. SE5
125 C12 D'Oyley St. SW1
126 E4 Draco St. SE17
127 D13 Dragoon Rd. SE8
127 J14 Drake Rd. SE4
127 J12 Drakefell Rd. SE4
127 H11 Drakefell Rd. SE14
126 L1 Dray Gdns. SW2
125 C10 Draycott Ave. SW3
125 C11 Draycott Pl. SW3
125 C11 Draycott Ter. SW3
120 G5 Drayford Clo. W9
124 A6 Drayson Ms. W8
124 D8 Drayton Gdns. SW10
122 A2 Drayton Pk. N5
123 E12 Driffield Rd. E3
120 G4 Droop St. W10
127 F9 Drover La. SE15
127 F9 Drovers Pl. SE15
126 A6 Druid St. SE1
121 F15 Drummond Cres. NW1
125 D15 Drummond Gate SW1
127 B9 Drummond Rd. SE16
121 G14 Drummond St. NW1
121 J16 Drury La. WC2
124 J3 Dryad St. SW15
124 J1 Dryburgh Rd. SW15
122 F6 Drysdale St. N1
122 D8 Dublin Cres. E8
124 A6 Duchess of Bedford's Wk. W8
121 H13 Duchess St. W1
122 L2 Duchy St. SE1
126 K1 Ducie St. SW4
123 G11 Duckett St. E1
120 E4 Dudley Rd. NW6
123 J15 Duff St. E14
122 G4 Dufferin St. EC1
125 A12 Duke of Wellington Pl. SW1
121 L14 Duke of York St. SW1
121 L14 Duke St. SW1
121 J12 Duke St. W1
124 A7 Dukes La. W8
122 J6 Dukes Pl. EC3
121 F15 Duke's Rd. WC1
120 K4 Dulford St. W11
125 L11 Dulka Rd. SW11
126 L2 Dulwich Rd. SE24
121 A11 Dunboyne Rd. NW3
122 G8 Dunbridge St. E2
123 D9 Duncan Rd. E8
122 E3 Duncan St. N1
122 E3 Duncan Ter. N1
121 K16 Duncannon St. WC2
127 J12 Dundalk Rd. SE4
127 H10 Dundas Rd. SE15
123 L9 Dundee St. E1
120 D3 Dundonald Rd. NW10
123 J11 Dunelm St. E1
127 F17 Dunloe St. E2
120 D4 Dunmore Rd. NW6
122 A7 Dunn St. E8
121 A14 Dunollie Rd. NW5
124 B3 Dunsany Rd. W14
120 C5 Dunster Gdns. NW6
122 D7 Dunston Rd. E8
125 J12 Dunston Rd. SW11
122 D7 Dunston St. E8
126 C7 Dunton Rd. SE1
126 G1 Durand Gdns. SW9
122 F8 Durant St. E2
123 H12 Durham Row E1
126 D1 Durham St. SE11
120 J7 Durham Ter. W2
124 G5 Durrell Rd. SW6
123 H9 Durward St. E1
123 K16 Duthie St. E14
127 G16 Dutton St. SE10
123 D14 Dye Ho. La. E3
124 K1 Dyers La. SW15
126 K5 Dylways SE5
124 J7 Dymock St. SW6
120 C4 Dyne Rd. NW6
120 C6 Dynham Rd. NW6
121 J15 Dyott St. WC1

E

122 H3 Eagle Ct. EC1
122 H1 Eagle St. WC1
122 E4 Eagle Wf. Rd. N1
121 E10 Eamont St. NW8
124 D6 Eardley Cres. SW5
126 D7 Earl Rd. SE1
122 H5 Earl St. EC2
124 K2 Earldom Rd. SW15
121 J15 Earlham St. WC2
124 C7 Earls Ct. Gdns. SW5
124 C6 Earls Ct. Rd. SW5
124 C6 Earls Ct. Rd. W8
124 D7 Earls Ct. Sq. SW5
124 B5 Earls Ter. W8
124 B6 Earls Wk. W8
122 C1 Earlsferry Way N1
120 F2 Earlsmead Rd. NW10
123 D9 Earlston Gro. E9
121 J15 Earnshaw St. WC2
124 C4 Earsby St. W14
123 J11 East Arbour St. E1
123 C13 East Cross Route E3
126 L6 East Dulwich Gro. SE22
126 K8 East Dulwich Rd. SE15
126 K7 East Dulwich Rd. SE22
127 C15 East Ferry Rd. E14
124 L7 East Hill SW18
123 J14 East India Dock Rd. E14
126 A8 East La. SE16
123 H9 East Mt. St. E1
122 F5 East Rd. N1
120 G4 East Row W10
122 K7 East Smithfield E1
126 D4 East St. SE17
126 F7 East Surrey Gro. SE15
122 J7 East Tenter St. E1
120 J8 Eastbourne Ms. W2
120 J8 Eastbourne Ter. W2
123 G11 Eastbury Ter. E1
121 J14 Eastcastle St. W1
122 K5 Eastcheap EC3

Gloucester Gate

126 H1 Eastcote St. SW9
127 K14 Eastern Rd. SE4
126 H4 Eastlake Rd. SE5
123 B13 Eastway E9
125 C12 Eaton Clo. SW1
126 K3 Eaton Dr. SW9
125 C12 Eaton Gate SW1
125 B13 Eaton La. SW1
125 B12 Eaton Ms. N. SW1
125 C12 Eaton Ms. S. SW1
125 C12 Eaton Ms. W. SW1
125 B12 Eaton Pl. SW1
125 B13 Eaton Row SW1
125 C12 Eaton Sq. SW1
125 C12 Eaton Ter. SW1
126 E1 Ebbisham Dr. SW8
120 A4 Ebbsfleet Rd. NW2
124 L7 Ebner St. SW18
122 G7 Ebor St. E1
125 D13 Ebury Bri. SW1
125 D13 Ebury Bri. Est. SW1
125 D12 Ebury Bri. Rd. SW1
125 C13 Ebury Ms. SW1
125 C12 Ebury Sq. SW1
125 C12 Ebury St. SW1
125 K11 Eccles Rd. SW11
122 C4 Ecclesbourne Rd. N1
125 C13 Eccleston Bri. SW1
125 B12 Eccleston Ms. SW1
125 C13 Eccleston Pl. SW1
125 C13 Eccleston Sq. SW1
125 C13 Eccleston St. SW1
122 E2 Eckford St. N1
125 K10 Eckstein Rd. SW11
120 G6 Edbrooke Rd. W9
124 H5 Eddiscombe Rd. SW6
127 L12 Eddystone Rd. SE4
122 A1 Eden Gro. N7
123 C11 Edenbridge Rd. E9
124 J5 Edenhurst Ave. SW6
124 H7 Edenvale St. SW6
123 F15 Edgar Rd. E3
124 G4 Edgarley Ter. SW6
125 J15 Edgeley Rd. SW4
121 G9 Edgware Rd. W2
125 A11 Edinburgh Gate SW1
120 F7 Edinburgh Ho. W9
121 D12 Edis St. NW1
124 E8 Edith Gro. SW10
124 C4 Edith Rd. W14
124 G7 Edith Row SW6
124 F8 Edith Ter. SW10
124 D5 Edith Vill. W14
125 J16 Edithna St. SW9
123 B12 Edmeston Clo. E9
126 F5 Edmund St. SE5
125 G10 Edna St. SW11
127 F11 Edric Rd. SE14
125 G16 Edrich Ho. SW4
127 E13 Edward Pl. SE8
127 E13 Edward St. SE8
127 F12 Edward St. SE14
124 B5 Edwardes Sq. W8
121 J12 Edwards Ms. W1
123 G10 Edwin St. E1
124 F6 Effie Pl. SW6
124 F6 Effie Rd. SW6
126 L2 Effra Par. SW2
126 K2 Effra Rd. SW2
127 D9 Egan Way SE16
121 D12 Egbert St. NW1
125 C10 Egerton Cres. SW3
127 G15 Egerton Dr. SE10
120 D2 Egerton Gdns. NW10
125 C10 Egerton Gdns. SW3
125 B10 Egerton Gdns. Ms. SW3
125 B10 Egerton Pl. SW3
125 B10 Egerton Ter. SW3
124 L8 Eglantine Rd. SW18
124 J2 Egliston Ms. SW15
124 J2 Egliston Rd. SW15
127 F11 Egmont St. SE14
121 A12 Elaine Gro. NW5
126 H3 Elam Clo. SE5
126 H3 Elam St. SE5
125 J11 Eland Rd. SW11
124 H8 Elbe St. SW6
125 F10 Elcho St. SW11
126 F8 Elcot Ave. SE15
122 H7 Elder St. E1
121 A9 Eldon Gro. NW3
124 B7 Eldon Rd. W8
122 H5 Eldon St. EC2
127 A11 Eleanor Clo. SE16
123 B9 Eleanor Rd. E8
123 F14 Eleanor St. E3
126 K2 Electric Ave. SW9
126 K2 Electric La. SW9
126 B3 Elephant & Castle SE1
127 A10 Elephant La. SE16
126 C4 Elephant Rd. SE17
123 K10 Elf Row E1
126 L4 Elfindale Rd. SE24
127 A12 Elgar St. SE16
120 G6 Elgin Ave. W9
120 K4 Elgin Cres. W11
120 G6 Elgin Est. W9
122 E3 Elia Ms. N1
122 E3 Elia St. N1
126 E2 Elias Pl. SW8
126 B5 Elim Est. SE1
127 H16 Eliot Hill SE13
127 H16 Eliot Pk. SE13
122 C4 Elizabeth Ave. N1
125 C13 Elizabeth Bri. SW1
126 E5 Elizabeth Est. SE17
121 B11 Elizabeth Ms. NW3
125 C12 Elizabeth St. SW1
120 H5 Elkstone Rd. W10
124 E3 Ellaline Rd. W6
127 K10 Elland Rd. SE15
122 J8 Ellen St. E1
124 G3 Ellerby St. SW6
120 A8 Ellerdale Rd. NW3
127 K15 Ellerdale St. SE13
120 L1 Ellerslie Rd. W12
125 K16 Ellerslie Sq. Ind. Est. SW2
127 H9 Ellery St. SE15
123 E12 Ellesmere Rd. E3
123 J15 Ellesmere St. E14
123 C9 Ellingfort Rd. E8
122 B2 Ellington St. N7
126 F3 Elliott Rd. SW9
121 C10 Elliott Sq. NW3
126 C3 Elliotts Row SE11
125 C11 Ellis St. SW1
123 F9 Ellsworth St. E2
126 H7 Elm Gro. SE15
125 D9 Elm Pk. Gdns. SW10
125 D9 Elm Pk. La. SW3
125 E9 Elm Pk. Rd. SW3
125 D9 Elm Pl. SW7
125 E15 Elm Quay Ct. SW8
122 G1 Elm St. WC1
121 F9 Elm Tree Clo. NW8
121 F9 Elm Tree Rd. NW8
125 J15 Elmhurst St. SW4
126 F5 Elmington Est. SE5
126 G5 Elmington Rd. SE5
127 J15 Elmira St. SE13
122 C5 Elmore St. N1
121 K9 Elms Ms. W2
125 L14 Elms Rd. SW4
124 G6 Elmstone Rd. SW6
126 L5 Elmwood Rd. SE24
122 B8 Elrington Rd. E8
123 H12 Elsa St. E1
123 B10 Elsdale St. E9
124 A4 Elsham Rd. W14
124 A4 Elsham Ter. W14
126 K7 Elsie Rd. SE22
127 L13 Elsiemaud Rd. SE4
125 J11 Elsley Rd. SW11
125 K11 Elspeth Rd. SW11
126 C5 Elsted St. SE17
127 H15 Elswick Rd. SE13
124 H8 Elswick St. SW6
121 C10 Elsworthy Ri. NW3
121 D10 Elsworthy Rd. NW3
121 C10 Elsworthy Ter. NW3
125 L9 Elsynge Rd. SW18
124 G6 Elthiron Rd. SW6
123 D13 Elton Ho. E3
122 A6 Elton Pl. N16
124 K8 Eltringham St. SW18
124 B8 Elvaston Ms. SW7
124 B8 Elvaston Pl. SW7
127 H15 Elverson Rd. SE8
125 C15 Elverton St. SW1
120 B2 Elvis Rd. NW2
122 F8 Elwin St. E2
125 D10 Elystan Pl. SW3
125 C10 Elystan St. SW3
126 A8 Emba St. SE16
124 H3 Embankment SW15
125 E11 Embankment Gdns. SW3
121 L16 Embankment Pl. WC2
127 K15 Embleton Rd. SE13
124 G7 Emden St. SW6
122 H1 Emerald St. WC1
122 L4 Emerson St. SE1
125 B14 Emery Hill St. SW1
123 E9 Emma St. E2
123 G12 Emmott Clo. E1
124 B7 Emperor's Gate SW7
124 D6 Empress Pl. SW6
126 E4 Empress St. SE17
123 G15 Empson St. E3
125 H13 Emu Rd. SW8
120 F4 Enbrook St. W10
121 J16 Endell St. WC2
121 G15 Endsleigh Gdns. WC1
121 G15 Endsleigh Pl. WC1
121 G15 Endsleigh St. WC1
127 H12 Endwell Rd. SE4
122 C6 Enfield Rd. N1
121 H11 Enford St. W1
127 K16 Engate St. SE13
121 B11 Englands La. NW3
122 C5 Englefield Rd. N1
123 G13 English St. E3
126 B7 Enid St. SE16
124 K2 Enmore Rd. SW15
123 G13 Ennerdale Ho. E3
125 A10 Ennismore Gdns. SW7
125 B10 Ennismore Gdns. Ms. SW7
125 B10 Ennismore Ms. SW7
125 B10 Ennismore St. SW7
122 K8 Ensign St. E1
124 K6 Enterprise Way SW18
127 C13 Enterprise Way SE8
124 F5 Epirus Rd. SW6
127 C14 Epping Clo. E14
124 G5 Epple Rd. SW6
122 G5 Epworth St. EC2
125 C15 Erasmus St. SW1
120 C6 Eresby Pl. NW6
123 G13 Eric St. E3
124 L6 Ericcson Clo. SW18
127 G11 Erlanger Rd. SE14
127 K15 Ermine Rd. SE13
123 G11 Ernest St. E1
124 J2 Erpingham Rd. SW15
120 G5 Errington Rd. W9
122 G4 Errol St. EC1
121 C11 Erskine Rd. NW3
126 C8 Esmeralda Rd. SE1
120 D5 Esmond Rd. NW6
124 K4 Esmond St. SW15
120 F6 Essendine Rd. W9
122 D3 Essex Rd. N1
124 A6 Essex Vill. W8
123 H12 Essian St. E1
124 F5 Estcourt Rd. SW6
125 J10 Este Rd. SW11
125 C15 Esterbrooke St. SW1
124 G2 Eternit Wk. SW6
125 G10 Ethelburga St. SW11
120 L1 Ethelden Rd. W12
127 E9 Ethnard Rd. SE15
121 C9 Eton Ave. NW3
121 B11 Eton College Rd. NW3
121 C11 Eton Rd. NW3
121 B11 Eton Vill. NW3
127 E12 Etta St. SE8
123 J16 Ettrick St. E14
127 C10 Eugenia Rd. SE16
124 F6 Eustace Rd. SW6
121 F15 Euston Gro. NW1
121 G13 Euston Rd. NW1
121 F15 Euston Sq. NW1
121 F14 Euston St. NW1
126 H2 Evandale Rd. SW9
127 J10 Evelina Rd. SE15
126 B8 Eveline Lowe Est. SE16
120 H2 Evelyn Fox Ct. W10
125 D9 Evelyn Gdns. SW7
127 D12 Evelyn St. SE8
122 E5 Evelyn Wk. N1
124 L4 Evenwood Clo. SW15
123 H16 Everest Pl. E14
122 D1 Everilda St. N1
124 E3 Everington St. W6
121 E14 Eversholt St. NW1
125 J11 Eversleigh Rd. SW11
126 J7 Everthorpe Rd. SE15
120 K3 Evesham St. W11
126 H2 Evesham Wk. SW9
125 J12 Evesham Way SW11
124 H5 Ewald Rd. SW6
123 E13 Ewart Pl. E3
121 B16 Ewe Clo. N7
122 L4 Ewer St. SE1
127 H16 Excelsior Gdns. SE13
122 H6 Exchange Arc. EC2
122 H6 Exchange Pl. EC2
122 H6 Exchange Sq. EC2
120 A4 Exeter Rd. NW2
126 G7 Exeter Rd. SE15
121 K16 Exeter St. WC2
127 F13 Exeter Way SE14
120 K2 Exhibition Clo. W12
125 A9 Exhibition Rd. SW7
120 H3 Exmoor St. W10
122 G2 Exmouth Mkt. EC1
123 C9 Exmouth Pl. E8
126 C6 Exon St. SE17
122 L2 Exton St. SE1
120 J2 Eynham Rd. W12
126 G2 Eythorne Rd. SW9
122 F7 Ezra St. E2

F

124 F5 Fabian Rd. SW6
127 D15 Factory Pl. E14
126 G2 Fairbairn Grn. SW9
122 J8 Fairclough St. E1
124 K1 Fairdale Gdns. SW15
120 C8 Fairfax Pl. NW6
120 C8 Fairfax Rd. NW6
124 L7 Fairfield Dr. SW18
123 E14 Fairfield Rd. E3
124 L7 Fairfield St. SW18
123 G14 Fairfoot Rd. E3
120 B7 Fairhazel Gdns. NW6
124 D4 Fairholme Rd. W14
122 G8 Fakruddin St. E1
125 J10 Falcon Gro. SW11
125 J10 Falcon La. SW11
125 H10 Falcon Rd. SW11
125 J10 Falcon Ter. SW11
127 C15 Falcon Way E14
120 F7 Falkirk Ho. W9
122 E6 Falkirk St. N1
121 A14 Falkland Rd. NW5
126 B4 Falmouth Rd. SE1
122 G4 Fann St. EC1
122 F6 Fanshaw St. N1
124 J2 Fanthorpe St. SW15
120 H4 Faraday Rd. W10
124 J2 Farlow Rd. SW15
124 E6 Farm La. SW6
121 K13 Farm St. W1
126 F3 Farmers Rd. SE5
126 A8 Farncombe St. SE16
126 D1 Farnham Royal SE11
124 B3 Faroe Rd. W14
123 J14 Farrance St. E14
121 C13 Farrier St. NW1
122 G2 Farringdon La. EC1
122 G2 Farringdon Rd. EC1
122 H3 Farringdon St. EC4
123 L12 Farrins Rents SE16
127 F10 Farrow La. SE14
122 H7 Fashion St. E1
122 B8 Fassett Rd. E8
122 B8 Fassett Sq. E8
127 G10 Faulkner St. SE14
124 G6 Favart Rd. SW6
125 H9 Fawcett Clo. SW11
124 E7 Fawcett St. SW10
124 K5 Fawe Pk. Rd. SW15
123 H15 Fawe St. E14
120 A7 Fawley Rd. NW6
126 L3 Fawnbrake Ave. SE24
122 G5 Featherstone St. EC1
126 J3 Featley Rd. SW9
124 G5 Felden St. SW6
124 C1 Felgate Ms. W6
120 F1 Felixstowe Rd. NW10
126 L7 Fellbrigg Rd. SE22
121 C9 Fellows Rd. NW3
124 J3 Felsham Rd. SW15
123 B13 Felstead St. E9
122 D5 Felton St. N1
122 J6 Fenchurch Ave. EC3
122 K6 Fenchurch St. EC3
126 B6 Fendall St. SE1
124 C5 Fenelon Pl. W14
126 F8 Fenham Rd. SE15
123 A10 Fenn St. E9
125 E16 Fentiman Rd. SW8
126 H1 Fenton Clo. SW9
126 J8 Fenwick Gro. SE15
125 J16 Fenwick Pl. SW9
126 J8 Fenwick Rd. SE15
121 C12 Ferdinand St. NW1
120 G5 Fermoy Rd. W9
123 G14 Fern St. E3
122 A8 Ferncliff Rd. E8
126 K1 Ferndale Rd. SW4
125 K16 Ferndale Rd. SW9
126 K4 Ferndene Rd. SE24
120 F5 Fernhead Rd. W9
127 L11 Fernholme Rd. SE15
124 G4 Fernhurst Rd. SW6
124 E8 Fernshaw Rd. SW10
122 A5 Ferntower Rd. N5
124 K7 Ferrier St. SW18
126 K8 Ferris Rd. SE22
127 D16 Ferry St. E14
124 J3 Festing Rd. SW15
122 J2 Fetter La. EC4
127 F14 Ffinch St. SE8
124 D4 Field Rd. W6
122 F1 Field St. WC1
122 H8 Fieldgate St. E1
120 F6 Fielding Ho. NW6
124 B3 Fielding Rd. W14
126 E4 Fielding St. SE17
122 C8 Fields Est. E8
122 A2 Fieldway Cres. N5
120 F4 Fifth Ave. W10
124 G4 Filmer Rd. SW6
124 D7 Finborough Rd. SW10
121 E9 Finchley Pl. NW8
120 A7 Finchley Rd. NW3
121 C9 Finchley Rd. NW8
126 A1 Finck St. SE1
123 J16 Findhorn St. E14
127 B12 Finland Quay SE16
127 J12 Finland Rd. SE4
127 B12 Finland St. SE16
124 G3 Finlay St. SW6
123 F9 Finnis St. E2
122 H5 Finsbury Circ. EC2
122 F2 Finsbury Est. EC1
122 G6 Finsbury Mkt. EC2
122 H5 Finsbury Pavement EC2
122 H5 Finsbury Sq. EC2
122 H5 Finsbury St. EC2
126 J4 Finsen Rd. SE5
120 J3 Finstock Rd. W10
123 L12 Fir Trees Clo. SE16
127 H9 Firbank Rd. SE15
120 G5 First Ave. W10
125 C10 First St. SW3
124 G4 Firth Gdns. SW6
122 K5 Fish St. Hill EC3
122 H1 Fisher St. WC1
127 A11 Fishermans Dr. SE16
121 G9 Fisherton St. NW8
121 G9 Fisherton St. Est. NW8
126 C1 Fitzalan St. SE11
124 C4 Fitzgeorge Ave. W14
121 J12 Fitzhardinge St. W1
124 C4 Fitzjames Ave. W14
121 A9 Fitzjohn's Ave. NW3
121 L13 Fitzmaurice Pl. W1
121 D12 Fitzroy Rd. NW1
121 G14 Fitzroy Sq. W1
121 G14 Fitzroy St. W1
125 J14 Fitzwilliam Rd. SW4
126 H2 Five Ways Rd. SW9
123 J12 Flamborough St. E14
123 B11 Flanders Way E9
126 J3 Flaxman Rd. SE5
121 F15 Flaxman Ter. WC1
121 A10 Fleet Rd. NW3
122 J2 Fleet St. EC4
126 E3 Fleming Rd. SE17
122 G6 Fleur de Lis St. E1
126 C5 Flint St. SE17
126 D6 Flinton St. SE17
126 G4 Flodden Rd. SE5
125 D10 Flood St. SW3
125 E10 Flood Wk. SW3
123 J15 Flora Clo. E14
121 K16 Floral St. WC2
127 G13 Florence Rd. SE14
122 C3 Florence St. N1
127 G13 Florence Ter. SE14
124 K4 Florian Rd. SW15
122 F8 Florida St. E2
124 H2 Floss St. SW15
124 A8 Flower Wk., The SW7
121 H14 Foley St. W1
122 H6 Folgate St. E1
123 J16 Follett St. E14
127 A16 Folly Wall E14
125 K12 Fontarabia Rd. SW11
123 D12 Ford Rd. E3
123 H9 Ford Sq. E1
123 D12 Ford St. E3
122 J8 Fordham St. E1
120 F5 Fordingley Rd. W9
122 H4 Fore St. EC2
127 C13 Foreshore SE8
122 B7 Forest Gro. E8
127 L9 Forest Hill Rd. SE22
122 B7 Forest Rd. E8
127 K9 Forester Rd. SE15
125 G12 Forfar Rd. SW11
120 G7 Formosa St. W9
121 J10 Forset St. W1
126 E3 Forsyth Gdns. SE17
126 C7 Fort Rd. SE1
122 H6 Fort St. E1
121 A13 Fortess Rd. NW5
125 K12 Forthbridge Rd. SW11
122 G4 Fortune St. EC1
124 H5 Foskett Rd. SW6
127 J14 Fossil Rd. SE13
122 J4 Foster La. EC2
121 J14 Foubert's Pl. W1
125 D9 Foulis Ter. SW7
123 L12 Foundry Clo. SE16
125 F15 Fount St. SW8
126 G2 Fountain Pl. SW9
122 H7 Fournier St. E1
120 F4 Fourth Ave. W10
125 J9 Fowler Clo. SW11
125 J10 Fownes St. SW11
123 G10 Fox Clo. E1
127 J12 Foxberry Rd. SE4
126 F2 Foxley Rd. SW9
125 G11 Foxmore St. SW11
127 J12 Foxwell St. SE4
122 A3 Framfield Rd. N5
123 C10 Frampton Pk. Est. E9
123 B10 Frampton Pk. Rd. E9
121 G9 Frampton St. NW8
127 L14 Francemary Rd. SE4
125 G12 Francis Chichester Way SW11
125 C14 Francis St. SW1
125 L15 Franconia Rd. SW4
126 L4 Frankfurt Rd. SE24
127 F14 Frankham St. SE8
127 C10 Frankland Clo. SE16
125 B9 Frankland Rd. SW7
125 D11 Franklin's Row SW3
126 A2 Frazier St. SE1
126 B8 Frean St. SE16
121 K10 Frederick Clo. W2
126 F3 Frederick Cres. SW9
122 F1 Frederick St. WC1
125 H11 Freedom St. SW11
121 A16 Freegrove Rd. N7
125 J12 Freke Rd. SW11
126 D6 Fremantle St. SE17
123 D10 Fremont St. E9
127 K12 Frendsbury Rd. SE4
126 E8 Frensham St. SE15
125 H10 Frere St. SW11
120 K3 Freston Rd. W10
120 K3 Freston Rd. W11
127 B16 Friars Mead E14
126 E8 Friary Est. SE15
126 F8 Friary Rd. SE15
122 K4 Friday St. EC4
122 F3 Friend St. EC1
127 H14 Friendly St. SE8
123 G11 Frimley Way E1
124 H7 Friston St. SW6
121 J15 Frith St. W1
120 L2 Frithville Gdns. W12
126 K7 Frogley Rd. SE22
124 L6 Frogmore SW18
120 A8 Frognal NW3
120 B8 Frognal Ct. NW3
120 A7 Frognal La. NW3
122 E4 Frome St. N1
125 H13 Froude St. SW8
124 F6 Fulham Bdy. SW6
124 H4 Fulham High St. SW6
124 E3 Fulham Palace Rd. SW6
124 D2 Fulham Palace Rd. W6
124 H5 Fulham Pk. Gdns. SW6
124 H5 Fulham Pk. Rd. SW6
125 D9 Fulham Rd. SW3
124 H4 Fulham Rd. SW6
125 D9 Fulham Rd. SW10
124 L8 Fullerton Rd. SW18
124 G7 Fulmead St. SW6
124 B1 Furber St. W6
126 F8 Furley Rd. SE15
122 B2 Furlong Rd. N7
124 H7 Furness Rd. SW6
122 J2 Furnival St. EC4
123 A10 Furrow La. E9
123 H14 Furze St. E3
126 J2 Fyfield Rd. SW9
125 C15 Fynes St. SW1

G

126 G6 Gables Clo. SE5
121 B9 Gabrielle Ct. NW3
126 A7 Gainsford St. SE1
126 H6 Gairloch Rd. SE5
121 B14 Gaisford St. NW5
127 B16 Galbraith St. E14
123 H14 Gale St. E3
124 C1 Galena Rd. W6
123 F9 Gales Gdns. E2
127 C9 Galleywall Rd. SE16
122 A3 Gallia Rd. N5
120 F4 Galton St. W10
124 L5 Galveston Rd. SW15
122 F4 Galway St. EC1
125 H13 Gambetta St. SW8
124 K3 Gamlen Rd. SW15
120 F8 Garden Rd. NW8
126 B3 Garden Row SE1
123 H11 Garden St. E1
123 E11 Gardeners Rd. E3
126 K8 Gardens, The SE22
120 A2 Gardiner Ave. NW2
125 J12 Garfield Rd. SW11
123 K14 Garford St. E14
122 K4 Garlick Hill EC4
120 B5 Garlinge Rd. NW2
123 K10 Garnet St. E1
121 A11 Garnett Rd. NW3
124 L7 Garratt La. SW18
124 K8 Garrick Clo. SW18
121 K16 Garrick St. WC2
127 J13 Garsington Ms. SE4
124 J8 Gartons Way SW11
120 J7 Garway Rd. W2
122 F7 Gascoigne Pl. E2
120 C6 Gascony Ave. NW6
123 C11 Gascoyne Rd. E9
123 K16 Gaselee St. E14
125 H16 Gaskell St. SW4
122 D3 Gaskin St. N1
124 E3 Gastein Rd. W6
127 B9 Gataker St. SE16
125 A10 Gate Ms. SW7
121 G10 Gateforth St. NW8
126 J1 Gateley Rd. SW9
126 E4 Gateway SE17
125 D13 Gatliff Rd. SW1
125 J15 Gauden Clo. SW4
125 H15 Gauden Rd. SW4
126 B4 Gaunt St. SE1
127 H10 Gautrey Rd. SE15
127 C14 Gaverick St. E14
123 F10 Gawber St. E2
120 A1 Gay Clo. NW2
120 H7 Gaydon Ho. W2
125 B16 Gayfere St. SW1
122 C8 Gayhurst Rd. E8
122 A1 Geary St. N7
126 B7 Gedling Pl. SE1
122 G4 Gee St. EC1
122 E7 Geffrye St. E2
127 F9 Geldart Rd. SE15
127 H10 Gellatly Rd. SE14
123 J9 Gelston Pt. E1
126 K2 Geneva Dr. SW9
124 L2 Genoa Ave. SW15
126 H4 Geoffrey Clo. SE5
127 J13 Geoffrey Rd. SE4
127 C13 George Beard Rd. SE8
126 A8 George Row SE16
121 J11 George St. W1
121 K12 George Yd. W1
122 A1 Georges Rd. N7
121 D14 Georgiana St. NW1
125 C12 Gerald Rd. SW1
124 L8 Geraldine Rd. SW18
126 B3 Geraldine St. SE11
127 D10 Gerards Clo. SE16
123 E12 Gernon Rd. E3
122 E3 Gerrard Rd. N1
121 K15 Gerrard St. W1
126 B2 Gerridge St. SE1
124 E8 Gertrude St. SW10
127 F9 Gervase St. SE15
122 B7 Ghent Way E8
123 C16 Gibbins Rd. E15
127 H10 Gibbon Rd. SE15
124 D5 Gibbs Grn. W14
122 F7 Gibraltar Wk. E2
126 C1 Gibson Rd. SE11
122 D2 Gibson Sq. N1
125 J12 Gideon Rd. SW11
127 F14 Giffin St. SE8
121 C16 Gifford St. N1
126 C2 Gilbert Rd. SE11
121 J12 Gilbert St. W1
121 A12 Gilden Cres. NW5
123 K13 Gill St. E14
123 G16 Gillender St. E3
123 G16 Gillender St. E14
122 A6 Gillett St. N16
121 E14 Gillfoot NW1
127 L15 Gillian St. SE13
121 A12 Gillies St. NW5
121 B10 Gilling Ct. NW3
125 C14 Gillingham St. SW1
124 H7 Gilstead Rd. SW6
124 D8 Gilston Rd. SW10
122 J3 Giltspur St. EC1
123 J15 Giraud St. E14
124 C3 Girdlers Rd. W14
124 F5 Gironde Rd. SW6
126 B3 Gladstone St. SE1
125 G13 Gladstone Ter. SW8
124 J3 Gladwyn Rd. SW15
120 C6 Gladys Rd. NW6
123 K10 Glamis Pl. E1
123 K10 Glamis Rd. E1
125 L16 Glanville Rd. SW2
120 E7 Glasgow Ho. W9
125 D14 Glasgow Ter. SW1
126 A3 Glasshill St. SE1
123 K11 Glasshouse Flds. E1
121 K14 Glasshouse St. W1
125 D16 Glasshouse Wk. SE11
120 A5 Glastonbury St. NW6
123 H15 Glaucus St. E3
124 C4 Glazbury Rd. W14
125 F9 Glebe Pl. SW3
124 C8 Gledhow Gdns. SW5
124 D4 Gledstanes Rd. W14
124 K3 Glegg Pl. SW15
123 A10 Glenarm Rd. E5
120 A6 Glenbrook Rd. NW6
126 K1 Glendall St. SW9
124 J3 Glendarvon St. SW15
125 C9 Glendower Pl. SW7
125 L16 Glenelg Rd. SW2
126 F3 Glenfinlas Way SE5
127 B16 Glengall Gro. E14
120 D5 Glengall Rd. NW6
126 D7 Glengall Rd. SE15
126 E7 Glengall Ter. SE15
127 C16 Glengarnock Ave. E14
126 L6 Glengarry Rd. SE22
121 B10 Glenilla Rd. NW3
121 B10 Glenloch Rd. NW3
121 B10 Glenmore Rd. NW3
124 H8 Glenrosa St. SW6
120 J2 Glenroy St. W12
127 J13 Glensdale Rd. SE4
124 C1 Glenthorne Rd. W6
121 G11 Glentworth St. NW1
127 F13 Glenville Gro. SE8
124 C4 Gliddon Rd. W14
123 L12 Globe Pond Rd. SE16
123 G11 Globe Rd. E1
123 F10 Globe Rd. E2
126 A5 Globe St. SE1
121 C12 Gloucester Ave. NW1
127 F16 Gloucester Circ. SE10
121 D13 Gloucester Cres. NW1
121 E13 Gloucester Gate NW1

Gloucester Gro.

126 E6 Gloucester Gro. Est. SE15
120 E6 Gloucester Ho. NW6
120 J8 Gloucester Ms. W2
121 G11 Gloucester Pl. NW1
121 H11 Gloucester Pl. W1
124 B8 Gloucester Rd. SW7
121 J9 Gloucester Sq. W2
125 D14 Gloucester St. SW1
120 J7 Gloucester Ter. W2
124 A6 Gloucester Wk. W8
122 F2 Gloucester Way EC1
125 J11 Glycena Rd. SW11
123 H15 Godalming Rd. E14
125 D10 Godfrey St. SW3
125 D16 Goding St. SE11
122 J4 Godliman St. EC4
127 H9 Godman Rd. SE15
120 L1 Godolphin Rd. W12
120 H4 Golborne Rd. W10
122 G4 Golden La. EC1
121 K14 Golden Sq. W1
120 C7 Goldhurst Ter. NW6
122 J8 Golding St. E1
121 E15 Goldington Cres. NW1
121 E15 Goldington Cres. Gdns. NW1
121 E15 Goldington St. NW1
122 G8 Goldman Clo. E2
120 G6 Goldney Rd. W9
125 G15 Goldsborough Rd. SW8
126 G8 Goldsmith Rd. SE15
122 E8 Goldsmith's Row E2
122 E8 Goldsmith's Sq. E2
127 C10 Goldsworthy Gdns. SE16
127 G10 Goldwin Clo. SE14
127 B10 Gomm Rd. SE16
120 A5 Gondar Gdns. NW6
127 E14 Gonson Pl. SE8
127 E15 Gonson St. SE8
121 H14 Goodge St. W1
123 K12 Goodhart Pl. E14
121 B16 Goodinge Clo. N7
122 J8 Goodman's Stile E1
122 K7 Goodmans Yd. E1
121 E16 Goods Way NW1
127 F12 Goodwood Rd. SE14
122 D5 Gopsall St. N1
120 J1 Gordon Ct. W12
126 H3 Gordon Gro. SE5
124 A6 Gordon Pl. W8
127 H9 Gordon Rd. SE15
121 G15 Gordon Sq. WC1
121 G15 Gordon St. WC1
127 L14 Gordonbrock Rd. SE4
123 D10 Gore Rd. E9
124 B8 Gore St. SW7
120 E6 Gorefield Pl. NW6
122 J6 Goring St. EC3
124 C4 Gorleston St. W14
122 F7 Gorsuch St. E2
121 H14 Gosfield St. W1
126 G2 Gosling Way SW9
121 A11 Gospel Oak Est. NW5
122 F7 Gosset St. E2
127 E12 Gosterwood St. SE8
122 E3 Goswell Rd. EC1
122 G1 Gough St. WC1
122 J7 Goulston St. E1
124 G4 Gowan Ave. SW6
120 B1 Gowan Rd. NW10
121 H15 Gower Ms. WC1
121 G14 Gower Pl. WC1
121 G14 Gower St. WC1
122 J8 Gower's Wk. E1
126 J8 Gowlett Rd. SE15
125 J12 Gowrie Rd. SW11
123 F15 Grace St. E3
122 K5 Gracechurch St. EC3
126 H5 Graces Ms. SE5
126 H6 Graces Rd. SE5
121 B13 Grafton Cres. NW1
121 F15 Grafton Pl. NW1
121 A12 Grafton Rd. NW5
125 J14 Grafton Sq. SW4
121 K13 Grafton St. W1
121 A11 Grafton Ter. NW5
121 G14 Grafton Way W1
121 G14 Grafton Way WC1
122 B8 Graham Rd. E8
122 E3 Graham St. N1
125 C12 Graham Ter. SW1
124 L1 Granard Ave. SW15
121 D15 Granary St. NW1
122 G7 Granby St. E2
121 E14 Granby Ter. NW1
122 D8 Grand Union Cres. E8
125 L11 Grandison Rd. SW11
125 G9 Granfield St. SW11
126 B7 Grange, The SE1
122 C7 Grange Ct. E8
122 B4 Grange Gro. N1
120 C6 Grange Pl. NW6
126 B8 Grange Pl. SE16
120 B1 Grange Rd. NW10
126 B6 Grange Rd. SE1
126 B6 Grange Wk. SE1
126 B7 Grange Yd. SE1
123 C9 Gransden Ave. E8
125 K9 Grant Rd. SW11
122 E3 Grantbridge St. N1
125 J16 Grantham Rd. SW9
123 F11 Grantley St. E1
120 F7 Grantully Rd. W9
122 D5 Granville Ct. N1
127 J16 Granville Gro. SE13
127 J16 Granville Pk. SE13
121 J12 Granville Pl. W1
120 E6 Granville Rd. NW6
122 F1 Granville Sq. WC1
122 F1 Granville St. WC1
124 B4 Gratton Rd. W14
121 F16 Gray's Inn Rd. WC1
125 H12 Grayshott Rd. SW11
121 J13 Great Castle St. W1
121 H11 Great Cen. St. NW1
121 J15 Great Chapel St. W1
124 D3 Great Ch. La. W6
125 B16 Great College St. SW1
121 J11 Great Cumberland Pl. W1
126 A5 Great Dover St. SE1
122 F6 Great Eastern St. EC2
125 A15 Great George St. SW1
122 L4 Great Guildford St. SE1
122 H1 Great James St. WC1
121 J14 Great Marlborough St. W1
122 L5 Great Maze Pond SE1
121 H16 Great Ormond St. WC1
122 F1 Great Percy St. WC1
125 B15 Great Peter St. SW1
121 G13 Great Portland St. W1
121 K14 Great Pulteney St. W1
121 J16 Great Queen St. WC2
121 J15 Great Russell St. WC1
121 L16 Great Scotland Yd. SW1
125 B15 Great Smith St. SW1
126 L6 Great Spilmans SE22
122 L3 Great Suffolk St. SE1
122 G3 Great Sutton St. EC1
121 H14 Great Titchfield St. W1
122 K6 Great Twr. St. EC3
120 H5 Great Western Rd. W9
120 H5 Great Western Rd. W11
122 J5 Great Winchester St. EC2
121 K15 Great Windmill St. W1
127 K14 Greatfield Clo. SE4
122 H8 Greatorex St. E1
121 J15 Greek St. W1
123 L9 Green Bank E1
126 L6 Green Dale SE22
126 E8 Green Hundred Rd. SE15
121 K11 Green St. W1
121 E10 Greenberry St. NW8
125 C14 Greencoat Pl. SW1
120 C7 Greencroft Gdns. NW6
122 H8 Greenfield Rd. E1
126 A2 Greenham Clo. SE1
127 C11 Greenland Quay SE16
121 D13 Greenland Rd. NW1
122 C4 Greenman St. N1
121 G13 Greenwell St. W1
127 E16 Greenwich Ch. St. SE10
127 G15 Greenwich High Rd. SE10
127 E16 Greenwich Mkt. SE10
127 G15 Greenwich S. St. SE10
127 B15 Greenwich Vw. Pl. E14
122 B8 Greenwood Rd. E8
122 L2 Greet St. SE1
124 A7 Gregory Pl. W8
123 K13 Grenade St. E14
121 G10 Grendon St. NW8
120 K3 Grenfell Rd. W11
120 K3 Grenfell Twr. W11
124 C8 Grenville Ms. SW7
124 C8 Grenville Pl. SW7
121 G16 Grenville St. WC1
126 J3 Gresham Rd. SW9
122 J4 Gresham St. EC2
121 H15 Gresse St. W1
126 G3 Greswell St. SW6
120 E7 Greville Hall NW6
120 E7 Greville Pl. NW6
120 E7 Greville Rd. NW6
122 H2 Greville St. EC1
122 H7 Grey Eagle St. E1
125 B15 Greycoat Pl. SW1
125 B15 Greycoat St. SW1
120 F1 Greyhound Rd. NW10
124 E3 Greyhound Rd. W6
124 E4 Greyhound Rd. W14
120 A1 Griffin Clo. NW10
124 H5 Grimston Rd. SW6
127 E14 Grinling Pl. SE8
127 D12 Grinstead Rd. SE8
120 G6 Grittleton Rd. W9
125 B12 Groom Pl. SW1
123 C11 Groombridge Rd. E9
122 A4 Grosvenor Ave. N5
125 A12 Grosvenor Cres. SW1
125 A12 Grosvenor Cres. Ms. SW1
125 C15 Grosvenor Est. SW1
120 A2 Grosvenor Gdns. NW2
125 B13 Grosvenor Gdns. SW1
121 K13 Grosvenor Hill W1
126 F4 Grosvenor Pk. SE5
125 A12 Grosvenor Pl. SW1
125 E13 Grosvenor Rd. SW1
121 K12 Grosvenor Sq. W1
121 K13 Grosvenor St. W1
126 E4 Grosvenor Ter. SE5
126 H6 Grove Cres. SE5
121 E9 Grove End Rd. NW8
126 J6 Grove Hill Rd. SE5
126 H6 Grove La. SE5
124 B2 Grove Ms. W6
126 H6 Grove Pk. SE5
123 D11 Grove Rd. E3
120 B2 Grove Rd. NW2
127 C13 Grove St. SE8
126 K6 Grove Vale SE22
123 K15 Grove Vill. E14
126 H6 Grovelands Clo. SE5
126 G1 Groveway SW9
126 G7 Grummant Rd. SE15
123 J15 Grundy St. E14
126 L3 Gubyon Ave. SE24
127 G15 Guildford Gro. SE10
125 G16 Guildford Rd. SW8
125 C14 Guildhouse St. SW1
122 G1 Guilford Pl. WC1
121 G16 Guilford St. WC1
126 C6 Guinness Bldgs. SE1
123 C12 Guinness Clo. E9
126 D3 Guinness Trust Bldgs. SE11
126 K3 Guinness Trust Est. SW9
124 H5 Guion Rd. SW6
127 B13 Gulliver St. SE16
122 H7 Gun St. E1
123 D12 Gunmakers La. E3
122 J2 Gunpowder Sq. EC4
124 E8 Gunter Gro. SW10
124 C4 Gunterstone Rd. W14
122 H7 Gunthorpe St. E1
123 L11 Gunwhale Clo. SE16
122 J4 Gutter La. EC2
126 A5 Guy St. SE1
127 L16 Guyscliff Rd. SE13
124 K3 Gwendolen Ave. SW15
124 L3 Gwendolen Clo. SW15
124 D4 Gwendwr Rd. W14
124 F8 Gwyn Clo. SW6
125 H9 Gwynne Rd. SW11
126 K5 Gylcote Clo. SE5

H

124 B3 Haarlem Rd. W14
122 F5 Haberdasher St. N1
126 G1 Hackford Rd. SW9
122 F7 Hackney Rd. E2
127 E16 Haddo St. SE10
127 C11 Haddonfield SE8
123 F10 Hadleigh St. E2
121 B13 Hadley St. NW1
125 K11 Hafer Rd. SW11
122 C7 Haggerston Rd. E8
127 K11 Hainford Clo. SE4
122 D6 Halcomb St. N1
122 H8 Halcrow St. E1
124 F5 Haldane Rd. SW6
124 L5 Haldon Rd. SW18
123 K15 Hale St. E14
127 F14 Hales St. SE8
127 J15 Halesworth Rd. SE13
122 E1 Half Moon Cres. N1
121 L13 Half Moon St. W1
124 E6 Halford Rd. SW6
125 B12 Halkin Pl. SW1
125 A12 Halkin St. SW1
121 G9 Hall Pl. W2
120 F8 Hall Rd. NW8
122 F3 Hall St. EC1
121 H13 Hallam St. W1
123 H12 Halley St. E14
122 C4 Halliford St. N1
125 C11 Halsey St. SW3
126 G3 Halsmere Rd. SE5
120 F3 Halstow Rd. NW10
122 C3 Halton Rd. N1
125 L14 Hambalt Rd. SW4
124 J7 Hamble St. SW6
121 F9 Hamilton Clo. NW8
121 F8 Hamilton Gdns. NW8
121 L12 Hamilton Pl. W1
120 E7 Hamilton Ter. NW8
126 J5 Hamlet, The SE5
123 G13 Hamlets Way E3
124 D1 Hammersmith Bri. SW13
124 D2 Hammersmith Bri. Rd. W6
124 C2 Hammersmith Bdy. W6
124 D2 Hammersmith Flyover W6
124 A2 Hammersmith Gro. W6
124 C3 Hammersmith Rd. W6
124 C3 Hammersmith Rd. W14
121 B14 Hammond St. NW5
126 G1 Hampson Way SW8
121 A10 Hampstead Grn. NW3
121 E14 Hampstead Rd. NW1
120 F6 Hampton Clo. NW6
126 C4 Hampton St. SE1
126 C3 Hampton St. SE17
122 H7 Hanbury St. E1
123 F16 Hancock Rd. E3
121 G16 Handel St. WC1
126 F2 Handforth Rd. SW9
123 D10 Handley Rd. E9
126 A5 Hankey Pl. SE1
124 F4 Hannell Rd. SW6
123 H10 Hannibal Rd. E1
125 J13 Hannington Rd. SW4
126 E2 Hanover Gdns. SE11
121 F10 Hanover Gate NW1
126 G8 Hanover Pk. SE15
120 C2 Hanover Rd. NW10
121 J13 Hanover Sq. W1
121 J13 Hanover St. W1
121 F10 Hanover Ter. NW1
125 B11 Hans Cres. SW1
125 B11 Hans Pl. SW1
125 B11 Hans Rd. SW3
126 L7 Hansler Rd. SE22
121 H14 Hanson St. W1
121 J15 Hanway St. W1
120 C8 Harben Rd. NW6
121 H9 Harbet Rd. W2
127 C15 Harbinger Rd. E14
124 G6 Harbledown Rd. SW6
124 G3 Harbord St. SW6
124 G8 Harbour Ave. SW10
127 A15 Harbour Ex. Sq. E14
126 J4 Harbour Rd. SE5
125 K9 Harbut Rd. SW11
127 K12 Harcourt Rd. SE4
121 H10 Harcourt St. W1
124 D7 Harcourt Ter. SW10
127 H9 Harders Rd. SE15
120 D1 Hardinge Rd. NW10
123 J10 Hardinge St. E1
122 F2 Hardwick St. EC1
123 E9 Hare Row E2
122 E6 Hare Wk. N1
122 B4 Harecourt Rd. N1
126 K4 Haredale Rd. SE24
127 J13 Harefield Ms. SE4
127 J13 Harefield Rd. SE4
121 G10 Harewood Ave. NW1
126 J6 Harfield Gdns. SE5
123 G12 Harford St. E1
126 J1 Hargwyne St. SW9
127 K11 Harlescott Rd. SE15
124 D8 Harley Gdns. SW10
123 F13 Harley Gro. E3
121 H13 Harley Pl. W1
121 C9 Harley Rd. NW3
121 H13 Harley St. W1
126 E1 Harleyford Rd. SE11
126 E2 Harleyford St. SE11
121 B13 Harmood St. NW1
126 D3 Harmsworth St. SE17
126 B6 Harold Est. SE1
126 B4 Harper Rd. SE1
123 F10 Harpley Sq. E1
125 G12 Harpsden St. SW11
122 H1 Harpur St. WC1
122 D8 Harriet Clo. E8
125 A11 Harriet Wk. SW1
124 C8 Harrington Gdns. SW7
125 C9 Harrington Rd. SW7
121 E14 Harrington Sq. NW1
121 F14 Harrington St. NW1
126 F5 Harris St. SE5
121 F16 Harrison St. WC1
123 K16 Harrow La. E14
122 J6 Harrow Pl. E1
120 F1 Harrow Rd. NW10
120 H6 Harrow Rd. W2
120 G5 Harrow Rd. W9
120 G4 Harrow Rd. W10
125 H9 Harroway Rd. SW11
121 J10 Harrowby St. W1
123 B12 Harrowgate Rd. E9
123 E14 Hartfield Ter. E3
121 A16 Hartham Clo. N7
121 A16 Hartham Rd. N7
125 G16 Hartington Rd. SW8
124 F5 Hartismere Rd. SW6
123 B11 Hartlake Rd. E9
121 C13 Hartland Rd. NW1
120 E5 Hartland Rd. NW6
123 F10 Hartley St. E2
127 G14 Harton St. SE8
127 F12 Harts La. SE14
127 L16 Harvard Rd. SE13
126 G5 Harvey Rd. SE5
122 D5 Harvey St. N1
120 E3 Harvist Rd. NW6
122 H6 Harwich La. EC2
124 F6 Harwood Rd. SW6
124 G7 Harwood Ter. SW6
126 H5 Hascombe Ter. SE5
125 K15 Haselrigge Rd. SW4
125 C10 Hasker St. SW3
122 C2 Haslam Clo. N1
123 B11 Hassett Rd. E9
126 F8 Hastings Clo. SE15
121 F16 Hastings St. WC1
127 G11 Hatcham Pk. Rd. SE14
127 E10 Hatcham Rd. SE15
127 F11 Hatfield Clo. SE14
122 L2 Hatfields SE1
120 J7 Hatherley Gro. W2
127 H9 Hathorne Clo. SE15
122 H2 Hatton Gdn. EC1
122 H2 Hatton Pl. EC1
122 H2 Hatton Wall EC1
127 A14 Havannah St. E14
121 D16 Havelock St. N1
125 F13 Havelock Ter. SW8
123 F12 Haverfield Rd. E3
121 B11 Haverstock Hill NW3
121 A12 Haverstock Rd. NW5
122 E3 Haverstock St. N1
126 F6 Havil St. SE5
122 C3 Hawes St. N1
123 H14 Hawgood St. E3
124 L1 Hawkesbury Rd. SW15
127 L11 Hawkslade Rd. SE15
124 E3 Hawksmoor St. W6
127 C10 Hawkstone Rd. SE16
121 C13 Hawley Cres. NW1
121 C13 Hawley Rd. NW1
121 C13 Hawley St. NW1
122 B6 Hawthorne Clo. N1
121 C10 Hawtrey Rd. NW3
123 J15 Hay Currie St. E14
121 K13 Hay Hill W1
122 D8 Hay St. E2
125 L16 Haycroft Rd. SW2
126 C3 Hayles St. SE11
121 K15 Haymarket SW1
126 E8 Haymerle Rd. SE15
121 L13 Hay's Ms. W1
125 L16 Hayter Rd. SW2
120 F1 Hazel Rd. NW10
127 L12 Hazeldon Rd. SE4
120 D5 Hazelmere Rd. NW6
120 G4 Hazelwood Cres. W10
124 H7 Hazlebury Rd. SW6
124 L1 Hazlewell Rd. SW15
124 B4 Hazlitt Rd. W14
123 J11 Head St. E1
125 A12 Headfort Pl. SW1
123 G9 Headlam St. E1
127 G13 Heald St. SE14
121 B13 Healey St. NW1
122 G6 Hearn St. EC2
125 H13 Heath Rd. SW8
122 G1 Heathcote St. WC1
125 J13 Heather Clo. SW8
120 B2 Heathfield Pk. NW2
124 G5 Heathmans Rd. SW6
125 J11 Heathwall St. SW11
126 J8 Heaton Rd. SE15
120 A3 Heber Rd. NW2
124 B1 Hebron Rd. W6
122 A1 Heddington Gro. N7
121 K14 Heddon St. W1
123 B12 Hedgers Gro. E9
126 E3 Heiron St. SE17
120 A1 Helena Rd. NW10
122 G4 Helmet Row EC1
123 C9 Helmsley Pl. E8
125 F15 Hemans St. SW8
125 J16 Hemberton Rd. SW9
122 D1 Hemingford Rd. N1
122 G8 Hemming St. E1
120 C6 Hemstal Rd. NW6
122 E6 Hemsworth St. N1
122 H7 Heneage St. E1
126 C7 Henley Dr. SE1
120 D2 Henley Rd. NW10
125 H12 Henley St. SW11
125 G10 Henning St. SW11
121 J13 Henrietta Pl. W1
123 A16 Henrietta St. E15
121 K16 Henrietta St. WC2
122 J8 Henriques St. E1
120 K3 Henry Dickens Ct. W11
124 J3 Henry Jackson Rd. SW15
127 L14 Henryson Rd. SE4
122 B5 Henshall St. N1
126 C5 Henshaw St. SE17
126 L8 Henslowe Rd. SE22
120 A2 Henson Ave. NW2
121 E10 Henstridge Pl. NW8
125 F10 Henty Clo. SW11
124 L1 Henty Wk. SW15
123 B14 Hepscott Rd. E9
122 G2 Herbal Hill EC1
120 D1 Herbert Gdns. NW10
121 B12 Herbert St. NW5
121 G16 Herbrand St. WC1
126 B1 Hercules Rd. SE1
120 E6 Hereford Ho. NW6
127 F13 Hereford Pl. SE14
120 J6 Hereford Rd. W2
124 C8 Hereford Sq. SW7
122 G8 Hereford St. E2
122 F3 Hermit St. EC1
122 L8 Hermitage Wall E1
124 L8 Herndon Rd. SW18
126 L4 Herne Hill SE24
126 J4 Herne Hill Rd. SE24
126 L3 Herne Pl. SE24
123 L12 Heron Pl. SE16
123 L14 Heron Quay E14
126 K4 Heron Rd. SE24
125 C15 Herrick St. SW1
120 E4 Herries St. W10
122 D6 Hertford Rd. N1
121 L12 Hertford St. W1
123 K14 Hertsmere Rd. E14
120 K4 Hesketh Pl. W11
124 D7 Hesper Ms. SW5
127 C15 Hesperus Cres. E14
123 J9 Hessel St. E1
125 F10 Hester Rd. SW11
124 H4 Hestercombe Ave. SW6
127 G14 Heston St. SE14
125 K16 Hetherington Rd. SW4
120 L1 Hetley Rd. W12
120 H3 Hewer St. W10
123 E12 Hewlett Rd. E3
125 F16 Heyford Ave. SW8
126 C4 Heygate St. SE17
124 J8 Hibbert St. SW11
127 L10 Hichisson Rd. SE15
125 J14 Hickmore Wk. SW4
125 J10 Hicks Clo. SW11
127 D12 Hicks St. SE8
125 C15 Hide Pl. SW1
121 J16 High Holborn WC1
123 E16 High St. E15
124 J4 High St. SW6
122 K4 High Timber St. EC4
122 B3 Highbury Cor. N5
122 A3 Highbury Cres. N5
122 A4 Highbury Est. N5
122 B3 Highbury Gro. N5
122 A4 Highbury New Pk. N5
122 B3 Highbury Pl. N5
122 B2 Highbury Sta. Rd. N1
122 A3 Highbury Ter. N5
122 A3 Highbury Ter. Ms. N5
120 H2 Highlever Rd. W10
126 H7 Highshore Rd. SE15
122 K8 Highway, The E1
123 K11 Highway, The E14
124 F7 Hilary Clo. SW6
126 H2 Hilda Ter. SW9
124 E6 Hildyard Rd. SW6
120 F2 Hiley Rd. NW10
120 C8 Hilgrove Rd. NW6
120 H2 Hill Fm. Rd. W10
120 E8 Hill Rd. NW8
121 K12 Hill St. W1
127 F10 Hillbeck Clo. SE15
121 A15 Hilldrop Cres. N7
121 A15 Hilldrop Est. N7
121 A15 Hilldrop La. N7
121 A15 Hilldrop Rd. N7
121 A10 Hillfield Ct. NW3
120 A5 Hillfield Rd. NW6
120 L6 Hillgate Pl. W8
120 L6 Hillgate St. W8
126 E3 Hillingdon St. SE5
126 E3 Hillingdon St. SE17
123 B9 Hillman St. E8
121 A16 Hillmarton Rd. N7
126 K3 Hillmead Dr. SW9
126 L6 Hillsborough Rd. SE22
120 E7 Hillside Clo. NW8
120 L5 Hillsleigh Rd. W8
120 C6 Hilltop Rd. NW6
127 J14 Hilly Flds. Cres. SE4
126 G2 Hillyard St. SW9
126 K8 Hinckley Rd. SE15
123 J14 Hind Gro. E14
121 J12 Hinde St. W1
126 L8 Hindmans Rd. SE22
123 A9 Hindrey Rd. E5
126 J3 Hinton Rd. SE24
120 K4 Hippodrome Pl. W11
123 E12 Hitchin Sq. E3
127 L16 Hither Grn. La. SE13
125 B13 Hobart Pl. SW1
124 L1 Hobbes Wk. SW15
123 H15 Hobday St. E14
124 E8 Hobury St. SW10
124 B3 Hofland Rd. W14
124 C7 Hogarth Rd. SW5
126 F8 Holbeck Row SE15
125 D12 Holbein Ms. SW1
125 C12 Holbein Pl. SW1
120 F1 Holberton Gdns. NW10
122 H2 Holborn EC1
122 H2 Holborn Viaduct EC1
124 D1 Holcombe St. W6
123 C10 Holcroft Rd. E9
125 H12 Holden St. SW11
127 L12 Holdenby Rd. SE4
122 F2 Holford St. WC1
125 J9 Holgate Ave. SW11
124 B4 Holland Gdns. W14
126 F2 Holland Gro. SW9
120 L4 Holland Pk. W11
120 L4 Holland Pk. Ave. W11
124 A4 Holland Pk. Gdns. W14
120 L5 Holland Pk. Ms. W11
124 B5 Holland Pk. Rd. W14
124 A3 Holland Rd. W14
122 L3 Holland St. SE1
124 A6 Holland St. W8
124 A4 Holland Vill. Rd. W14
124 A5 Holland Wk. W8
121 J15 Hollen St. W1
121 J13 Holles St. W1
126 L4 Hollingbourne Rd. SE24
126 H7 Holly Gro. SE15
122 B7 Holly St. E8
122 C7 Holly St. Est. E8
123 F9 Hollybush Gdns. E2
126 K3 Hollybush Wk. SW9
127 G10 Hollydale Rd. SE15
127 G9 Hollydene SE15
127 G16 Hollymount Clo. SE10
124 E8 Hollywood Rd. SW10
125 H9 Holman Rd. SW11
122 A4 Holmcote Gdns. N5
120 A6 Holmdale Rd. NW6
126 L4 Holmdene Ave. SE24
124 F7 Holmead Rd. SW6
121 B10 Holmefield Ct. NW3
121 B13 Holmes Rd. NW5
126 A2 Holmes Ter. SE1
124 K2 Holroyd Rd. SW15
123 G11 Holton St. E1
125 K15 Holwood Pl. SW4
123 F14 Holyhead Clo. E3
126 C3 Holyoak Rd. SE11
124 F2 Holyport Rd. SW6
122 G6 Holywell La. EC2
122 G6 Holywell Row EC2
125 H10 Home Rd. SW11
127 L11 Homeleigh Rd. SE15
127 C14 Homer Dr. E14
123 B12 Homer Rd. E9
121 H10 Homer Row W1
121 H10 Homer St. W1
123 A11 Homerton Gro. E9
123 A10 Homerton High St. E9
123 A12 Homerton Rd. E9
123 A10 Homerton Row E9
127 L10 Homestall Rd. SE22
124 F5 Homestead Rd. SW6
120 A7 Honeybourne Rd. NW6
120 C3 Honeyman Clo. NW6
120 E5 Honiton Rd. NW6
122 K8 Hooper St. E1
125 J9 Hope St. SW11
120 E4 Hopefield Ave. NW6
126 F5 Hopewell St. SE5
126 F5 Hopewell Yd. SE5
122 L3 Hopton St. SE1
126 E5 Hopwood Rd. SE17
122 E8 Horatio St. E2
120 K6 Horbury Cres. W11
124 G4 Horder Rd. SW6
120 G5 Hormead Rd. W9
121 C9 Hornby Clo. NW3
124 H2 Horne Way SW15
122 A1 Hornsey St. N7
127 E10 Hornshay St. SE15
124 A6 Hornton St. W8
121 L16 Horse Guards Ave. SW1
121 L15 Horse Guards Rd. SW1
127 E16 Horseferry Pl. SE10
123 K11 Horseferry Rd. E14
125 C15 Horseferry Rd. SW1
122 A2 Horsell Rd. N5
126 A7 Horselydown La. SE1
126 L1 Horsford Rd. SW2
126 E5 Horsley St. SE17
127 L13 Horsmonden Rd. SE4
124 F8 Hortensia Rd. SW10
123 B9 Horton Rd. E8
127 J15 Horton St. SE13
122 H3 Hosier La. EC1
124 J2 Hotham Rd. SW15
126 D2 Hotspur St. SE11
122 J6 Houndsditch EC3
120 A4 Hoveden Rd. NW2
124 L1 Howards La. SW15
127 J10 Howbury Rd. SE15
126 J8 Howden St. SE15
125 B14 Howick Pl. SW1
125 F10 Howie St. SW11
121 B10 Howitt Rd. NW3
121 H14 Howland St. W1
127 A12 Howland Way SE16

Loftie St.

120 H8 Howley Pl. W2
122 E7 Hows St. E2
127 K12 Howson Rd. SE4
122 F6 Hoxton Sq. N1
122 D6 Hoxton St. N1
125 J16 Hubert Gro. SW9
123 H13 Huddart St. E3
120 B1 Huddlestone Rd. NW2
125 C13 Hugh St. SW1
124 J7 Hugon Rd. SW6
124 L8 Huguenot Pl. SW18
127 A11 Hull Clo. SE16
124 E4 Humbolt Rd. W6
126 D7 Humphrey St. SE1
122 L1 Hungerford Bri. SE1
122 L1 Hungerford Bri. WC2
121 B15 Hungerford Rd. N7
127 F11 Hunsdon Rd. SE14
120 L3 Hunt St. W11
121 G16 Hunter St. WC1
122 C1 Huntingdon St. N1
121 G14 Huntley St. WC1
122 H8 Hunton St. E1
123 E16 Hunts La. E15
126 C6 Huntsman St. SE17
124 J5 Hurlingham Ct. SW6
124 J5 Hurlingham Gdns. SW6
124 H5 Hurlingham Rd. SW6
121 C10 Huson Clo. NW3
127 A14 Hutchings St. E14
127 L13 Huxbear St. SE4
120 F4 Huxley St. W10
121 L10 Hyde Pk. W2
125 A12 Hyde Pk. Cor. W1
121 J10 Hyde Pk. Cres. W2
121 K9 Hyde Pk. Gdns. W2
124 A8 Hyde Pk. Gate SW7
121 J10 Hyde Pk. Sq. W2
121 J10 Hyde Pk. St. W2
122 D6 Hyde Rd. N1
127 E9 Hyndman St. SE15

I

123 D14 Iceland Rd. E3
123 J16 Ida St. E14
127 F14 Idonia St. SE8
124 B1 Iffley Rd. W6
124 E7 Ifield Rd. SW10
120 F3 Ilbert St. W10
120 K7 Ilchester Gdns. W2
124 B5 Ilchester Pl. W14
127 F10 Ilderton Rd. SE15
127 D9 Ilderton Rd. SE16
126 D3 Iliffe St. SE17
125 K10 Ilminster Gdns. SW11
122 D5 Imber St. N1
125 B9 Imperial College Rd. SW7
124 G7 Imperial Rd. SW6
124 G7 Imperial Sq. SW6
123 F16 Imperial St. E3
127 A14 Indescon Ct. E14
120 K1 India Way W12
125 G13 Ingate Pl. SW8
125 H13 Ingelow Rd. SW8
120 L1 Ingersoll Rd. W12
126 H2 Ingleborough St. SW9
124 G3 Inglethorpe St. SW6
126 H2 Ingleton St. SW9
127 C14 Inglewood Clo. E14
120 A6 Inglewood Rd. NW6
126 G3 Inglis St. SE5
125 J9 Ingrave St. SW11
121 B13 Inkerman Rd. NW5
121 F12 Inner Circle NW1
120 K7 Inverness Pl. W2
121 D13 Inverness St. NW1
120 J7 Inverness Ter. W2
127 K11 Inverton Rd. SE15
126 D5 Inville Rd. SE17
125 H10 Inworth St. SW11
124 G6 Irene Rd. SW6
122 F4 Ironmonger Row EC1
126 H1 Irving Gro. SW9
124 B3 Irving Rd. W14
121 K15 Irving St. WC2
120 D1 Irwin Gdns. NW10
126 G1 Isabel St. SW9
123 A10 Isabella Rd. E9
122 L3 Isabella St. SE1
127 B16 Isambard Ms. E14
124 K2 Isis Clo. SW15
122 D3 Islington Grn. N1
122 E3 Islington High St. N1
122 C2 Islington Pk. St. N1
121 A14 Islip St. NW5
126 J7 Ivanhoe Rd. SE5
124 D5 Ivatt Pl. W14
123 D11 Iveagh Clo. E9
125 H14 Iveley Rd. SW4
124 B6 Iverna Ct. W8
124 B6 Iverna Gdns. W8
120 B5 Iverson Rd. NW6
125 C10 Ives St. SW3
122 F8 Ivimey St. E2
121 G11 Ivor Pl. NW1
121 C14 Ivor St. NW1
127 K13 Ivy Rd. SE4
122 E6 Ivy St. N1
127 J11 Ivydale Rd. SE15
125 C10 Ixworth Pl. SW3

J

123 D9 Jackman St. E8
126 A7 Jacob St. SE1
126 A7 Jamaica Rd. SE1
126 B8 Jamaica Rd. SE16
123 H10 Jamaica St. E1
120 A2 James Ave. NW2
121 J12 James St. W1
120 L6 Jameson St. W8
121 D13 Jamestown Rd. NW1
127 B14 Janet St. E14
126 A8 Janeway St. SE16
127 C10 Jarrow Rd. SE16
123 A13 Jarrow Way E9
124 A8 Jay Ms. SW7
123 E14 Jebb St. E3
125 K12 Jedburgh St. SW11
125 H16 Jeffreys Rd. SW4
121 C14 Jeffreys St. NW1
125 H16 Jeffreys Wk. SW4
126 L2 Jelf Rd. SW2
124 E1 Jenner Pl. SW13
123 J15 Jeremiah St. E14
121 L14 Jermyn St. SW1
127 H12 Jerningham Rd. SE14
121 G10 Jerome Cres. NW8
127 J15 Jerrard St. SE13
122 J7 Jewry St. EC3
124 K7 Jew's Row SW18
120 A1 Jeymer Ave. NW2
122 L3 Joan St. SE1
122 H1 Jockey's Flds. WC1
123 D13 Jodrell Rd. E3
121 K16 John Adam St. WC2
122 A6 John Campbell Rd. N16
122 K3 John Carpenter St. EC4
126 A8 John Felton Rd. SE16
122 K8 John Fisher St. E1
125 D15 John Islip St. SW1
127 G15 John Penn St. SE13
121 J13 John Princes St. W1
126 B8 John Roll Way SE16
126 F3 John Ruskin St. SE5
122 B3 John Spencer Sq. N1
122 G1 John St. WC1
122 G1 John's Ms. WC1
122 D8 Johnson Clo. E8
125 D14 Johnson's Pl. SW1
126 D1 Jonathan St. SE11
123 G13 Joseph St. E3
126 L1 Josephine Ave. SW2
125 H11 Joubert St. SW11
126 F7 Jowett St. SE15
127 B16 Jubilee Cres. E14
125 D10 Jubilee Pl. SW3
123 J10 Jubilee St. E1
121 F16 Judd St. WC1
125 F10 Juer St. SW11
127 D15 Julian Pl. E14
125 J10 Junction App. SW11
122 E4 Junction Wf. N1
123 K10 Juniper St. E1
127 E11 Juno Way SE14
122 B1 Jupiter Way N7
123 D16 Jupp Rd. W. E15
126 C1 Juxon St. SE11

K

125 J9 Kambala Rd. SW11
125 G11 Kassala Rd. SW11
125 J11 Kathleen Rd. SW11
125 H16 Kay Rd. SW9
122 E8 Kay St. E2
122 J1 Kean St. WC2
123 L11 Keel Clo. SE16
122 J1 Keeley St. WC2
127 B9 Keetons Rd. SE16
125 K11 Keildon Rd. SW11
120 J2 Kelfield Gdns. W10
126 K2 Kellett Rd. SW2
121 B13 Kelly St. NW1
125 H15 Kelman Clo. SW4
126 K8 Kelmore Gro. SE22
125 L10 Kelmscott Rd. SW11
122 G8 Kelsey St. E2
124 B7 Kelso Pl. W8
127 B16 Kelson Ho. E14
124 F5 Kelvedon Rd. SW6
127 L11 Kelvington Rd. SE15
122 J1 Kemble St. WC2
126 J4 Kemerton Rd. SE5
123 A12 Kemeys St. E9
120 E3 Kempe Rd. NW6
124 D6 Kempsford Gdns. SW5
126 C2 Kempsford Rd. SE11
124 G6 Kempson Rd. SW6
127 C12 Kempthorne Rd. SE8
126 H4 Kenbury St. SE5
125 F16 Kenchester Clo. SW8
126 F3 Kendal Clo. SW9
121 J10 Kendal St. W2
127 G10 Kender St. SE14
125 K15 Kendoa Rd. SW4
125 C9 Kendrick Pl. SW7
124 J3 Kenilworth Ct. SW15
123 E12 Kenilworth Rd. E3
120 D5 Kenilworth Rd. NW6
120 F1 Kenmont Gdns. NW10
123 A9 Kenmure Rd. E8
125 G12 Kennard St. SW11
120 G5 Kennet Rd. W9
122 L8 Kennet St. E1
120 A1 Kenneth Cres. NW2
122 D6 Kenning Ter. N1
126 D2 Kennings Way SE11
125 D16 Kennington La. SE11
126 E1 Kennington Oval SE11
126 E2 Kennington Pk. Pl. SE11
126 E2 Kennington Pk. Rd. SE11
126 B2 Kennington Rd. SE1
126 B2 Kennington Rd. SE11
120 G3 Kensal Rd. W10
124 A7 Kensington Ch. Ct. W8
120 L6 Kensington Ch. St. W8
124 A7 Kensington Ch. Wk. W8
124 A7 Kensington Ct. W8
124 B7 Kensington Ct. Pl. W8
120 J7 Kensington Gdns. Sq. W2
124 B8 Kensington Gate W8
124 A8 Kensington Gore SW7
124 B6 Kensington High St. W8
124 B5 Kensington High St. W14
120 L6 Kensington Mall W8
120 L7 Kensington Palace Gdns. W8
120 K5 Kensington Pk. Gdns. W11
120 J5 Kensington Pk. Rd. W11
120 L6 Kensington Pl. W8
124 A8 Kensington Rd. SW7
124 A7 Kensington Rd. W8
124 A7 Kensington Sq. W8
122 E7 Kent St. E2
121 F10 Kent Ter. NW1
121 C13 Kentish Town Rd. NW1
121 B13 Kentish Town Rd. NW5
123 B11 Kenton Rd. E9
121 G16 Kenton St. WC1
124 C7 Kenway Rd. SW5
123 A12 Kenworthy Rd. E9
125 K15 Kenwyn Rd. SW4
124 G3 Kenyon St. SW6
125 K16 Kepler Rd. SW4
121 H15 Keppel St. WC1
123 J15 Kerbey St. E14
126 G5 Kerfield Pl. SE5
125 J10 Kerrison Rd. SW11
125 H11 Kersley Ms. SW11
125 H11 Kersley St. SW11
120 E3 Keslake Rd. NW6
126 J8 Keston Rd. SE15
126 L3 Kestrel Ave. SE24
124 L4 Keswick Rd. SW15
126 L1 Kett Gdns. SW2
123 G9 Key Clo. E1
125 E16 Keybridge Ho. SW8
120 A3 Keyes Rd. NW2
126 B3 Keyworth St. SE1
125 H10 Khyber Rd. SW11
126 F1 Kibworth St. SW8
120 C5 Kilburn High Rd. NW6
120 F4 Kilburn La. W9
120 F3 Kilburn La. W10
120 F6 Kilburn Pk. Rd. NW6
120 D6 Kilburn Pl. NW6
120 D7 Kilburn Priory NW6
120 J6 Kildare Gdns. W2
120 J6 Kildare Ter. W2
125 L16 Kildoran Rd. SW2
124 H8 Kilkie St. SW6
122 E1 Killick St. N1
123 B11 Killowen Rd. E9
125 H14 Killyon Rd. SW8
124 F4 Kilmaine Rd. SW6
124 C2 Kilmarsh Rd. W6
123 H14 Kilner St. E14
120 F4 Kilravock St. W10
124 G4 Kimbell Gdns. SW6
127 H9 Kimberley Ave. SE15
120 D4 Kimberley Rd. NW6
125 H16 Kimberley Rd. SW9
126 G5 Kimpton Rd. SE5
127 A11 Kinburn St. SE16
127 F9 Kincaid Rd. SE15
126 D4 King & Queen St. SE17
127 F10 King Arthur Clo. SE15
125 A15 King Charles St. SW1
123 K10 King David La. E1
122 J4 King Edward St. EC1
126 B2 King Edward Wk. SE1
123 D9 King Edwards Rd. E9
127 F16 King George St. SE10
122 A6 King Henry St. N16
121 C10 King Henry's Rd. NW3
122 B6 King Henry's Wk. N1
126 A3 King James St. SE1
123 H11 King John St. E1
122 J4 King St. EC2
121 L14 King St. SW1
121 K16 King St. WC2
122 K5 King William St. EC4
127 E16 King William Wk. SE10
120 B4 Kingdon Rd. NW6
127 C16 Kingfield St. E14
124 A4 Kingham Clo. W11
126 D6 Kinglake St. SE17
121 K14 Kingly St. W1
125 L16 King's Ave. SW4
121 C10 Kings College Rd. NW3
122 F1 King's Cross Rd. WC1
127 G9 Kings Gro. SE15
122 G1 King's Ms. WC1
120 C1 Kings Rd. NW10
125 C12 King's Rd. SW1
125 E9 King's Rd. SW3
124 F7 King's Rd. SW6
124 F8 King's Rd. SW10
120 J2 Kingsbridge Rd. W10
122 B6 Kingsbury Rd. N1
122 B6 Kingsbury Ter. N1
120 B5 Kingscroft Rd. NW2
120 L3 Kingsdale Gdns. W11
120 J3 Kingsdown Clo. W10
121 A11 Kingsford St. NW5
120 C6 Kingsgate Pl. NW6
120 C6 Kingsgate Rd. NW6
123 C10 Kingshold Rd. E9
122 B6 Kingsland Grn. E8
122 B7 Kingsland High St. E8
122 F6 Kingsland Rd. E2
122 D6 Kingsland Rd. E8
120 D5 Kingsley Rd. NW6
125 J11 Kingsley St. SW11
121 E9 Kingsmill Ter. NW8
121 D12 Kingstown St. NW1
122 J1 Kingsway WC2
120 D4 Kingswood Ave. NW6
124 F4 Kingwood Rd. SW6
125 A12 Kinnerton St. SW1
124 E4 Kinnoul Rd. W6
126 J8 Kinsale Rd. SE15
126 A5 Kipling Est. SE1
126 A5 Kipling St. SE1
127 B9 Kirby Est. SE16
126 A6 Kirby Gro. SE1
123 F10 Kirkwall Pl. E2
127 H9 Kirkwood Rd. SE15
125 F14 Kirtling St. SW8
126 F3 Kirwyn Way SE5
123 F14 Kitcat Ter. E3
126 F5 Kitson Rd. SE5
127 H11 Kitto Rd. SE14
123 G14 Knapp Rd. E3
124 C7 Knaresborough Pl. SW5
126 H3 Knatchbull Rd. SE5
127 K12 Kneller Rd. SE4
125 A11 Knightsbridge SW1
125 A10 Knightsbridge SW7
125 A11 Knightsbridge Grn. SW1
124 E6 Knivet Rd. SW6
123 D15 Knobs Hill Rd. E15
124 L8 Knoll Rd. SW18
123 F10 Knottisford St. E2
126 J2 Knowle Clo. SW9
125 J14 Knowles Wk. SW4
125 H11 Knowsley Rd. SW11
121 H11 Knox St. W1
120 C6 Kylemore Rd. NW6
124 B8 Kynance Pl. SW7

L

122 D7 Laburnum St. E2
123 E14 Lacey Wk. E3
122 H5 Lackington St. EC2
126 K8 Lacon Rd. SE22
124 K3 Lacy Rd. SW15
120 K5 Ladbroke Gdns. W11
120 G3 Ladbroke Gro. W10
120 J4 Ladbroke Gro. W11
120 L5 Ladbroke Rd. W11
120 K5 Ladbroke Sq. W11
120 K5 Ladbroke Ter. W11
120 L5 Ladbroke Wk. W11
121 A14 Lady Margaret Rd. NW5
127 J15 Ladycroft Rd. SE13
127 L15 Ladywell Rd. SE13
126 A7 Lafone St. SE1
123 L11 Lagado Ms. SE16
124 B3 Lakeside Rd. W14
124 H4 Lalor St. SW6
123 C9 Lamb La. E8
122 H7 Lamb St. E1
125 L16 Lambert Rd. SW2
122 C2 Lambert St. N1
125 C16 Lambeth Bri. SE1
125 C16 Lambeth Bri. SW1
126 C1 Lambeth High St. SE1
122 K4 Lambeth Hill EC4
126 B1 Lambeth Palace Rd. SE1
126 B1 Lambeth Rd. SE1
126 C1 Lambeth Wk. SE11
121 A12 Lamble St. NW5
121 B10 Lambolle Pl. NW3
121 B10 Lambolle Rd. NW3
125 J13 Lambourn Rd. SW4
124 G4 Lambrook Ter. SW6
122 G1 Lamb's Conduit St. WC1
122 H5 Lamb's Pas. EC1
127 E14 Lamerton St. SE8
124 C1 Lamington St. W6
123 C11 Lammas Rd. E9
124 E8 Lamont Rd. SW10
120 G8 Lanark Pl. W9
120 E7 Lanark Rd. W9
127 B15 Lanark Sq. E14
127 K11 Lanbury Rd. SE15
124 F5 Lancaster Ct. SW6
121 B10 Lancaster Dr. NW3
120 K8 Lancaster Gate W2
121 B9 Lancaster Gro. NW3
120 K8 Lancaster Ms. W2
122 K1 Lancaster Pl. WC2
120 J4 Lancaster Rd. W11
126 A3 Lancaster St. SE1
121 K9 Lancaster Ter. W2
120 K8 Lancaster Wk. W2
120 F5 Lancefield St. W10
125 A11 Lancelot Pl. SW7
122 D6 Lancresse Ct. N1
126 L7 Landcroft Rd. SE22
124 J2 Landford Rd. SW15
127 E11 Landmann Way SE14
125 B11 Landon Pl. SW1
123 L16 Landons Clo. E14
125 J16 Landor Rd. SW9
124 H5 Landridge Rd. SW6
123 E12 Lanfranc Rd. E3
123 G10 Lang St. E1
126 E4 Langdale Clo. SE17
127 F16 Langdale Rd. SE10
122 A8 Langford Clo. E8
126 J6 Langford Grn. SE5
120 E8 Langford Pl. NW8
121 H13 Langham Pl. W1
121 H13 Langham St. W1
120 A7 Langland Gdns. NW3
120 E2 Langler Rd. NW10
125 E16 Langley La. SW8
121 J16 Langley St. WC2
124 G3 Langthorne St. SW6
126 F3 Langton Rd. SW9
124 E8 Langton St. SW10
120 D7 Langtry Rd. NW8
120 G6 Lanhill Rd. W9
123 J15 Lansbury Est. E14
123 J16 Lansbury Gdns. E14
120 K5 Lansdowne Cres. W11
122 B8 Lansdowne Dr. E8
125 G16 Lansdowne Gdns. SW8
120 K4 Lansdowne Ri. W11
120 K4 Lansdowne Rd. W11
121 G16 Lansdowne Ter. WC1
120 L5 Lansdowne Wk. W11
125 G15 Lansdowne Way SW8
126 A4 Lant St. SE1
127 A14 Lanterns Ct. E14
127 H10 Lanvanor Rd. SE15
120 G5 Lapford Clo. W9
126 C4 Larcom St. SE17
123 D10 Lark Row E2
125 H15 Larkhall La. SW4
125 J14 Larkhall Ri. SW4
124 E3 Larnach Rd. W6
124 L2 Larpent Ave. SW15
125 H11 Latchmere Rd. SW11
125 H11 Latchmere St. SW11
123 J11 Latham Ho. E1
120 J2 Latimer Pl. W10
120 H2 Latimer Rd. W10
126 E8 Latona Rd. SE15
124 C3 Latymer Ct. W6
120 F7 Lauderdale Rd. W9
124 B8 Launceston Pl. W8
127 B16 Launch St. E14
124 E4 Laundry Rd. W6
122 B7 Laurel St. E8
127 G12 Laurie Gro. SE14
123 D11 Lauriston Rd. E9
127 G10 Lausanne Rd. SE15
125 K11 Lavender Gdns. SW11
122 C8 Lavender Gro. E8
125 K11 Lavender Hill SW11
123 L12 Lavender Rd. SE16
125 J9 Lavender Rd. SW11
125 K11 Lavender Sweep SW11
125 K11 Lavender Wk. SW11
124 C7 Laverton Pl. SW5
122 L3 Lavington St. SE1
126 B5 Law St. SE1
122 C6 Lawford Rd. N1
121 B14 Lawford Rd. NW5
123 K15 Lawless St. E14
127 A16 Lawn Ho. Clo. E14
125 E16 Lawn La. SW8
121 A11 Lawn Rd. NW3
123 F14 Lawrence Clo. E3
125 E10 Lawrence St. SW3
123 F12 Lawton Rd. E3
126 F3 Laxley Clo. SE5
127 C9 Layard Rd. SE16
127 C9 Layard Sq. SE16
122 B2 Laycock St. N1
122 G2 Laystall St. EC1
122 E2 Layton Rd. N1
123 B14 Leabank Sq. E9
122 J6 Leadenhall St. EC3
126 A4 Leake St. SE1
120 H5 Leamington Rd. Vill. W11
124 C1 Leamore St. W6
127 G14 Leander Ct. SE8
122 H2 Leather La. EC1
126 A6 Leathermarket St. SE1
125 K11 Leathwaite Rd. SW11
127 H15 Leathwell Rd. SE8
124 L6 Lebanon Gdns. SW18
124 L6 Lebanon Rd. SW18
120 B1 Lechmere Rd. NW2
125 D9 Lecky St. SW7
127 F9 Ledbury Est. SE15
120 J5 Ledbury Rd. W11
126 F8 Ledbury St. SE15
127 J16 Lee Bri. SE13
123 A13 Lee Conservancy Rd. E9
122 D7 Lee St. E8
122 F1 Leeke St. WC1
127 B16 Leerdam Dr. E14
121 K12 Lees Pl. W1
126 K2 Leeson Rd. SE24
127 D13 Leeway SE8
123 E16 Leggatt Rd. E15
127 L16 Legge St. SE13
122 C2 Legion Clo. N1
121 K15 Leicester Sq. WC2
120 E2 Leigh Gdns. NW10
121 G16 Leigh St. WC1
120 E1 Leighton Gdns. NW10
121 A14 Leighton Gro. NW5
121 A14 Leighton Pl. NW5
121 A14 Leighton Rd. NW5
120 J8 Leinster Gdns. W2
120 K8 Leinster Ms. W2
120 J8 Leinster Pl. W2
120 J6 Leinster Sq. W2
120 K8 Leinster Ter. W2
122 J7 Leman St. E1
124 B2 Lena Gdns. W6
125 J15 Lendal Ter. SW4
120 B2 Lennon Rd. NW2
125 B11 Lennox Gdns. SW1
125 B11 Lennox Gdns. Ms. SW1
122 C7 Lenthall Rd. E8
127 F9 Leo St. SE15
122 G5 Leonard St. EC2
126 F8 Leontine Clo. SE15
123 H13 Leopold St. E3
125 L15 Leppoc Rd. SW4
126 C6 Leroy St. SE1
125 L13 Lessar Ave. SW4
127 G16 Lethbridge Clo. SE13
124 G5 Lettice St. SW6
126 H6 Lettsom St. SE5
125 H16 Levehurst Way SW4
123 H16 Leven Rd. E14
122 F3 Lever St. EC1
121 A14 Leverton St. NW5
123 G13 Lewey Ho. E3
127 J16 Lewis Gro. SE13
121 B13 Lewis St. NW1
127 H16 Lewisham Hill SE13
127 L16 Lewisham Pk. SE13
127 G15 Lewisham Rd. SE13
127 H14 Lewisham Way SE4
127 G13 Lewisham Way SE14
124 C6 Lexham Gdns. W8
124 C6 Lexham Ms. W8
121 K14 Lexington St. W1
121 C13 Leybourne Rd. NW1
127 F11 Leylang Rd. SE14
127 E12 Liardet St. SE14
122 B3 Liberia Rd. N5
126 G1 Liberty St. SW9
123 D13 Libra Rd. E3
126 A3 Library St. SE1
123 F12 Lichfield Rd. E3
126 H2 Lidcote Gdns. SW9
120 E2 Liddell Gdns. NW10
120 B6 Liddell Rd. NW6
121 E14 Lidlington Pl. NW1
124 K3 Lifford St. SW15
127 A14 Lightermans Rd. E14
126 C1 Lilac Pl. SE11
121 G10 Lilestone St. NW8
126 H3 Lilford Rd. SE5
124 E3 Lillie Rd. SW6
124 E6 Lillie Yd. SW6
125 J13 Lillieshall Rd. SW4
122 H2 Lily Pl. EC1
124 G5 Lilyville Rd. SW6
125 K11 Limburg Rd. SW11
122 L8 Lime Clo. E1
124 A2 Lime Gro. W12
122 K6 Lime St. EC3
127 B15 Limeharbour E14
123 K13 Limehouse Causeway E14
123 H12 Limehouse Flds. Est. E14
124 E8 Limerston St. SW10
127 K16 Limes Gro. SE13
127 K9 Limes Wk. SE15
127 K11 Limesford Rd. SE15
124 D3 Linacre Ct. W6
120 B1 Linacre Rd. NW2
125 C11 Lincoln St. SW3
122 J1 Lincoln's Inn Flds. WC2
127 H14 Lind St. SE8
127 L13 Lindal Rd. SE4
120 E3 Linden Ave. NW10
120 L2 Linden Ct. W12
120 K6 Linden Gdns. W2
127 J9 Linden Gro. SE15
120 K6 Linden Ms. W2
120 A8 Lindfield Gdns. NW3
123 J14 Lindfield St. E14
123 H10 Lindley St. E1
125 K11 Lindore Rd. SW11
124 H8 Lindrop St. SW6
125 D15 Lindsay Sq. SW1
127 G16 Lindsell St. SE10
122 C4 Lindsey Ms. N1
122 H3 Lindsey St. EC1
125 G14 Linford St. SW8
127 K16 Lingards Rd. SE13
125 H16 Lingham St. SW9
121 G11 Linhope St. NW1
123 A10 Link St. E9
126 H6 Linnell Rd. SE5
125 K16 Linom Rd. SW4
126 C8 Linsey St. SE16
120 C6 Linstead St. NW6
122 D4 Linton St. N1
124 H5 Linver Rd. SW6
126 H7 Linwood Clo. SE5
126 G7 Lisford St. SE15
124 C5 Lisgar Ter. W14
121 K15 Lisle St. WC2
121 F10 Lisson Grn. Est. NW8
121 G10 Lisson Gro. NW1
121 G9 Lisson Gro. NW8
121 H10 Lisson St. NW1
125 J14 Liston Rd. SW4
121 K15 Litchfield St. WC2
120 B8 Lithos Rd. NW3
124 D7 Little Boltons, The SW10
122 H3 Little Britain EC1
125 B13 Little Chester St. SW1
126 A4 Little Dorrit Ct. SE1
121 K15 Little Newport St. WC2
121 J14 Little Portland St. W1
121 H16 Little Russell St. WC1
121 L14 Little St. James's St. SW1
125 J15 Littlebury Rd. SW4
127 L16 Littlewood SE13
122 D7 Livermere Rd. E8
126 D5 Liverpool Gro. SE17
122 C2 Liverpool Rd. N1
122 A2 Liverpool Rd. N7
122 H6 Liverpool St. EC2
123 D16 Livingstone Rd. E15
125 J9 Livingstone Wk. SW11
122 F4 Lizard St. EC1
122 F1 Lloyd Baker St. WC1
122 F2 Lloyd Sq. WC1
122 F2 Lloyd St. WC1
122 J6 Lloyd's Ave. EC3
127 H14 Loampit Hill SE13
127 J15 Loampit Vale SE13
124 E2 Lochaline St. W6
123 H16 Lochnagar St. E14
127 D15 Lockesfield Pl. E14
122 B1 Lockhart Clo. N7
123 G13 Lockhart St. E3
125 G13 Lockington Rd. SW8
127 J16 Lockmead Rd. SE13
123 J13 Locksley Est. E14
123 H13 Locksley St. E14
127 B9 Lockwood Sq. SE16
123 C10 Loddiges Rd. E9
127 F10 Loder St. SE15
121 F9 Lodge Rd. NW8
123 J16 Lodore St. E14
126 A8 Loftie St. SE16

Lofting Rd.

122 C1 Lofting Rd. N1
120 L1 Loftus Rd. W12
124 C6 Logan Ms. W8
124 C6 Logan Pl. W8
126 C2 Lollard St. SE11
126 A3 Loman St. SE1
122 C7 Lomas Ct. E8
122 H8 Lomas St. E1
125 H9 Lombard Rd. SW11
122 J5 Lombard St. EC3
126 F5 Lomond Gro. SE5
126 E6 Loncroft Rd. SE5
126 K5 London Bri. EC4
122 L5 London Bri. SE1
122 L5 London Bri. St. SE1
123 C9 London Flds. E8
123 C9 London Flds. E. Side E8
122 C8 London Flds. W. Side E8
123 C9 London La. E8
126 B3 London Rd. SE1
121 J9 London St. W2
122 H4 London Wall EC2
121 K16 Long Acre WC2
122 H3 Long La. EC1
126 A5 Long La. SE1
125 K13 Long Rd. SW4
122 F7 Long St. E2
122 G1 Long Yd. WC1
125 J11 Longbeach Rd. SW11
127 L16 Longbridge Way SE13
126 C7 Longfield Est. SE1
121 G13 Longford St. NW1
125 H12 Longhedge St. SW11
126 E6 Longhope Clo. SE15
126 C8 Longley St. SE1
125 C14 Longmoore St. SW1
123 F11 Longnor Rd. E1
124 C6 Longridge Rd. SW5
127 C13 Longshore SE8
120 D5 Lonsdale Rd. NW6
120 J5 Lonsdale Rd. W11
122 D2 Lonsdale Sq. N1
120 H7 Lord Hills Rd. W2
125 B16 Lord N. St. SW1
122 F1 Lorenzo St. WC1
124 B2 Loris Rd. W6
126 H1 Lorn Rd. SW9
124 A3 Lorne Gdns. W11
126 E3 Lorrimore Rd. SE17
126 E3 Lorrimore Sq. SE17
122 J5 Lothbury EC2
126 G3 Lothian Rd. SW9
120 F4 Lothrop St. W10
124 F8 Lots Rd. SW10
120 D8 Loudoun Rd. NW8
122 A1 Lough Rd. N7
126 K3 Loughborough Pk. SW9
126 H2 Loughborough Rd. SW9
126 D1 Loughborough St. SE11
123 G11 Louisa St. E1
125 K9 Louvaine Rd. SW11
122 J4 Love La. EC2
126 H5 Love Wk. SE5
126 D8 Lovegrove St. SE1
123 L16 Lovegrove Wk. E14
127 E10 Lovelinch Clo. SE15
122 D8 Lovell Ho. E8
120 B5 Loveridge Rd. NW6
121 L12 Lover's Wk. W1
126 K4 Lowden Rd. SE24
123 J12 Lowell St. E14
124 A4 Lwr. Addison Gdns. W14
125 B13 Lwr. Belgrave St. SW1
123 A10 Lwr. Clapton Rd. E5
124 J1 Lwr. Common S. SW15
125 B13 Lwr. Grosvenor Pl. SW1
124 D1 Lwr. Mall W6
126 A1 Lwr. Marsh SE1
121 C10 Lwr. Merton Ri. NW3
124 J1 Lwr. Richmond Rd. SW15
127 C11 Lwr. Rd. SE8
127 B10 Lwr. Rd. SE16
125 C12 Lwr. Sloane St. SW1
122 K5 Lwr. Thames St. EC3
120 C6 Lowfield Rd. NW6
125 B12 Lowndes Clo. SW1
125 B12 Lowndes Pl. SW1
125 A11 Lowndes Sq. SW1
125 B11 Lowndes St. SW1
126 H4 Lowth Rd. SE5
127 F10 Lubbock St. SE14
125 C10 Lucan Pl. SW3
127 G14 Lucas St. SE8
126 B8 Lucey Rd. SE16
122 J3 Ludgate Bdy. EC4
122 J3 Ludgate Hill EC4
127 F12 Ludwick Ms. SE14
127 H9 Lugard Rd. SE15
123 J9 Luke Ho. E1
122 G6 Luke St. EC2
123 J10 Lukin St. E1
127 H9 Lulworth Rd. SE15
121 J12 Lumley St. W1
125 D13 Lupus St. SW1
124 E3 Lurgan Ave. W6
125 G12 Lurline Gdns. SW11
125 F16 Luscombe Way SW8
120 E1 Lushington Rd. NW10
127 F16 Luton Pl. SE10
121 G9 Luton St. NW8
124 L1 Luttrell Ave. SW15
121 H12 Luxborough St. W1
124 C3 Luxemburg Gdns. W6
127 C11 Luxford St. SE16
127 G13 Luxmore St. SE4
126 J4 Luxor St. SE5
123 E12 Lyal Rd. E3
125 B12 Lyall Ms. SW1
125 B12 Lyall St. SW1
120 B2 Lydford Rd. NW2
120 G5 Lydford Rd. W9
125 J14 Lydon Rd. SW4
125 L16 Lyham Rd. SW2
121 C14 Lyme St. NW1
120 B7 Lymington Rd. NW6
126 F8 Lympstone Gdns. SE15
125 K13 Lyncott Cres. SW4
120 A6 Lyncroft Gdns. NW6
121 A9 Lyndhurst Gdns. NW3
126 H6 Lyndhurst Gro. SE15
121 A9 Lyndhurst Rd. NW3
126 G7 Lyndhurst Sq. SE15
121 A9 Lyndhurst Ter. NW3
126 G7 Lyndhurst Way SE15
120 D5 Lynton Rd. NW6
126 C7 Lynton Rd. SE1
121 G9 Lyons Pl. NW8
124 C4 Lyons Wk. W14
124 F3 Lysia St. SW6
126 L7 Lytcott Gro. SE22
126 D5 Lytham St. SE17
124 L3 Lytton Gro. SW15

M

121 F15 Mabledon Pl. WC1
124 F4 Mablethorpe Rd. SW6
123 A12 Mabley St. E9
125 J13 Macaulay Ct. SW4
125 J13 Macaulay Rd. SW4
125 K13 Macaulay Sq. SW4
127 G16 Macauley Ms. SE13
124 D1 Macbeth St. W6
121 E10 Macclesfield Bri. NW1
122 F4 Macclesfield Rd. EC1
125 G12 Macduff Rd. SW11
123 E11 Mace St. E2
120 L2 Macfarlane Rd. W12
127 J10 Machell Rd. SE15
125 J13 Mackay Rd. SW4
121 E10 Mackennal St. NW8
122 B1 Mackenzie Rd. N7
121 J16 Macklin St. WC2
126 C8 Macks Rd. SE16
121 F14 Mackworth St. NW1
126 D4 Macleod St. SE17
124 B4 Maclise Rd. W14
127 D15 Maconochies Rd. E14
127 C15 Macquarie Way E14
120 F5 Macroom Rd. W9
123 G15 Maddams St. E3
121 K13 Maddox St. W1
122 B2 Madras Pl. N7
126 F3 Madrigal La. SE5
126 D6 Madron St. SE17
122 L6 Magdalen St. SE1
126 E2 Magee St. SE11
125 L16 Magnolia Pl. SW4
126 A7 Maguire St. SE1
123 L12 Mahogany Clo. SE16
120 H8 Maida Ave. W2
120 E7 Maida Vale W9
121 C15 Maiden La. NW1
121 K16 Maiden La. WC2
127 G16 Maidenstone Hill SE10
127 F15 Maitland Clo. SE10
121 B11 Maitland Pk. Est. NW3
121 B11 Maitland Pk. Rd. NW3
121 B11 Maitland Pk. Vill. NW3
125 C10 Makins St. SW3
127 A14 Malabar St. E14
124 K1 Malbrook Rd. SW15
123 G10 Malcolm Pl. E2
123 G10 Malcolm Rd. E1
121 B12 Malden Cres. NW1
121 A11 Malden Rd. NW5
122 D4 Maldon Clo. N1
126 J6 Maldon Clo. SE5
121 G15 Malet Pl. WC1
121 G15 Malet St. WC1
126 J6 Malfort Rd. SE5
121 L14 Mall, The SW1
124 D1 Mall Rd. W6
123 B13 Mallard Clo. E9
125 L10 Mallinson Rd. SW11
125 E9 Mallord St. SW3
127 K12 Mallory Clo. SE4
121 G10 Mallory St. NW8
123 F13 Malmesbury Rd. E3
123 B9 Malpas Rd. E8
127 H13 Malpas Rd. SE4
126 E8 Malt St. SE1
126 B7 Maltby St. SE1
124 G7 Maltings Pl. SW6
120 H5 Malvern Clo. W10
125 C9 Malvern Ct. SW7
120 E5 Malvern Gdns. NW6
120 F5 Malvern Pl. NW6
122 C8 Malvern Rd. E8
120 F6 Malvern Rd. NW6
122 D2 Malvern Ter. N1
127 L15 Malyons Ter. SE13
127 J9 Manaton Clo. SE15
124 E2 Manbre Rd. W6
120 G4 Manchester Dr. W10
127 D16 Manchester Gro. E14
127 D16 Manchester Rd. E14
121 J12 Manchester Sq. W1
121 H12 Manchester St. W1
126 A5 Manciple St. SE1
125 L14 Mandalay Rd. SW4
121 D14 Mandela St. NW1
126 F2 Mandela St. SW9
126 C6 Mandela Way SE1
121 J12 Mandeville Pl. W1
125 L16 Mandrell Rd. SW2
121 J15 Manette St. W1
124 L5 Manfred Rd. SW15
121 B16 Manger Rd. N7
127 A14 Manilla St. E14
121 D12 Manley St. NW1
127 H13 Manor Ave. SE4
127 C9 Manor Est. SE16
127 E10 Manor Gro. SE15
120 C3 Manor Ho. Dr. NW6
127 H13 Manor Ms. SE4
126 D3 Manor Pl. SE17
125 D10 Manresa Rd. SW3
122 J7 Mansell St. E1
121 A11 Mansfield Rd. NW3
121 H13 Mansfield St. W1
122 E8 Mansford St. E2
124 C8 Manson Ms. SW7
125 C9 Manson Pl. SW7
120 A4 Manstone Rd. NW2
127 J12 Mantle Rd. SE4
125 J9 Mantua St. SW11
123 G10 Mantus Rd. E1
127 L13 Manwood Rd. SE4
123 G9 Mape St. E2
120 C4 Mapesbury Rd. NW2
121 H14 Maple St. W1
122 C8 Mapledene Rd. E8
123 F13 Maplin St. E3
120 F5 Marban Rd. W9
121 K11 Marble Arch W1
122 L8 Marble Quay E1
124 E5 Marchbank Rd. W14
121 G16 Marchmont St. WC1
126 F6 Marchwood Clo. SE5
126 C6 Marcia Rd. SE1
125 L9 Marcilly Rd. SW18
124 B1 Marco Rd. W6
123 A9 Marcon Pl. E8
126 K2 Marcus Garvey Way SE24
127 B9 Marden Sq. SE16
123 H12 Mardon St. E14
123 D9 Mare St. E8
120 A8 Maresfield Gdns. NW3
121 J13 Margaret St. W1
125 E10 Margaretta Ter. SW3
125 L16 Margate Rd. SW2
122 F2 Margery St. WC1
124 D3 Margravine Gdns. W6
124 D3 Margravine Rd. W6
123 G11 Maria Ter. E1
123 E9 Marian Pl. E2
127 A9 Marigold St. SE16
124 H7 Marinefield Rd. SW6
123 G13 Maritime St. E3
125 K11 Marjorie Gro. SW11
122 K6 Mark La. EC3
121 B16 Market Rd. N7
125 D11 Markham Sq. SW3
125 D10 Markham St. SW3
124 K7 Marl Rd. SW18
122 D8 Marlborough Ave. E8
125 C10 Marlborough Bldgs. SW3
124 C6 Marlborough Ct. W8
126 D8 Marlborough Gro. SE1
120 D8 Marlborough Hill NW8
120 E8 Marlborough Pl. NW8
121 L14 Marlborough Rd. SW1
125 C10 Marlborough St. SW3
124 B7 Marloes Rd. W8
120 C3 Marlow Ct. NW6
127 A11 Marlow Way SE16
121 D9 Marlowes, The NW8
125 K12 Marmion Rd. SW11
126 G8 Marmont Rd. SE15
120 F4 Marne St. W10
125 K12 Marney Rd. SW11
127 L13 Marnock Rd. SE4
123 H12 Maroon St. E14
122 B4 Marquess Est. N1
122 B5 Marquess Rd. N1
121 B15 Marquis Rd. NW1
127 K15 Marsala Rd. SE13
126 J7 Marsden Rd. SE15
121 B12 Marsden St. NW5
123 A12 Marsh Hill E9
123 L14 Marsh Wall E14
121 J14 Marshall St. W1
126 A4 Marshalsea Rd. SE1
125 B15 Marsham St. SW1
127 B16 Marshfield St. E14
123 C15 Marshgate La. E15
126 D3 Marsland Clo. SE17
123 C9 Martello St. E8
123 C9 Martello Ter. E8
123 J9 Martha St. E1
123 K10 Martineau Est. E1
124 F5 Marville Rd. SW6
127 E14 Mary Ann Gdns. SE8
126 G5 Mary Datchelor Clo. SE5
126 G5 Mary Datchelor Pl. SE5
120 D7 Mary Grn. NW8
120 K4 Mary Pl. W11
122 D4 Mary St. N1
120 G6 Marylands Rd. W9
121 H12 Marylebone High St. W1
121 J12 Marylebone La. W1
121 H13 Marylebone Ms. W1
121 H10 Marylebone Rd. NW1
121 H12 Marylebone St. W1
126 C1 Marylee Way SE11
124 B3 Masbro Rd. W14
124 K3 Mascotte Rd. SW15
125 G10 Maskelyn Clo. SW11
126 C5 Mason St. SE17
122 F4 Mason's Pl. EC1
123 G11 Massingham St. E1
127 C14 Mast Ho. Ter. E14
123 H11 Masters St. E1
127 A14 Mastmaker Rd. E14
126 K7 Matham Gro. SE22
124 C5 Matheson Rd. W14
122 D1 Matilda St. N1
126 K4 Matlock Clo. SE24
123 J12 Matlock St. E14
120 G3 Matthew Clo. W10
125 A15 Matthew Parker St. SW1
125 H11 Matthews St. SW11
122 A5 Matthias Rd. N16
126 G6 Maude Rd. SE5
125 L16 Mauleverer Rd. SW2
125 C15 Maunsel St. SW1
120 J1 Maurice St. W12
123 D14 Maverton Rd. E3
126 D7 Mawbey Est. SE1
126 D7 Mawbey Pl. SE1
125 F16 Mawbey St. SW8
126 J7 Maxted Rd. SE15
124 F7 Maxwell Rd. SW6
126 L3 Mayall Rd. SE24
120 B1 Maybury Gdns. NW10
121 L13 Mayfair Pl. W1
125 L15 Mayfield Clo. SW4
122 C7 Mayfield Rd. E8
125 J16 Mayflower Rd. SW9
122 E1 Maygood St. N1
120 B5 Maygrove Rd. NW6
125 K9 Maysoule Rd. SW11
120 C6 Mazenod Ave. NW6
126 B2 McAuley Clo. SE1
125 J10 McDermott Clo. SW11
126 J8 McDermott Rd. SE15
126 G4 McDowall Rd. SE5
120 H5 McGregor Rd. W11
126 G8 McKerrell Rd. SE15
124 C7 McLeod's Ms. SW7
127 E14 McMillan St. SE8
126 H6 McNeil Rd. SE5
123 B10 Mead Pl. E9
126 E3 Meadcroft Rd. SE11
126 E1 Meadow Ms. SW8
125 F16 Meadow Pl. SW8
126 F1 Meadow Rd. SW8
126 B4 Meadow Row SE1
121 C11 Meadowbank NW3
124 F2 Meadowbank Clo. SW6
126 B6 Meakin Est. SE1
121 J15 Meard St. W1
125 G13 Meath St. SW11
122 G1 Mecklenburgh Pl. WC1
122 G1 Mecklenburgh Sq. WC1
121 E15 Medburn St. NW1
123 A10 Median Rd. E5
126 G4 Medlar St. SE5
120 B6 Medley Rd. NW6
123 E12 Medway Rd. E3
125 B15 Medway St. SW1
126 K1 Medwin St. SW4
127 G9 Meeting Ho. La. SE15
123 B10 Mehetabel Rd. E9
127 G15 Melba Way SE13
126 K6 Melbourne Gro. SE22
126 G2 Melbourne Ms. SW9
122 K1 Melbourne Pl. WC2
124 B5 Melbury Ct. W8
124 B5 Melbury Rd. W14
121 G10 Melbury Ter. NW1
121 H11 Melcombe Pl. NW1
121 G11 Melcombe St. NW1
122 A2 Melgund Rd. N5
121 F9 Melina Pl. NW8
124 A1 Melina Rd. W12
126 A5 Melior St. SE1
127 B14 Mellish St. E14
124 L8 Melody Rd. SW18
126 G8 Melon Rd. SE15
120 A1 Melrose Ave. NW2
124 B2 Melrose Gdns. W6
124 A2 Melrose Ter. W6
125 C9 Melton Ct. SW7
121 F14 Melton St. NW1
124 J8 Mendip Rd. SW11
124 F4 Mendora Rd. SW6
123 C9 Mentmore Ter. E8
122 L1 Mepham St. SE1
121 J16 Mercer St. WC2
123 G9 Merceron St. E1
124 C2 Mercers Pl. W6
123 F13 Merchant St. E3
127 K16 Mercia Gro. SE13
124 L4 Mercier Rd. SW15
127 E11 Mercury Way SE14
127 K15 Mercy Ter. SE13
120 A2 Meredith Ave. NW2
127 K12 Meretone Clo. SE4
127 A16 Meridian Gate E14
124 K4 Merivale Rd. SW15
126 A5 Mermaid Ct. SE1
123 L13 Mermaid Ct. SE16
126 B4 Merrick Sq. SE1
124 E6 Merrington Rd. SW6
127 L13 Merritt Rd. SE4
126 E4 Merrow St. SE17
124 E1 Merthyr Ter. SW13
121 C10 Merton Ri. NW3
124 L6 Merton Rd. SW18
127 L11 Mertins Rd. SE15
126 K2 Mervan Rd. SW2
120 C6 Messina Ave. NW6
125 K12 Meteor St. SW11
126 D2 Methley St. SE11
120 H3 Methwold Rd. W10
122 L8 Mews St. E1
124 L5 Mexfield Rd. SW15
122 L3 Meymott St. SE1
123 C11 Meynell Cres. E9
123 C11 Meynell Gdns. E9
123 C11 Meynell Rd. E9
125 J9 Meyrick Rd. SW11
122 F4 Micawber St. N1
124 G7 Michael Rd. SW6
124 E6 Micklethwaite Rd. SW6
121 D9 Middle Fld. NW8
120 G4 Middle Row W10
122 J2 Middle Temple La. EC4
122 H6 Middlesex St. E1
127 A11 Middleton Dr. SE16
121 A16 Middleton Gro. N7
122 C7 Middleton Rd. E8
123 F9 Middleton St. E2
121 E15 Midland Rd. NW1
123 H12 Midlothian Rd. E3
124 D8 Milborne Gro. SW10
123 B10 Milborne St. E9
126 A3 Milcote St. SE1
122 B5 Mildmay Ave. N1
122 A5 Mildmay Gro. N1
122 A5 Mildmay Pk. N1
122 A5 Mildmay Rd. N1
122 B5 Mildmay St. N1
123 G11 Mile End Pl. E1
123 H10 Mile End Rd. E1
123 G12 Mile End Rd. E3
125 E16 Miles St. SW8
122 K1 Milford La. WC2
123 K10 Milk Yd. E1
126 G4 Milkwell Yd. SE5
126 L3 Milkwood Rd. SE24
120 A4 Mill La. NW6
122 D6 Mill Row N1
124 G2 Mill Shot Clo. SW6
126 A7 Mill St. SE1
121 K14 Mill St. W1
125 C16 Millbank SW1
125 C16 Millbank Twr. SW1
126 J3 Millbrook Rd. SW9
127 C10 Millender Wk. SE16
121 E14 Miller St. NW1
122 A7 Millers Ave. E8
122 A7 Millers Ter. E8
124 A2 Millers Way W6
125 G12 Millgrove St. SW11
127 B15 Millharbour E14
122 G1 Millman Ms. WC1
122 G1 Millman St. WC1
127 H12 Millmark Gro. SE14
126 A7 Millstream Rd. SE1
127 B14 Millwall Dock Rd. E14
120 E3 Milman Rd. NW6
125 E9 Milmans St. SW10
122 D2 Milner Pl. N1
122 C3 Milner Sq. N1
125 C11 Milner St. SW3
124 B3 Milson Rd. W14
126 C7 Milton Clo. SE1
127 E12 Milton Ct. Rd. SE14
122 H5 Milton St. EC2
120 C2 Milverton Rd. NW6
126 D2 Milverton St. SE11
124 G5 Mimosa St. SW6
126 D6 Mina Rd. SE17
122 K6 Mincing La. EC3
125 C12 Minera Ms. SW1
126 F2 Minerva Clo. SW9
123 E9 Minerva St. E2
126 H3 Minet Rd. SW9
124 A3 Minford Gdns. W14
123 K14 Ming St. E14
122 J7 Minories EC3
123 D11 Minson Rd. E9
120 A4 Minster Rd. NW2
122 E5 Mintern St. N1
124 F5 Mirabel Rd. SW6
126 G8 Mission Pl. SE15
122 G4 Mitchell St. EC1
122 B5 Mitchison Rd. N1
126 A2 Mitre Rd. SE1
122 J6 Mitre St. EC3
120 G1 Mitre Way NW10
126 J1 Moat Pl. SW9
127 A14 Moiety Rd. E14
124 G6 Molesford Rd. SW6
127 K16 Molesworth St. SE13
121 H10 Molyneux St. W1
127 H10 Mona Rd. SE15
125 B15 Monck St. SW1
126 K5 Monclar Rd. SE5
126 H8 Moncrieff St. SE15
123 C14 Monier Rd. E3
126 C2 Monkton St. SE11
120 J6 Monmouth Rd. W2
121 J16 Monmouth St. WC2
126 D8 Monnow Rd. SE1
127 F11 Monson Rd. SE14
121 H11 Montagu Ms. N. W1
121 H11 Montagu Pl. W1
121 H11 Montagu Sq. W1
121 J11 Montagu St. W1
127 K13 Montague Ave. SE4
122 L5 Montague Clo. SE1
121 H15 Montague Pl. WC1
122 A8 Montague Rd. E8
122 H4 Montague St. EC1
121 H16 Montague St. WC1
127 J9 Monteagle Way SE15
125 H13 Montefiore St. SW8
123 D13 Monteith Rd. E3
126 D2 Montford Pl. SE11
124 L1 Montolieu Gdns. SW15
121 A14 Montpelier Gro. NW5
125 B10 Montpelier Pl. SW7
127 G9 Montpelier Rd. SE15
125 A10 Montpelier Sq. SW7
125 B10 Montpelier St. SW7
125 B10 Montpelier Wk. SW7
122 K1 Montreal Pl. WC2
120 E4 Montrose Ave. NW6
125 A9 Montrose Ct. SW7
125 A12 Montrose Pl. SW1
124 K4 Montserrat Rd. SW15
127 L16 Monument Gdns. SE13
122 K5 Monument St. EC3
123 K10 Monza St. E1
127 B10 Moodkee St. SE16
123 F11 Moody St. E1
122 D3 Moon St. N1
122 H5 Moor La. EC2
124 F7 Moore Pk. Rd. SW6
125 C11 Moore St. SW3
122 H5 Moorfields EC2
122 H5 Moorgate EC2
120 J6 Moorhouse Rd. W2
126 K3 Moorland Rd. SW9
126 K2 Moorlands Est. SW9
122 F4 Mora St. EC1
123 K14 Morant St. E14
126 G1 Morat St. SW9
123 F10 Moravian St. E2
126 J1 Mordaunt St. SW9
127 H16 Morden Clo. SE13
127 H16 Morden Hill SE13
127 G16 Morden La. SE13
127 G15 Morden St. SE13
124 C3 More Clo. W14
123 H11 Morecambe Clo. E1
126 C4 Morecambe St. SE17
122 F3 Moreland St. EC1
125 H13 Moresby Wk. SW8
125 D14 Moreton Pl. SW1
125 D14 Moreton St. SW1
125 D14 Moreton Ter. SW1
122 A2 Morgan Rd. N7
120 H5 Morgan Rd. W10
123 F12 Morgan St. E3
122 L6 Morgans La. SE1
124 K7 Morie St. SW18
127 K16 Morley Rd. SE13
126 B2 Morley St. SE1
126 H4 Morna Rd. SE5
123 B10 Morning La. E9
124 C5 Mornington Ave. W14
121 E14 Mornington Cres. NW1
123 F14 Mornington Gro. E3
126 G4 Mornington Ms. SE5
127 F13 Mornington Rd. SE8
121 E13 Mornington St. NW1
121 E13 Mornington Ter. NW1
126 A6 Morocco St. SE1
123 D11 Morpeth Gro. E9
123 D10 Morpeth Rd. E9
123 F11 Morpeth St. E2
125 B14 Morpeth Ter. SW1
123 H15 Morris Rd. E14
123 J9 Morris St. E1
125 J12 Morrison St. SW11
120 F6 Morshead Rd. W9
120 D7 Mortimer Cres. NW6
120 D7 Mortimer Est. NW6
120 D7 Mortimer Pl. NW6
122 C6 Mortimer Rd. N1
120 F2 Mortimer Rd. NW10
121 J14 Mortimer St. W1
122 C4 Morton Rd. N1
126 L2 Morval Rd. SW2
123 E14 Morville St. E3
120 K7 Moscow Rd. W2
125 J10 Mossbury Rd. SW11
123 G13 Mossford St. E3
125 C10 Mossop St. SW3
120 F3 Mostyn Gdns. NW10
123 E14 Mostyn Gro. E3
126 G2 Mostyn Rd. SW9
125 B12 Motcomb St. SW1
123 C10 Moulins Rd. E9
122 G2 Mount Pleasant WC1
120 C2 Mount Pleasant Rd. NW10
121 K13 Mount Row W1
121 K12 Mount St. W1
123 K16 Mountague Pl. E14
120 C4 Mowbray Rd. NW6
123 E9 Mowlem St. E2
126 F2 Mowll St. SW9
121 H12 Moxon St. W1
124 G4 Moylan Rd. W6
120 F5 Mozart St. W10
125 E9 Mulberry Wk. SW3
124 E5 Mulgrave Rd. SW6
126 A5 Mulvaney Way SE1
125 L11 Muncaster Rd. SW11
124 D5 Mund St. W14
124 C4 Munden St. W14
122 F6 Mundy St. N1
120 H4 Munro Ms. W10
125 E9 Munro Ter. SW10
124 F4 Munster Rd. SW6
121 F13 Munster Sq. NW1
126 C4 Munton Rd. SE17
127 E9 Murdock St. SE15
122 D1 Muriel St. N1
126 A2 Murphy St. SE1
122 E4 Murray Gro. N1
121 C15 Murray Ms. NW1
121 C15 Murray St. NW1
126 G1 Mursell Est. SW8
124 E4 Musard Rd. W6
123 J10 Musbury St. E1
124 E4 Muscal W6
126 J7 Muschamp Rd. SE15
121 H16 Museum St. WC1
124 F6 Musgrave Cres. SW6
127 G11 Musgrove Rd. SE14
120 D6 Mutrix Rd. NW6
126 G3 Myatt Rd. SW9
126 H2 Myatt's Flds. S. SW9
122 F2 Myddelton Sq. EC1
122 F2 Myddelton St. EC1
127 E11 Myers La. SE14
122 E2 Mylne St. EC1
122 H8 Myrdle St. E1
127 J16 Myron Pl. SE13
122 E6 Myrtle Wk. N1
125 J11 Mysore Rd. SW11

N

123 H16 Nairn St. E14
126 L5 Nairne Gro. SE24
121 D16 Naish Ct. N1
123 J14 Nankin St. E14
125 K12 Nansen Rd. SW11
124 K8 Nantes Clo. SW18
127 D14 Napier Ave. E14
124 J5 Napier Ave. SW6
122 E4 Napier Gro. N1
124 B5 Napier Pl. W14
120 F1 Napier Rd. NW10
124 B4 Napier Rd. W14
122 B3 Napier Ter. N1
125 L14 Narbonne Ave. SW4

Powis Sq.

120 J5 Powis Sq. W11
120 J5 Powis Ter. W11
122 D8 Pownall Rd. E8
125 H11 Poyntz Rd. SW11
123 E9 Poyser St. E2
121 J9 Praed St. W2
125 L16 Prague Pl. SW2
125 H12 Prairie St. SW8
121 D14 Pratt St. NW1
126 C1 Pratt Wk. SE11
122 D4 Prebend St. N1
122 K7 Prescot St. E1
125 J15 Prescott Pl. SW4
127 A16 Prestons Rd. E14
122 L3 Price's St. SE1
122 F1 Prideaux Pl. WC1
125 J16 Prideaux Rd. SW9
126 F2 Prima Rd. SW9
121 B10 Primrose Gdns. NW3
121 C11 Primrose Hill Ct. NW3
121 C11 Primrose Hill Rd. NW3
122 H6 Primrose St. EC2
121 D12 Prince Albert Rd. NW1
121 F10 Prince Albert Rd. NW8
120 A8 Prince Arthur Rd. NW3
124 B8 Prince Consort Rd. SW7
123 B13 Prince Edward Rd. E9
125 F13 Prince of Wales Dr. SW8
125 G10 Prince of Wales Dr. SW11
125 A10 Prince of Wales Gate SW7
121 B12 Prince of Wales Rd. NW5
127 E13 Prince St. SE8
120 L4 Princedale Rd. W11
122 H7 Princelet St. E1
123 K9 Princes Ct. E1
125 B9 Princes Gdns. SW7
125 A10 Princes Gate SW7
125 B9 Princes Gate Ms. SW7
120 L4 Princes Pl. W11
127 H16 Princes Ri. SE13
120 K7 Princes Sq. W2
122 J5 Princes St. EC2
121 J13 Princes St. W1
127 B13 Princess Ct. SE16
121 D12 Princess Rd. NW1
120 E6 Princess Rd. NW6
126 B3 Princess St. SE1
120 H7 Princethorpe Ho. W2
122 H1 Princeton St. WC1
122 B3 Prior Bolton St. N1
127 F16 Prior St. SE10
126 B5 Prioress St. SE1
125 G15 Priory Ct. SW8
122 E1 Priory Grn. Est. N1
125 G16 Priory Gro. SW8
125 G16 Priory Ms. SW8
120 D5 Priory Pk. Rd. NW6
120 D7 Priory Rd. NW6
120 D7 Priory Ter. NW6
124 D8 Priory Wk. SW10
122 E8 Pritchard's Rd. E2
126 B8 Priter Rd. SE16
126 L2 Probert Rd. SW2
122 H1 Procter St. WC1
123 L10 Prospect Pl. E1
124 F4 Prothero Rd. SW6
121 K12 Providence Ct. W1
122 E5 Provost Est. N1
121 C11 Provost Rd. NW3
122 E5 Provost St. N1
123 L9 Prusom St. E1
122 K5 Pudding La. EC3
123 D15 Pudding Mill La. E15
126 J1 Pulross Rd. SW9
123 D13 Pulteney Clo. E3
122 D1 Pulteney Ter. N1
124 F6 Pulton Pl. SW6
123 F9 Pundersons Gdns. E2
124 F3 Purcell Cres. SW6
122 E6 Purcell St. N1
121 E15 Purchese St. NW1
123 G15 Purdy St. E3
124 G5 Purser's Cross Rd. SW6
120 E1 Purves Rd. NW10
124 J4 Putney Bri. SW6
124 J4 Putney Bri. SW15
124 J4 Putney Bri. App. SW6
124 K4 Putney Bri. Rd. SW15
124 L6 Putney Bri. Rd. SW18
124 J2 Putney Common SW15
124 K3 Putney High St. SW15
124 K1 Putney Pk. La. SW15
122 A5 Pyrland Rd. N5
126 J6 Pytchley Rd. SE22

Q

121 A11 Quadrant Gro. NW5
122 G7 Quaker St. E1
124 H6 Quarrendon St. SW6
127 A14 Quarterdeck, The E14
127 A11 Quebec Way SE16
123 B11 Queen Anne Rd. E9
121 H13 Queen Anne St. W1
125 A15 Queen Anne's Gate SW1
124 D2 Queen Caroline Est. W6
124 D2 Queen Caroline St. W6
126 A7 Queen Elizabeth St. SE1
122 A6 Queen Margarets Gro. N1
127 B13 Queen of Denmark Ct. SE16
121 G16 Queen Sq. WC1
122 K4 Queen St. EC4
121 L13 Queen St. W1
122 K3 Queen Victoria St. EC4
122 K4 Queenhithe EC4
124 E4 Queens Club Gdns. W14
121 B12 Queens Cres. NW5
120 J8 Queens Gdns. W2
124 B8 Queen's Gate SW7
124 B8 Queen's Gate Gdns. SW7
124 B8 Queen's Gate Ms. SW7
124 B8 Queen's Gate Pl. SW7
124 B8 Queen's Gate Pl. Ms. SW7
124 B8 Queen's Gate Ter. SW7
121 D9 Queen's Gro. NW8
122 D3 Queen's Head St. N1
120 F3 Queens Pk. Ct. W10
127 G9 Queens Rd. SE14
127 G9 Queens Rd. SE15
126 E5 Queen's Row SE17
121 D9 Queen's Ter. NW8
121 L14 Queen's Wk. SW1
125 C9 Queensberry Pl. SW7
120 K7 Queensborough Ter. W2
122 C7 Queensbridge Rd. E2
122 C7 Queensbridge Rd. E8
122 C4 Queensbury St. N1
120 L3 Queensdale Cres. W11
120 L4 Queensdale Pl. W11
120 L3 Queensdale Rd. W11
120 L4 Queensdale Wk. W11
120 C6 Queensgate Pl. NW6
121 D9 Queensmead NW8
124 F3 Queensmill Rd. SW6
125 E13 Queenstown Rd. SW8
120 J7 Queensway W2
122 A1 Quemerford Rd. N7
124 H8 Querrin St. SW6
120 D6 Quex Rd. NW6
122 E3 Quick St. N1
124 K3 Quill La. SW15
122 F8 Quilter St. E2
126 K6 Quorn Rd. SE22

R

124 E6 Racton Rd. SW6
120 H4 Raddington Rd. W10
127 L16 Radford Rd. SE13
124 G5 Radipole Rd. SW6
121 D10 Radlett Pl. NW8
124 B6 Radley Ms. W8
121 J10 Radnor Pl. W2
120 D4 Radnor Rd. NW6
126 F8 Radnor Rd. SE15
122 F4 Radnor St. EC1
124 C5 Radnor Ter. W14
125 D10 Radnor Wk. SW3
125 F10 Radstock St. SW11
125 K16 Raeburn St. SW2
121 B13 Raglan St. NW5
121 A14 Railey Ms. NW5
126 K2 Railton Rd. SE24
122 L5 Railway App. SE1
127 A10 Railway Ave. SE16
121 E16 Railway St. N1
127 D15 Rainbow Ave. E14
126 F6 Rainbow St. SE5
123 L9 Raine St. E1
120 F2 Rainham Rd. NW10
123 F14 Rainhill Way E3
127 C12 Rainsborough Ave. SE8
124 E2 Rainville Rd. W6
123 L16 Raleana Rd. E14
122 D3 Raleigh St. N1
124 L7 Ram St. SW18
121 J14 Ramillies Pl. W1
125 D15 Rampayne St. SW1
122 G8 Ramsey St. E2
125 G10 Randall Clo. SW11
127 F16 Randall Pl. SE10
126 D1 Randall Rd. SE11
121 D16 Randell's Rd. N1
120 E7 Randolph Ave. W9
120 G8 Randolph Cres. W9
120 E7 Randolph Gdns. NW6
120 G8 Randolph Ms. W9
120 G8 Randolph Rd. W9
121 C14 Randolph St. NW1
124 J5 Ranelagh Ave. SW6
124 J5 Ranelagh Gdns. SW6
125 D12 Ranelagh Gro. SW1
124 E2 Rannoch Rd. W6
123 D13 Ranwell St. E3
125 A11 Raphael St. SW7
123 J11 Ratcliffe Cross St. E1
123 J12 Ratcliffe La. E14
123 K11 Ratcliffe Orchard E1
121 H15 Rathbone Pl. W1
121 H14 Rathbone St. W1
126 K2 Rattray Rd. SW2
126 G8 Raul Rd. SE15
123 H9 Raven Row E1
124 L3 Ravenna Rd. SW15
127 H15 Ravensbourne Pl. SE13
124 C1 Ravenscourt Pl. W6
124 C1 Ravenscourt Rd. W6
122 E7 Ravenscroft St. E2
126 D2 Ravensdon St. SE11
120 A5 Ravenshaw St. NW6
120 F1 Ravensworth Rd. NW10
126 C1 Ravent Rd. SE11
125 C11 Rawlings St. SW3
122 F3 Rawstorne St. EC1
122 G2 Ray St. EC1
127 C9 Raymouth Rd. SE16
124 L4 Rayners Rd. SW15
124 C1 Raynham Rd. W6
123 B9 Reading La. E8
123 L9 Reardon Path E1
123 L9 Reardon St. E1
127 F11 Reaston St. SE14
127 E10 Record St. SE15
122 D4 Rector St. N1
125 J14 Rectory Gdns. SW4
125 J14 Rectory Gro. SW4
123 H11 Rectory Sq. E1
127 D11 Reculver Rd. SE16
122 J2 Red Lion Ct. EC4
126 E4 Red Lion Row SE17
122 H1 Red Lion Sq. WC1
122 H1 Red Lion St. WC1
126 L5 Red Post Hill SE21
126 K5 Red Post Hill SE24
120 J7 Redan Pl. W2
124 B3 Redan St. W14
126 F6 Redbridge Gdns. SE5
125 E11 Redburn St. SW3
126 F4 Redcar St. SE5
123 K10 Redcastle Clo. E1
122 G7 Redchurch St. E2
124 D7 Redcliffe Gdns. SW10
124 D7 Redcliffe Ms. SW10
124 E8 Redcliffe Pl. SW10
124 D8 Redcliffe Rd. SW10
124 D7 Redcliffe Sq. SW10
124 E7 Redcliffe St. SW10
126 A4 Redcross Way SE1
126 E8 Reddins Rd. SE15
125 E10 Redesdale St. SW3
124 C6 Redfield La. SW5
124 J3 Redgrave Rd. SW15
121 E13 Redhill St. NW1
123 H10 Redman's Rd. E1
124 C1 Redmore Rd. W6
127 B12 Redriff Est. SE16
127 B11 Redriff Rd. SE16
123 D10 Redruth Rd. E9
123 L12 Redwood Clo. SE16
125 C9 Reece Ms. SW7
126 H8 Reedham St. SE15
126 C2 Reedworth St. SE11
122 D4 Rees St. N1
121 K12 Reeves Ms. W1
123 G15 Reeves Rd. E3
125 H11 Reform St. SW11
122 E6 Regan Way N1
125 C15 Regency St. SW1
123 F15 Regent Sq. E3
121 F16 Regent Sq. WC1
121 K15 Regent St. SW1
121 J13 Regent St. W1
125 F16 Regents Bri. Gdns. SW8
121 E11 Regents Pk. NW1
121 C11 Regents Pk. Rd. NW1
122 D8 Regents Row E8
127 F14 Reginald Rd. SE8
127 F14 Reginald Sq. SE8
121 A13 Regis Rd. NW5
120 L2 Relay Rd. W12
126 J8 Relf Rd. SE15
122 E3 Remington St. N1
127 A10 Renforth St. SE16
126 C3 Renfrew Rd. SE11
127 J16 Rennell St. SE13
127 C9 Rennie Est. SE16
122 L3 Rennie St. SE1
124 G4 Reporton Rd. SW6
123 J12 Repton St. E14
127 H12 Reservoir Rd. SE4
123 B10 Retreat Pl. E9
127 J12 Revelon Rd. SE4
126 C8 Reverdy Rd. SE1
124 F8 Rewell St. SW6
127 L10 Reynolds Rd. SE15
122 D4 Rheidol Ter. N1
125 H16 Rhodesia Rd. SW9
123 H12 Rhodeswell Rd. E14
123 F12 Rhondda Gro. E3
121 B12 Rhyl St. NW5
123 J15 Ricardo St. E14
123 K13 Rich St. E14
126 F1 Richborne Ter. SW8
124 A2 Richford St. W6
122 D1 Richmond Ave. N1
120 B2 Richmond Ave. NW10
122 D1 Richmond Cres. N1
122 C3 Richmond Gro. N1
122 C7 Richmond Rd. E8
125 A16 Richmond Ter. SW1
124 A3 Richmond Way W12
124 A3 Richmond Way W14
124 E6 Rickett St. SW6
123 E14 Ridgdale St. E3
126 J3 Ridgeway Rd. SW9
124 L7 Ridgmount Rd. SW18
121 H14 Riding Ho. St. W1
122 A7 Ridley Rd. E8
120 A2 Riffel Rd. NW2
120 L3 Rifle Pl. W11
123 H15 Rifle St. E14
124 H4 Rigault Rd. SW6
123 J15 Rigden St. E14
125 K15 Rigge Pl. SW4
126 B7 Riley Rd. SE1
125 F9 Riley St. SW10
121 K9 Ring, The W2
122 A2 Ringcroft St. N7
124 L5 Ringford Rd. SW18
124 G4 Ringmer Ave. SW6
122 C1 Ripplevale Gro. N1
122 E1 Risinghill St. N1
125 E16 Rita Rd. SW8
122 E2 Ritchie St. N1
122 B8 Ritson Rd. E8
123 B10 Rivaz Pl. E9
122 C4 River Pl. N1
122 F2 River St. EC1
124 C1 Rivercourt Rd. W6
124 J5 Rivermead Ct. SW6
125 E15 Riverside Ct. SW8
124 D1 Riverside Gdns. W6
123 E16 Riverside Rd. E15
120 F5 Riverton Clo. W9
124 E1 Riverview Gdns. SW13
122 F6 Rivington St. EC2
123 C14 Roach Rd. E3
127 F15 Roan St. SE10
121 J12 Robert Adam St. W1
126 C4 Robert Dashwood Way SE17
127 F11 Robert Lowe Clo. SE14
124 G3 Robert Owen Ho. SW6
121 F13 Robert St. NW1
122 F8 Roberta St. E2
123 D16 Robertson Rd. E15
125 J13 Robertson St. SW8
126 C8 Robin Ct. SE16
123 J16 Robin Hood La. E14
123 E10 Robinson Rd. E2
126 H1 Robsart St. SW9
125 K9 Rochelle Clo. SW11
121 C14 Rochester Ms. NW1
121 B14 Rochester Pl. NW1
121 B14 Rochester Rd. NW1
125 C14 Rochester Row SW1
121 C14 Rochester Sq. NW1
125 B15 Rochester St. SW1
121 B14 Rochester Ter. NW1
121 A11 Rochford St. NW5
126 B4 Rockingham Est. SE1
126 B4 Rockingham St. SE1
124 K4 Rockland Rd. SW15
124 A3 Rockley Rd. W14
121 H11 Rodmarton St. W1
126 C4 Rodney Pl. SE17
126 C4 Rodney Rd. SE17
122 E1 Rodney St. N1
127 A16 Roffey St. E14
122 G1 Roger St. WC1
127 H13 Rokeby Rd. SE4
124 D8 Roland Gdns. SW7
126 D5 Roland Way SE17
127 E10 Rollins St. SE15
126 D7 Rolls Rd. SE1
126 L4 Rollscourt Ave. SE24
127 E12 Rolt St. SE8
123 F10 Roman Rd. E2
123 E12 Roman Rd. E3
122 B1 Roman Way N7
127 L16 Romborough Gdns. SE13
127 L16 Romborough Way SE13
122 H8 Romford St. E1
121 K15 Romilly St. W1
127 E16 Romney Rd. SE10
125 B16 Romney St. SW1
122 A2 Ronalds Rd. N5
120 A4 Rondu Rd. NW2
122 K6 Rood La. EC3
125 K14 Rookery Rd. SW4
127 B12 Rope St. SE16
127 A12 Ropemaker Rd. SE16
122 H5 Ropemaker St. EC2
123 G13 Ropery St. E3
122 E8 Ropley St. E2
124 F4 Rosaline Rd. SW6
124 C8 Rosary Gdns. SW7
124 F5 Rosaville Rd. SW6
122 L4 Rose All. SE1
123 E13 Rosebank Gdns. E3
122 B7 Roseberry Pl. E8
127 C9 Roseberry St. SE16
122 G2 Rosebery Ave. EC1
124 H7 Rosebury Rd. SW6
120 D3 Rosedene NW6
124 E3 Rosedew Rd. W6
123 K14 Rosefield Gdns. E14
126 F7 Rosemary Rd. SE15
120 B8 Rosemont Rd. NW3
125 C11 Rosemoor St. SW3
125 G10 Rosenau Cres. SW11
125 G10 Rosenau Rd. SW11
127 L11 Rosenthorpe Rd. SE15
127 A16 Roserton St. E14
123 A11 Rosina St. E9
124 J3 Roskell Rd. SW15
120 K4 Rosmead Rd. W11
122 F2 Rosoman St. EC1
124 K2 Rossdale Rd. SW15
121 D14 Rossendale Way NW1
127 D9 Rossetti Rd. SE16
121 G10 Rossmore Rd. NW1
124 G5 Rostrevor Rd. SW6
123 C13 Rothbury Rd. E9
122 C4 Rotherfield St. N1
127 D9 Rotherhithe New Rd. SE16
127 C11 Rotherhithe Old Rd. SE16
127 A10 Rotherhithe St. SE16
123 L11 Rotherhithe Tunnel E1
123 K12 Rotherhithe Tunnel App. E14
127 A10 Rotherhithe Tunnel App. SE16
124 J3 Rotherwood Rd. SW15
126 B6 Rothsay St. SE1
121 D11 Rothwell St. NW1
125 A10 Rotten Row SW7
127 B16 Rotterdam Dr. E14
126 B8 Rouel Rd. SE16
123 G14 Rounton Rd. E3
122 L2 Roupell St. SE1
121 C14 Rousden St. NW1
124 F4 Rowallan Rd. SW6
122 C7 Rowan Ct. E8
124 C3 Rowan Rd. W6
124 F2 Rowberry Clo. SW6
126 D7 Rowcross St. SE1
125 H12 Rowditch La. SW11
120 C1 Rowdon Ave. NW10
123 A10 Rowe La. E9
125 H10 Rowena Cres. SW11
120 H7 Rowington Clo. W2
121 A10 Rowland Hill St. NW3
120 D7 Rowley Way NW8
123 D16 Rowse Clo. E15
121 A15 Rowstock Gdns. N7
124 E6 Roxby Pl. SW6
125 D11 Royal Ave. SW3
121 C14 Royal College St. NW1
120 L3 Royal Cres. W11
122 J5 Royal Ex. EC3
127 F16 Royal Hill SE10
125 E11 Royal Hospital Rd. SW3
122 K7 Royal Mint Ct. EC3
122 K7 Royal Mint St. E1
127 F13 Royal Naval Pl. SE14
123 B9 Royal Oak Rd. E8
127 F16 Royal Pl. SE10
126 E3 Royal Rd. SE17
126 B1 Royal St. SE1
123 E11 Royal Victor Pl. E3
123 E10 Royston St. E2
122 D6 Rozel Ct. N1
125 J14 Rozel Rd. SW4
127 E9 Ruby St. SE15
120 E6 Rudolph Rd. NW6
121 D16 Rufford St. N1
122 G1 Rugby St. WC1
123 K14 Rugg St. E14
123 K10 Rum Clo. E1
124 F7 Rumbold Rd. SW6
126 J1 Rumsey Rd. SW9
120 K4 Runcorn Pl. W11
126 H3 Rupert Gdns. SW9
120 E5 Rupert Rd. NW6
121 K15 Rupert St. W1
125 J12 Rush Hill Rd. SW11
126 K2 Rushcroft Rd. SW2
127 L14 Rushey Mead SE4
122 E5 Rushton St. N1
126 A3 Rushworth St. SE1
126 J5 Ruskin Pk. Ho. SE5
126 L4 Ruskin Wk. SE24
124 B4 Russell Gdns. W14
124 A4 Russell Gdns. Ms. W14
126 G2 Russell Gro. SW9
124 B4 Russell Rd. W14
121 G16 Russell Sq. WC1
121 K16 Russell St. WC2
123 L12 Russia Dock Rd. SE16
123 E10 Russia La. E2
126 F5 Rust Sq. SE5
123 D13 Ruston St. E3
125 C15 Rutherford St. SW1
125 A10 Rutland Gdns. SW7
125 A10 Rutland Gate SW7
124 D1 Rutland Gro. W6
120 B2 Rutland Pk. NW2
123 D10 Rutland Rd. E9
125 B10 Rutland St. SW7
127 G11 Rutts Ter. SE14
124 J3 Ruvigny Gdns. SW15
121 L14 Ryder St. SW1
127 K10 Rye Hill Est. SE15
127 K10 Rye Hill Pk. SE15
126 H8 Rye La. SE15
126 J8 Rye Pas. SE15
127 K11 Rye Rd. SE15
127 L16 Ryecroft Rd. SE13
124 G7 Ryecroft St. SW6
121 B13 Ryland Rd. NW5
124 E5 Rylston Rd. SW6
125 B11 Rysbrack St. SW3

S

125 J11 Sabine Rd. SW11
121 K14 Sackville St. W1
122 H2 Saffron Hill EC1
126 C1 Sail St. SE11
126 E3 St. Agnes Pl. SE11
124 B7 St. Albans Gro. W8
122 D3 St. Alban's Pl. N1
127 E16 St. Alfege Pas. SE10
125 K15 St. Alphonsus Rd. SW4
122 H2 St. Andrew St. EC4
122 K3 St. Andrew's Hill EC4
120 B1 St. Andrews Rd. NW10
124 E4 St. Andrews Rd. W14
123 G15 St. Andrews Way E3
123 J13 St. Anne's Row E14
124 L7 St. Ann's Hill SW18
120 K3 St. Anns Rd. W11
125 B15 St. Ann's St. SW1
121 E9 St. Ann's Ter. NW8
120 L3 St. Anns Vill. W11
127 J11 St. Asaph Rd. SE4
121 C15 St. Augustines Rd. NW1
127 H16 St. Austell Rd. SE13
125 D12 St. Barnabas St. SW1
123 A11 St. Barnabas Ter. E9
125 G16 St. Barnabas Vill. SW8
122 J7 St. Botolph St. EC3
122 J3 St. Bride St. EC4
121 F16 St. Chad's Pl. WC1
121 F16 St. Chad's St. WC1
120 H4 St. Charles Sq. W10
122 B2 St. Clements St. N1
122 B2 St. Clements St. N7
122 H2 St. Cross St. EC1
120 B5 St. Cuthberts Rd. NW2
124 H5 St. Dionis Rd. SW6
127 G13 St. Donatts Rd. SE14
122 K6 St. Dunstan's Hill EC3
124 D3 St. Dunstans Rd. W6
121 D10 St. Edmunds Ter. NW8
127 A11 St. Elmos Rd. SE16
120 H5 St. Ervans Rd. W10
126 K6 St. Francis Rd. SE22
120 A3 St. Gabriels Rd. NW2
121 K13 St. George St. W1
126 B3 St. Georges Circ. SE1
125 C13 St. George's Dr. SW1
121 J10 St. Georges Flds. W2
126 B2 St. Georges Rd. SE1
123 K12 St. Georges Sq. E14
127 C13 St. Georges Sq. SE8
125 D15 St. George's Sq. SW1
125 D15 St. George's Sq. Ms. SW1
126 E6 St. Georges Way SE15
125 L14 St. Gerards Clo. SW4
121 J15 St. Giles High St. WC2
126 F6 St. Giles Rd. SE5
127 C11 St. Helena Rd. SE16
120 H3 St. Helens Gdns. W10
120 D3 St. Hildas Clo. NW6
124 E1 St. Hilda's Rd. SW13
123 E10 St. James Ave. E2
120 L4 St. James Gdns. W11
127 B16 St. James Ms. E14
124 D2 St. James St. W6
127 G12 St. James's SE14
125 B14 St. James's Ct. SW1
126 J2 St. James's Cres. SW9
125 A14 St. James's Pk. SW1
121 L14 St. James's Pl. SW1
126 D8 St. James's Rd. SE1
126 B8 St. James's Rd. SE16
121 L15 St. James's Sq. SW1
121 L14 St. James's St. SW1
121 D11 St. James's Ter. Ms. NW8
122 G3 St. James's Wk. EC1
122 E2 St. John St. EC1
124 L3 St. John's Ave. SW15
123 A10 St. John's Ch. Rd. E9
126 J2 St. John's Cres. SW9
122 E5 St. Johns Est. N1
120 K4 St. Johns Gdns. W11
125 K9 St. John's Hill SW11
125 K9 St. John's Hill Gro. SW11
122 G3 St. John's La. EC1
125 K10 St. John's Rd. SW11
127 H14 St. Johns Vale SE8
121 E9 St. John's Wd. High St. NW8
121 D9 St. John's Wd. Pk. NW8
121 G9 St. John's Wd. Rd. NW8
121 E9 St. John's Wd. Ter. NW8
122 A6 St. Jude St. N16
123 E9 St. Jude's Rd. E2
120 D6 St. Julian's Rd. NW6
122 L8 St. Katharine's Way E1
120 D3 St. Laurence Clo. NW6
123 L16 St. Lawrence St. E14
120 H4 St. Lawrence Ter. W10
126 H2 St. Lawrence Way SW9
123 H15 St. Leonards Rd. E14
121 B12 St. Leonards Sq. NW5
123 F15 St. Leonards St. E3
125 D11 St. Leonard's Ter. SW3
125 E10 St. Loo Ave. SW3
125 K15 St. Luke's Ave. SW4
122 F5 St. Luke's Est. EC1
120 H5 St. Lukes Rd. W11
125 D10 St. Luke's St. SW3
120 F5 St. Luke's Yd. W9
124 L1 St. Margarets Cres. SW15
120 F2 St. Margaret's Rd. NW10
127 K13 St. Margarets Rd. SE4
125 A16 St. Margaret's St. SW1
122 J7 St. Mark St. E1
121 D12 St. Marks Cres. NW1
124 E7 St. Mark's Gro. SW10
120 J4 St. Marks Pl. W11
122 A7 St. Marks Ri. E8
120 H3 St. Marks Rd. W10
120 J4 St. Marks Rd. W11
121 D14 St. Martin's Clo. NW1
121 K16 St. Martin's La. WC2
121 K16 St. Martin's Pl. WC2
126 H1 St. Martin's Rd. SW9
122 J4 St. Martin's-le-Grand EC1
124 B5 St. Mary Abbots Pl. W8
124 B5 St. Mary Abbots Ter. W14
122 K6 St. Mary at Hill EC3
122 J6 St. Mary Axe EC3
127 A10 St. Marychurch St. SE16
126 C2 St. Mary's Gdns. SE11
122 B3 St. Mary's Gro. N1
124 J1 St. Mary's Gro. SW13
121 H9 St. Marys Mans. W2
122 D3 St. Marys Path N1
127 G10 St. Mary's Rd. SE15
121 H9 St. Marys Sq. W2
121 H9 St. Marys Ter. W2
126 C2 St. Mary's Wk. SE11
126 K1 St. Matthew's Rd. SW2
122 F8 St. Matthew's Row E2
124 G5 St. Maur Rd. SW6
126 H1 St. Michael's Rd. SW9
121 J9 St. Michaels St. W2
127 K12 St. Norbert Grn. SE4
127 L11 St. Norbert Rd. SE4
124 F4 St. Olaf's Rd. SW6
126 D1 St. Oswald's Pl. SE11
121 C14 St. Pancras Way NW1
122 D4 St. Paul St. N1
120 B2 St. Paul's Ave. NW2
123 L11 St. Paul's Ave. SE16
122 J3 St. Paul's Chyd. EC4
121 C15 St. Pauls Cres. NW1
122 B5 St. Paul's Pl. N1
122 B3 St. Pauls Rd. N1
122 B5 St. Paul's Shrubbery N1
123 H13 St. Pauls St. E3
123 H13 St. Pauls Way E3
122 E8 St. Peter's Clo. E2
122 D3 St. Peters St. N1
124 F5 St. Peters Ter. SW6
122 C6 St. Peter's Way N1

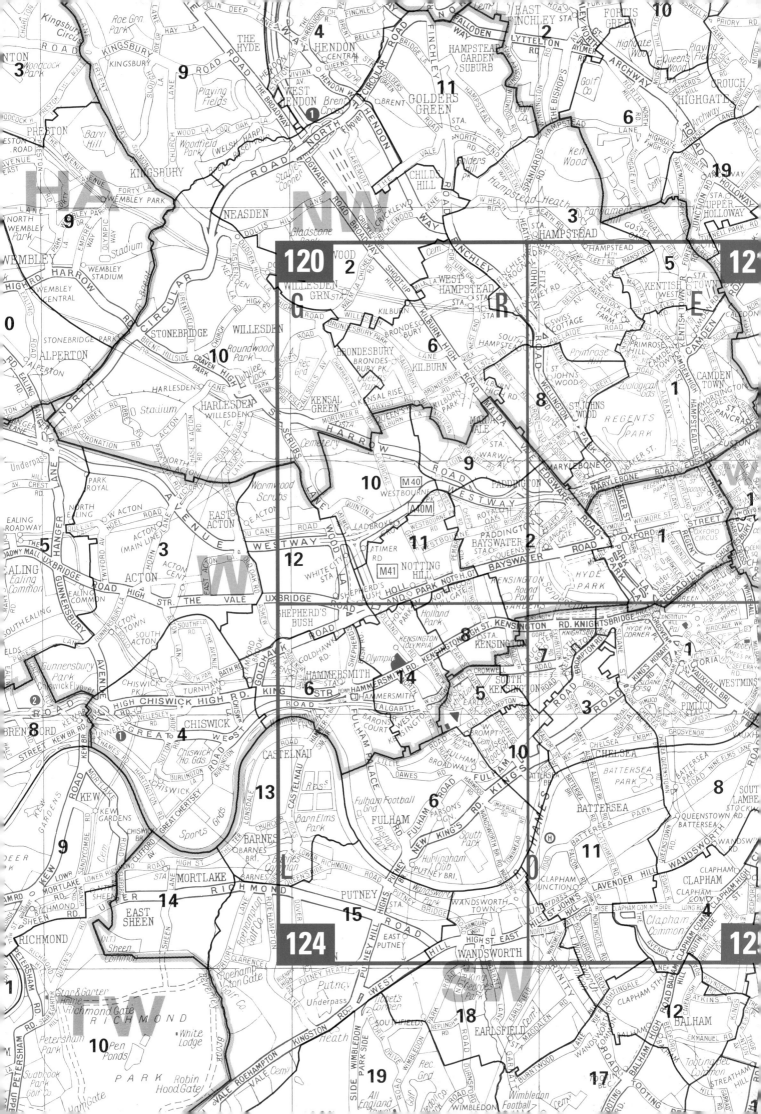